CIVILIZATION

PAST & PRESENT

CIVILIZATION:
FROM THE INDUSTRIAL REVOLUTION TO THE PRESENT

INCLUDES SELECTED CHAPTERS FROM
CIVILIZATION: PAST AND PRESENT, VOLUME II 8E

T. WALTER WALLBANK (LATE)
Emeritus, University of Southern California

ALASTAIR M. TAYLOR
Emeritus, Queen's University

NELS M. BAILKEY
Emeritus, Tulane University

GEORGE F. JEWSBURY
Oklahoma State University

CLYDE J. LEWIS
Emeritus, Eastern Kentucky University

NEIL J. HACKETT
Oklahoma State University

Addison Wesley Longman
Higher Education Publishing Group

Our custom books consist of products that are produced from camera-ready copy. Peer review, class testing, and accuracy are primarily the responsibility of the author(s).

You can order a copy at your local bookstore or call the publisher directly at 1-800-782-2665.

Custom Book Manager: Lisa Wunderle
Production Administrator: Nicole DuCharme
Cover Design: Zina Scarpulla

CIVILIZATION: FROM THE INDUSTRIAL REVOLUTION TO THE PRESENT

Includes selected chapters from Civilization: Past & Present Volume II, 8E ISBN (0-673-99431-7)

ISBN: 0-673-67628-5

96 97 3 2 1

BRIEF CONTENTS

DETAILED CONTENTS

Maps

Documents

Preface

Originally published in 1942, *Civilization Past & Present* was the first text of its kind. Its objective was to present a survey of world cultural history, treating the development and growth of civilization not as a unique European experience but as a global one through which all the great culture systems have interacted to produce the present-day world. The book attempted to include all the elements of history—social, economic, political, religious, aesthetic, legal, and technological.

The purposes of *Civilization Past & Present*, as envisaged in the first edition five decades ago, have even more significance today. A knowledge of Western civilization is an essential aim of education, but this alone is no longer adequate. With the accelerating tempo of developments in communication and technology, every day each part of the world is brought into closer contact with other parts; the world is now truly a "global village." Perhaps the most significant happening in our time is the political and cultural reemergence of the world's non-Western peoples. They have played an important role in world affairs, and in the future their role will be even more important. Hence, these people, their cultures, and their civilizations must be known and understood.

NEW TO THE EIGHTH EDITION

The eighth edition maintains the strengths that have made *Civilization Past & Present* a widely popular introductory textbook. The authors have sought to profit from the many helpful suggestions that have come from users and reviewers, to utilize the latest historical scholarship, and to extend the historical narrative to the present day. While the eighth edition retains the basic organization and approach of its predecessors, all chapters have been reviewed and revised in the light of new developments. Many chapters have been completely rewritten, and there are some new chapters. Chapter 5, new to this edition, describes the beginning and spread of Christianity,

the end of the Roman Empire in the West, the beginning and flowering of Byzantium, and the spread and development of civilization in eastern Europe and Russia.

Chapters 9 and 10 have been thoroughly revised to integrate better the social, political, economic, cultural, religious, and intellectual history of the European Middle Ages. Better integration was also the goal for the revisions of Chapters 21 through 25, which examine the Napoleonic and Industrial Revolutions; the revolutions of the mid-nineteenth century, their ideological underpinnings, and the cultural responses to them; and European politics through the nineteenth century to the brink of World War I. Chapters 34, 35, and 36, which cover the period since the end of World War II, have also been thoroughly revised to reflect the changes resulting from the end of the Cold War, the fall of Communist regimes in Eastern Europe, the collapse of the Soviet Union, and the rise of the global economy and transnational economic unions. Finally, the Epilogue offers a brief retrospective on the twentieth century and a prospective on what may lie ahead in the twenty-first century.

FEATURES

This text has been developed with the dual purpose of helping students acquire a solid knowledge of past events and, equally important, of helping them think more constructively about the significance of those events for the difficult times in which we now live. Several features assist students toward achievement of those goals.

The Maps

Each chapter begins with a two-color map designed to help students see at a glance the geographical focus of the chapter. The brief caption accompanying the map highlights the significance of the map and its relevance to the topics that will be discussed in the chapter. In addition, other two-color maps are distributed liberally throughout the text. Some are designed to make clear the nature of a single distinctive event; others illustrate larger trends. The 14 full-color maps at the back of the book constitute an atlas of historical reference maps. The notes accompanying the maps in the Historical Atlas describe the principal features and significance of each of the reference maps.

Chapter-Opening Timelines and Outlines

At the beginning of each chapter is a timeline highlighting the significant events of the era covered in the chapter, along with an opening outline listing the major topics to be discussed. The chapter-opening maps, timelines, and outlines provide students with geographical, chronological, and topical reference frames for their study of each chapter.

The Document Excerpts

Each chapter includes one or more excerpts from documents of the era under discussion. The excerpts have been selected from a variety of documents—political, economic, legal, intellectual, popular—to show students the kinds of materials historians use to understand and interpret the past. Reading the excerpts will permit students to experience at first hand the voices and records of the past.

Suggestions for Reading

Each chapter ends with an annotated bibliography listing special historical studies, biographies, and some collections of source materials. The works listed are intended to provide students with ample sources from which to prepare special reports or with which to expand their understanding of a particular subject.

The Color Plates

Eight inserts of full-color art reproductions appear throughout the text. The works of art have been carefully selected to illustrate some facet of a culture pattern discussed in the text. These reproductions, with the accompanying commentary, constitute a capsule history of world art.

The Pronunciation Key

In the general index, the correct pronunciation is given for most proper names. Thus students will find it easy, as well as helpful, to look up the correct pronunciation of the names and places referred to in the text. The index also provides pronunciation guides for many unfamiliar, difficult, or foreign words.

The pedagogical features of the eighth edition, along with the text narrative, are intended to provide the reader with an understanding of the contribution of past eras to the shaping of subsequent events and to illuminate the manner in which the study of global history affords insights into the genesis, nature, and direction of our civilization. As we approach the end of the twentieth century, the need for this kind of historical perspective has never been greater.

SUPPLEMENTS

The following supplements are available for use in conjunction with this book.

For the Student

Student Study Guide in two volumes. Volume I (Chapters 1 through 18) and Volume II (Chapters 17 through 37) prepared by David G. Egler, Sterling J. Kernek, and Charles O'Brien of Western Illinois University. Each chapter includes chapter overviews, lists of themes and concepts, map exercises, multiple-choice practice tests, and critical thinking and essay questions.

World History Map Workbook in two volumes. Volume I (to 1600) and Volume II (from 1600) prepared by Glee Wilson of Kent State University. Each volume includes over 40 maps accompanied by over 120 pages of exercises. Each volume is designed to teach the location of various countries and their relationship to one another. Also included are numerous exercises aimed at enhancing students' critical thinking abilities.

SuperShell II Computer Tutorial. An interactive program for computer-assisted learning, prepared by George Jewsbury of Oklahoma State University. Features multiple-choice, true-false, and completion quizzes; comprehensive chapter outlines; "flash cards" for key terms and concepts; and diagnostic feedback.

Timelink: World History Computerized Atlas by William Hamblin of Brigham Young University. A highly graphic, Hypercard-based computerized atlas and historical geography tutorial for the Macintosh.

Mapping World Civilizations: Student Activities. A free student workbook by Gerald Danzer, University of Illinois, Chicago. Features numerous map skill exercises written to enhance students' basic geographical literacy. The exercises provide ample opportunities for interpreting maps and analyzing cartographic materials as historical documents. The instructor is entitled to one free copy of *Mapping World Civilizations: Student Activities* for each copy of the text purchased from HarperCollins.

For the Instructor

Instructor's Resource Manual by George Jewsbury of Oklahoma State University. Includes chapter outlines, discussion suggestions, critical thinking exercises, map exercises, primary source analysis suggestions, term paper and essay topics. Special "Instructor's Tool Kit" includes numerous audio-visual suggestions. Includes six essays on teaching African history written by Robert Edgar of Howard University and six essays on teaching about genocide written by George Jewsbury of Oklahoma State University.

Guide to Advanced Media and Internet Resources for World History by Richard M. Rothaus of Oklahoma State University. This pamphlet provides a comprehensive review of CD-ROM, software, and Internet resources for world civilization including a list of the primary sources, syllabi and articles, and discussion groups available on-line.

Discovering World History Through Maps and Views, Second Edition, by Gerald Danzer, University of Illinois, Chicago, winner of the AHA's James Harvey Robinson Award for his work in the development of map transparencies. The second edition of this set of 100 four-color transparencies is completely updated and revised to include the newest reference maps and the most useful source materials. These transparencies are bound with introductory materials in a three-ring binder, including an introduction on teaching history with maps and detailed commentary on each transparency. The collection includes source and reference maps, views and photos, urban plans, building diagrams, and works of art.

Test Bank by George Jewsbury of Oklahoma State University. A total of 2000 questions, including 50 multiple-choice questions and five essay questions per chapter. Each test is referenced by topic, type, and text page number.

TestMaster Computerized Testing System. A test-generation software package available for DOS and Macintosh computers. Allows users to add, delete, and print test items.

Map Transparencies A set of 48 two-color and four-color text map transparencies from *Civilization Past & Present*.

Grades. A grade-keeping and classroom management software program that maintains data for up to 200 students.

The HarperCollins World Civilization Media Program. A wide variety of media enhancements for use in teaching world civilization texts.

ACKNOWLEDGMENTS

To the following reviewers who gave generously of their time and knowledge to provide thoughtful evaluations and many helpful suggestions for the revision of the text, the authors express their gratitude.

Michael L. Carrafiello
East Carolina University

J. R. Crawford
Montreat-Anderson College

Edward R. Crowther
Adams State College

William Edward Ezzell
DeKalb College–Central Campus

Robert B. Florian
Salem-Teikyo University

Robert J. Gentry
University of Southwestern Louisiana

Donald E. Harpster
College of St. Joseph

Gordon K. Harrington
Weber State University

Geoff Haywood
Beaver College

Roger L. Jungmeyer
Lincoln University of Missouri

Bernard Kiernan
Concord College

Harral E. Landry
Texas Women's University

Marsha K. Marks
Alabama A&M University

Eleanor McCluskey
Broward Community College

Arlin Migliazzo
Whitworth College

William C. Moose
Mitchell Community College

Wayne Morris
Lees-McRae College

John G. Muncie
East Stroudsburg University

Sr. Jeannette Plante, CSC
Notre Dame College

Chad Ronnander
University of Minnesota

William M. Simpson
Louisiana College

Terrence S. Sullivan
University of Nebraska at Omaha

Leslie Tischauser
Prairie State College

Arthur L. Tolson
Southern University

Joseph A. Tomberlin
Valdosta State University

Thomas Dwight Veve
Dalton College

Prologue →

PERSPECTIVE ON HUMANITY

If the time span of our planet—now estimated at some 5 billion years—were telescoped into a single year, the first eight months would be devoid of any life. The next two months would be taken up with plant and very primitive animal forms, and not until well into December would any mammals appear. In this "year," members of *Homo erectus*, our ancient predecessors, would mount the global stage only between 10 and 11 P.M. on December 31. And how has the human species spent that brief allotment? Most of it—the equivalent of more than half a million years—has been given over to making tools out of stone. The revolutionary changeover from food-hunting nomads to farmers who raised grain and domesticated animals would occur in the last 60 seconds. And into that final minute would be crowded all of humanity's other accomplishments: the use of metal; the creation of civilizations; the mastery of the oceans; and the harnessing of steam, then gas, electricity, oil, and, finally, in our lifetime, nuclear energy. Brief though it has been, humanity's time on the globe reveals a rich tapestry of science, industry, religion, and art. This accumulated experience of the human species is available for study. We call it *history*.

PAST AND PRESENT

As we read and learn about early societies and their members, we discover them to be very different from us and the world in which we live. And yet, we are linked by more than curiosity to our ancient predecessors. Why? Because we are of the same species, and we share a fundamental commonality that connects present with past: the human-environment nexus. It is the dynamic interplay of environmental factors and human activities that accounts for the terrestrial process known as history. The biological continuity of our species, coupled with humanity's unflagging inventiveness, has enabled each generation to build on the experiences and contributions of its forebears—so that continuity and change in human affairs proceed together.

The Universal Culture Pattern

In the interplay of men and women with their environment and fellow beings, certain fundamental needs are always present. Six needs, common to people at all times and in all places, form the basis of a "universal culture pattern" and deserve to be enumerated.

1. *The need to make a living.* Men and women must have food, shelter, clothing, and the means to provide for their offsprings' survival.
2. *The need for law and order.* From earliest times, communities have had to keep peace among their members, defend themselves against external attack, and protect community assets.
3. *The need for social organization.* For people to make a living, raise families, and maintain law and order, a social structure is essential. Views about the relative importance of the group and the individual within it may vary with any such social structure.
4. *The need for knowledge and learning.* Since earliest times, humankind has transmitted knowledge acquired through experience, first orally and then by means of writing systems. As societies grow more complex, there is increasing need to preserve knowledge and transmit it through education to as many people as possible.
5. *The need for self-expression.* People have responded creatively to their environment even before the days when they decorated the walls of Paleolithic caves with paintings of the animals they hunted. The arts appear to have a lineage as old as human experience.
6. *The need for religious expression.* Equally old is humanity's attempt to answer the "why" of its existence. What primitive peoples consid-

ered supernatural in their environment could often, at a later time, be explained by science in terms of natural phenomena. Yet today, no less than in archaic times, men and women continue to search for answers to the ultimate questions of existence.

Culture Change and Culture Lag

When people in a group behave similarly and share the same institutions and ways of life, they can be said to have a common *culture*. Throughout this text we will be looking at a number of different cultures, some of which are designated as *civilizations*. (If all tribes or societies have culture, then civilization is a particular *kind* of culture.) "A culture is the way of life of a human group; it includes all the learned and standardized forms of behavior which one uses and others in one's group expect and recognize. . . . Civilization is that kind of culture which includes the use of writing, the presence of cities and of wide political organization, and the development of occupational specialization."[1]

Cultures are never wholly static or wholly isolated. A particular culture may have an individuality that sets it off sharply from other cultures, but invariably it has been influenced by external contacts. Such contacts may be either peaceful or warlike, and they meet with varying degrees of acceptance. Through these contacts occurs the process of culture *diffusion*. Geography, too, has profoundly influenced the development of cultures, although we should not exaggerate its importance. Environmental influences tend to become less marked as people gain technological skill and mastery over the land. The domestication of animals and cereals, for example, took place in both the Old and New Worlds, but the animals and grains were different because of dissimilar ecological factors. Invention is another important source of culture change, although it is not clear to what extent external physical contact is required in the process of invention. Perhaps it may be possible for men and women in different times and places to hit on similar solutions to the challenges posed by their respective environments—resulting in the phenomenon known as *parallel invention*.

Some parts of a culture pattern change more rapidly than others, so that one institution sometimes becomes outmoded in relation to others in a society. When different parts of a society fail to mesh harmoniously, the condition is often called *culture lag*. Numerous examples of this lag could be cited: the exploitation of child laborers during the nineteenth century, the failure to allow women to vote until this century, and the tragedy of hunger in the midst of plenty.

PAST AND PRESENT AS PROLOGUE

What can the past and present—as history—suggest to us for tomorrow's world? In the first place, changes in the physical and social environments will probably accelerate as a result of continued technological innovation. These changes can result in increased disequilibrium and tensions among the various segments comprising the universal culture pattern—in other words, in increased culture lag.

Has the past anything to tell the future about the consequences of cultural disequilibrium—anything that we might profitably utilize in present-day planning for the decades ahead? Because our planet and its resources are finite, at some point our society must expect to shift progressively from exponential growth toward an overall global equilibrium. By that term, we mean the setting of maximal levels on the number of humans who can inhabit this planet with an assured minimal standard of life and on the exploitation of the earth's resources required to provide that standard. Otherwise, environmental disaster on an unprecedented scale could result in the decades ahead. Past and present conjoin to alert us to the need to engage in new forms of planning for the years ahead and also to the need to rethink our existing social goals and value systems. We need as long and as accurate a perspective as possible to make realistic analyses and to take the proper actions to improve our quality of life.

THE "HOW" OF HISTORY

History is the record of the past actions of humankind, based on surviving evidence. History shows that all patterns and problems in human affairs are the products of a complex process of growth. By throwing light on that process, history provides a means for profiting from human experience.

History as a Science

There is more than one way to treat the past. In dealing with the American Revolution, for example, the historian may describe its events in narrative form or, instead, analyze its general causes and compare its stages with the patterns of revolutions in other countries. Unlike the scientist who attempts to verify hypotheses by repeating experiments under controlled conditions in the laboratory and to classify phenomena in a general group or category, the historian has to pay special attention to the *uniqueness* of data, because each event takes place at a particular time and in a particular place. And since that time is now past, conclusions cannot be verified by duplicating the circumstances in which the event occurred.

Nevertheless, historians insist that history be written as scientifically as possible and that evidence be analyzed with the same objective attitude employed by the scientist examining natural phenomena. This scientific spirit requires historians to handle evidence according to established rules of historical analysis, to recognize biases and attempt to eliminate their effects, and to draw only such conclusions as the evidence seems to warrant.

The Historical Method

To meet these requirements, historians have evolved the "historical method." The first step is the search for *sources*, which may be material remains, oral traditions, pictorial data, or written records. From the source the historian must infer the facts. This process has two parts. *External criticism* tests the genuineness of the source. In *internal criticism* the historian evaluates the source to ascertain the author's meaning and the accuracy of the work.

The final step in the historical method is *synthesis*. Here the historian must determine which factors in a given situation are most relevant to the purpose at hand, since obviously not everything that occurred can be included. This delicate process of selection underscores the role

that subjectivity plays in the writing of history. Furthermore, the more complex the events involved, the more crucial becomes the historian's judgment.[2]

Periodization

Can we really categorize history as "ancient," "medieval," or "modern"? Clearly, what is "modern" in the twentieth century could conceivably be considered "medieval" in the twenty-fifth century, and eventually "ancient" in the thirty-fifth century A.D. Yet not to break up the account would be akin to reading this book without the benefit of parts, chapters, paragraphs, or even separate sentences. Like time itself, history would then become a ceaseless flow of consciousness and events. To simplify the task and to manage materials more easily, the historian divides time into periods. The divisions chosen and the lines drawn reveal the distinctive way in which the historian regards the past—namely, in terms of patterns that seem logical and meaningful.

THE "WHY" OF HISTORY

The historian seeks to describe not only *what* has happened and *how* it happened, but also *why* society undergoes change. Any search of this kind raises a number of fundamental questions: the roles of Providence, the individual, and the group in history; the extent to which events are unique or, conversely, can fit into patterns; and the problem of progress in human affairs. The answers vary with different philosophical views of the universe and the human role therein.

Those who hold the teleological view see in history the guidance of a Divine Will, directing human destinies according to a cosmic purpose. Other thinkers have exalted the role of the individual in the historical process—such as Thomas Carlyle, who contended that major figures chiefly determined the course of human events. Opponents of Carlyle's thesis often contend that history is determined by "forces" and "laws" and by the actions of entire societies. Sociologists approach history primarily by analyzing the origins, institutions, and functions of groups. Economists tend to look at the historical record from the standpoint of group action and especially the impact of economic forces.

To Karl Marx irresistible economic forces governed human beings and determined the trend of events. Marx contended that the shift from one economic stage to another—such as the shift from feudalism to capitalism—is attained by upheavals, or revolutions, which occur because the class controlling the methods of production eventually resists further progress in order to maintain its vested interests.

Numerous other attempts have been made to explain societal processes according to a set of principles. Oswald Spengler maintained that civilizations were like organisms; each grew with the "superb aimlessness" of a flower and passed through a cycle of spring, summer, autumn, and winter. Charles Darwin's evolutionary hypothesis made a strong impact on nineteenth-century thought and gave rise to the concept that the principle of "survival of the fittest" must also apply to human societies. This line of thought—known as social Darwinism—raises social and ethical questions of major importance.

Does history obey impersonal laws and forces so that its course is inevitable? Or, at the other extreme, since every event is a unique act, is history simply the record of unforeseen and unrelated episodes? Can this apparent dilemma be avoided? We believe it can. Although all events are, in various respects, unique, they also contain elements that invite comparison. The comparative approach permits us to seek relationships between historical phenomena and to group them into movements or patterns or civilizations. We eschew any "theory" of history, preferring to see merit in a number of basic concepts. These include the effects of physical environment on social organization and institutions; the roles played by economic, political, and religious factors; and the impact exerted by men and women occupying key positions in various societies.

THE CHALLENGE OF HISTORY

Progress and growth is a continuous factor. It depends on, and contributes to, the maintenance of peace and security, the peaceful settlement of international disputes, and worldwide improvement in economic and social standards. Surely an indispensable step toward solving contemporary humanity's dilemma—technology without the requisite control and power without commensurate wisdom—must be a better understanding of how the world and its people came to be what they are today. Only by understanding the past can we assess both the perils and the opportunities of the present—and move courageously and compassionately into the future.

NOTES

1. David G. Mandelbaum, "Concepts of Civilization and Culture," *Encyclopaedia Britannica*, 1967 ed., Vol. 5, p. 831A.
2. See P. Gardiner, *The Nature of Historical Explanation* (London: Oxford University Press, 1952), p. 98.

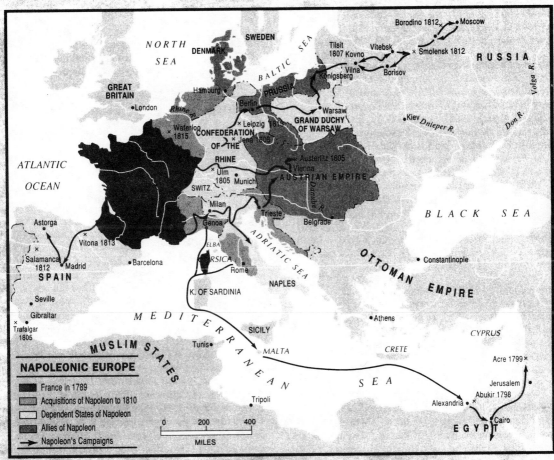

NAPOLEONIC EUROPE

- ■ France in 1789
- ■ Acquisitions of Napoleon to 1810
- □ Dependent States of Napoleon
- ■ Allies of Napoleon
- → Napoleon's Campaigns

0 200 400
MILES

→ Napoleon combined the military advances of the *Ancien Régime* and the unleashed democratic forces of the Revolution to achieve in ten years what Louis XIV had failed to accomplish in a half-century, the domination of Europe.

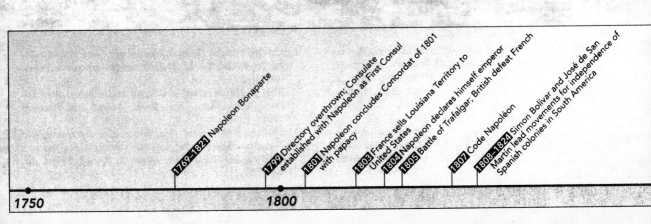

1769–1821 Napoleon Bonaparte

1799 Directory overthrown; Consulate established with Napoleon as First Consul

1801 Napoleon concludes Concordat of 1801 with papacy

1803 France sells Louisiana Territory to United States

1804 Napoleon declares himself emperor

1805 Battle of Trafalgar; British defeat French

1807 Code Napoléon

1808–1824 Simon Bolívar and José de San Martín lead movements for independence of Spanish colonies in South America

1750   1800

The Napoleonic World Revolution, 1800–1825

Even as a student, Napoleon considered himself to be a man of destiny, and he worked hard to construct the image he wanted to project to the future. As soon as the ship carrying him to exile in St. Helena set sail, his partisans and detractors began the debate over his career that continues to the present day. Whatever the viewpoint of the participants in that debate, all—with rare exceptions—agree that few people have as decisively affected their times and set in motion developments that so profoundly altered the future as Napoleon Bonaparte.

He spread the values of the French Revolution throughout the Continent as his armies marched through Europe, even as he stifled them in France. Through his military and political policies he set in motion the major social and political upheavals that dominated the nineteenth century. By his foreign policies he inaugurated modern Latin American history and enabled the United States to double in size. He rearranged the Holy Roman Empire and set in motion the development of modern Germany. The breadth and nature of his conquests sparked the growth of modern nationalism throughout the Continent. His economic policies changed

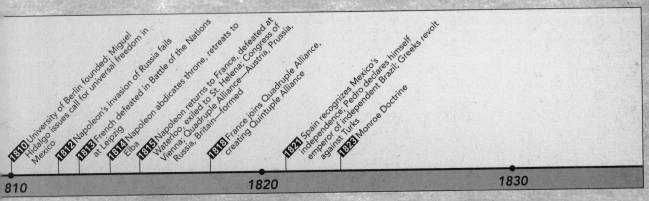

1810 University of Berlin founded; Miguel Hidalgo issues call for universal freedom in Mexico

1812 Napoleon's invasion of Russia fails

1813 French defeated in Battle of the Nations at Leipzig

1814 Napoleon abdicates throne, retreats to Elba

1815 Napoleon returns to France, defeated at Waterloo, exiled to St. Helena; Congress of Vienna; Quadruple Alliance—Austria, Prussia, Russia, Britain—formed

1818 France joins Quadruple Alliance, creating Quintuple Alliance

1821 Spain recognizes Mexico's independence; Pedro declares himself emperor of independent Brazil; Greeks revolt against Turks

1823 Monroe Doctrine

810   1820   1830

the flow of capital and stimulated industrialization in Britain and economic reform throughout Europe.

NAPOLEON AND FRANCE

Revolutions favor the bright, the ambitious, and the lucky. Napoleon Bonaparte (1769–1821) had all three qualities in abundance. He was born in Corsica to a low-ranking Florentine noble family in 1769—the year after control of that island passed from Genoa to France. At the age of ten his father placed him in the military academy at Brienne. Six years later he received his officer's commission. At the beginning of the French Revolution he was a 20-year-old officer doomed by his family's modest standing and the restrictions of the Old Regime to a mediocre future. Ten years later, he ruled France. The revolution gave him the opportunity to use his brains, ability, charm, and daring to rise rapidly.

A potent mixture of eighteenth-century rationalism, romanticism, and revolutionary politics dominated his thought. He learned constantly, reading the classics, absorbing Enlightenment tracts, and constantly talking to people who could teach him. As an outsider from Corsica, he was tied to no particular faction in France and pursued his own interests with a fresh point of view. He drew close first to the men of 1789, then to the Jacobins, and later to the Directory. Never did he allow control of his fate to escape from his own hands, pragmatically choosing whatever political, social, or religious option that could serve his goals.[1]

He never doubted that fate had chosen him to accomplish great things. Equipped with a vast reserve of energy to match his enormous ego, Napoleon worked and studied ceaselessly, running on very little sleep. He was disciplined in his use of time and gifted in public relations skills. He pitched his messages and dreams to all levels of society and had the ability to inspire and gain the maximum sacrifice from his nation and his armies.

The Opportunist

Napoleon came at the right time—a generation earlier or later and the situation would not have allowed him to gain power. He took advantage of the gutting of the old officer class by the revolutionary wars and the Jacobins to rise quickly to a prominent position from which he could appeal to the Directory. That self-interested group of survivors asked the Corsican to break up a right-wing uprising in October 1795. The following year the Directory gave Napoleon command of the smallest of the three armies sent to do battle with the Austrians.

The two larger forces crossed the Rhine on their way to attack the Habsburgs while Napoleon's corps went over the Alps into Italy as a diversionary move. Contrary to plan, the main forces did little while Napoleon, who was supposed to be no more than bait, crushed the Sardinians and then the Austrians in a brilliant series of campaigns. As he marched across northern Italy he picked off Venice and was well on the road to Vienna where the Austrians approached him to make peace. Without instructions from his government, Napoleon negotiated the Treaty of Campo Formio (1797) and returned home a hero.

→ This heroic portrait by Antoine Jean Gros shows the 27-year-old Napoleon leading his troops at the battle of Arcola in northern Italy in November 1796.

After considering an invasion of Britain in the first part of 1798—a cross-Channel task he deemed impossible—Napoleon set out with the Directory's blessing to strike at Britain's economy by attacking its colonial structure. He would invade Egypt, expose the weakness of the Ottoman Empire, and from there launch an attack on India. The politicians were as much impressed by this grand plan as they were relieved to get the increasingly popular Napoleon out of town. He successfully evaded the British fleet in the Mediterranean, landed in Egypt, and took Alexandria and Cairo in July. The British Admiral Horatio Nelson (1758–1805) found the French fleet and sank it at Aboukir on August 1, 1798. Even though their supply lines and access to France were cut off, Napoleon's forces fought a number of successful battles against the Turks in Syria and Egypt.[2]

However, the fact remained that the French armies were stranded in Egypt and would be forced to remain there until 1801, when a truce allowed them to come home. This development would normally be regarded as a defeat, yet when Napoleon abandoned his army in August 1799, slipped by the British fleet, and returned to Paris, he was given a frenzied, triumphant homecoming. In public appearances, he adopted a modest pose and gave addresses on the scientific accomplishments of the expedition, such as the finding of the Rosetta stone, a discovery which provided the first clue in the deciphering of Egyptian hieroglyphics.

Napoleon, his brothers, and the Abbé Sieyès sought to take advantage of the political crisis surrounding the Directory. A coalition including Russia, Great Britain, Austria, Naples, Portugal, and the Ottoman Empire threatened France from the outside, while a feverlike inflation ravaged the economy domestically. Various political factions courted Napoleon, whose charisma made him appear to be the likely savior of the country. In the meantime, he and his confederates planned their course. They launched a clumsy, though successful, coup in November 1799 and replaced the Directory with the Consulate. The plotters shared the cynical belief that "constitutions should be short and obscure" and that the nature of democracy consisted of the fact that the rulers rule, and the people obey.

The takeover ended the revolutionary decade. France remained, in theory, a republic, but nearly all power rested with the 31-year-old Napoleon, who ruled as first Consul. Still another constitution was written and submitted to a vote of the people. Only half of the eligible voters went to the polls, but an overwhelming majority voted in favor of the new constitution: 3,011,007 in favor versus 1,526 against.[3]

France to 1804: New Foundations

Ten years of radical change made France ready for one-man rule—but of a type much different from that exercised by the Bourbon monarchy. The events of 1789 had overturned the source of legitimate political power. It no longer came from God, but from the people. The social structure of the Old Regime was gone and with it the privileges of hereditary and created nobility. The Church no longer had financial or overt political power. The old struggles between kings and nobles, nobles and bourgeoisie, peasants and landlords, and Catholics and Protestants were replaced by the rather more universal confrontation between rich and poor.

Ten years of revolution had seen three attempts to rebuild the French system: the bourgeois-constitutional efforts to 1791; the radical programs to 1794; and the rule to 1799 by survivors who feared both the right and the left. Although each attempt had failed, each left valuable legacies to the new France. The first attempt established the power of the upper middle classes; the second showed the great power of the state to mobilize the population; and the third demonstrated the usefulness of employing former enemies in day-to-day politics.

Being the pragmatic tactician that he was, Napoleon used elements from the Old Regime and the various phases of the revolution to reconstruct France. He built an autocracy far more powerful than Louis XVI's government. He took advantage of the absence of old forms of competition to central power from the nobility and the feudal structure that had been destroyed in the name of liberty, equality, and fraternity. He used the mercantile policies, military theories, and foreign policy goals of the Old Regime, the ambitions of the middle class, and the mobilization policies of the

Jacobins. All he asked from those who wished to serve him was loyalty. Defrocked priests, renegade former nobles, reformed Jacobins, small business-men, and enthusiastic soldiers all played a role. His unquestioning acceptance of the ambitious brought him popularity because ten years of constant change had compromised most politically active people in some form of unprincipled, immoral, or illegal behavior.

Napoleon built his state on the *philosophes'* conception of a system in which all French men would be equal before the law. The revolution destroyed the sense of personal power of a sovereign and substituted what the British historian Lord Acton would later in the century call the "tyranny of the majority." The French state accordingly could intervene more effectively than ever before, limited only by distance and communications problems.[4]

The mass democratic army created by the total mobilization of both people and resources was one of the best examples of the new state system. A revolutionary society had fought an ideological war, and the experience changed the nature of combat forever. Because advancement and success were based on valor and victory, rather than bloodlines or privilege, the army profited from the new social structure and sought to preserve and extend it. The army best symbolized the great power of the French nation unleashed by the Revolution. Many of the economic and diplomatic problems that preceded the Revolution remained, but Napoleon's new state structure provided inspired solutions.

Taking advantage of his military supremacy, Napoleon gained breathing space for his domestic reforms by making peace with the Second Coalition by March 1802. He then set about erecting the governing structure of France that remains with few changes to this day. He developed an administration that was effective in raising money, assembling an army, and exploiting the country's resources. His centralized government ruled through prefects, powerful agents in the provinces who had almost complete control of local affairs and were supported by a large police force. He then established a stable monetary policy based on an honest tax-collecting system, backed by up-to-date accounting procedures. The Bank of France that he created remains an institution regarded as a model of sound finance.

Napoleon knew that the country he ruled was overwhelmingly Catholic and that national interest dictated that he come to terms with the papacy. Through the Concordat of 1801 with Pope Pius VII the pope gained the right to approve the bishops whom the First Consul appointed to the reestablished Catholic Church. The state permitted seminaries to be reopened and paid priests' salaries. Pius regained control of the Papal States and saw his church recognized as the "religion of the majority of Frenchmen." The Church thus resumed its position of prominence, but without its former power and wealth.

Napoleon viewed education as a way to train useful citizens to become good soldiers and bureaucrats, and he pursued the development of mass education by trying to increase the number of elementary schools, *lycées* (secondary schools), and special institutes for technical training. The schools were to be used to propagandize the young to serve the state through "directing political and moral opinion." Overarching the entire system was the University of France, which was more an administrative body to control education than a teaching institution. Napoleon had neither the time nor the resources to put mass education in place during his lifetime, although he did gain immediate success in training the sons of the newly arrived middle classes to become state functionaries.[5]

Perhaps Napoleon's greatest accomplishment came in the field of law. Building on reforms begun ten years earlier, he put a talented team of lawyers to work to bring order to the chaotic state of French jurisprudence. At the time he took power the country was caught in the transition from the old legal system of 366 separate local systems to a uniform code. By 1804, the staff had compiled a comprehensive Civil Law Code (called the Code Napoléon after 1807) that was a model of precision and equality when compared to the old system. The Code ensured the continuation of the gains made by the middle classes in the previous decade and emphasized religious toleration and the abolition of the privileges held under the old order. Unfortunately, the Code perpetuated the inferior status of women in the areas of civil rights, financial activities, and divorce. Nonetheless it has served as the basis for law codes in many other countries.

The price France paid for all of this was rule by police state that featured censorship, secret police, spies, and political trials, which sent hundreds to their deaths and thousands into exile. Order did prevail, however, and for the first time in ten years it was safe to travel the country's roads. Napoleon also reduced the "representative assemblies" to meaningless rubber stamps. Liberty, equality, and fraternity meant little in a land where the First Consul and his police could deny a person's freedom and right of association because of a perceived intellectual or political conflict.

To consolidate all of the changes, Napoleon proclaimed himself emperor in December 1804. Fifteen years after the outbreak of the revolution, France had a new monarch. The nation approved the change in a plebiscite by 3,572,329 to 2,579. As Napoleon took the crown from Pope Pius VII, who had come from Rome for the occasion, and crowned himself, the First French Republic came to an end.

→ The artist Jacques Louis David, an ardent admirer of Napoleon, painted several pictures glorifying him. This is a preliminary sketch for David's coronation painting of the emperor.

NAPOLEON AND THE WORLD

Since 1792, war had been France's primary occupation, and on the whole it had been a profitable one. The French had gained much land and money, as well as the opportunity to export the Revolution. Napoleon's reforms helped make his country even stronger in battle. At the end of 1804 Napoleon embarked on a series of campaigns designed to show France's invincibility. A key to French success was the emperor himself, who employed his own remarkable genius to lead his strong and wealthy country.

Military Superiority

Napoleon brought equal parts of intellectual strength, sensitivity to mood and opportunity, and undoubted bravery to the task of making war. He had been trained in the most advanced methods of his day, and he had better, more mobile artillery and more potent powder to blow holes through the enemy's lines. He worked well with a talented command staff to which he gave much responsibility to wield their divisions as conditions dictated. Finally, he was the ultimate leader. Whether as lieutenant, general, first consul, or emperor, Napoleon inspired masses of soldiers in a dramatic way. At the same time he mobilized the home front through the use of the press and skillfully written dispatches.

Beneath this image making, the supreme commander was extremely flexible in his use of resources, always changing his tactics. He was pragmatic, moved rapidly, and lived off the land—until the Russian campaign. He won the loyalty of his men by incentives and rewards, not brutal discipline. He set many military precedents, among them the use of ideological and economic warfare as well as the rapid simultaneous movement of a large number of columns. These columns could quickly converge on a given point with devastating results, breaking the will of the enemy. Finally, he personally led his troops into battle, exposing himself to incredible dangers with little regard for his own safety.[6]

His nemesis was Great Britain, and during 1803 and 1804 he prepared a cross-Channel invasion, but the inability of the French navy to control the Channel and the formation of the Third Coalition (Great Britain, Russia, Austria, and

Sweden) forced him to march eastward. In October 1805 Admiral Nelson and the British ended Napoleon's hopes of dominating the seas by destroying the joint French-Spanish fleet at the Battle of Trafalgar.

France did far better on land, gaining mastery over the Continent by the end of 1807. Napoleon totally demoralized the Third Coalition in the battles at Ulm (October 1805) and Austerlitz (December 1805). He then annihilated the Prussians who had entered the conflict in the battles at Jena and Auerstadt (October 1806). He occupied Berlin, where he established the Continental System, a blockade of the Continent that was an effort to defeat Britain by depriving it of trade with the rest of Europe. Finally in June 1807, he defeated the Russians at the battle of Friedland and forced Tsar Alexander I to sign the Tilsit Treaty in July. This treaty, ratified on a raft anchored in the middle of the Nieman River, brought the two major land powers of Europe together in an alliance against Britain.

At the beginning of 1808 Napoleon stood supreme in Europe, leading France to a dominance it had never experienced before or since. Several of his relatives occupied the thrones of nearby countries. The rest of the continent appeared to be mere satellites revolving around the Napoleonic sun.[7]

Napoleon's Revolution in Europe

As he achieved his military goals, Napoleon set in motion a chain reaction of mini-revolutions that had a profound impact on the rest of the century. British sea power stood in the way of France's total mastery of the Continent. Even though their economy suffered under the impact of the Continental System (exports dropped by 20 percent with a resultant cutback in production and rise in unemployment), the damage was not permanent. The Continental System inadvertently contributed to Britain's economic development by forcing it to industrialize quickly as it sought new markets and methods. Safe behind their wall of ships, the British turned out increasing quantities of goods as they passed through the early phases of industrialization.

Napoleon's armies carried French ideological baggage and institutional reforms with them across the Continent. Even though the emperor consolidated the Revolution in a conservative way in France, he broke apart his opponents' fragile social and governmental structures when he marched across the Rhine. Napoleon consciously spread the messages of liberty, fraternity, and equality with all of the antifeudal, antiprivilege, and antirepressive themes inherent in the revolutionary triad. Where the French governed directly, they used the Code Napoléon and the reformed administrative practices. After 1815 the changes may have been repressed by the restored governments, but they set the precedents that bore fruit throughout most of Europe by 1848.

The French presence triggered a hostile wave. Many Europeans saw Napoleon as an imperialist, and the people he had "emancipated" began to realize that they had exchanged an old for a new form of despotism. By posing as the champion of the Revolution, Napoleon sowed the seeds of the opposition that would work against him later, especially in Prussia. With the exception of the Poles, who had labored under Russian dominance and now served Napoleon well, the rest of Europe reacted against the French yoke.

The most significant rebellion took place in Portugal and Spain. His entry into those countries to topple the passive Bourbons and strengthen the leaky Continental System was uncharacteristically shortsighted. Napoleon had a serious fight on his hands in the Peninsular War that followed. Guerrilla uprisings soon broke out, supported by a British expeditionary force and supplies. These bloody wars tied down from 200,000 to 300,000 French troops over a period of five years and drained the French treasury. The invasion of Spain also prompted a series of uprisings in the New World that gave birth to modern Latin American history.

The social and political changes the French triggered in Germany were equally profound. When he redrew the map of Europe after his victories, Napoleon destroyed the remnants of the Holy Roman Empire, and in so doing erased 112 states of that ancient league. Only six of the former 50 free cities retained their status. Further, by changing the territorial arrangements of other areas, he reduced the number of German political units from more than 300 to 39. The historian Hajo Holborn wrote that "it was the French invasion and the rule of Napoleon that finally led German intellectuals to the problem of the state." All over Germany a wave of nationalism stirred the politically conscious population and prepared the way for the liberation movement. Prussia in particular underwent a rebirth after 1806 to enable it to compete with France, and many German nationalists thereafter began to look to Berlin for strength and leadership. Prussian reform politicians such as Baron Heinrich vom und zum Stein (1757–1831) and Prince Karl von Hardenberg (1750–1822) initiated a program of social change that included the abolition of serfdom—without turning land over to the peasants—a degree of self-government in the cities, and emancipation of the Jews. Although Napoleon had limited the Prussian army to 42,000 men, the Berlin authorities undermined this restriction by a subterfuge—as soon as one army was trained it was placed on reserve and a new army was called up for training. In this way Prussia managed to build a force of 270,000 men. These efforts gained the support of Prussian intellectuals who used education as a means of nationalistic propaganda. The University of Berlin, founded in 1810, became a strong center for national movements.[8]

The Invasion of Russia

Opposition to Napoleon grew in both Austria and Russia. After the valiant but unsuccessful campaigns against the French in 1809, culminating in the bloody battle of Wagram, Vienna became a docile though not a dependable ally. Napoleon's marriage to Marie Louise, the daughter of Francis I of Austria, proved to be only a tenuous tie between the French emperor and the Habsburgs. In Russia, the Tilsit Treaty had never been popular, and the economic hardships brought on by the Continental System made a break in the alliance virtually inevitable. By the end of 1810 France and Russia prepared to go to war against one another.

Napoleon understood the shaky base on which his dominance rested. Involvement in Spain had drained France. The Continental System was not working against Britain. Alexander I proved to be an increasingly undependable ally. Finally, after two years of preparations, Napoleon launched a massive invasion of Russia in 1812 to put an end to at least one of his problems.

The emperor prepared carefully for his attack on Russia. Food supply would be a major problem for the 611,000 troops in the first and second lines of the invasion because his forces would be too large to live off the land. Furthermore the French troops took with them over 200,000 animals, which required forage and water. The invasion force delayed its march until late June to ensure that the Russian plains would furnish sufficient grass to feed the animals. The well-thought-out, massive preparations for the invasion proved inadequate to the problems posed by the 600-mile march from the Nieman River to Moscow.

Although Napoleon's 12-nation army made almost constant headway, the Russian forces remained intact. Because they were outnumbered nearly three to one, the tsar's armies under the leadership of General Barclay de Tolly (1761–1818) and later General Mikhail Kutuzov (1745–1813) continually retreated into the vastness of their land rather than face almost certain defeat at the hands of the invaders. The Russians destroyed everything of possible use to Napoleon's forces—the so-called scorched earth policy—continually harassed the advancing columns, and threatened the French supply lines. When the Russians finally stood their ground at Borodino (September 7, 1812), the effects of distance and disease had taken their toll among the French, and the numbers of the opposing forces were nearly equal. After a brutal conflict in which 75,000 of the total 200,000 combatants were left dead or wounded, the road to Moscow was open to the victorious French.

The Russian campaign was both a success and a failure for Napoleon. The French did gain their objective—the former capital city of Moscow—but the Russians refused to surrender. Shortly after the French occupied Moscow, fires broke out, destroying three-fourths of the city. After spending 33 days in the burned shell of the former capital waiting in vain for the tsar, who was 400 miles north in St. Petersburg, to agree to peace, Napoleon gave orders to retreat. He left the city on October 19. To remain would have meant having his lines cut by winter and being trapped with no supplies. His isolation in Moscow would have encouraged his enemies in Paris. Leaving the city, as it turned out, condemned most of his men to death.[9]

As the remnant of Napoleon's forces marched west in October and November, they were forced to retrace virtually the same route they had used in the summer. They suffered the attacks of the roving bands of partisans, starvation, and the continual pressure of Kutuzov's forces. Thousands perished daily, and by the end of November only about 100,000 of the original force had made

➔ An engraving commemorating the signing of the Treaty of Tilsit by Napoleon and Tsar Alexander I of Russia after the French defeated the Russians at the battle of Friedland in June 1807. The two monarchs conducted their negotiations on a lavishly equipped barge moored midstream in the Nieman River. The peace they concluded failed to last, and Napoleon's invasion of Russia in 1812 did not end as successfully for the French as had the battle of Friedland.

their escape from Russia. Thirteen years earlier Napoleon had abandoned an army in Egypt to return to Paris. In November 1812 he abandoned another army, this time in Russia, and returned home to pursue his fortunes.

Napoleon's Defeat

Russia, which had stood alone against the French at the beginning of 1812, was soon joined by Prussia, Austria, and Britain in 1813 and 1814 in what came to be known as the "War of Liberation." While British armies under the Duke of Wellington (1769–1852) helped clear the French forces out of Spain, the allied troops pushed Napoleon's forces westward. A combination of Napoleon's genius and the difficulties in coordinating the allied efforts prolonged the war, but in October 1813 the French suffered a decisive defeat at Leipzig in the Battle of the Nations, one year to the day after Napoleon had fled Moscow.

The allies sent peace offers to Napoleon, but he refused them, pointing out that "you sovereigns who were born to the throne may get beaten 20 times, and yet return to your capitals. I cannot. For I rose to power through the camp."[10] After Leipzig the Napoleonic empire rapidly disintegrated, and by the beginning of 1814 the allies had crossed the Rhine and invaded France. At the end of March, the Russians, Austrians, and

Prussians took Paris. Two weeks later Napoleon abdicated his throne, receiving in return sovereignty over Elba, a small island between Corsica and Italy.

Napoleon arrived in Elba in May and established his rule over his 85-square-mile kingdom. He set up a mini-state, complete with an army, navy, and court. Boredom soon set in and in February 1815 he eluded the British fleet and returned to France. His former subjects, bored with the restored Bourbon, Louis XVIII, gave him a tumultuous welcome. Napoleon entered Paris and raised an army of 300,000 men and sent a message to the allies gathered to make peace at Vienna that he desired to rule France and only France. The allies, who were on the verge of breaking up their alliance, united, condemned Napoleon as an enemy of peace, and sent forces to France to put him down once and for all.

At the Battle of Waterloo on June 18, 1815, the Duke of Wellington, supported by Prussian troops under Field Marshall Gebhard von Blücher (1749–1819), narrowly defeated Napoleon. The vanquished leader sought asylum with the British, hoping to live in exile either in England or the United States. But the allies, taking no chances, shipped him off to the bleak south Atlantic island of St. Helena, 5000 miles from Paris. Here he set about writing his autobiography. He died of cancer in 1821 at the age of 51.

Even with the brief flurry of the One Hundred Days, Napoleon had no hope of re-creating the grandeur of his empire as it was in 1808. The reasons for this are not hard to find. Quite simply, Napoleon was the heart and soul of the empire, and after 1808 his physical and intellectual vigor began to weaken. Administrative and military developments reflected this deterioration, as Napoleon began to appoint sycophants to positions of responsibility. Further, by 1812 the middle classes on whom he depended began suffering the economic consequences of his policies. The Continental System and continual warfare made their effects deeply felt through decreased trade and increased taxes. Even though some war contractors profited, the costs of Napoleon's ambitions began to make Frenchmen long for peace.

Outside France, the growth of national resistance on the Continent worked against the dictator who first stimulated it by exporting the call for liberty, equality, and fraternity. Equally important, the 25 years of French military superiority disappeared as other nations adopted and improved on the new methods of fighting. Finally, the balance of power principle made itself felt. France could not eternally take on the whole world.

Napoleon and the Americas

The forces generated by the French Revolution and Napoleon deeply affected the Americas in the 50 years after 1776. The former English colonies south of Canada had gained their independence with French assistance and the new government had close relations with Paris until the outbreak of the revolutionary wars, when President George Washington proclaimed neutrality. When relations with the British began to improve during the 1790s, the French waged a virtual war on American shipping, taking over 800 ships in the last three years of the century. The United States benefitted from one aspect of Napoleon's activities. In 1803, the emperor sold the region known as Louisiana for $15 million;

Napoleon on His Place in History

In his conversations with the Count de Las Cases, Napoleon clearly expressed *his* notion of his place in history.

"I closed the gulf of anarchy and cleared the chaos. I purified the Revolution, dignified Nations and established Kings. I excited every kind of emulation, rewarded every kind of merit, and extended the limits of glory! This is at least something! And on what point can I be assailed on which an historian could not defend me? Can it be for my intentions? But even here I can find absolution. Can it be for my despotism? It may be demonstrated that the Dictatorship was absolutely necessary. Will it be said that I restrained liberty? It can be proved that licentiousness, anarchy, and the greatest irregularities, still haunted the threshold of freedom. Shall I be accused of having been too fond of war? It can be shown that I always received the first attack. Will it be said that I aimed at universal monarchy? It can be proved that this was merely the result of fortuitous circumstances, and that our enemies themselves led me step by step to this determination. Lastly, shall I be blamed for my ambition? This passion I must doubtless be allowed to have possessed, and that in no small degree; but at the same time, my ambition was of the highest and noblest kind that ever, perhaps, existed—that of establishing and of consecrating the empire of reason, and the full exercise and complete enjoyment of all the human faculties!"

And here the historian will probably feel compelled to regret that such ambition should not have been fulfilled and gratified! Then after a few moments of silent reflection: "This," said the Emperor, "is my whole history in a few words."

From *Memoirs of the Life, Exile, and Conversations of the Emperor Napoleon*, edited by the Count de Las Cases. (New York: Eckler, 1900).

this Louisiana Purchase increased the land area of the new country by 200 percent. Unfortunately, the United States suffered considerable commercial losses as it became caught up in the French-British conflict.

The French overthrow of the Spanish Bourbons in 1808 encouraged the revolts that created 13 republics in Spanish America by 1824. The charismatic leader who stepped into the void was Simon Bolívar (1783–1830), hailed as "the Liberator" of South America. After completing his rationalist education in Paris during the last years of the Directory, he returned to his native Venezuela to exploit colonial resistance to the Napoleonic takeover of Spain in 1808. Convinced after the disaster at Trafalgar that transatlantic ambitions were pointless, Napoleon left the Spanish colonial empire to its own complex fate.[11]

Loyal at first to the deposed Spanish Bourbons and newly filled with refugees from the parent country, Spain's colonies soon began to entertain the idea that they had their own destinies to fulfill as new nations. The American-born elite of European blood, the *Creoles*, were especially attracted to the prospect of expelling the controlling *peninsulares*, Spaniards of European birth who usually returned to Spain after a profitable term of colonial service.[12]

Bolívar stepped into this situation by issuing a series of inflammatory and visionary messages calling for the liberation of Venezuela and of a larger unit then called Gran Colombia (modern-day Colombia, Panama, Ecuador, and Venezuela), which he hoped would expand to include all of Spanish South America. He was frequently defeated by Spanish loyalist forces, yet he kept fighting and made use of skills as an orator and as a tactician. He eventually forced the remnants of the Spanish military and administrative personnel to go home. He proposed a constitution that favored the elite of the new nations, a document that was much like the one written by the Directory. He dreamed of a continental state split into the nation-states of Venezuela, Colombia, Ecuador, Peru, and Bolivia, but he ran afoul of liberal critics and regional loyalties and eventually died in exile in British Jamaica.

Argentina, Uruguay, and Chile were liberated in comparable fashion by the stoic, Spanish-educated Creole officer José de San Martín (1778–1850) who was as austere and reserved as Bolívar was flashy and outgoing. The two could never forge an alliance, partly because of personality differences and partly because of San Martín's preference for a constitutional monarchy like that of Britain or the French Constitution of

→ Simon Bolívar and his army battle the Spanish at Araure in Venezuela. Although the Spanish were better trained and equipped, Bolívar led his soldiers with such personal valor that he managed to liberate four countries.

THE AMERICAS
1800–1826

Louisiana Purchase

UNITED KINGDOM

UNITED STATES

ATLANTIC
OCEAN

Colorado R.

Rio Grande

GULF OF
MEXICO

MEXICO

CUBA (Sp.)   Hispaniola

BR. HONDURAS HAITI   PUERTO RICO
                        (Sp.)

UNITED PROVS. OF   Mosquito Coast   GUIANA
CENTRAL AMERICA   (Br.)   (Dutch)

VENEZUELA   (Fr.)

COLOMBIA

GALAPAGOS IS.

ECUADOR   Amazon R.

PACIFIC
OCEAN

PERU   EMPIRE OF
Lima   BRAZIL

Paraguay R.
Paraná R.

PARAGUAY

ARGENTINE
CONFEDERATION

CHILE   Buenos   URUGUAY
        Aires

Patagonia

1000   2000

MILES

ISLAS MALVINAS
(Arg.)

The Mexican revolution began earlier and produced more extreme consequences than its South American counterpart. The Mexican middle class was even smaller than that of the rest of Spanish America and far more conservative. Between 1808 and 1810 anti-Bonapartist sentiment shifted to a general rejection of the European monarchy in Creole circles throughout the vice-royalty of New Spain.

The revolution was actually begun by an enlightened provincial Creole priest, Miguel Hidalgo (1753–1811), who on September 16, 1810, issued a call for universal freedom (the date is celebrated in Mexico today as the *Dia del Grito*, the Day of the Call). Hidalgo led his ragged army of Indians and idealists to the gates of Mexico City but hesitated to take the city fearing the bloodbath that would follow. Although Hidalgo was condemned by the colonial bishops and executed for treason six months after his uprising began, his cause was taken up by others, including José Maria Morelos (1765–1815), a radical *mestizo* (mixed-blood) parish priest who became an effective guerrilla leader. Finally, in August 1821, the last Spanish viceroy recognized the independence of Mexico, whose ruling classes promptly fell to squabbling over the constitution.

While men of ideas argued, military opportunists took power. Two would-be Napoleons, Augustín de Iturbide (1783–1824) and Antonio López de Santa Anna (1794–1876), dominated politics for the next quarter-century, at the end of which Mexico lost the northern half of its territory to the United States. Iturbide, a Creole landowner and officer who had fought as a Spanish loyalist until 1816, became emperor of Mexico for a turbulent ten-month reign in 1822–1823. Santa Anna, who emulated Napoleon's opportunism more successfully than many of the Frenchman's other qualities, became president or dictator of the Mexican republic 11 times between 1833 and 1855. His career as a military leader included several disastrous incidents, notably his humiliating defeat and capture by Texan rebels at San Jacinto in April 1836—six weeks after he had exterminated their comrades at the secularized Franciscan mission in San Antonio known as the Alamo and a month after he had mercilessly massacred Texan prisoners at Goliad.[13]

1791. The Spanish colonies he had freed rejected his desires, but the Portuguese in Brazil accepted them. King John VI of Portugal had fled his country in 1807 and ruled the Portuguese empire from Rio de Janeiro for the next 14 years. Returning to Lisbon in 1821, the king left his son Dom Pedro as regent of Brazil. Impatient with the reactionary behavior of the Lisbon government, Pedro declared himself emperor of an independent Brazil, which he and his son Pedro II ruled as a constitutional monarchy for nearly seventy years.

The social and economic consequences of the Latin American revolutions were far different from those in North America and Europe. The area was much poorer and more divided. The new nations of Latin America quickly fell to the commercial dominance of the British Empire. Their economies, exploited by speculators in North America and Europe, have been subject to drastic fluctuations ever since, based as they are on exportation of raw materials. The conditions of the Indian population declined as the new liberal regimes confiscated the large landholdings of the religious orders, which had served to insulate the surviving Indians from direct confrontations with the Europeans' economic and technological dominance. As in every country since the Reformation where Church property was bought up by the monied classes, the local population was reorganized into a new labor force more profitable to the new owners. In this case, the owners simply reorganized the Indian communities into a labor force and drove those who were not productive and the mestizos off the land. This movement in some countries has continued in one form or another to the present day.

The Latin American Church, staffed largely by *peninsulares*, was shattered by the national revolutions. When reconstituted with greatly reduced property and clerical personnel, the Church desperately sought to win the protection of the more conservative elements in the Creole elite by opposing liberalism in any form. Since the Church had been the exclusive instrument of education and social welfare before liberation, and since the ruling classes showed little interest in providing for the continuation of schools, orphanages, and relief for the lower classes, the misery of the Latin American poor grew more acute throughout the nineteenth century.

The legal and social standing of women rose momentarily and then fell, as it did in France. Individual Creole women, such as Bolívar's astute mistress, Manuela Sanches, made major contributions to the revolution, but the adoption of the Napoleonic Code in the 1820s had the same impact on women's legal status as in Europe at the same time.

It can be argued that in the wake of Napoleon's deposing the Spanish Bourbons, Latin America suffered a decline in political stability and internal economic health. The peasants and urban laborers of Indian and mixed-blood descent, the culture-shaping Church, and women of all classes paid a heavy price for liberation from the Spanish and Portuguese overlords. The single group to gain was the secular, male Creole leadership. Nevertheless, what Napoleon had destroyed was gone, and no serious attempt was made to restore the old colonial regime. The political independence of the new nations of Latin America was guaranteed, at least in theory, by the United States in the proclamation of the Monroe Doctrine in 1823.

THE IDEOLOGICAL LEGACY OF AN AGE OF CHANGE

The artists and philosophers caught up in the romantic movement redefined their place in society in the late 1700s. They found little comfort in socially approved standards. They rejected eighteenth-century classicism and the cold logic of the Enlightenment. They preferred to look far to the past, to long-forgotten civilizations—imprecisely recalled—and commemorated them in simulated ruins. They also studied the hazy examples of the medieval world, especially myths and folklore. By stressing an individual's past, uniqueness, emotions, and creativity, the romantics had a profound effect on the arts (see Chapter 23) and politics.

In the wake of forces unleashed by the French Revolution and Napoleon, political theorists constructed varied responses to the changes through which they were living. The "isms"—nationalism, liberalism, conservatism, socialism, and communism—all came into use in the first half of the nineteenth century. As the romantic artists and philosophers tried to find new ways to express their creativity, the political theorists sought new formulas to express their hopes and goals for society.

Nationalism

The romantics investigated history, folklore, linguistics, and myths to define their own uniqueness. They revived the Scandinavian sagas, the French *Chanson de Roland,* and the German *Nibelungen* stories. During a time of uncertainty, change, and stress, it was both comforting and uplifting to look to the past, even an imagined one. The romantics' search for their own cultural roots coincidentally helped give birth to nationalism.

After the Revolution in 1789, this new ideological force dominated the cultural and political activities of France. The spirit of fraternity projected by the French Revolution united the French people. Unique conditions in different parts of Europe produced different variants of nationalism. However, common to them all was a populace consciously embracing a common land, language, folklore, history, enemies, and religion. These elements are the ingredients of the nation's and the individual's identity and pull the members into an indivisible unity.

Nationalism can exist where there is no state structure and can thrive in a state where the nation is repressed. Nationalism, unlike patriotism, does not need flags and uniforms. All that is needed is a historical and emotional unity around which the members of the nation can gather: a unity that entails the cultural and political loyalty to the nation.

On the Continent, romantics reacted against the French and Napoleonic dominance and helped bring people together in nationalistic opposition, especially in Germany. George Wilhelm Friedrich Hegel (1770–1831) later built on the movement in his lectures and writings at the University of Berlin. For Hegel, history was a process of evolution in which the supremacy of primitive instincts would give way to the reign of clear reason and freedom—the "world spirit"—that would be manifested in the state. Hegel believed that the Prussia of his day offered the best example of the state as a spiritual organism, because in Prussia the individual had the greatest "freedom"—defined not as the individual escaping from society but as a condition in which there is no conflict between the individual and society. The Prussian state, in Hegel's eyes, blended the proper proportions of national identity and structure to enable its individuals to gain their greatest growth. His high regard for the state was not shared by most romantics, but his exaltation of the Prussian state at a time when Germany was still fragmented had a powerful unifying influence. This was the beginning of the belief in the uniqueness and superiority of Germany that had such drastic consequences in the twentieth century.

The research and writings of the Germans Johann Gottfried von Herder (1744–1803) and Jacob (1785–1863) and Wilhelm Grimm (1786–1859) provided historical support and linguistic bases for the Slavic nationalist movements. Herder conceived of a world spirit (*Weltgeist*) made up of component parts of the various national spirits (*Volksgeist*). Each of these national spirits was seen as playing an essential role in the world process, and Herder believed that the Slavs were soon to make an important contribution. The Grimm brothers' philological work aided the literary and linguistic revivals of many Slavic groups. Romantic nationalism was also found in the writings of history by Leopold von Ranke in Germany, Jules Michelet in France, Frantisek Palacky in Bohemia-Moravia, and George Bancroft in the United States.

Romantic nationalism in Britain reacted strongly against the human costs of industrialization and the pretensions of the new merchant classes. It focused on the medieval roots of Britain, as well as on movements such as philhellenism (the love of ancient Greece). In France, Spain, Italy, Russia, and other parts of the Continent the romantic movement made important contributions to the growth of national identity. In Italy, for example, Giuseppe Mazzini (1805–1872) and Alessandro Manzoni (1785–1873) played important roles in the unification struggle of the country.[14]

Conservatism

The reaction to the French Revolution, especially as expressed by Edmund Burke, provided the basis of nineteenth-century European conservatism. There were many thinkers who did not believe in the revolutionary slogan of liberty, equality, and fraternity. They did not believe that liberation could be gained by destroying the historically evolved traditions of the Old Regime. Freedom could be found only in order and maintained solely by continual reference to precedents. A legitimate political and social life needed the framework of tradition to survive.

The conservatives did not have faith in the individual nor did they share the romantics' love of pure emotion and spontaneity. Beginning with Burke and continuing through the first part of the nineteenth century to the Frenchman Joseph

→ Ogilby's *Britannia* was one of a number of geographical works celebrating the glories of England. The two riders make their way past thriving urban industry toward prosperous farms while in the distance merchant ships depart for the colonial empire. The illustration is from the title page of the 1675 edition of the work.

ence to history. They believed that the welfare and happiness of humanity resided in the slowly evolving institutions of the past. Industrialization and the consequences of the French Revolution severed the connection with the past and were therefore dangerous. The conservatives were backward-looking, finding their standards and values in the proven events of the past, not in the untried reforms of the present.

Liberalism

The rising middle and commercial classes found their interests and ideals best expressed in the doctrine of liberalism. Liberalism affirmed the dignity of the individual and the "pursuit of happiness" as an inherent right. The ideology's roots were set firmly in the eighteenth-century soil of constitutionalism, laissez-faire economics, and representative government. Liberals thought in terms of individuals who shared basic rights, were equal before the law, and used parliament to gain power and carry out gradual reform. In addition, liberals believed that individuals should use their power to ensure that each person would be given the maximum amount of freedom from the state or any other external authority.

In economics, liberals believed in fair competition among individuals responding to the laws of supply and demand with a minimum of governmental regulation or interference. Scottish economist Adam Smith (1723–1790) best expressed this view in his *The Wealth of Nations*. Liberals agreed with Smith that society benefitted more from competition among individuals motivated by their self-interest than from governmental regulation. The most intelligent and efficient individuals would gain the greatest rewards, society would prosper, and the state would be kept in its proper place—that of protecting life and property.[15]

Liberals fought foes from above and below as they translated their ideas into public policy. Nobles and the landed gentry still controlled most countries in Europe, so throughout the century the middle classes fought to gain political power commensurate with their economic strength. While they were trying to increase their own influence, they sought to limit the political base of the emerging working classes. By the end of the century the middle classes had consolidat-

de Maistre (1753–1821), the Russian Nicholas Karamzin (1766–1826), and the Spaniard Juan Donoso-Cortés (1809–1853) there was a body of intellectuals who found strength, not weakness, in the church and monarchy of the Old Regime; danger, not liberation, in the nationalistic movements; and degradation, not exaltation, in the new romantic art forms.

Conservatism took many forms during the nineteenth century, ranging from the romantic to the patriotic to the religious to the secular. Whatever their approach, conservatives stressed the need to maintain order through a constant refer-

Adam Smith, *The Wealth of Nations*

The ideological mainstream guiding the industrializing middle classes was Adam Smith's *The Wealth of Nations*.

Every individual is continually exerting him-self to find out the most advantageous employment for whatever capital he can command. It is his own advantage, indeed, and not that of the society, which he has in view. But the study of his own advantage naturally, or rather necessarily, leads him to prefer that employment which is most advantageous to the society.

As every individual, therefore, endeavours as much as he can both to employ his capital in the support of domestic industry and so to direct that industry that its produce may be of the greatest value, every individual necessarily labours to render the annual revenue of the society as great as he can. He generally, indeed, neither intends to promote the public interest nor knows how much he is promoting it. By preferring the support of domestic to that of foreign industry, he intends only his own security; and by directing that industry in such a manner as its produce may be of the greatest value, he intends only his own gain, and he is in this, as in many other cases, led by an invisible hand to promote an end which was no part of his intention. Nor is it always the worse for the society that it was no part of it. By pursuing his own interest he frequently promotes that of the society more effectually than when he really intends to promote it. I have never known much good done by those who affected to trade for the public good. It is an affectation, indeed, not very common among merchants, and very few words need be employed in dissuading them from it.

→ Adam Smith, engraving by James Tassie, 1787. Smith outlined his theory of the division of labor, prices, wages, and distribution in *An Inquiry into the Nature and Causes of the Wealth of Nations (1776)*, a work which laid the foundation for the science of political economy. The influence of *Wealth of Nations*, in both politics and economics, is equaled by few other books.

From Adam Smith, *The Wealth of Nations* (Oxford: Clarendon Press, 1880).

ed their control over the industrialized world. This was perhaps the major political achievement of the century.

Liberals were sufficiently liberated from the demands of manual labor and possessed enough wealth to spend their spare time in public pursuits. They had the time and leisure to work in government to control state policy to protect their own interests. They gained sufficient security that they undertook the enactment of social reform to head off revolution. They became the dominant voices in the press and universities and gained commanding authority over public opinion. The liberals' most important contributions came in the areas of civil rights, promotion of the rule of law, government reform, and humanitarian enterprises.

The main interpreters of liberalism came from Britain, and during the first half of the century Jeremy Bentham (1748–1832) and John Stuart Mill (1806–1873) adapted some liberal theories to modern reality. Bentham devised the concept of utilitarianism, or philosophical radicalism, based on the two concepts of utility and happiness. He connected these two by noting that each individual knows what is best for himself or herself and that all human institutions should be measured according to the amount of happiness they give. Bentham built on these two eighteenth-century concepts to form the pain-and-pleasure principle. He believed that government's function was to gain as great a degree of individual freedom as possible, for freedom was the essential precondition of happiness. Utilitarianism in government was thus the securing of the "greatest happiness for the greatest number." If society could provide as much happiness and as little pain as possible it would be working at maximum efficiency. Bentham recognized what later liberals would eventually espouse—that the government would have to work at all levels—but he left no precise prescription as to how to proceed.

Mill spoke more to this issue. He began by noting that in industry the interests of the owners and workers did not necessarily coincide. He proposed the theory that government should, if necessary, pass legislation to remedy injustice, pointing out that when the actions of business owners harm the people, the state must step in to protect the citizenry. He challenged the liberal theory of minimal government interference in the economic life of the nation and pointed out that humanitarianism is more important than profit margin. He accepted that maximum freedom should be permitted in business and that natural law should dictate insofar as possible the relationship of citizens.

He also pointed out that the distribution of wealth depends on the laws and customs of society and that these can be changed by human will. The rights of property and free competition, therefore, should be upheld but within reasonable limits. Mill pointed out that the liberty of the individual is not absolute—it has to be placed under the wider interests of society. His ideas had within them the germ of the welfare state, but he had little effect on affairs in his own day.

In the late twentieth century the word *liberalism* has undergone some change in meaning. The term still implies reform, but liberals today advocate an active governmental role in minimizing the extremes of wealth, in balancing the great power enjoyed by business and labor, and in conserving natural resources. Today's liberals also

→ Plan for a model prison, called the Panopticon, designed by Jeremy Bentham. The circular arrangement allowed a centrally located guard to monitor all outside cells. The Panopticon was never built, but the plan influenced the design of later prisons.

advocate the state's intervention to help the individual by providing social security and in opposing racial, sexual, and age discrimination.

Socialism

The working classes of Europe, heartened by the French Revolution's call for equality and afflicted by the hardships inherent in the first phase of industrialization found that socialism best expressed their values and goals. Socialists attacked the system of laissez-faire capitalism as unplanned and unjust. They condemned the increasing concentration of wealth and called for public or worker ownership of business. The nature of the industrial system, dividing worker and owner, also raised serious problems, and socialists insisted that harmony and cooperation, not competition, should prevail.

Socialists believed that human beings are essentially good, and with the proper organization of society there would be a happy future with no wars, crimes, administration of justice, or government. In this perfectly balanced world there would also be perfect health and happiness. As one prophet foretold, "every man with ineffable ardor, will seek the good of all."[16] Karl Marx (see Chapter 23) later derisively labeled socialists who sought such a world as "Utopians."

The first prominent Utopian socialist was the French noble Claude Henri de Rouvroy, Count de Saint-Simon (1760–1825). He defined a nation as "nothing but a great industrial society" and politics as "the science of production." He advocated that humanity should voluntarily place itself under the rule of the paternalistic despotism of scientists, technicians, and industrialists who would "undertake the most rapid amelioration possible of the lot of the poorest and most numerous class."[17]

Francois Marie Charles Fourier (1772–1837), another French utopian, believed that the future society must be cooperative and free. He worked out a communal living unit of 1620 people called a "phalanstery." The members of the group chose voluntarily those tasks that appealed to them to do the work needed to ensure the phalanstery's survival. Although his plan was endorsed by many prominent people, attempts made to found cooperative Fourierist communities were unsuccessful. The famous Brook Farm colony in Massachusetts was one such short-lived experiment.

Robert Owen (1771–1858), a successful mill owner in Scotland, was a more practical utopian socialist. His New Lanark, the site of his textile mills, was a model community. Here, between 1815 and 1825, thousands of visitors saw rows of neat, well-kept workers' homes, a garbage collection system, schools for workers' children, and clean factories where workers were treated kindly and no children under age 11 were employed. In 1825 Owen moved to the vicinity of Evansville, Indiana, where he established a short-lived community at New Harmony.

Their optimism blinded the utopians to the nature of humanity and the world in which they lived. Brook Farm and New Harmony were based on the notion that human beings naturally love one another or could be brought to that level. The basic impracticality of the experiments doomed them to failure. However, the notion that capitalism was inherently corrupt and that it

→ Artist's rendering of Robert Owen's utopian community at New Harmony, Indiana. Square, fortresslike buildings surround the community's interior gardens and exercise grounds. The community was established in 1825, but internal dissension forced its dissolution three years later.

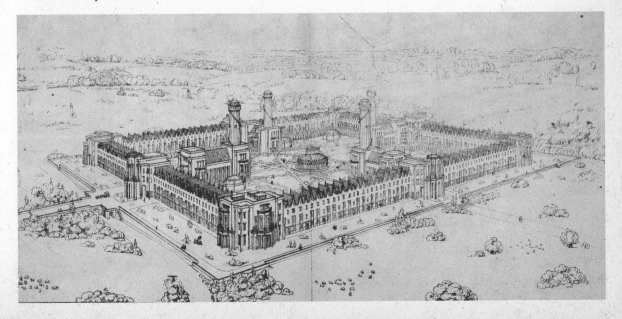

was essential to remove the system remained an article of faith for subsequent socialists, including Karl Marx, who had a far more comprehensive and hard-headed plan that will be examined in Chapter 23.

THE VIENNA SETTLEMENT: 1815

Once Napoleon was "safely" exiled to Elba, representatives of all the European powers except the Ottoman Empire gathered in September at Vienna. They had the imposing task of building a new political and diplomatic structure for Europe after a quarter century of wars and revolutions. The factor that had brought the British, Prussians, Austrians, and Russians together—Napoleon—was gone, and wartime unity dissolved into peacetime pursuit of self-interest.

Work went slowly during the ten-month span of the Congress of Vienna. The leaders who gathered at Vienna—Lord Castlereagh of Great Britain, Count von Hardenberg of Prussia, Prince Klemens von Metternich of Austria, Tsar Alexander I of Russia, and Prince Charles Maurice de Talleyrand of France—met in small secret conferences to decide the future of Europe. Metternich came to dominate the conference, as much by his diplomatic skills as by his ability to impress on the participants the need for stability.

The Congress dealt with numerous issues: the status of France, the new political boundaries, the response to liberal and national attitudes sweeping the continent, the fate of those powers who had lost territory during the previous 25 years, and the future of dispossessed dynasties. The solutions proposed were moderate. France was allowed to return to its 1792 boundaries; however, after Napoleon's return and the One Hundred Days, the allies cut back the boundaries and imposed penalties. They virtually ignored the democratic, liberal, and nationalistic forces in favor of a more traditional solution to the upheavals of the past 25 years.[18]

Allied Dilemmas

The events since 1789 had drastically altered the map of Europe. For example, the thousand-year-old Holy Roman Empire had disappeared. In an attempt to restore some balance, the Congress followed four principles: legitimacy, encirclement of France, compensation, and balance of power. The Congress ruled that royal houses that had been expelled, such as the Bourbons in France, Spain, and Naples, the House of Savoy in Sardinia-Piedmont, and the House of Orange in Holland, would be replaced on their thrones. The redrawn map of Europe resembled the 1789 configuration, except that the Holy Roman Empire remained dissolved. In its place were the 39 states of the German Confederation, dominated by Austria. The redrawing of boundaries created a protective belt of states around France to make future aggression more difficult. The principle of compensation assured that no important power

➔ This cartoon, *La Balance Politique*, lampoons the balance of power politics played out at the Congress of Vienna. Here, Wellington places money on the scales opposite the king of Prussia and Metternich. At right, Tsar Alexander I confers with Talleyrand.

Metternich on His Political Principles

In the aftermath of the Napoleonic age, waves of change threatened the structure erected at the Congress of Vienna. Metternich had a precise notion of what was happening.

Kings have to calculate the chances of their very existence in the immediate future; passions are let loose, and league together to overthrow everything which society respects as the basis of its existence; religion, public morality, laws, customs, rights, and duties, all are attacked, confounded, overthrown, or called in question. The great mass of the people are tranquil spectators of these attacks and revolutions, and of the absolute want of all means of defense. A few are carried off by the torrent, but the wishes of the immense majority are to maintain a repose which exists no longer, and of which even the first elements seem to be lost.

Having now thrown a rapid glance over the first causes of the present state of society, it is necessary to point out in a more particular manner the evil which threatens to deprive it, at one blow, of the real blessings, the fruits of genuine civilisation, and to disturb it in the midst of its enjoyments. This evil may be described in one word—presumption; the natural effect of the rapid progression of the human mind towards the perfecting of so many things. This it is which at the present day leads so many individuals astray, for it has become an almost universal sentiment.

Religion, morality, legislation, economy, politics, administration, all have become common and accessible to everyone. Knowledge seems to come by inspiration; experience has no value for the presumptuous man; faith is nothing to him; he substitutes for it a pretended individual conviction, and to arrive at this conviction dispenses with all inquiry and with all study; for these means appear too trivial to a mind which believes itself strong enough to embrace at one glance all questions and all facts. Laws have no value for him, because he has not contributed to make them, and it would be beneath a man of his parts to recognise the limits traced by rude and ignorant generations.

Power resides in himself; why should he submit himself to that which was only useful for the man deprived of light and knowledge? That which, according to him, was required in an age of weakness cannot be suitable in an age of reason and vigour amounting to universal perfection, which the German innovators designate by the idea, absurd in itself, of the Emancipation of the People! Morality itself he does not attack openly, for without it he could not be sure for a single instant of his own existence; but he interprets its essence after his own fashion, and allows every other person to do so likewise, provided that other person neither kills nor robs him.

From *Memoirs of Prince Metternich, 1815–1829*, vol. III, translated by Mrs. Alexander Napier. (New York: Charles Scribner's Sons, 1881).

---

suffered a loss as the result of the Congress's work. Austria was compensated for the loss of the Austrian Netherlands by gaining territory in Italy and along the Adriatic. Sweden received Norway in return for permitting Russia to keep Finland.

The desire to construct an effective balance of power remained at the center of the Congress's attention. Each power, however, had its own idea of what constituted a proper balance. Russia's ambitions in Poland almost broke up the conference Britain believed that an enlarged Russia threatened peace. Prussia wanted all of Saxony. Austria feared a growing Prussia. While the four wartime allies split, the clever French representative Talleyrand negotiated a secret treaty among the French, Austrians, and British that pledged mutual assistance to restrain the Russians and Prussians. Russia and Prussia eventually reduced their demands for land in Poland and Saxony, and the sought-after balance of power was achieved.

Although the Congress has received criticism for ignoring the growth of liberty, equality, and fraternity in Europe, it has received praise for finding a general settlement of a complex series of problems, especially from scholars who favorably compare its work to that of the victorious allies at

Versailles after World War I.[19] The representatives were not totally, blindly reactionary, however; many of the changes of the previous 25 years were retained. The 40 years of general peace that followed, flawed though they may have been, are testimony to the success of Metternich and his colleagues in gaining stability. But, by ignoring the forces of change expressed in the new ideologies, the representatives at Vienna ensured the ultimate failure of the system they created.

The Congress System and Revolution

The Vienna negotiators set out to coordinate their policies to maintain stability. The first proposal for postwar consultation was symbolic and quixotic. In the fall of 1815, Tsar Alexander I proposed the formation of a Holy Alliance to be based on "the precepts of justice, Christian charity, and peace." No one was quite sure what the tsar meant by this pact, but every ruler in Europe signed it except the British king, the Turkish sultan, and the pope. Castlereagh dismissed the Holy Alliance as "a piece of sublime mysticism and nonsense." In November 1815 Austria, Prussia, Russia, and Britain signed the Quadruple Alliance, which became the Quintuple Alliance when France joined in 1818. Under this agreement the powers pursued their goals through what came to be known as the Congress System,

EUROPE IN 1815

— Boundary of the German Confederation

→ Prince Klemens von Metternich, portrait by Sir Thomas Lawrence. At the height of his powers during the Congress of Vienna, Metternich was largely responsible for the balance of European power agreement worked out at the Congress.

a Europe-wide network to maintain order, peace, and stability. This was the first truly functional experiment in collective security.

The Congress System's dedication to the 1815 status quo was challenged in 1820 and 1821 by nationalistic and liberal revolts in the Germanies, Greece, Spain, Italy, and Latin America. The most violent revolutions occurred in Spain and Italy. Spanish liberals rebelled against the misgovernment of the restored Bourbon King Ferdinand VII, and their insurrection spread to the army, which mutinied. The general uprising that followed forced the king to give into the liberals' demands for a constitution and representative government. The Spaniards' success sparked rebellions in Naples and Sicily, governed by the Neapolitan Bourbon King Ferdinand I. The Italian revolt ran much the same path as that in Spain, and with much the same result—a constitution based on the Spanish model.

Metternich arranged for the Congress allies to meet at Troppau in 1820, Laibach in 1821, and Verona in 1822 to deal with the uprisings. Ferdinand I came to Laibach, supported Congress Sys-

tem intervention, and reneged on granting a constitution; Austrian troops invaded Italy and placed him back on his throne. In 1822 the Congress allies met to consider the Spanish problem, and the French volunteered to restore the status quo. They sent their armies in to crush the liberals. The repression of the revolts in Spain and Italy marked the high point of the Congress System's success.

Britain began its withdrawal from the Continent into "splendid isolation" in 1820, and the ardent support of British liberals for the 1821 Greek revolt against the Turks further weakened London's interest in cooperating with its former allies. When the Congress System discussed restoring the Spanish king's authority in Latin

→ Although Britain escaped the violent revolutions that occurred elsewhere in Europe during the nineteenth century, British critics, like the cartoonist whose work is pictured here, passionately lamented corruption in government and the loss of liberty suffered by British working-class citizens.

America, the British objected. Further, U.S. President James Monroe warned the Europeans in 1823 that their intervention into the Western hemisphere would be regarded as an unfriendly act. By the middle of the decade the Congress System had withered to an Austrian-Russian alliance in which Metternich set the agenda and the Russians acted as the "gendarme of Europe."

CONCLUSION

Through his wars and foreign policies Napoleon broadcast the revolution that had occurred in France to the world and made necessary a wholesale redrawing of political boundaries both in Europe and the Americas. The French emperor changed the nature of warfare and increased the efficiency and reach of state power. For a quarter-century the monarchies of Europe faced the battering ram of revolutionary energies, and by 1815 the framers of the Vienna settlement had to admit that Europe could not be returned to its pre-1789 condition.

The French ideals of individualism, freedom of thought, pride in nation, and equality under the law that had appeared after 1789 took the form of ideologies in the first half of the nineteenth century. The middle classes and underprivileged throughout the continent began aggressively to pursue the rights and liberties inherent in these ideals. The Congress of Vienna made a valiant effort to restore stability to Europe, but its efforts were doomed by these currents.

→ Suggestions for Reading

Napoleon has attracted the attention of a broad range of historians. See, for example, P. Geyl, *Napoleon: For and Against* (Humanities Press, 1974). F. Markham, *Napoleon and the Awakening of Europe* (Collier, 1965) is a convenient introduction to the period. The best surveys dealing with Napoleon's activities are R. B. Holtman, *The Napoleonic Revolution* (Lippincott, 1967) and Owen Connelly, *French Revolution/Napoleonic Era* (Holt, Rinehart & Winston, 1979). See also Jean Tulard, *Napoleon: The Myth of the Saviour* (Weidenfeld and Nicholson, 1984).

The military art of the era is well described in Gunther Rothenberg, *The Art of Warfare in the Age of Napoleon* (Indiana Univ., 1978). David G. Chandler's *The Campaigns of Napoleon* (Macmillan, 1966) is comprehensive and well written. One of Napoleon's opponents receives excellent coverage in E. Longford, *Wellington, the Years of the Sword*

(Harper, 1969). Leo Tolstoy's *War and Peace* gives an incomparably vivid coverage of the 1812 campaign. For those wanting complete bibliographic reference, see Donald D. Howard, ed., *Napoleonic Military History* (Garland, 1986).

G. Brunn's *Europe and the French Imperium* (Harper, 1938) is a classic. See also essays in Hajo Holborn's *Germany and Europe: Historical Essays* (Doubleday, 1971) for insights into the French emperor's impact in central Europe. Hans Kohn's *Prelude to Nation-States: The French and the German Experience, 1789–1815* (Van Nostrand, 1967) is useful.

The French influence on the Americas is reviewed in Alexander de Conde, *The Quasi-War: The Politics and Diplomacy of the Undeclared War with France 1797–1801* (Scribner, 1966). R. A. Humphreys and John Lynch edited a useful series of essays and primary documents in *The Origins of the Latin American Revolutions, 1806–1826* (Knopf, 1967). See also Irene Nicholson, *The Liberators: A Study of Independence Movements in Spanish America* (Praeger, 1969) for an essential volume in understanding the revolutionary period. The first chapters of David Bushnell and Neill Macaulay, *The Emergence of Latin America in the Nineteenth Century* (Oxford, 1988) provide essential social, economic, and political background.

H. D. Aiken, ed., *The Age of Ideology: The Nineteenth Century Philosophers* (Mentor, 1962) explores selections from the works of Hegel, Mill, and others. Jonathan Beecher's *Charles Fourier: The Visionary and His World* (Univ. of California, 1986), performs the invaluable task of taking Fourier's ideas seriously and placing them in the context of the France of his day. For a lively survey of the economic thinkers, see Robert L. Heilbroner's *The Worldly Philosophers* (Touchstone, 1970). One of the best surveys of nineteenth-century European thought is G. L. Mosse, *The Culture of Western Europe: The Nineteenth and Twentieth Centuries* (Rand McNally, 1974).

H. Nicolson, *The Congress of Vienna: A Study of Allied Unity, 1812–1822* (Compass, 1961) is a civilized analysis of diplomatic interaction and a good companion to Henry A. Kissinger, *A World Restored: Metternich, Castlereagh, and the Problems of Peace, 1812–1822* (Sentry, 1957). The following are excellent on the general background to the period: A. J. May, *The Age of Metternich, 1814–1848* (Holt, Rinehart, and Winston, 1967), E. Hobsbawm, *The Age of Revolution, Europe 1789–1848* (Mentor, 1969), J. Talmon, *Romanticism and Revolt: Europe 1815–1948* (Harcourt Brace Jovanovich, 1967).

→ Notes

1. Herbert Butterfield, *Napoleon* (New York: Collier Books, 1977), pp. 20–25.
2. Gunther E. Rothenberg, *The Art of Warfare in the Age of Napoleon* (Bloomington: Indiana University Press, 1980), pp. 31–45.

3. Alfred Cobban, *A History of Modern France*, vol. II (Harmondsworth: Penguin, 1970), pp. 9–13.

4. George LeFebvre, *The French Revolution: From 1793 to 1799*, vol. II, trans. by J. H. Steward and J. Friguglietti (New York: Columbia University Press, 1964), pp. 259–317.

5. Owen Connelly, *French Revolution/Napoleonic Era* (New York: Holt, Rinehart and Winston, 1979), pp. 236–237.

6. Robert B. Holtman, *The Napoleonic Revolution* (New York: J. B. Lippincott, 1967), pp. 38–40.

7. Rothenberg, *The Art of Warfare*, pp. 42–52.

8. Hajo Holborn, *Germany and Europe: Historical Essays* (New York: Doubleday, 1971), p. 9.

9. For a view from the Russian side, see Michael and Diana Josselson, *The Commander: A Life of Barclay de Tolly* (Oxford: Oxford University Press, 1980).

10. H. A. L. Fisher, *A History of Europe*, vol. III (Boston: Houghton Mifflin, 1936), p. 891.

11. C. K. Webster, "British, French, and American Influences," in R. A. Humphreys and J. Lynch, eds., *The Origins of the Latin American Revolution, 1800–1826* (New York: Alfred A. Knopf, 1967), p. 78.

12. David Bushnell and Neill Macaulay, *The Emergence of Latin America in the Nineteenth Century* (New York: Oxford University Press, 1988), pp. 3–9.

13. Bushnell and Macaulay, *The Emergence of Latin America*, pp. 55–82.

14. Peter F. Sugar, "External and Domestic Roots of Eastern European Nationalism," in Peter F. Sugar and Ivo J. Lederer, eds., *Nationalism in Eastern Europe* (Seattle: University of Washington Press, 1969), pp. 3–21.

15. Robert L. Heilbroner, *The Worldly Philosophers* (New York: Simon and Schuster, 1972), pp. 40–72.

16. W. Godwin, "Political Justice," in Sidney Hook, *Marx and the Marxists: The Ambiguous Legacy* (Princeton: Van Nostrand, 1955), p. 28.

17. Quoted in E. R. A. Seligman, ed., *Encyclopedia of the Social Sciences*, vol. XIII (New York: The Macmillan Company, 1935), p. 510a.

18. Geoffrey Bruun, *Europe and the French Imperium* (New York: Harper & Row, 1938), p. 38.

19. L. C. B. Seaman, *From Vienna to Versailles* (New York: Harper & Row, 1963), p. 8.

CHAPTER 22

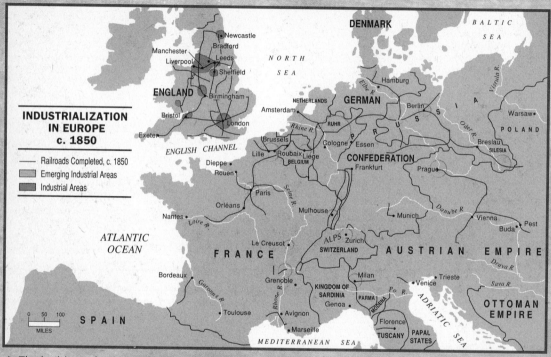

INDUSTRIALIZATION IN EUROPE c. 1850

— Railroads Completed, c. 1850
▢ Emerging Industrial Areas
▢ Industrial Areas

→ The building of railroads characterized the first phase of industrialization. By serving as the veins and arteries of industry and commerce, the railroads assured the successful launching of the second phase of modernization.

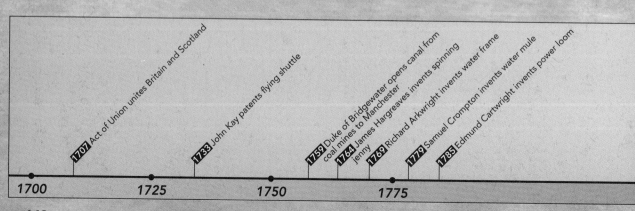

1707 Act of Union unites Britain and Scotland

1733 John Kay patents flying shuttle

1759 Duke of Bridgewater opens canal from coal mines to Manchester

1764 James Hargreaves invents spinning jenny

1769 Richard Arkwright invents water frame

1779 Samuel Crompton invents water mule

1785 Edmund Cartwright invents power loom

| 1700 | 1725 | 1750 | 1775 |

Industrialization and European Global Hegemony, 1825–1914

Chapter Outline

Industrialization brought new tools and power sources to do work formerly performed by humans and animals. The huge increase in productivity made possible by using machines can be shown in the amount of raw cotton British cloth makers imported in 1760 and 1850: whereas in 1760 they imported a bit over 1000 tons, in 1850 the number had risen to over 222,000 tons.

The story behind the growth of the textile industry is one of a continual "catch-up" game between the spinners and weavers to respond to an expanding market. After the 1707 Act of Union with Scotland, Britain possessed an increasing population with a larger per capita income than that of any other European state.[1] This development provided a growing domestic source of both customers and workers.

As the nineteenth century progressed, industrialists in other economic sectors used machines to do work formerly performed by humans and animals. Productive capacity grew geometrically, permitting factories to turn out more and better quality goods at cheaper prices.

Even more than Napoleon, the inventors of the new machines changed Europeans' lives. The

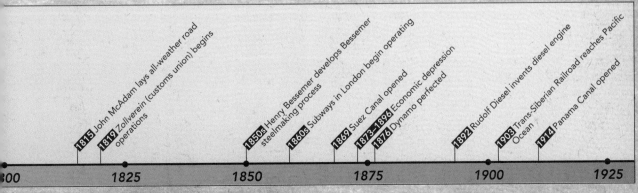

1815 John McAdam lays all-weather road operations

1819 Zollverein (customs union) begins

1850s Henry Bessemer develops Bessemer steelmaking process

1860s Subways in London begin operating

1869 Suez Canal opened

1873–1896 Economic depression

1876 Dynamo perfected

1892 Rudolf Diesel invents diesel engine

1903 Trans-Siberian Railroad reaches Pacific Ocean

1914 Panama Canal opened

1800   1825   1850   1875   1900   1925

French leader spread the forces of revolution to the world and made necessary a wholesale redrawing of political boundaries. But the people who devised new tools and new ways to do old jobs set in process the transition from an agrarian to a modern, urbanized society.

INDUSTRIALIZATION: THE FIRST PHASE

The transition from a rural agrarian to an urban life-style merits applying the term *revolutionary* to the process of industrialization. The incremental steps that led to increased textile production were repeated and continue to be repeated in the production of other goods as well. Liberation from the productive limitations imposed by dependence on human and animal power is the great gift of industrialization. Industrialization has enabled nations to satisfy more efficiently their citizens' essentially unlimited demand for goods.

The Revolution in Making Cloth

Practical people seeing the need for greater output solved the practical problems of increasing production. In the many steps from the raw cotton to the finished cloth, there were bottlenecks—primarily in making yarn and weaving the strands together. In 1733, John Kay (1704–1764), a spinner and mechanic, patented the first of the great machines—the flying shuttle. This device made it possible for one person to weave wide bolts of cloth by using a spring mechanism that sent the shuttle across the loom. This invention upset the balance between the weavers of cloth and the spinners of yarn: ten spinners were required to produce enough yarn needed by one weaver.

James Hargreaves (d. 1778), a weaver and carpenter, eliminated that problem in 1764 with his spinning jenny, a mechanical spinning wheel that allowed the spinners to keep up with the weavers. Five years later, a barber named Richard Arkwright (1732–1792) built the water frame that made it possible to spin many threads into yarn at the same time. Ten years after that, Samuel Crompton (1753–1827), a spinner, combined the spinning jenny and water frame into the water mule, which, with some variations, is used today. By this time the makers of yarn were outpacing the weavers, but in 1785, Edmund Cartwright (1743–1823) invented the power loom that mechanized the weaving process. In two generations what had once been a home-based craft became an industry.

The appetite of the new machines outran the supply of cotton. Since most of the material came from the United States, the demand exceeded the capability of the slave-based southern economy to create the supply. The best worker could not

→ Skilled workers in an English calico printing works. Most skilled workers, who represented only a small fraction of the work force, were men; the larger work force of ordinary factory workers was made up of men, women, and children.

prepare more than five or six pounds of cotton a day because of the problems of the seeds. American inventor Eli Whitney (1765–1825), among others, devised the cotton gin, a machine that enabled a worker to clean more than fifty times as much cotton a day. This device coincidentally played a major role in the perpetuation of slavery in the United States.

Finally, the textile industry became so large that it outgrew the possibilities of its power source: water power. Steam came to drive the machines of industrializing Britain. In the first part of the eighteenth century, mechanic Thomas Newcomen (1663–1729) made an "atmospheric engine" in which a piston was raised by injected steam. As the steam condensed, the piston returned to its original position. Newcomen's unwieldy and inefficient device was put to use pumping water out of mines. James Watt (1736–1819), a builder of scientific instruments at the University of Glasgow, perfected Newcomen's invention. Watt's steam engine also was first used to pump water out of mines. It saved the large amounts of energy lost by the Newcomen engine and led to an increase in coal productivity. After 1785, it was also used to make cloth and drive ships and locomotives. The application of steam to weaving made it possible to expand the use of cloth-making machines to new areas, and after 1815 hand looms began to disappear from commercial textile making, replaced by the undoubted superiority of the cloth-making machines.

These inventors made their contributions in response to the need to solve particular problems. Their machines and the new power sources expanded productivity and transformed society in ways never before imagined.

Britain's Dominance

Industrialization began in Britain in the eighteenth century for a number of reasons. Neither the richest nor the most populous country in western Europe, it did, nevertheless, possess at virtually all levels of society a hard-working, inventive, risk-taking private sector that received strong support from the government. Industrialization could not begin and grow without individual business owners who took a chance on something new. The British maintained this close tie between private initiative and creative governmental support throughout the eighteenth and nineteenth centuries.

Thanks to early governmental support of road improvements and canal construction, Britain had a better transportation network than any other country in Europe. The British also had mastery of the seas, excellent ports, and a large merchant fleet. They enjoyed the advantage of living safely on their island, away from the carnage of war, even during the Napoleonic wars. The chance to industrialize in stable conditions gave them the opportunity to profit from war contracts between 1792 and 1815. They developed their industrial capacity without fear of damage from battle or loss of life.

Probably the most important factor was the relative flexibility of the British social and political systems. Members of the elite, unlike their colleagues on the Continent, pursued their wealth in the new industrial framework with great energy. They worked closely with the middle classes and workers, even to the point during the nineteenth century of sponsoring gradual reform efforts to stifle any chance of revolution from below.

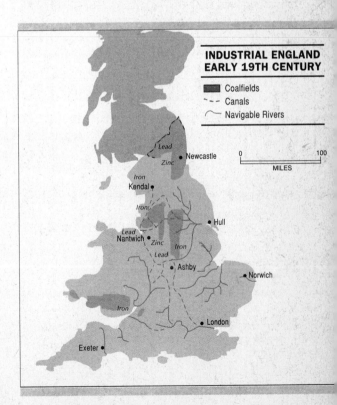

INDUSTRIAL ENGLAND
EARLY 19TH CENTURY

Coalfields
Canals
Navigable Rivers

The combination of inventiveness, growing markets, governmental support, and social flexibility made Britain the world's dominant economic power until the end of the nineteenth century. Napoleon's interference had hurt British economic growth, but had also spurred the British to look for new manufacturing methods and markets. Once the wars were over, Britain flooded the Continent and the Americas with high-quality, inexpensive goods. No nation could compete against British efficiency. When Britain began industrializing before 1789, there were isolated areas on the Continent such as the French Le Creusot works that could have served as the base for similar growth. However, 26 years of revolution and mercantile policies made that competition impossible.[2]

The industrialized cotton textile production continued to increase in Britain and was supplemented by the arrival of the modern Iron Age. In 1800 Russia and Sweden had exported iron to Britain. By 1815 Britain exported more than five times as much iron as it imported. By 1848 the British produced more iron than the rest of the world combined. As in textile production, a number of inventions appeared in ironmaking in response to problems. Improved refining of brittle cast iron made it more malleable and tough so it could be used in more products. At the same time more efficient mining processes for both coal and iron ore were used to ensure a dependable supply of raw materials.

To further help Britain dominate the metals market, in the 1850s Henry Bessemer (1813–1898) developed a process to make steel, a harder and more malleable metal than iron, quickly and cheaply. So effective was the process that between 1856 and 1870 the price of British steel fell to one half the amount formerly charged for the best grade of iron. The drastic reduction in price due to innovations in production, a mark of industrialization, had a positive impact on all areas of the economy.

In the period after the mid-century, Britain produced more than two-thirds of the world's coal and more than half of the world's iron and cloth. Industrial development encouraged urbanization, and by 1850 more than half of the population lived in cities and worked in industries. The British continued to enjoy the highest per capita income in the world, and the island nation stood head and shoulders above the world in terms of economic and material strength.

INDUSTRIALIZATION: THE SECOND PHASE

The second phase of industrialization brought new products and power sources to the Continent. Increased food production and improved health standards and diet led to a population explosion that promised both economic gains and bureaucratic burdens. The rapid and massive growth of cities brought with it the social problems of urbanization. Workers united to fight for their interests, while the middle classes extended their wealth and influence. The actions of both groups changed the nature of social and political life.

Food and Population Increases

Liberated from many of the restraints of the past by the French, Napoleonic, and Industrial Revolutions, most Europeans made the transition from a society based on agriculture to a modern urban society. The spectacular growth of the industrial sector makes it easy to overlook the great strides made in food production during the nineteenth century. Because of the improved global transportation network and better farming methods, the expanding number of city dwellers had more and better food to eat in 1914 than they had had in 1815.

It is estimated that in 1815, around 60 percent of the money and 85 percent of the European people were tied to farming. These large quantities of capital and labor were not used effectively because the advances made in Holland and Britain in the seventeenth and eighteenth centuries had not spread on the Continent. However, progressive landowners gradually introduced these improved methods when they saw the money to be made by feeding the growing populations of the cities.

By the end of the nineteenth century, farmers on the Continent were plowing new lands and using higher yielding crop varieties to survive in the worldwide agricultural competition. Industrial nations such as Britain, in which only 10 percent of the population was engaged in farming, imported more than a fourth of its food. Farmers in the Americas, Australia, and New Zealand competed with each other in the cut-throat export market. The peasants of Ireland and southern and eastern Europe were unable to produce efficiently enough to prosper in this new setting. Russia, where the peasantry comprised 70 percent of the population, had to export to bring in foreign capital to finance industrialization. When the country had to compete with efficient foreign farmers, the tsarist minister of finance stated, "We may go hungry, but we will export."[3]

The expanded food supply supported the growth in European population from 175 million to 435 million.[4] This 130 percent increase between 1800 and 1910 partially disproved the views the British clergyman Thomas Robert Malthus (1766–1834) set forth in his *Essay on Population*. Malthus asserted that human reproduction could easily outrun the earth's ability to produce food.[5] In his own day he could point to the limited food supply and rapidly increasing population. From this evidence he concluded that the inevitable fate of humanity was misery and ruin, since the number of people would rise geometrically while food supply would grow only arithmetically. The experience of the next two centuries has at least temporarily disproved Malthus's thesis.

A gradual decline in mortality rates, slightly better medical care, more food, earlier marriages, and better sanitary conditions contributed to the population increase. The number of people grew so rapidly in Europe that although 40 million Europeans emigrated throughout the world, the Continent still showed a population increase in one century that was greater than that of the previous 2000 years. Where the economies were advanced, such as in northern and western Europe, the population growth could be absorbed. But in the poorer countries of southern and eastern Europe, the masses faced the choices of overcrowding and starvation or emigration.

The Ties That Bind: New Networks

To bring the increased food supply to the growing population, to distribute new resources to larger markets, and to connect augmented capital with essential information, Europeans built the most complete and far-reaching transportation and communication networks ever known. Without rapid and dependable transport and contact the Industrial Revolution could not have occurred, cities would not have grown, factories could not have functioned, and the new millions of Europeans would not have been fed. The new networks became the arteries and nervous system of Europe.

The Duke of Bridgewater made a major step forward in water transportation in 1759 when he built a seven-and-one-half mile long canal from his mines to Manchester. Water transport cut the price of his coal in half and gave Britain a vivid lesson in the benefits of canals. Nearly 4000 miles of improved rivers and canals were built, with strong governmental support by the 1830s, making it possible to ship most of the country's products by water. Following the British example, canal building spread through Europe and North America and then to Egypt with the Suez Canal in 1869 and Latin America with the Panama Canal in 1914. The first project cut the sailing time between London and Bombay India by nearly half, while the second did away with the need to sail around South America to reach the Pacific Ocean.

Until 1815 most roads were muddy, rutted paths that were impassable during spring thaws and autumn rains. In that year a Scotsman, John McAdam, created the all-weather road by placing small stones in compact layers directly on the road bed. The pressure of the traffic moving over the highway packed the stones together to give a fairly smooth surface. This practical solution cut the stagecoach time for the 160 miles from London to Sheffield from four days in the 1750s to 28 hours.

Steam-powered vessels replaced the graceful though less dependable sailing ships in ocean commerce. Clipper ships are among the most beautiful objects ever built, but they cannot move without wind. Sturdy, awkward-looking steamships carried larger cargo with greater regularity and thereby revolutionized world trade. The price of American wheat on the European market dropped by three-fourths in the last part of the century, thanks in considerable degree to the savings made possible by the large, reliable steamships. Transatlantic passenger and mail

→ Building the Suez Canal requires a massive investment in up-to-date technology. The canal, completed in 1869, linked the Indian Ocean to the Mediterranean Sea by way of the Red Sea.

services were also improved by the use of steam to power seagoing vessels.

The most important element in the European arterial network was the railroad. Between 1830 and 1860 rails linked every major market in Europe and in the United States. By 1903 the Russians had pushed the Trans-Siberian railroad to the Pacific Ocean. Railroads cheaply and efficiently carried people and large amounts of material long distances and knit countries and continents closer together. Within cities, urban rail lines and trolleys were widespread by the end of the century; these had an impressive effect on housing and business patterns by permitting a wider diffusion of workers. In the 1860s London was the first city to establish subways, followed by Budapest in 1896 and Paris in 1900.

Connected with the growth of transportation networks and technological innovation, major improvements came in the area of communications. Postal agreements among the various countries made cheap and dependable mail service possible. The modern postage stamp as well as improved transportation systems brought astronomical increases in the number of letters and packages mailed after 1850.[6] Starting in the 1840s the electric telegraph, undersea cable, telephone, wireless telegraph, and typewriter expanded the ability to exchange ideas and information. No longer would distance be a critical obstacle after the transportation and communi-cations revolutions. The world became a smaller, if not more unified, place.

The Continent Industrializes

The Continent faced many hurdles to economic growth after 1815. Obstacles to mobility, communication, and cooperation among the classes prevented the social structures there from adapting as easily to change as had the British. The farther south and east the social system, the more repressive was the structure. In many parts of the Continent, the restored nobilities reclaimed their power, and they were intellectually, financially, or politically prepared to support industrial development. Fragmented political boundaries, geographical obstacles, and toll-takers along primary river and road systems hampered growth, especially in central Europe. In eastern Europe, the middle classes were weaker and more isolated than in the west.

At the end of the Napoleonic wars, the initial stages of industrialization were evident in Belgium, France, and Germany. In Sweden, Russia, and Switzerland there were pockets of potential mechanized production, but the total of these activities was tiny compared to Britain's economy. In 1850 only Belgium could compete with British products in its own markets. There a combination of favorable governmental policies, good transportation, and stability brought some success.

Governments and businesses sent officials and representatives to Britain to try to discover the secrets of industrialization. The British tried to protect their advantage by banning the export of machines and processes and limiting foreign access to their factories. Industrial espionage existed then as now, and Continental competitors did uncover some secrets. Britain's success could be studied, components of it stolen, and its experts hired, but no country on the Continent could combine all the factors that permitted Britain to dominate.

After the mid-century, a long period of peace, improved transportation, as well as strategic government assistance encouraged rapid economic growth in France and the German states. Population increased 25 percent in France and nearly 40 percent in the Germanies, which provided a larger market and labor supply. Two generations of borrowed British technology began to be applied and improved upon; but the two most important developments came in banking and customs and toll reforms.

After 1815, aggressive new banking houses appeared across Europe, strengthened by the profits they had made by extending loans to governments during the Napoleonic wars. They saw the money to be made investing in new industries, such as railroads, and worked with both governments and major capitalists. Firms such as Hope and Baring in London, the Rothschilds in Frankfurt, Paris, Vienna, and London, and numerous Swiss bankers were representative of the private financiers who had well-placed sources and contacts throughout the state and business communities.[7]

Banking changed radically during this period to satisfy the growing demands for money. Long-range capital needs were met by the formation of investment banks, while new institutions were created to fill the need for short-term credit. The ultimate source of financial liquidity was the middle classes—the thousand of little people who put their money in banks to make their own profits through interest earned. More money could be gained from the many small investors than from the few rich families who used to dominate banking.

The Germans led the way in the other major development, the *Zollverein* (customs union), that began under Prussian leadership in 1819. This arrangement helped break down the physical and financial barriers imposed at the various state boundaries and in the next 23 years came to include most of central and northern Germany. Instead of the more than 300 divisions fragmenting the Germans in 1800, there was a virtual free trade market, something Britain had enjoyed since the union of Scotland and England in 1707—and which the European Economic Community created across the Continent in 1993. The significance of the *Zollverein* was that it allowed goods to circulate free of tolls and tariffs, thus reducing prices and stimulating trade.

In the second half of the century, industrialization on the Continent grew rapidly, aided by

→ The increasing volume of trade between the English industrial towns of Liverpool and Manchester (in the early 1820s the traffic of goods was estimated to be approximately 1000 tons per week) and the demand for a method of transport speedier than the canal led to the building of a railroad between the two towns. Although the original purpose for the railroad was the traffic in goods, passenger traffic soon became important as well.

the increased flow of credit and the elimination of many internal barriers. Tariff walls throughout the area fell to a degree not matched until after World War II. Major firms, such as the German Krupp works and the French silk industries, controlled portions of the European market and competed effectively with Britain throughout the world.

Technological Growth and Advances

Another reason for the Continent's economic emergence was a wide range of new technologies using new materials, processes, and transportation. New competitors began with state-of-the-art factories that allowed them to outproduce Britain, whose older factories were less productive.

The basic change in the second phase of industrialization was the use of electricity in all aspects of life. Scientists had discovered electricity's basic principles a century earlier, but it was difficult to generate and transmit power across long distances. When the first dependable dynamo, a device that changed energy from mechanical into electrical form, was perfected in 1876, it became possible to generate electricity almost anywhere. Inventors, such as the American Thomas A. Edison, began to use the new resource in industry, transportation, entertainment, and the home. Humanity had finally found a source of power that could be transmitted and used easily. The British took the lead in applying electricity to home use. The Germans made the most advanced application of electric technology to industry.

Another fundamental change came in the use of gas and oil in the newly devised internal combustion engine. Steam power's use was limited by its appetite for huge amounts of fuel and its sheer bulk. Gottlieb Daimler (1834–1900) perfected the internal combustion engine used in most automobiles today. In 1892 Rudolf Diesel invented the engine that bears his name. It burned fuel instead of harnessing the explosions that drove the Daimler engine.

These new developments led directly to the search for and use of petroleum and the beginning of the passenger car industry. By 1914 the making of cars was a key part of the Italian, Russian, German, French, and American economies. Automobile manufacturing called for a number of spin-off industries such as tire, ball bearing, and windshield manufacturing—the list extends to hundreds of items. Leaving aside the passenger car's economic contribution, the world's cities and people felt the complex impact of this new form of transportation, with consequences such as expanding the range of an individual's world and increased noise levels and pollution that changed the character of urban areas.

Other new machines also changed the quality of life. Bicycles became commonplace in the 1890s, as did sewing machines, cameras, and typewriters, to name a few items. Never before had people had the ability to transform ideas almost instantly into products accessible to the average person. This was another dividend of industrialization and a symbol of a rapidly changing Europe.

The Human Costs of Industrialization

Industrialization drove society from an agricultural to an urban way of life. The old system, in which peasants worked the fields during the summer and did their cottage industry work in the winter to their own standards and at their own pace, slowly disappeared. In its place came urban life tied to the factory system. The factory was a place where people did repetitive tasks using machines over long hours to process large amounts of raw materials. This was an efficient way to make a lot of high-quality goods at cheap cost. But the factories were often dangerous places and the life-style connected to them had a terrible effect on the human condition.

In the factory system, the workers worked and the owners made profits. The owners wanted to make the most they could from their investment and to get the most work they could from their employees. The workers, in turn, felt that they deserved more of the profits because their labor made production possible. This was a situation guaranteed to produce conflict, especially given the wretched conditions the workers faced in the first stages of industrialization.

The early factories were miserable places, featuring bad lighting, lack of ventilation, dangerous machines, and frequent breakdowns. Safety standards were practically nonexistent and workers in various industries could expect to contract serious diseases; for example, laborers working with lead paint developed lung problems, pewter workers fell ill to palsy, miners suffered black lung disease, and those using primi-

→ Children who worked in the English mines were called "hurriers." This illustration of children working in the mines appeared in a book entitled *The White Slaves of England*, published in 1853.

tive machines lost many fingers, hands, and even lives. Not until late in the century did health and disability insurance come into effect. In some factories workers who suffered accidents were deemed to be at fault, and since there was little job security, a worker could be fired for virtually any reason.

The demand for plentiful and cheap labor led to the widespread employment of women and children. Girls as young as six years old were used to haul carts of coal in Lancashire mines, and boys and girls of four and five years of age worked in textile mills—their nimble little fingers could easily untangle jammed machines. When they were not laboring, the working families lived in horrid conditions in such wretched industrial cities as Lille, France, and Manchester, England. There were no sanitary, water, or medical services for the workers and working families were crammed twelve and fifteen to a room in damp, dark cellars. Bad diet, alcoholism, cholera, and typhus led to a reduced life span in the industrial cities. Simultaneous with, and perhaps part of, the industrialization process was the vast increase in illegitimate births. Up to mid-century, corresponding to the time of maximum upheaval, continent-wide figures indicate that at least one-third of all births were out of wedlock.[8]

Industrialization and Children

Early industrialization demanded huge sacrifices, especially from children.

Sarah Gooder, aged 8 years

I'm a trapper [work] in the Gawber pit. It does not tire me, but I have to trap without a light and I'm scared. I go at four and sometimes half past three in the morning, and come out at five and half past. I never go to sleep. Sometimes I sing when I've light, but not in the dark; I dare not sing then. I don't like being in the pit. I am very sleepy when I go sometimes in the morning. I go to Sunday-schools and read *Reading made Easy*. [She knows her letters and can read little words.] They teach me to pray. [She repeated the Lord's Prayer, not very perfectly, and ran on with the following addi-

tion.] "God bless my father and mother, and sister and brother, uncles and aunts and cousins, and everybody else, and God bless me and make me a good servant. Amen. I have heard tell of Jesus many a time. I don't know why he came on earth, I'm sure, and I don't know why he died, but he had stones for his head to rest on. I would like to be at school far better than in the pit."

From *Parliamentary Papers* (London, 1842).

Later generations profited from the sacrifices made by the first workers in the industrialization. Factory owners came to understand that they could make more profit from an efficient factory staffed by contented and healthy workers.

Urban Crises

Huge population increases and industrialization prompted a massive growth of European cities in the nineteenth century, as can be seen in the following table.[9]

Nineteenth Century Urban Growth

CITY	1800	1910
London	831,000	4,521,000
Paris	547,000	2,888,000
Berlin	173,000	2,071,000
Vienna	247,000	2,030,000
St. Petersburg	220,000	1,907,000

In addition, new towns sprang up throughout the Continent and soon reached the level of more than 100,000 inhabitants. Even in agrarian Russia, where 70 percent of the population worked on the land, there were 17 cities of more than 100,000 by the end of the century.

Political leaders faced serious problems dealing with mushrooming city growth. The factory system initially forced families to live and work in squalor, danger, and disease, a condition to be found today in countries undergoing the first stages of industrialization. City leaders had the responsibility to maintain a clean environment, provide social and sanitation services, enforce the law, furnish transportation, and—most serious of all—build housing. They uniformly failed to meet the radical challenges of growth.

Until mid-century, human waste disposal in some parts of Paris was taken care of by dumping excrement into the gutters or the Seine River or through street-corner manure collections. Not until Baron Georges Haussman's (1809–1891) urban renewal in the 1850s and 1860s (see Chapter 24) did the city get an adequate garbage, water, and sewage system. Police protection remained inadequate or corrupt. Other cities shared Paris's problems to a greater or lesser degree. The industrial towns that had sprung up were in even worse condition than the older centers.

By the end of the century, however, governments began to deal effectively with urban prob-

→ This illustration, *Over London—By Rail*, vividly depicts the problems that accompanied urbanization—cramped living spaces, crime, and air and water pollution.

lems. By 1914, most major European cities began to make clean running water, central heat, adequate street lighting, mass public education, dependable sewage systems, and minimal medical care available for their people.

NEW FORCES AND THE STATE

Since 1500 the European state system had been going through a process of competition and concentration; in the four centuries after 1500 the number of political units declined from around 500 to roughly 25.[10] The six largest survivors—Britain, Germany, France, Russia, Italy, and the Austro-Hungarian monarchy—took advantage of their new material and economic power and adjusted more or less successfully to the challenges and opportunities presented by the times.

Industrialization gave some of these states immense material strength, economic power, and technology that affected the everyday lives of their citizens. The states vastly expanded their

An Industrial Town

The terrible life in the industrial towns touched observers such as novelist Charles Dickens, who in his book *Hard Times* described a typical British factory town.

It was a town of red brick, or of brick that would have been red if the smoke and ashes had allowed it; but as matters stood, it was a town of unnatural red and black, like the painted face of a savage. It was a town of machinery and tall chimneys, out of which interminable serpents of smoke trailed themselves for ever and ever, and never got uncoiled. It had a black canal in it, and a river that ran purple with ill-smelling dye, and vast piles of building full of windows where there was a rattling and trembling all day long, and where the piston of the steam engine worked monotonously up and down, like the head of an elephant in a state of melancholy madness. It contained several large streets all very like one another, and many small streets still more like one another, inhabited by people equally like one another, who all went in and out at the same hours, with the same sound upon the same pavement, to do the same work, and to whom every day was the same as yesterday and tomorrow, and every year the counterpart of the last and the next.

From Charles Dickens, *Hard Times* (London: Thomas Nelson and Sons, n.d.), p. 26.

---

activities in building up their armed forces, controlling the food supply, overseeing the economy, training technical personnel, increasing police functions, and compiling statistical records.

During the second half of the nineteenth century, major European states turned their full attention to education. The increase in literacy and the corresponding growth of the mass circulation press during the latter part of the era brought politics to the common people and changed the nature of political life.

By the end of the nineteenth century the major European states had transformed themselves to head off "inevitable" class conflict and to tap into the forces that raised the general level of prosperity. The states became richer, more powerful, and more effective than ever before. New technology enabled them to intervene in the lives of their citizens in new ways. They formed huge conscript armies, increased taxation, established universal education, improved medical and social support services, and installed communications networks. The states initiated activity that fueled Europe's imperialist expansion across the globe while improving the material lives of citizens at home.

The Committee of Public Safety during the French Revolution and later Napoleon Bonaparte had recognized the essential need for mass public education.[11] The state could not tolerate illiterates as industrial workers or as useful citizens. By 1900 all of the major states had invested heavily in education, and the evolution of the popular press to profit from mass literacy helped change the nature of political life. Politics went from the reasoned discourse of the drawing rooms of the elite to the crude rhetoric of mass movements that reflected working-class and middle-class values.

With the increased effectiveness of communications brought by railroads, the telephone and telegraph, nations became much more unified, and governments regulated each individual's life. They kept statistics and records of each citizen's life and exercised control over such matters as food supply and public order. As wealth and population grew, so did the number of bureaucracies. The postal service and railroads in Germany saw the number of their employees soar from 245,000 in 1880 to nearly 700,000 in 1910.[12] Further, military conscription touched the lives of most young men, except in Britain. By 1897 France and Germany each had nearly 3.5 million men in the field or on reserve, and these soldiers were better and more expensively armed than ever before.

The states tapped an increasing tax base to finance their augmented functions. The German empire's income grew from 263 million marks in 1873 to over 1200 million marks in 1909.[13] Other

governments, even the poorest, registered comparable increases. By 1914, the states that were the most flexible—Britain, Germany, and France—were the most powerful and broadcast their power to the rest of the world. Russia, Italy, and the Austro-Hungarian monarchy, meanwhile, struggled to remain great powers.

THE FOUNDATIONS OF EUROPEAN GLOBAL DOMINANCE

The word *imperialism* has come to mean many things to many people. Broadly speaking, the term refers to the extension of authority or control, whether direct or indirect, of one nation over another. But we use the term imperialism in a more restricted sense to refer to the period in the latter part of the nineteenth century when western Europe, which controlled much of the world's finance, commerce, military power, and intellectual life, extended its power over many of the peoples of the world.

Building on the foundations of their industrial economies and their efficient state structures, Europeans gained control of most of Asia, Africa, and the Americas in the nineteenth century. They achieved their domination by sending their people to settle, their armies to conquer, and/or their merchants to trade. Scientific and economic superiority harnessed to efficient state structures provided the strength for European expansion and domination. The nations of western Europe justified their imperialism with a

number of rationalizations. Imperialism was variously defended as an attempt to spread civilization, to bring Christianity to the "heathen," and to introduce progress to the "less fortunate." Some inventive thinkers distorted scientific discoveries and theories to devise self-serving arguments for the supposed inevitability and eternal nature of their dominance.

Economic Bases for Imperialism

The global economy imposed demands for more money and better management on Europe's firms. Industrialists came to live or die by their efficiency, and efficiency often meant consolidation. Large firms could make more products at a cheaper cost than small firms because they could raise the money to buy the resources, install the newest technology, and train and employ more workers. Large firms carried more political clout than did small ones and lobbied for state policies and regulations that favored them. Some firms, such as that of Alfred Nobel (1833–1896), the Swedish industrialist and inventor of dynamite, set up branches in many different countries. Others tried to control an entire market in one country, as did the Standard Oil firm of John D. Rockefeller (1839–1937) in the United States. Whatever the strategy, the gigantic firm became the dominant industrial force.

With the need for more capital, firms began to sell stock to the middle classes. Joint stock companies were not new, but they had not been favored because if an enterprise failed the investors were liable for its debts. Britain, followed by other industrial states, adopted statutes, or limited liability laws, that protected investors from business failure. As middle-class wealth increased, more people began to play the stock market.

New Structures

Businesses developed new strategies to dominate individual sectors of the market. One new development was the *trust*, an arrangement in which a body of trustees held a majority of stock in a given industry and could thereby control wages, prices, and merchandising policies of several companies. Another tactic was the *holding company*, in which a corporation incorporated to gain the same control as it would with the less-formal trust. In Europe these alliances took the form of huge industrial combinations known as *cartels*. The cartel, often secret, controlled prices and markets in fundamentally important goods such as rubber or steel. The ultimate way to dominate an area of business, however, was the *monopoly*, in which one firm gained control of the total economic cycle of a product.

The new generations of industrialists developed more efficient management methods. American engineer Frederick W. Taylor (1856–1912) devised the scientific management system, which recommended breaking down each stage of the industrial process to its most minute segment and studying the efficiency of each step of work to establish the optimum speed of productivity. Improved methods such as the use of interchangeable parts and the introduction of the assembly line brought productivity to a high level by 1914. New production methods and organizational structures were better able to satisfy the infinite desires of the world market.

The New World Economy

From the fifteenth through the eighteenth centuries, a large part of Europe had expansionist ambitions. Prevailing mercantilist theories encouraged the seeking of colonies and monopolies in overseas trade. A combination of political and economic factors, however, slowed down the imperialistic drive in the half century after 1815. Britain's desire for an empire had been diminished after the loss of the 13 American

→ Assembling magnetos on the assembly line at the Ford Motor Company in Highland Park, Michigan. One worker could assemble a single magneto in 29 minutes; 29 workers, properly arranged, could assemble a magneto in 5 minutes.

colonies in 1783, and France had lost nearly all of its overseas possessions by the end of the Napoleonic wars. In addition, the laissez-faire school of economics argued against the possession of colonies.

France reignited the drive for a world empire during Louis Napoleon's reign, and the scramble for colonies heated up after 1870. In his six years as British prime minister, Disraeli annexed Fiji and Cyprus, fought a war against the Zulus in southeastern Africa, purchased a controlling interest in the Suez canal shares, and proclaimed Queen Victoria empress of India. The other major powers, to a greater or lesser degree, followed Britain's lead and the race to carve up the globe began in earnest. It has been estimated that in 1800, fully half of the world was not known to Europeans. By 1900, more land had been explored and acquired by them

"NEW CROWNS FOR OLD ONES!"

→ In this 1876 cartoon from *Punch*, Queen Victoria exchanges her royal crown for a new imperial crown proclaiming her empress of India.

than in the previous four centuries. The nations of the small, northwest peninsula of the Eurasian landmass claimed control of 60 percent of the earth's surface.

In 1914 Great Britain, with its far-flung empire, was the world's richest nation. Even though it imported more goods than it exported, it earned nearly a billion dollars a year from overseas investments, shipping fees, and banking and insurance services. Germany had become the Continent's economic giant. Its population had risen from 41 million to 65 million between 1871 and 1910. Close cooperation between government and private industry paid dividends. The state established protectionist tariffs after 1879, supported technical education, and encouraged industrial cartels. France lagged behind Germany in both population and industrial output, but it was still an economic power.

In the 50 years before World War I, international trade rose from $7 billion to $42 billion.

European nations were by and large their own best customers, even with the tariff barriers that were erected on the Continent after 1879. Europe became the chief supplier of world capital: Britain invested heavily in its empire and the United States; France made huge loans to Russia, and Germany and England extended large loans to the Ottoman Empire. The European economic primacy was felt in the far corners of the world. Soon the Argentinean *gaucho*, the Australian sheep man, and the American cowboy— each a symbol of the free man in the mythology of his own country—were cogs in the global economic machine of constantly circulating raw materials and finished goods.

The international economy tied the world to the rhythms of the booms and busts of Europe. Economic historians differ in their interpretations of the frequency and causes of the stages of economic expansion and contraction in the business cycle. Whether one believes in a ten-year, twenty-year, or century-long cycle, the fact remains that economies throughout the world increasingly became extensions of Europe's economic changes.[14] The depression that lasted from 1873 to 1896 is symbolic of the impact of economic events in Europe on the world. Overall, prices fell by roughly 30 percent in all products. Around the world, suffering was severe, especially in those areas that depended on the shipment of their raw materials to cities or abroad and that had no control over the price their products could demand. But by 1896, there had been a readjustment, and the period to 1914 was generally prosperous.

Political Implications

The internationalization of the economy placed diplomacy and finances into a common harness. The developing countries needed money to compete in the new world economic system. The industrialized countries looked on the rest of the world as a supplier of labor and raw materials, a market for finished goods, and a place for capital investments.

For creditors, investments abroad fell into three logical groupings. Lenders could purchase the bonds of strong nations—a safe investment but with a low rate of return. They could make

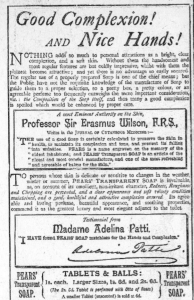

Good Complexion! AND Nice Hands!

NOTHING adds so much to personal attractions as a bright, clear complexion, and a soft skin. Without them the handsomest and most regular features are but coldly impressive, whilst with them the plainest become attractive; and yet there is no advantage so easily secured. The regular use of a properly prepared Soap is one of the chief means; but the Public have not the requisite knowledge of the manufacture of Soap to guide them to a proper selection, so a pretty box, a pretty colour, or an agreeable perfume too frequently outweighs the more important consideration, viz. : the *Composition of the Soap itself*, and thus many a good complexion is spoiled which would be enhanced by proper care.

A most Eminent Authority on the Skin,

Professor Sir Erasmus Wilson, F.R.S.,

Writes in the JOURNAL of CUTANEOUS MEDICINE :—

"THE use of a good Soap is certainly calculated to preserve the Skin in "health, to maintain its complexion and tone, and prevent its falling "into wrinkles. PEARS is a name engraved on the memory of the "oldest inhabitant; and PEARS' Transparent Soap is an article of the "nicest and most careful manufacture, and one of the most refreshing "and agreeable of balms for the skin."

TO persons whose skin is delicate or sensitive to changes in the weather, winter or summer, PEARS' TRANSPARENT SOAP is invaluable, as, on account of its emollient, non-irritant character, Redness, Roughness and Chapping are prevented, and a clear appearance and soft velvety condition maintained, and a good, healthful and attractive complexion ensured. Its agreeable and lasting perfume, beautiful appearance, and soothing properties, commend it as the greatest luxury and most elegant adjunct to the toilet.

Testimonial from

Madame Adelina Patti.

"I HAVE found PEARS' SOAP matchless for the Hands and Complexion."

Adelina Patti

| PEARS' Transparent SOAP. | TABLETS & BALLS: 1s. each. Larger Sizes, 1s. 6d. and 2s. 6d. *(The 2s. 6d. Tablet is perfumed with Otto of Roses.)* A smaller Tablet (unscented) is sold at 6d. | PEARS' Transparent SOAP. |

THE FORMULA OF BRITISH CONQUEST

PEARS' SOAP IS THE BEST

PEARS' SOAP IN THE SOUDAN.

"Even if our invasion of the Soudan has done nothing else it has at any rate left the Arab something to puzzle his fuzzy head over, for the legend PEARS' SOAP IS THE BEST, inscribed in huge white characters on the rock which marks the farthest point of our advance towards Berber, will tax all the wits of the Dervishes of the Desert to translate."—Phil Robinson, War Correspondent *(in the Soudan) of the Daily Telegraph in London, 1884.*

→ Shrinking national markets sparked the drive for expansion into international markets for manufactured goods. The advertisement for Pears' Soap is inscribed on the rock marking the farthest point of the British advance in the Sudan.

loans to underdeveloped countries—a riskier venture but with a much higher rate of return. Finally, the financial powers could put their money into stable countries that needed capital in specialized areas. This would ensure a good return on a safe investment. Within these categories were many variations, all of which held the promise of a handsome payoff, usually both in financial and political terms.

For debtors, however, loans could be helpful or devastating, depending on the circumstances. The United States was able to get needed capital with a minimum infringement on its sovereignty. At the opposite extreme was the case of the Ottoman Empire, which received its first loan in 1854. Twenty-two years later the Turks were so deeply in debt that they had to put a major portion of their tax base in foreign hands just to pay the interest. Unlike the Americans, the Turks put just 10 percent of the borrowed funds to productive use. Other countries had similar results. Russia by 1914 had a funded debt of 9 billion rubles, half of which was owed to foreigners. Hungary had to use 10 percent of its gross national product to pay foreign investors to cover loans and interest in the pre-war period.[15] Foreign investments of this type were just one facet of the great powers' financial dominance. Economic control implied a profound political impact on the debtor country and represented the most efficient form of imperialism.

CONCLUSION

In Britain, artisans brought practical solutions to bottlenecks in the making of cotton cloth to successfully overcome the limits of animal and human power and to increase output. The island nation possessed the proper balance of population, money, governmental support, internal markets, and a risk-taking entrepreneurial class to accomplish the first revolution in industrialization. The results achieved in textiles were reproduced in iron and steel, as Britain came to dominate the world economically by mid-century.

The second phase of industrialization brought new wealth and a whole new range of products to the Continent and carried the urban problems already experienced in Britain across the Channel. The rapid growth of cities strained the capabilities of local and national authorities to respond to the challenges of providing utilities, education, law enforcement, and social services. Industrialization demanded great sacrifices from the first generation of men, women, and children caught up in it.

Strengthened by increased tax revenues and improved technology, the governments of Europe expanded their scope and influence, while providing an outlet for public opinion. By the early twentieth century, Europe had brought together the material strength, intellectual vitality, and governmental flexibility to dominate the planet. The explosive increase in productivity made possible by industrialization and Europe's massive population growth contributed the power and personnel to extend economic and political control from the western tip of the Eurasian landmass to the entire world.

✦ Suggestions for Reading

David Landes's *The Unbound Prometheus: Technological Change and Industrial Development in Western Europe from 1750 to the Present* (Cambridge, 1969) is a well-written and excellent survey of the entire sweep of industrialization. For Britain specifically, see T. Ashton, *The Industrial Revolution: 1760–1830* (Oxford, 1949), P. Mathias, *The First Industrial Nation* (Methuen, 1983), Phyllis Deane, *The First Industrial Revolution* (Cambridge, 1979), and John Rule, *The Vital Century: England's Developing Economy, 1714–1815* (Longman, 1992). Also recommended is S. B. Clough, *Economic History of Europe* (Walker, 1968). C. Singer et al., eds., *The Late Nineteenth Century, 1850–1900*, vol. 5, in the series *A History of Technology* (Oxford, 1958) is lavishly illustrated and clearly written. See also W. O. Henderson, *The Industrialization of Europe: 1780–1914* (London, 1969) and *The Rise of German Industrial Power* (Berkeley, 1975), J. C. Chambers and G. E. Mingay, *The Agricultural Revolution* (Schocken, 1966), and Carlo Cipolla, ed., *The Fontana Economic History of Europe: The Emergence of Industrial Societies* (Fontana Books, 1973). Rondo E. Cameron's *France and the Economic Development of Europe: 1800–1914* (Octagon, 1961) gives another perspective along with A. S. Milward and S. B. Saul, *The Economic Development of Continental Europe 1780–1870* (Allen & Unwin, 1973). For a useful survey of German developments, see T. Hammerow, *Restoration, Revolution, Reaction: Economics and Politics in Germany* (Princeton, 1958). William Blackwell provides useful background on tsarist developments in his *Industrialization of Russia* (Crowell, 1970). A useful volume on international economic growth is Sidney Pollard, *European Economic Integration* (Harcourt Brace Jovanovich, 1974). Francis Sheppard's *London 1808–1970: The Internal War* (Univ. of California, 1971) is a fine account of a city experiencing the challenge of growth.

The social impact of industrialization can be seen in the novels of Charles Dickens, especially *Hard Times*. T. K. Rabb and R. I. Rotberg include several selections on the social impact of industrialization in *The Family in History* (Harper & Row, 1973). Asa Brigg's *Victorian Cities* (Harper & Row, 1968) and *Victorian People* (Univ. of Chicago, 1959) are vivid portrayals. Peter Stearns, *European Society in Upheaval* (Macmillan, 1967), and W. L. Langer, *Political and Social Upheaval, 1832–1852* (Harper & Row, 1969) are valuable surveys. Louise A. Tilly and Joan W. Scott, *Women, Work, and Family* (Holt, Rinehart, and Winston, 1978) is a seminal work on the change in the work and family life of women wrought by industrialization.

For background on the factors aiding Europe's expansion abroad, see in addition to suggestions provided in Chapter 23: Carl Cipolla, *The Economic History of World Population* (Penguin, 1962); Thomas McKeown, *The Modern Rise of Population* (Academic, 1976); George Lichtheim, *Imperialism* (Praeger, 1971); Heinz Gollwitzer, *Europe in the Age of Imperialism: 1880–1914* (Harcourt Brace Jovanovich, 1979); Roger Price, *The Economic Modernisation of France* (John Wiley, 1975); Sidney Pollard, *European Economic Integration: 1815–1970* (Harcourt Brace Jovanovich, 1974); D. Fieldhouse, *Colonialism: 1870–1945* (London, 1981); W. J. Mossman, *Theories of Imperialism* (London, 1981); Alan Hodgart, *The Economics of European Imperialism* (Norton, 1978); G. H. Nadela and P. Curtis, eds., *Imperialism and Colonialism* (Macmillan, 1965). Daniel R. Headrick's *The Tools of Empire: Technology and European Imperialism in the Nineteenth Century* (Oxford, 1981) gives a thorough examination of the decisive role played by European technology in the establishment of economic control over the world.

✦ Notes

1. J. D. Chambers, "Enclosures and the Labour Supply in the Industrial Revolution," *Economic History Review*, 2nd series, V, 1953, pp. 318–343, as cited in David Landes, *The Unbound Prometheus: Technological Change and Industrial Development in Western Europe from 1750 to the Present* (Cambridge: Cambridge University Press, 1969), p. 115.
2. E. J. Hobsbawm, *The Age of Revolution, 1789–1848* (New York: New American Library, 1964), pp. 44–73.
3. I. Vyshnegradsky, quoted in William L. Blackwell, *The Industrialization of Russia: An Historical Perspective* (New York: Thomas Y. Crowell, 1970), p. 24.
4. Fernand Braudel, *Capitalism and Material Life: 1400–1800* (New York: Harper & Row, 1975), p. 11; William Langer, "Checks on Population Growth: 1750–1850," *Scientific American* 226 (1972), pp. 92–99.
5. Thomas R. Malthus, "An Essay on Population," in *Introduction to Contemporary Civilization in the West*, vol. II (New York: Columbia University Press, 1955), p. 196.
6. Eugen Weber, *A Modern History of Europe* (New York: W. W. Norton, 1971), p. 988.
7. Sidney Pollard, *European Economic Integration: 1815–1970* (New York: Harcourt Brace Jovanovich, 1974), pp. 56–62.
8. Edward Shorter, "Illegitimacy, Sexual Revolution, and Social Change in Modern Europe," in Theodore K. Rabb and Robert I. Rotberg, eds., *The Family in History* (New York: Harper & Row, 1973), pp. 48–84.

9. Heinz Gollwitzer, *Europe in the Age of Imperialism: 1880–1914* (New York: Harcourt Brace Jovanovich, 1969), p. 20.

10. Charles Tilly, "Reflections on the History of European State-Making," in Charles Tilly, ed., *The Formation of National States in Western Europe* (Princeton: Princeton University Press, 1975), p. 15.

11. Edward H. Reisner, *Nationalism and Education Since 1789* (New York: Macmillan, 1923), pp. 35, 145, 211.

12. Robert Schnerb, "Le XIXe Siècle: L'Apogée de L'Expansion Européene (1815–1914)," *Histoire Générale des Civilisations*, Vol. 6 (Paris: Presses Universitaires de France, 1955), p. 235.

13. Gabriel Ardant, "Financial Policy and Economic Infrastructure of Modern States and Nations," in Charles Tilly, ed., *The Formation of National States in Western Europe* (Princeton: Princeton University Press, 1975), pp. 219–222.

14. David S. Landes, *The Unbound Prometheus: Technological Change and Industrial Development in Western Europe from 1750 to the Present* (Cambridge: Cambridge University Press, 1969), p. 233.

15. Sidney Pollard, *European Economic Integration: 1815–1970* (New York: Harcourt Brace Jovanovich, 1974), pp. 74–78.

CHAPTER 23

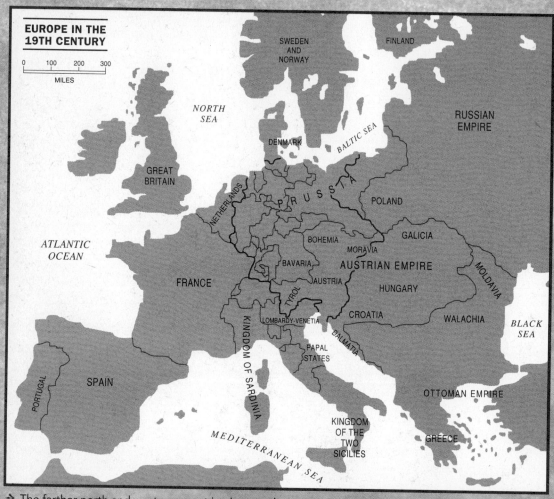

EUROPE IN THE 19TH CENTURY

0 100 200 300
MILES

NORTH SEA

SWEDEN AND NORWAY

FINLAND

RUSSIAN EMPIRE

DENMARK

BALTIC SEA

GREAT BRITAIN

NETHERLANDS

PRUSSIA

POLAND

ATLANTIC OCEAN

BOHEMIA

MORAVIA

GALICIA

BAVARIA

AUSTRIAN EMPIRE

MOLDAVIA

FRANCE

AUSTRIA

HUNGARY

TYROL

LOMBARDY-VENETIA

CROATIA

WALACHIA

BLACK SEA

KINGDOM OF SARDINIA

DALMATIA

PAPAL STATES

PORTUGAL

SPAIN

OTTOMAN EMPIRE

KINGDOM OF THE TWO SICILIES

GREECE

MEDITERRANEAN SEA

→ The farther north and west one went in nineteenth-century Europe, the stronger and more influential were the middle classes. Farther south and east, on the contrary, the weaker the middle classes, their influence, and their economic contribution.

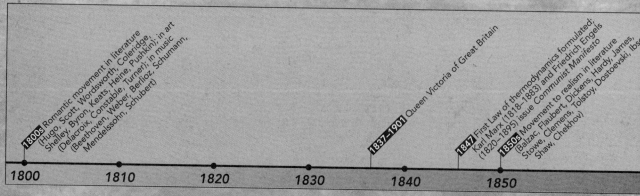

1800s Romantic movement in literature (Hugo, Scott, Wordsworth, Coleridge, Shelley, Byron, Keats, Heine, Pushkin); in art (Delacroix, Constable, Turner); in music (Beethoven, Weber, Berlioz, Schumann, Mendelssohn, Schubert)

1837–1901 Queen Victoria of Great Britain

1847 First Law of thermodynamics formulated; Karl Marx (1818–1883) and Friedrich Engels (1820–1895) issue Communist Manifesto

1850s Movement to realism in literature (Balzac, Flaubert, Dickens, Hardy, James, Stowe, Clemens, Tolstoy, Dostoevski, Ibsen, Shaw, Chekhov)

1800   1810   1820   1830   1840   1850

The Cultural Dominance of the European Middle Classes, 1815–1914

CHAPTER OUTLINE

The greatest beneficiaries of industrialization were the middle classes of western Europe, who profited directly from controlling all aspects of the industrial economy. Their newfound wealth, harnessed to the social and legal changes resulting from the French Revolution and the reform movement in Britain, allowed them to dominate all aspects of political life by 1900. Both literate and numerous, they also shaped religious, scientific, and cultural affairs.

While it is difficult to give a strict definition of the bourgeoisie, it is easier to say who was *not* middle class. Neither factory workers nor peasants nor the aristocracy were included. Those closer to the laboring classes were called the lower middle classes, or the *petit bourgeoisie*, while those near the elite were the upper middle classes, or the *haute bourgeoisie*. Included in the lower middle classes were skilled artisans, bureaucrats, clerks, teachers, shopkeepers, and clergy. They realized how little separated them from the laboring masses and were constantly trying to climb socially. Later in the century they benefit-

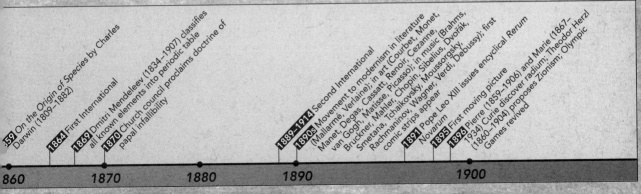

ted most from the compulsory education laws and were avid consumers of the books written by the new wave of authors, the penny-press newspapers, and state propaganda. In general, the farther south and east one went in Europe, the less numerous and weaker were the middle classes.

The *haute bourgeoisie* gained most of the wealth created by industrialization. It was not easy to break into this level of society, but money, taste, and aggressiveness could open the doors for the bankers, factory owners, lawyers, architects, occasional professors, doctors, or high governmental officials who tried. Once admitted, they gained many of the benefits of the aristocracy such as access to the best schools. Because of their wealth and leisure time they controlled politics, the press, and the universities.

The British upper middle class was a group riddled with contradictions. The age in which they lived came to be labeled the Victorian period, after Victoria (1837–1901), the long-reigning English queen. On the surface the Victorians had little doubt about what was right and wrong, moral and immoral, and most importantly, proper and improper. Underneath this surface propriety some members of the leading families of the *haute bourgeoisie* pursued a life marked by a pursuit of diverse sexual pleasure and drug addiction. One of the prime ministers of the era, William Gladstone, devoted considerable attention to "reforming" prostitutes. At the same time, the Victorian literary establishment concentrated on "cleaning up" Shakespeare's plays and toning down some parts of Gibbon's *Decline and Fall of the Roman Empire*.

The British upper middle class employed more than two and a half million servants at the century's end—nearly a million people more than farmed the land—and led crusades against slavery, alcohol, pornography, and child labor. Their efforts led to the passage of a series of reforms limiting the employment of young children, setting maximum working hours for teenagers, and regulating working conditions for women—even when the factory owners argued that such changes were bad for the country because they violated the freedom of contract between the worker and the employer. The British upper middle class set the tone to be imitated by their peers across the Continent.[1]

CHRISTIANITY IN THE INDUSTRIAL AGE

After the Reformation, Christianity continued to be buffeted by serious intellectual, political, and social challenges. The Scientific Revolution and the Enlightenment ate away at the authority of the traditional church. Darwin's theories challenged the traditional Christian view of the origins of the world as presented in the Bible. The Christian churches were reeling under the challenges posed by industrialization and urbanization during the nineteenth century. The demographic changes that resulted from rapid growth of cities forced the church to respond to different audiences facing more difficult problems than those of an earlier, simpler age. Yet Christianity endured and adapted, deeply affected by the ambitions and values of the ascending middle classes, especially in the rapidly growing Methodist Church.

During the nineteenth century, middle-class European missionaries went forth in their centuries-old function as self-proclaimed messengers of the word of God. Once the European states began competing for land around the globe, the missionaries often complemented national policy in their religious work. Buttressed by their complacent sense of cultural superiority, they felt justified in undermining the cultures of the peoples with whom they came in contact—especially if that was the price to be paid for eternal salvation.

Changes in the Catholic Church

In 1864 Pope Pius IX (1846–1878), who had become extraordinarily reactionary after having been expelled from Rome in 1848 and in the wake of the Italian unification movement (see p. 694), issued the *Syllabus of Errors*, a document that attacked the critical examination of faith and doctrine. In 1870 he called a general council of the church to proclaim the doctrine of papal infallibility, which states that when speaking *ex cathedra* (from the chair) on issues concerning religion and moral behavior, the pope cannot err.

Pius' successor, Leo XIII (1879-1903) was more flexible and less combative and helped bring the church into the modern age. In his

ACCORDING TO THE IDEAS OF OUR MISSIONARY MANIACS.

→ This 1895 cartoon satirizes the missionary mania of the age of imperialism. According to the caption, "The Chinaman *must* be converted even if it takes the whole military and naval forces of the two greatest nations of the world [Great Britain and the United States] to do it."

encyclical *Rerum Novarum* ("Concerning new things") issued in 1891, Leo condemned Marxism and upheld capitalism but severely criticized the evils affecting the working classes. By pointing out some of the Christian elements of socialism, Leo placed the church on the side of the workers who were suffering the greatest ills resulting from industrialization. Leo worked to improve relations with Germany, encouraged the passage of social welfare legislation, and supported the formation of Catholic labor unions and political parties.

A New Spirit

Spiritual life among the intellectual elite in England received a powerful stimulus from the Oxford Movement. At the beginning of the nineteenth century, a core of spiritual activists at Oxford, including the future Cardinal John Henry Newman (1801–1890) met to defend the church from the various secular and political forces that were besieging it. During the 1830s the group split, some members remaining within the Anglican church, and others—including Newman—joining the Catholic church. During the rest of the century, the Oxford Movement brought new life to the church in England through its missionary work, participation in

social concerns, and improvement of the intellectual level of the faith. Similar developments occurred across the Continent.

SCIENTIFIC SUPERIORITY

Europe's world dominance in basic scientific research began with Copernicus in the 1500s and extended through the nineteenth century. The major difference between sixteenth-century work and modern discoveries was that the effects of the latter research had almost immediate and widespread economic applications as well as intellectual implications.

Darwin and Evolution

In the mid-nineteenth century Charles Darwin (1809–1892) formulated a major scientific theory in *On the Origin of Species by Means of Natural Selection* (1859). This theory of evolution, stating that all complex organisms developed from simple forms through the operation of natural causes, challenged traditionalist Christian beliefs on creation and altered views of life on earth. The theory contended that no species is fixed and changeless. Classical thinkers first stated this view, and contemporary philosophers such as

Pope Leo XIII, *Rerum Novarum*

Pope Leo XIII responded to the radical changes affecting Europe in his encyclical *Rerum Novarum*, issued May 15, 1891. The document addressed the challenges facing Christians and advised them how to respond. See, for example, Leo's advice on unions.

Associations in immense variety and especially unions of workers are now more common than they have ever been. This is not the place to enquire into the origins of most of them, their aims or the methods they employ. There is plenty of evidence to confirm the opinion that many are in the hands of secret leaders and are used for purposes which are inconsistent with both Christian principles and the social good. They do all that they can to ensure that those who will not join them shall not eat. In this state of affairs Christian workers have but two alternatives: they can join these associations and greatly endanger their religion; or they can form their own and, with united strength, free themselves courageously from such injustice and intolerable oppression. That the second alternative must be chosen cannot be doubted by those who have no desire to see men's highest good put into extreme danger.

High praise is due to the many Catholics who have informed themselves, seen what is needed and tried to learn from experience by what honourable means they might be able to lead unpropertied workers to a better standard of living. They have taken up the workers' cause, seeking to raise the incomes of families and individuals, introduce equity into the relations between workers and employers and strengthen among both groups regard for duty and the teaching of the Gospel—teaching which inculcates moderation, forbids excess and safeguards harmony in the state between very differently situated men and organizations. We see eminent men coming together to learn from each other about these things and unite their forces to deal with them as effectively as possible. Others encourage different groups of workers to form useful associations, advise them, give them practical help and enable them to find suitable and well-paid employment. The bishops offer their goodwill and support.

From Leo XIII, *Rerum Novarum*, translated by Joseph Kirwan (London: Catholic Society, 1983).

Hegel had used the concept of evolutionary change. In the century before Darwin, other research supported the concept of change, both biological and social.

Darwin built on the work of Sir Charles Lyell (1797–1875) and Jean Baptiste Lamarck (1744–1829) when he began his investigations. Lyell's three-volume *Principles of Geology* (1830–1833) confirmed the views of the Scottish geologist James Hutton (1726–1797), who stated that the earth developed through natural rather than supernatural causes. Lyell helped popularize the notion of geological time operating over a vast span of years. This understanding is essential to the acceptance of any theory of biological evolution, based as it is on changes in species over many thousands of generations. Lamarck, a naturalist, argued that every organism tends to develop new organs to adapt to the changing conditions of its environment. He theorized that these changes are transmitted by heredity to the descendants, which are thereafter changed in structural form.

Though he had originally studied medicine at Edinburgh and prepared for the ministry at Cambridge University, Darwin lost interest in both professions and became a naturalist while in his twenties. From 1831 to 1836 he studied the specimens he had collected while on a five-year surveying expedition aboard the ship *Beagle*, which had sailed along the coast of South America and among the Galapagos Islands. The works of his predecessors, plus questions that he had about the theories of Thomas Robert Malthus, as presented in Malthus's *Essay on Population*, helped him define the problem he studied. When Darwin's book finally appeared, it changed many basic scientific and social assumptions.

In his revolutionary work, Darwin constructed an explanation of how life evolves that upset the literal interpretation of the Bible taught in most Christian churches.

> *Species have been modified, during a long course of descent chiefly through the natural selection of numerous successive, slight, favorable variations; aided in an important manner by the direct action of external conditions, and by variations which seem to us in our ignorance to arise spontaneously.*[2]

His explanation radically affected the views of the scientific community about the origin and evolution of life on the planet. The hypothesis, in its simplified form, states that all existing plant and animal species are descended from earlier and, generally speaking, more primitive forms. The direct effects of the environment causes species to develop through the inheritance of minute differences in individual structures. As the centuries passed, the more adaptable, stronger species lived on, while the weaker, less flexible species died out. Additionally, a species may also be changed by the cumulative working of sexual selection, which Darwin saw to be the "most powerful means of changing the races of man."

After the announcement of Darwin's theories, others, such as the German biologist August Weismann (1834–1914) and the Austrian priest Gregor Mendel (1822–1884), worked along similar lines to explore the genetic relationships among living organisms. Weismann proved that acquired characteristics cannot be inherited. Mendel's investigations into the laws of heredity, based on his experiments with the crossing of garden peas, proved to be invaluable in the scien-

THE MODERN THEORY OF THE DESCENT OF MAN.

→ In *The Descent of Man* (1871), Charles Darwin theorized that humans evolved from lower life forms. Using Darwin's theory, Ernst Haeckel prepared this schematic history of the process of evolution showing the progression from the simplest single-cell organisms to present-day human beings.

tific breeding of plants and animals and demonstrated that the evolution of different species was more complex than Darwin had concluded. Based on their work, biologists hypothesized that there are chromosomes that carry the characteristics of an organism. Darwin had hinted at and now further research supported the mutation theory, which states that sudden and unpredictable changes within a chromosome can be transmitted by heredity to produce new species. Scientists began to work with the very fundamental building blocks of life and established the groundwork of contemporary biotechnical research.

Darwin and other investigators carefully researched and cautiously stated their findings. Unlike earlier discoveries, however, their work came to be widely reported in popular journals and applied by commentators and politicians. The newly ascendant middle classes responded enthusiastically to their understanding of evolutionary theory, finding in it a comfortable reassurance of the "rightness" of their own upward mobility and Europe's dominance in the world.

Medicine, Chemistry, and Physics

Important advances in medicine, chemistry, and physics contributed to a population explosion on the Continent and had significant economic implications, further strengthening the bases of Europe's dominance. At the beginning of the nineteenth century, medical practices were making a slow transition away from the indiscriminate use of leeches and bleeding. In the 1840s, physicians began to use ether and chloroform to reduce pain during operations. The Scottish surgeon Joseph Lister (1827–1912) developed new antiseptic practices that made major advances against the spread of infection. By 1900, fairly sophisticated and much safer surgical procedures were available.

Probably the most important single advance came with the substantiation of the germ theory of disease by Louis Pasteur (1822–1895) and Robert Koch (1843–1910). During his search for a cure to anthrax—a disease that in the late 1870s destroyed more than 20 percent of the sheep in France—Pasteur established the principle that the injection of a mild form of disease bacterium causes the body to form antibodies

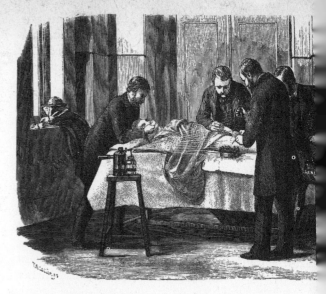

→ This 1882 engraving shows the Lister carbolic spray being used as an antiseptic as the surgeons perform an operation.

that prevents the vaccinated individual from getting the severe form of the particular disease. Koch discovered the specific organisms that caused 11 diseases, including tuberculosis. The work of Pasteur and Koch placed the sciences of bacteriology and immunology on a firm footing and gave promise that the end of such deadly diseases as typhoid and smallpox might be in sight.

Modern chemistry gained its foundations during the nineteenth century, founded on the atomic theory advanced by an English Quaker schoolmaster, John Dalton (1766–1844). In 1869 Russian chemist Dmitri Mendeleev (1834–1907) drew up a periodic table in which all known elements were classified according to their weights and properties. From gaps in this table, chemists were able to deduce the existence of undiscovered elements. Other researchers made advances in the field of nutrition and discovered the significance of vitamins. Biochemical research threw light on the presence and function of the ductless (endocrine) glands. Chemotherapy advanced with the discovery of a chemical that could destroy the syphilis bacteria and with procedures that would lead to the discovery of sulfa drugs, penicillin, and other antibiotics.

Revolutionary strides in physics came in the areas of electricity and thermodynamics, of which the First Law was formulated in 1847.

Michael Faraday (1791–1867) prepared the way for the dynamo, a device that made possible changes in communications, the transmission of current over long distances, and the development of the electric motor. The Scottish scientist James Clerk Maxwell (1831–1879) and the German Heinrich Hertz (1857–1894) conducted basic research into the nature of electromagnetic phenomena such as light, radiant heat, and ultraviolet radiation.

Pierre (1859–1906) and Marie (1867–1934) Curie made major strides toward the discovery of the X ray and radioactivity. When they extracted radium from uranium ore in 1896 the scientific world became aware of the strength of radioactivity. Marie Curie was the first person to be awarded two Nobel Prizes, one in physics and one in chemistry.

→ Marie Curie, born Manya Skłodowska in Warsaw, Poland, shared with her husband, Pierre, the 1903 Nobel Prize in physics for their work on radioactivity, a term of Marie coined in 1898. She won the 1911 Nobel in chemistry for her discovery of radium and polonium and isolation of pure radium. Irène Curie, the daughter of Marie and Pierre, shared with her husband, Frédéric Joliot, the 1935 Nobel in chemistry for their work in synthesizing new radioactive isotopes of various elements.

At the beginning of the twentieth century, the British physicist Ernest Rutherford (1871–1937) helped develop electron theory. It had been postulated that the atom contains particles known as electrons. Rutherford contributed the idea that each atom has a central particle, or nucleus, that is positively charged and separate from the negatively charged electrons. These discoveries destroyed one of the foundations of traditional physics—that matter is indivisible and continuous.

NEW CERTAINTIES

The territory opened up by the scientists seemed to complement the ambitions of the middle classes. The optimism generated by science in the laboratory and Europe's advance across the globe supported the commonly held belief in inevitable progress. It also buttressed the theories of a new breed of social scientists known as the positivists. Positivism is a mechanistic way of thinking that uses the methods and principles of science to define the laws of a strictly material world that presumably may be scientifically verified.

Auguste Comte (1798–1857), an engineer who was formerly secretary to Saint-Simon, established the foundations for the philosophical approach known as positivism in a series of lectures and publications in the 1830s and 1840s. He stated that one could find and verify the laws that controlled society in the same way that a scientist discovered physical laws. For Comte humanity was a part of a machine, which possessed neither free will nor a divinely infused spark of life. Comte's goal was to understand the machine and devise a science to discover the laws of history and society. He developed the social science of sociology and stated that when humanity could base itself on science, and not on opinion, harmony would arise.

The New Science and Modern Racism

Darwin's hypotheses were very attractive to the positivists, who, along with their imitators, distorted the British scientist's findings by applying them to areas Darwin never dreamed of discussing—human social, economic, and political activities—to justify the fantasies of eternal

→ Auguste Comte. Comte developed the theory of positivism, according to which science is totally objective and value-free.

progress, the dominance of science, the perfectibility of humanity through obedience to the supposedly unchanging laws of society, and the assumption of Anglo-Saxon racial dominance. The Social Darwinists, positivists, and others of their kind followed a simplistic approach to the world based on their comforting belief that humanity is a cog in a machine and that the possibilities of individuals are predetermined by their place in the larger scheme of things.

The most popular Social Darwinist was the English philosopher Herbert Spencer (1820–1903), who applied Darwin's theories to all aspects of human social and political life. Spencer had a deep influence in both Europe and the United States. As a convenient doctrine to justify the actions and philosophies of those newly arrived at the top of the social and political structure, Social Darwinism dominated Western social thought in the late nineteenth century.

Stressing the role of change and chance in nature, the broadly applied Darwinian theory reinforced the trend away from absolute standards and procedures. The American physicist Charles Sanders Peirce (1839–1914) broke new

William Graham Sumner on Socialism

The nineteenth century was the prime age of the "fit." Darwin's scientific theories were applied to, among other things, political theory. William Graham Sumner saw socialism as retrograde.

The origin of socialism, which is the extreme development of the sentimental philosophy, lies in the undisputed facts which I described at the outset. The socialist regards this misery as the fault of society. He thinks that we can organize society as we like and that an organization can be devised in which poverty and misery shall disappear. He goes further even than this. He assumes that men have artificially organized society as it now exists. Hence if anything is disagreeable or hard in the present state of society, it follows, on that view, that the task of organizing society has been imperfectly and badly performed, and that it needs to be done over again. These are the assumptions with which the socialist starts, and many socialists seem also to believe that if they can destroy belief in an Almighty God who is supposed to have made the world such as it is, they will then have overthrown the belief that there is a fixed order in human nature and human life which man can scarcely alter at all, and, if at all, only infinitesimally.

The truth is that the social order is fixed by laws of nature precisely analogous to those of the physical order. The most that man can do is by ignorance and self-conceit to mar the operation of social laws.

From William Graham Sumner, *The Challenge of Facts*, 1914.

philosophical ground in this area. In the late 1890s, William James (1842–1910) popularized Peirce's approaches in his philosophy of pragmatism. James stated that "an idea is true so long as to believe it is profitable to our lives." In effect, the pragmatists rejected any concept of truth or reality as an absolute and favored a more flexible, result-oriented approach.

The rapid political, social, economic, philosophical, and intellectual changes that shook Europe and the world led to new ways of defining individuals and groups. Even before Darwin publicized his theory of evolution, pseudoscientists such as Joseph Arthur de Gobineau (1816–1882) laid the foundations of modern racism, justifying the domination of one group over another for "scientific" reasons. Gobineau applied biological theory to politics, regarding nations as organisms. He argued that different races are innately unequal in ability and worth and that the genius of a race depended upon heredity, not external factors. Gobineau stated a widely held belief among Europeans that white people alone were capable of cultural creativity and that intermixture with other races would destroy that creativity. Social Darwinist arguments and Gobineau's theories in support of white superiority gave "rational" justifications to blatant bigotry and provided a reassuring sanction for European domination over Asians and Africans.

Supported by the new pseudoscience and the belief that Europeans alone bore the burdens of progress, European imperialism took on a more blatant and bellicose form. Aggressive nationalism was adhered to almost as a religion; it served as a powerful vehicle for politicians to mobilize their constituents. Nationalistic pressures became especially strong in eastern Europe and the Balkans, where political instability and economic underdevelopment created insecure conditions.

One of the manifestations of the identities was the Anglo-Saxon movement. In Britain and Germany writers and speakers presented the case for the superiority of northern Europeans. They stated that world leadership should naturally reside in London and Berlin because the people living there possessed the proper combination of religion, racial qualities, and culture to enable them to dictate the world's future. People

→ In a work published in 1854–1855, Joseph Arthur de Gobineau advanced the theory that the Aryan is the superior race among human beings. The theory would have ominous consequences later in the twentieth century.

as diverse as Kaiser William II and U.S. President Woodrow Wilson were affected by this outlook.

"Pan" Movements and Anti-Semitism

Another manifestation of a regrouping on the basis of new principles came with the so-called pan-cultural movements. Pan-Slavic movements had begun before 1850. These were based either around the Orthodox Slavs' foundation in Moscow or the Catholic Slavs' center at Prague. In the latter part of the century the Russians would use their Pan-Slavic movement to expand their influence into the Balkans in pursuit of their "destiny" to create and rule a great Slavic empire. The Pan-Germanic League was organized in Berlin in the 1890s to spread the belief in the superiority of the German race and culture.

Houston Stewart Chamberlain on the Characteristics of the German Race

Houston Stewart Chamberlain had no doubts about the superiority of the Germans. His views found their way into Hitler's beliefs.

Let us attempt a glance into the depths of the soul. What are the specific intellectual and moral characteristics of this Germanic race? Certain anthropologists would fain teach us that all races are equally gifted; we point to history and answer: that is a lie! The races of mankind are markedly different in the nature and also in the extent of their gift, and the Germanic races belong to the most highly gifted group, the group usually termed Aryan. Is this human family united and uniform by bonds of blood? Do these stems really all spring from the same root? I do not know and I do not much care; no affinity binds more closely than elective affinity, and in this sense the Indo-European Aryans certainly form a family.

Physically and mentally the Aryans are pre-eminent among all peoples; for that reason they are by right, as the Stagirite expresses it, the lords of the world. Aristotle puts the matter still more concisely when he says, "Some men are by nature free, others slaves"; this perfectly expresses the moral aspect. For freedom is by no means an abstract thing, to which every human being has fundamentally a claim; a right to freedom must evidently depend upon capacity for it, and this again presupposes physical and intellectual power. One may make the assertion, that even the mere conception of freedom is quite unknown to most men. Do we not see the *homo syriacus* develop just as well and as happily in the position of slave as of master? Do the Chinese not show us another example of the same nature? Do not all historians tell us that the Semites and half-Semites, in spite of their great intelligence, never succeeded in founding a State that lasted, and that because every one always endeavoured to grasp all power for himself, thus showing that their capabilities were limited to despotism and anarchy, the two opposites of freedom?

From Houston Stewart Chamberlain, *Foundations of the Nineteenth Century*, 1900.

Anti-Semitism—hatred of the Jews—had been a part of European history since the legalization of Christianity. But the movement attained a new strength and vigor in the last part of the nineteenth century. In Germany, the historian Heinrich von Treitschke (1834–1896) stated that "the Jews are our calamity." In France, anti-Semitism played a significant role in the Dreyfus affair. In eastern Europe, the Jews suffered many injustices, while in Russia many Jews died in organized pogroms. Anti-Semitism became stronger because of the economic dislocation that modernization introduced and of the work of bigoted cranks who turned out pseudo-scientific tracts and forgeries such as the *Protocols of the Elders of Zion*.

In response, a desire for a homeland grew among the Jews. In 1896 Theodor Herzl (1860–1904) came forward with the program of Zionism, which had as its purpose the creation of an independent state within Palestine. The first general congress of Zionists was held in Switzerland in 1896, and a small-scale emigration to Palestine, which had been settled for centuries by Arabs, began. In the first decade of the twentieth century, the election of Karl Leuger (1844–1910), who ran and stayed in power as mayor of Vienna on an anti-Semitic platform, foretold the tragic genocide that would occur later in the century. It was in this atmosphere that the young Adolf Hitler spent some of his formative years, reading racist, Social Darwinist, and Pan-Germanic tracts.

SOCIALIST RESPONSES TO MIDDLE-CLASS DOMINANCE

The middle of the nineteenth century did not in any way mark the arrival of workers as a major political force in Europe, but it was then that Karl Marx (1818–1883) made a major contribution to their cause through his ideological work. Marx and his colleague, Friedrich Engels (1820–1895), wrote the *Communist Manifesto* in late 1847. In it they outlined the theory of scientific socialism, sketched a wide-ranging program that advocated violent revolution, preached the inevitable conflict of the bourgeoisie and the proletariat, rejected traditional morality and religion, and condemned contemporary governments. In so doing, they made the transition from a philosophical approach to social problems to a basis for modern socialist and communist movements. In the next three decades Marx conceptualized the framework he and Engels erected in the *Manifesto*.

The Marxian Analysis

Karl Marx was born in Trier, Germany, to middle-class Jewish parents who had converted to Protestantism. He attended the University of Berlin as a doctoral candidate in philosophy, instead of law as his father desired. At the university he joined a circle that followed some aspects of Hegel's thought. After finishing his degree, he could not find a university position and so returned to the Rhineland where he began writing for a local liberal newspaper. The injustices he saw around him and his reading of the French socialists Henri de Saint-Simon and Pierre Joseph Proudhon led him to concentrate on the economic factors in history. He went to Paris to continue his studies, met Engels, and was expelled by the authorities in 1845. From there he went first to Belgium and finally to England where, after 1848, he spent most of the rest of his life.

An uncompromising hostility to capitalism drove Marx's work. He stated in the *Manifesto* that communists "openly declare that their ends can be attained only by the forcible overthrow of all existing social conditions." Virtually every day he made his way to the British Museum where he waged intellectual war on capitalism by doing research for his major works, especially *Das Kapital*.

At night he returned home to write, enduring difficult living conditions and the death of three of his children in the 1850s. He wrote prolifically, although suffering from boils, asthma, spleen and liver problems, and eye strain. His constant inability to handle money drove him into fits of rage against his creditors. He was increasingly intolerant of those who disagreed with him and became an embittered recluse; yet his vision and theories inspired reformers for the next century. Marx gave the oppressed an explanation for their difficult position and a hope for their future.

A materialistic view of history shaped his approach. He wrote that economic forces drove history. He did not deny the existence or importance of spiritual or philosophical values; nor did he doubt that the occasional genius could alter the flow of events. However, the material aspects of life were much more important. Marx believed that "it is not the consciousness of men which determines their existence, but on the contrary, it is the existence which determines their consciousness." As an economic determinist he believed that when the means of production of a

→ Karl Marx with his daughter. After being expelled from several European countries, Marx settled in England where he devoted himself to the development of his theory of scientific socialism.

given era changed, the whole social and ideological structure was transformed.

Marx identified the productive forces of society as the key factor in history. The world was driven by class conflict between those who controlled the means of production and those who did not, whether master against slave in ancient Greece, patrician against plebeian in Rome, lord against serf in the middle ages, noble against bourgeois in the early modern times, or capitalist against the proletarian in the modern world. The world's history moved in this zigzag pattern through class struggle, a reflection of the Hegelian dialectic.

Hegel had written that history is made up of a number of cultural periods, each one the expression of a dominant spirit or idea. After fulfilling its purpose, a given period is replaced by a period of contradictory ideas or set of values. The original thesis is negated, and that negation in turn is also negated after it has run its course. Where Hegel saw history driven through a historical dialectic in cultural terms to a final phase, Marx saw history moving to its conclusion of the workers controlling the means of production.

The bourgeoisie, who had erected the new capitalist society by gaining control of the means of production through organizing trade and industry, created its opposition in the proletariat, the class-conscious workers. This group would be, according to Marx, "the seeds of the bourgeoisie's own destruction." According to the dialectic, when the workers recognized their true power they would overthrow the bourgeoisie. Out of this conflict would come the final act of the dialectical process, the classless society in which "each person would work according to his ability and receive according to his need." An interim dictatorship might have to occur, because a number of features of the old order would remain and the proletariat would have to be protected. However, as the classless society evolved, the state would wither away.

Through his research, Marx identified a number of defects that foretold the inevitable overthrow of the bourgeoisie, among them alienation and surplus value. The factory system turned workers into cogs in the larger machine and deprived them of satisfaction in their work. In addition, Marx charged that owners did not pay workers for the value they created. A worker could, for example, produce in seven hours the necessary economic value to supply one individual's needs, but the owner would keep the worker laboring for twelve hours. The owner thereby stole the "surplus value" of five working hours from workers, thus robbing them of the fruits of their work.

Finally, Marx noted that in the capitalist system the rich got richer and fewer and the poor got poorer and more numerous. This produced huge discontent and increased the chance of revolution. Further, the masses would be unable to buy all of the goods they produced and economic crises of overproduction and unemployment would become the rule. In time, once the bourgeois phase of dominance had run its course, the contradictions between the classes would become so great that the proletariat would rise up and take over the means of production.

Marx was the last of the great universal theorists. As is the case with other ideologists in the rationalist eighteenth-century tradition, he built on the foundations erected by others and made a creative synthesis that has had worldwide appeal. As was also the case with other major thinkers, his thoughts, which were often hypotheses, have been frozen in dogma or revised in various countries to take forms he would have trouble recognizing. It is not surprising that the rapidly changing age in which he lived would outrun many of his projections, especially those concerning the rigidity of the capitalists.

Labor Movements

Well before Marx conceived his theories, the British economy suffered through a difficult time after the end of the Napoleonic wars. High unemployment struck skilled workers, especially hand loom weavers. In frustration, some of them fought back and destroyed textile machines, the symbol of the forces oppressing them. Strikes, demonstrations, and incidents such as the Peterloo massacre, August 16, 1819, at St. Peter's Fields in which soldiers closed down a political meeting, killing eleven and injuring hundreds, vividly expressed the workers' rage. Not until the British reformers came forward in the 1820s did the laborers begin to gain some relief.

Their efforts to form labor unions received an important boost in 1825 when the Combina-

Portfolio Six

Nineteenth-Century Art of the Western World

→ Rejecting the historical, religious, and mythological themes of the painters who preceded him, Gustave Courbet chose to portray what he saw—the contemporary life of the world around him. For this he was soundly criticized by his contemporaries. Critics attacked *Young Ladies Giving Alms to a Cowherd* (1851–1852) for its "ugliness," vulgarity, lack of perspective, and violation of tradition. Yet it is these same attributes that made Courbet a revolutionary figure in the history of art.

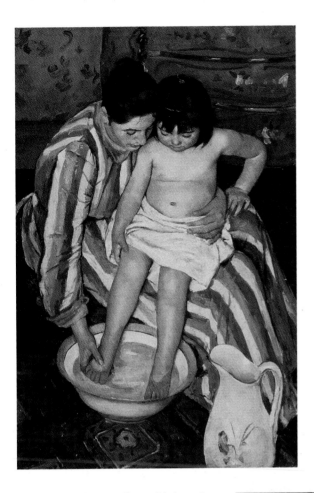

→ A concern for the effects of light and color united the French impressionists, yet each also developed a personal style. Often regarded as the boldest innovator was Claude Monet, who did series of paintings of the same subject, such as *Water Lilies* (1906), opposite page. U.S.-born Mary Cassatt, who studied in Paris, specialized in paintings of mothers and children, as in *The Bath* (1891–1892), above left. With its vibrant color and shimmering light, *On the Terrace* (1881), above right, is a typical example of the work of Pierre Auguste Renoir. Careful control of line, calculated design, and off-center composition are hallmarks of the works of Edgar Degas, evident in *A Woman with Chrysanthemums* (completed in 1865), right

→ Another artist whose work provoked public outcry was Edouard Manet. A barrage of hostility greeted Manet's *Luncheon on the Grass* (1863), with the frank nudity of the female model juxtaposed with the two clothed male figures. Although the models and the setting seem realistic, Manet was in fact little concerned with subject matter; he believed that the artist's reality lies in the brush strokes and color used, rather than in the objects represented in the painting. This attitude later coalesced in the "art for art's sake" school of thought.

→ Katarina Ivanovic (1811–1882), *The Conquest of Belgrade in 1806*. Throughout history, it has been the rare woman who has achieved success or even recognition in painting. Two areas in which women did achieve some modest success were miniature painting and portraiture; this work by Ivanovic is quite atypical in that regard. Most women artists, excluded from art schools and academies, were likely to be dismissed as amateurs.

→ James Tissot was born in France but later moved to England and then Palestine. His genre paintings of scenes of fashionable life combine painstakingly realistic detail with a sentimental romanticism. The figures in the foreground of *The Last Evening* (1873), which records the end of a shipboard romance, are the artist himself and his beloved Mrs. Kathleen Newton. A few years after Tissot completed this work, Mrs. Newton died, at age 28 a victim of tuberculosis. Her death devastated the artist.

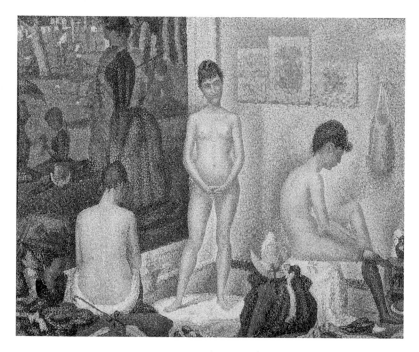

→ Georges Seurat, *The Models* (1888). Another artist who departed from the impressionists was Seurat, who developed a style he termed Divisionism (it has also been called neo-impressionism or pointillism). Rather than mixing pigments on the palette, Seurat covered his canvases systematically with dots of color. Viewed from a distance, the dots were to blend in the beholder's eye into tints more luminous, more subtle, and richer than those that could be obtained through traditional methods.

→ Vincent van Gogh was less interested in the photographic reproduction of nature than in the re-creation of his vision of what he saw, expressed through his use of brilliant, intense, unmodulated color and dynamic brush strokes. The swirling, exploding stars in *The Starry Night* (1889), painted at the sanitarium at St. Rémy during one of van Gogh's lucid periods, seem to express the artist's turbulent emotions.

✦ Originally associated with the impressionists, Paul Cézanne became dissatisfied with the limitations of impressionist style and began a relentless search for the structure and form beneath the color. *Montagne Sainte-Victoire* (1904) is one of a long series Cézanne painted of a mountain scene near his home in Aix-en-Provence. It was works like this that had such a profound influence on the cubists and expressionists who followed Cézanne.

→ A growing disenchantment with the values and traditions of Western civilization led Paul Gauguin to Tahiti, where he spent a number of years living in accord with the local lifestyle. In its carved look, bold pattern, tropical colors, and subject matter drawn from primitive life, *The Red Dog* (1892) is typical of Gauguin's later works in which the origins of modern primitivism can be found.

Karl Marx and Friedrich Engels, *Manifesto of the Communist Party*

The *Manifesto* had little effect on the revolutionary year of 1848. However, in the twentieth century it became one of the most widely read tracts in world history.

A spectre is haunting Europe—the spectre of Communism. All the Powers of old Europe have entered into a holy alliance to exorcise this spectre; Pope and Czar, Metternich and Guizot, French Radicals and German police-spies.

The first step in the revolution by the working class is to raise the proletariat to the position of ruling class, to win the battle of democracy.

The proletariat will use its political supremacy to wrest, by degrees, all capital from the bourgeoisie, to centralise all instruments of production in the hands of the State, i.e., of the proletariat organized by the ruling class; and to increase the total of productive forces as rapidly as possible.

In the most advanced countries the following will be pretty generally applicable:

1. Abolition of property in land and application of all rents of land to public purposes.
2. A heavy progressive or graduated income tax.
3. Abolition of all right of inheritance.
4. Confiscation of the property of all emigrants and rebels.
5. Centralisation of credit in the hands of the State, by means of a national bank with State capital and an exclusive monopoly.
6. Centralisation of the means of communication and transport in the hands of the State.
7. Extension of factories and instruments of production owned by the State; the bringing into cultivation of waste lands, and the improvement of the soil generally in accordance with a common plan.
8. Equal liability of all to labour. Establishment of industrial armies, especially for agriculture.
9. Combination of agriculture with manufacturing industries; gradual abolition of the distinction between town and country, by a more equable distribution of the population over the country.
10. Free education for all children in public schools. Abolition of children's factory labour in its present form. Combination of education with industrial production, etc., etc.

When, in the course of development, class distinctions have disappeared, and all production has been concentrated in the hands of a vast association of the whole nation, the public power will lose its political character. Political power, properly so called, is merely the organised power of one class for oppressing another. If the proletariat during its contest with the bourgeoisie is compelled, by the force of circumstances, to organise itself as a class, if, by means of a revolution, it makes itself the ruling class, and, as such, sweeps away by force the old conditions of production, then it will, along with these conditions, have swept away the conditions for the existence of class antagonisms, and of classes generally, and will thereby have abolished its own supremacy as a class.

In place of the old bourgeois society, with its classes and class antagonisms, we shall have an association in which the free development of each is the condition for the free development of all.

From Karl Marx and Friedrich Engels, *Manifesto of the Communist Party* (International Press, 1911).

---

tion Acts, passed in 1799 against the formation of workers' associations, were repealed. The first unions, such as the half-million strong Grand National Consolidated Trades Union, were weak and disorganized, split by the gulf between skilled workers and common laborers. Nonetheless, the workers laid the foundations for the powerful unions that defended them by the end of the century.

As industry became more sophisticated and centralized, so too did the labor movement. Across Europe the workers could choose anarchist, socialist, or conservative paths to follow. Some unions centered on a particular occupa-

→ This plate commemorates a protest meeting of the Trades Union Congress held April 21, 1834, to present a petition to the king.

tion—the trade or the craft unions. Others found their focus in the various productive stages of an industry, while still others, such as the English Trade Unions Congress, were nationwide and all-encompassing, wielding great power. Whatever the choice, by 1900 unions had made important advances through their solidarity in launching paralyzing strikes.

Socialist parties in the second half of the century helped the workers' movements by providing a theoretical basis and an aggressive public statement of their case. Karl Marx, who spent his life researching and writing in the defense of the proletariat—even though he had precious little contact with them—organized the International Organization of Workers, the First International, in London in 1864. The First International included labor activists ranging from English trade unions to East European refugees to anarchists to German theorists.

Not much came of the First International's efforts because of constant arguing among the factions and Marx's vindictiveness toward other major figures, such as the Russian anarchist Bakunin. Defeat of the Paris Commune in 1871 delivered a devastating blow to the French socialist movement. However, the Social Democrats—Marxian socialists—made important gains in Germany, forcing Bismarck to make concessions. It became the largest party in the country and the strongest socialist party in Europe under the

leadership of its founder, Ferdinand Lassalle. In 1871 there were two socialists in the *Reichstag*; by 1912 the number had risen to 110.

In the three decades after Marx's death in 1883 his theories dominated the European workers' movements, even if those movements themselves were not united. The French split into three distinct socialist groups. Some British socialists were greatly influenced by the maxims of Christianity, while the Fabian Society—among whose members were George Bernard Shaw, H. G. Wells, and Sidney and Beatrice Webb—pursued a more prosaic political path. With the spread of industrialization, workers and their leaders found important support in Marx's work even in places such as Russia, where Marx had never foreseen his thoughts having any influence.

Because of the widespread impact of Marx's ideas in the social sciences and the labor movement, the period of the Second International (1889–1914) may be called without any exaggeration the "golden age of Marxism."[3] A broad spectrum of thinkers among the twelve million members of the Second International claimed Marx as their inspiration, even though they might differ on the role of the state, the functions of unions, the crisis of capitalism, or the role of the proletariat. There was not a single, monolithic Marxist movement in Europe. Yet despite their doctrinal differences, the Social Democrats in all countries could agree on essential needs for the workers: an eight-hour day, the need to replace standing armies with militias, and the welfare state buttressed by universal suffrage.

The socialist movement strengthened labor unions, and the workers achieved substantial progress by 1914. Whether by working within the various states' legislatures or by raising the specter of revolution, the unions and their socialist allies helped bring about substantial reforms in the economy, labor practices, civil rights, the courts, and education. They pushed the capitalists to reform, thus avoiding the apocalyptic revolution forecast by Marx.

By 1914, although the workers could not negotiate on an equal basis with the owners, they had vastly improved their position over that endured by their grandparents. The British movement had four million members and was a powerful force, while German unions benefitted members in a broad number of areas from life insurance to travel. The income gap between rich and poor began to narrow by 1914. Working hours were shortened and living conditions improved. The real wages of workers, that is, the amount of goods that their income could actually buy, increased by 50 percent in the industrial nations in the last 30 years of the nineteenth century.

MODERN CULTURAL RESPONSES

The romantic movement unleashed sensitivities that played a major role in forming the literary, artistic, and musical changes of the nineteenth century. The romantics' emphasis on the individual is apparent in the novels of Wolfgang von Goethe (1749–1832) and Friedrich von Schiller (1759–1805). Goethe's *The Sorrows of Young Werther* (1774) tells the story of a sensitive, feeling, outcast young man who kills himself with the pistol of his rival after failing to gain his true love. Schiller's *Wilhelm Tell* (1804) describes the heroic struggle of the Swiss patriots in their drive for independence against tyranny. Unlike the brittle wit and irony of the authors of the Enlightenment, such as Voltaire, these stories were sentimental and emotional descriptions of people acting in response to overwhelming and impossible social and/or political dilemmas, who did what their hearts told them was right. It was better to experience a moving young death or to rise up against impossible odds than to look dispassionately and rationally at life.

The romantic movement's emphasis on the individual created among some of its participants a truly picturesque life-style. For every Victor Hugo (1802–1885) who lived a long, full, and respectable life, there were artists, writers, and musicians from London to Moscow who were deeply affected by romanticism. To most romantics such as Keats it was better to live briefly and intensely according to the commandments of the heart than to die old, fat, rich, bored, and bourgeois.

Literature

The novel came into prominence in the eighteenth century, but it became the dominant literary form of the nineteenth. Writers such as Vic-

→ Eugène Delacroix's illustration for the Prologue of Goethe's *Faust* portrays the archfiend Mephistopheles as a winged devil.

tor Hugo and Sir Walter Scott mined the myths and legends of France and Britain respectively to write vastly successful works for the ever-expanding middle-class audiences. Hugo's *Notre Dame de Paris* (1831) and Scott's *Ivanhoe* (1819) detailed their nations' past so effectively that both books were imitated, and sequels and imitations appeared into the twentieth century. By mid-century a variety of social and psychological themes challenged the historical novel along with the gently critical works of William Makepeace Thackeray (1811–1863) who in works such as *Vanity Fair* (1848) poked fun through deft characterizations of the nouveau riche social climbers that dominated society.

Poets responded far more pointedly to the challenges thrown down by the Napoleonic and Industrial Revolution. In 1798, two young British poets, William Wordsworth (1770–1850) and Samuel Taylor Coleridge (1772–1834), published a volume of verse called *Lyrical Ballads*. Wordsworth wrote in the preface that poetry was "the spontaneous overflow of powerful feelings recollected in tranquillity." Wordsworth sought to express "universal passions" and the "entire world of nature" through simple, unladen vocabulary. He stressed the intuitive and emotional contemplation of nature as a path to creativity. In an 1802 sonnet he expressed his love of nature and country.

> *Oft have I looked round*
> *With joy in Kent's green vales; but never found*
> *Myself so satisfied in heart before.*
> *Europe is yet in bonds; but let that pass*
> *Thought for another moment. Thou are free,*
> *My Country! and 'tis joy enough and pride*
> *For one hour's perfect bliss, to tread the grass*
> *Of England once again.*

In his *Rime of the Ancient Mariner* (1798) and *Kubla Khan* (1816) Coleridge pursued the supernatural and exotic facets of life. His vivid descriptions of distant subjects and nonrational elements of human life served as the precedent for later artists as they examined the areas of fantasy, symbolism, dream states, and the supernatural. The French poet Alphonse de Lamartine (1790–1869) led the way in making the transition from classicism to romanticism and had an impact across the Continent.

The British poets George Gordon (Lord Byron) (1788–1824) and Percy Bysshe Shelley (1792–1822) rebelled against the constraints of their society and expressed their contempt for the standards of their time through their lives and works. Byron gloried in the cult of freedom, and when the Greeks rose up against the Turks in 1821 he joined their cause. He died of fever soon after his arrival. Shelley believed passionately that human perfectibility was possible only through complete freedom of thought and action. On the Continent, Heinrich Heine (1797–1856), who was, like Byron, a cutting satirist and, like Shelley, a splendid lyricist, shared their romantic ideals. Heine is best remembered for his *Buch der Lieder*, songs which were put to music by Franz Schubert (1797–1828) and Felix Mendelssohn (1809–1847).

John Keats (1795–1821) was neither social critic nor rebel; for him, the worship and pursuit

➔ In Gustave Doré's illustration for Coleridge's *Rime of the Ancient Mariner*, the seaman bears the terrible burden of the albatross, hung around his neck as a curse for killing the bird of good luck.

of beauty were of prime importance. In *Ode on a Grecian Urn* (1821) he states

> *Beauty is truth, truth beauty—that is all*
> *Ye know on earth, and all ye need to know.*

Keats advocated for art and beauty's sake in themselves, instead of the classical formulas of an earlier age or the socialist realism of the latter part of the century.

Alexander Pushkin (1799–1837), Russia's greatest poet, liberated his nation's language from the foreign molds and traditions forced upon it in the eighteenth century. While serving as the transition between the classical and romantic ages, Pushkin helped create a truly Russian literature, one that expressed profound depth of his love for his country.

Art and Architecture

The age of change brought new tendencies to painting as well as to other art forms. There is a great contrast between the precise draftsmanship and formal poses of the classical painters and the unrestrained use of color and new effects of the romantic artists (see Portfolio Five following p. 544). Some artists such as the French master Eugène Delacroix (1798–1863) received major critical resistance. Conservative critics panned his *Massacre of Chios,* a flamboyant work painted in 1824 under the direct impact of receiving the news of the Turks' slaying of Christians on Chios, as the "Massacre of painting."

Less flashy but equally part of the romantic transition are the works of the British painter John Constable (1776–1837). Deeply influenced by romanticism's emphasis on nature, Constable was in some respects the originator of the mod-

→ Lord Byron in Greek dress. One of the leading Romantic poets, Byron lived the life of the romantic hero he created in his writing. He lived passionately and died tragically of fever in 1824 while he was in Greece fighting with the Greek insurgents.

ern school of landscape painting. His choice of colors was revolutionary, as he used greens freely in his landscape, an innovation considered radical by critics who favored brown tones. Constable's countryman, J. M. W. Turner (1775–1851), sparked controversy with his use of vivid colors and dramatic perspectives, which gave him the ability to portray powerful atmospheric effects.

Around 1830 romanticism's fascination with the medieval period led to a shift from Greek and Roman models to a Gothic revival, in which towers and arches became the chief architectural characteristics. Sir Walter Scott's romances played a major role in this development, and his house at Abbotsford was a model as it was designed along Scottish baronial lines. In France Eugène Viollet-le-Duc (1814–1879) spearheaded the movement by writing, teaching, and restoring properties under the aegis of the Commission on Historical Monuments. Victor Hugo's *Notre Dame de Paris* popularized the revival with its discussion of fifteenth-century life. For the next few decades, architecture was dominated by styles that looked back especially to the Gothic and rococo styles, which were sometimes combined in esthetically disastrous presentations.

Music

Ludwig van Beethoven (1770–1827) served as a bridge between the classical and romantic periods. The regularity of the minuet, the precision of the sonata, and the elegant but limited small chamber orchestra—all forms he mastered—were not sufficient to express the powerful forces of the age. A comparison of his relatively measured and restrained First Symphony with the compelling and driven Fifth or the lyrical, nature-dominated Sixth Symphonies dramatically reveals the changes that he underwent. Beethoven was the ultimate romantic—a lover of nature, passionate champion of human rights, and fighter for freedom. Beethoven spoke to the heart of humanity through his music.

The momentum of the forces that Beethoven set in motion carried through the entire century. Carl Maria von Weber (1786–1826), Hector Berlioz (1803–1869), Robert Schumann (1810–1856), and Felix Mendelssohn (1809–1847) and Franz Schubert (1797–1828) made major contri-

→ In the hands of Beethoven, formal music, which had previously reflected the polished and artificial manners of the salon, became a vehicle for expressing deep human emotions.

butions in developing the musical repertoire of Europe by mid-century.

FROM REALISM TO MODERNISM IN THE ARTS

After the middle of the nineteenth century, artists and writers responded to the new age in the realist movement. Artists, especially the French, who were among the most notable early proponents of realism, focused on the concrete aspects of life. From the end of the century until and beyond 1914 the artistic community experimented with a range of new forms and structures in the modernist movement. At the same time that these movements were developing, a huge new group of consumers, the lower and middle classes, were becoming participants in the new mass culture. They might find little to admire in the fine arts, but through their buying power and

their numbers they would come to have a great effect on some parts of the creative community.

Realism

In literature and art as in politics, realism replaced romanticism after mid-century. To the realists it was no longer enough to be true to one's instincts and emotions. Now they must faithfully observe and graphically report all aspects of life in a dispassionate, precise manner in order to depict individuals in their proper setting. In this age of change, there was much for writers and artists to portray, and a much larger public now had the leisure time and political interests to respond to their work.

The trend toward the realistic novel had been foreshadowed in the work of Honoré de Balzac (1799–1850), the author of the 90-volume *La Comédie Humaine (The Human Comedy)*, which depicts French life in the first half of the nineteenth century. Balzac, a master of characterization, described life in such detail that his work is a valuable reference on social history for twentieth-century scholars. Gustave Flaubert (1821–1880) was the first French realist writer. His masterpiece, *Madame Bovary* (1856), exhaustively described how the boredom of a young romantic provincial wife led her into adultery, excess, and ultimately, suicide.

British novelist Charles Dickens (1812–1870) protested social conditions in his works characterizing the everyday life of the middle classes and poor. In such works as *Oliver Twist* (1838), *Dombey and Son* (1847–1848), and *Hard Times* (1854), he describes some of the worst excesses of industrial expansion and social injustice. Later, in novels such as *Far from the Madding Crowd* (1874) Thomas Hardy (1840–1928) dealt with the struggle—almost always a losing one—of the individual against the impersonal, pitiless forces of the natural and social environment.

American writers such as Henry James (1843–1916), Samuel Clemens (1835–1910), and Harriet Beecher Stowe (1811–1896) made important contributions to the realist tradition. James tried to catch the "atmosphere of the mind" through an almost clinical examination of the most subtle details. Clemens, perhaps better known as Mark Twain, used humor and accurate descriptions of the Midwest and Far West to underscore social injustice. Stowe, through her detailed work *Uncle Tom's Cabin* (1852), captured the American public's attention and strongly influenced the antislavery movement.

The Russian novelists Leo Tolstoy (1828–1910) and Feodor Dostoevski (1821–1881) produced the most developed presentation of the realistic novel. Tolstoy stripped every shred of glory and glamour from war in *War and Peace* (1869) and gave an analytical description of the different levels of society. Dostoevski devised a chilling, detailed view of life in St. Petersburg in *Crime and Punishment* (1866), and *Brothers Karamazov* (1880) offered a painstaking analysis of Russian life during a period of change.

Drama was deeply influenced by realism, as could be seen in the works of the Norwegian Henrik Ibsen (1828–1906), the Irishman George Bernard Shaw (1856–1950), and the Russian Anton Chekhov (1860–1904). In *A Doll's House* (1879) Ibsen through his exhausting, quiet, tension-filled work assailed marriage without love as being immoral. Though his characters are not heroic in their dimensions, Ibsen captures the quiet desperation of normal life. Shaw used satire and nuance to shock the British public into reassessing their conventional attitudes. Finally, Chekhov's *Cherry Orchard* (1904) showed the changes wrought by emancipation of the serfs on the lives of a gentry family. Lacking obvious plot and action, the play depends on portrayal of detail to build a subtle, exhausting tension.

Modernism

Romanticism broke the classical forms and opened the way for diversity in forms, styles, and themes. Romantics followed their emotions, while realists advocated a more objective way of portraying the world by stressing accuracy and precision. By the end of the century a new movement—modernism—which was fragmented, disorganized, and united only in its reaction to the past came to dominate Europe's writers, artists, and musicians.

Modernism freed the writer from all rules of composition and form and all obligations to communicate to a large audience. Poetry was especially affected by this new tendency. Toward the end of the century, in reaction to the demands of realism, French poets Stéphane Mal-larmé (1842–1898) and Paul Verlaine (1844–1896) inaugurated the symbolist movement. Poetry rather than prose best fit the symbolists' goal of conveying ideas by suggestion rather than by precise, photographic word-pictures.

In a sense, all modern literature stems from the symbolist movement. By increasing the power of the poet to reach the readers' imagination through expanded combinations of allusion, symbol, and double meaning, symbolism gave new life to the written word. But in exploring new poetic realms and possibilities, the symbolists left behind the majority of readers who had been trained to see clarity, precision, simplicity, and definition as positive aspects of literature.

Modernism freed painters from the need to communicate surface, photographic reality. Gustave Courbet (1819–1877) consciously dropped all useless adornments and instead boldly painted the life of the world in which he lived. He was soon surpassed by his countrymen who became preoccupied with problems of color, light, and atmosphere (see Portfolio Six following p. 672). Artists such as Claude Monet (1840–1926), Edouard Manet (1832–1882), Edgar Degas (1834–1917), Mary Cassatt (1845–1926), and Pierre Auguste Renoir (1841–1919) tried to catch the first impression made by a scene or an object on the eye, undistorted by intellect or any subjective attitude. They were called impressionists and worked in terms of light and color rather than solidity of form.

The impressionists found that they could achieve a more striking effect of light by placing one bright area of color next to another without any transitional tones. The also found that shadows could be shown not as gray but as colors complementary to those of the objects casting the shadow. At close range an impressionist painting may seem little more than splotches of unmixed colors, but at a proper distance the eye mixes the colors and allows a vibrating effect of light and emotion to emerge. The impressionists' techniques helped revolutionize art.

One of the weaknesses of the impressionists' work was that they sacrificed much of the clarity of the classical tradition to gain their effects. Paul Cézanne (1839–1903) addressed that problem. He tried to simplify all natural objects by stressing their essential geometric structure. He believed that everything in nature corresponded to the shape of a cone, cylinder, or sphere. Proceeding from this theory, he was able to get below the surface and give his objects the solidity that had eluded the impressionists, yet he kept the impressionists' striking use of color.

The Dutch artist Vincent van Gogh (1853–1890), while adapting the impressionist approach to light and color, painted using short strokes of heavy pigment to accentuate the underlying forms and rhythms of his subjects. He achieved intensely emotional results, as he was willing to distort what he saw to communicate the sensations he felt. His short life of poverty and loneliness was climaxed by insanity and suicide.

Before 1914 other modernist-inspired forms emerged. French artist Henri Matisse (1869–1954) painted what he felt about an object, rather than just the object itself. He had learned to simplify form partly from his study of African primitive art and the color schemes of oriental carpets. The Spanish artist Pablo Picasso (1881–1974) and others helped develop the school called cubism. Cubists would choose an object, then construct an abstract pattern from it, giving the opportunity to view it simultaneously from several points. Such a pattern is evident in Picasso's *Three Musicians* (1921).

Music

After mid-century, Johannes Brahms (1833–1897), Anton Bruckner (1824–1896), and Gustav Mahler (1860–1911) built on the momentum of forces that Beethoven had set in motion and made lyrical advances in composition and presentation. Each made unique use of the large symphony orchestra, and Brahms also composed three exquisite string quartets.

In addition, many composers turned to their native folk music and dances for inspiration. Beethoven had used native themes as had Schubert and Schumann in Austria and Germany. Frederick Chopin (1810–1849), even though he did most of his work in France, drew heavily on Polish folk themes for his mazurkas and polonaises. Jean Sibelius (1865–1957) in Finland, Anton Dvorák (1841–1904) and Bedrich Smetana (1824–1884) in Bohemia-Moravia, and Russians Peter Ilich Tchaikovsky (1840–1893), Modest Moussorgsky (1835–1881), and Sergei Rachmaninov (1873–1943) all incorporated folk music in

→ Pablo Picasso, *Three Musicians* (1921). The work is one of the great masterpieces of the Cubist style. The separate pieces of the painting resemble architectural blocks, but the artist's primary concern is with the whole image, not its individual parts.

their work. This use of folk themes was aesthetically satisfying and pleasing to the audiences.

Romanticism and nationalism, plus the increasing number of enthusiasts, sparked developments in opera during the century. In his fervid Germanic works, Richard Wagner (1813–1883) infused old Teutonic myths and German folklore with typically romantic characteristics such as emphasis on the supernatural and the mystical. Wagner's *Ring* cycle was the culmination of a long and productive career. His descendants still manage the *Festspielhaus*, a theater in Bayreuth, Germany, that he designed and his admirers financed.

The greatest operatic composer of the century was Giuseppi Verdi (1813–1901) who composed such masterpieces as *Aida*, *Rigoletto*, *Il Trovatore*, *La Forza del Destino*, and many others. His operas, along with those of Wagner, form the core of most of today's major opera house repertoires.

Modernism affected music as it had affected poetry and art. The French composer Claude Debussy (1862–1918) tried in his music to imitate what he read in poetry and saw in impressionist paintings. He engaged in "tone painting" to achieve a special mood or atmosphere. This device can be seen in his *Prélude à l'aprés midi d'un faune (Prelude to the Afternoon of a Faun)*, which shocked the musical world when it was first performed in 1892. The impressionist painters had gained their effects by juxtaposing widely different colors. The composers juxtaposed widely separate chords to create similarly brilliant, shimmering effects.

The music world rarely dealt with social problems or harsh realism. Its supporters were by and large the newly ascendant middle classes who had benefitted from the economic growth triggered by industrialization. They used the wealth derived from their commercial prosperity to finance the building of new opera and symphony halls and maintain the composers and orchestras. Major soloists were the idols of their day, as they showed their virtuosity in compositions that made use of romantic subject matter infused with sentiment and, not infrequently, showmanship. The drew capacity audiences of contented listeners.

Popular Culture

The urban working and lower middle classes began to be important consumers of the popular cultural products of their countries. With increasing literacy these classes provided a huge audience for publishers. More leisure time and money enabled them to fill the music halls and

public sporting arenas. They would rarely be found in the concert halls, art galleries, or in serious bookstores. Rather they read the penny press and the "dime novel," both of which featured simple vocabulary and easy-to-follow information and plots. The penny press served many functions: to inform, entertain, and sell goods. Sensationalism, whether the confessions of a "fallen woman" or the account of some adventurer, was the main attraction of the dime novel. Comic strips first appeared in central Europe in the 1890s.

There was a level of literature between great novels and the penny press, and that was the comforting, light, and entertaining literature such as the works of Scottish author Samuel Smiles (1812–1904). Smiles's *Self Help* (1859) sold 20,000 copies its first year and 130,000 over the next 30 years. Titles of Smiles's other works—*Thrift*, *Character*, and *Duty*—form a catalog of Victorian virtues. In the United States, Horatio Alger (1834–1899) wrote more than a hundred novels following similar themes: virtue is rewarded, the good life will win out in the struggle with temptation, and the heroes—usually poor but pure-hearted youths—will come to enjoy wealth and high honor.

A number of technological advances—coated celluloid film, improved shutter mechanisms, reliable projectors, and a safe source of illumina-

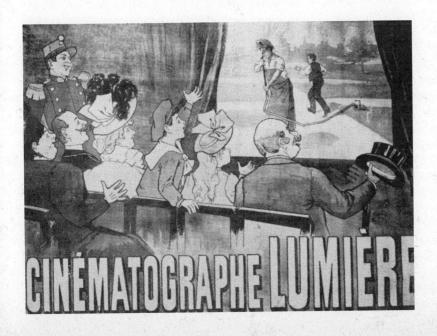

→ Pioneers in the motion picture industry were the French brothers Auguste and Louis-Jean Lumière. They invented both the color photography process that bears their name and the Cinématographe, an early motion picture camera. This poster is for one of their first films, *L'arroseur arrosé* (1896).

tion—were combined to introduce the cinema, or the movies, to the world. These developments seem to have come together almost simultaneously in France, Britain, and the United States. The first public moving picture performances took place in Paris in 1895 and soon after in London and New York. Even though another 20 years passed before feature-length films were produced, movies proved to be an immediate success, attracting an infinitely larger audience than live performances could ever reach.

Sports, including football in its North American and European forms, bicycle racing, cricket, baseball, and boxing, captured the popular imagination. Pierre de Coubert (1863–1937) revived the Olympic games of ancient Greece in 1896 in Athens. Thirteen nations took part in an event that instantly caught the international public's imagination.[4]

In the new society of early twentieth-century Europe, the popular culture of mass literature, movies, and sports played as important a role as did high culture. In a simpler way, purveyors of popular culture communicated values and lessons that bound a nation together much more than did the serious writers and artists of the age. The gulf between "high" and "popular" culture has yet to be bridged.

CONCLUSION

The middle classes came to dominance in western Europe, where they established life-styles and attitudes imitated throughout the rest of the world. They helped shape and extend the Christian faith, especially Protestantism, and defended the faith from attack while extending it by missionary work throughout the world.

The middle classes made significant discoveries in the fields of biology, chemistry, physics, and medicine, and European scientists made fundamental discoveries that greatly expanded the frontiers of knowledge. Charles Darwin's work not only upset the understanding of the development of organisms, its popularization had immense, if misdirected, social implications.

The progress made in economics and science encouraged many of the bourgeoisie to believe that they were inherently superior and had the right to pursue their destiny. A range of pseudoscientific and racist theories came to be espoused, with terrible consequences.

In the latter half of the nineteenth century, the workers and their proponents responded to the middle class dominance of the public arena. They struggled, with the help of the socialist parties, for just treatment in the modern, industrial world. To a greater or lesser degree, their political programs were affected by the ideological work of Karl Marx.

At all levels of European society, life-styles, aesthetic standards, and the means for self-expression changed dramatically by the end of the nineteenth century. Cultural activities were no longer the sole preserve of the elite and elect, all of whom shared a common classical conception of "good" and "bad." At the end of the century, cultural activities were as fragmented and diverse as was the European world. The classicism of the eighteenth century at least had the advantage of unifying the participants in cultural activities. By 1900, in art, music, poetry, prose, and architecture it would have been difficult to gain a consensus between the artist and the audience on what was "good" and "bad."

Never before had the creators of poetry, art, prose, music, and architecture had a greater opportunity to communicate to such a large audience. The cinema and vastly increased publishing facilities held out great opportunity to artists and writers. Unfortunately, by the end of the century the modernist writers, artists, and musicians were seemingly able to communicate only with a finely trained elite. In a sense, what was needed was a new series of classical definitions, forms, and functions upon which all could agree. But the romantic drive to individualism, which came to full flower in the century, made that impossible. Even today, the vast gulf between mass culture and the fine arts continues to grow.

✦ Suggestions for Reading

See Stephen F. Mason, *A History of Sciences* (Collier, 1962) and Rupert Hall and Marie Boas Hall, *A Brief History of Science* (Signet, 1964) for clear and concise surveys of the development of science. The literature on Darwin and his times are voluminous. Darwin's *Origin of Species* and *Voyage of the Beagle* are available in a number of editions. C. C. Gillespie nicely sets the stage for the period in *Genesis and Geology* (Harvard Univ., 1951). G. Himmelfarb's *Dar-*

win and the Darwinian Revolution (Norton, 1968) and W. Irvin's Ape, Angels & Victorians: The Story of Darwin, Huxley, & Evolution (McGraw-Hill, 1955) are excellent studies. R. Hofstadter's Social Darwinism in American Thought (Beacon, 1955) is a fascinating study of how a subtle theory can be misapplied. Dubois's Louis Pasteur: Free Lance of Science (Little, Brown, 1950) is an example of a biography that is sound both as history and literature. J. Bronowski's The Ascent of Man (Little, Brown, 1974) is a humane, wise overview of the development of science through the ages.

George F. Mosse provides a valuable overview of intellectual developments during the nineteenth century in The Culture of Western Europe, the Nineteenth and Twentieth Centuries: An Introduction (Rand McNally, 1974). Franklin L. Baumer's Modern European Thought, Continuity and Change in Ideas: 1600–1950 (Macmillan, 1977) is a classic analysis of the development of Western thought and a helpful guide through the nineteenth century.

Among the immense number of works dealing with Karl Marx, the following are clear and valuable introductions for the student: I. Berlin, Karl Marx: His Life and Environment (Oxford, 1963); George Lichtheim, Marxism (Praeger, 1961); and Alexander Balinsky, Marx's Economics (Heath, 1970). E. P. Thompson's The Making of the English Working Class (Random House, 1966) remains a classic study of worker adaptation to industrialization.

Useful guides to nineteenth-century cultural developments are D. S. Mirsky, A History of Russian Literature (Vintage, 1958); H. L. C. Jaffe, The Nineteenth and Twentieth Centuries, Vol. 5, The Dolphin History of Painting (Thames & Hudson, 1969); C. Edward Gauss, Aesthetic Theories of French Artists: From Realism to Surrealism (Johns Hopkins, 1949); and H. C. Colles, Ideals of the Nineteenth and Twentieth Century, Vol. 3, The Growth of Music (Oxford, 1956).

→ Notes

1. J. H. Plumb, "The Victorians Unbuttoned," Horizon, XI, n. 4, 1969, pp. 16–25. See also S. Marcus, The Other Victorians: A Study of Sexuality and Pornography in Mid-Nineteenth Century England (New York: Basic Books, 1966).
2. C. Darwin, "The Origin of Species," in Introduction to Contemporary Civilization in the West, II (New York: Columbia University Press, 1955), pp. 453–454.
3. Leszek Kolakowski, Main Currents of Marxism, Vol. 2., P. S. Falla, trans. (Oxford: Oxford University Press, 1978), p. 1.
4. Robert Schnerb, "Le XIXe Siècle: L'Apogée de L'Expansion Européene (1815–1914)," Histoire Générale des Civilisations, vol. 6 (Paris: Presses Universitaires de France, 1955), pp. 468–469.

CHAPTER 24

CENTERS OF REVOLUTION 1848–1849

German Confederation

0   100   200
MILES

UNITED KINGDOM
OF GREAT BRITAIN
AND IRELAND

NORTH SEA

SWEDEN

DENMARK

BALTIC SEA

NETHERLANDS

Elbe

Berlin ★

RUSSIA

Vistula R.

BELGIUM

PRUSSIA

Rhine R.

HESSE CASSEL

SAXONY

Frankfurt ★

Krakow •

ATLANTIC

OCEAN

GERMAN

STATES

BOHEMIA

Prague ★

HUNGARY

BAY

OF

BISCAY

FRANCE

Loire R.

Seine R.

Paris ★

Garonne R.

SWITZERLAND

Novara ★ Milan ★
Turin ★

Rhone R.

LOMBARDY

Vienna ★

EMPIRE OF AUSTRIA

Buda •• Pest

Drava R.

VENETIA

Venice ★
Custozza ★

Danube R.

SERBIA

Douro R.

SPAIN

Ebro R.

KINGDOM OF SARDINIA

Florence ★

PAPAL
STATES

OTTOMAN

MONTENEGRO

PORTUGAL

Tagus R.

CORSICA

Rome ★

EMPIRE

GREECE

BALEARIC IS.

Naples ★ NAPLES

AND

MEDITERRANEAN SEA

Palermo ★
SICILY

→ Like a political plague, the 1848 revolutions broke out in those governmental centers that had failed either to adapt to the new social and economic conditions of Europe or had lost the ability to impose force effectively on their people.

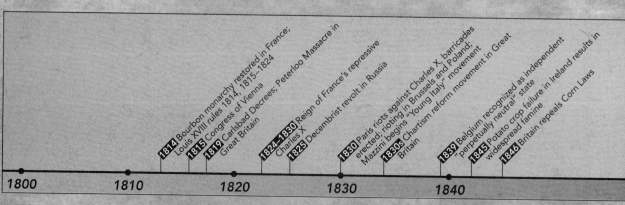

1814 Bourbon monarchy restored in France; Louis XVIII rules 1814, 1815–1824

1815 Congress of Vienna

1819 Carlsbad Decrees; Peterloo Massacre in Great Britain

1824–1830 Reign of France's repressive Charles X

1825 Decembrist revolt in Russia

1830 Paris riots against Charles X barricades erected; rioting in Brussels and Poland; Mazzini begins "Young Italy" movement

1830s Chartism reform movement in Great Britain

1839 Belgium recognized as independent "perpetually neutral" state

1845 Potato crop failure in Ireland results in widespread famine

1846 Britain repeals Corn Laws

1800   1810   1820   1830   1840

European Politics, 1815–1871

The allies who defeated Napoleon attempted to build an international structure to maintain stability after 1815. Almost immediately, liberal and nationalistic forces sought to revise the definition of the status quo. Until 1848, the combined efforts of the Russians and the Austrians sufficed to keep the lid on the boiling pot of political and economic pressures for change. But in that year, a wave of revolutions spread across the Continent and put an end to the structure created at Vienna.

The revolutionaries, because of their conflicting goals, failed to turn their ideals into sustained state policy. After 1848, continental politics would be built on the basis of *Realpolitik*, that is, realism in politics. *Realpolitik* disregards theory or idealism and emphasizes the practical application of power to gain state goals, no matter the damage to ethics or morality. The European map changed once again as Cavour consolidated Italy and Bismarck united Germany.

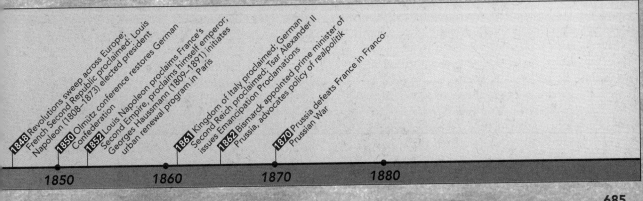

1848 Revolutions sweep across Europe; French Second Republic proclaimed; Louis Napoleon (1808–1873) elected president

1850 Olmütz conference restores German Confederation

1852 Louis Napoleon proclaims France's Second Empire, proclaims himself emperor; Georges Haussmann (1809–1891) initiates urban renewal program in Paris

1861 Kingdom of Italy proclaimed; German Second Reich proclaimed; Tsar Alexander II issues Emancipation Proclamations

1862 Bismarck appointed prime minister of Prussia, advocates policy of realpolitik

1870 Prussia defeats France in Franco-Prussian War

1850   1860   1870   1880

RESTORATION AND REVOLUTION: FROM 1815 TO 1848

The political structure built at the Congress of Vienna could not control the currents of individualism, freedom of thought, pride in nation, and equality under the law that had been unleashed after 1789. Although Europe was at peace by 1815, a new type of upheaval began as the middle and lower classes pursued the promises of the revolutionary era.

The Return of the Bourbons

The restored Bourbon monarch Louis XVIII (1814, 1815–1824) was an unhappy choice for the French throne. The new king, a brother of the guillotined Louis XVI, was ill-equipped to lead France out of a quarter-century of revolution and Napoleonic charisma. Dull and unpopular, he had been the target of a Talleyrand epigram that "the Bourbons have learned nothing and forgotten nothing." Nonetheless, he tried to hold the country together by blending elements of the revolutionary period with remnants of the old regime. Unfortunately, the mixture helped create the instability that plagued the country throughout the century.

Louis began by "granting" his subjects a charter that established a form of constitutional monarchy in which he kept all executive power, controlled lawmaking, and influenced the makeup of the legislature. The restored Bourbon made little attempt to return to the institutions of the old regime and accepted Napoleon's Civil Code, the Concordat with the papacy, and the governmental reforms. For nine years he suffered the fate of moderates trying to navigate between two extremes—he was attacked by both sides. The right wing assailed the charter for giving too much to the middle classes while the liberals and radicals said that he had not gone far enough in his policies. Louis was succeeded by his brother, Charles X (1824–1830), who cared nothing about maintaining political balance.

Charles did not accept any of the changes of the age. In 1829 he announced that he "would rather saw wood than be a king of the English type." So out of tune was he with the times that

→ In the July Revolution of 1830, Parisians took to the streets to protest the restrictive laws of Charles X.

in July 1830 he drove the usually submissive legislature to the point that it refused to support his proposed ultraroyalist ministry. When elections went badly for him, he issued a set of laws censoring the press and further limiting the already heavily restricted right to vote. These repressive acts drove liberals, radicals, and their journalist allies to revolt. They barricaded the narrow streets of Paris with overturned carts, boxes, tables, and paving stones. Fighting behind these obstacles and from rooftops, they held off the army. Three days later a less reactionary faction took power after Charles fled across the Channel to exile in Great Britain.

The new government represented the upper middle classes and landed gentry, and represented a compromise between the French republicans—led by the aging Marquis de Lafayette, hero of the American Revolution—and the relatively liberal monarchist supporters of the Orléans branch of the Bourbons. The new king, Louis Philippe (1830–1848), who claimed the title of "the citizen king," resolutely supported the interests of the wealthy.

Louis Philippe took great pains to portray a "bourgeois" image. He received the crown from "the people" and replaced the white Bourbon flag with the revolutionary tricolor. However, Louis Philippe's policies consistently favored the upper bourgeoisie and gentry and shut the workers and middle classes out of the political arena. Of the 32 million French citizens, only 200,000 wealthy male property owners were allowed to vote.

Workers protested that the government was ignoring their interests. Louis Philippe and his advisers were more interested in pursuing a policy of divide-and-conquer and ignored most suggestions for reform. Restrictive legislation such as the September Laws were passed in 1835 to control the growing radical movement. The government kept control but, under the calm surface, serious pressures were building. By 1848 France faced a serious crisis.

The French Influence in Belgium and Poland

Liberals across the Continent were encouraged by the Paris uprising of 1830, but only in Belgium were there any lasting results. The Vienna Congress had placed the Belgians under the Dutch crown, but this settlement ignored the cultural, economic, religious, and linguistic differences between the two people. The Belgians were primarily French-speaking Catholic farmers and workers while the people of Holland were Dutch-speaking Protestant seafarers and traders.

Belgian liberals asked the Dutch King William I of Orange to grant them their own administration in August 1830. When he refused, rioting broke out in Brussels, which the Dutch troops were unable to put down. After expelling the troops, the Belgians declared their independence and drew up a liberal constitution. William asked in vain for help from Tsar Nicholas I. The principle of legitimacy as a pretext for intervention was dead. Stalemate ensued until the summer of 1831 when the Belgian national assembly met in Brus-

➔ The citizen king, Louis Philippe, shown here strolling through Paris, attempted some reform, but it was not enough to stop the revolution of 1848.

sels and chose Prince Leopold of Saxe-Coburg-Gotha as king. Eight years later the international status of the new state was settled. Belgium was recognized to be a perpetually neutral state.

The French rebellion had an impact in Poland, where Poles in and around Warsaw rose up in the name of liberal and national principles. After the Congress of Vienna, Poles in this region gained a special status. The area known as Congress Poland had its own constitution and substantial local autonomy. The winds of change and the repressive tendencies of Tsar Nicholas I combined to push the Poles into rebellion in the winter of 1830–1831. The rebels suffered from internal division and the numerically and militarily superior Russians crushed them. Their major accomplishment was to tie down the Russian troops, whom Nicholas wanted to send to help the Dutch king, for six months and perhaps save the Belgian revolution.[1]

German and Italian Nationalism

The forces of nationalism influenced central Europe from the tip of Italy through the Habsburg lands of central and eastern Europe to the Baltic Sea. Napoleon had performed a great, though unwitting, service for the Germans and Italians through his direct governing in the area and also by revising the European map. After 1815, the region knew the positive effects of a different style of governing and was divided into a much more rational set of political units.

Metternich had ensured that the Vienna Congress made Austria the dominant partner in the German Confederation. To preserve his country's dominance both in the Confederation and throughout the Habsburg monarchy he knew that he had to fight continually against nationalism. The currents of romanticism found forceful expression in the works of German poets and philosophers and in lectures in German classrooms. Nationalism and liberalism found many followers among the young. For example, in the great patriotic student festival that took place in October 1817 (the tercentenary of the Reformation) at Wartburg where Luther had taken refuge, liberal students burned reactionary books on the great bonfire to protest their discontent with the status quo. Protests spread both openly and secretly in the *Burschenschaften* (liberal societies). Metternich moved harshly against the students. He pushed through the Diet of the German Confederation the Carlsbad Decrees (1819). These acts dissolved student associations, censored the press, and restricted academic freedom. However, the decrees failed to stop the forces of liberalism and nationalism, which grew during the next twenty years.

Italy, which Metternich saw as being only a "geographic expression" and not a nation, also posed special problems. The Congress of Vienna, in accord with the principles of legitimacy and compensation, had returned Italy to its geographic status of 1789, divided into areas dominated by the Bourbons, the Papal States, and the Austrians. This settlement ignored the fact that in the interim the Italians had experienced more liberty and better government than ever before. The return to the old systems was also a return to high taxes, corruption, favoritism, and banditry.

It was perhaps ironic that this fragmented, individualistic land should produce the most notable romantic nationalist in Europe, Giuseppe Mazzini. After the Austrians put down the Italian revolutionary movements in 1820 and 1821, Mazzini began to work actively for independence. In 1830 he was implicated in an unsuccessful revolution against the Sardinian royal government and thrown into jail for six months. Once released, he went to London and started a patriotic society that he called "Young Italy." This organization sent appeals to students and intellectuals to form an Italian nationalist movement. In the meantime, the reactionary forces weathered nationalist pressures.

Metternich also feared nationalism in the Habsburg realm, a mosaic composed of many different nationalities, languages, and religions. If nationalism and the desire for self-rule became strong among the Magyars, Czechs, southern

Mazzini on the Duties of the Individual

Giuseppe Mazzini saw the individual's obligation to the human family to be transcendent.

Your first duties—first as regards importance—are, as I have already told you, towards Humanity. You are men before you are either citizens or fathers. If you do not embrace the whole human family in your affection, if you do not bear witness to your belief in the Unity of that family, consequent upon the Unity of God, and in the fraternity among the peoples which is destined to reduce that unit to action; if, wheresoever a fellow-creature suffers, or the dignity of human nature is violated by falsehood or tyranny—you are not ready, if able, to aid the unhappy, and do not feel called upon to combat, if able, for the redemption of the betrayed or oppressed—you violate your law of life, you comprehend not that Religion which will be the guide and blessing of the future.

From Emilie A. Venturi, *Joseph Mazzini: A Memoir* (London, 1875).

Slavs, and Italians, the Habsburg Empire would fall apart. Nationalism threatened the Germans who controlled the Empire yet constituted only 20 percent of its population.

By understanding the complex and combustible nature of the region in which Metternich exercised his power, we can begin to appreciate his dread of democratic government and nationalism and his obsession with maintaining the status quo. Liberalism and nationalism would destroy his power. In a world that was rapidly industrializing, Metternich's power rested on a backward system. Only in Bohemia and the areas immediately around Vienna was there any middle class. A great majority of the inhabitants were peasants, either powerless serfs as in Hungary, or impoverished tenant farmers who owed one-half of their time and two-thirds of their crop to the landlord. Government was autocratic, and the regional assemblies had little power and represented mainly the nobility. The social, political, and economic structures were extremely vulnerable to the winds of change that came in 1848.[2]

THE REVOLUTIONARY YEAR OF 1848

As it had before, France once again opened a revolutionary era, and the events there set a precedent for what was to occur throughout Europe in 1848. The overthrow of the old order came first in Paris in February and then spread to Berlin, Vienna, Prague, and Budapest in March. Never before had France—or Europe—seen such a fragmented variety of political and social pressures at work at the same time (see map on p. 684). Romantics, socialists, nationalists, middle classes, peasants, and students could all agree that the old structure had to be abandoned, but each group had a different path to that goal and a separate view of what the new world should be. Louis Philippe fled Paris, Metternich abandoned Vienna, and the Prussian King Frederick William IV gave in. But the movements in France and elsewhere fell apart as soon as they had won because of their diversity, lack of experience, and conflicting goals.

France and the Second Republic

The pressures building since 1830 and strengthened by economic depression in 1846 and 1847 erupted in Paris in February 1848 in a series of banquets. In this seemingly harmless social arena, liberals and socialists pushed for an end to corruption and reforms of the electoral system. The government tried to block the banquet scheduled for February 22, and in response the opposition threw up more than 1500 barricades to block the streets of Paris. When violence broke out, republican leaders took the opportunity to

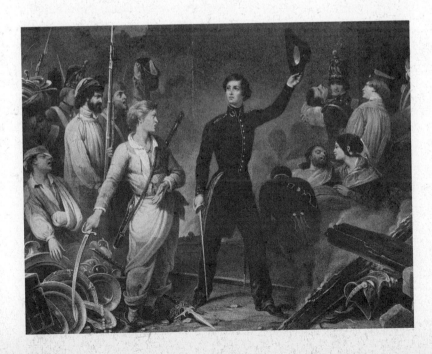

→ This painting, *24 Février 1848*, celebrates the revolutionary spirit of the mid-nineteenth century. A young French hero encourages his fellow citizens to fight for liberty.

set up a provisional revolutionary government and proclaimed the introduction of universal manhood suffrage. Louis Philippe fled to exile in England.

The new government, the Second Republic, had a brief (1848–1851) and dreary existence. Neither the new leaders nor the voters had any experience with representative government. The forces that united to overthrow the king soon split into moderate and radical wings. The first group wanted middle-class control within the existing social order, while the latter faction desired a social and economic revolution. By the summer the new government faced a major crisis over the issue of national workshops sponsored by the socialist Louis Blanc (1811–1882). The workshops were to be the state's means to guarantee every laborer's "right to work." The moderate-dominated government voiced its belief in Blanc's principle of full employment, but the leaders gave the plan's administration to men who wanted to ridicule it. As a result, the workshops became a national joke. Laborers were assigned "make-work" jobs such as carrying dirt from one end of a park to the other on one day, and then carrying it back the next.

The disbanding of the workshops incited a violent insurrection known as the "June Days." The unemployed workers raised a red flag as a sign of revolution—the first time that the red flag had been used as a symbol of the proletariat. With the cry of "bread or lead," the demonstrators rebuilt the barricades and tried to overthrow the government. The most bloody fighting Paris had seen since the Reign of Terror gave the insurgents far more lead than bread, and the movement was crushed. After that, the bourgeoisie and the workers would be on the opposite sides of the political strife.

Germany and the Frankfurt Assembly

The example of the French February revolution quickly crossed the Rhine River and spread to central Europe. At public assemblies throughout Germany patriotic liberals demanded unification. Rapid changes came with minimal casualties, thanks largely to the humane response of the Prussian King Frederick William IV. When his subjects erected barricades in Berlin on March 15, he decided to make concessions rather

→ The artillery attempts to demolish a barricade in this scene of the street fighting during the Frankfurt insurrection of 1848.

than unleash further violence and bloodshed. He ordered the regular army troops out of Berlin and tried to make peace with his "dear Berliners" by promising a parliament, a constitution, and a united Germany. Upon learning of this development, the rulers of the other German states agreed to establish constitutional governments and guarantee basic civil rights.

The Frankfurt Assembly opened its first session on May 18. More than 500 delegates attended, coming from the various German states, Austria, and Bohemia. The primarily middle-class membership of the assembly included about 200 lawyers, 100 professors, and many doctors and judges. Popular enthusiasm reached a peak when the assembly's president announced that "We are to create a constitution for Germany, for the whole Empire." The assembly deliberated at length over the issues of just what was meant by Germany and what form of government would be best for the new empire. Some debaters wanted a united Germany to include all Germans in central Europe, even Austria and Bohemia. Others did not want the Austrians included, for a variety of religious and political reasons. Another issue of contention was whether the new imperial crown should be given to the Habsburgs in Vienna or the Hohenzollerns in Berlin.

Germany's history changed tragically when the Assembly failed to unite and bring a liberal solution to political problems. From May to December the Assembly wasted time in splendid debates over nonessential topics. As the participants talked endlessly, they threw away their chance to take decisive action and contributed to the failed dreams of 1848. Gradually, the conservatives recovered from the shock of the spring revolts and began to rally around their rulers, exhorting them to undo the reformers' work. In Prussia the king regained his confidence, as the army remained loyal and the peasants showed little interest in political affairs. The Berlin liberals soon found themselves isolated and the king was able to regain control.

Even though the anti-liberal forces were at full tide, the Frankfurt Assembly continued its work. It approved the Declaration of the Rights of the German People, an inspiring document that articulated the progressive political and social ideals of 1848. In April 1849, the Assembly approved a constitution for a united Germany that included an emperor advised by a ministry and a legislature elected by secret ballot. Austria was excluded when it refused to join the new union.

When the leadership of the new German Reich (nation) was offered to Frederick William, he refused to accept it, later declaring that he could not "pick up a crown from the gutter." After this contemptuous refusal, most of the Assembly's members returned home. Outbreaks against the conservative domination continued, but the Prussian army effectively put them down. Thousands of prominent middle-class liberals fled, many emigrating to the United States.

Italy

The news of the revolutions in Paris and Vienna triggered a rash of uprisings on the Italian peninsula. In Sicily, Venice, and Milan revolutionaries demanded an end to foreign domination and despotic rule. In response, King Charles Albert of Sardinia voluntarily granted a new liberal constitution. Other states, such as Tuscany, also issued constitutions. In the Papal States, meanwhile, reform had begun as early as 1846. Absolute government in Italy almost disappeared.

As in the rest of Europe, the liberal and nationalist triumphs and reforms were quickly swept away by the reactionary tide. The Austrians regained their mastery in the north of Italy in July when they defeated Charles Albert at the decisive battle of Custozza. Another defeat a year later forced him to abdicate in favor of his oldest son, Victor Emmanuel II. Austria helped restore the old rulers and systems of government in Italy to their pre-1848 conditions.

The final blow to the Italian movements came in November 1848 when Pope Pius IX, who had begun a program of reform, refused to join in the struggle against Catholic Austria for a united Italy. His subjects forced him to flee from Rome, and the papal lands were declared a republic, with Mazzini as the head. The pope's flight prompted a hostile reaction from conservative Europe, and the French sent in an army to crush the republic in July 1849. When the pope returned to Rome, he remained bitterly hostile to all liberal causes and ideas until his death in 1878.

The Habsburg Monarchy

The events of 1848 took a tragic toll in the Habsburg territories. When the news of the February uprising reached Vienna, Prague, and Budapest, reformers immediately called for change. In Budapest, the nationalist liberal Louis Kossuth (1802–1894) attacked the Habsburg ruler's "stagnant bureaucratic system" and spoke of the "pestilential air blowing from the Vienna charnel house and its deadening effect upon all phases of Hungarian life." He demanded parliamentary government for the whole of the empire.

In Vienna, Kossuth's speech inspired some Austrian students and workers to demonstrate in the streets. The movement soon gained the force of a rebellion and the frightened Austrian emperor forced Metternich, the symbol of European reaction, to resign. Meanwhile, the Hungarian Diet advocated a liberal, parliamentary government under a limited Habsburg monarchy. The Vienna-controlled Danubian region, that mosaic of nationalities, appeared to be on the verge of being transformed into a federation.

The empire's diversity soon became mirrored in a characteristic of the revolutionary movements, as the various nationalities divided

→ In this satiric cartoon, Pope Pius IX removes his liberal "saviour's" mask to reveal his true nature after his refusal to support the revolution in Italy.

regroup and suggested to them the obvious tactic to follow to regain their former dominance: Divide and conquer the subject nationalities. In June demonstrations broke out in the streets of Prague, barricades were thrown up, and fighting began. The Austrians lobbed a few shells, Prague surrendered, and any hope for an autonomous kingdom of Bohemia ended.

In Hungary, Kossuth announced that he would offer civil rights, but not national independence, to the minority nationalities under his control. In protest, the South Slavs under the Croat leader Joseph Jellachich (1801–1859) attacked the Magyars, and civil war broke out. The Austrians took advantage of the situation and made Jellachich an imperial general. Following his attack against the Magyars, he was ordered to Vienna where in October he forced the surrender of the liberals who controlled the capital.

By the end of the year the weak and incapable emperor Ferdinand I abdicated in favor of his nephew Franz Joseph. The Austrians began to repeal their concessions to the Hungarians, arguing that their new emperor was not bound by the acts of his predecessor. The Magyars, outraged by this maneuver, declared complete independence for their country. The Austrians, aided by 100,000 Russian troops sent by Tsar Nicholas I, defeated the Hungarians in a bloody and one-sided struggle. By the summer of 1849 Kossuth fled the country and the Hungarian revolution reached its tragic conclusion.[3]

among themselves. The Hungarians wrote a new constitution that was quite liberal, calling for a guarantee of civil rights, an end to serfdom, and the destruction of special privileges. In theory, all political benefits guaranteed in the constitution were to extend to all citizens of Hungary, including non-Magyar minorities. The emperor accepted these reforms and promised, in addition, a constitution for Austria. He also promised the Czechs in Bohemia the same reforms granted the Hungarians.

By summer the mood suddenly shifted. German and Czech nationalists began to quarrel and the Magyars began to oppress the Slavic nationalities and Romanians after they, in turn, demanded their own political independence. Divisions among the liberal and nationalistic forces gave the conservatives in Vienna time to

NEW POLITICAL FORMS IN FRANCE, ITALY, AND GERMANY

The revolutions of 1848 dealt a death blow to the idealistic liberals, nationalists, and romantics who had failed in the pursuit of their various goals. In France, some moderates learned that a revolution in the name of liberal principles could unleash forces that would threaten the middle classes. In the Habsburg monarchy the assorted nationalities which had tried to free themselves from Vienna's control found that the nationalism that motivated each of them could also doom their struggle for freedom by making a unified advance impossible. By the end of the revolutionary year, the leaders of Germany and Italy were able to discard most of the demands of their liberal opponents, but they would build on the potent nationalistic forces that would lead eventually to unification.

France's Second Empire

In France, the violence of the June Days moved the conservatives in the countryside and the moderates in the cities to elect Louis Napoleon (1808–1873), nephew of Napoleon I, to the presidency of the Second Republic. Although he had failed miserably in his attempts to overthrow the king in 1836 and 1840, he was sure that destiny intended great things for him. When he came back to Paris after the revolution he was untainted by any involvement in the June Days and appeared to be a unifying force.

The republic's constitution gave strong powers to the president, but limited the office to only one term. Louis Napoleon took advantage of the authority given him and his strong majority to fortify his position. He and his conservative allies dominated France for the next two years, becoming strong enough to overthrow the constitution in a coup d'état in December 1851. Louis Napoleon and his allies brutally put down the workers and peasants who opposed the coup and engineered a plebiscite that gave him virtually unanimous support. In 1852 he proclaimed himself Emperor Napoleon III, and the Second Empire replaced the Second Republic.

During its eighteen-year span the Second Empire accomplished a great deal. Industrialization brought prosperity to France. Production doubled. France supported the building of the Suez Canal, and railway mileage increased by 500 percent. The partial legalization of labor unions and guarantee of the right to strike improved workers' conditions. Baron Georges Haussmann transformed Paris in an ambitious urban renewal that featured broad boulevards, unified architecture, modern utilities, and improved traffic flow.

The price for the order and stability needed to build this prosperity came in the form of political control. The government remained, in theory, a parliamentary regime. The emperor's agents rigged the elections to ensure a majority in the powerless legislature for the emperor. The secret police hounded opponents—both real and potential—and the state censored the press, which accordingly rarely reported bad news.

At first the emperor brought glory to France through an interventionist and imperialist foreign policy. He continually claimed to be a man of peace, but he allied with Britain in the Crimean War, supported Cavour, briefly, in Italy,

➔ View of the Champs-Elysées after the rebuilding of Paris. In a mere 20 years, Baron Georges Haussmann transformed Paris from a city of narrow streets and dark and dirty slums to a beautiful city crisscrossed by broad, tree-lined boulevards, open spaces, and a number of small neighborhood parks. Haussmann's renovations had political as well as aesthetic aims; destruction of many small and narrow streets eliminated places where revolutionaries might easily erect barricades and the wide boulevards permitted the rapid deployment of troops to put down rebellions.

expanded French influence to assure a foothold in Indochina, raised the French flag over Tahiti, and penetrated West Africa along the Senegal River. Foreign affairs soured for him in the 1860s when he made an ill-advised attempt to take advantage of the confusion caused by the U.S. Civil War to establish a foothold in the Americas. He placed Maximilian, a Habsburg prince, on the Mexican throne and sent 40,000 troops to support him. Mexican patriots expelled the forces and executed the prince. After 1866 Louis Napoleon met his match in the Prussian Chancellor Otto von Bismarck (1815–1898), when his blundering ambition contributed to a quick Prussian victory over Austria. Finally, in 1870 he gambled on a successful war against Prussian and lost. With this defeat the Second Empire ended.[4]

Cavour Unites Italy

After 1848, the Italian unification movement came to be centered in the Kingdom of Sardinia, where the young monarch Victor Emmanuel II refused to withdraw the liberal constitution granted by his father. The prime minister, Count Camillo Benso di Cavour (1810–1861), a liberal influenced by what he had seen in Switzerland, France, and Britain, assumed leadership of the drive to unify the peninsula.

After 1852, when he became prime minister, Cavour concentrated on freeing his country from Austrian domination. He knew, however, that Sardinia needed allies to take on the Habsburgs. To that end, in 1855 Sardinia joined Britain and France in their fight against Russia in the Crimean War. This step enabled Cavour to speak at the peace conference after the war, where he stated Italy's desire for unification.

Cavour's presentation won Napoleon III's support, and the two opportunists found that they could both make gains if they could draw the Austrians into war. They agreed that if Cavour could entice the Vienna government into war, France would come to Sardinia's aid and help eject the Austrians from Lombardy and Venetia. In return, France would receive Nice and Savoy from Sardinia. The plan worked to perfection. In April 1859, Cavour lured the Austrians into declaring war. The French and Sar-

→ Count Camillo Benso di Cavour, the leader of the movement for Italian unification.

dinians defeated them at Magenta and Solferino and drove them out of Lombardy. At the same time, revolts broke out in Tuscany, Modena, Parma, and Romagna. Napoleon received praise and was proclaimed the savior and liberator of Italy.

Upon receiving his share of the agreement, Napoleon III reversed himself and made peace with Austria, before the allies could invade Venetia. The massing of Prussian troops on French borders as well as his second thoughts about the implications of a united Italy drove Napoleon to this move. The Sardinians were outraged, but there was little they could do but agree to a peace settlement. The agreement awarded Lombard to Sardinia; restored the exiled rulers of Parma, Modena, Tuscany, and Romagna; and set up an Italian confederation in which Austria was included.

France's duplicity did not stop Cavour. A year later, appealing to the British, he made major changes in the peace settlement. Plebiscites were held in Tuscany, Modena, and Parma, and they voted to join Sardinia. Even with the loss of Nice and Savoy to France, the addition of the three areas made Sardinia the dominant power in the peninsula.

With the consolidation of power in the north, Giuseppe Garibaldi (1807–1882) became the major figure in the unification struggle. This follower of Mazzini, secretly financed by Cavour, led his 1000 tough adventurers—the Red Shirts—to conquer Sicily and Naples. He then prepared to take the Papal States. This move prompted Cavour, who feared that a march on the pope's holdings might provoke French intervention, to rush troops to Naples. He convinced Garibaldi to surrender his power to Victor Emmanuel II, thus ensuring Sardinian domination of the unification movement. By November 1860, Sardinia had annexed the former kingdom of Naples and Sicily, and all the papal lands, except Rome and its environs.

A meeting at Turin in March 1861 formally proclaimed the existence of the Kingdom of Italy, a new nation of 22 million people. But Austrian control of Venetia and the pope's jurisdiction over Rome were problems that remained unsolved until after Cavour's death in 1861. Italy gained Venetia in 1866, through acting as Prussia's ally in the Austro-Prussian war. When the Franco-Prussian war broke out in 1870, the French could do little to help the pope. Italian forces took control of Rome, and in 1871 it became the capital of a unified Italy.

The opportunistic methods used by the Sardinians have been criticized. Cavour made no attempt to hide the true nature of his policies. He once said "if we did for ourselves what we do for our country, what rascals we should be."[5] He fully understood the rules of the *Realpolitik* game in the post-1848 state system. His skill in playing that game and in gaining Italian unification cannot be doubted.

Germanic Competition

Conservative forces regained control in Vienna and Berlin after 1848, but the Austrian Habsburgs operated from a position much weaker than that of the Prussian Hohenzollerns. The Habsburg victory over the Hungarians brought only temporary comfort. The collapse of the liberal and nationalistic movements in the Habsburg empire was followed by a harsh repression that did little to address the basic political problems facing Vienna. Centralizing and Germanizing tendencies stimulated nationalist sentiments in the empire. After their losses to the French and Sardinians in 1859, the Austrians considered moving toward a federal system for their lands. The Hungarians, however, demanded equality with Vienna.

Prussia, on the other hand, went from strength to strength. Facing a different range of problems in a much more unified state, King Frederick William issued a constitution in 1850 that paid lip service to parliamentary democracy but kept real power in the hands of the king and upper classes. The Berlin court wanted to form a confederation of north German states, without Austria. This plan frightened the Austrians and made the Russians uneasy as well. A meeting of the three powers at Olmütz in 1850 forced the Prussians to withdraw their plan. Instead, the 1815 German Confederation was affirmed, with

UNIFICATION OF ITALY 1859–1870

Kingdom of Sardinia to 1859
Kingdom of Sardinia, 1860
Annexed to Kingdom of Sardinia, 1861; Establishes Kingdom of Italy
Kingdom of Italy, 1866
Kingdom of Italy, 1870

THE UNIFICATION OF GERMANY
1815–1871

- Prussia, 1815–1866
- Annexed by Prussia, 1866
- Joined Prussia in Forming the North German Confederation, 1867
- Joined with Prussia to Form the German Empire, 1871
- Alsace-Lorraine Ceded to German Empire by France, 1871
- German Confederation, 1815–1866

0
MILES

Vienna recognized as the major German power. The embittered Prussians returned to Berlin, pledging revenge for the "humiliation of Olmütz."

Despite this diplomatic setback, Prussia gained success in other areas. Berlin kept the Austrians out of the *Zollverein*, the customs union of German states, and fought off their efforts to weaken it. The government, dominated by the nobles, was modern and efficient, especially when compared with that in Vienna. The Prussians extended public education to more of their citizenry than in any other European state. At the end of the 1850s, a new ruler, William I (1861–1888), came to power. He had a more permissive interpretation of the 1850 constitution

and allowed liberals and moderates the chance to make their voices heard.

Bismarck and German Unification

A stalemate occurred in 1862 when the king wanted to strengthen his army, but the Chamber of Deputies would not vote the necessary funds. The liberals asserted the constitutional right to approve taxes, while the king equally strongly expressed his right to build up his forces. As the king struggled with this constitutional crisis, he called Otto von Bismarck (1815–1898) home from his post as Prussian ambassador in France and made him prime minister.

Bismarck advised the king to ignore the legislature and collect the needed taxes without the Chamber's approval. Bismarck knew the necessity of armed strength in order to gain Prussia's diplomatic goals. Ironically, his later military victories would gain him the support of many of the liberals whom he had encouraged the king to defy.

Bismarck's arrival in Berlin strengthened not only the king but also the hopes of those who wanted a united German state. Unification appealed to virtually all segments of German society, from the liberals to the conservatives, such as the historian Heinrich von Treitschke who stated, "There is only one salvation! One state, one monarchic Germany under the Hohenzollern dynasty."[6] Berlin, through its leadership of the *Zollverein*, sponsorship of the confederation of north German states, and efficient bureaucracy, was the obvious choice for the capital of a unified German state. With the arrival of Bismarck, the Prussians gained the necessary leadership for unification.

The prime minister was a master of the art of *Realpolitik*. He had the intelligence to assess accurately the actual state of conditions, the insight to gauge the character and goals of his opponents, and the talent to move skillfully and quickly. Unlike most of his colleagues, he was a master image maker, so effective that historians have used his epithet "blood and iron" to describe his career. Few statesmen have ever accomplished so much change with such a comparatively small loss of life in a controlled use of war. Bismarck was a master politician who knew that force was the final card to be played, to be used as the servant of diplomacy and not its master.[7]

Some historians have attributed his successes to mere luck, whereas others have deemed them products of genius. An example is his approach to Russia. Bismarck knew that he would have to solidify relations with Russia, and he achieved this in 1863 by promising the Russians that he would aid them in all Polish-related problems. Giving up virtually nothing, he gained a secure eastern flank and thus set up three wars that brought about German unification.

→ Otto von Bismarck, the "Iron Chancellor," was the shrewd and masterful prime minister of Prussia from 1862 and the first chancellor of the united Germany from 1871 to 1890.

The Danish and Austrian Wars

In 1864 Bismarck invited Austria to join Prussia and wage war on Denmark. The cause of the conflict was the disputed status of two duchies bordering on Prussia and Denmark. These two duchies of Schleswig and Holstein were claimed by both the Germans and the Danes. The two Germanic powers overwhelmed the modest Danish forces and split the duchies: Austria took Holstein, and Schleswig went to Prussia. With his eastern and northern flanks stabilized, Bismarck set out to isolate Austria.

Italy was already hostile to the Austrians and remained so when Bismarck promised it Venetia in return for its assistance in the future war. He encouraged the French to be neutral by intimating that Prussia might support France should it seek to widen its borders. Severe domestic crises with the Hungarians absorbed Austria, which soon found itself isolated. The Prussian leader provoked war with Vienna by piously expressing alarm at the manner in which the Austrians were ruling Holstein and sending troops into the province. Austria took the bait, entered the war, and was devastated by the Prussians at the battle of Sadowa. In this Seven Weeks' War, the Prussians avenged the "humiliation of Olmütz."

Prussia offered a moderate peace settlement that ended the old German Confederation. In its place Bismarck formed the North German Confederation, with Austria and the south German states excluded. Prussia annexed several territories such as Hanover, Mecklenberg, and other states north of the Main River in this penultimate stage in the unification of Germany.

The War with France

After 1867 Bismarck turned his attention westward to France and Napoleon III. The French leader had allowed himself to be talked into neutrality in 1866 because he anticipated a long war between his German neighbors that would weaken both of them and because he hoped to expand into the neutral state of Belgium. In August 1866 Napoleon approached Bismarck for his share of the fruits of victory, but the German leader refused to agree to French demands. Frustrated and offended, Napoleon III insisted that Prussia approve France's annexation of Luxembourg and Belgium. In a crafty move Bismarck invited the French envoy to Berlin to put these demands into writing but still avoided giving a definite response. Four years later Bismarck sent the document to the British in order to gain their sympathy for the upcoming war with the French. After France's active participation in the Crimean War, there was no chance that Russia would come to Napoleon's aid. Bismarck let the Austrians know about France's cooperation with the Prussians during the 1866 war, and Italy was not about to help Napoleon III after his activities in 1859. By 1870 France was isolated. It was simply a question now of Bismarck maneuvering the French into war.

The immediate controversy centered on the succession to the Spanish throne left vacant after a revolution had overthrown the reactionary queen Isabella. The Spaniards asked Leopold, a Hohenzollern prince, to become the constitutional king of their country. France saw this as an unacceptable extension of Prussian influence, and Leopold withdrew his candidacy. But this was not enough for Paris. The French sent their ambassador to Ems, where the Prussian king was vacationing, to gain from him a pledge that he would not again permit Leopold to seek the Spanish throne. This was not a reasonable request, and the king refused to agree to it. After the interview he directed that a message be sent to Bismarck, describing the incident. Bismarck altered the message of this "Ems dispatch" to give the impression that the French ambassador had insulted the Prussian king and that the king had returned the insult. The rumor was leaked to the press and infuriated both the Germans and the French.

France declared war in July. The two countries' forces appeared to be evenly matched in equipment, but the Germans had a better trained and more experienced army. In two months the Prussians overwhelmed the French, delivering the crowning blow at the battle of Sedan, where the emperor and his army were surrounded and forced to surrender. Forces of the north and south German states besieged France for four months before the final French capitulation. By the Treaty of Frankfurt, France lost Alsace and a part of Lorraine to Germany and was required to pay a large indemnity. In the Hall of Mirrors at Versailles, the Second Reich was proclaimed, and William I was crowned German emperor. The call for revenge of France's defeat and humiliation became a major issue in French politics.

RUSSIA AND BRITAIN: THE EXTREMES OF EUROPE

Russia avoided the revolutionary currents after 1815, but unlike Britain, Russia had neither the economic strength nor the social and political flexibility to change. Tsar Alexander I (1801–1825) understood the major problems facing his empire, especially those of serfdom and the need to reform the autocratic system. His grandmother, Catherine II, had educated him in the traditions and assumptions of the Enlightenment, and for the first four years of his reign he attempted major reforms in the areas of education, government, and social welfare.

Bismarck and the Ems Despatch

Bismarck knew how to manipulate public opinion through press leaks and doctored documents. See how he altered the Ems despatch to achieve his goals vis-à-vis France.

I made use of the royal authorization communicated to me through Abeken, to publish the contents of the telegram; and in the presence of my two guests I reduced the telegram by striking out words, but without adding or altering, to the following form:

> After the news of the renunciation of the hereditary Prince of Hohenzollern had been officially communicated to the imperial government of France by the royal government of Spain, the French ambassador at Ems further demanded of his Majesty the King that he would authorize him to telegraph to Paris that his Majesty the King bound himself for all future time never again to give his consent if the Hohenzollerns should renew their candidature. His Majesty the King thereupon decided not to receive the French ambassador again, and sent to tell him through the aide-de-camp on duty that his Majesty had nothing further to communicate to the ambassador.

The difference in the effect of the abbreviated text of the Ems telegram as compared with that produced by the original was not the result of stronger words but of the form, which made this announcement appear decisive, while Abeken's version only would have been regarded as a fragment of a negotiation still pending, and to be continued at Berlin.

After I had read out the concentrated edition to my two guests, Moltke remarked: "Now it has a different ring; it sounded before like a parley; now it is like a flourish in answer to a challenge."

From *Bismarck, The Man and the Statement*, translated by A. J. Butler, 2 vol. (New York, 1899).

→ Following France's defeat in the Franco-Prussian War, the Second Reich of the German Empire (the first Reich was the Holy Roman Empire) was proclaimed on January 21, 1871, in the Hall of Mirrors at the Palace of Versailles outside Paris. The new emperor William I stands on the dais, but the central figure in the painting is the white-coated Otto von Bismarck, the first chancellor of the new empire.

Russia, however, possessed neither the inventive and flexible ruling classes nor the economic wealth of Britain. Its problems were far more harsh. Serfdom, a system that held millions of Russians in its grip, was socially repressive and economically inefficient. The autocratic system simply was inadequate to govern efficiently the world's largest state.

Obstacles to Reform in Russia

Alexander's experiments with limited serf emancipation, constitutionalism, and federalism demonstrated his desire for change. The tsar was all-powerful in theory, but in reality he depended on the nobles who, in turn, gained their wealth from serfdom. Carrying out the necessary reforms would destroy the foundations of Alexander's power. The fact that his father and grandfather had been killed by nobles made him cautious. Further, it was his misfortune to rule during the Napoleonic wars, and for the first 15 years of his reign he had to devote immense amounts of money and time to foreign affairs. His reform plans were never carried through to completion, and not until the 1850s, when it was almost too late, would there be another tsar willing to make the fundamental social and political reforms needed to make Russia competitive in the industrializing world.[8]

In the reactionary decade after 1815 reformers fell from favor. However, the open discussion of the need for change in the first part of Alexander's reign, the experiences of the soldiers returning from western Europe and the activities of the expanding number of secret societies kept the dream of change alive. When Alexander failed to respond, the intensity of the reformers' discussions increased. Alexander died in December 1825, and there was confusion over which of his two brothers would succeed to the throne. The days between his death and the confirmation of his younger brother Nicholas I (1825–1855) gave a small circle of liberal nobles and army officers the chance to advance their ill-defined demands for a constitution. The officers who led this revolt had been infected with liberal French thought. They sought to end serfdom and establish representative government and civil liberties in Russia. On December 26 these liberals led a small uprising in St. Petersburg. This Decembrist Revolt, as it was called, lasted less than a day and could have been put down even earlier had Nicholas been more decisive. This abortive, ill-planned attempt doomed any chance of liberal or democratic reform in Russia for thirty years.

Nicholas I and Reaction

The Decembrist incident shook Nicholas badly, and throughout his reign he remained opposed to liberal and revolutionary movements. He sponsored "Official Nationalism," whose foundations were "Autocracy, Orthodoxy, and Nationalism"— the Romanov dynasty, the Orthodox church, and a glorification of a putative Russian spirit. He carried out a thorough policy of censorship that included the screening of foreign visitors, publications, even musical compositions. The government closely monitored both students' activities and curricula in schools and universities. Finally, some 150,000 "dangerous" people were exiled to Siberia. Millions of non-Russians in the empire began to experience limitations on their identities through a forced adherence to Russian customs called "Russification." These activities strengthened Nicholas's immediate control and stopped potential upheaval, but he failed to address adequately the important social and political reforms Russia so badly needed.

Despite his efforts to control intellectual and political currents, Nicholas failed. Reformist activity may have been repressed, but the Russian intellectual circles were creative, tuned as they were to the works of the German philosophers and poets. In the 1840s and 1850s a new breed of intellectuals appeared, thinkers devoted to achieving political goals. Although they would not make their strength felt until after the 1860s, these thinkers, known as the intelligentsia, established strong roots during Nicholas's reign. Alexander Herzen (1812–1870) and Michael Bakunin (1814–1876) were the pioneers of this peculiarly Russian movement. Herzen was a moderate socialist who advocated freeing the serfs, liberalizing the government, and freeing the press. In 1847 he went into exile in London where he founded his famous paper, the *Kolokol* ("Bell"), ten years later. It was widely read in Russia, supposedly appearing mysteriously on the tsar's table. Bakunin, the father of Russian anarchism, was more radical. He believed reform of

Russia was useless and advocated terrorism. He preached that anarchy—complete freedom—was the only cure for society's ills. He too went into exile in the West.

The Russian intellectuals debated many questions, most important of which was whether Russia should imitate all aspects of European life or pursue its own tradition of orthodoxy and a single-centered society. The question had been posed since the reign of Peter the Great. The Westerners argued that if Russia wished to survive it had to adopt basic aspects of the West and renounce much of its own past. The Slavophiles, on the other side of the dialogue, renounced Europe and the West, and regarded it as materialistic, pagan, and anarchic.

Nicholas was able to maintain control to the extent that the 1830 and 1848 revolutions had little influence or impact on Russia. Some aspects of industrialization were introduced, as the first Moscow-to-St. Petersburg rail line was put into operation. The government appointed commissions to examine the questions of serfdom and reform, but these were extremely secret considerations.[9] Still, basic doubts about Russia's future remained. Dissident intellectuals, economic and social weakness, and autocratic stagnation were indicators that difficult times were in store for the country.

Alexander II and the Great Reforms

Russia's inept performance in the Crimean War spotlighted the country's weaknesses and the need for reform. When Alexander II (1855–1881) came to the throne, even the conservatives among his subjects acknowledged the need for major change. The new tsar moved quickly to transform the basis of the autocratic structure—the institution of serfdom—but ran into delay from the nobility. Alexander appointed a committee, which after five years of deliberation, drew up the Emancipation Proclamations, issued in March 1861. By this reform, 32 million state peasants and 20 million serfs who had no civil rights, could not own property, and owed heavy dues and services to the nobility began the transition to land ownership and citizenship.

The government paid the landlords a handsome price for the land that was to be turned over to the peasants. In return, the peasants had to pay the government for the land over a period of 49 years by making payments through their village commune, the *mir*. The drawn-out nature of the land transfer disappointed the former serfs, who had expected a portion of the lords' lands to be turned over to them without charge. Instead, the peasants were trapped in their village communes, which received and allocated all of the land—much of it poor—and divided it among the various families and paid taxes. Even though they were granted ownership of their cottages, farm buildings, garden plots, domestic animals, and implements, the restrictions placed on the peasants by confining them to their villages constituted a serious problem. New generations of peasants increased the population, but there was no corresponding increase in their share of the land.

→ When attempts to settle the Decembrist revolt peacefully failed, Tsar Nicholas ordered troops to fire on the rebels. More than 60 people were killed in the brief fight. Putting down the Decembrist revolt also sounded the death knell for liberal reform in Russia.

The emancipation of the serfs was the single most important event in the domestic history of nineteenth-century Russia. In its wake it brought about thoroughgoing reforms of the army, judiciary, municipal government, and system of local self-government. One of the most important reforms came in 1864 when local government was transformed by the *Zemstvo* law. In the countryside the gentry, middle classes, and peasants elected representatives to local boards *(zemstvos).* These boards collected taxes for and maintained roads, asylums, hospitals, and schools. The *zemstvos* became one of the most successful governmental organizations in Russia.[10]

British Flexibility

Like Russia, Britain did not directly experience the revolutionary upheaval that afflicted the Continent, even though the island nation felt many of the same pressures as France during the same period. The postwar period was the most difficult time for Britain, as the transition back to a peacetime economy and the wrenching changes caused by industrialization made their effects felt. Some traditional workers lost their jobs due to the increasing use of machines, and in response, workers smashed the machines and destroyed some factories. Violence broke out when some working-class groups and radicals pushed for rapid reforms. The worst incident took place in August 1819 in what became known as the Peterloo Massacre. In Manchester, a crowd of 60,000 gathered at St. Peter's Fields to push for parliamentary reforms. When the army was sent to disband the meeting, several people were killed and hundreds injured.

Britain's ruling class, in power since the 1770s, were conservatives who were blind to the hardships of their workers. They continued to respond to the long-departed excesses of the French Revolution. Instead of dealing with the misfortunes of the poor and unemployed, they declared that the doctrine of "peace, law, order, and discipline" should be their guide. To that end, they pushed through a series of repressive acts after 1815 that suspended the Habeas Corpus Act, restricted public meetings, repressed liberal newspapers, and placed heavy fines on literature considered to be dangerous. Massive conflict between the rich and poor appeared inevitable.

The Duke of Wellington's failure to acknowledge the need for reforms in the 1830s so aroused the public that the "Iron Duke" and the Tories (Conservatives) were forced to resign. They were replaced by a more liberal group, the Whigs. The drive toward self-interested reform by the upper classes had begun in the 1820s, led by Robert Peel (1788–1850) and George Canning (1770–1827), who started the modern British reform tradition that continued to 1914. When Wellington was voted out of office, Lord Charles Grey (1764–1845), leader of the Whig party, became head of government. In 1832 Grey pushed immediately to reform Parliament.[11]

Britain's political abuses were plain for all to see. Representation in the House of Commons was not at all proportional to the population. Three percent of the people dictated the election of members. The rapidly growing industrial towns such as Manchester and Birmingham—each with more than 100,000 citizens—had no representatives, while other areas, virtually without population, had delegates. After being blocked by aristocratic interests, first in the House of Commons and then in the House of Lords, reform bills responding to these electoral abuses were finally passed. But this occurred only because King William IV threatened to create enough new members of the House of Lords who would vote for the bills in order to pass them. Grey's reform bills did not bring absolute democracy, but they pointed the way toward a more equitable political system.

The Reformist Tide

Beginning in the 1820s reformers pushed through laws that ended capital punishment for more than a hundred offenses, created a modern police force for London, recognized labor unions, and repealed old laws that kept non-Anglican Protestants from sitting in Parliament. They also passed the Catholic Emancipation Act that gave Roman Catholics voting rights and the rights to serve in Parliament and most public offices. The reform tide increased in the 1830s and 1840s. Abolitionist pressures brought about the ending of slavery in the British empire in 1833. Parliament passed laws initiating the regulation of working conditions and hours. In 1835 the Municipal Corporations Bill introduced a

→ Chartists march their Grand Petition, calling for broader voting rights, to the House of Commons in 1842. Parliament rejected the petition as it had in 1839 and would again in 1848.

uniform system of town government by popular elections.

Britain's government was far from being a democracy, and in the 1830s and 1840s a strong, popular movement known as Chartism developed. Its leaders summarized the country's needs in six demands: universal manhood suffrage, secret voting, no property qualifications for members of Parliament, payment of Parliament members so that the poor could seek election, annual elections, and equal districts. In 1839, 1842, and 1848 the Chartists presented their demands, backed by more than a million signatures on their petitions. But each time they failed to gain their goals, and the movement declined after 1848. By the end of the century, however, all of their demands, except that for annual parliamentary elections, had been put into law.

Mirroring the ascendancy of the middle classes, economic liberalism became dominant. A policy of free trade came to be favored because, given Britain's overwhelming economic superiority, the country could best profit from that approach. The Corn Laws' protective duties on imported grain, which had favored the gentry since 1815, no longer suited the industrializing British economy. These laws had been designed to encourage exports and to protect the British landowners from foreign competition. By the middle of the century the population had grown to such an extent that British farmers could no longer feed the country and the price of bread rose alarmingly.

The potato crop famine in Ireland in 1845 that led to the death of perhaps a half million people spotlighted the situation and the need for low-priced food from abroad. Repeal of the Corn Laws made possible the import of cheaper food for the masses. Soon Britain abandoned customs duties of every kind. The economy boomed under the stimulus of cheap imports of raw materials and food.

For the next 20 years an alliance of the landed gentry and the middle classes worked together to dominate the government and to keep the lower classes "in their stations." The newly ascendant middle classes believed that political reforms had gone far enough, and the Whig government of Lord Palmerston who served as prime minister from 1855 to 1865 reflected this view.

CONCLUSION

The Congress of Vienna dealt with the challenges of liberalism and nationalism as much as it confronted the classic problems of balance of power and compensation. The epidemic of revolutions in the 1820s, 1830s, and 1840s showed that the European patterns laid out in 1815 could not be maintained. In 1848 the legacy of the French Revolution and the process of industrialization combined to overpower the political structures of France, Germany, Italy, and the Habsburg empire.

The 1848 revolutions enjoyed brief, spectacular successes and tragic, lasting failures. The leaders of the revolutions had little or no experience, and they acted under a total infatuation with their ideals. The force of nationalism, so powerful an enemy of autocracy, soon proved to be a fragmenting force among the various liberated nationalities. These factors doomed the idealistic revolutionaries and introduced a new range of political alternatives.

The postrevolutionary generation in France turned to Louis Napoleon in a search for stability and prosperity. The French gained both—for a time—at the price of reduced liberty and military and diplomatic defeat. The Italians achieved unification under the leadership of Cavour in Sardinia. The Habsburg empire, after nearly 20 years of trying to deal successfully with its fractious nationalities, redefined itself as the Dual Monarchy in 1867. In Prussia, after a period of reaction, a constitutional crisis in 1862 led to the rise to power of Otto von Bismarck and the achievement of German unification by 1871.

Russia and Britain avoided the revolutionary upheavals, the first through a policy of repression that failed to respond effectively to its overwhelming problems and the second because of an improving standard of living and a flexible, self-interested political leadership. Throughout the half century after Waterloo, however, the advanced nations of Europe underwent the trau-

mas of industrialization, which had as devastating an effect on the old idealism as had the political upheavals of 1848.

→ Suggestions for Reading

H. Nicolson, *The Congress of Vienna: A Study of Allied Unity, 1812–1822* (Compass, 1961) is a civilized analysis of diplomatic interaction and a good companion to Henry A. Kissinger, *A World Restored: Metternich, Castlereagh, and the Problems of Peace, 1812–1822* (Sentry, 1957). The following are excellent on the general background to the period: A. J. May, *The Age of Metternich, 1814–1848* (Holt, Rinehart, and Winston, 1967), E. Hobsbawm, *The Age of Revolution, Europe 1789–1848* (Mentor, 1969), J. Talmon, *Romanticism and Revolt: Europe 1815–1948* (Harcourt Brace Jovanovich, 1967), P. Stearns, *European Society in Upheaval* (Macmillan, 1967), R. C. Binkley, *Realism and Nationalism: 1852–1871* (Torchbooks, 1935), W. E. Mosse, *Liberal Europe* (Harcourt Brace Jovanovich, 1974), John Weiss, *Conservatism in Europe* (Harcourt Brace Jovanovich, 1977).

Volume 4 of A. Cobban's *A History of Modern France* (Penguin, 1970) is a useful survey. For greater detail see F. Artz, *France Under the Bourbon Restoration, 1814–1830* (Russell, 1931); T. Howarth, *Citizen King: The Life of Louis-Philippe, King of the French* (Verry, 1961); G. Duveau, *1848: The Making of a Revolution* (Vintage, 1967), and F. A. Simpson, *Louis Napoleon and the Recovery of France* (Greenwood, 1975).

Two valuable surveys on Britain are Asa Briggs, *The Making of Modern England, 1783–1867: The Age of Improvement* (Torchbooks, 1959) and E. L. Woodward, *The Age of Reform, 1815–1870* (Oxford, 1962). The tragedy of the Irish famine is thoroughly analyzed in Joel Mokyr's *Why Ireland Starved: A Quantitative and Analytical History of the Irish Economy, 1800–1850* (Allen & Unwin, 1983). *The Chartists: Popular Politics in the Industrial Revolution* (Pantheon Books, 1984) shows the widespread foundations of the English reform movement. Derek Bayles gives the most thorough coverage of the Italian unification movement in *The Risorgimento and the Unification of Italy* (Allen & Unwin, 1982).

A. J. P. Taylor, *The Course of German History* (Capricorn, 1962) is a short, controversial essay on German national history since the French Revolution. T. Hamerow, *Restoration, Revolution, Reaction: Economics and Politics in Germany, 1815–1871* (Princeton, 1966) is highly praised. L. Namier's *1848: The Revolution of the Intellectuals* (Anchor, 1946) is critical of the liberals at Frankfurt. E. Eyck's balanced *Bismarck and the German Empire* (Norton, 1964) is offset by Taylor's hostile *Bismarck: The Man and the Statesman* (Alfred A. Knopf, 1955). O. Pflanze's *Bismarck and the Development of Germany: The Period of Unification, 1815–1871* (Princeton, 1963) is first-rate. Barbara Jelavich's *The Habsburg Empire in European Affairs* (Rand McNally,

1969) is an excellent, brief history. C. A. Macartney's *The Habsburg Empire: 1790–1918* (Weidenfeld and Nicholson, 1968) is thorough, but pro-Hungarian. Alan Sked, *The Decline and Fall of the Habsburg Empire 1815–1918* (London: Longman, 1989) provides a fresh view of unexpected strengths and weaknesses of the Vienna-based empire.

J. N. Westwood's *Endurance and Endeavour: Russian History 1812–1986* (Oxford, 1988) is the best new survey, replacing Hugh Seton-Watson's *The Russian Empire 1801–1917* (Oxford, 1967). Allen McConnell's *Tsar Alexander I* (Cromwell, i970) remains the best short biography. W. Bruce Lincoln's *In the Vanguard of Reform* (Northern Illinois, 1982) sets the standard for scholarship on Nicholas I. Deep insights into Russian intellectual development are to be found in N. Berdyaev's *The Russian Idea* (Beacon, 1962). The best introductory book on nineteenth-century Russia is Marc Raeff's *Understanding Imperial Russia* (Columbia, 1984).

✢ Notes

1. Norman Davies, *Heart of Europe: A Short History of Poland* (Oxford: Oxford University Press, 1987), pp. 166–167.

2. Barbara Jelavich, *The Habsburg Empire in European Affairs: 1814–1918* (Chicago: Rand McNally & Co., 1969), pp. 21–39.

3. Jorg K. Hoensch, *A History of Modern Hungary: 1867–1986* (London: Longman, 1988), pp. 4–10.

4. For vivid characterizations of this period see Roger L. Williams, *The World of Napoleon III: 1851–1870* (New York: Collier Books, 1962).

5. Quoted in J. S. Schapiro, *Modern and Contemporary European History: 1815–1940* (Boston: Houghton Mifflin Co., 1940), p. 222.

6. Quoted in K. S. Pinson, *Modern Germany* (New York: The Macmillan Company, 1954), p. 116.

7. L. C. B. Seaman, *From Vienna to Versailles* (New York: Harper and Row, 1962), pp. 96–129.

8. See Allen McConnell's biography *Tsar Alexander I: Paternalistic Reformer* (New York: Crowell, 1970), for a clear treatment of this most complex personality.

9. W. Bruce Lincoln, *In the Vanguard of Reform* (DeKalb: Northern Illinois University Press, 1982), pp. 139–167.

10. J. N. Westwood, *Endurance and Endeavour: Russian History 1812–1986* (Oxford: Oxford University Press, 1987), pp. 79–103.

11. G. Bingham Powell, Jr., "Incremental Democratization: The British Reform Act of 1832," in G. A. Almond, S. C. Flanagan, and R. J. Mundt, eds., *Crisis, Choice, and Change* (Boston: Little, Brown, 1973), p. 149.

CHAPTER 25

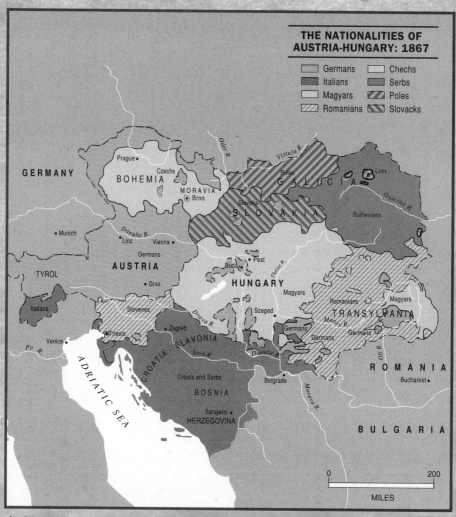

THE NATIONALITIES OF
AUSTRIA-HUNGARY: 1867

- Germans
- Italians
- Magyars
- Romanians
- Chechs
- Serbs
- Poles
- Slovacks

→ Contemporary critics of the *Ausgleich*, the governing statute in Austria-Hungary after 1867, derided its ineffectiveness in dealing with the many ethnic groups in its realm. In 1995, observers noted that few improvements had been made in governing the area.

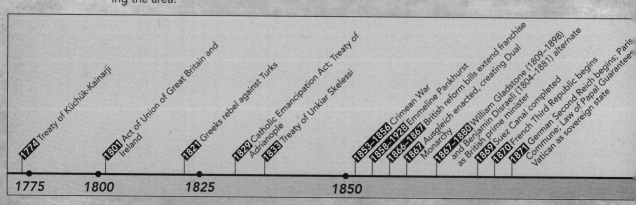

1774 Treaty of Küchük-Kainarji

1801 Act of Union of Great Britain and Ireland

1821 Greeks rebel against Turks

1829 Catholic Emancipation Act; Treaty of Adrianople

1833 Treaty of Unkiar Skelessi

1853–1856 Crimean War

1858–1928 Emmeline Pankhurst

1866–1867 British reform bills extend franchise

1867 Ausgleich enacted, creating Dual Monarchy

1867–1880 William Gladstone (1809–1898) and Benjamin Disraeli (1804–1881) alternate as British prime minister

1869 Suez Canal completed

1870 French Third Republic begins

1871 German Second Reich begins; Paris Commune, Law of Papal Guarantees, Vatican as sovereign state

1775   1800   1825   1850

European Politics, 1871–1914

CHAPTER OUTLINE

MAPS

DOCUMENT

After 1871, six countries dominated European politics: Great Britain, Germany, France, Russia, Italy, and Austria-Hungary. Each power claimed a glorious past, strong culture, and rich resources. Yet the leaders of only three of the "great powers," those in London, Berlin, and Paris, actually possessed a power base capable of supporting pretensions of grandeur.

Great Britain, Germany, and France adjusted more or less successfully to the opportunities presented by industrialization, scientific advances, and mass participation politics after 1871. They built modern political systems that effectively tapped the resources of their countries while responding efficiently to the demands of their people.

If a full-scale war broke out, the leaders in Russia, Italy, and Austria-Hungary could not compete effectively. They did not have the industrial and scientific establishments to fuel their drives to become "great powers." Their political infrastructures presented obstacles to effective government. Russia limped along, an autocracy attempting to modernize itself; Italy suffered from regional fragmentation and economic weakness; Austria-Hungary remained paralyzed in nationalistic discord.

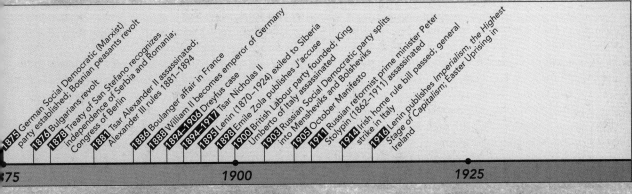

1875 German Social Democratic (Marxist) party established; Bosnian peasants revolt
1876 Bulgarians revolt
1878 Treaty of San Stefano recognizes independence of Serbia and Romania; Congress of Berlin
1881 Tsar Alexander II assassinated; Alexander III rules 1881–1894
1886 Boulanger affair in France
1888 William II becomes emperor of Germany
1894–1906 Dreyfus case
1894–1917 Tsar Nicholas II
1895 Lenin (1870–1924) exiled to Siberia
1898 Emile Zola publishes J'accuse
1900 British Labour party founded; King Umberto of Italy assassinated
1903 Russian Social Democratic party splits into Mensheviks and Bolsheviks
1905 October Manifesto
1911 Russian reformist prime minister Peter Stolypin (1862–1911) assassinated
1914 Irish home rule bill passed; general strike in Italy
1916 Lenin publishes Imperialism, the Highest Stage of Capitalism; Easter Uprising in Ireland

1875   1900   1925

For the previous five hundred years, the Ottoman Turks had controlled the Balkans. As the Sultan's grip on southeastern Europe weakened in the eighteenth and nineteenth centuries, the nations that had labored under Turkish domination began their drive for independence. The "Eastern Question," that is, the question of what to do with the region, attracted the attention of all six great powers during the nineteenth century. Their inability to answer the question would have dreadful results in 1914.

BRITAIN AND DEMOCRACY

Blessed by its wealth and adaptability, Britain built a truly democratic political structure by 1914. The state continued to support business even as it became more intimately involved in matters affecting the welfare of its citizens. Two great statesmen, William Ewart Gladstone (1809–1898), a Liberal, and Benjamin Disraeli (1804–1881), a Conservative, dominated the first part of this period with their policies of gradual reform. They alternated as prime minister from 1867 to 1880. After Disraeli's death, Gladstone prevailed until he retired in 1894.

Gladstone and Disraeli

The two leaders came from sharply contrasting backgrounds. The son of a rich Liverpool merchant, Gladstone had every advantage that wealth and good social position could give him. He entered Parliament in 1833 and quickly became one of the greatest orators of his day. He began as a Conservative, working in the tradition of the Tory reformer Robert Peel. Gradually he shifted his alliance to the newly formed Liberal party in the 1850s and became a strong supporter of laissez-faire economics and worked to keep government from interfering in business. He was far more effective as a political reformer than as a social or economic one.

Disraeli had few of Gladstone's advantages. The son of a Jew who became a naturalized British subject in 1801, Disraeli was baptized an Anglican. He first made a name for himself as the author of the novel *Vivian Grey* (1826). In contrast to Gladstone, Disraeli went from liberalism to conservatism in his philosophy. He stood for office as a Conservative throughout his career and became the leader of the party.

→ In this *Punch* cartoon, political rivals William Gladstone (left) and Benjamin Disraeli (right) are ready to sling mud at each other. The cartoon's caption reads, "A Bad Example."

Both Liberals and Conservatives had to face the fact that the complacency of government during the "Victorian Compromise" from 1850 to 1865 could not continue. The alliance of landed gentry and middle classes may have successfully kept the lower classes "in their stations" but serious problems plagued the country. Only one adult male in six was entitled to vote. Both parties felt the pressure to make the political system more representative. Both parties also knew that reform must come, and each hoped to take the credit and gain the resultant strength for extending the vote.

The Liberals' turn came first. In 1866 they introduced a moderate reform bill enfranchising city workers. Some Conservatives opposed it, fearful that increasing the franchise would bring the day of revolution closer. When the proposal failed to pass, political agitation and riots rocked the country. The outbreaks evidently impressed the members of Parliament, and when the Conservatives came to power in 1867, Disraeli successfully sponsored the Second Reform Bill, which added more than a million city workers to the voting rolls. The measure increased the electorate by 88 percent, although women and farm laborers were still denied the vote.

Even though the Conservatives passed the voter reform bill, the new elections in 1868 brought the Liberals back to power, and Gladstone began his so-called Glorious Ministry, which lasted until 1874. With the granting of the vote to the urban masses it became imperative to educate their children. The Education Act of 1870 promoted the establishment of local school boards to build and maintain state schools. Private schools received governmental subsidies if they met certain minimal standards. Elementary school attendance, which was compulsory between the ages of 5 and 14, jumped from 1 to 4 million in ten years.

Other reforms included a complete overhaul of the civil service system. Previously, in both the government and military, appointments and promotions depended on patronage and favoritism. But in 1870, this method was replaced by open examinations. The government also improved the military by shortening enlistment terms, abolishing flogging, and stopping the sale of officers' rank. Gladstone's government successfully revamped the justice system and introduced the secret ballot. Finally, some restrictions on labor unions' activities were removed. By 1872 the Glorious Ministry had exhausted itself, and Disraeli referred to Gladstone and his colleagues in the House of Commons as a "range of exhausted volcanoes."

Disraeli's government succeeded the Glorious Ministry in 1874, and he stated that he was going to "give the country a rest." He was no stand-pat Conservative, however. He supported an approach known as Tory democracy, which attempted to weld an alliance between the landed gentry and the workers against the middle class. Even during this "time of rest" Disraeli's government pushed through important reforms in public housing, food and drug legislation, and union rights to strike and picket peacefully.

Gladstone returned to power in 1880 and continued the stream of reforms with the Third Reform Bill, which extended the vote to agricultural workers. This act brought Britain to the verge of universal male suffrage. Gladstone also

secured passage of the Employers' Liability Act, which gave workers rights of compensation in case of accidents on the job.

The Irish Problem

One dilemma escaped and continues to escape the solutions of well-meaning reformers in Britain, that of the British role in Ireland. The present-day crisis in Northern Ireland originated in the seventeenth century. The British placed large numbers of Scottish emigrants in the province of Ulster in northern Ireland, which built a strong colony of Protestants—the so-called Orangemen, or Scotch-Irish. In the eighteenth century the British passed a number of oppressive laws against the Irish Catholics, restricting their political, economic, and religious freedom and effectively taking their lands. Passage of the Act of Union in 1801 forced the Irish to send their representatives to the Parliament in London, not Dublin. A large part of the Irish farmland passed into the hands of parasitic landlords who leased their newly gained lands in increasingly smaller plots to more and more people. Many peasants could not pay their rent and were evicted from the land. The Irish lost both their self-government and their livelihood.

In 1845 the potato crop, the main staple of diet, failed and a terrible famine ensued, which led to a tremendous decline in population. Hundreds of thousands emigrated to the United States; perhaps as many as 500,000 people died. Between 1841 and 1891 the population fell by more than 40 percent, from 8.8 million to less than 5 million.

The Irish gained a few concessions from the British during the century in the form of the Catholic Emancipation Act (1829) and also received protection from arbitrary eviction for tenants during the Glorious Ministry. The Irish Anglican Church lost its favored position when Roman Catholics were freed of the obligation to pay tax support to a church they did not attend. In 1881 Gladstone pushed through an act that allowed the Irish peasants the chance gradually to regain land that had once been theirs.

None of these concessions made up for the lack of home rule, and in 1874 the Irish patriot Charles Stewart Parnell (1846–1891) began to work actively to force the issue through Parliament. Gladstone introduced home rule bills in

1886 and 1893, but both were defeated. A home rule bill was finally passed in 1914, but by this time the Ulsterites strongly opposed the measure and prepared to resist their forced incorporation into Catholic Ireland. The outbreak of war with Germany postponed civil strife, but it was only a two-year delay until the Easter Uprising of 1916. Not until 1921 did southern Ireland finally gain the status of a British dominion. The home rule bill never went into effect.

The New Liberals

Gladstone's fight for Irish home rule split his party and paved the way for a decade of Conservative rule in Britain (1895–1905). Partly because of foreign and imperial affairs, the Conservatives departed from the reformist traditions of Tory democracy. By 1905 the need for social and political reform again claimed the attention of the parties.

More than 30 percent of the adult male laborers earned a weekly wage equivalent to seven dollars. Such an unacceptably low wage made it impossible to save for periods of unemployment and emergencies. Workers demonstrated their discontent in a number of strikes. Partially in response to the workers' needs and at the prompting of the Fabian Socialists, the Labour party was founded in 1900, under the leadership of J. Ramsay MacDonald (1866–1937), a self-made intellectual who had risen from humble

status, and the Scottish miner Keir Hardie (1856–1915). The liberals found themselves threatened on both their left and right flanks. They decided to abandon their laissez-faire economic concepts and embrace a bold program of social legislation. The radical Welsh lawyer Lloyd George portrayed their program. "Four spectres haunt the poor: Old Age, Accident, Sickness, and Unemployment. We are going to exorcise them."[1]

Led by Prime Minister Herbert Asquith, Lloyd George, and the young Winston Churchill, who had defected from the Conservatives, the Liberal party—with the aid of the Labour bloc—put through a broad program. It provided for old-age pensions, national employment bureaus, workers' compensation protection, and sickness, accident, and unemployment insurance. In addition, labor unions were relieved of financial responsibility for losses caused by strikes. Members of the House of Commons, until that time unpaid, were granted a modest salary. This last act allowed an individual without independent wealth to pursue a political career.

The House of Lords tried to block the Liberal reform plan by refusing to pass the 1909–1910 budget, which laid new tax burdens, including an income tax, on the richer classes in order to pay for the new programs. The Liberals and Labour fought back by directly attacking the rationale for the Lords' existence. They argued that a hereditary, irresponsible upper house was an anachronism in a democracy. The result was the

EJECTMENT OF IRISH TENANTRY.

THE EJECTMENT.

→ Wracked by poverty and famine, Ireland was further tormented during the 1840s by the mass eviction of tenant farmers. After the evictions, cottages were burned down at once to prevent other homeless farmers from occupying them.

→ Emmeline Pankhurst, in white scarf, at a rally protesting a government unresponsive to women's issues. After 1910 the women's suffrage movement turned increasingly militant.

Parliament Bill of 1911 that took away the Lords' power of absolute veto. Asquith announced that the king had promised to create enough new peers to pass the bill if needed (a tactic used with the 1832 Reform Bill). The Lords had to approve and thereafter could only delay and force reconsideration of legislation.

By 1914 the evolutionary path to democracy and a modern democratic state structure had been largely completed, except for women's suffrage. In the previous generation some effort had been put in to gain the vote for women, but by and large the effort had been unsuccessful. Women's suffrage was not a major concern for the major parties, whose leaders—for the most part—felt that women's proper place was in the home. At the turn of the century the most effective group working for women's rights was the Women's Social and Political Union (WSPU), whose members were the first to be known as suffragettes. The founder of the group, Emmeline Pankhurst (1858–1928), first agitated, then disturbed, and then challenged the order and stability of England in the decade before World War I. Pankhurst and her colleagues traveled and worked constantly to make their case, and in 1910 the WSPU abandoned traditional rhetoric in favor of mass marches, hunger strikes, and property damage. In 1913 a young suffragette martyred herself by running in front of the king's horse at the Derby.[2] With the outbreak of the war, the WSPU backed the national effort against the Germans, and finally in 1918 women age 30 and over were granted the vote. Ten years later, they gained equal voting rights with men.

THE SECOND REICH TO 1914

Within the brief span of one lifetime, the fragmented German areas of central Europe successfully united under Prussian, that is, Hohenzollern, leadership to challenge Britain for world leadership. Bismarck provided the initial genius to bring about unification, but the source of German strength was found in its rapid economic growth, population increase, and efficient political structure. Prussia's success drew the enthusiastic support of prominent businessmen, intellectuals, and artists and the increasing concern of its neighbors.

The Second Reich came into existence at a ceremony in January 1871 in the Hall of Mirrors at the Palace of Versailles. There King William I became emperor of a federal union of 26 states with a population of 41 million. The bicameral (two-house) legislature of the new empire consisted of a *Bundesrat*, representing the ruling houses of the various states, and a *Reichstag*, representing the people through its 397 members elected by male suffrage. The dominant power rested with the emperor, who controlled military and foreign affairs and the 17 votes in the *Bundesrat* needed to veto any constitutional change. The actual head of government was the chancellor who was appointed by the kaiser and responsible to him only. This arrangement allowed the chancellor to defy or ignore the legislature if it served his purpose. However, he had to operate within the constraints of the federal state structure in which large powers of local government were given to the member states.

Bismarck as Chancellor

As chancellor, Otto von Bismarck built modern Germany on his belief in the inherent efficiency of a state based on one faith, one law, and one ruler. He distrusted those institutions that did not fit that tripartite formula: specifically the Catholic Church and the Socialist party. Bismarck was more constrained in domestic than in foreign affairs. It is not surprising, therefore, that he fared better in foreign matters.

The Catholic political party had sent a large bloc of representatives to the *Reichstag* in 1871, and these members supported the complete independence of the church from state control, denounced divorce, objected to secular education, and questioned freedom of conscience. Many Catholics strongly supported the new dogma of papal infallibility. Within the Protestant Prussian part of Germany, Bismarck introduced anti-Catholic policies that triggered a conflict known as the *Kulturkampf* (the struggle for civilization). These so-called May laws made it an offense for the clergy to criticize the government, regulated the educational activities of the religious orders, and expelled the Jesuits from the country. The state also required civil marriages and dictated that all priests study theology at state universities. Pope Pius IX declared these

acts null and void and told loyal Catholics to refuse to obey them. Many of the chancellor's laws applied equally to Protestants, who actively protested them.

As opposition spread, Bismarck struck hard at the Catholics, imprisoning priests, confiscating church property, and closing down pulpits. When the tide did not turn in his favor, he realized that he could not afford to create millions of martyrs. Showing his shrewd sense of power, he cut his losses, retreated, and repealed most of the anti-Catholic laws.

The Social Democratic (Marxist) movement posed a greater challenge to Bismarck's rule. The party's founder, Ferdinand Lassalle (1825–1864), rejected violence as a means to gain power and instead advocated working within the existing political structure. After his death the movement retained its nonviolent nature. The party's popularity soared when it was officially established in 1875, and its leaders pushed for true parliamentary democracy and wider ranging social programs. In 1878 Bismarck used two attempts on the emperor's life as an excuse to launch an all-out campaign to weaken the Social Democrats, even though they had no connection with the assassination attempts. He dissolved extralegal socialist organizations, suppressed their publications, and threw their leaders in jail. Despite these measures the socialists continued to gain support.

When he failed to weaken the socialists by direct confrontation, the chancellor changed tactics. He decided to undercut them by taking over their program. Through the 1880s he implemented important social legislation that provided wage earners with sickness, accident, and old-age insurance. He sponsored other laws that responded to many of the abuses workers encountered. Still, the Social Democrats continued to grow in size and influence. However, by creating the first welfare state, the pragmatic Prussian chancellor defused a potential revolution.

Kaiser William II

In 1888 William II, the grandson of the emperor, became head of the Reich. Just as Bismarck had dominated European affairs since 1862, the new emperor would play a key role until 1918. Here was a person who, without Bismarck's finesse,

Kaiser William II's Naval Ambitions

Kaiser William knew Germany had a grand future, an expanding future. He also wanted Germans to travel on the high seas, to the dismay of the British.

In spite of the fact that we have no such fleet as we should have, we have conquered for ourselves a place in the sun. It will now be my task to see to it that this place in the sun shall remain our undisputed possession, in order that the sun's rays may fall fruitfully upon our activity and trade in foreign parts, that our industry and agriculture may develop within the state and our sailing sports upon the water, for our future lies upon the water. The more Germans go out upon the waters, whether it be in the races of regattas, whether it be in journeys across the ocean, or in the service of the battle-flag, so much the better will it be for us. For when the German has once learned to direct his glance upon what is distant and great, the pettiness which surrounds him in daily life on all sides will disappear.

From C. Gauss, *The German Kaiser as Shown in His Public Utterances* (New York: Charles Scribner's Sons, 1915).

---

advocated a policy of "blood and iron." Where Bismarck knew the limits and uses of force and appreciated the nuances of public statements, William was a militarist and a bully. Serving in a modern age, the new emperor still believed in the divine right of kings and constantly reminded his entourage that "he and God" worked together for the good of the state. With such a contrast in styles, it is not surprising that William saw Bismarck not as a guide but as a threat. He once stated that "it was a question of whether the Bismarck dynasty or the Hohenzollern dynasty should rule."[3] Finally, in March 1890, Bismarck resigned.

At the beginning of the twentieth century Germany presented a puzzling picture to the world. On the one hand the blustering kaiser made fiery and warlike statements. He encouraged militarism and the belief that *Alles kommt von oben* ("Everything comes down from above"). On the other hand his thoroughly advanced country made great scientific and cultural strides. Observers of German affairs noted that one-third of the voters supported the Social Democrats, an indication of a healthy parliamentary system. A commonly held pride in Germany's accomplishments knit the country together.

More important than William's behavior was the fact that by the beginning of the new century the Germans competed actively in all areas with the British. Although Germany did not outproduce Britain, long-term projections showed that the island nation's growth had leveled out and that in the next generation the Reich would surpass it. The Germans dominated the world market in the chemical and electrical industries and were making strides in other areas. They boasted a more efficient organization of their industries, a higher literacy rate for their workers, better vocational training, and a more aggressive corps of businessmen. German labor unions were less combative than the British, while the government gave more support to industry than did Parliament.

THE FRENCH THIRD REPUBLIC TO 1914

The defeat of France's Second Empire at the battle of Sedan in 1870 gave birth to the Third Republic. The humiliating peace terms, which stripped France of a part of Lorraine and all of Alsace and imposed a huge indemnity on the country, created a desire for revenge. The spectacle of the Germans crowning their emperor and proclaiming the Second Reich at Versailles, the symbol of French greatness, left a bitter taste.

Persistent class conflicts, covered over during Louis Napoleon's reign, also contributed to many years of shaky existence before the republic gained a firm footing. A new, overwhelmingly royalist national assembly was elected to construct a new, conservative government after the signing of the peace. This, added to the shock of the defeat, touched off a revolutionary outburst that led to the Paris Commune (1871).

Shaky Beginnings

Parisians had suffered such severe food shortages during the siege of the city that some had been forced to eat rats and zoo animals. When it turned out that their sacrifices had been in vain, republican and radical Parisians joined forces in part of the city to form a commune, in the tradition of the 1792 Paris Commune, to save the republic. The Communards advocated government control of prices, wages, and working conditions (including stopping night work in the bakeries). After several weeks of civil strife, the commune was savagely put down. Class hatred split France further yet.

Because the two monarchist factions that constituted a majority could not agree on an acceptable candidate for the monarchy, they finally settled on a republic as the least disagreeable form of government. The national assembly approved the new republican constitution in 1875. Under the new system, members of the influential lower house—the Chamber of Deputies—was elected by direct suffrage. There was also a Senate, whose members were elected indirectly by electoral colleges in the departments. The constitution established a weak executive, elected by the legislature. The ministry exercised real power, but its authority depended on whatever coalition of parties could be assembled to form a tenuous majority in the legislature.

The Boulanger and Dreyfus Affairs

The stormy tenure of the Third Republic was marked by a series of crises such as increased anarchist violence leading up to a series of bombings in 1893, financial scandals such as the notorious Panama Canal venture that implicated a wide range of leading figures, and lesser scandals. The two most serious threats were the Boulanger and Dreyfus affairs.

The weak and traumatized republic was both threatened and embarrassed by the public cries for vengeance uttered in 1886 by General Georges Boulanger (1837–1891), the minister of war. This charismatic, war-mongering figure made a series of speeches, which he ended by emotionally proclaiming: "Remember, they are waiting for us in Alsace." The considerable number of anti-republicans saw him as a man on horseback who would sweep away the republic in a coup d'état, much as Louis Napoleon had done in 1851, and bring back French grandeur. The government finally ordered Boulanger's arrest on a charge of conspiracy, and he fled the country. Later, he committed suicide.

The Dreyfus case was far more serious because it polarized the entire country, divided and embittered French opinion by the anti-Semitic fervor it unleashed, and challenged the fundamental ideals of French democracy. Captain Alfred Dreyfus (1859–1935), the first Jewish officer on the French general staff, was accused in 1894 of selling military secrets to Germany. His fellow officers tried him, found him guilty, stripped him of his commission, and condemned him to solitary confinement on Devil's Island, a dreadful convict settlement off the northeast coast of South America. Even with the case supposedly settled, military secrets continued to leak to the Germans, and subsequently a royalist, spendthrift officer named Major Esterhazy was accused, tried, and acquitted.

The case became a cause célèbre in 1898 when the French writer Emile Zola (1840–1902) wrote his famous letter *J'accuse* ("I accuse"), in which he attacked the judge for knowingly allowing the guilty party to go free while Dreyfus remained in jail. The next year Esterhazy admitted his guilt, but by that time the entire country had split into two camps. On the one side were the anti-Dreyfusards—the army, church, and royalists; on the other side were the pro-Dreyfusards—the intellectuals, socialists, and republicans. The case was once again placed under review in the military courts, and even though Esterhazy had confessed, the court continued to find Dreyfus guilty. Finally, the French president pardoned him and in 1906 the highest civil court in France found him innocent.

The case had greater significance than just the fate of one man. Those who had worked against Dreyfus, especially the church, would pay dearly for their stand. Many republicans believed that the church, a consistent ally of the monar-

ing rapidity. Yet France was strong, prosperous, and one of only two republics among the world's great powers.

RUSSIA: REFORMERS, REACTIONARIES, REVOLUTIONARIES

While Alexander II pushed through the "Great Reforms," the revolutionary movement grew stronger. In the 1850s the nihilist movement developed, questioning all old values, championing the freedom of the individual, and shocking the older generation. At first the nihilists tried to convert the aristocracy to the cause of reform. Failing there, they turned to the peasants in an almost missionary frenzy. Some of the idealistic young men and women joined the movement to work in the fields with the peasants, while others went to the villages as doctors and teachers to preach the message of reform. This "go to the people" campaign was known as the populist, or *narodnik*, movement. Not surprisingly, the peasants largely ignored the outsiders' message.

→ Captain Alfred Dreyfus had to pass through this "Guard of Dishonor" each day on his way to the courtroom during his second trial in 1899.

chists, was the natural enemy of democratic government. They demanded an end to the church's official ties to the state. In 1904 and 1905 the government closed all church schools and repudiated the Napoleonic Concordat. All ties between church and state were formally ended.

After weathering forty difficult years, by 1914 the Third Republic had gained prosperity and stability. Workers had gained their voice in the country as the various trade and local union groups came together in the *Confédération Générale du Travail*, the General Confederation of Labor. Monarchists and other right-wing parties still had considerable influence, although the Dreyfus affair had weakened them.

French republicanism had wide support across the political spectrum. Most French citizens enjoyed basic democratic rights, which they exercised through the extremely complex multiparty political system of the republic. The various ministries that were constructed from the fragile coalitions came and went with bewilder-

Revolutionary Response

Frustrated by this rejection, the idealistic young people turned more and more to terrorism. The radical branch of the nihilists, under the influence of Bakunin's protégé Sergei Nechaev (1847–1882), pursued a program of the total destruction of the status quo, to be accomplished by the revolutionary elite. In his *Revolutionary Catechism* Nechaev stated that "everything that promotes the success of the revolution is moral and everything that hinders it is immoral." The soldiers in the battle, the revolutionaries, were "doomed men," having "no interests, no affairs, no feelings, no habits, no property, not even a name."[4] The revolution dominated all thoughts and actions of these individuals.

For the 20 years after his emancipation of the serfs, Alexander suffered under increasing revolutionary attack. It was as though the opposition saw each reform not as an improvement but as a weakness to be exploited. In Poland the tsar had tried to reverse the Russification program of his father and in return saw the Polish revolt of 1863. Would-be assassins made a number of attempts on him, and the violence expanded throughout the 1870s as a number of his officials were attacked by young terrorists such as Vera Zasulich (1851–1919). Finally Alexander was assassinated in 1881, on the very day he had approved a proposal to call a representative assembly to consider new reforms.

Reaction: 1881–1905

The slain tsar's son, Alexander III (1881–1894), could see only that his father's reforms had resulted in increased opposition and, eventually, death. During his reign he tried to turn the clock back and reinstate the policy of "Autocracy, Orthodoxy, and Nationalism." Under the guidance of his chief adviser, Constantine Pobedonostsev (1827–1907), Alexander pursued a policy of censorship, regulation of schools and universities, and increased secret police activities. Along with renewing Russification among the minorities, he permitted the persecution of Jews, who were bullied and sometimes massacred in attacks called pogroms. Alexander may have been successful in driving the revolutionaries underground or executing them and the nationalities may have been kept in their place, but under Alexander III Russia lost 13 valuable years in its attempt to become economically and politically competitive with western Europe.

Succeeding Alexander was his son, Nicholas II (1894–1917), a decent but weak man. He inherited and retained both his father's advisers and policies. Larger forces overwhelmed him. Industrialization and rural overpopulation exerted a wide range of political pressures, and the autocratic structure could not cope.

Political Alternatives to Autocracy

Russia lacked a tradition of gradual reform and the habits of compromise such as existed in England. After the assassination of Alexander II, the government increasingly used brutal force to keep order. At the same time it did little to help the people suffering in the transition from an agrarian to an industrial society. The regime worked energetically to eliminate the opposition by placing secret agents among them, launching violent assaults, and carrying on diversionary anti-Semitic activities with bands of thugs called the Black Hundreds.

By attacking the opposition, the tsarist government concentrated on a symptom of Russia's problems, rather than their causes—the repeated failures to carry out effective reform. Despite the best efforts of the tsars to crush all opposition movements, political parties opposing the autocracy flourished.

The Liberal party (Constitutional Democrats, or *Kadets*) wanted a constitutional monarchy and peaceful reform on the British model. Although limited in numbers, because of the elevated social standing of most of their members, the Kadets were a powerful voice for change in Russia. The much more numerous Social Revolutionaries combined non-Marxian socialism with the *narodnik* tradition and simplistically called for "the whole land for the whole people." These agrarian socialists wanted to give the land to the peasants. However, they lacked a unified leadership and a well-thought-out program.

In this troubled environment, the solutions proposed by Karl Marx attracted a number of supporters. Marx himself did not believe that Russia would be a favorable laboratory for his theories. He expressed surprise when *Das Kapital* was translated into Russian in 1872 but was pleased when he learned of the broad impact of his theories. Not until 1898, however, was there an attempt to establish a Russian Social Democratic party made up of radical intellectuals and politically active city workers.

The Russians did not experience the most demanding parts of industrialization until the end of the century and then on a different basis from that of the western European countries. Russia remained an overwhelmingly agrarian society in which the state paid for building factories by using grain produced by the peasants for export on the depressed world market. The Social Democrats looked to Marx to show them the way to a complete social, economic, and political revolution. However, the urban, industrial emphasis of Marx's theories sparked debate over the way in which they applied to Russia. The thinker and actor who would eventually apply and implement Marxist theory was Vladimir Ilich Ulyanov (1870–1924), who later took the name of Lenin.

Born in Ulyanovsk, formerly Simbirsk, a small city along the Volga River, Lenin grew up in the moderate and respectable circumstances provided by his father, a school administrator and teacher. In 1887, the government arrested and executed Lenin's brother, Alexander, in St. Petersburg for plotting against the life of the tsar. Shortly thereafter Lenin began to master the writings of Marx and to study the situation in which Russia found itself. He overcame major obstacles from tsarist officials and passed his law exams at St. Petersburg University without formally attending classes. After 1893 he began to compile his theories of tactics and strategy that would form the basis of the Communist Party in Russia until its death in 1991.

In 1895 a court sentenced him to exile in Siberia for his political activities. Although in exile, he enjoyed complete liberty of movement in the district and could hunt, fish, swim, study, read, and keep up a large correspondence. His comrade, Nadezhda Krupskaia, joined him and they were married. Later they translated Sidney and Beatrice Webb's *The History of Trade Unionism*. Lenin's exile ended in 1900 when he and Krupskaia went to Switzerland where they joined other Russian Social Democrats in exile in founding the newspaper *Iskra* ("Spark"), whose motto was "From the Spark—the conflagration."

→ Lenin, the main force of the Russian Revolution from which emerged the Soviet Union, spent years studying Marx's theories and adapting them to conditions in Russia.

Lenin Splits the Social Democrats

In applying Marx to Russian conditions, Lenin found it necessary to sketch in several blank spots. Lenin's methods differed greatly from those of western European Marxists, as did his theories. Lenin advocated the formation of a small elite of professional revolutionaries, the vanguard of the proletariat. These professionals, subject to strict party discipline, would anticipate the proletariat's needs and best interests and lead them through the oxymoronic theory of "democratic centralism."

The Social Democrats met in 1903 in London and split into two wings—the Bolsheviks and the Mensheviks—over the questions of the timing of the revolution and the nature of the party. (In Russian, Bolshevik means "majority" and Menshevik means "minority," the names stemming from a vote on party policies in 1903 when the Bolsheviks did prevail. On most occasions until the summer of 1917, however, the Bolsheviks were in fact in a distinct minority among the Social Democrats.) The two factions differed sharply on strategy and tactics. The Bolsheviks, following Lenin's revisionist views, were prepared to move the pace of history along through "democratic centralism." The Mensheviks believed that Russian socialism should grow gradually and peacefully in accord with Marxist principles of development and historical evolution, and they were prepared to work within a framework dominated by bourgeois political parties. They knew that their victory was inevitable, given the historical dialectic, and that the proletariat would play the lead role, assisted by the party. After their split in 1903, the two factions never reconciled.

After 1903 Lenin had little success in changing the political conditions of Russia, beyond affecting the most sophisticated part of the workers' movement. However, he continued to make significant doctrinal contributions. Lenin recommended a socialism whose weapon was violence and whose tactics allowed little long-range compromise with the bourgeoisie. However, he also saw the advantages of flexibility and encouraged temporary deviations that might serve the goals of the working class. He took little for granted and reasoned that the development of class unity to destroy the capitalists among the Russian workers might require some assistance. To that end he refined his notion of the way in which the elite party would function. In revolution the elite party would infiltrate the government, police, and army while participating in legal workers' movements; in government the party would enforce its dictates on the populace with iron discipline.

Lenin looked out at the undoubted strength of the advanced technological nation-state and marveled at its extension of power. In *Imperialism, the Highest Stage of Capitalism* (1916) he forecast that the modern capitalist states would destroy themselves. He argued that the wages of the workers did not represent enough purchasing power to absorb the output of the capitalists' factories, and that the vast amounts of capital that were accumulated could not be invested profitably in the home country. Therefore, the states would engage in an inevitable competition for markets, resources, and capital that would drive them from cutthroat competition to outright war and their ultimate destruction. At that point, he reasoned, his elite party would be ready to pick up the pieces from the blindly selfish powers.

The Revolution of 1905 and Its Aftermath

Once again, as in 1854 at Crimea, a failure in war—this time a "splendid little war" against Japan—exposed the weaknesses of the autocratic tsarist regime. Strikes and protests spread throughout the land in response to the military failure in the last days of 1904. On January 22, 1905, the Cossacks opened fire on a peaceful crowd of workers who had advanced on the Winter Palace in St. Petersburg carrying a petition asking for the tsar's help. In response, a general strike broke out with the strikers demanding a democratic republic, freedom for political prisoners, and the disarming of the police. Soviets—councils of workers—appeared in the cities to direct revolutionary activities. Most business and government offices closed, and the whole machinery of Russian economic life creaked to a halt. The country was virtually paralyzed.

After a series of half-measures and stalling in response to strikes and revolutionary activities, the tsar found himself pushed to the wall. Unable to find a dictator to impose order, he was forced to issue the October Manifesto of 1905, which promised "freedom of person, conscience, assembly, and union." A national Duma (legislature) was to be called without delay. The right to vote would be extended, and once in session, no law could be enacted without the Duma's approval. The October Manifesto split the moderate from the socialist opposition and kept Nicholas on the throne, although he was heartbroken for having made the compromise. The socialists tried to start new strikes, but the opposition was now totally split apart.

Most radical forces boycotted the first Duma meeting in the spring of 1906. As a result, the Kadets became the dominant force. Even with this watered-down representation, the tsar was upset by the criticism of the government's handling of the Russo-Japanese War, treatment of minorities, handling of political prisoners, and economic policies. Claiming that the representatives "would not cooperate" with the government, Nicholas dissolved the first Duma. The Russian people turned a cold shoulder to the Kadets' appeals for support. Sensing the decline of political fervor, Nicholas appointed a law-and-order conservative, Peter Stolypin (1862–1911) as prime minister. He cracked down on a number of the radicals, ruling under the emergency Article Number 87.

Unlike previous tsarist appointees, Stolypin knew that changes had to be made, especially in the area of agriculture. Stolypin created the process to develop a class of small farmers, even without Nicholas's full support. He pushed through reforms that abolished all payments still owed by the peasants under the emancipation law and permitted peasants to withdraw from the commune and claim their shares of the land and other wealth as private property. He also opened lands east of the Urals to the peasants and extended financial aid from the state. He was well on the way to finding a solution to that most enduring of Russian problems, the peasant

→ On January 22, 1905, Russian imperial troops opened fire on the crowd of peaceful demonstrators gathered outside the Winter Palace in St. Petersburg. The day is known in history as Bloody Sunday.

problem, before he was assassinated in 1911 by a Social Revolutionary, who was also an agent of the secret police.[5]

In spite of a reactionary tsar and nobility, Russia made major gains in the nine years after 1905 toward becoming a constitutional monarchy. The nation made great economic and social progress in that time. Industrialization increased and generated new wealth. Increased political and civil rights spawned an active public life. Stolypin's death, however, deprived the country of needed leadership. The coming First World War gave Russia a test it could not pass.

THE LESSER GREAT POWERS

Italy, united in 1861 and territorially completed by 1870, and the Austro-Hungarian monarchy faced overwhelming problems. The Italians had to deal with economic, political, and cultural differences between the northern and southern parts of the country, a lack of natural resources, and a politically inexperienced population. It also had too many people. The Austro-Hungarian monarchy had to work through a cumbersome structure to govern a mosaic of nationalities.

Italy

Italy's most troubling problem was the question of the papacy, which seriously weakened the state. The pope, the spiritual father of most Italians, refused to accept the incorporation of Rome into the new nation. He called himself the "prisoner of the Vatican," and encouraged—with little effect—his Italian flock not to vote. In an attempt to satisfy the pope, the government passed the Law of Papal Guarantees (1871), which created the Vatican as a sovereign state and allocated the pope an annual sum of $600,000 (roughly the amount of money he had received from his previously held lands). Pius IX rejected the offer, but the state refused to repeal the law.

Despite conflicting and unstable political parties, the new state carried on an impressive program of railroad building, naval construction, and attempts at social and welfare legislation.

→ Unification realized a dream for Italian patriots but failed to solve Italy's problems. Regional differences separated the industrial north from the agrarian south, suffrage was severely restricted, and the parliamentary system was frequently corrupt. For most Italians, the cartoonist implies, unification meant vastly increased taxes to pay for the new building and social welfare programs.

But major problems remained, especially with the peasantry in the south. Radical political parties made their presence felt after the turn of the century in the form of widespread strikes. In 1900 an anarchist assassinated King Umberto, who had taken the throne in 1878. Change proceeded slowly after that, and not until 1912 did the country gain universal manhood suffrage, a time when there was still widespread illiteracy.

The Italian leaders' ambition to make Italy a world power placed a great burden on the nation. Money spent on the army came at the expense of needed investments in education and social services. National resources were squandered in an unsuccessful attempt to build an empire in Africa.

Up to the beginning of World War I, Italy faced severe economic crises and labor unrest. In June 1914 a general strike spread through the central part of the peninsula. Benito Mussolini, editor of a socialist journal, played a key role in this movement. Attempts to achieve compulsory education, freedom of the press, and better working conditions did little to ease the economic hardships and high taxes that had driven thousands to emigrate to the United States. The south especially suffered, because it had not shared in the industrial gains of the northern part of the country.

The Austro-Hungarian Monarchy

After the Austrians' disastrous defeat by Prussia, Franz Joseph was forced to offer the Hungarians an equal partnership with Vienna in ruling the empire. The offer was accepted and in 1867 the constitution known as the *Ausgleich* (compromise) was enacted. Under this document the Dual Monarchy came into existence in which the Habsburg ruler was both the king of Hungary and the emperor of Austria—that is, the area that was not a part of Hungary. Each country had its own constitution, language, flag, and parliament. Ministers common to both countries handled finance, defense, and foreign affairs, but they were supervised by "Delegations," which consisted of sixty members from each parliament who did not meet together, except in emergency circumstances. The *Ausgleich* was to be renegotiated every ten years.

The Dual Monarchy contained 12 million Germans, 10 million Hungarians, more than 24 million Slavs, and 4 million Romanians, among other nationalities. Although the Germans of Austria had recognized the equality of the Hungarians, the rest of the nationalities continued to live under alien rule. Now, instead of having to deal with one dominant national group, they had to cope with two. In some cases, such as in the prospering, cosmopolitan, and sophisticated area of Bohemia-Moravia, the people wanted an independent state or, at the very least, more rights within the Habsburg realm. Other groups, such as the Serbs, sought the goal of joining their countrymen living in adjacent national states. The nationalities question remained an explosive problem for the authorities in Vienna and Budapest.

The functioning of the Dual Monarchy was best symbolized by the official bank notes, which were printed in eight languages on one side and in Hungarian on the other. In the Hungarian part of the Dual Monarchy the aristocracy governed under the Kossuth constitution of 1848. The Hungarians refused to share rule with the minorities in their kingdom. A small, powerful landed oligarchy dominated the mass of backward, landless peasants. The conservative leadership carried out a virtual process of Magyarization with their minorities, while they continually squabbled with the Austrians.

In the Austrian portion, wealthy German businessmen and the landed aristocracy dominated political life. But even with this concentration of power, the government was much more democratic, especially after 1907 when the two-house legislature was elected by universal manhood suffrage. Here, too, nationalism was a serious problem, and political parties came to be based not on principle but on nationality. Each nationality had to work with the Germans, even though it might detest them. The nationalities frequently disliked one another, and this prevented the formation of any coalitions among them. By 1914 the Austrians had extended their subject nationalities' substantial local self-government, but this concession did little to quiet discontent.

The *Ausgleich* functioned poorly, yet its defenders could still tell themselves that they were, after all, citizens of a "great" empire. The Dual Monarchy occupied a strategic geographical location and had enough military strength to be very influential in the Balkans. In addition, the area had great economic potential with Hungarian wheat, Croatian and Slovenian livestock, Czech banks and industry, and Austrian commerce. But Franz Joseph ruled over a disjointed conglomeration of peoples whose economic and political strength could not compare with that of Germany or even France.

THE FAILED TEST: THE EASTERN QUESTION

One of the key geopolitical questions facing the Europeans was the Eastern Question: What was to be done about the disintegrating Ottoman Empire? At the beginning of the nineteenth century, the Turks had sovereignty over the strategic eastern Mediterranean and North African regions. However, they did not possess the power to rule this broad realm effectively, and parts of the area were virtual power vacuums. The Eastern Question would test whether Europe's political wisdom had kept pace with its increase in material strength.

The Balkans Awaken

By the end of the eighteenth century, Ottoman power had substantially declined in the Balkans, just at a time when the various peoples began to experience the waves of nationalism. In 1799, Sultan Selim III acknowledged the independence of the mountainous nation of Montenegro, after its long and heroic defense of its liberty. Further proof of Ottoman weakness came in 1804 when some renegade Turkish troops in Belgrade went on a rampage, disobeyed the sultan's orders, and forced the Serbian people to defend themselves. This initial act of self-protection blossomed into a rebellion that culminated, after 11 difficult years, with the Serbs gaining an autonomous position under the Turks.

Turkish weakness attracted both Russian and British interests. Russia had made a substantial advance toward the Mediterranean during the reign of Catherine II. By the Treaty of Küchük Kainarji (1774) the Russians gained the rights of navigation in Turkish waters and the right to intervene in favor of Eastern Orthodox Christians in the Ottoman Empire. The British protested these gains, and in 1791 Prime Minister William Pitt the Younger denounced Russia for its supposed ambitions to dismember Turkey. Only the common threat of Napoleon from 1798 to 1815 diverted Great Britain and Russia from their competition in the eastern Mediterranean.

The forces of nationalism in Greece took advantage of the chaotic administration of the Turks in 1821. Unlike the Serbian rebellion, the Greek revolution gained substantial outside support from Philhellenic societies of Great Britain. Even though Metternich hoped the revolt would burn itself out, the Greeks were able to take advantage of intervention by the great powers to gain their independence.

During the Greek revolt, the British feared that Russia would use the Greek independence movement as an excuse for further expansion at Turkish expense. The British intervened skillfully, and the Greeks were able to gain their independence without a major Russian advance toward the Straits. Tsar Nicholas I wanted to weaken Turkey in order to pave the way for Russia to gain control over the Dardanelles and the Bosporus. So much did he want this expansion of his realm that he set aside his obligations to support the European balance of power. Britain became alarmed at this policy, and the upshot was an agreement in 1827 in which Britain, France, and Russia pledged themselves to secure Greek independence. Russia eventually defeated the Turks, and in 1829 the Treaty of Adrianople gave the Greeks the basis for their independence while Serbia received autonomy. The Danubian Principalities of Moldavia and Wallachia, the basis of the future state of Romania, became Russian protectorates.

By the 1830s it became apparent that the Turks were to be an object of, rather than a subject in, European diplomacy. The sultan's government had few admirers in Europe, but the European powers agreed—at least for the present—to prop up the decaying Ottoman Empire rather than allow one nation to gain dominance in the strategic area.

In 1832 Mehemet Ali, the virtually independent governor of Egypt, attacked the sultan, easily putting down the forces of the empire. To prevent the establishment of a new and probably stronger government at the Straits, Nicholas I sent an army to protect Constantinople. The Treaty of Unkiar Skelessi (1833) made Turkey a virtual protectorate of Russia.

Britain could not tolerate Russia's advantage and for the next ten years worked diplomatically to force the tsar to renounce the treaty and sign a general agreement of Turkish independence. This diplomatic game did little to improve the Ottoman Empire's condition. In 1844, while visiting Britain, Nicholas referred to Turkey as a "dying man" and proposed that the British join in a dissection of the body.

The Crimean War

The Crimean War, which lasted from 1853 to 1856, was a major turning point in the course of the Eastern Question. The immediate origins of the war were to be found in a quarrel over the

management and protection of the holy places in Palestine. Napoleon III, in a move to gain support from Catholics and the military in France, upheld the Roman Catholics' right to perform the housekeeping duties. On the other side, acting under the terms of the treaty signed to Küchük Kainarji in 1774, Nicholas stated that the Orthodox faithful should look after the holy places.

From this obscure argument the Crimean War eventually emerged, as the great powers all intervened in the discussions to protect their interests. The tsar's ambassador to the Turks tried to use the dispute to improve Russia's position in the empire, while the British told the sultan to stand firm against the Russians. After the Russians occupied the Danubian Principalities in an attempt to show the Turks the seriousness of their demands, the Turks declared war on the

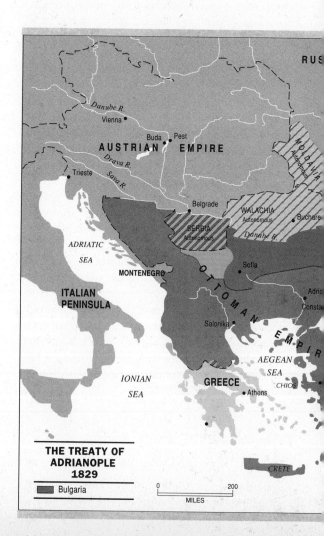

THE TREATY OF ADRIANOPLE 1829

Bulgaria

0   200

MILES

Russians in October 1853. By the next summer the French, Sardinians, and British had joined the Turks. Napoleon III saw the war as a chance to enhance his dynasty's reputation, and the Sardinians found an opportunity to gain allies in their drive for Italian unification. Under the impact of anti-tsarist public opinion, the British took steps to stop the Russians. The stated aim of all the allies was, of course, the defense of the sultan. A combination of the allies' military strength and the tsarist forces' inefficiency stalemated the Russians. Austria, a former close ally of Russia, took advantage of Russia's difficulties to extend Austrian influence into the Balkans.

The Russians sued for peace and the Treaty of Paris (1856) once again attempted to resolve the Eastern Question. The treaty affirmed the integrity of the Ottoman Empire. The Black Sea was to be a neutral body of water, and the Straits were closed to foreign warships. The treaty declared that no power had the right to intervene on behalf of the sultan's Christian subjects. Russian control of the Principalities was ended. The Crimean War momentarily stopped the Russian advance into the Balkans, but the problems posed by the "sick man of Europe" remained. Further, the various Balkan nations became even more inflamed with the desire for self-rule.

The Unanswered Question

In the generation after the Crimean War the problems posed by the disintegrating Ottoman Empire became more severe. To the north, the Russians, who could do little militarily in the Balkans during this period of intense internal reforms, broadcast the message of Pan-Slavic solidarity to their "Orthodox" brothers in the Balkans. The Austrians, their appetites whetted by their part in the Crimean War, kept a wary and opportunistic eye on developments in the Balkans. British loans to the Turks cut into the Turkish tax base and led to the destruction of the indigenous Ottoman textile industry. In addition, with the completion of the Suez Canal in 1869, the eastern Mediterranean came to be even more essential to British interests. Finally, the Germans began to increase their influence in the area after 1871.

Nationalism further inflamed the unresolved Eastern Question. The Bulgarians, who had been under the Turkish yoke since the fourteenth century, started their national revival in the late eighteenth century. By the 1860s they had formed a liberation movement, which was strengthened in 1870 by the founding of the Bulgarian Exarchate, a Bulgarian wing of the Greek Orthodox faith. The Bulgarians took strength from the example of the Romanians, who after centuries of Turkish dominance and a quarter century as a Russian protectorate had gained their independence in 1861, largely as a result of great power influence. Also, during the 1860s the Serbian leader Michael Obrenovich had worked toward a Balkan union against the Turks. Amid this maneuvering and ferment, the Turks were unable to strengthen their rule over areas theoretically under their control.

The crisis came to a head in 1875 when peasants revolted in the district of Bosnia, a Turkish-governed province populated by a religiously diverse group of Slavs. Following this insurrection Serbia and Montenegro declared war on the Turks. In the summer of 1876 the Bulgarians revolted, but the Ottoman forces put down the rebellion. When highly emotional accounts of the Turkish massacres were published in western Europe, the incident became known as the "Bulgarian horrors" and drew British attention to the Balkans. The Pan-Slav faithful in Moscow and St. Petersburg were naturally thrilled at the exploits of their "little brothers," and money and "volunteers" flowed southward.

The series of nationalistic uprisings in the improperly governed Ottoman provinces had captured the attention of the great powers, and by the end of 1875 the Eastern Question was once again the main focus of international diplomacy. The "sick man of Europe" was still strong enough to devastate the Serbs and Montenegrins in the field. The insurgents were forced to sue for peace, a move that drew Tsar Alexander II and the Russians into war with Turkey in 1877. After a hard-fought campaign, the Russians broke through early in 1878 and were close to achieving their final goal of taking Constantinople, when the sultan sued for peace.

The resulting Treaty of San Stefano in March 1878 recognized the complete independence of Serbia and Romania from the theoretical Ottoman sovereignty and reaffirmed Montenegro's independence. A large Bulgarian state was set up, nominally tributary to Turkey but actually dominated by Russia. The Straits were effectively

THE TREATY OF SAN STEFANO 1878

▮ Bulgaria as Proposed by the Treaty

0   100
MILES

THE CONGRESS OF BERLIN 1878

▮ Bulgaria as Amended by the Congress of Berlin

0   100
MILES

under Russian control, as the Bulgarian state would have a coast on the Aegean. The Eastern Question was almost solved.

Britain and Austria, however, correctly perceived a major shift of the balance of power in Russia's favor, and the two of them forced a reconsideration of the San Stefano treaty at the Congress of Berlin in June and July of 1878. Held under the supervision of Bismarck, the self-styled "honest broker," the congress compelled Russia to agree to a revision of Bulgaria's status. The large state created in March was broken into three parts: the northernmost section would be independent, paying tribute to the Turks, while the other two parts would be under Turkish control. Austria got the right to "occupy and administer" the provinces of Herzegovina and Bosnia.

The congress turned back the Russian advance, stymied the national independence movement, and did little to impel Turkey to put its house in order. The Austrian gains caused great bitterness among the Serbs and Russians, a mood that added to the tension in the Balkans. The Eastern Question remained unanswered, and the Balkans remained an arena of local nationalistic conflicts that would appeal to the imperialistic designs of the great powers, especially the Russians and Austro-Hungarian monarchy.[6]

CONCLUSION

By 1914 Great Britain ruled a world empire based on its effective, flexible governmental structure, industrial strength, strong financial institutions, and strong navy. On the Continent,

Germany's economic and military power could not be doubted. Despite a bellicose emperor, German society was dynamic and creative and its governmental system maintained stability while being responsive to the varied needs of its constituents. France had endured crises, "musical chairs" governments, and a contentious group of ideological competitors. Yet, it remained the strongest democracy on the Continent, and its future appeared to be bright.

Russia, Italy, and Austria-Hungary struggled unsuccessfully to equal the economic and military strength wielded by the governments in London, Berlin, and Paris. The Russians, Italians, and the diverse population of the Dual Monarchy faced an array of overwhelming, insoluble problems that prevented them from reaching the level of the truly great powers.

Ultimately, the attentions of all the European capitals came to be directed to and dominated by the Eastern Question. Running like a thread through the century, the Eastern Question, the fate of the disintegrating Ottoman Empire, was transformed from a balance-of-power question to one of small-power nationalism and great-power expansion. The failure to resolve this question would lead to World War I.

✦ Suggestions for Reading

D. Thomson, *England in the Nineteenth Century, 1815–1914* (Penguin, 1964) and J. Conacher, ed., *The Emergence of Parliamentary Democracy in Britain in the Nineteenth Century* (Wiley, 1971) are valuable brief accounts. See also F. Ensor, *England, 1870–1914* (Oxford, 1936); G. Kitson Clark, *The Making of Victorian England* (Atheneum, 1967); George M. Young, *Victorian England, Portrait of an Age* (Galaxy, 1954); P. Magnus, *Gladstone* (Dutton, 1954); and Robert Blake, *Disraeli* (Anchor, 1969). G. Dangerfield's *The Strange Death of Liberal England 1910–1914* (Capricorn, 1935) describes the inability of the Liberals to deal with major problems. Susan Kent's *Sex and Suffrage in Britain: 1860–1914* (Princeton University, 1987) performs the useful service of portraying the interconnection between the individual goals of the major suffragettes and the society in which they lived.

D. W. Brogan, *The French Nation: From Napoleon to Pétain* (Colophon, 1957) is a good survey. See also B. Gooch, *The Reign of Napoleon III* (Rand McNally, 1970); D. Thomson, *Democracy in France Since 1870* (Oxford, 1946); Stewart Edwards, *The Paris Commune, 1871* (Quadrangle, 1970); and Douglas Johnson, *France and the Dreyfus Affair* (Walker). See also John McManners, *Church and State in France,*

1870–1914 (Harper & Row, 1972). Eugen Weber, *Peasants into Frenchmen* (Univ. of California, 1976) and T. Zeldin, *France: 1848–1945* (Oxford, 1973–1975) are two brilliant, conflicting social surveys.

Michael Balfour, *The Kaiser and His Times* (Houghton Mifflin, 1964) describes the impact of William II on Germany and Europe. See also A. Rosenberg, *Imperial Germany: The Birth of the German Republic, 1871–1918* (Oxford, 1970). F. Stern's *Gold and Iron* (Vintage, 1979) is a fascinating study of the interaction of capital and politics.

Events in Russia have been thoroughly studied in L. H. Haimson, ed., *The Politics of Rural Russia: 1905–1914* (Indiana, 1979); Philip Pomper, *Sergei Nechaev* (Rutgers, 1979); D. W. Treadgold, *The Great Siberian Migration* (Princeton, 1957); Paul Avrich, *The Russian Anarchists* (Norton, 1978); A. Yarmolinsky, *The Road to Revolution* (Collier, 1962); and B. D. Wolfe, *Three Who Made a Revolution* (Beacon, 1974). A fine collection of translation documents giving a first-hand view of the huge changes Russia underwent at this time is G. L. Freeze, *From Supplication to Revolution* (Oxford, 1988). A well-written and penetrating biography of Lenin is L. Fischer, *The Life of Lenin* (Harper & Row, 1965).

A notion of the complexity of the nationalities question in the Habsburg realm can be found in the chapters of P. F. Sugar and I. Lederer, eds., *Nationalism in Eastern Europe* (Univ. of Washington, 1969). C. E. Shorske's *Fin de Siècle Vienna: Politics and Culture* (Vintage, 1981) is a classical intellectual history of the Dual Monarchy in its decline. Jorg K. Hoensch discusses Hungary's motivations and programs in Chapter 2 of *A History of Modern Hungary* (Longman, 1988). Christopher Seton-Watson's *Italy from Liberalism to Fascism: 1870–1925* (Methuen, 1967) is clear and concise.

M. S. Anderson's *The Eastern Question, 1774–1923* (St. Martin's, 1966) is the best treatment of the Balkans dilemma. For the nationalities conflicts in the region see Barbara Jelavich, *History of the Balkans*, I (Cambridge, 1983).

✦ Notes

1. Quoted in F. Owen, *Tempestuous Journey: Lloyd George, His Life and Times* (London: Hutchinson, 1954), p. 186.
2. Emmeline Pankhurst, *My Own Story* (New York: Source Book Press, 1970).
3. Quoted in C. G. Robinson, *Bismarck* (London: Constable, 1918), p. 472.
4. Quoted in Basil Dmystryshyn, ed., *Imperial Russia: A Source Book, 1700–1917* (New York: Holt, Rinehart, & Winston, 1967), p. 241.
5. Hans Rogger, *Russia in the Age of Modernisation and Revolution: 1881–1917* (London: Longman, 1988), pp. 243–247.
6. See M. S. Anderson, *The Eastern Question, 1774–1923* (New York: St. Martin's Press, 1966).

CHAPTER 26

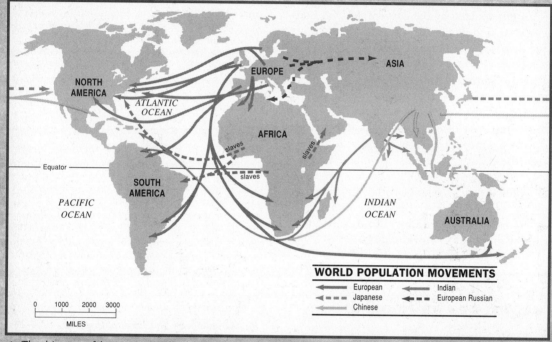

→ The history of humanity is the history of population movement. Perhaps the most significant movement of people on a global scale took place between 1600 and 1900, sometimes with tragic results for the indigenous peoples.

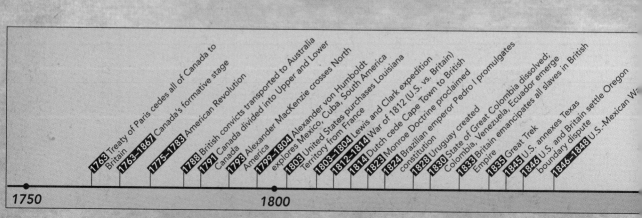

Transplanted Europes, 1815–1914

CHAPTER OUTLINE

The greatest population movement in history took place between 1500 and 1914 when millions of Europeans crossed the oceans to make new homes for themselves. At the same time, the slave trade brought vast numbers of Africans to the Americas. These immigrants, whether voluntary or forced, brought with them their languages, religions, cultures, political institutions, and laws.

No matter where they settled—the Americas, South Africa, Australia, and New Zealand—the Europeans faced the same challenges of unexplored lands: racial diversity, isolation, and the search for new identities. The newly ascendant middle classes with their generally liberal politics dominated, usually at the expense of the indigenous population or the African slaves.

Although the challenges were the same, the results were unique to each region. Canada, Australia, New Zealand, and the Union of South Africa illustrate the transplantation of British culture to the far corners of the globe. The United States developed the political stability and strong economy that allowed it to grow and prosper, though not without the tragedies of the Civil War, the oppression of its black population, and

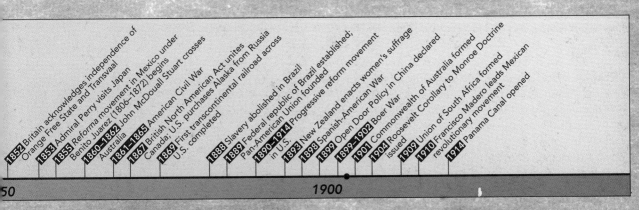

1852 Britain acknowledges independence of Orange Free State and Transvaal
1853 Admiral Perry visits Japan
1855 Reforma movement in Mexico under Benito Juárez (1806–1872) begins
1860–1862 John McDouall Stuart crosses Australia
1861–1865 American Civil War
1867 British North American Act unites Canada; U.S. purchases Alaska from Russia
1869 First transcontinental railroad across U.S. completed
1888 Slavery abolished in Brazil
1889 Federal republic of Brazil established; Pan-American Union founded
1890–1914 Progressive reform movement in U.S.
1893 New Zealand enacts women's suffrage
1898 Spanish-American War
1899 Open Door Policy in China declared
1899–1902 Boer War
1901 Commonwealth of Australia formed
1904 Roosevelt Corollary to Monroe Doctrine issued
1909 Union of South Africa formed
1910 Francisco Madero leads Mexican revolutionary movement
1914 Panama Canal opened

50   1900

the devastation of native American culture. Latin America faced fundamental challenges of racial and social diversity, economic exploitation, and political instability.

COMMON DENOMINATORS

In distinctive ways, each of the new lands reflected nineteenth-century movements that had originated in western Europe—nationalism, democracy, and imperialism. In addition, they had problems and opportunities which sprang from conditions specific to their environments. One was the assimilation of the tremendous tide of immigrants entering the new lands. But before the settlers and slaves came, vast spaces had to be explored, paths to the interior mapped, and natural resources located.

Exploration

In what is now Canada, Alexander Mackenzie in 1789 traveled to the Great Slave Lake, then down the river that now bears his name to the shores of the Arctic. Four years later he crossed the Rocky Mountains to the Pacific and thereby became the first European to cross North America at its greatest width.

In the United States, Meriwether Lewis and William Clark started from St. Louis in the winter of 1803–1804, blazed a trail through the unknown Northwest, and reached the Pacific two years later. For a half century the process of exploration and mapping continued, reaching its climax in John Frémont's expeditions to Oregon and California.

The most famous figure in the exploration of South America was the German naturalist Alexander von Humboldt, who from 1799 to 1804 explored Mexico, Cuba, and South America. He investigated the valley of the Orinoco, crossed the Andes, and studied the sources of the Amazon.

The continent of Australia was not crossed from north to south until the middle of the nineteenth century. Between 1860 and 1862 John McDouall Stuart made three attempts before he successfully completed the journey from Adelaide to Van Diemen's Gulf. The penetration of the interior of South Africa differed from explorations in the other new lands. It was achieved by the gradual expansion of white settlement in such movements as the Great Trek rather than by exploratory expeditions.

Immigration

The poor and landless people of Europe settled the vast and often fertile lands found by the explorers. The increase in European population from 200 million to 460 million during the nineteenth century provided the pool of 40 million immigrants who crossed the oceans. By 1914, the number of people of European background living abroad totaled 200 million—a figure almost equal to Europe's population in 1815.

For some 350 years this movement from Europe was accompanied by an equally significant forced migration from West Africa to the Americas. The number transported in the slave trade ran into the millions, and many died from ill treatment at the time of capture and during the forty-day voyage across the Atlantic. This trade cost Africa perhaps 15 million people, not including the Arab slave trade from the East African coast.

Black Africans in the New Lands

In general, the liberal and egalitarian trends in western Europe took root in the new lands. However, the millions of Africans seized and forcibly transplanted to the Americas had little chance to benefit from those ideals.

The slave trade in Latin America began shortly after 1502. Because many native Americans died from European diseases such as smallpox and measles, the local population could not fill the mounting demand for labor on the plantations. To meet that demand, the influx of black slaves increased geometrically. The first slaves imported into Brazil arrived in 1538. By 1600 they formed the basis of the economy there, as well as along the Peruvian coast, in Mexico's hot lands, in Santo Domingo, in Cuba, and in the mines of Colombia. By 1800 the population of Haiti was predominantly black or mulatto, and the African element was substantial in Brazil and Cuba. There were smaller, though still significant, black populations in the Dominican Republic, Panama, Venezuela, and Colombia.

A Slave's Memoir

Olaudah Equiano captured the misery of transported slaves in his *Travels*.

One day, when all our people were gone out to their work as usual and only I and my dear sister were left to mind the house, two men and a woman got over our walls, and in a moment seized us both, and without giving us time to cry out or make resistance they stopped our mouths and ran off with us into the nearest wood. Here they tied our hands and continued to carry us as far as they could till night came on, when we reached a small house where the robbers halted for refreshment and spent the night.

The first object which saluted my eyes when I arrived on the coast was the sea, and a slave ship which was then riding at anchor and waiting for its cargo. These filled me with astonishment, which was soon converted into terror when I was carried on board. I was immediately handled and tossed up to see if I were sound by some of the crew, and I was now persuaded that I had gotten into a world of bad spirits and that they were going to kill me. Their complexions too differing so much from ours, their long hair and the language they spoke (which was very different from any I had ever heard) united to confirm me in this belief. Indeed such were the horrors of my views and fears at the moment that, if ten thousand worlds had been my own, I would have freely parted with them all to have exchanged my condition with that of the meanest slave in my own country. When I looked around the ship too and saw a large furnace or copper boiling and a multitude of black people of every description chained together, every one of their countenances expressing dejection and sorrow, I no longer doubted my fate; and quite overpowered with horror and anguish, I fell motionless on the deck and fainted. When I recovered a little I found some black people about me, who I believed were some of those who had brought me on board and had been receiving their pay; they talked to me in order to cheer me, but all in vain. I asked them if we were not to be eaten by those white men with horrible looks, red faces, and loose hair. They told me I was not, and one of the crew brought me a small portion of spirituous liquor in a wine glass, but being afraid of him I would not take it out of his hand.

The stench of the hold while we were on the coast was so intolerably loathsome that it was dangerous to remain there for any time, and some of us had been permitted to stay on the deck for the fresh air; but now that the whole ship's cargo were confined together it became absolutely pestilential. The closeness of the place and the heat of the climate, added to the number in the ship, which was so crowded that each had scarcely room to run himself, almost suffocated us. This produced copious perspirations, so that the air soon became unfit for respiration from a variety of loathsome smells, and brought on a sickness among the slaves, of which many died, thus falling victims to the improvident avarice, as I may call it, of their purchasers. This wretched situation was again aggravated by the galling of the chains, now become insupportable, and the filth of the necessary tubs, into which the children often fell and were almost suffocated. The shrieks of the women and the groans of the dying rendered the whole a scene of horror almost inconceivable. Happily perhaps for myself I was soon reduced so low here that it was thought necessary to keep me almost always on deck, and from my extreme youth I was not put in fetters.

At last we came in sight of the island of Barbados, at which the whites on board gave a great shout and made many signs of joy to us.

From Paul Edwards, ed., *Equiano's Travels: His Autobiography, The Interesting Narrative of the Life of Olaudah Equiano or Gustavus Vassa the African* (London: Heinemann Educational Books, 1967).

A century after Africans were brought to Latin America, they appeared in the English colonies to the north. The first blacks landed in Jamestown in 1619, but their status was uncertain for some fifty years. Between 1640 and 1660 there is evidence of slavery, and after the latter date the slave system was defined by law in several of the colonies. White indentured servants, at first an important part of the work force, were soon replaced by African slaves, who provided a lifetime of work to the plantation owner. In 1790 when the white population was just over 3 million, there were some 750,000 African-Americans in the United States.

During the American Revolution, serious questions arose about the morality of slavery. Some people saw an embarrassing contradiction between human bondage and the ideals of the Declaration of Independence. This antislavery sentiment temporarily weakened as fear grew over a bloody slave insurrection in Santo Domingo, unrest among American slaves, and the unsettling economic and social consequences of the French Revolution. Slave rebellions in the early 1800s shocked many Americans.

The Industrial Revolution played a large role in harnessing slavery to the economy of the southern states. English textile mills required an

→ Slaves rose up against the French in Saint Domingue in 1791. Napoleon sent an army to restore slavery in 1799, but many of the French soldiers died of yellow fever, and the rebels defeated the decimated French army in 1803.

increased supply of cotton. New technology and new lands made the plantation system more profitable, creating an additional demand for slaves even as their importation ended in 1808.

Race Problems in the New Lands

The imposition of European hegemony over native inhabitants in the far corners of the globe and the slave trade created tragic racial conflicts. It is difficult to gain an accurate estimate of the number of Indians in North America, but it is generally held that before European settlement there were around 200,000 in Canada and 850,000 in the United States. Since the arrival of white settlers, the number of Indians in the two North American areas has been reduced by approximately half, largely through disease and extermination. While in modern time attempts have been made to help Native Americans make a place for themselves in urban society, these efforts have generally been inadequate. Even though in the past two centuries Canada has compiled a much more humane record dealing with Native Americans than the United States, Indians remain the most neglected and isolated minority in North America.

The aborigines of Australia and Tasmania—numbering possibly 300,000 at the time of the arrival of the Europeans—were also decimated by the diseases and liquors brought by the white settlers. The native inhabitants could not adjust to the new ways of life brought about by the disappearance of their hunting grounds. At times they were treated brutally: in some places they were rounded up in gangs and shot. Sometimes the Europeans encouraged drunkenness among the natives, then gave them clubs to fight each other for the entertainment of the "civilized" spectators. The natives of Tasmania are now extinct, and the aborigines of Australia are a declining race.

In New Zealand the native Maoris were better able to stand up to the whites. After serious wars in the 1860s peace was finally secured and the Maoris slowly accommodated themselves to the new world created by the whites. Since 1900 the Maoris have shared the same political rights and privileges as the white settlers and have obtained the benefits of advanced education. The

The thousand years of contact between the Spanish and Portuguese with the dark-skinned Moorish people and their early African explorations helped prevent the development of the virulent form of racism found in North America. There was also a difference in the status of the slave in North and South America. In North America the slave was regarded as a piece of property, with no legal or moral rights. In Latin America, because of the traditions of Roman law and the Catholic Church, slaves had a legal personality and moral standing.

Even though slave status was generally considered to be perpetual, gaining freedom was not as difficult in Latin America as in North America. By 1860 free blacks outnumbered slaves two to one in Brazil while slaves outnumbered free blacks eight to one in the United States. Finally, there has been greater racial mixing in Latin America. The greatest meld of races—red, white, and black—in the history of the world has taken place there. This intermingling has gone a long way to ease racial tensions.[1]

✦ This 1816 pictograph was meant to demonstrate to Australian aborigines the evenhandedness of British justice.

✦ This family picture of a *mestizo* father, a Spanish mother, and their daughter, known as a *castiza*, was part of a racial chart of Mexican peoples.

Maoris now constitute about 9 percent of the population and their numbers are increasing.

In two areas colonized by Europeans, Latin America and South Africa, the indigenous peoples greatly outnumbered the white settlers. Some authorities, for example, estimate that the population of Latin America in pre-Colombian days was at least 25 million. While a large percentage of these people died following the initial European impact because of disease, war, and famine, in the long run their numbers substantially increased. There was much racial mixing between the Indians and the Europeans. This *mestizo*, or mixed race, strain, together with the Indians, outnumbered the white population. In the early twentieth century, there were estimated to be 20 million Indian, 30 million *mestizo*, 26 million black and mulatto, and 34 million white. Only in Argentina, Chile, and a few smaller states such as Costa Rica, Cuba, and Uruguay have European stocks overwhelmed the Indians.

In South Africa the indigenous people were not exterminated, but they were denied the opportunity to share in European civilization. The fierce fighting between the European frontier people (mainly the Dutch) and the Africans led to constant misunderstanding and fear. Despite many political and economic disabilities, in the nineteenth century the South African natives showed a substantial increase in numbers. By 1904 the population breakdown of the roughly 8 million people comprised 21.6 percent European, 67.4 percent African, 2.4 percent Asiatic, and 8.6 percent "coloured." Unlike the situation in Latin America, the European minority resolutely opposed any mixing with the nonwhites and enforced unyielding segregation, or *apartheid*, until 1991.

The Search for a New Nationality

The transplanted Europeans generally focused their energies on domestic matters and left world affairs to the European states. Those under the British flag generally accepted British leadership in world affairs and depended on London's fleet for protection. The United States devoted considerable energy to exploiting its vast natural resources and Americanizing the millions of immigrants who flocked to its shores. Latin America was politically unstable but rich in natural resources. The region managed to avoid the cruder imperialistic partitions and outright annexations so evident in Africa, China, and Southeast Asia. This lack of total exploitation owed more to luck rather than to the virtue of the outside powers. The economic interests of the United States, and to some extent of Britain, coincided with the preservation of the status quo in Latin America.

Among all the transplanted Europeans, the United States found the quest for independence the easiest. Its power, size, resources, and heritage of freedom and the rule of law contributed to a distinctive and recognizable national ideal that survived the threat of the Civil War. The search for national unity has not been as successful in Canada, given the split between the closely knit French Canadian minority and the majority English-speaking population.

Nationalism has burned brightly in each of the Latin American nations, sometimes at the expense of political stability. The eight major administrative divisions in the late colonial era have fragmented into 19 states—a process frequently accompanied by insurrection, rebellion, and war.

Australia and New Zealand have found the search for a new nationality difficult. Because they are remote from Europe, inhabitants of these islands have clung to the traditions and life of their ancestors, even to the point that the New Zealanders claim to be more British than the British. More difficult is the situation in South Africa where the white majority are the Boers rather than the British. These Afrikaners have developed a distinctive, unbending culture based on rigid Calvinism and the Dutch tongue.

THE BRITISH DOMINIONS

The British Dominions became self-governing without breaking their political ties to Great Britain. With the exception of South Africa, these new nations were predominantly British in stock, language, culture, and governmental traditions. In the case of Canada, however, a strong French Canadian minority in Quebec, inherited from the original French regime, persisted and preserved its French heritage. In South Africa, following a confused history of rivalry and war between the British and Dutch settlers, a shaky union was achieved. There were no complications of rival Europeans in Australia and New Zealand, which were settled by the British in the beginning and did not have to adjust to an influx of other Europeans. Both Australia and Canada attained political unity by merging a number of colonies into a single government.

South Africa

The first European contact in the area later known as the Union of South Africa, located at the southern tip of Africa, occurred in 1487 when Bartholomew Diaz reached the Cape of Good Hope. Ten years later Vasco da Gama rounded the Cape on his way to the Indies. Two centuries later, large fleets of Dutch ships made their way around Africa to the Indies to trade for spices and oriental wares. The Cape became a strategic place to get fresh water and replenish supplies.

In 1651 the Dutch established a settlement at the Cape of Good Hope, named Cape Town, which grew slowly. As the Dutch settlers pushed inland, they came into conflict with the Bantu-speaking Africans, who strongly resisted white expansion. The Dutch period of South African history came to an end in 1814 when the Dutch ceded the colony to Great Britain.

Friction between the British and the Boers, or Dutch burghers, quickly developed over the treatment of the native peoples. The Dutch had many slaves and resented the attitudes of the missionaries, who accused the Dutch of abusing the natives. Britain's emancipation of all slaves in the empire in 1833 exacerbated ill feeling.

Two years later 12,000 Boers undertook an epic journey in their ox-drawn wagons to a new country where they could pursue their way of life without interference. This Great Trek was a folk movement comparable to the covered wagon epic of the American West.[2] Finally on the high plateau, or *veldt,* the Boers established two little republics, the Orange Free State and the Transvaal. The British, in the meantime, extended their settlement along the eastern coast north of the Cape and founded the colony of Natal.

The Great Trek did little to resolve the Boers' difficulties. In the mid-nineteenth century there was much fighting with the Africans, who resisted the incursions of both Boers and British. In 1852 the British government made treaties with the Boers, acknowledging the independence of the Orange Free State and the Transvaal but retaining a shadowy right to have a voice in the foreign affairs of the two republics.

The Boer War and the Creation of the Union of South Africa

The discovery of diamonds in 1868 on the borders of the Cape and of gold in 1885 in the Transvaal attracted thousands of Englishmen and people of other nations to the mines. The president of the Transvaal, Paul Kruger, was determined that these newcomers would not gain control. He was passionately devoted to the Boer way of life, which was simple, mainly rural, and uncomplicated. To curb the growing power of the *Uitlanders* (outlanders), Kruger began to impose heavy taxes on them, while the Boers paid practically nothing. English was banned in the courts and public schools. It was almost impossible for the *Uitlanders* to become naturalized citizens of the Transvaal.

Kruger's main adversary was Cecil Rhodes, a man of driving ambition both for himself and for British imperial interests. Born in 1853, he had a frail constitution and as a young man emigrated to South Africa to improve his health. He became fabulously wealthy in the diamond fields, the leading figure in the DeBeers diamond syndicate and the owner of many gold mining properties in the Transvaal. Rhodes was determined to thwart Kruger by uniting a self-governing South Africa within the British Empire.

To forestall Kruger's plans, Rhodes persuaded Britain to annex territory on the Transvaal's eastern and western borders. He prevented Boer expansion to the north by gaining extensive settlement and mining right in the high and fertile

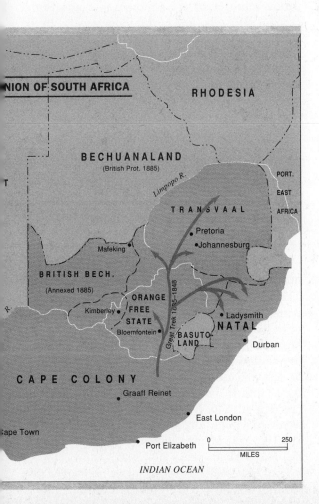

→ Cecil Rhodes. He once declared that his lifelong ambition was to "bring the whole civilized world under British rule, to make the Anglo-Saxon race into an empire."

plateau through which flowed the Zambezi River. In 1890 the town of Salisbury was founded, becoming the capital of the region named Rhodesia.

Meanwhile, the *Uitlanders* began to plot an insurrection. At the close of 1895, a group of Rhodesian mounted police invaded the Transvaal, but they were quickly forced to surrender to a force of Boer commandos. This incident alienated the Dutch population in the Cape, pushed the Orange Free State into an alliance with the Transvaal, and strengthened Kruger's policies.

The South African crisis now moved from the area of covert *Uitlander* plots to British diplomacy. Britain did not want totally independent Boer states. British statesmen also feared that a hostile Transvaal, with its immense mining wealth and consequent economic power, would be able to dominate all South Africa. From 1896 to the spring of 1899 continuous efforts were made to reconcile Boer and British differences but without success. Britain began to send troops, and the Transvaal and the Orange Free

State prepared for war. Hostilities erupted in the fall of 1899.

The world was amazed at the war that followed. The Boers were crack shots and expert horsemen. Knowing every inch of ground on which they fought, they frequently outmaneuvered the British troops. But the tide turned in 1900 when the British inflicted several disastrous defeats on the Boers.

After the Boers surrendered in 1902, the British treated them magnanimously. They gave them loans to rebuild burned farmhouses and buy cattle, and more significantly, they extended the right of self-government to the Transvaal in 1906 and to the Orange Free State two years later. The Liberal government in Great Britain permitted the Boer and English states to unite and form the Union of South Africa in 1909. Only seven years after the war, Boer and Briton joined hands to create a new self-governing dominion. The first prime minister of the Union was Louis Botha (1863–1919), who had been a Boer general in the war. Botha's primary purpose was to create neither an English nor a Boer nationality but a blend of the two in a new South African patriotism.

Australia

The discovery of Australia dates back to the seventeenth century when Dutch explorers sighted its shores. Captain Cook's South Seas voyage in 1769, however, paved the way for British settlement. In 1788 Britain transported a group of convicts to Australia and settled them at Sydney. From the parent colony of Sydney, later called New South Wales, five other settlements were founded.

Although a majority of the first Europeans in Australia were prisoners, most of them were political prisoners and debtors, rather than hardened criminals. After seven years of servitude many were liberated and as "emancipists" became citizens. Quite early in the nineteenth century, many free settlers also came to Australia. They began to protest the dumping of convicts in their new home, and Britain took the first steps to end the practice in 1840. By 1850 the Australian colonies were enjoying a liberal form of self-government.

The Australian colonies grew slowly during the first half of the nineteenth century. Sheep raising became the basis of the economy. The discovery of gold in 1851 quickened the tempo of

Sidney Low on Cecil Rhodes

During his time, Cecil Rhodes stood as the foremost European imperialist in Africa. The journalist Sidney Low captured Rhodes's philosophical essence.

Whatever inconsistency there may have been in his actions, his opinions, so far as I could perceive, did not vary. In fact, he repeated himself a good deal, having a kind of apostolic fervour in expatiating on the broad simple tenets of the Rhodesian religion. His cardinal doctrines I should say were these: First, that insular England was quite insufficient to maintain, or even to protect, itself without the assistance of the Anglo-Saxon peoples beyond the seas of Europe. Secondly, that the first and greatest aim of British statesmanship should be to find new areas of settlement, and new markets for the products that would, in due course, be penalised in the territories and dependencies of all our rivals by discriminating tariffs. Thirdly, that the largest tracts of unoccupied or undeveloped lands remaining on the globe were in Africa, and therefore that the most strenuous efforts should be made to keep open a great part of that continent to British commerce and colonisation. Fourthly, that as the key to the African position lay in the various Anglo-Dutch States and provinces, it was imperative to convert the whole region into a united, self-governing, federation, exempt from meddlesome interference by the home authorities, but loyal to the Empire, and welcoming British enterprise and progress. Fifthly, that the world was made for the service of man, and more particularly of civilised, white, European men, who were most capable of utilising the crude resources of nature for the promotion of wealth and prosperity. And, finally, that the British Constitution was an absurd anachronism, and that it should be remodelled on the lines of the American Union, with federal self-governing Colonies as the constituent States.

From Sidney Low, "Contemporary Recollections," in *The Nineteenth Century and After*, 1902.

---

development, but agriculture continued to be the mainstay of Australia's economy. Railway mileage was expanded, and large investments of foreign capital helped the young nation to develop its resources. In 1850 the population of the country was about 400,000; a decade later it had nearly doubled. In the decade before 1914 the population increased from just under 4 million to 5 million people.

In 1901 the six Australian colonies formed a federal union known as the Commonwealth of Australia, which bears many resemblances to the American system of government. The legislature is composed of a House of Representatives and a Senate. Each state elects six senators, while the lower house is made up of members elected by each state in accordance with its population. In the Commonwealth government the chief executive is the prime minister, who is responsible to the legislature and thus does not possess the fixed term guaranteed the American president.

New Zealand

About a thousand miles from the Australian mainland is a group of islands, two of which are of particular importance. These lonely projections of British influence in the South Pacific constitute the self-governing Dominion of New Zealand. The total population of this country, which has an area five-sixths the size of Great Britain, is just over 3.3 million. The earliest white settlers were desperate convicts who had escaped from penal settlements in Australia. The activity of other colonizers forced the British government to assume protection of the islands in 1840, and British agents signed a treaty guaranteeing certain rights, especially land rights, to the Maoris.

New Zealand gradually became a rich pastoral, farming, and fruit-raising country. The chief export, then as now, was wool. The development of refrigeration enabled large quantities of

→ Because it was considered too far from England to be attractive to free settlers, Australia was first used as a penal colony for English convicts. Although many of the convicts were sentenced to deportation for relatively minor offenses, they often suffered great cruelty and hardships in the prison camps. Here, English convicts plow an Australian field while the guard cracks his whip over their heads.

meat and dairy products to be shipped to foreign markets, especially to Great Britain.

Both New Zealand and Australia have been seen as sociological laboratories because of their pioneering activities in democratic government and social welfare legislation. As early as 1855, the state of Victoria in Australia introduced the secret ballot in elections. The "Australian ballot" was later adopted in Great Britain, the United States, and other parts of the world. Women's suffrage was introduced in New Zealand in 1893 and in Australia nine years later. In New Zealand a program of "land for the people" was implemented through the imposition of heavy taxes on large tracts of land held by absentee landlords. New Zealand also led the world in the adoption of noncontributory old-age pensions in 1878 and the establishment of a national infant welfare system in 1907. Before 1914 Australia had passed similar measures.

Canada

From 1534, when Jacques Cartier sailed up the Saint Lawrence River and claimed the area for France, until 1763, Canada was part of the French empire. Unlike the English colonies in the New World, the French colony of Canada was rigidly supervised by Paris. The home government supervised all trade activities, and the

Catholic Church monopolized education. Few Protestants were allowed to settle in New France.

The French king granted huge tracts of land to nobles, who in turn parceled out their estates to peasant farmers. This introduction of a version of European feudalism seriously hampered development in Canada. It limited expansion by denying free land to pioneers, and it also subjected the population to restrictive control by royal officials, priests, and nobles.

Canada became caught up in the worldwide French–British competition. In addition to Britain's interest in its Atlantic seaboard colonies, its fishermen frequently landed at Newfoundland. In 1670 the Company of Gentlemen Adventurers of England Trading into Hudson's Bay was chartered to engage in the fur trade with the Indians. When war broke out in Europe between France and Britain, their colonies in the New World also went to war. Britain's ultimate victory was anticipated in the Treaty of Utrecht (1713) in which France gave up Acadia (later known as Nova Scotia), surrendered claims to Newfoundland, and recognized the Hudson's Bay Company territory as English.

The last of the four colonial wars ended in a complete victory for Britain. In 1763, by the Treaty of Paris, the British gained all of Canada. London tried to ensure the loyalty of the French Canadians by issuing a royal proclamation guaranteeing the inhabitants' political rights and their freedom to worship as Roman Catholics. These guarantees were strengthened in 1774 when the British government passed the Quebec Act, called the "Magna Carta of the French Canadian race." This act reconfirmed the position of the Catholic Church and perpetuated French laws and customs. However, there was no provision for a representative assembly, such as existed in English-speaking colonies. At that time the French lacked both the interest and experience in self-government.

Canada's Formative Stage

The period from 1763 to 1867 is known as the formative stage of Canada. A number of developments took place during this period: the growth of the English-speaking population, the defeat of an attempted conquest by the United States, the grant of local self-government, and finally the confederation of Canada into a dominion.

The major source of growth of the English-speaking population was the American Revolution. Although the rebellious colonists tried to conquer Canada, the Canadians remained loyal to Britain largely because of the liberal provisions of the Quebec Act, and the invasion failed. Those inhabitants of the thirteen colonies not in favor of separation from Great Britain suffered at the hands of the victorious patriots, and a large number of them fled to Canada. The immigrants, known as United Empire Loyalists, settled in Nova Scotia, along the Saint Lawrence River, and north of the Great Lakes.

The newcomers resented the absence of political representation in their new home and pushed for a measure of self-government. Numerous struggles arose between the French Canadians and the newly arrived Loyalists. To meet this situation the British in 1791 divided British North America into two separate provinces called Upper and Lower Canada and granted each province a representative assembly. The quarrel between the English- and French-speaking populations has continued to the present day.

Open rebellion in 1837 was put down militarily, and in response, the British government sent a special commissioner, Lord Durham (1792–1840), to study the Canadian situation and make recommendations. A statesman with vision, Durham realized that a much larger degree of self-government had to be granted if the home country wished its colonies to remain loyal. He recommended that certain matters of imperial concern, such as foreign relations, should be directed from London, but that Canada alone should control its own domestic affairs. By the mid-nineteenth century London granted self-government to Canada. Unlike the thirteen colonies that severed their connection with the parent country by revolution, Canada achieved

→ The Loyalist encampment at Johnston, a settlement on the banks of the St. Lawrence River in Canada, founded on June 6, 1784.

virtual independence peacefully and remained loyal to Britain.

Fear of the United States, the need for a common tariff policy, and a concerted effort to develop natural resources led Canadians into confederation. A plan of union, the British North American Act, was approved by the British government and passed by the Parliament in London in 1867. This act united Canada—until then divided into the provinces of Quebec and Ontario, Nova Scotia, and New Brunswick—into a federal union of four provinces. The new government had some similarities to the political organization of the United States, but it adopted the British cabinet system with its principle of ministerial responsibility. As a symbol of its connection with Great Britain, provision was made for a governor-general who was to act as the British monarch's representative to Canada.

Modern Canada

The new nation encountered many problems from the first. Its vast size caused communications problems, which became even more acute in 1869 when the dominion purchased the territories of the Hudson's Bay Company extending from present-day Ontario to the Pacific coast, south to the Columbia River. In 1871 the new colony of British Columbia joined the dominion on the promise of early construction of a transcontinental railroad to link the west coast with eastern Canada.

Another disturbing problem was the lack of good relations with the United States. After the Civil War, Irish patriots in the United States, seeking revenge against the British for their treatment of Ireland, launched armed incursions over the border. However, in 1871 the major differences between the two countries were ironed out in the Treaty of Washington, a landmark in the use of arbitration.

The country developed rapidly under the leadership of the dominion's first prime minister, Sir John A. Macdonald (1815–1891), who served from 1867 to 1873 and again from 1878 to 1891. Canadians developed their country through encouraging new industry, building a railroad across the country in 1885, and attracting immigrants. Sir Wilfrid Laurier (1841–1919), who served as prime minister from 1896 to 1911, con-

tinued Macdonald's work. Between 1897 and 1912, Canada received 2.25 million new citizens, bringing the total population to more than 7 million. Internal restructuring created new provinces out of the former Hudson's Bay Company holdings, so that in 1914 the dominion consisted of nine provinces. At the same time, the country had to deal with the consequences of its rapid growth: labor discontent, corruption, and agrarian unrest. Canada was becoming a mature nation, with all of the accompanying problems of depressions, unequal distribution of wealth, and governmental restraint of business.

A long-lasting challenge has been the bicultural nature of the country. In 1761, the entire country was French, but a momentous change began with the American Revolution when English-speaking American Loyalists wishing to keep their British allegiance fled to Canada. In 1761 there were only 65,000 people in New France; by 1815 the population of all the British North American colonies had increased to 600,000, of whom only 250,000 were French. Between 1815 and 1850 a second wave of immigrants from Britain brought the entire population to 2.4 million, of whom fewer than one-third were French. During the nineteenth century and indeed to the present, the population of French origin has remained between 28 and 31 percent of the total.

From the first arrival of significant numbers of British to the latter part of the twentieth century, the relations between the French and English speakers have been strained. Lord Durham saw this clearly in 1837 when he wrote "I found two nations warring in the bosom of a single state; I found a struggle not of principles but of races." Durham singled out the most persistent and disturbing problem facing Canada.

This cultural conflict is based on the French resentment of the British victory two centuries ago and the British pride in that accomplishment. There was also a clash in the field of religion. New France was highly conservative, ruled by an authoritarian regime. When this political authority was removed, the Catholic Church in Quebec became the main defender and citadel of French Catholic culture. The English-speaking Canadians, however, tended to be antagonistic to the Church's role.

Further complicating relations was the fact that the French portion remained largely agricul-

THE GROWTH OF MODERN
CANADA

Canada in 1841
Canada Today

tural with a high rate of illiteracy. The British were more urban and technologically educated, and consequently the English-speaking part became richer and dominant. Although the federal constitution sought to create a bilingual society and a dual school system, the French continued to be bitter over the progressive erosion of this guaranteed equality in the western provinces, where no appreciable French population developed. The English-speaking Canadians assumed a pose of superiority and ridiculed French culture, while making little effort to learn the French language.

At the end of the nineteenth century, while Canada was a united federation in political structure, a common Canadianism had not been achieved. The French had no intention of being absorbed by the culture of the majority. At the end of the twentieth century the question of how to create a single nationality comprised of two separate but officially equal cultures remained Canada's major problem.

THE UNITED STATES

The revolutionary movements in Europe during the nineteenth century fought either aristocratic domination or foreign rule—or both. The nineteenth-century struggles in the United States were not quite the same. Instead, there were two major related problems. One was the annexation, settlement, and development of the continent;

the other was slavery. Free land and unfree people were the sources of the many political confrontations that culminated in the Civil War, the greatest struggle of nineteenth-century America.

At the conclusion of its successful revolution in 1783, the United States was not a democracy. When the Constitution of the new nation was ratified, only one male in seven had the vote. Religious requirements and property qualifications ensured that only a small elite participated in government. These restrictions allowed patricians from established families in the South and men of wealth and substance in the North to control the country for nearly half a century.

Democratic Influences

The influence of the western frontier helped make America more democratic. Even before the Constitution was ratified, thousands of pioneers crossed the Appalachian Mountains into the new "western country." In the West, land was to be had for the asking, social caste did not exist, one person was as good as another. Vigor, courage, self-reliance, and competence counted, not birth or wealth. Throughout the nineteenth century the West was the source of new and liberal movements that challenged the conservative ideas prevalent in the East.

Until the War of 1812, democracy grew slowly. In 1791 Vermont had been admitted as a manhood suffrage state, and the following year Kentucky followed suit; but Tennessee, Ohio, and Louisiana entered the Union with property and tax qualifications for the vote. After 1817 no new state entered the Union with restrictions on male suffrage except for slaves. Most appointive offices became elective, and requirements for holding office were liberalized.

Andrew Jackson changed the tone and emphasis of American politics. In 1828 he was elected to the presidency following a campaign that featured the slogan "Down with the aristocrats." He was the first president produced by the West; the first since George Washington not to have a college education; and the first to have been born in poverty. He owed his election to no congressional clique, but to the will of the people, who idolized "Old Hickory" as their spokesman and leader.

The triumph of the democratic principle in the 1830s set the direction for political development. With Jackson's election came the idea that any man, by virtue of being an American citizen, could hold any office in the land. Governments widened educational opportunities by enlarging the public school system. With increased access to learning, class barriers became less important. The gaining and keeping of political power came more and more to be tied to satisfying the needs of the people who voted.

Simultaneous with the growth of democracy came the territorial expansion of the country. The Louisiana territory, purchased from France for about $15 million in 1803, doubled the size of the United States. In 1844, Americans, influenced by "manifest destiny," the belief that their domination of the continent was God's will, demanded "All of Oregon or none." The claim led to a boundary dispute with Great Britain over land between the Columbia River and 54'40" north latitude. In 1846 the two countries accepted a boundary at the 49th parallel, and the Oregon territory was settled. The annexation of Texas in 1845 was followed by war with Mexico in 1846. In the peace agreement signed two years later Mexico ceded California, all title to Texas, and the land between California and Texas to the United States. As a result of these acquisitions, by 1860 the area of the United States had increased by two-thirds over what it had been in 1840.

The addition of the new territories forced the issue of whether slavery should be allowed in those areas. Paralleling developments in Great Britain, abolitionists in the United States, particularly New England, vigorously condemned slavery. Henry Clay's Missouri Compromise of 1820 permitted slavery in Missouri but forbade it in the rest of the Louisiana Purchase. This settlement satisfied both sides for only a short time. The antislavery forces grew more insistent. In the senatorial campaigns of 1858, candidate Abraham Lincoln declared:

> A house divided against itself cannot stand. I believe this government cannot endure permanently half slave and half free. I do not expect the Union to be dissolved—I do not expect the house to fall—but I do expect it will cease to be divided. It will become all one thing, or all the other.[3]

Slavery was an important issue; it served as a focus for the differences and tensions separating

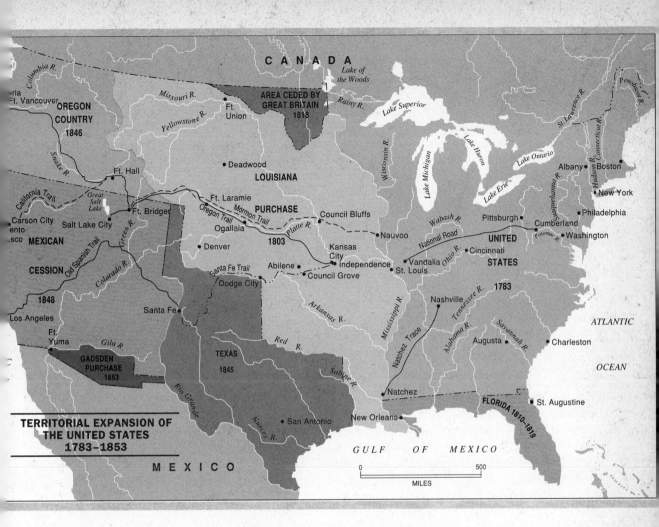

TERRITORIAL EXPANSION OF THE UNITED STATES 1783–1853

the North from the South. However, a more fundamental cause of conflict was that, in a sense, the two sections had become separate societies. The former was industrial, urban, and democratic; the latter was mainly agricultural, rural, and dominated by a planter aristocracy. The South strongly opposed the North's desire for higher tariffs, government aid for new railroads, and generous terms for land settlement in the West. These fundamental differences brought North and South to war. Slavery served as a moral irritant.

The Civil War and Its Results

Soon after Abraham Lincoln was inaugurated as president, the southern states seceded from the Union and formed the Confederate States of America. The first shot of the Civil War was fired at Fort Sumter, South Carolina, in 1861, initiat-

ing the bloodiest war experienced by any Western nation to that time. Four agonizing years of conflict, in which more than one-half million men died, ended when General Robert E. Lee surrendered to General Ulysses S. Grant at Appomattox Courthouse in Virginia in April 1865. A few days later, the nation was stunned by the assassination of President Lincoln, who had just begun his second term.

With the final collapse of the Confederacy before the overwhelming superiority of the Union in manpower, industrial resources, and wealth, the Civil War became the grand epic of American history in its heroism, romance, and tragedy. The victorious North used military occupation to try to force the South to extend voting and property rights to the former slaves. Eventually, this so-called Reconstruction period (1865–1877) was ended by a tacit agreement between the northern industrial and the southern white leaders that enabled the latter to regain political control and to deprive blacks of their newly won rights. Southerners invoked Social Darwinist arguments to justify their actions in denying full "blessings of freedom" to the former slaves.

Southern politicians deprived blacks of their voting rights by enacting state laws or employing devices such as poll taxes, literacy tests, property qualifications, and physical threats. Racial segregation in schools, restaurants, parks, and hotels was effectively applied. Laws prohibiting interracial marriage were enacted and blacks were generally excluded from unions. Between 1885 and 1918, more than 2500 blacks were lynched in the United States. As second-class citizens, freed but landless, the former slaves essentially formed a sharecropping class, mired in poverty and deprived of equal educational opportunity.[4]

It took more than a century after the Civil War for black Americans to gain a politically equal footing. Despite all of the obstacles they encountered in the half century after the Emancipation Proclamation, by 1914 black Americans had made some substantial achievements: the creation of a professional class estimated at 47,000; a 70 percent literacy rate; ownership of 550,000 homes, 40,000 businesses, and savings of some $700 million. Black churches, banks, and insurance companies evolved into substantial institutions. In addition black individuals made major contributions to a number of different fields: Henry Ossawa Tanner (1859–1937) was recognized as a distinguished painter; George Washington Carver (1865–1943) made substantial contributions in the field of agricultural chemistry; and W. E. B. DuBois (1868–1963), a social scientist of national stature, began the first effective black political protest early in the century.

If the causes and consequences of the American Civil War are complex, the all-important result was simple. It settled the issue of whether the United States was an indivisible sovereign nation or a collection of sovereign states. The sacrifice of hundreds of thousands of lives preserved the Union, but the inhuman treatment of blacks remained.

Development, Abuse, and Reform

The North's victory was a boost for industrialization as well as a result of it—and the economic revolution in the United States that followed was

→ American artist Henry Ossawa Tanner demonstrated remarkable talent to create a strong and memorable mood, as is evident in *The Banjo Lesson* (1893).

more significant than the conflict itself. Railroads were built across broad prairies and the first transcontinental line, the Union Pacific, was completed in 1869.

Settlers swarmed west. Between 1850 and 1880 the number of cities with a population of 50,000 or more doubled. The number of men employed in industry increased 50 percent. In 1865 there were 35,000 miles of railroads in the country. By 1900 the trackage was estimated to be about 200,000—more than in all of Europe. In 1860 a little more than a billion dollars was invested in manufacturing; by 1900 this figure had risen to 12 billion. The value of manufactured products increased proportionately. In 1870 the total production of iron and steel in the United States was far below that of France and Britain. Twenty years later the United States had outstripped them and was producing about one-third of the world's iron and steel.

In the age of rapid industrialism and materialistic expansion, many who pursued profits lost sight of ethical principles both in business and government. In five years, between 1865 and 1870, the notorious Tweed Ring cost the city of New York at least $100 million. Ruthless financiers, such as Jay Gould and Jim Fisk, tampered with the basic financial stability of the nation. The administration of President Ulysses Grant was tainted by scandals and frauds. A new rich class failed to appreciate its responsibilities to society. Corruption was a blatant feature of the new order.

For roughly a century the gospel for the new nation of America had been rugged individualism. As in Europe, governmental interference in business was unwelcome because of the strong belief that individuals should be free to follow their own inclinations, run their own businesses, and enjoy the profits of their labors. In an expanding nation where land, jobs, and opportunity beckoned, there was little to indicate that the system would not work indefinitely. By 1880, however, the end of the frontier was in sight. Free land of good quality was scarce, and the frontier

→ Railroad companies distributed elaborately illustrated brochures and broadsides to lure people to the West, where they would settle on land owned by the railroad.

→ George Washington Carver. As director of agricultural research at Tuskegee Institute, he derived many new products from southern crops.

could no longer serve as a safety valve to release the economic and social pressures of an expanding population.

Between 1850 and 1900 the United States became the most powerful state in the Western Hemisphere, increased its national wealth from $7 billion to $88 billion, established an excellent system of public education, and fostered the spread of civil liberties. But there were many disturbing factors in the picture. Unemployment, child labor, and industrial accidents were common in the rapidly growing cities. Slums grew and served as breeding places for disease and crime. Strikes, often accompanied by violence, brought to a head the tension between labor and capital.

In response, the wide-ranging Progressive reform movement developed between 1890 to 1914. This movement was rooted partly in the agrarian protests against big business sparked by the Populists of the Midwest and South. The Progressives effectively mobilized the middle classes to work to eliminate sweatshops, the exploitation of labor, and the abuse of natural resources.

The success of the Progressive movement was reflected in the constitutions of the new states admitted to the Union and in their introduction of the direct primary, the initiative and referendum, and the direct election of senators. All these measures tended to give the common people more effective control of the government. After the enactment of the Interstate Commerce Act in 1887, which introduced federal regulation over railroads, a steady expansion of governmental regulation of industry began.

As president of the United States from 1901 to 1909, Theodore Roosevelt launched an aggressive campaign to break up the trusts, conserve natural resources, and regulate railroads, food, and drugs. In 1913 President Woodrow Wilson started a militant campaign of reform called the "New Freedom." His administration reduced the tariff because it was too much the instrument of special economic privilege, enacted banking reform with the Federal Reserve Act of 1913, and regulated businesses in the public interest through the Clayton Antitrust Act and the establishment of the Federal Trade Commission, both in 1914.

In 1914 the United States was the richest, most populous, and most influential nation in the West. The country's first census, taken in 1790, counted a population of just under 4 million; by 1910 the number was 99 million. During the nineteenth century more than 25 million immigrants had made their way to America. Since the days of George Washington, the national wealth had increased at least a hundredfold. Once the producer of raw materials only, the United States by 1914 was the world's greatest industrial power, producing more steel than Britain and Germany combined. A single company—United States Steel—was capitalized for $1.46 billion, a sum greater than the total estimated wealth of the country in 1790.

The United States and the World

From the first, U.S. foreign policy pursued three goals: national security, trade, and the spread of democracy. During its first quarter century, the United States fought a brief naval war with France, became embroiled with Britain in the War of 1812, and sent two expeditions to the Mediterranean to deal with the Barbary pirates. These complications notwithstanding, Americans spent the next century developing their country. Thomas Jefferson summarized the country's foreign policy with these words: "Peace, commerce, and honest friendship with all nations—entangling alliances with none."[5]

Early in the 1820s the policy of noninvolvement was seriously challenged when conservative members of the Quadruple Alliance offered to help the Spanish king regain control of Latin America. Both Britain and the United States viewed this possibility with alarm. George Canning, the British foreign secretary, suggested that his government and the United States make a joint declaration warning against European intervention in South America. U.S. President James Monroe seriously considered the invitation, but decided against it.

Instead Monroe offered a unilateral doctrine in his message to Congress in December 1823. He warned the European powers against any attempt to impose their system in the Western Hemisphere and also declared that the United States had no intention of interfering in European affairs. In 1823 the United States could "have its cake and eat it too." The shield of the British fleet stood behind the Monroe Doctrine, with or without a formal alliance between Washington and London, and the United States avoided the complications and dangers inherent in European intervention.

It was sometimes difficult to reconcile the desire for isolation with the country's stated love of freedom; for example, much sympathy was expressed for the Greeks as they fought against Turkish tyranny in the 1820s, but there was little active support. When the country established new foreign contacts, it went across the Pacific. In 1844 the United States made its first treaty with China, opening certain ports to American trade and securing the rights of American merchants and sailors to be tried in American tribunals in China. In 1853 Commodore Matthew Perry visited Japan, and by his show of force, persuaded the Japanese to open some of their harbors to American ships. By 1854 the United States was considering the annexation of the Hawaiian Islands, and in 1867 it purchased Alaska from Russia for the amazingly low price of $7.2 million.

Emperor Napoleon III tested the Monroe Doctrine during the Civil War by sending over Maximilian to establish the Mexican empire. While the war raged, U.S. protests did little to sway the French. But after 1865, the 900,000 veterans backing up the protests plus the actions of the Mexican patriots forced Napoleon to withdraw his military and financial support. In 1867 a Mexican firing squad executed Maximilian.

Foreign affairs were virtually forgotten for the next generation, and one New York newspaper recommended the abolition of the foreign service. However, as productivity increased, the United States was forced to seek new outlets for its goods, especially now that the frontier had disappeared. Foreign trade increased from $393 million in 1870 to more than $1.33 billion in 1900. During the same period, investments abroad went from virtually nothing to $500 million. At the same time American missionary activity greatly expanded in Africa, the Middle East, and Asia. Like their European counterparts, many American leaders were influenced by the theory of Social Darwinism, especially when it was applied to foreign affairs. The slogan "survival of the fittest" had its followers in the U.S. Congress as well as in the British Parliament, French Chamber of Deputies, and German Reichstag. In order to be truly great, many argued, the United States must expand and assume a vital role in world politics. This argument was instrumental in the United States's acquisition of a global empire.

Roosevelt the Activist

The United States began building a modern navy in 1883, and by 1890 the buildup had accelerated greatly. Care was taken not to alarm the country, however, and the new ships were officially known as "seagoing coastline battleships," a handy nautical contradiction. When this naval program was initiated, the U.S. Navy ranked twelfth among the powers; by 1900 it had advanced to third place.

The growing international stature of the United States received startling confirmation in the border dispute between Britain and Venezuela in 1895. When Britain delayed before agreeing to submit the issue to arbitration, the State Department of the United States took the initiative and drafted a blunt note to London. The note warned the British that refusal to accept arbitration would have grave consequences. The State Department noted U.S. dominance in the Western Hemisphere and boasted that America's "geographical position protected it from European Pressures." Britain was preoccupied with the Boers in South Africa, the Germans on the Continent, and the French in the Sudan and thus could not argue too strenuously against the message. The British agreed to resolve the dispute through arbitration.

There were signs of the new dynamism in American foreign policy in Asia as well. In 1899 U.S. Secretary of State John Hay initiated a policy for maintaining equal commercial rights in China for the traders of all nations, and the Open Door Policy in China became a reality. In the melodrama of the Boxer Rebellion, the United States again was a leader rather than a follower.

This heightened activity of the United States is best symbolized by the ideas and actions of

→ The execution of Maximilian by firing squad in 1867. The protests of the United States against France's violation of the Monroe Doctrine helped convince Napoleon III to withdraw French military support of Maximilian's empire in Mexico. Without this support the empire soon collapsed.

Theodore Roosevelt. In his terms as president he was one of the leading figures on the world stage. At the request of the Japanese he assumed the role of peacemaker in the Russo-Japanese War. The peace conference, which met in 1905 at Portsmouth, New Hampshire, successfully concluded a treaty, and in 1910 Roosevelt received the Nobel Peace Prize.

Roosevelt was not always a man of peace, however. When he believed the legitimate interests of the United States to be threatened, he did not hesitate to threaten or use force, as could be seen in Panama. In 1901 the British conceded to the United States the exclusive right to control any canal that might be dug through the isthmus. For $40 million the United States bought the rights of a private French company that had already begun work on the canal. A lease was negotiated with Colombia, through whose territory the canal would be built, but that country's senate refused to ratify the treaty, claiming the

compensation was too small. Roosevelt is reputed to have responded, "I did not intend that any set of bandits should hold up Uncle Sam." The upshot was a revolution, financed with money borrowed from banker and financier John Pierpont Morgan. Panama, the new republic that seceded from Colombia in 1903, concluded a canal treaty with the United States, and in 1914 the canal was opened. The United States had moved far from its traditional place on the periphery of world affairs.

LATIN AMERICA

The new nations of Latin America faced a complex of dilemmas that bequeathed a frustrating century of political instability and foreign economic domination. Civil wars, revolutions, and regimes came and went with alarming and costly regularity. Progressive leaders who tried to modernize their countries had to face the opposition of powerful, traditional institutions and massive and complex social problems.

The Creation of the Latin American States

In the first decades of the nineteenth century, the Latin American colonies pursued an irresistible movement for independence. By 1825, Spanish and Portuguese power was broken in the Western Hemisphere, and nine new political units emerged in Latin America. Mexico, Guatemala, Great Colombia, Peru, Bolivia, Paraguay, Argentina, and Chile were free of Spain, and Brazil had gained its independence from Portugal. Once free of those powers, however, the new nations of Latin America were hampered by European and North American dominance over their economic and political affairs.

For most of the new Latin American nations their first half century was a time of decline and disappointment. The great liberators could not maintain control of the nations they had freed. The liberal, urban Creoles who had begun the independence movements were inexperienced and unable to make the political compromises necessary to govern new countries. They soon lost power to crude military leaders, or *caudillos*, whose armed gangs struggled for power in a con-

→ President Theodore Roosevelt visited the Culebra Cut at the Panama Canal in November 1916. Here he is shown sitting on a 95-ton steam shovel.

fusing series of upheavals. A growing sectionalism accompanied these coups. Mammoth states broke up into tiny republics, which in turn were threatened by localism.

In part, Latin America's problems resulted from the Spanish colonial system that had offered native-born whites little opportunity or responsibility in government. The tradition of autocracy and paternalism was a poor precedent for would-be democratic republics. The emphasis on executive power inspired presidents, generals, landowners, and church officials to wield authority with arrogant disregard for public opinion and representative government.

The colonial economic system, based on raw materials rather than industry, encouraged concentration of land and other forms of wealth in a few hands. The church with its vast properties, monopoly on education and welfare agencies, and command over cultural life complicated the politics of every new nation.

In addition, the new states were cursed by problems associated with the wars of independence. Some of the most productive areas were devastated. Hatred and division remained. Many men who had fought the royalists remained armed, predisposed to a life of violence and pillage and likely to group themselves about the *caudillos*, who promised adventure or profit in revolutions.

The final problem facing the new states was that of racial disunity. In 1825 there were from 15 to 18 million people in the former Spanish empire. About 3 million of them were whites, the wealthiest and most educated population. That figure remained constant until the last third of the century, when immigration from Europe increased drastically. There were about the same number of *mestizos*, who scorned the Indians but were not accepted by whites. Their numbers steadily increased, as did their ambition. During the nineteenth century at least half of the population in some states was Indian. Deprived of the small protection once offered by the Spanish crown, they either sank into peonage or lived in semi-independence under their tribal rulers. Finally, in Brazil and most of the Caribbean islands, blacks were a large majority. Conflicts of interest quickly developed between these broad racial groups, particularly between the Creoles and the *mestizos*. The pernicious effects of these divisive factors were played out in each nation.

Mexico

Despite its promising beginning in 1821, Mexico suffered a half century of turmoil. Iturbide's empire lasted only a few months, to be replaced by a federal republic. In less than ten years, however, a coup brought to power as dictator a preposterous military leader named Antonio Lopez de Santa Anna (1795–1876). Under his notorious rule, the defenders of the Alamo were massacred in 1836 and Mexico's political life was generally debased. His conduct of the war with the United States (1846–1848) humiliated Mexico. The overthrow of this corrupt, incompetent *caudillo* in 1855 brought more thoughtful and circumspect men into politics.

The liberals, under the leadership of Benito Juarez (1806–1872), set out to implement a reform program known as the *Reforma*. They planned to establish a more democratic republic, destroy the political and economic force of the Church, and include the *mestizos* and Indians in political life. A terrible civil war followed their anticlerical measures; it ended in 1861 with Juarez's apparent victory. The European powers invaded when Mexico was unable to meet the payments on its debts owed to foreigners, and a French puppet regime was established. By 1867 popular uprisings and pressure from the United States had driven French troops from Mexican soil.

Juarez again set out to institute the *Reforma*, but the poverty of the country hampered progress. After he died, one of his adherents, Porfirio Diaz (1830–1915), took power. Under Diaz, who served as president from 1877 to 1880 and again from 1884 to 1911, Mexican politics stabilized. Foreign capital entered in large amounts. Factories, railroads, mines, trading houses, plantations, and enormous ranches flourished, and Mexico City became one of the most impressive capitals in Latin America.

Diaz's rule, though outwardly conforming to the constitution, was a dictatorship. If there was much encouragement of arts and letters, there was no liberty. The Indians sank lower and lower into peonage or outright slavery. In spite of the anticlerical laws of the Juarez period, the Church was quietly permitted to acquire great wealth, and foreign investors exploited Mexico, creating a long-lasting hatred of foreigners.

In 1910 the critics of Diaz found a spokesman in a frail, eccentric man named Francisco

→ Benito Juarez, an Indian from southern Mexico, led the liberal reform group that successfully implemented the reform constitution of 1857. The new constitution curtailed the rights of the military and the Church in an effort to break the power of these two influential groups.

Madero (1873–1913) who undertook to lead a revolutionary movement and surprised the world by succeeding. Madero was murdered in 1913, and Mexico suffered another period of turmoil during which the country was controlled mainly by self-styled local rulers. Still, a determined group was able to organize a revolutionary party and to bring about the only genuine social revolution that Latin America experienced until the First World War.

Argentina

Until the 1970s, Argentina was probably the most advanced Spanish-speaking country in the world. It attained this position in a period of sudden growth that followed a half century of sluggishness. Its beginning as a free nation was promising. Soon, however, the bustling port city of Buenos Aires, whose energetic population sought to encourage European capital and commerce, found itself overawed by the *caudillos*, the great ranchers of the interior, and their retainers, the *guachos*— the colorful, nomadic cowboys and bandits whose way of life has been romanticized in literature and folklore. The *caudillos* intimidated the supporters of constitutional government in Buenos Aires, and until mid-century, Argentina was not a republic but rather a *gaucho* paradise, isolated and ruled by men who wanted to keep European influences out.

In 1852 a combination of progressive elements overthrew the *gaucho* leader. Commerce with Europe was revived and within ten years Argentina had become a united republic of admirable stability. The constitution was usually observed and individual rights were respected to a high degree. Immigrants poured in, and soon the population of Argentina became the most

European of the New World republics, for it contained few Indians or blacks.

Foreign capital, especially British, brought about amazing developments; port facilities, railroads, light industry, and urban conveniences were among the most advanced in the world. Buenos Aires became by far the largest and most beautiful city in Latin America, despite its location on a monotonous, flat plain beside a muddy estuary.

The flat plain, or pampas, is perhaps the richest land in the world for grass and wheat, and livestock have been multiplying there for centuries. The introduction of refrigerated ships around 1880 made it feasible to transport enormous quantities of fresh beef to Britain in exchange for capital and finished goods. About 1900 wheat joined beef as a major Argentine export. This intimate commercial relationship with Britain, which lasted until after World War II, affected nearly every aspect of Argentine life.

Nevertheless, although elite society was dominated by leaders who were pro-British in business and pro-French in culture, a true Argentine nationalism was developing. Along with the growth of this powerful sentiment came demands for more democracy and a wider distribution of wealth.

Brazil

For many years this former Portuguese colony escaped the turbulence and disorders that befell its Spanish-speaking neighbors, probably because it had achieved independence without years of warfare and military dominance and because it enjoyed the continuity and legitimacy afforded by a respected monarchy. The first emperor, Pedro I (1822–1831), promulgated a constitution

Francisco Madero, The Plan of San Luis Potosí

The Mexican revolutionary movement received its most eloquent definition in the plan of San Luis Potosí, written by Francisco Madero from his exile in San Antonio, Texas.

Peoples, in their constant efforts for the triumph of the ideal of liberty and justice, are forced, at precise historical moments, to make their greatest sacrifices.

Our beloved country has reached one of those moments. A force of tyranny which we Mexicans were not accustomed to suffer after we won our independence oppresses us in such a manner that it has become intolerable. In exchange for that tyranny we are offered peace, but peace full of shame for the Mexican nation. . . .

It may almost be said that martial law constantly exists in Mexico; the administration of justice, instead of imparting protection to the weak, merely serves to legalize the plunderings committed by the strong; the judges instead of being the representatives of justice, are the agents of the executive, whose interests they faithfully serve; the chambers of the union have no other will than that of the dictator; the governors of the States are designated by him and they in their turn designate and impose in like manner the municipal authorities.

From this it results that the whole administrative, judicial, and legislative machinery obeys a single will, the caprice of General Porfirio Dìaz, who during his long administration has shown that the principal motive that guides him is to maintain himself in power and at any cost.

For this reason the Mexican people have protested against the illegality of the last election and, desiring to use successively all the recourses offered by the laws of the Republic, in due form asked for the nullification of the election by the Chamber of Deputies, notwithstanding they recognized no legal origin in said body and knew beforehand that, as its members were not the representatives of the people, they would carry out the will of General Dìaz, to whom exclusively they owe their investiture.

In such a state of affairs the people, who are the only sovereign, also protested energetically against the election in imposing manifestations in different parts of the Republic; and if the latter were not general throughout the national territory, it was due to the terrible pressure exercised by the Government, which always quenches in blood any democratic manifestation, as happened in Puebla, Vera Cruz, Tlaxcala, and in other places.

But this violent and illegal system can no longer subsist.

I have very well realized that if the people have designated me as their candidate for the Presidency it is not because they have had an opportunity to discover in me the qualities of a statesman or of a ruler, but the virility of the patriot determined to sacrifice himself, if need be, to obtain liberty and to help the people free themselves from the odious tyranny that oppresses them.

Therefore, and in echo of the national will, I declare the late election illegal and, the Republic being accordingly without rulers, provisionally assume the Presidency of the Republic until the people designate their rulers pursuant to the law. In order to attain this end, it is necessary to eject from power the audacious usurpers whose only title of legality involves a scandalous and immoral fraud.

From United States Congress, Senate Subcommittee on Foreign Relations, *Revolutions in Mexico*, 62nd Congress, 2nd Session (Washington, DC.: Government Printing Office, 1913).

in 1824, and the accession to the throne of Pedro II in 1840 initiated a period of political liberty and economic and cultural progress that lasted throughout his 50-year reign.

Immigrants were attracted to this peaceful land, and foreign investments were heavy but without the massive exploitation that Mexico experienced under Diaz. Economic growth tended to favor the southeastern part of the country at the expense of the great sugar plantations in the tropical north. The abolition of slavery in 1888 hurt the sugar lords economically, and they rose up against the emperor. Joining them were army officers, who resented the civilian nature of Pedro's regime, and a small number of ideological republicans. In 1889 the aging emperor was forced to abdicate.

For nearly ten years the new federal republic of Brazil underwent civil wars and military upheavals, much like those experienced by other Latin American countries. Finally, the republic was stabilized with the army in control, and Brazil resumed its progressive course. Foreign capital continued to enter, and immigration from Europe remained heavy. By 1914 Brazil was generally stable and prosperous, with a growing tradition of responsible government.

Other Latin American Nations

Political turmoil, geographical handicaps, and racial disunity all played a part in the development of the other new nations in Latin America. Bolivia, named so hopefully for the Liberator Simon Bolívar, underwent countless revolutions. Peru's course was almost as futile. The state of Great Colombia dissolved by 1830, and its successors—Colombia, Venezuela, and Ecuador—were plagued by instability and civil wars. Paraguay endured a series of dictatorships and Uruguay, created in 1828 as a buffer between Argentina and Brazil, long suffered from interventions by those two countries.

An exception to the prevailing pattern of political chaos was the steady growth of the republic of Chile. In 1830 Chile came under the control of a conservative oligarchy. Although this regime proved to be generally enlightened, the country was kept under tight control for a century and was ruled for the benefit of the large landlords and big business.

Central America narrowly escaped becoming part of Mexico in 1822. After a 15-year effort to create a Central American confederation, Guatemala, San Salvador, Honduras, Nicaragua, and Costa Rica asserted their independence. Except for Costa Rica, where whites comprised the bulk of the population, racial disunity delayed the development of national feeling. In the Caribbean the Dominican Republic, after decades of submission to the more populous but equally underdeveloped Haiti, maintained a precarious independence.

Foreign Dominance

The Industrial Revolution came into full stride just after the Latin American republics were born. The great industries of western Europe and the United States demanded more and more raw materials and new markets in which to sell finished products. Capital accumulated, and invest-

→ Nitrates being loaded at Pisagua, the northernmost nitrate port of Chile. Economic development of the new Latin American republics depended to a large extent on the export trade, especially the export of minerals and other raw materials to the industrial markets of western Europe and the United States. Control of the valuable export trade could occasionally lead to war, as it did in the War of the Pacific (1879–1883) in which Chile defeated Peru and Bolivia for control of the nitrate fields.

ors eagerly sought opportunities to place their money where they could obtain high rates of interest. This drive for markets, raw materials, and outlets for surplus capital led to classic examples of economic imperialism.

The continual disorder and the lack of strong governments in Latin America gave businesses the opportunity to obtain rich concessions and float huge loans. Many of the Latin American government leaders, brought to power through revolution and interested only in personal gain, often resorted to the vicious practice of selling concessions to foreign corporations for ready cash. Political bosses bartered away the economic heritage of their lands, for Latin America was rich in minerals, oil, and other important resources. Foreign investors sometimes acted in good faith, providing capital at a reasonable rate of interest to Latin American regimes which, it became apparent, had no intention of fulfilling the contract. On other occasions unscrupulous capitalists took full advantage of officials in ignorant or helpless governments.

Injured foreign investors usually appealed to their government to intercede in their behalf, generating an unending stream of diplomatic correspondence over debt claims. The United States, Great Britain, Germany, France, Italy, and Spain—the chief investor states—would not permit their citizens to be mistreated in their ventures in foreign investments.

In 1902–1903 a dispute between Venezuela and a coalition formed by Germany, Great Britain, and Italy provoked the three European powers into blockading the Latin American country and even firing on some of the coastal fortifications to remind the Venezuelan dictator of his obligations to some of their nationals. U.S. President Theodore Roosevelt at first stood by, watching Venezuela take its punishment. Then he became suspicious of German motives and began to match threat with threat, forcing the Europeans to back down and place the issue into international arbitration.

In 1904 Roosevelt issued the Roosevelt Corollary to the Monroe Doctrine, an addition that was a frank statement that chronic wrongdoing on the part of Latin American governments might force the United States to exercise an international police power. The Roosevelt pronouncement was picturesquely described as the policy of "speaking softly but carrying a big stick." The United States established a customs receivership in the Dominican Republic and exercised similar control in Nicaragua and Haiti. The Roosevelt Corollary expanded the Monroe Doctrine from its original purpose of keeping out European political interference in Latin America to enlarging the commercial interests of the United States.

In 1898 the United States had gone to war with Spain over the way the Spaniards ruled Cuba: the mistreatment of the Cubans also affected

→ Nearly one-quarter of the invasion force that sailed for Cuba was made up of black troops. This illustration of the Battle of Quasimas near Santiago, Cuba, on June 24, 1898, shows the 9th and 10th Colored Cavalry supporting the Rough Riders in the battle against the Spanish. Black soldiers also helped the Rough Riders take San Juan Hill.

American commercial interests. Victory in the brief, dramatic, and well-publicized Spanish-American War brought the United States recognition as a world power and possession of a conglomeration of islands in the Pacific Ocean as well as in the Caribbean. The United States annexed Puerto Rico and placed the Philippines, which were halfway around the world, under American rule. Sensitive to accusations of imperialism in Cuba, the U.S. government offered Cuba an imperfect, closely tutored independence in which the Cubans were obliged by law to acknowledge the right of the United States to intervene for the "preservation of Cuban independence" and the "maintenance of a government adequate for the protection of life, property, and individual liberty." These and other restrictions on Cuban independence were embodied in the Platt Amendment (1901) to the new Cuban constitution. Thus the United States established its first American protectorate. Panama soon became another protectorate of the United States. Generally both American business and the local population profited from these arrangements.

Roosevelt oversaw the introduction of what has been called Dollar Diplomacy—the coordinated activities of American foreign investors and the U.S. State Department to obtain and protect concessions for the investors. From 1890 this policy won for Americans concessions for Latin American

President William McKinley on Imperialism

Even the Americans joined the imperialistic race. Unlike the Europeans, who propounded intellectually sophisticated rationalizations, the Americans moved for different, often celestial, reasons. McKinley noted:

I have been criticized a good deal about the Philippines, but I don't deserve it. The truth is, I didn't want the Philippines, and when they came to us, as a gift from the gods, I did not know what to do with them. When the Spanish war broke out, Dewey was at Hongkong, and I ordered him to go to Manila, and he had to; because, if defeated, he had no place to refit on that side of the globe, and if the Dons were victorious they would likely cross the Pacific and ravage our Oregon and California coasts. And so he had to destroy the Spanish fleet, and did it. But that was as far as I thought then. When next I realized that the Philippines had dropped into our lap, I confess that I did not know what to do with them. I sought counsel from all sides—Democrats as well as Republicans—but got little help. I thought first we would take only Manila; then Luzon; then other islands, perhaps all. I walked the floor of the White House night after night until midnight; and I am not ashamed to tell you, gentlemen, that I went down on my knees and prayed Almighty God for light and guidance more than one night.

And one night late it came to me this way—I don't know how it was, but it came: (1) That we could not give them back to Spain—that would be cowardly and dishonorable; (2) that we could not turn them over to France or Germany—that would be bad business and discreditable; (3) that we could not leave them to themselves—they were unfit for self-government—and they would soon have anarchy and misrule over there worse than Spain's was; and (4) that there was nothing left for us to do but to take them all, and to educate the Filipinos, and uplift and civilize and Christianize them, and, by God's grace, do the very best we could by them, as our fellowmen for whom Christ also died. And then I went to bed, and went to sleep, and slept soundly, and next morning I sent for the chief engineer of the War Department (our map-maker), and told him to put the Philippines on the map of the United States (pointing to a large map on the wall of his office); "and there they are, and there they will stay while I am president!"

From G. A. Malcolm and M. M. Kalw, *Philippine Government* (Boston, 1932).

A Critic of Imperialism

Francisco Garcia Calderón saw not only the great powers' political impact but also the debilitating cultural problems.

Interventions have become more frequent with the expansion of frontiers. The United States have recently intervened in the territory of Acre, there to found a republic of rubber gatherers; at Panama, there to develop a province and construct a canal: in Cuba, under cover of the Platt Amendment, to maintain order in the interior; in Santo Domingo, to support the civilising revolution and overthrow the tyrants; in Venezuela, and in Central America, to enforce upon these nations, torn by intestine disorders, the political and financial tutelage of the imperial democracy. In Guatemala and Honduras the loans concluded with the monarchs of North American finance have reduced the people to a new slavery. Supervision of the customs and the dispatch of pacificatory squadrons to defend the interests of the Anglo-Saxon have enforced peace and tranquility: such are the means employed. The New York American announces that Mr. Pierpont Morgan proposes to encompass the finances of Latin America by a vast network of Yankee banks. Chicago merchants and Wall Street financiers created the Meat Trust in the Argentine. The United States offer millions for the purpose of converting into Yankee loans the moneys raised in London during the last century by the Latin American States; they wish to obtain a monopoly of credit. It has even been announced, although the news hardly appears probable, that a North American syndicate wished to buy enormous belts of land in Guatemala, where the English tongue is the obligatory language. The fortification of the Panama Canal, and the possible acquisition of the Galapagos Island in the Pacific, are fresh manifestations of imperialistic progress. . . .

Warnings, advice, distrust, invasion of capital, plans of financial hegemony all these justify the anxiety of the southern peoples. . . . Neither irony nor grace nor scepticism, gifts of the old civilizations, can make way against the plebeian brutality, the excessive optimism, the violent individualism of the [North American] people.

All these things contribute to the triumph of mediocrity; the multitude of primary schools, the vices of utilitarianism, the cult of the average citizen, the transatlantic M. Homais, and the tyranny of opinion noted by Tocqueville; and in this vulgarity, which is devoid of traditions and has no leading aristocracy, a return to the primitive type of the redskin, which has already been noted by close observers, is threatening the proud democracy. From the excessive tensions of wills, from the elementary state of culture, from the perpetual unrest of life, from the harshness of the industrial struggle, anarchy and violence will be born in the future. In a hundred years men will seek in vain for the "American soul," the "genius of America," elsewhere than in the undisciplined force or the violence which ignores moral laws. . . .

Essential points of difference separate the two Americas. Differences of language and therefore of spirit; the difference between Spanish Catholicism and multiform Protestantism of the Anglo-Saxons; between the Yankee individualism and the omnipotence of the State natural to the nations of the South. In their origin, as in their race, we find fundamental antagonism; the evolution of the North is slow and obedient to the lessons of time, to the influences of custom; the history of the southern peoples is full of revolutions, rich with dreams of an unattainable perfection.

From Francisco Garcia Calderón, *Latin America: Its Rise and Progress* (London: T. F. Unwin, 1913).

products such as sugar, bananas, and oil from more than a dozen Latin American republics.

In the face of such activities, the pious assertions of those espousing the Pan-American philosophy—that the nations of the Western Hemisphere were bound by common geography and democratic political ideals—gained little acceptance. The "Colossus of the North," as the Latin American nations referred to the United States, clearly acted in its own self-interest. Sarcastic observers referred to the Pan-American Union, founded in 1889, as "the Colonial Division of the Department of State." By 1914 Latin America's relations with the rest of the world were neither healthy nor comforting. After a century of independence, Latin America still lingered on the margins of international life. Left to shift for itself in the face of a future shaded by U.S. imperialism, Latin America saw only a hard road ahead in its relations with the outside world.

CONCLUSION

From the seventeenth through the nineteenth centuries the greatest human migration from the smallest continent, Europe, had taken place. This migration surpassed in scope such momentous human wanderings of the past as those of the Indo-Europeans into India and southern Europe and the incursions of the Germanic tribes into the Roman Empire. Transoceanic in character, this mass movement originated in Europe, which during this period, forged ahead of the rest of the world in industry, technology and science, wealth, and military power.

This dispersal of Europeans has been treated mainly in the history of the British Dominions, the United States, and Latin America. However, equally affected were the African peoples, shipped by the million in a vicious slave trade to develop the vast natural resources of the new lands. They contributed substantially to the cultures and economies of their new societies, especially in Latin America and the United States, but paid an incredible cost—especially in the United States.

The United States with its profound varieties of development, despite a common European heritage, was by far the most important of the new lands of the nineteenth century. The frontier and slavery both influenced the formation of a distinctive society, and the latter bequeathed to the country the most intractable of its twentieth-century domestic problems. The Civil War had more "revolutionary" consequences—socially, economically, and politically—than any other event occurring in the new lands.

→ Suggestions for Reading

R. W. Logan, *The Negro in the United States . . . The Nadir, 1877–1901* (Anvil, 1954) traces the plight of blacks in post-reconstruction America. See also C. Vann Woodward, *The Strange Career of Jim Crow* (Oxford, 1974); J. Forbes Munroe, *Africa and the International Economy* (London, 1976); and E. D. Genovese, *Roll Jordan, Roll: The World the Slaves Made* (Random House, 1976). See H. E. Driver, *Indians of North America* (Chicago, 1969) for an overview of the Native Americans' contact with and overwhelming by the whites and Basil Davidson, *Black Mother: The Years of the African Slave Trade* (Little, Brown, 1961).

A. R. M. Lower's *Colony to Nation: a History of Canada* (Toronto, 1946) is a history of Canada from the British conquest to 1850. For two important aspects of Canadian history, see Bruce Hutchinson, *The Struggle for the Border* (Longman, 1955) and D. M. L. Faar, *The Colonial Office and Canada* (Toronto, 1948). See also L. Lipson, *Politics of Equality* (Chicago, 1948). For provocative studies of history and society, see O. H. K. Spate, *Australia* (Praeger, 1968) and Douglas Pike, *Australia* (Cambridge, 1969). See M. Wilson and L. Thompson, eds., *The Oxford History of South Africa* (1969). Also recommended is E. Roux, *Time Longer than Rope, A History of the Blackman's Struggle for Freedom in South Africa* (Wisconsin, 1964).

For a brief and stimulating survey of the first half of U.S. history, see M. Cunliffe, *The Nation Takes Shape: 1789–1837* (Univ. of Chicago, 1959). Also recommended is A. M. Schlesinger's classic *The Age of Jackson* (Mentor, 1945). Paul H. Buck's *The Road to Reunion 1865–1900* is a good survey of the consequences of the Civil War (Little, Brown, 1937). A good chance to read great literature and fine biography is Carl Sandburg's three-volume biography of Lincoln (many editions).

A critique of the American scene that has become a classic is Alexis de Tocqueville's *Democracy in America* (Mentor). George E. Mowry skillfully characterized *The Era of Theodore Roosevelt* (Torchbooks, 1958). See also Arthur S. Link, *Woodrow Wilson and the Progressive Era* (Torchbooks, 1963).

Some useful studies of Latin America in the nineteenth and early twentieth centuries are Miron Burgin, *The Economic Aspects of Argentinean Federalism, 1820–1852* (Harvard, 1946); J. R. Scobie, *Revolution on the Pampas: A Social History of Argentine Wheat* (Texas, 1964); Jonathan C. Brown, *A Socioeconomic History of Argentina: 1776–1860;* R. L. Gilmore, *Caudillism and Militarism in Venezuela 1810–1910* (Ohio Univ. 1964); T. L. Karnes, *The Failure of Union: Central America 1824–1960* (Univ. of North Carolina, 1961); and M. C. Meyer and W. L. Sherman, *The Course of Mexican History* (Oxford, 1979). See also D. Bushnell and N. Macauley, *The Emergence of Latin America in the Nineteenth Century* (Oxford, 1988).

→ Notes

1. Hubert Herring, *History of Latin America* (New York: Alfred A. Knopf, 1956), p. 97.
2. Alfred L. Burt, *The British Empire and Commonwealth* (Boston: D. C. Heath, 1956), p. 286.
3. C. Van Doren, ed., *The Literary Works of Abraham Lincoln* (New York: Limited Editions Club, 1941), p. 65.
4. S. E. Morison, *The Oxford History of the American People* (London: Oxford University Press, 1965), p. 793.
5. Quoted in F. R. Dulles, *America's Rise to World Power* (New York: Harper & Row, 1955), p. 4.

CHAPTER 27

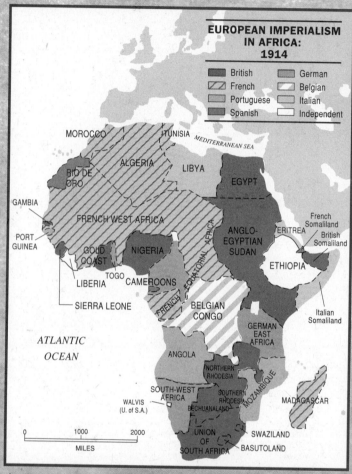

EUROPEAN IMPERIALISM IN AFRICA: 1914

- British
- French
- Portuguese
- Spanish
- German
- Belgian
- Italian
- Independent

MOROCCO
TUNISIA
MEDITERRANEAN SEA
RIO DE ORO
ALGERIA
LIBYA
EGYPT
GAMBIA
FRENCH WEST AFRICA
PORT GUINEA
GOLD COAST
NIGERIA
FRENCH EQUATORIAL AFRICA
ERITREA
French Somaliland
British Somaliland
TOGO
LIBERIA
CAMEROONS
ETHIOPIA
SIERRA LEONE
BELGIAN CONGO
Italian Somaliland
ATLANTIC OCEAN
GERMAN EAST AFRICA
ANGOLA
NORTHERN RHODESIA
SOUTH-WEST AFRICA
SOUTHERN RHODESIA
MOZAMBIQUE
MADAGASCAR
WALVIS (U. of S.A.)
BECHUANALAND
UNION OF SOUTH AFRICA
SWAZILAND
BASUTOLAND
ANGLO-EGYPTIAN SUDAN

0   1000   2000
MILES

→ The thoughtless carving up of Africa into imperial holdings on the basis of longitude and latitude lines created a legacy of ethnic rivalries that would plague Africa throughout the twentieth century.

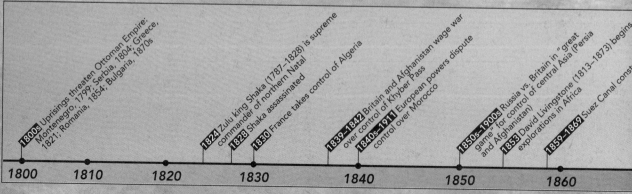

1800s Uprisings threaten Ottoman Empire: Montenegro, 1799; Serbia, 1804; Greece, 1821; Romania, 1854; Bulgaria, 1870s

1824 Zulu king Shaka (1787–1828) is supreme commander of northern Natal

1828 Shaka assassinated

1830 France takes control of Algeria

1839–1842 Britain and Afghanistan wage war over control of Khyber Pass

1840s–1911 European powers dispute control over Morocco

1850s–1900s Russia vs. Britain in "great game" for control of central Asia (Persia and Afghanistan)

1853 David Livingstone (1813–1873) begins explorations in Africa

1859–1869 Suez Canal constr

1800   1810   1820   1830   1840   1850   1860

Africa and the Middle East, 1800~1914

CHAPTER OUTLINE

Sub-Saharan Africa

North Africa

The Middle East

MAPS

European Imperialism in Africa, 1914

The Ottoman Empire, c. 1900

The Persian Gulf Area, c. 1900

DOCUMENTS

Lord Lugard Justifies European Imperialism
in Africa

The Earl of Cromer on Egypt

In the eighteenth and nineteenth centuries, Europeans steadily advanced into the Middle East and Africa. Europe's economic, technological, and military superiority overwhelmed the diverse, complex civilizations and made them targets in the competition for an empire.

In Sub-Saharan Africa the diversity of tribes made a unified political response to the Europeans impossible. By the beginning of the twentieth century Africans found themselves living within political boundaries imposed by the Europeans without regard for the existing ethnic distribution of peoples. They began the painful process of altering their life-styles to survive in the industrialized world.

The Islamic world retained its religious strength and sophisticated cultures and continued to expand in the face of the European onslaught. However, the disintegration of the Ottoman Empire brought about massive political change. Whether in North Africa or in central Asia, Muslims found themselves caught up in assorted great power rivalries.

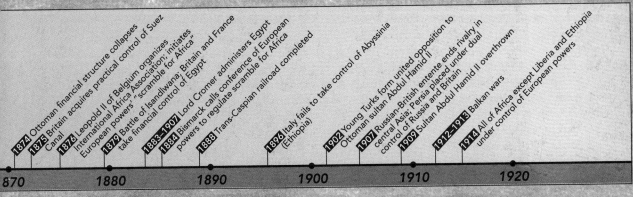

1874 Ottoman financial structure collapses

1875 Britain acquires practical control of Suez Canal

1876 Leopold II of Belgium organizes International Africa Association; initiates European powers' "scramble for Africa"

1879 Battle of Isandlwana; Britain and France take financial control of Egypt

1883–1907 Lord Cromer administers Egypt

1884 Bismarck calls conference of European powers to regulate scramble for Africa

1888 Trans-Caspian railroad completed

1896 Italy fails to take control of Abyssinia (Ethiopia)

1902 Young Turks form united opposition to Ottoman sultan Abdul Hamid II

1907 Russian-British entente ends rivalry in central Asia; Persia placed under dual control of Russia and Britain

1909 Sultan Abdul Hamid II overthrown

1912–1913 Balkan wars

1914 All of Africa except Liberia and Ethiopia under control of European powers

870   1880   1890   1900   1910   1920

SUB-SAHARAN AFRICA

Until the nineteenth century the great continent of Africa, many times the size of Europe, was virtually unknown to most Europeans. Still less was known in Europe about the 150 million people living in Africa. But this state of affairs changed rapidly as a result of the intrepid investigations of some European explorers. The most successful of this group was David Livingstone (1813–1873), a Scottish missionary who crossed the vast region from the Cape of Good Hope to Lake Tanganyika. He began his explorations in 1853 and "discovered" Victoria Falls and the Zambezi River. After his death in 1873, his work in the interior was carried on by Henry M. Stanley (1841–1904), the British explorer and journalist who had located Livingstone in 1871 and had with classic British understatement greeted him, "Dr. Livingstone, I presume."

The European Onslaught

The comparative ease with which Europeans took and divided the continent may give the impression that there were few effective leaders among the Africans. There were many, especially among the Bantu people of southeastern Africa. But African tribes and nations lacked sufficient unity to mount an effective resistance to the Europeans in the nineteenth century.

Toward the end of the eighteenth century the Bantus made contact with the white civilization that spread from the Cape. After 1820, as black populations increased and room for expansion diminished, 2 million people became engulfed in a vast, bloody terror. In this fiery crucible, newly emerging black rulers forged many scattered clans into a few powerful states. The mightiest of these strong men was Shaka, king of the Zulus.

Born in 1787, an illegitimate son of a minor chief, Shaka spent a miserable childhood as an outcast among his mother's relatives. As a youth he became a warrior in the army of Dingiswayo, a powerful chief, who had learned some military tactics from the English and traded with the Portuguese. In his first battle Shaka distinguished himself and was promoted to captain. He soon became supreme commander, succeeded his father as chief, and later became supreme commander of northern Natal. By 1824 he governed

→ Shaka, Zulu chief and military and political leader, holds the traditional Zulu *assagai*, or sword.

250,000 people along the coast between the Pongola and Umzimbubu Rivers.

Shaka was a complex and magnetic personality. He dabbled in magic and witchcraft as well as capricious statecraft. He was customarily attended by executioners who were casually ordered to dispose of those who displeased him. He also was responsible for incidents of mass murder. Yet Zulu traditions have always portrayed him as a folk hero, one who cared for his soldiers and his people and who could cover 80 miles a day and celebrate all night. Whites who encountered him were appalled by his cruelty and amazed by his dignity, honesty, and intelligence.

Hundreds of isolated clans were drawn into his nation. Shaka revolutionized the Zulu army by introducing the "stabbing spear," using mass, disciplined infantry tactics, and perfecting the regimental organization begun under Dingiswayo. He tried to transform the ancient pattern of his society, based on kinship, into a territorial state under one absolute ruler, whose subchiefs lost most of their power. He was well on the way to leading his people beyond family and clan loyalty to national consciousness when he was assassinated in 1828.

His empire successfully resisted expanding white civilization for half a century after his death, and his legacy lived on to enable his successors to wage the most successful wars ever fought by blacks against Europeans. In 1879 the Zulus under King Cetshwayo defeated a British force, killing 700 soldiers, 130 colonists, and hundreds of their African allies, at Isandlwana.

In 1870 the Europeans controlled only 10 percent of the continent. The two most important foreign holdings were at the geographical extremes of the continent: French-administered Algeria in the north, and the Cape Colony, governed by Great Britain, in the south. Most of the other European holdings were mere coastal ports along West Africa. There were also strong political forces in Africa. In present-day Nigeria there was the Muslim Fulani Empire, created by Usman dan Fodio (1754–1817). In Ethiopia, Theodore II and Menelik II built a united state. However, after 1870 there were neither enough Shakas nor Zulus to block the advancing Europeans.

One of the first European leaders to act was King Leopold II of Belgium. In 1876 he organized the International Africa Association and brought the explorer Stanley into his service. The association, composed of scientists and explorers from all nations, ostensibly was intended to serve humanitarian purposes. But the crafty king had other motives. Representing the association, Stanley went to the Congo where he made treaties with several African chiefs and, by 1882, obtained over 900,000 square miles of territory.[1]

Britain's occupation of Egypt and the Belgian acquisition of the Congo moved Bismarck in 1884 to call a conference of the major European powers to discuss potential problems of unregulated African colonization. The assembly, meeting in Berlin, paid lip service to humanitarianism by condemning the slave trade, prohibiting the sale of liquor and firearms in certain areas, and expressing concern for proper religious instruction for the Africans. Then the participants moved to matters that they considered to be much more important.

They set down the rules of competition by which the great powers were to be guided in their search for colonies. They agreed that the area along the Congo River was to be administered by Leopold of Belgium, but that it was to be a neutral territory with free trade and navigation. No nation was to stake out claims in Africa without first notifying the other powers of its intention. No territory could be claimed unless it was effectively occupied, and all disputes were to be settled by arbitration.

In spite of these declarations, the competitors often ignored the rules. On several occasions, war was barely avoided. The humanitarian

→ Zulu warriors under Cetshwayo, Shaka's nephew and king of the Zulus from 1873 to 1879, attacked and destroyed the British garrison at Isandlwana in 1879.

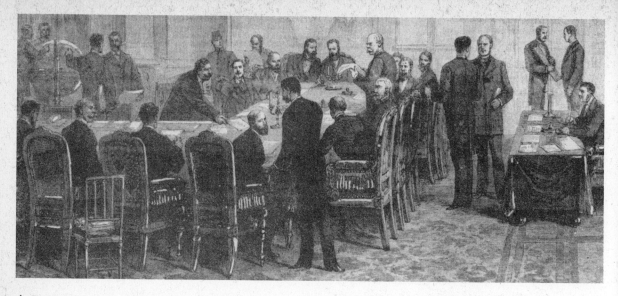

→ Representatives of 14 nations, including the United States, met in Berlin in 1884 to set new rules to govern their "scramble for Africa." No representative from Africa participated in the conference.

rules were generally ignored. The methods Europeans used to acquire lands continued in many cases to involve the deception of the Africans. European colonists got huge land grants by giving uneducated chiefs treaties they could not read and whose contents they were not permitted to understand. In return, the natives were rewarded with bottles of gin, red handkerchiefs, and fancy dress costumes. The comparison between the European treaty methods and those of the Americans in the negotiations with the Native American tribes is all too apparent.

The ethical and cultural differences between the Africans and the Europeans were especially vast regarding the subject of land ownership. Since in many cases Africans reserved ownership of the land to tribes, allowing individuals only the use of it, chiefs granted land to European settlers with no idea that they were disposing of more than its temporary use. When the settlers later claimed ownership of the land, the natives were indignant, feeling that the tribe had been robbed of land, contrary to tribal law.

Division of Africa

14 European imperialists divided Africa themselves, with two exceptions. Only d Ethiopia remained independent.

Shortly after the Berlin conference, King Leopold organized his African territories into the African Free State, subject to his control alone. He began to exploit the colony's economic resources by granting concessions to private companies, reserving for his own administration an extensive rubber-producing area ten times as large as Belgium. A system of forced labor was introduced, and soon stories of filthy work camps, horrible whippings, and other atrocities leaked out of the "Free State," which was undergoing the process of "civilization" as the Belgians referred to it. In the face of a rising tide of international outrage, Leopold was forced to turn the "Free State" over to the Belgian government in 1908. The conditions of the colony, renamed the Belgian Congo, improved under the direct administration of the government.

In the 1880s Germany acquired three colonies on the west coast of Africa: German Southwest Africa, Togoland, and Cameroons. They made their most important gains, however, on the east coast of the continent. German penetration there was largely the work of one man, Carl Peters, a student of British colonization methods. In 1884 he and three other colonial enthusiasts disguised as British workers and set out on a secret mission to eastern Africa. Peters succeeded in obtaining treaties from local chiefs, which

Lord Lugard Justifies European Imperialism in Africa

Lord Lugard gave as eloquent and effective a rationale for European imperialism in Africa as one can find. His argument is a model of elevated self serving.

The "Scramble for Africa" by the nations of Europe—an incident without parallel in the history of the world—was due to the growing commercial rivalry, which brought home to civilised nations the vital necessity of securing the only remaining fields for industrial enterprise and expansion. It is well, then, to realise that it is for our *advantage*—and not alone at the dictates of duty—that we have undertaken responsibilities in East Africa. It is in order to foster the growth of the trade of this country, and to find an outlet for our manufactures and our surplus energy, that our far-seeing statesmen and our commercial men advocate colonial expansion.

There are some who say we have no *right* in Africa at all, that "it belongs to the natives." I hold that our right is the necessity that is upon us to provide for our ever-growing population—either by opening new fields for emigration, or by providing work and employment which the development of over-sea extension entails—and to stimulate trade by finding new markets, since we know what misery trade depression brings at home.

While thus serving our own interests as a nation, we may, by selecting men of the right stamp for the control of new territories, bring at the same time many advantages to Africa. Nor do we deprive the natives of their birthright of freedom, to place them under a foreign yoke. It has ever been the key-note of British colonial method to rule through and by the natives, and it is this method, in contrast to the arbitrary and uncompromising rule of Germany, France, Portugal, and Spain, which has been the secret of our success as a colonising nation, and has made us welcomed by tribes and peoples in Africa, who ever rose in revolt against the other nations named. In Africa, moreover, there is among the people a natural inclination to submit to a higher authority. That intense detestation of control which animates our Teutonic races does not exist among the tribes of Africa, and if there is any authority that we replace, it is the authority of the Slavers and Arabs, or the intolerable tyranny of the "dominant tribe."

From Captain F. D. Lugard, *The Rise of Our East African Empire*, vol. I (London: William Blackwood and Sons, 1893).

---

gave him control of 60,000 square miles. The next year, Bismarck proclaimed the region to be German East Africa.

The British had been laying claims to the region directly north of Peters's concessions. Contradictory German and British claims were settled amicably in 1886 and 1890. After the agreements, which included the British concession of the strategic Helgoland Island in the North Sea, the British held Uganda along the shores of Lake Victoria, British East Africa (later known as Kenya), the rich spice island of Zanzibar, and the area of Nyasaland. Germany's claim to its protectorate in East Africa (later called Tanganyika, now Tanzania) was recognized by the British.

Meanwhile, by 1884 the British had gained control over a stretch of African coast fronting on the Gulf of Aden. This protectorate (British Somaliland) was of great strategic value since it guarded the lower approach to the Suez Canal. Equally important were the headwaters of the Nile, situated in the area known later as the Anglo-Egyptian Sudan. In 1898 the British gained control of this area. Among the British acquisitions on the west coast of Africa, the most important were the territories around the mouth of the Niger, stretching back toward the Sudan. These British possessions included Gambia, Sierra Leone, the Gold Coast, and Nigeria.

During this same period British influence in southern Africa had expanded northward from

→ An 1892 cartoon from *Punch* captures the dream of empire builder Cecil Rhodes for British domination of Africa from "Cape to Cairo."

Cape Colony to German East Africa. The main force behind this drive came from the capitalist Cecil Rhodes, who dreamed of an uninterrupted corridor of British territory from the Cape of Good Hope to Cairo.

If overpopulation, lack of trade, and widespread poverty had been the most compelling reasons for gaining colonies, Italy should have obtained the most extensive areas in Africa. But Italy emerged from the scramble for colonies with very little territory. The Italians gained a piece of the Red Sea coast and a slice of barren and desolate land on the Indian Ocean. But these areas were of little value without the rich plateau

of Abyssinia (Ethiopia) in the hinterland. An attempt to take the ancient empire in 1896 ended in the humiliating destruction of a 20,000-man Italian army.

Building on Louis Napoleon's ambitions, France continued in 1884 developing a colonial program by acquiring a large section of equatorial Africa along the right bank of the Congo River. From trading posts along the west coast of the continent, France pushed into the interior and obtained most of the basins of the Senegal and Niger Rivers. Expeditions from France's north African holdings penetrated the Sahara. Although France did not succeed in getting to the Nile, by 1900 it controlled the largest empire in Africa, one that stretched eastward from the Atlantic to the western Sudan and southward to the Congo River. The French also took control of the large island of Madagascar in the south Indian Ocean. They completed their colonial gains in 1911—over German protests—by making Morocco a French protectorate.

Costs and Benefits

Africa's wealth surpassed the hopes of the most avid imperialist. By the first decade of this century the continent was the world's greatest producer of gold and diamonds. Rich resources of tin, phosphates, and copper had also been discovered. Africa supplied large amounts of rubber, coffee, and cotton. European imperialists gained not only huge territories and vast reserves of raw materials; they also gained the labor of millions of Africans.

The Africans who came under European domination had to make severe adjustments. The impact of European imperialism was profound and widespread. European imperialists divided Africa by drawing lines on a map with total disregard for traditional political and social structures. For the first time, many villagers were forced to pay money taxes to a distant central authority. In most cases, Africans had lived within a small tribal area of law and political affiliation. With the advent of imperial rule, dozens of formerly distinct—and often antagonistic—tribes were brought together, as in the case of Nigeria, into one colony. In other cases of imperialism, large tribes were split into two or three European colonial segments. Colonies were not usually unified nations, a fact that would have bloody consequences as they became independent after World War II.

The colonization process in Africa, undertaken by a dynamic, self-confident, and technologically advanced civilization, severely disrupted cultures that had been isolated from the mainstream of world affairs. Kinship and family ties were weakened when villagers sought jobs in distant towns and mines. In some areas as many as 50 percent of the young males sought employment in order to pay the new hut taxes or to buy cheap but enticing European wares.

Their mothers, wives, and sisters left behind received a double shock. They had to carry on the increased work load and maintain the family unit single-handedly, with an enormous increase in their hours per week of labor to feed their families. However, they also saw their roles diminished as European notions of the "woman's place" displaced them from their traditional positions of social influence. In the new export markets, men monopolized the raising of cash crops, cutting

→ An Ethiopian painting of the Battle of Adowa in 1896 in which the army of Emperor Menelik II defeated the invading Italians. At the top of the painting, Saint George intercedes for the Ethiopians.

women out of economic opportunities. Undoubtedly, wages from absent husbands did help raise standards of living, but the effect on family ties and tribal loyalties was destructive.

The old ways of life were most disrupted in colonies that attracted European settlement, such as Kenya and Southern Rhodesia. In such areas, Africans were confined to "native reserves" or to segregated areas in the towns. On occasion large tracts of land were allocated exclusively for European use. It was in these societies that racial tensions most rapidly developed.

For a half century after the scramble for colonies began, the incidence of social change was uneven. In some remote areas, Africans may never have seen white persons, let alone worked for them. But tribal life was gradually transformed by the introduction of new forms of land tenure, enforcement of alien systems of law, and the growth of the money economy. In an attempt to imitate the technologically and militarily superior Europeans, many Africans tried to adopt the ways of their new rulers. As a result, some of them became "detribalized", and often bewildered, as they were also alienated from much of their traditional culture but unable to understand fully and be part of the new. Although the transformation of Africa was probably inevitable at some point, it was unfortunate that this revolutionary change occurred so quickly, and at the hands of intruders whose motives were so selfish. Much too frequently the imperialists disparaged all African culture, dismissing the Africans as barbarous and uncivilized.

Colonialism may have been an abrupt and rude awakening to the new day of the industrialized world, but it did bring several benefits. The arrival of Europeans introduced more peace between the tribes by imposing more efficient law enforcement methods. The international slave trade ended. The Europeans brought in material and technological advances, such as telegraph and telephone communications, railroads, improved harbors, and improved medical standards. European organizational and educational techniques were introduced in the form of better administrative systems, widespread schools, and a money economy. All of these things may have been necessary to enable Africa to enter the modern age, but they came at a very high price.

NORTH AFRICA

At the beginning of the nineteenth century, the Ottoman Empire controlled—albeit tenuously—all of the African coast along the Mediterranean, with the exception of Morocco. The decline of Turkish power, however, made the area virtually self-governing or subject to European pressures. By 1914 all of North Africa from Casablanca to Cairo had come under direct European control.

Egypt

Europe had long been fascinated by Egypt, and Napoleon's invasion of that country had increased interest in both its historic sights and its economic potential. As the Ottoman control declined in the first quarter of the century, Mehmet Ali came to be the dominant figure in the country. He was able to increase his authority in the theoretically Turkish-controlled land and carry out economic and agricultural changes. By the 1830s he had expanded his power to the point where the great powers had to step in to save the Turks from his forces.

The dynamism of Mehmet Ali, however, did not touch the life of the Egyptian *fellah* (peasant), who lived amid poverty, disease, and ignorance. Most Egyptians continued to depend on the narrow green strip along the Nile River for survival, just as they had for thousands of years. Mehmet Ali's successes did not bring Egypt prosperity.

In the 1850s the government had to borrow a substantial amount of money from Great Britain to provide basic services. Dependence on foreign finance increased as the Egyptians tried to build railroads, schools, and factories to improve their economy. One of the foremost projects undertaken was that of the Suez Canal, built in cooperation with the French from 1859 to 1869. The more the Egyptians built however, the more their debts increased. By 1875 financial difficulties forced Ismail, ruler of Egypt, to sell his block of 175,000 shares in the Suez Canal. The stock was snapped up by Disraeli, the astute prime minister of Great Britain. This maneuver gave Britain virtual control of this essential water link between Europe and the East.

When Ismail tried to repudiate his debts in 1879, Great Britain and France took over financial control of Egypt. The British and French forced Ismail to abdicate in favor of his son. The Egyptian ruling classes and officer corps did not want foreign rule, and violence broke out in 1881 and 1882. The worst outbreak came at Alexandria, where many Europeans lost their lives during rioting. The British, acting unilaterally, then routed the Egyptians at Tell el-Kebir. After that, the British took responsibility for the running of the country.

To reorganize Egyptian finances, eliminate corruption from the administration, and improve the all-important (for the British) cotton industry, Sir Evelyn Baring, later named Lord Cromer, was sent to Egypt to oversee the country's affairs from 1883 to 1907. He overhauled the system of government, curbed the use of forced labor, and carried out substantial public works projects. Some authorities have maintained that the best record of British imperialism is to be found in Egypt. European technology, governmental expertise, and financial practices aided the country's development. Despite this, in the first years of the twentieth century, Egyptians were voicing a growing demand for self-government.

Other States of North Africa

In Tripoli, Tunis, Algeria, and Morocco, the Europeans also made steady inroads during the nineteenth century. These four areas lacked the fertile green belt along a river such as Egypt possessed along the Nile. They also lacked both the economic basis and political leaders to attempt such grandiose projects as those pursued by the Egyptians. By the end of the century the rest of the north coast of Africa came under the control of the Italians and the French.

The area around Tripoli had gained its independence from the Turks in the first part of the eighteenth century. For the rest of the century the area served as a base for Mediterranean pirates. In 1835 it once again came under Turkish control where it remained until the Italians focused their attention on the area at the end of the century. The Italians declared war on the Turks, after having gained the consent of the great powers. After a more difficult campaign than the Italians had expected, the Turks ceded the area to them in 1912.

The Ottomans had taken control of Tunis in 1575 and held on to it until the French estab-

The Earl of Cromer on Egypt

The Earl of Cromer looked back after his career in Egypt and claimed the following benefits of European domination.

No one can fully realise the extent of the change which has come over Egypt since the British occupation took place unless he is in some degree familiar with the system under which the country was governed in the days of Ismail Pasha. The contrast between now and then is, indeed, remarkable. A new spirit has been instilled into the population of Egypt. Even the peasant has learnt to scan his rights. Even the Pasha has learnt that others besides himself have rights which must be respected. The courbash may hang on the walls of the Moudirieh, but the Moudir no longer dares to employ it on the backs of the fellaheen. For all practical purposes, it may be said that the hateful corvèe system has disappeared. Slavery has virtually ceased to exist. The halcyon days of the adventurer and the usurer are past. Fiscal burthens have been greatly relieved. Everywhere law reigns supreme. Justice is no longer bought and sold. Nature, instead of being spurned and neglected, has been wooed to bestow her gifts on mankind. She has responded to the appeal. The waters of the Nile are now utilised in an intelligent manner. Means of locomotion have been improved and extended. The soldier has acquired some pride in the uniform which he wears. He has fought as he never fought before. The sick man can be nursed in a well-managed hospital. The lunatic is no longer treated like a wild beast. The punishment awarded to the worst criminal is no longer barbarous. Lastly, the schoolmaster is abroad, with results which are as yet uncertain, but which cannot fail to be important.

All these things have been accomplished by the small body of Englishmen who, in various capacities, and with but little direct support or assistance from their Government or its representative, have of late years devoted their energies to the work of Egyptian regeneration. They have had many obstacles to encounter. Internationalism and Pashadom have stood in the path at every turn. But these forces, though they could retard, have failed to arrest the progress of the British reformer. The opposition which he has had to encounter, albeit very embarrassing, merely acted on his system as a healthy tonic. An eminent French literary critic has said that the end of a book should recall its commencement to the mind of the reader. Acting on this principle, I may remind those who have perused these pages that I began this work by stating that, although possibly counter-parts to all the abuses which existed, and which to some extent still exist in Egypt, may be found in other countries, the conditions under which the work of Egyptian reform has been undertaken were very peculiar. The special difficulties which have resulted from those conditions have but served to bring out in strong relief one of the main characteristics of the Anglo-Saxon race. Other nations might have equally well conceived the reforms which were necessary. It required the singular political adaptability of Englishmen to execute them. A country and a nation have been partially regenerated, in spite of a perverse system of government which might well have seemed to render regeneration almost impossible.

From Earl of Cromer, *Modern Egypt*, vol. 2 (New York: Macmillan, 1908).

lished a protectorate there in 1881. As in the case with Tripoli, the power of the local government was weak, and the coastline harbored pirates and thieves. As had been the case in Egypt, the Tunisian government became indebted financially to European lenders, even before the French took over. After 1881 most of the country's wealth went abroad, and most of the population lived in desperate poverty.

Algeria's coastline also served as a base for piracy from the sixteenth to the nineteenth centuries. In the 1820s the French complained forcefully of the pirates' activities along the French coast. When in 1827 the Algerian ruler insulted the French consul in public by hitting him with a fly swatter, France used the incident as a suitable pretext to enter the country. Paris sent down a large army to occupy Algeria, but it took 17 years to put down the fierce Berber tribesmen. Algeria was then incorporated as an integral part of the French state.

From the 1840s to the end of the century French interests also dominated in Morocco, the first country to experience overseas expansion by Europe. But European states contested the area until 1911, and the Moroccan question increased tensions between Germany and France up to the beginning of World War I.

In general, the North African countries west of Egypt lacked the vigorous leadership, strong economies, and unified populations needed to stand off the European advances. Geographical obstacles were perhaps the major issue, as a nomadic population had to search continuously for the scarce means of existence.

THE MIDDLE EAST

In 1800 the Islamic world stretched from the Atlantic Ocean to the Pacific, in a broad band that reached across North Africa, the Middle East, central Asia, and down to Indonesia. The Islamic religion retained its original vigor, and the Islamic world followed similar religious and cultural forms. This came from a way of life based on the Koran emphasizing daily prayers, fasting, and pilgrimages to Mecca. By the late nineteenth century, more than 175 million Muslims performed daily religious duties. Whatever their race or nationality, Muslims shared the same sacred language, law, morality, social structure, and institutions. Every year the number of believers traveling to Mecca grew. It is estimated that by 1900 more than 50,000 Indians and 20,000 Malays were making the trip each year.

The Islamic world mirrored the great diversity of peoples, environments, and external pressures that affected the faithful from Ceuta in Morocco to Djakarta in Indonesia. Even in religious matters, doctrinal differences split devout Muslims into rival sects, and these differences were as devastating as those afflicting Christianity.

Political fragmentation, economic weakness, and inadequate communications and transportation links made it difficult for the Islamic world to compete with the Europeans. The diverse populations within the Islamic world, including Arabs, Indians, Berbers, and Egyptians, shared religion, culture, and language, but not political unity. An equally serious problem was economic weakness. Consisting principally of deserts and arid lands, the Islamic world clung to outdated agricultural techniques long abandoned by the West. Islam's prohibition of usury hampered the growth of modern capitalist institutions (banks, for example) and the evolution of a middle class. Despite the fact that Muslims occupied such strategic locations as areas around the Bosporus and the Dardanelles, the Suez, the overland route to India, and the Persian Gulf region, the Islamic world suffered from poor communications and transportation systems.

During the nineteenth century, the Ottoman Empire, Persia, and Afghanistan could not build an adequate political or economic base from which to defend themselves against Britain or Russia. The modern state structure—with its professional bureaucrats, broadly based nationalism and patriotism, ideologies, mass literacy, and civil law structure—did not exist in the Islamic world.

To a large degree the major occupations of nineteenth-century western Europe, including research scientist, party politician, state functionary, technologist, and industrial worker, and social flexibility for men and women were not present among the Muslim nations either. Instead, the function of warrior remained primary, and political life fluctuated between the despotic and the nonchalant. Corruption, social decay, lack of education and literacy also blocked effective government. In short, the Middle Eastern states could not effectively mobilize their resources or move their citizens. The Europeans moved in to take advantage of the Islamic world's vulnerability.[2]

The Disintegrating Ottoman Empire

Even though the Ottoman Empire had been in a state of decline since the end of the seventeenth century, 200 years later it was still the largest and most prestigious realm in the Islamic world. The

Sultan ruled territory extending from North Africa to the Indian Ocean. But the sultan's control over 40 million people living there was often weak and sporadic.

The lines of power and communication to the empire's far corners were not dependable. The farther one went from Constantinople the less secure was Turkish control. At its inception in the sixteenth century the Ottoman administration had been a model of effectiveness. Over the next two centuries it declined as bribery and favoritism replaced the merit basis for administration. The armed forces, once the most feared in all Europe, lacked discipline and came to be as much a threat to the sultan as to foreign enemies.

More than most, the Ottoman state was based on war, and to ensure its stability the Turks needed the momentum of continuous victory. However, their very success as fighters doomed them. They had pushed Ottoman control to its extreme limits of the Atlas and Caucasus mountains. Short-range wars of conquest were no longer possible, and the warrior class became more concerned with its land and privi-

leges than defense of the faith. In addition, by the late seventeenth century the Europeans had become stronger and for the first time were able to defeat the Turks. Europe profited from the Scientific Revolution, the Enlightenment, and industrialization. The Ottoman Empire chose not to pursue these developments, nor did it look to take advantage of the forces of nationalism and patriotism to mobilize its diverse populations. As the western states improved their strength, the Turks could not change quickly enough to remain competitive.[3]

Discontent with the Turks' rule resulted in revolts in the 1630s (the Druse), the 1740s (the Wahhabi), and 1769 (the revolt led by Ali Bey Al-Kabir). Instead of addressing the causes of these major rebellions, the Turks rededicated themselves to the maintenance of their 500-year-old foundation of life and law—Islam.[4] In the nineteenth century this was not a sufficiently flexible basis for competition in the international arena.

From the 1790s on, attempts were made to reform the Turkish system. The Koran was the foundation for Islam, and although it was the

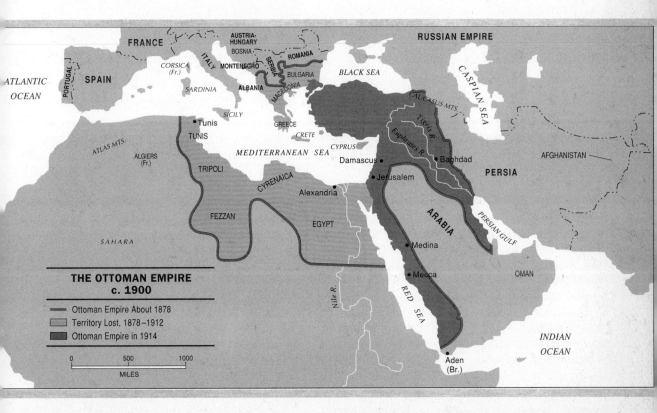

THE OTTOMAN EMPIRE
c. 1900

— Ottoman Empire About 1878
▢ Territory Lost, 1878–1912
■ Ottoman Empire in 1914

0   500   1000
MILES

most important basis for a Muslim's daily existence, it did not contain all of the answers to the questions of technological change. Firearms and artillery had been accepted from the infidel for centuries because they could be used in defense of the faith, yet the clock and the printing press, two symbols of Western advance, were not allowed. No printing by Muslims was allowed in Istanbul in either Turkish or Arabic until 1729, and then the publication of books was sporadic until the end of the century.

After the 1780s, foreign influences were increasingly felt in the Ottoman Empire: military advisers and diplomats operated more and more in Constantinople and the sultans began establishing permanent diplomatic posts in Europe. As is the case with developing states today, the military in the empire came to be the most advanced element in society. The training it received in modern technology necessitated the learning of foreign languages and political theory. A whole new group emerged, trained to look beyond the Koran for their information, and even their inspiration.[5]

The power of tradition and the faith made the drive for reform a hesitant one at best. Those who went too fast, such as Sultan Selim III (1789–1807) were overthrown. Later in the nineteenth century, sultans who wanted to become more competitive with the Europeans were hampered in their reform attempts by the administrative chaos of the empire. Reforms rarely reached further than a day's ride from Istanbul.

Perhaps sensing the weakening at the center and taking advantage of the changes brought by the Napoleonic era, the peoples of the Balkans began to work for independence. The Montenegrins, who never acknowledged Ottoman domination, received recognition of their independent status in 1799. In response to a breakdown of Ottoman administration, the Serbs rose in revolt in 1804, followed by the Greeks in 1821, the Romanians in the 1850s, and the Bulgarians in the 1870s. Russia continued to pressure the Turks while the other powers intruded more and more on the sultan's affairs. Vassals in Albania, Egypt, and Macedonia rebelled. Particularly serious was Mehmet Ali's challenge in the 1820s and 1830s when he took Crete and Syria. Not only did he threaten Istanbul, he pushed his gains to the Persian Gulf and Indian Ocean. By the 1840s a

→ Eugène Delacroix, *Massacre of Chios* (1824). European liberals and romantics such as Delacroix supported the Greeks in their struggle for independence from the Turks, who were seen as cruel oppressors.

combination of the great powers pushed him back to Egypt, where he remained as a viceroy.

The empire's weakness was especially exposed in the prelude to the Crimean War when Russia and France squabbled over the holy places of Christianity. Istanbul served merely as an arena in which Europe's diplomats debated the Turks' fate. Even though the Turks emerged from the turmoil with their great power status guaranteed, it was apparent to all that the empire was kept alive only because the Europeans could think of no other alternative for the strategic state. In 1860 France gained the right to intervene in Syria. In 1874 the Ottoman financial structure collapsed under the pressure of huge foreign loans, just at the time of renewed uprisings in the Balkans.

Portfolio Seven

Art of the Americas, Australia, Africa, and Asia

→ Although he is probably best known as the inventor of the telegraph, Samuel F. B. Morse also studied painting and longed for recognition as an artist. In the *Exhibition Gallery of the Louvre* (1832–1833), Morse has copied in miniature a number of the museum's masterpieces, including works by Leonardo, Titian, Raphael, Rubens, Van Dyck, and others. Visitors and copyists occupy the foreground of the painting. Eventually Morse abandoned painting to pursue his interests in science and mechanics.

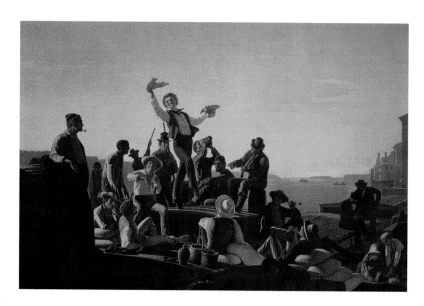

The democratic genre art of the 1830s in the United States expressed the romantic adventure of the rapidly expanding frontier of Jacksonian America. George Caleb Bingham graphically portrayed lively images of frontier life in his paintings of riverboatmen, local politicians, and domestic scenes. *The Jolly Flatboatmen in Port* (1857) is one of a series of paintings of the same subject.

Asher Durand was a founder, along with Thomas Cole, of the Hudson River school of American art. The name is applied to a number of nineteenth-century U.S. landscape painters who worked mainly in the region of the Catskill Mountains and the Hudson River. Characteristic of their work is careful attention to detail and a sense of wonder at the breathtaking beauty of the unfolding American landscape. *Kindred Spirits* (1849) is Durand's memorial to Cole. In the work, Cole and the poet William Cullen Bryant are seen admiring the beauty of the Catskills.

⤍ The great American architect of the twentieth century, Frank Lloyd Wright adapted the structure, materials, and plan of a building to its natural setting so that the land and the building became a unified whole. In the Kaufman House, *Falling Water*, at Bear Run, Pennsylvania (1936), the overhanging concrete slabs blend harmoniously with the rocky ledges, while the interior of the house is a continuous flow of interrelated and interpenetrating areas.

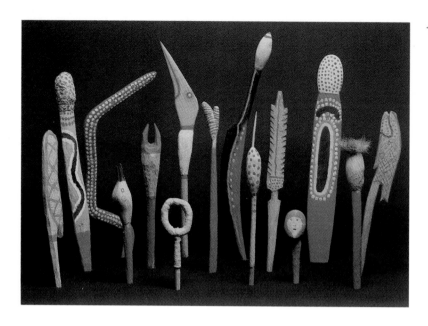

→ These Australian aboriginal sculptures were discovered near Lake Eyre in southern Australia in the early part of the twentieth century. The style of the figures suggests that aboriginal art was free of outside influence but did reflect the close bond the aborigines acknowledged between themselves and nature.

→ Diego Rivera, *Father Hidalgo and Other Famous Mexicans* (detail from the mural *Independence and Revolution*). Mexican painter and muralist Diego Rivera integrated European and native Amerindian artistic methods and traditions in his works of social realism. As artist of the Mexican Revolution, Rivera used his mural to glorify the traditional Mexican cultural heritage, to teach the Mexican people the history of their political struggle, and to celebrate the accomplishments of the revolution.

This carved wooden figure represents King Glé Glé of Abomey, a slaving center and capital of the native African kingdom of Dahomey (now Benin). Glé Glé, a warrior-king who massacred thousands of prisoners, boasted, "I am like the young lion who spreads terror as soon as his teeth grow."

The experience of European imperialism affected all aspects of African life, including art. In the car shown here, an early twentieth-century work from the Congo, a Belgian magnate reclines in the backseat while the African chauffeur drives.

→ This figure is from an album of illustrations of the Javanese *wayang*, or shadow theater. All attributes of the highly stylized figures—facial features, hairstyle, costume, and ornaments—indicate the physical and mental qualities of the character represented. The illustrations were probably drawn as a guide to the *wayang* characters, of which there were more than 600, for European observers. The figure shown here is that of the nobleman Raden Djaya Erawan. Shadow play stories derived both from Javanese sources and Hindu religious traditions.

→ Phoenix robe, an embroidered satin gown made for Tzu Hsi, Empress Dowager of China, known near the end of her reign as the Old Buddha. The robe, which dates from the end of the nineteenth century, would have been worn over some and under other embroidered gowns and jackets of silk and satin.

➷ This contemporary Japanese woodcut records the events surrounding the arrival of Commodore Matthew Perry in Japan in 1853. The panels surrounding the map at center depict Perry's landing at the seaport of Uraga, an American warship anchored in the harbor, Perry's men on parade, a group of *samurai* in battle attire, and a sumo wrestling contest.

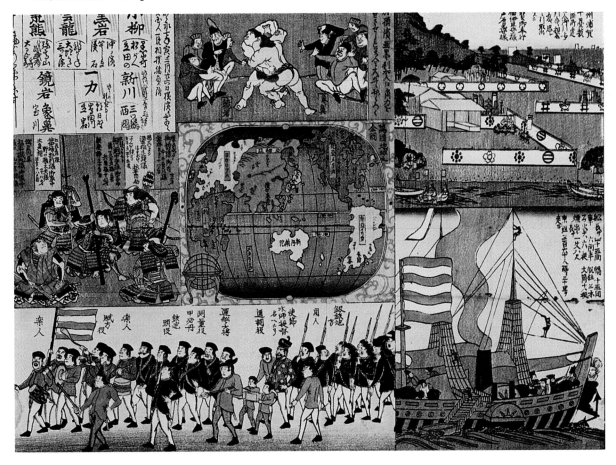

→ Kawai Gyokudo, *Colored Rain* (1940). This landscape painting, in color on silk, is characteristic of Gyokudo's style, which combines traditional Japanese techniques with Western methods of depiction. The mistlike rain falling over the scene helps to suggest the poetic atmosphere of the Japanese landscape.

Young Turks

In 1876 Midhat Pasha, a dedicated reformer and provincial governor, unveiled a plan for a new, Western-style political structure in the Ottoman Empire. Under his scheme the empire was declared to be a unitary state with the guarantees of free press, freedom of conscience, equality under the law, and equal taxation. In addition, he proposed the creation of an Ottoman citizenship, a step away from the traditional theocratic basis of power. The plan was proclaimed in Istanbul in December 1876 and Midhat Pasha became grand vizir. Unfortunately for the empire, Abdul Hamid II—the new sultan who came to the throne soon after—destroyed the reform plans, dismissed Midhat Pasha as grand vizir, and suspended the parliament.

By the spring of 1877, Abdul Hamid was trying to rule as his predecessors had four centuries earlier—absolutely. Spies spread throughout the country to track down liberals and other opponents. Censorship was applied and those who had worked for reforms disappeared mysterious-

→ Abdul Hamid II. Widespread discontent with his oppressive rule lent strength to the reform movement of the Young Turks, who ultimately deposed the sultan in 1909.

ly or were forced into exile. At a time when he needed unity and change to preserve his crumbling holdings, Abdul Hamid chose to split up potential opponents and destroy them. The sultan's basic problem was not the reform movement, but the reactionary nature of his policies.

The sultan faced severe challenges on all fronts. Throughout his realm nationalist movements threatened his rule. The European powers continued their economic and political pressures on his holdings: France annexed Tunis in 1881, Britain occupied Egypt in 1882, and Italy reached for Tripoli in 1900. Remaining under Turkish rule were the Arabs of the Middle East, primarily Muslim in religion, with significant Christian minorities in some areas. They were beginning to be affected by the same nationalistic spirit that had spread throughout nineteenth-century Europe. They joined the Balkan nations in pushing for concessions from the weak Ottoman structure. By the beginning of the twentieth century, opposition to the sultan's tyranny and misrule was widespread among his many subjects.

A nucleus of opposition formed among a group of exiled reformers who had been educated in western European universities. In 1902 these opponents, called the Young Turks, and other national groups oppressed by the sultan met in Paris to form a united opposition to Abdul Hamid. They advocated a modernized, Western state with a professional police force, a sound economic policy, and substantial social reforms. They adopted the European clock and recommended broad-ranging educational opportunities and revised dress codes to bring women out of seclusion.

At the same time a number of young army officers joined the Young Turks, giving the movement the military power and coordination it needed for a successful rebellion. In 1908 the Young Turks told the sultan to put the 1876 constitution into effect or else face an armed uprising. Abdul Hamid saw the weakness of his position and agreed to the demands. But after gaining their initial goals, the revolutionaries split deeply over the question of the status of non-Turks in the new regime. Some of the Young Turks wanted to grant full political rights to the minorities, while others advocated severe restrictions. The new parliament that came into existence after the restoration immediately bogged

Young Turks march in triumph after their successful coup and overthrow of the despot Abdul Hamid II and his reactionary government.

down over the rights of subject nationalities. Encouraged by the division within the parliament, the sultan attempted a counterrevolution to regain power. When he turned against the Young Turks—who by this time had gained substantial popular support—he was overthrown in 1909.

Arabs in Syria, Lebanon, and the vast Arabian peninsula were not happy with the new regime. Along with the Albanians in the Balkans, they were repelled by the Young Turks' program of Turkish supremacy and their policy of centralization, which would obviously leave no hopes for Arab home rule. When World War I broke out in 1914, the British, once an Allied victory was assured, had little difficulty in turning the Arab nations against the Turkish sultan.

Other parts of the empire fell away during and after the Young Turk revolt. Between 1908 and 1913, Austria-Hungary annexed Bosnia and Herzegovina, Greece annexed Crete, and Italy—in the course of a short but difficult war—seized Tripoli and Cyrenaica. Finally, in 1912 and 1913, the Balkan nations fought two wars, which resulted in the partitioning of Macedonia. The once mighty Ottoman Empire was finally destroyed.

The "Great Game"

The area between the Caspian Sea and the Persian Gulf served as the focus of conflict between Britain and Russia during the nineteenth century. The attention of these two major powers could not have been welcomed by the two nations caught in the cross fire, Persia and Afghanistan.

Persia (now Iran), one of the more strategically located areas of the Islamic world, contained many different peoples (Turks, Arabs, Persians, Kurds, Jews, and Armenians) and religions (Islam, Zoroastrianism, Judaism, and Armenian Christianity). Ruling over this crossroads area was the Kajar Dynasty, which had to deal with the Russians to the North and the British to the south.

Afghanistan, which lay to the east of Persia, controlled the Khyber Pass, the most direct land route from Russia to British-controlled India. The mountainous country had been divided previously between the Mongols and Persians. By the nineteenth century the shah in Kabul, Afghanistan's capital city, ruled over the tribal confederations that roamed the country.

Russia had begun its advance toward the region in the middle of the sixteenth century. From that time to the present, the Russians have had a deep and abiding interest in the Islamic world to the south. Russia had several motives in pursuing control of this region: it needed a warm-water port, a direct trade route to India, and a defensive buffer zone between European Russia and Asia. Throughout the eighteenth and nineteenth centuries the Russians extended their control across the Black Sea, the Caucasus, and into central Asia to the frontiers of Persia and Afghanistan. Their advance drew the worried attention of the British.

Britain wanted to maintain control of the sea lanes of the eastern Mediterranean, and after 1869 it sought sole access to the Suez Canal. European power politics in the 1840s, 1850s, and 1870s had helped the British thwart the Russian drive to control the Straits, Constantinople, and the eastern Mediterranean. But Russia's expansion across the Urals threatened the British from another flank—through central Asia. British foreign policy in the nineteenth century focused equally on defense of India's land frontiers to the north and protection of the Suez Canal, Red Sea, and the Persian Gulf.

During the first half of the century, Persia and Afghanistan were caught up in armed conflicts with the Russians and the British. The Persians, defeated by the Russians in two wars, lost large amounts of territory and had to pay substantial indemnities. In an attempt to gain control of the Khyber Pass, the British fought the Afghans from 1839 to 1842. In the first part of the conflict a British force numbering about 3000 was massacred. Later, British troops from India took control of the region. Britain's advances were gained by a strong army and controlled by a well-trained colonial government. Persia and Afghanistan weakened as the two major European forces extended their power from north and south.

While Britain consolidated its hold on India, Russia expanded toward the southeast. Many indigenous peoples, such as the Mongols, Afghans, Turkomans, and Tatars, came within Russia's sphere of influence. Their cities—Samarkand, Tashkent, and Bokhara—became tsarist administrative centers.

Russia's advance was won not only by its army, but also by the construction of the Trans–Caspian Railway, which at its completion in 1888 reached 1064 miles into the heart of Asia. The Orenburg–Tashkent railway, completed in 1905, stretched 1185 miles farther. Both lines vastly increased Russia's ability to maintain military pressure on and economic superiority over the area. Inspired by the feats of both the army and the engineers, some Russian imperialists dreamed of conquering Afghanistan and penetrating India itself. The central Asian thrust was part of the "Great Game" between Britain and Russia—Russian pressure against India was designed primarily as a counter against Britain in other areas.[6]

At the end of the nineteenth century Afghanistan and Tibet continued to be serious areas of tension. Effective British pressure blocked Russia's design on Afghanistan and a British military expedition to Lhasa in 1904 countered Russian influence in Tibet. Persia, however, remained a more difficult problem.

The Persian Dilemma

Britain made economic inroads into Persia during the nineteenth century, gaining control of most of the area's mineral wealth and banking operations. The British completed a telegraph line from Lon-

E PERSIAN GULF AREA c. 1900

ssian Territory
tish Territory
ilroads
oposed Russian Railroads

RUSSIA
Kazalinsk
ARAL SEA
Tashkent
Andizhan
Khiva
Bokhara
Samarkand
CASPIAN SEA
Merv
Gunib
Territory given to Afghanistan by Russia and Britain
Kabul
KHYBER PASS
Meshed
y
d
sia
rkey
Tehran
Area under Russian control
AFGHANISTAN
PERSIA
BALUCHISTAN
Kerman
Area under British control
BRITISH INDIA
KUWAIT
Bushire
Bender
PERSIAN GULF
BAHRAIN
QATAR
OMAN
ARABIA
INDIAN OCEAN
0   500
MILES

→ This 1885 cartoon from *Punch* shows the British lion and the Indian tiger watching apprehensively as the Russian bear attacks the Afghan wolf.

don to Persia in 1870, symbolizing the direct tie between Britain and that far-off land.

During the last part of the century, the Persians attempted a program of westernization, complete with a new capital at Tehran. They made major investments to establish hospitals, a school system, as well as an army. But all of this cost money, which the Persians borrowed from the British and the Russians. The great powers, in their turn, gained control of a large part of the country's economy.

The British may have blocked the Russians in other areas, but Persia remained an area of competition. The Royal Navy, based at Aden, was charged with keeping communications routes open from India to the Suez and with protecting the entry to the Red Sea. Along the Arabian coast the British gained control, through treaties with a number of friendly, minuscule sheikdoms such as Muscat, Oman, Bahrain, and Kuwait. The maintenance of this sphere of influence effectively blocked German and French efforts to gain footholds along the Persian Gulf.

Germany had tried unsuccessfully to build a terminus on the Persian Gulf for its projected Berlin-to-Baghdad railroad. In 1903 the British foreign secretary issued what has been called a British Monroe Doctrine over the area: "I say it without hesitation, we should regard the establishment of a naval base or a fortified port in the Per-

→ A contemporary Russian drawing of a construction train on the Trans–Caspian Railway. Completion of this railway allowed Russia to transport and supply troops to central Asia and extend its economic influence in that area.

sian Gulf by any other power as a very grave menace to British interests, and we should certainly resist it by all means at our disposal."[7] Although Britain had discouraged German attempts to build a railroad to Persia, there was still the possibility that the Russian Trans-Caucasian Railway might be extended south through Persia to the warm waters of the Persian Gulf. In this event the tsar's government might not profit commercially only but might also build a naval base that would threaten the British sea route to India.

Persia was in no position to resist Russian pressure. Its government was corrupt and inefficient, and Russia took advantage of its weakness. By the beginning of the twentieth century parts of northern Persia were in the control of the Russians. Tsarist forces trained the Persian army, put up telegraph lines, established a postal system, and developed trade. Some Persian workers crossed into Russia to work in the Caucasus oil fields. The Russian ministry of finance even set up a bank—The Discount and Loan Bank of Persia—with branches in many parts of the nation. This bank loaned the Persian government 60 million rubles and provided 120 million rubles to Persian merchants to enable them to buy Russian goods.

The British government had no desire to see Russia gain power along the Persian Gulf. To counter this threat to the British–Indian lifeline, the British set up the Imperial Bank of Persia in southeastern Persia. At the same they gained a profitable tobacco monopoly.

Persian patriotic reformers carried out a successful revolution in 1906. They established a parliament and initiated reforms, aided by American advisers. This development, plus the changing diplomatic situation in western Europe brought on by the increase in tensions with the Germans brought the two competitors—Britain and Russia—together in 1907 to sign an agreement to end their rivalry in central Asia.

By the terms of the Anglo–Russian entente, Russia agreed to deal with the sovereign of Afghanistan only through the British government. Great Britain agreed to refrain from occupying or annexing Afghanistan so long as it fulfilled its treaty obligations. Persia became an Anglo–Russian holding, split up into three zones: the northern part was a Russian sphere of influence, the middle section was a neutral zone, and the southern portion was under British control.

The partnership was, however, only a marriage of convenience brought on by larger pressures in Europe. Russia continued intervening in Persian domestic politics, throwing its support to the shah, who was willing to do its bidding. Though upset by the Russians' activities, the British chose not to alienate them because they needed to build an alliance to counter Germany. Britain needed Russia's help and abided by the compromise arrangement in Persia.

The nineteenth-century extension of European state power over the Middle East reflected each great power's views of its own trade and defense needs. But the colonial powers ignored the desires, goals, and legitimate demands of the indigenous population.

CONCLUSION

By 1914 the European states had established their primacy over Africa and the Middle East. There was no doubting the nature and extent of Europe's material and technological dominance over the region. While thousands of Africans worked in European-owned mines, thousands of Persians crossed into Russia to work in tsarist oil fields. Both groups were begrudging witnesses to and labor sources for Europe's economic strength. While financiers in London, Berlin, and Paris skimmed the profits off the top of their newly controlled areas, European officials and diplomats dictated policy for most of the region.

Even before 1914, however, the forces that would eventually remove European dominance in the next half century were at work. These forces gained strength from European ideals. All of the apologists in Europe who spoke of carrying the "white man's burden" or of spreading "civilization" to the "lesser peoples" had a major blind spot in their world view. They confused technological and material strength with cultural strength. There could, of course, be no doubting the European material superiority over the Middle East and Africa. There was no military, economic, or technological arena in which the non-Europeans could claim superiority by 1914.

Yet the identities of the peoples caught under European dominance did not disappear. Rather, under the influence of—and in friction with—the European ideologies and political structures that accompanied the diplomats and industrialists, their identities became more sharply defined.

The rapid expansion of European primacy over Africa and the Middle East failed to establish firm roots. Europeanization remained a surface phenomenon, affecting mainly the material aspects of life. Islam retained its strength and the African peoples the essence of their identities. The contact of both areas with European state systems was immediately tragic, but not fatal. Armed with the technological, intellectual, and political lessons they learned from the Europeans, the Middle East and Africa could hope, someday, to compete on an equal basis.

→ Suggestions for Reading

Kenneth Ingham, *A History of East Africa* (Longman, 1962) and J. D. Fage, *An Introduction to the History of West Africa* (Cambridge, 1969) are useful studies, as is J. B. Webster and A. A. Boahen, *History of West Africa* (Praeger, 1967). See also R. Hallett, *Africa to 1975* (Michigan, 1974); J. D. Fage, *History of West Africa* (Cambridge, 1969); Ronald Robinson and J. Gallagher, *Africa and the Victorians* (St. Martin's, 1969); and Peter Duignan and L. H. Gann, eds., *Colonialism in Africa* (Cambridge, 1969), which contains perceptive essays on the motivations for imperialism. John D. Omer-Cooper, *The Zulu Aftermath* (Northwestern, 1966) remains the best study of Shaka and

his drive to build a united country. A clear and concise coverage of the European carving up of Africa is Thomas Pakenham, *The Scramble for Africa* (Random House, 1991). The nature of Britain's imperial mission in Africa is shown in the lives of three men: F. Gross, *Rhodes of Africa* (Praeger, 1957); Lord Elton, *Gordon of Khartoum* (Knopf, 1955); and M. Perham, *Lugard, The Years of Adventure* (Archon, 1968).

R. H. Davison, *Turkey* (Prentice-Hall, 1968) is a brief, well-written survey. Bernard Lewis provides excellent analyses in *The Emergence of Modern Turkey*, 2nd ed. (Oxford, 1968). William Miller, *The Ottoman Empire and Its Successors, 1801–1927* (Octagon, 1966) and L. S. Stavrianos, *The Balkans Since 1453* (Holt, Rinehart & Winston, 1961) provide thorough treatment of the multiethnic challenge facing the Turks. P. Coles, *The Ottoman Impact on Europe* (Harcourt Brace Jovanovich, 1968) is a wise survey.

→ Notes

1. L. H. Gann and P. Duignan, *Burden of Empire* (New York: Praeger, 1967), p. 286.
2. Robert Schnerb, "Le XIXe Siècle: L'Apogée de L'Expansion Européene (1815–1914)," *Histoire Générale des Civilisations*, VI (Paris: Presses Universitaires de France, 1955), pp. 347–352.
3. L. S. Stavrianos, *The Balkans Since 1453* (New York: Holt, Rinehart & Winston, 1961), pp. 135–136.
4. Bernard Lewis, *The Emergence of Modern Turkey* (Oxford: Oxford University Press, 1968), pp. 1–17.
5. Lewis, *The Emergence of Modern Turkey*, pp. 41–64.
6. Peter Fleming, *Bayonets to Lhasa* (New York: Harper & Row, 1961), p. 21.
7. Quoted in N. D. Harris, *Europe and the East* (Boston: Houghton Mifflin, 1926), p. 285.

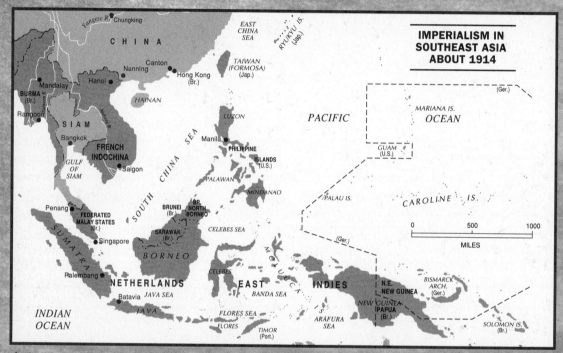

CHAPTER 28

IMPERIALISM IN SOUTHEAST ASIA ABOUT 1914

→ Europeans and Americans expanded their domains into Southeast Asia in the latter nineteenth century. In return for short-term gains in wealth and prestige, however, they left behind local— and often bloody—discord and international wars.

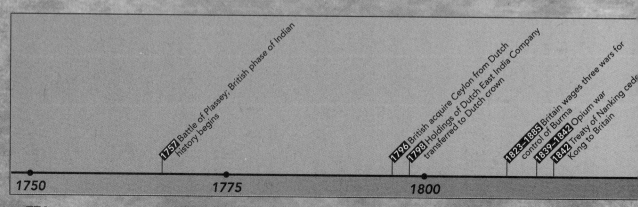

1757 Battle of Plassey, British phase of Indian history begins

1796 British acquire Ceylon from Dutch

1798 Holdings of Dutch East India Company transferred to Dutch crown

1823–1885 Britain wages three wars for control of Burma

1839–1842 Opium war

1842 Treaty of Nanking cede[s] [Hong] Kong to Britain

1750   1775   1800

Asia, 1800–1914

The large countries of south and east Asia—
India, China, and Japan—and their smaller neighbors faced decisive challenges from the Western
powers in the nineteenth century. Only Japan possessed the adaptability to meet the Europeans on
their own terms before 1914. As for the rest, their
religious, cultural, and political characteristics
combined with technological and economic
underdevelopment doomed their efforts to resist
the Western advance. Mughul rule was extremely
weak in the Indian subcontinent; the Indochinese
peninsula and the islands of the Pacific and Indian oceans had long been subjected to European
influence; and China with its unbending sense of
superiority refused to recognize a changing world.

All of south and east Asia shared similar geographic problems and challenges. The area contained many regions of densely populated territory that made large-scale agriculture impossible.
Large cities were few in number, and most people lived in small villages. In nineteenth-century
India, for example, roughly 80 percent of the
people lived in communities of fewer than 2000
inhabitants. The area was and still is vulnerable
to natural disasters such as tidal waves, earth-
quakes, and occasional droughts. These conditions produced a population suffering poor living

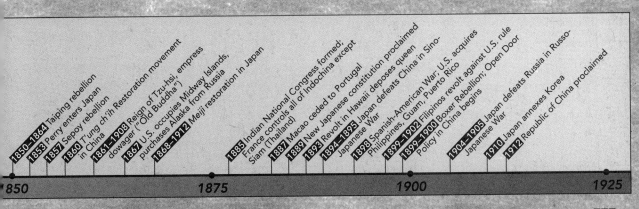

1850–1864 Taiping rebellion
1853 Perry enters Japan
1857 Sepoy rebellion
1860 T'ung ch'ih Restoration movement in China
1861–1908 Reign of Tzu-hsi, empress dowager ("Old Buddha")
1867 U.S. occupies Midway Islands, purchases Alaska from Russia
1868–1912 Meiji restoration in Japan
1885 Indian National Congress formed; France controls all of Indochina except Siam (Thailand)
1887 Macao ceded to Portugal
1889 New Japanese constitution proclaimed
1893 Revolt in Hawaii deposes queen
1894–1895 Japan defeats China in Sino-Japanese War
1898 Spanish-American War; U.S. acquires Philippines, Guam, Puerto Rico
1899–1902 Filipinos revolt against U.S. rule
1899–1900 Boxer Rebellion; Open Door Policy in China begins
1904–1905 Japan defeats Russia in Russo-Japanese War
1910 Japan annexes Korea
1912 Republic of China proclaimed

1850   1875   1900   1925

conditions, high infant mortality rates, endemic diseases, and inadequate nutrition.

INDIA TO 1914

The decline of Mughul power proved to be a great opportunity for the British and French, who through the late seventeenth and most of the eighteenth centuries competed for dominance in India. They fought through their trading companies and agents who sought local allies. India, like North America, was part of the world struggle for empire between the two European powers. The British victory over Bengal in the battle of Plassey (1757) ushered in the British phase of Indian history. Britain's naval supremacy and the superior discipline of its European-led armies enabled Britain to defeat France in 1760. French influence in India soon disappeared.

Dual Control Under the British

The traders became rulers, assuming the dual roles of businessmen and representatives of a

sovereign state. Anarchy spread until 1818 when the British East India Company stepped in to become the subcontinent's police force. Some local rulers accepted the company's rule but others who resisted lost their land. Administration of the subcontinent was divided into two sections: British India was ruled directly by London, while in Indian India the local dynasties ruled under British supervision. The British Parliament, concerned that a profit-seeking company controlled the lives of millions of people, enacted legislation in 1773 and 1784 that gave it power to control company policies and appoint the governor-general, the highest company official in India.

The system of dual control lasted until 1858 and brought several benefits to the peninsula, especially to women. The practice of *suttee* in which widows burned themselves on the funeral pyres of their deceased husbands was prohibited. The company also worked against the practice of killing female infants. Further, steps were taken to end the seclusion of women from society. A secret police force broke up the brutal system of banditry and murder called *thuggee* (hence our

→ This drawing by a British officer of a Bengal regiment shows a British magistrate settling a court case in 1853, during the period of dual control when the British East India Company and the British government shared authority over India.

→ The storming of the Kashmir Gate at Delhi during the Sepoy rebellion of 1857.

word *thug*). The British also introduced a comprehensive, multilevel educational system.

Rebellion and Reform

In the spring of 1857 a serious rebellion interrupted the flow of liberal reforms. Indian troops who formed the bulk of the company's armed forces, called *sepoys*, started the uprising when they complained that a new cartridge issued to them was smeared with the fat of cows and pigs. This outraged both the Hindus, for whom the cow was a sacred animal, and the Muslims, who considered the pig unclean. Fortunately for the British, many areas remained loyal or at least calm. But in the affected areas there was fierce fighting and many lives were lost.

The Sepoy rebellion marked the final collapse of the Mughuls. The mutineers had proclaimed as their leader the last of the Mughul emperors permitted to maintain a court at Delhi. After the British put down the revolt, they exiled him to Burma. The rebellion also put an end to the system of dual control under which the British government and the East India Company shared authority. Parliament removed the company's political role, and after 258 years, the East India Company ended its rule.

Under the new system, the governor-general gained additional duties and a new title—viceroy.

The viceroy was responsible to the secretary of state for India in the British cabinet. In the subcontinent, the British maintained direct control of most of the high positions in government, while Indians were trained to carry out administrative responsibilities in the provincial and subordinate systems. London reorganized the courts and law codes, along with the army and public services. English became the administrative language of the country. Only on rare occasions could native civil officials rise to higher positions in the bureaucracy.

India was governed by and for the British, who viewed themselves as the only people able to rule. By 1900 there was still 90 percent illiteracy among native men and 99 percent among women. Few schools existed at the village level to remedy that situation. The masses of the rural poor paid for the government through taxes on beverages and salt. India provided rich resources and vast markets for the British. In return the British introduced improved health standards, better water systems, and political stability.

The English language and British railroads introduced more unity to the country than it had ever known. But the imperial rulers took advantage of the subcontinent's diversity of religions, castes, and principalities (over 700 separate political units) to rule by a policy of divide and conquer. The British justified their political policies and economic dominance over India by pointing out that they were improving the lives of nearly one-fifth of the human race—almost 300 million people. This rationale could not remove the fact that the contrasts between the European and Asiatic ways of life in cities like Bombay, Delhi, and Calcutta were as great as the difference between night and day.

Resentment against British rule led to the rapid growth of the Indian nationalist movement. In 1885, with the help of several Englishmen who had Indian political ambitions, the Indian National Congress was formed. The British educational system, although it touched only a minority of the people, served as one of the most potent forces behind the new movement, as the Indians embraced many of the liberal causes popular in England. Especially strong was the drive for women's equality and freedom, away from their traditional position of depen-

dence, in which women's legal standing and power derived from their ties to men.

As Indians learned the history of the rise of self-government in England, their desire for political freedom in their own land grew. The system of British control prevented Indians from rising above a certain level. At the same time, newly educated Indian youths, for social and cultural reasons, disdained manual labor. The result was a pool of thousands of frustrated and unemployed educated Indian youths who turned angrily against the government.

The British responded to the spread of violence with a major shift in policy between 1907 and 1909. They allowed the various provincial legislatures to elect Indian majorities, and an Indian was seated in the executive council of the governor-general. The central government's legislature, however, remained under British control. These concessions satisfied moderates, for the time being, but did not appease the more radical protesters. In the twentieth century the spirit of nationalism would become even more insistent.

SOUTHEAST ASIA TO 1914

Southeast Asia includes the lands wedged between India and China and the multitude of islands in the Indian and Pacific oceans. It is a complex, diverse area whose fragmentation rendered it unable to resist the Europeans' incursions, which had begun in the sixteenth century.

European Incursions

Throughout the area European investors established a plantation economy to grow coffee, tea, pepper, and other products demanded by the world market. They also discovered and exploited important mineral deposits. The Europeans attempted to introduce law and order for the purpose of limiting the chronic civil war and banditry that plagued the area. As was the case in India, the impact of European ways of life, especially Western education, created a new generation of nationalists. In the Dutch East Indies, French Indochina, and the Philippines, young intellectuals aspired to complete independence for themselves and their countries.

In the eighteenth and nineteenth centuries Great Britain gained control of Ceylon, Malaya,

BRITISH INDIA
1914

☐ British Territory
☐ Dependent States

RUSSIA

CHINA

Kabul

AFGHANISTAN
KASHMIR
PUNJAB
Lahore
BALUCHISTAN
Indus R.
TIBET
Lhasa

Delhi
NEPAL
RAJPUTANA
Lucknow
Ganges R.
BHUTAN
Karachi
Benares
ASSAM
Akhmadabad
BENGAL
Dacca
Nagpur
ORISSA
Calcutta
BURMA
Bombay
Cuttack
HYDERABAD
Hyderabad
Rangoon
GOA
(Port.)
MYSORE
MADRAS
Bangalore
Madras
BAY
Pondichéry
OF
(Fr.)
BENGAL

600
MILES
CEYLON
Colombo

RABIAN
SEA

INDIAN OCEAN

and Burma. The first colony, taken from the Dutch in 1796, became one of the most valuable British holdings, producing such prized commodities as tea, rubber, lead, and sapphires. The Malay peninsula, with the important island of Singapore, provided a vantage point from which Britain could dominate the seas surrounding southern Asia and export valuable supplies of tin and rubber. The British conquered Burma in three wars between 1823 and 1885 and annexed it to India.

After a century-long absence, France returned to southeast Asia in the nineteenth century. French commercial and religious interests had been established as early as the seventeenth century, but British power in the Indian Ocean prevented France from stabilizing its position at that time. Not until the mid-nineteenth century did France increase its presence in Indochina. Anti-Christian persecutions in the area in 1856 and the fear that Catholicism would be eliminated if France did not go to its aid moved the French to join the British against China and Vietnam.

France took Saigon in 1860 and from that base expanded its influence and power through treaties, exploration, and outright annexation.

The French took Hanoi in 1882, governed Cochin China as a direct colony, and held Annam (central Vietnam), Tonkin, and Cambodia as protectorates in one degree or another. Laos too was soon brought under French "protection." By the beginning of the twentieth century France had created an empire in Indochina nearly 50 percent larger than the parent country. Only Siam (Thailand) managed to hold off the French advance and keep its independence.

Late in the sixteenth century the Dutch had taken most of the East Indies from the Portuguese, and in 1602 the Dutch East India Company was organized to exploit the resources of the Spice Islands. In 1798 the company's holdings were transferred to the Dutch crown. For some time the spice trade had been declining, and early in the nineteenth century the Dutch set about raising new products.

In the 1830s the so-called culture system was introduced, under which one-fifth of all native land was set aside to raise crops for the government. One-fifth of all the natives' time was also required to work the lands. As a result, the production of sugar, tobacco, coffee, tea, and other products increased tremendously. In the long run,

→ In 1859, on the pretext of preserving Catholicism in Indochina, a French and Spanish expeditionary force stormed and captured the fortress of Saigon.

the culture system gave the islands a prosperous system of raising crops, but it also often deprived the natives of sufficient land for their own use. Conditions for the natives improved in 1900 when the Dutch abandoned the culture system. Less favorable for the local population was the Dutch neglect of higher education and the failure to prepare them for eventual self-government.

American Imperialism

While the Europeans were pursuing their interests in the Far East, a new imperial power was emerging in the Pacific—the United States. In 1867 the Americans occupied the Midway Islands and purchased Alaska from the Russians. The next step was in the Hawaiian Islands.

During the nineteenth century, Americans and Europeans had developed large sugar plantations on the mid-Pacific islands. The United States poured capital into them, and by 1881 the U.S. secretary of state referred to the islands as part of the "American system." In 1893, a revolt, engineered with the assistance of the marines, deposed the Hawaiian queen and set up a republic designed to ensure U.S. control in the islands. Five years later both houses of Congress issued a joint declaration to annex the islands.

The United States's successful war against Spain in 1898 affected both Cuba and the Philippines. In May of that year Admiral George Dewey destroyed the Spanish fleet at Manila and the first American soldiers began operations in the Philippines. By the treaty of December 1898, Spain ceded the Philippines, Guam, and Puerto Rico to the United States. One year later the Americans occupied the small Pacific outpost of Wake Island.

Some of the liberal Filipino patriots who had rebelled against the Spanish in 1896 assisted the Americans, but they had no wish to exchange one master for another. When it became evident that they would not quickly gain self-rule, fighting broke out. The hostilities that began in 1899 lasted for three years. The ironic spectacle of American forces being used in a second conquest of the Philippines brought about a strong revulsion against imperialism in many quarters of the United States. A New York newspaper responded to Rudyard Kipling, an apologist for imperialism, in this way:

> We've taken up the white man's burden
> Of ebony and brown:
>
> Now will you kindly tell us, Rudyard,
> How we may put it down.[1]

American colonial administration in the Philippines proved to be liberal and well-intentioned for the most part. In 1913 the legislature became dominantly native, although final authority in the most important matters was still reserved to the U.S. Congress. The Philippine tariff was shaped to favor American trade, and large amounts of capital from the United States were invested in the islands. Increased educational opportunities strengthened the desire for independence among many Filipinos. In their eyes, American government in the Philippines, no matter how efficient or humanitarian, was no substitute for self-government.

There could be no doubt that by 1900 the United States sat astride the Pacific basin as did no other power. The consequences of this Pacific imperial posture were to become a major and costly constituent of American life in the twentieth century. A massive conflict with Japan, another in Korea, and the tragic war in Vietnam lay in the future. Whether such involvement was essential for American basic interests was to become a crucial and painful question.

THE CENTRAL KINGDOM

At the end of the 1800s China's four million square miles held 450 million people, up from 200 million a century earlier. The ruling dynasty was the Ch'ing, established by Manchus from Manchuria, who in 1644 had superseded the Ming. These descendants of the Tatars appreciated Chinese civilization and adopted a conciliatory attitude toward their subjects. They refused, however, to allow intermarriage with the Chinese, for they realized that only their blood difference kept them from being assimilated and conquered. By and large, however, the Manchus gradually became Chinese in their attitudes and habits.

The Manchu emperors were remarkably successful. The reign of Ch'ien-lung (1736–1795) was a time of great expansion. The Manchus gained Turkestan, Burma, and Tibet. By the end of the eighteenth century Manchu power extended even into Nepal, and the territory under the Ch'ing control was as extensive as under any previous dynasty.

The Perils of Superiority

The prevailing attitude of superiority to the cultures of all other peoples was an obstacle to China's leaders. They regarded with contempt rather than admiration advances in other parts of the world. Evidence of China's problems could be found in the eighteenth-century revolts in Formosa, Kansu, Hunan, Kueichou, and Shantung. All of them were suppressed, but clearly China faced serious difficulties.

In the first part of the nineteenth century, China continued to act imperiously toward foreigners. Merchants from western Europe came to China in increasing numbers, pursuing their trade in the face of great difficulties. Trade restrictions confined the foreign merchants to Canton and the Portuguese colony of Macao. In Canton, the Chinese controlled both trade and taxes. In spite of these obstacles, the foreigners made enough profit to compensate for their being treated as inferiors by the Chinese government.[2]

The Manchus would neither recognize nor receive diplomatic representatives of foreign powers. In addition, China knew that the foreigners needed Asian products more than the Chinese required European goods. In 1793 the imperial court responded to the British request for a permanent trade representative in Peking in this manner:

> To send one of your nationals to stay at the Celestial Court to take care of your country's trade with China . . . is not in harmony with the state system of our dynasty and will definitely not be permitted . . . there is nothing we lack, as your principal envoy and others have themselves observed. We have never set such store on strange or ingenious objects, nor do we have need of any more of your country's manufactures.[3]

The Western Response

The foreigners were especially irritated by the high customs duties the Chinese forced them to pay and by the attempts of Chinese authorities to stop the growing import trade in opium. The drug had long been used to stop diarrhea, but in the seventeenth and eighteenth centuries people in all classes began to use it recreationally. Most opium came from Turkey or India, and in 1800 its import was forbidden by the imperial government. Despite this restriction, the opium trade continued to flourish. Privately owned vessels of many countries, including the United States, made huge profits from the growing number of Chinese addicts. The government in Peking noted that the foreigners seemed intent on dragging down the Chinese by encouraging opium addiction.

→ The Canton waterfront in a nineteenth-century painting. Canton was the first Chinese port regularly visited by European traders. The Portuguese arrived in 1511, followed by the British in the seventeenth century, and the French and Dutch in the eighteenth.

→ The stacking room at an opium factory in Patna, India. Opium smuggling upset the balance of trade and destroyed China's economy.

In the meantime, the empire faced other problems. Corruption spread through the army, and tax farmers defrauded the people. The central bureaucracy declined in efficiency, and the generally weak emperors were unable to meet the challenges of the time. The balance of trade turned against the Chinese in the 1830s, and the British decided to force the issue of increased trade rights. The point of conflict was the opium trade. By the late 1830s more than 30,000 chests of opium, each of which held about 150 pounds of the extract, were being brought in annually by the various foreign powers. Some authorities assert that the trade in opium alone reversed China's formerly favorable balance of trade. In the spring of 1839 Chinese authorities at Canton confiscated and burned the opium. In response, the British occupied positions around Canton.

In the war that followed, the Chinese could not match the technological and tactical superiority of the British forces. In 1842 China agreed to the provisions of the Treaty of Nanking. Hong Kong was ceded to Great Britain, and other ports, including Canton, were opened to British residence and trade. It would be a mistake to view the conflict between the two countries simply as a matter of drug control; it was instead the acting out of deep cultural conflicts between East and West.[4]

The French and Americans approached the Chinese after the Nanking Treaty's provisions became known, and in 1844 gained the same trading rights as the British. The advantages granted the three nations by the Chinese set a precedent that would dominate China's relations with the world for the next century. The "most favored nation" treatment came to be extended so far that China's right to rule in its own territory was limited. This began the period referred to by the Chinese as the time of unequal treaties—a time of unprecedented degradation for China. The humiliation the Central Kingdom suffered is still remembered and strongly affects important aspects of its foreign policy. Meanwhile, the opium trade continued to thrive.

The British and French defeated China in a second opium war in 1856. By the terms of the Treaty of Tientsin (1858) the Chinese opened new ports to trading and allowed foreigners with passports to travel in the interior. Christians gained the right to spread their faith and hold property, thus opening up another means of Western penetration. The United States and Russia gained the same privileges in separate treaties.

The Manchu empire appeared to be well on the way to total physical dismemberment and economic collapse. Three provisions of these treaties caused long-lasting bitterness among the Chinese: extraterritoriality, customs regulations, and the right to station foreign warships in Chinese waters. *Extraterritoriality* meant that in a dispute with the Chinese, Westerners had the right to be tried in their own country's consular court. Europeans argued that Chinese concepts of justice were more rigid and harsh than those in the West. But the Chinese viewed extraterritoriality as not only humiliating to China's sovereignty, but also discriminatory in favor of Western nations. The other two provisions greatly weakened China's fiscal and military structure. After 1860 China was a helpless giant.

China's Response

The Chinese competition with the Westerners had been carried on in military and economic terms. But the basic conflict was in the realm of civilization and values. The Chinese could note the obvious—that the Europeans possessed technological and military superiority. The question they faced was how to adapt the strength of Europe to the core of Chinese civilization in order to become

Lin Tse-hsu on the Opium Trade

Lin Tse-hsu saw that the opium trade, which gave Europe such huge profits, undermined his country. He asked Queen Victoria to put a stop to the trade.

After a long period of commercial intercourse, there appear among the crowd of barbarians both good persons and bad, unevenly. Consequently there are those who smuggle opium to seduce the Chinese people and so cause the spread of the poison to all provinces. Such persons who only care to profit themselves, and disregard their harm to others, are not tolerated by the laws of heaven and are unanimously hated by human beings. His Majesty the Emperor, upon hearing of this, is in a towering rage. He has especially sent me, his commissioner, to come to Kwangtung, and together with the governor-general and governor jointly to investigate and settle this matter.

All those people in China who sell opium or smoke opium should receive the death penalty. If we trace the crime of those barbarians who through the years have been selling opium, then the deep harm they have wrought and the great profit they have usurped should fundamentally justify their execution according to law. We take into consideration, however, the fact that the various barbarians have still known how to repent their crimes and return to their allegiance to us by taking the 20,183 chests of opium from their storeships and petitioning us, through their consular officer [superintendent of trade], Elliot, to receive it. It has been entirely destroyed and this has been faithfully reported to the Throne in several memorials by this commissioner and his colleagues.

Fortunately we have received a specially extended favor from His Majesty the Emperor, who considers that for those who voluntarily surrender there are still some circumstances to palliate their crime, and so for the time being he has magnanimously excused them from punishment. But as for those who again violate the opium prohibition, it is difficult for the law to pardon them repeatedly. Having established new regulations, we presume that the ruler of your honorable country, who takes delight in our culture and whose disposition is inclined towards us, must be able to instruct the various barbarians to observe the law with care. It is only necessary to explain to them the advantages and disadvantages and then they will know that the legal code of the Celestial Court must be absolutely obeyed with awe.

We find that your country is sixty or seventy thousand *li* [three *li* make one mile] from China. Yet there are barbarian ships that strive to come here for trade for the purpose of making a great profit. The wealth of China is used to profit the barbarians. That is to say, the great profit made by barbarians is all taken from the rightful share of China. By what right do they then in return use the poisonous drug to injure the Chinese people? Even though the barbarians may not necessarily intend to do us harm, yet in coveting profit to an extreme, they have no regard for injuring others. Let us ask, where is your conscience? I have heard that the smoking of opium is very strictly forbidden by your country; that is because the harm caused by opium is clearly understood. Since it is not permitted to do harm to your own country, then even less should you let it be passed on to the harm of other countries—how much less to China!

From Lin Tse-hsu, Letter to Queen Victoria, 1839.

able to compete effectively with the West. In Chinese terms, this was the *t'i-yung* concept. *T'i* means substance and *yung* means use.

Combining the two elements presented the severe problem of gaining a proper balance. Those who wanted to keep the old culture opposed those who wanted to modernize the country. In 1860 the *T'ung ch'ih* Restoration movement attempted to strengthen the Manchus. Serious attempts were made to preserve Chinese culture while trying to make use of Western technology. Had these attempts at adaptation been carried out in a time of peace, perhaps the Chinese could have adjusted, but China did not enjoy the luxury of tranquillity. The concessions to the "foreign devils" resulted in a great loss of prestige for the Manchus.

More dangerous for the Manchus than the West was the spate of revolts in the north, west, and south of the country. The most tragic was the Taiping rebellion that lasted from 1850 to 1864. The uprising, fought to attain the Heavenly Kingdom of Great Peace (T'ai-p'ing t'ien-kuo), stemmed from widespread discontent with the social and economic conditions of Manchu rule and the perception of a lack of authority in Peking. The revolt began near Canton and centered on the plans of Hung Hsiu-ch'uan, a person who was driven to desperation by consistently failing the lowest examination to gain entry into the civil service. After contact with American missionaries and some reading of Christian tracts, he came to identify himself as a son of God, Jesus' little brother. His task was to bring salvation to China.

He attracted followers, especially from the poor, and prepared to fight. For ten years, he and his forces controlled the southern part of China from Nanking, and he set out to create a new society, totally detached from the traditional Chinese fabric. Hung struck out at vice, Confucianism, private property, and the landlords. By taking on all that was established in China, he ensured his defeat. The Taiping rebellion was one of the most costly movements in history. It reached into seventeen of China's eighteen provinces. Estimates of the number of deaths range between 20 and 30 million.[5]

After the external buffeting from the west and the internal uprising, the Manchu dynasty limped along for another half century, led by a conservative coalition of Manchu and Chinese officials who advised the empress dowager, Tzu-hsi, who served from 1861 until her death in 1908. Known first as Orchid, then as Yehonala, then as the Yi Concubine, then as Tzu-hsi, and finally as the Old Buddha, she followed the most direct path for a bright and ambitious Manchu female—she entered court circles as a concubine. After receiving the traditional training in court, she honed her political skills. She understood the intricate ceremonial life and mastered the intrigue of palace politics. When the senior concubine failed to give birth to a healthy heir to the throne, Tzu-hsi bore the emperor a strong and healthy child.

→ Tzu-hsi, the Empress Dowager or Old Buddha. The Boxer Rebellion near the end of her reign indicated the degree to which the central government had lost power in China.

Her position as mother of the heir-apparent opened the door to power, and during the reigns of the next three emperors she was a dominant power, either as co-regent or regent. She built a network of powerful allies and informers that helped her to crush internal revolts and restore a measure of prestige to China during a brief period of tranquillity from 1870 to 1895. She and her circle were so removed from the world that she used funds earmarked for the navy to rebuild her summer house, in honor of her sixtieth birthday. At a time when the Japanese were rapidly modernizing and foreign powers introduced many forms of new technology in their factories, railroads, and communications, China held to the policies based on tradition and custom.

Carving Up China

During the first wars against the Europeans, the Chinese began the process of ceding territory and spheres of influence to foreigners. By 1860, as a result of the Treaty of Peking, Russia gained the entire area north of the Amur River and founded the strategic city of Vladivostok. In 1885 France took Indochina and Britain seized Burma. In 1887 Macao was ceded to Portugal. China was too weak to resist these encroachments on its borders. But the crowning blow came not from the Western nations, but from Japan—a land the Chinese had long regarded with amused contempt.

Trouble had long brewed between China and Japan, especially over the control of Formosa and Korea. War broke out in 1894 in a dispute over China's claims on Korea. The brief Sino-Japanese struggle resulted in a humiliating defeat for China. By the treaty of Shimonoseki (1895), China was forced to recognize the independence of Korea and hand over the rich Liao-tung peninsula and Formosa to Japan.

The Chinese defeat was the signal for the renewal of aggressive actions by Western powers, who forced Japan to return the strategic Liao-tung peninsula to China. Shortly thereafter, the European powers made their own demands of China. Germany demanded a 99-year lease to Kiaochow Bay and was also given exclusive mining and railroad rights throughout Shantung province. Russia obtained a 25-year lease to Dairen and Port Arthur and gained the right to build a railroad across Manchuria, thereby achieving complete domination of that vast territory. In 1898 Britain obtained the lease of Weihaiwei, a naval base, and France leased Kwangchowan in southern China.

The United States, acting not from any high-minded desires but rather from the fear that American business was being excluded from China, brought a halt, or at least a hesitation, to the process of dismemberment. In 1899 Secretary of State John Hay asked the major powers to agree to a policy of equal trading privileges. In 1900 several powers did so, and the Open Door policy was born.

The humiliation of the defeat by Japan had incensed young Chinese intellectuals who agitated for liberation from foreign dominance. Led by enlightened and concerned patriots such as Kang yu-wei, the liberals proposed a wide-ranging series of economic, social, political, and educational reforms, and the young emperor, Tzu-hsi's nephew, approved them. What followed came to be known as the "hundred days of reform."

Tzu-hsi and her advisers encouraged anti-foreign sentiment and opposed the patriots' attempts to bring about basic democratic reforms on a Confucianist basis. The reform attempts threatened the interests of the Tzu-hsi's supporters, and she came out of retirement in 1898, imprisoned her nephew, and revoked all of the proposed reforms.

After the suppression of the reform movement, a group of secret societies united in an organization known as the Righteous Harmony Fists, whose members were called Boxers by the Westerners. At first they were strongly anti-Manchu, but by 1899 the chief object of their hatred had become the foreign nations who were stripping China of land and power. The Boxers started a campaign to rid China of all "foreign devils." Many Europeans were killed and the legations at Peking were besieged. In August 1900 an international army forced its way to Peking and released the prisoners. China was forced to apologize for the murder of foreign officials and pay a large indemnity.

By this time, even the Old Buddha acknowledged the need for change. After 1901 she sanctioned reforms in the state examination system, education and governmental structure, and eco-

RUSSIAN EMPIRE

0   600
MILES

MONGOLIA

MANCHURIA

Amur R.

1905

LIAOTUNG
PENINSULA

Vladivostok
(Rus.)

SEA OF
JAPAN

Peking

Port Arthur
(Rus.)

Dairen
(Rus.)

Weihaiwei
(Br.)

Huang Ho

SHANTUNG
PROVINCE

Kiaochow
Bay (Ger.)

KOREA

1910

JAPAN

EAST
CHINA
SEA

Yangtze R.

CHINA

1895

PACIFIC
OCEAN

TAIWAN
(FORMOSA)

Hong Kong
(Br.)

BURMA

Kwangchowan
(Fr.)   HAINAN

Macao
(Port.)

Mekong R.

FRENCH
INDOCHINA

SOUTH
CHINA
SEA

PHILIPPINE
ISLANDS

SIAM

**IMPERIALISM
IN CHINA
ABOUT 1900**

The "Benefits" of Imperialism

Imperialism provided a previously unattainable standard of living for Europeans, as a letter from Miss Eden proves.

I wish you could see my passage sometimes. The other day when I set off to pay George a visit I could not help thinking how strange it would have seemed at home. It was a rainy day, so all the servants were at home. The two tailors were sitting in one window, making a new gown for me, and Rosina by them chopping up her betel-nut; at the opposite window were my two Dacca embroiderers working at a large frame, and the sentry, in an ecstasy of admiration mounting guard over them. There was the bearer standing upright, in a sweet sleep, pulling away at my punkah. My own five ser-vants were sitting in a circle, with an English spelling-book, which they were learning by heart; and my *jemadar*, who, out of compliment to me, has taken to draw, was sketching a bird. Chance's [Miss Eden's dog] servant was waiting at the end of the passage for his "little excellency" to go out walking, and a Chinese was waiting with some rolls of satin that he had brought to show.

From *The Sahibs*, edited by Hilton Brown (London: William Hodge & Company Limited, 1948).

nomic life; she even approved the drive to end the binding of girls' feet—all to no avail.

Only a decade after the conclusion of the Boxer rebellion, a revolution broke out all over China, and in 1912 the Republic of China was proclaimed with Sun Yat-Sen as president. The revolutionary Chinese leaders knew that there had to be radically different approaches taken in China to allow it to survive and compete. As one official wrote in the 1890s:

> Western nations rely on intelligence and energy to compete with one another. To come abreast of them China should plan to promote commerce and open mines; unless we change, the Westerners will be rich and we poor. We should excel in technology and the manufacture of machinery; unless we change, they will be skillful and we clumsy. . . . Unless we change, the Westerners will cooperate with each other and we shall stand isolated; they will be strong and we shall be weak.[6]

THE JAPANESE ALTERNATIVE

Western powers gained effective control of India, southeast Asia, and China by the end of the nineteenth century. Japan, however, responded to the Western advance in an alert and united manner, successfully adapting elements of strength from the West to the core of its own structures and ways of life.

At the beginning of the eighteenth century Japan was ruled from Edo (now Tokyo), the largest city in the country, by the head of the Tokugawa clan, whose leaders had declared themselves *shogun* since 1603. As the military dictator with a retinue of feudal lords and warriors, the *shogun* kept the country united and at peace. The Tokugawa strengthened the feudal framework of unity and stability that helped give Japan the basis for a successful response to the European challenge.

The Japanese emperor, in residence at Kyoto, served as a figurehead with no real function other than as a symbol around which the nation could rally. The Tokugawa ruled the country through their feudal lords, the *daimyo*. These officials in turn governed their regions with the aid of the *samurai*, the soldiers who also acted as administrators and governed and taxed the peasants. Below the peasants on the social scale were the artisans and merchants who lived in the cities, a reflection of the fact that the Tokugawa saw agriculture as the foundation of politics and society.

The stratified society may well have ensured the power of the Tokugawa, but over a period of two centuries it was tested by peasant uprisings in the countryside and discontent in the cities. The peasant rebellions could be put down by force. But in the cities in the late eighteenth and early nineteenth centuries, remarkable economic growth accompanied the rapid urbanization. New social and political forces posed difficulties for the Tokugawa structure. The spread of education and the increase in wealth helped spur the growth of a new urban class drawn from young, aggressive merchants and intellectuals. Those at the lower end of the social scale became wealthier than many of the *samurai*. These social forces could not be dealt with so easily by the Tokugawa governmental structure.

By the nineteenth century the shogunate lost much of its force and authority. The once-efficient government had become lax, especially in the realm of tax collection. Changing conditions in the cities and the flow of Western information from the open port of Nagasaki worked to undermine the traditional system.

The Western Challenge

Both European and American merchants and diplomats tried to open relations with Japan during the first part of the nineteenth century, but even at mid-century foreign traders and missionaries found their ability to move throughout the country greatly limited. Within the country the question of how and when to open up to the West was discussed. European inventions such as the daguerreotype and new manufacturing tech-

niques had already made their appearances. But Japanese policy toward foreigners would not be defined until 1853. On July 7 of that year the U.S. ships under the command of Matthew Perry sailed into Edo Bay.

Perry, with a force of two steam frigates and two sloops-of-war, had been sent by the American government to convince the Japanese that a treaty opening trade relations between the two countries would be of mutual interest. He had been instructed to be tactful and to use force only if necessary. After delivering a letter from the U.S. president, he remained in port ten days. When he departed, he told the authorities in Edo that he would return in a year for an answer. He actually came back eight months later, in February 1854. The Americans returned with more ships before the deadline because they feared that the French or the Russians might gain concessions sooner from the Japanese.

The *shogun*, after a period of intense debate within his country, agreed to Perry's requests. The Treaty of Kanagawa, the first formal agreement between Japan and a Western nation, was signed. By its terms, shipwrecked sailors were to be well treated and two ports were to be opened for provisioning ships and a limited amount of

→ Commodore Perry meeting the imperial commissioners at Yokohama. In 1854 Perry secured a treaty in which Japan agreed to permit foreign vessels to obtain provisions within Japanese territory and to allow U.S. ships to anchor in the ports at Shimoda and Hakodate.

→ Westerners and Japanese gather at the Foreign Merchants' Building in Yokohama, a major trading port.

trade. European traders soon obtained similar privileges, plus the right of extraterritoriality.

The entry of the West placed a severe strain on the already weakened Japanese political structure. Antiforeign sentiment grew, even as many Japanese recognized that accommodation with the West was bound to come. Western representatives in Japan were caught in the middle, and there were a number of attacks against them. By 1867, after a time of strife and confusion, Japan reached the point of revolution. European and American fleets had bombarded Kagoshima and Shimonoseki in 1863 and 1864, thereby convincing some of the antiforeign elements of the hopelessness of their position. In 1867 the system of dual government, with the emperor at Kyoto and the *shogun* at Edo, was abandoned. The capital was moved from Kyoto to Edo, which was renamed Tokyo (eastern capital).

The Meiji Restoration

The next generation of Japanese leaders accomplished what no other non-Western leaders were able to do—they adapted the Europeans' strengths to their own situation and successfully competed against the West. The new leaders who oversaw the end of the dual power system were young and most were of *samurai* origin. They understood the nature of Western power and the threat it posed to their country. They proposed as Japan's best defense the forming of a "rich coun-

try and strong military," based on Western technology and institutions adapted to their country's needs. The young emperor, whose rule was known as the *Meiji* (enlightened government), reigned from 1868 to 1912. During that time Japan became a dynamic, modern power the West had to recognize as an equal.

Centuries earlier the Japanese had gained a great deal from China. Now they set out to learn from the West the lessons of how to construct an industrialized, bureaucratized state. For the next generation, the results of those lessons would be applied in a broad variety of areas. The voluntary abolition of feudal rights accompanied and facilitated the restoration of the emperor's supreme authority. In 1871 the end of the feudal system was officially announced, although it was far from actual fact. At the same time the government established a new administrative division and reformed the education and mail systems.

In 1882 a commission went out to study the world's various governmental systems in order to write a new constitution for Japan. The committee members were particularly impressed by Bismarck's German system, and the new constitution proclaimed in 1889 gave the premier a position analogous to that held by the chancellor in Germany. Under the new system the cabinet was responsible to the emperor alone. Only the army and the navy could appoint their respective ministers. Since no statesman could form a cabinet without a war minister, and the army could overthrow any cabinet by simply withdrawing its minister, ultimate control of policies rested with military interests. The constitution provided for a Diet, which wielded financial influence through its refusal power over unpopular budgets in peacetime. Under the new system the emperor, who held sovereign power, was considered "sacred and inviolable."

The Japanese adapted the lessons they learned from the West in other areas. In 1876 national conscription went into effect, and a modern military structure was created. German and French advisers trained army officers while naval officers received their instructions from the British. The government initiated the founding of banks, factories, and business concerns. Later, when they became successful, these establishments were turned over to private ownership and management. Japan also changed to the modern calendar, symbolizing its entry into the modern age.

Although the Japanese went to the West to find the best ways to modernize their country, they themselves, and not foreigners, made the major changes. Foreigners built the railways, telegraphs, lighthouses, dockyards, and warships. But the authorities in Tokyo initiated a constitution that firmly maintained their control.

→ Modern and traditional Japan meet in this 1905 photo. Farmers wheel their carts through the streets while, above them, workers install electric power lines.

Japan's Success

On the surface the Japanese government was liberal and parliamentary. In reality it was ultraconservative, giving the emperor and the cabinet dominant power. Though Japan was the first Asian nation to achieve a high degree of literacy, education remained the tool of the government, and one of its chief functions was to produce docile servants of the state. The press was subjected to wide control and censorship. The army was used as a means of instilling conscripts with unquestioning loyalty and obedience to the emperor. In army barracks young soldiers learned that the noblest fate was death on the battlefield. Unlike the Chinese, who revered the scholar most of all, the Japanese admired the soldier—warfare was the supreme vocation.

The Japanese were ready to seize the new methods and ideas of the west to serve their own military ends. It should not be forgotten, however, that ultimately it was through a display of military power that the West forced home the notion of its own superiority on Asia.

In adopting many of the aspects of the Western state system—universal conscription, professional bureaucracy, mass literacy, state ideology—some Japanese institutions were forced to change. The *samurai*, who had formerly made their living as warriors or by serving their feudal lords, had to change their life-styles. Many of them made the transition to the new system effortlessly. The conservative *samurai* were upset when the government passed a law in 1876 that diminished their financial advantages and also forbade the carrying of swords in public. Civil war broke out in some districts, and the government's forces put down the stubborn *samurai* and their armies.

The oligarchy that carried out the revolution through which Japan passed was able to keep a fair amount of control. They brought all of the people into the new system in one form or another. They could accomplish such a major revolution with a minimum of turmoil because all the changes were done within the confines of traditional reverence for the emperor.

Ito Hirobumi on the New Japanese Constitution

The Japanese were the only non-Europeans quickly to adopt, choose, and use European concepts successfully for their own purpose. Ito Hirobumi's thoughts on drafting the new Japanese constitution represent one instance of how this system worked.

It was in the month of March 1882, that His Majesty ordered me to work out a draft of a constitution to be submitted to his approval. No time was to be lost, so I started on the 15th of the same month for an extended journey to different constitutional countries to make as thorough a study as possible of the actual workings of different systems of constitutional government, of their various provisions, as well as of theories and opinions actually entertained by influential persons on the actual stage itself of constitutional life. I sojourned about a year and a half in Europe, and having gathered the necessary materials, in so far as it was possible in so short a space of time, I returned home in September 1883. Immediately after my return I set to work to draw up the Constitution. . . .

It was evident from the outset that mere imitation of foreign models would not suffice, for there were historical peculiarities of our country which had to be taken into consideration. For example, the Crown was, with us, an institution far more deeply rooted in the national sentiment and in our history than in other countries. It was indeed the very essence of a once theocratic State, so that in formulating the restrictions on its prerogatives in the new Constitution, we had to take care to safeguard the future realness or vitality of these prerogatives, and not to let the institution degenerate into an ornamental crowning piece of the edifice. At the same time, it was also evident that any form of constitutional régime was impossible without full and extended protection of honor, liberty, property, and personal security of citizens, entailing necessarily many important restrictions on the powers of the Crown. . . .

Another difficulty equally grave had to be taken into consideration. We were just then in an age of transition. The opinions prevailing in the country were extremely heterogeneous, and often diametrically opposed to each other. We had survivors of former generations who were still full of theocratic ideas, and who believed that any attempt to restrict an imperial prerogative amounted to something like high treason. On the other hand there was a large and powerful body of the younger generation educated at the time when the Manchester theory was in vogue, and who in consequence were ultra-radical in their ideas of freedom. Members of the bureaucracy were prone to lend willing ears to the German doctrinaires of the reactionary period, while, on the other hand, the educated politicians among the people having not yet tasted the bitter significance of administrative responsibility, were liable to be more influenced by the dazzling words and lucid theories of Montesquieu, Rousseau, and other similar French writers. A work entitled *History of Civilization,* by Buckle, which denounced every form of government as an unnecessary evil, became the great favorite of students of all the higher schools, including the Imperial University. On the other hand, these same students would not have dared to expound the theories of Buckle before their own conservative fathers. At that time we had not yet arrived at the stage of distinguishing clearly between political opposition on the one hand, and treason to the established order of things on the other. The virtues necessary for the smooth working of any constitution, such as love of freedom of speech, love of publicity of proceedings, the spirit of tolerance for opinions opposed to one's own, etc., had yet to be learned by long experience.

Permission to reprint selections from *Sources of Japanese Tradition*, edited by William T. de Bary (Columbia University Press, 1958), provided by the publisher.

Through Shintoism, virtually the state religion, the restoration leaders devised the ultimate political and religious ideology. In Shinto the emperor, directly descended from the Sun Goddess, can demand unlimited loyalty to himself. He expresses the gods' will. As a former president of the privy council, Baron Hozumi, wrote:

> The Emperor holds the sovereign power, not as his own inherent right, but as an inheritance from his Divine Ancestor. The government is, therefore, theocratical. The Emperor rules over his country as the supreme head of the vast family of the Japanese nation. The government is, therefore patriarchal. The Emperor exercises the sovereign power according to the Constitution, which is based on the most advanced principles of modern constitutionalism. The government is, therefore, constitutional. In other words, the fundamental principle of the Japanese government is theocratic-patriarchal-constitutionalism.[7]

The process of industrialization coincided with this fundamental social and political revolution. In its rapid economic growth, Japan faced the same problems of demographic and urban growth the West faced. Social and cultural discontent naturally followed from such a rapid transformation. But the ideological and political structure constructed in the Meiji restoration was enough to hold the country together while at the same time repelling the Europeans and the Americans.

In the eyes of Western diplomats, Japanese prestige had begun to increase soon after the conclusion of the Sino-Japanese war of 1894–1895. In 1902 Japan scored a diplomatic triumph in allying itself with Great Britain, an alliance viewed by both nations as a deterrent to Russian expansion. When a year later the Russians rebuffed Japanese attempts to negotiate a sphere-of-influence agreement over Korea and Manchuria, the Tokyo government attacked Port Arthur and bottled up Russia's fleet, without a formal declaration of war. The quick series of Japanese victories that followed forced the Russians to agree to the Treaty of Portsmouth in September 1905. Japan gained half the island of Sakhalin, the leaseholds on the Liaotung peninsula and Port Arthur, and various Russian railway and mining rights in southern Manchuria. Japan's paramount position in Korea was also

→ During the Meiji period, Japan undertook a successful program of industrialization, as is evident in this 1905 photo of a Japanese silk-weaving factory.

conceded, paving the way for its annexation of that nation in 1910.

Japan's victory in the war with Russia in 1904–1905 astounded the world. Japan had successfully met the challenge of European primacy and was now accepted as a first-class power in its own right.

CONCLUSION

European incursions of the eighteenth and nineteenth centuries in the Indian subcontinent, southeast Asia, China, and Japan prompted a variety of reactions. In India the Mughul Dynasty was unable to control the myriad of peoples and religions over which it ruled, and the resulting instability furnished a convenient pretext for the ultimate imposition of British control. Only Siam (Thailand) maintained its independence in southeast Asia, and that only because the French and British wanted a buffer state between their holdings in the region. China suffered a distressing decline in the nineteenth century from its position as Central Kingdom to a helpless giant split into spheres of influence. Japan alone was able to adapt and successfully compete with the Western nations.

Japan had a number of advantages, compared to its neighbors. The Confucian base of

Japanese culture promoted a rational consideration of Western technological and intellectual advantages that might be useful. It also emphasized hard work, self-sacrifice, loyalty, and the role of the family. Japan's island location helped it resist direct foreign rule. Its leadership in the last one-third of the century was in the hands of a group of aggressive young officials who embraced the theories and practices of a modern economy. The Japanese brought back from the West the best and most useful elements of a modern economy and applied them to their cultural and social base. The speed with which they accomplished this transformation, barely 40 years after the fall of the *shogun*, is an impressive indication of the strength of Japanese society.

The Japanese defeat of the Russians in 1905 did not alter any basic power relationships. Yet it was the first step in a new direction. The nineteenth century, by and large, saw the West expand its holdings over colonies worldwide, building on sheer technological and economic superiority. At the same time the foreigners' successes did not fundamentally change the cultural basis of the native peoples. The Japanese showed one example the non-Western world could follow, by adapting the strong technology of the West to its own strong culture. They paved the way for other countries during the course of the twentieth century who would find their own paths to reassert their self-rule, after they too had mastered some of the Western tools.

✦ Suggestions for Reading

For valuable insights into British rule and its consequences see M. Edwards, *British India* (Taplinger, 1968) and S. Gopal, *British Policy in India* (Cambridge, 1965). P. Speare provides a good short history in *The Oxford History of Modern India: 1740–1795* (Oxford, 1979). Two good studies of British imperial rule are P. Woodruff, *The Men Who Ruled India*, 2 vols. (St. Martin's, 1954) and J. Morris, *Pax Britannica* (Harcourt Brace Jovanovich, 1980).

The Americans' entry into the Pacific is outlined in F. R. Dulles, *America's Rise to World Power* (Harper & Row, 1955). Recommended surveys of Southeast Asia are D. G. E. Hall, *A History of Southeast Asia* (St. Martin's, 1968); and H. J. Benda and J. A. Larkin, *The World of Southeast Asia* (Harper & Row, 1967).

Li Chien-nung, *The Political History of China* (Van Nostrand, 1956), is a fine history of nineteenth-century China. For a good discussion of the transition China faced, see A. Feuerwerker, ed., *Modern China* (Prentice-Hall, 1964). Another useful study of China is Immanuel Hsu, *The Rise of Modern China* (Oxford, 1975). A key study on China's greatest rebellion is Franz Michael, *The Taiping Rebellion* (Univ. of Washington, 1972). P. W. Fay's *The Opium War, 1840–1842* (Norton, 1976) is a fine study. For views on the stresses of the late imperial period, see D. H. Bays, *China Enters the Twentieth Century . . .* (Michigan, 1978).

W. B. Beasley, *The Modern History of Japan* (Holt, Rinehart & Winston, 1973) is a useful overview. For an investigation into the early contacts between Europe and Asia, see George B. Sansom, *The Western World and Japan* (Knopf, 1974) and *Japan: A Short Cultural History* (Stanford, 1952). Thomas Haber, *The Revolutionary Origins of Modern Japan* (Stanford, 1981) and G. M. Beckmann, *The Modernization of China and Japan* (Harper & Row, 1962) are essential to an understanding of the Meiji programs.

✦ Notes

1. Quoted in T. A. Bailey, *The American Pageant* (Lexington: D. C. Heath, 1956), p. 630.
2. K. S. Latourette, *A Short History of the Far East* (New York: Macmillan, 1947), p. 184.
3. Quoted in F. H. Michael and G. E. Taylor, *The Far East in the Modern World* (New York: Holt, Rinehart & Winston, 1956), p. 122.
4. Li-Chien-nung, *The Political History of China, 1840–1928*, trans. by Sau-yu Teng and J. Ingalls (Princeton: D. Van Nostrand Co., 1956), p. 29.
5. Michael and Taylor, *The Far East in the Modern World*, p. 183.
6. Quoted in Ch'u Chai and Winberg Chai, *The Changing Society of China* (New York: Mentor Books, 1962), p. 189.
7. Michael and Taylor, *The Far East in the Modern World*, pp. 253–256.

CHAPTER 29

DIPLOMATIC CRISES 1905–1914

0 100 200
MILES

NORWAY
SWEDEN
DENMARK
Stockholm
Moscow
Riga
Smolensk
Minsk
RUSSIA
GREAT BRITAIN
Glasgow
NORTH SEA
BALTIC SEA
British Ultimatum to Germany Aug. 1914
Hamburg
Berlin
GERMANY
Warsaw
POLAND
Kiev
Kharkov
Rostov
Don R.
Vistula R.
Dnieper R.
Russian Mobilization 1914
London
NETHERLANDS
BELGIUM
Cologne
LUX.
Rhine
Elbe R.
Prague
Munich
Dniester R.
ATLANTIC OCEAN
Paris
FRANCE
Loire R.
SWITZ.
Danube R.
Budapest
AUSTRIA-HUNGARY
Austrian Annexation of Bosnia 1908
Austrian Ultimatum to Serbia July 1914
ROMANIA
Bucharest
SEA OF AZOV
BLACK SEA
BAY OF BISCAY
Bordeaux
Rhône
Milan
Trieste
Po R.
Sarajevo 1914
Belgrade
SERBIA
BULGARIA
Sofia
Constantinople
Ankara
Kizil R.
Douro R.
Ebro R.
Madrid
Barcelona
CORSICA
Rome
ITALY
ADRIATIC SEA
MONTE-NEGRO
ALBANIA
GREECE
AEGEAN SEA
Smyrna
OTTOMAN EMPIRE
PORTUGAL
Lisbon
Tagus R.
SPAIN
SARDINIA
Naples
Athens
CYPRUS
BALEARIC IS.
Marseille
Tangier 1905
Algeciras 1906
Casablanca
Fez
Algiers
SICILY
CRETE
MEDITERRANEAN SEA
Tunis
TUNISIA (Fr.)
MALTA (Br.)
Agadir 1911
MOROCCO
ALGERIA (Fr.)
Tripoli
LIBYA (It.)
Bengasi
Alexandria
Cairo
Nile R.
EGYPT (Br. Prot.)

→ By 1905 there were not many parts of the globe left to attract Europe's imperial interests. Instead, the great powers, now grouped into two competing alliance systems, looked closer to home: North Africa and the Balkans.

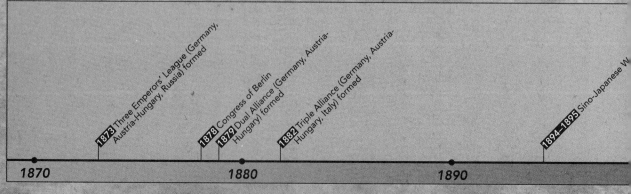

1873 Three Emperors' League (Germany, Austria-Hungary, Russia) formed

1878 Congress of Berlin

1879 Dual Alliance (Germany, Austria-Hungary) formed

1882 Triple Alliance (Germany, Austria-Hungary, Italy) formed

1894–1895 Sino-Japanese W

1870
1880
1890

World War and Tragic Peace

In 1914 Europeans had many reasons to be optimistic about the future. The growth produced by the previous three generations was supported by a sturdy belief in progress. Business and labor leaders had avoided the explosive class conflicts that Marx had forecast. Statesmen made serious efforts toward international cooperation, as could be seen by the establishment of the Hague Tribunal to arbitrate international disputes.

There were, however, danger signs for the Continent. Within Europe the competitive energies generated by the states came to be harnessed in two conflicting alliance systems. The nagging Eastern Question eventually dragged the alliances into war. In the four years of bloodshed that began in 1914, over 13 million Europeans died. Europe lost a generation of the best and bravest of its sons and substantial portions of the Continent suffered massive damage. The world economy lost what little equilibrium remained. Four empires—the German, the Austro-Hungarian, the Russian, and the Ottoman—either disappeared or were in the process of disappearing. Europe's golden age was brought to an end by a combination of tragic forces: militarism, rival alliances, economic imperialism, secret diplomacy, and narrow, bellicose nationalism. The bitter-

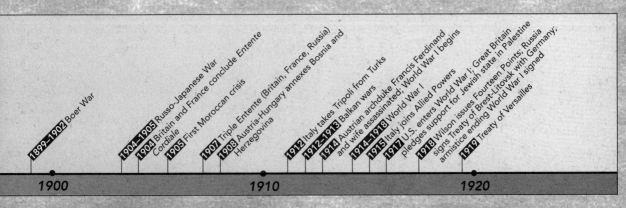

1899–1902 Boer War

1904–1905 Russo-Japanese War

1904 Britain and France conclude Entente Cordiale

1905 First Moroccan crisis

1907 Triple Entente (Britain, France, Russia)

1908 Austria-Hungary annexes Bosnia and Herzegovina

1912 Italy takes Tripoli from Turks

1912–1913 Balkan wars

1914 Austrian archduke Francis Ferdinand and wife assassinated; World War I begins

1914–1918 World War I

1915 Italy joins Allied Powers

1917 U.S. enters World War I; Great Britain pledges support for Jewish state in Palestine

1918 Wilson issues Fourteen Points; Russia signs Treaty of Brest-Litovsk with Germany; armistice ending World War I signed

1919 Treaty of Versailles

1900   1910   1920

ness engendered by the war made the establishment of a lasting peace impossible. World War I set in motion the forces that made the twentieth century the most bloody one in the history of humanity.

STATE COMPETITION AND DIPLOMATIC FAILURE

Europe's greatest danger came not from critics or the occasional radical group, but from competition among the great powers. Europe's militarism, rival alliances, secret diplomacy, imperialism, and nationalism were the underlying, long-range causes of the First World War. These elements had long been present on the European scene, but at the turn of the century they were made even more explosive by the ambitions and policies of Germany.

The Elements of Competition

At the beginning of the twentieth century, European politics remained much the same as it had in the previous three centuries—a competition among states. The main difference in 1900 was that there were some 25 independent political units instead of about 500. The laws were the same as those established at Westphalia in 1648. The states recognized no authority above themselves and followed international law only when it suited their interests. They were ready to take advantage of a neighbor's weakness and threaten war if the prize to be won was substantial enough. War, whether the threat or the reality, remained the prime instrument of national policy. This "extension of politics" was frequently used whenever peaceful methods did not work.

Military force was the ultimate arbiter in international affairs. By the end of the 1870s, five of the six major powers had introduced compulsory military training. Although the British had not done so, they were in the process of expanding their fleet. By the first decade of this century the great powers had nearly 4.5 million men in the military and spent annually more than $2 billion on arms. The weapons industry became an important part of the European economy.

Economic rivalry and tariff restrictions heightened the competitions between states. In the new mercantilism, states acted as aggressive champions for their own businesses. In some cases economic rivalry led to fighting: Japanese designs on the Asian mainland caused war with China in 1894; Great Britain fought the Boer War in South Africa from 1899 to 1902; Japan and Russia fought over Manchuria from 1904 to 1905; and Italy took Tripoli from Turkey in 1912.

Nationalism was the greatest force fueling the rise in tensions on the Continent. As used by Europe's politicians, the spirit of nationalism took on narrow, blatant, and warlike qualities to

➜ This cartoon portrays international power politics as a deadly billiard game in which the players use rifles and swords as cue sticks to strike the cannonballs. Bombs are stacked beneath the table, which is covered with a map of Europe. The snake-haired figure at center is identified as Diplomacy.

unite the populations of Europe behind the policies of their leaders. Among both ruling groups and state minorities, nationalism became a new religion and an essential tool of power politics. The greatest danger to peace came in the nationalistic ambitions of the Balkan nations. Proud of their new freedom, they were determined to extend it to their compatriots still under the Turks or Austrians. Serbia in particular was ready to liberate the other Slavs. However, there was no reason that this local problem should have plunged Europe into war.

In this atmosphere of international anarchy, most states did not feel strong enough to rely solely on their own resources for defense. Nations whose interests ran along parallel lines joined together. In response, nations outside an alliance formed unions to match their competitors. The creation of the two major rival alliances—the Triple Alliance (Germany, Austria-Hungary, and Italy) and the Triple Entente (Britain, France, and Russia)—was the key fact in European diplomacy before 1914. However, the alliances brought no assured peace. Rather, they increased the possibility of major war because it was impossible now to localize a problem such as that of the Balkan Slavs.

Closely tied to the system of alliances was the practice of secret diplomacy. Some diplomats threatened, intimidated, and jockeyed for power. The traditional activities of spies with their secret reports and unscrupulous methods poisoned the atmosphere even further. The increase in tension overwhelmed the efforts of decent and honorable statesmen to keep peace.

The End of Bismarck's System

From 1870 to 1890 the German chancellor Otto von Bismarck dominated European diplomacy. He built a foreign policy devoted to the diplomatic isolation of France by depriving it of potential allies. He reasoned that the French would try to take revenge on Germany and regain Alsace and Lorraine, but he knew they could do little without aid from the Austrians or Russians. In 1873 Bismarck made an alliance, known as the Three Emperors' League (Dreikaiserbund), with Russia and Austria-Hungary.

The conflicts between the Austrians and Russians in the Balkans soon put a strain on the League, and at the Congress of Berlin (1878) Bismarck was forced to choose between the conflicting claims of Vienna and St. Petersburg. He chose to support Austria-Hungary for a number of reasons, including fear of alienating Great Britain if he backed the Russians. In addition, he felt that he could probably dominate Austria more easily than Russia. This momentous shift paved the way for a new arrangement. In 1879 Bismarck negotiated the Dual Alliance with the Austro-Hungarian monarchy; in 1882 a new partner—Italy—joined the group, which was now called the Triple Alliance.

The choice of Austria over Russia did not mean that Bismarck abandoned his ties with the tsars. In 1881 the Three Emperors' League was renewed. Rivalries between the Dual Monarchy and Russia in the Balkans put an effective end to the arrangement, and the Dreikaiserbund collapsed for good in 1887. Bismarck negotiated a separate agreement with Russia called the Reinsurance Treaty, in which both sides pledged neutrality—except if Germany attacked France or Russia attacked Austria—and support of the status quo.

Under Bismarck's shrewd hand, Germany kept diplomatic control for 20 years. Bismarck chose his goals carefully and understood the states with which he worked. He made every effort to avoid challenging Britain's interests and to continue isolating France. As a result, Germany was not surrounded by enemies. The chancellor kept from alienating Russia while maintaining his ties with Austria.

In the 1890s, however, the rash actions of the new kaiser, William II, destroyed Germany's favorable position. He dismissed Bismarck in 1890, took foreign policy in his own hands, and frittered away the diplomatic advantages the chancellor had built up. France had been attempting to escape from its isolation for some time, and through its loans had begun to make important inroads into Russia, even before Bismarck retired. When the kaiser allowed the Reinsurance Treaty to lapse, the Russians sought new allies. By 1894 France got what it had wanted for 20 years—a strong ally. The Triple Alliance of Germany, Italy, and Austria-Hungary was now confronted by the Dual Alliance of Russia and France. Germany's worst fears had come to pass as it was now encircled by enemies.

Friedrich von Bernhardi Summarizes Germany's Intentions

Friedrich von Bernhardi stated German dreams and frustrations a full two years before the outbreak of World War I.

Duties of the greatest importance for the whole advance of human civilization have thus been transmitted to the German nation, as heir of a great and glorious past. It is faced with problems of no less significance in the sphere of its international relations. These problems are of special importance, since they affect most deeply the intellectual development, and on their solution depends the position of Germany in the world.

The German people has always been incapable of great acts for the common interest except under the irresistible pressure of external conditions, as in the rising of 1813, or under the leadership of powerful personalities, who knew how to arouse the enthusiasm of the masses, to stir the German spirit to its depths, to vivify the idea of nationality, and force conflicting aspirations into concentration and union.

We must therefore take care that such men are assured the possibility of acting with a confident and free hand in order to accomplish great ends through and for our people.

Within these limits, it is in harmony with the national German character to allow personality to have a free course for the fullest development of all individual forces and capacities, of all spiritual, scientific, and artistic aims. "Every extension of the activities of the State is beneficial and wise, if it arouses, promotes, and purifies the independence of free and reasoning men; it is evil when it kills and stunts the independence of free men." This independence of the individual, within the limits marked out by the interests of the State, forms the necessary complement of the wide expansion of the central power, and assures an ample scope to a liberal development of all our social conditions.

We must rouse in our people the unanimous wish for power in this sense, together with the determination to sacrifice on the altar of patriotism, not only life and property, but also private views and preferences in the interests of the common welfare. Then alone shall we discharge our great duties of the future, grow into a World Power, and stamp a great part of humanity with the impress of the German spirit. If, on the contrary, we persist in that dissipation of energy which now marks our political life, there is imminent fear that in the great contest of the nations, which we must inevitably face, we shall be dishonourably beaten; that days of disaster await us in the future, and that once again, as in the days of our former degradation, the poet's lament will be heard:

O Germany, the oaks still stand,
But thou art fallen, glorious land!
Körner

From Friedrich von Bernhardi, *Germany and the Next War,* translated by Allen H. Powles (New York: Longmans, Green, and Co., 1914).

Britain Ends Its Isolation

At the end of the nineteenth century Britain found itself involved in bitter rivalries with Russia, both in the Balkans and in the Middle East, and with France in Africa. During the Boer War, all of the great powers in Europe were anti-British. However, the supremacy of the British fleet helped discourage intervention. As the new century began, London became concerned that its policy of splendid isolation might need to be abandoned. In these circumstances, the most normal place for Britain to turn would be to Germany.

On the surface, nothing seemed more natural than that these two dominant European powers should adjust their national interests to avoid conflict. From the 1880s to 1901 both sides made several approaches to investigate an "understanding" between the major sea power, Britain, and the strongest land power, Germany. Tradition and dynastic relations spoke in favor of a

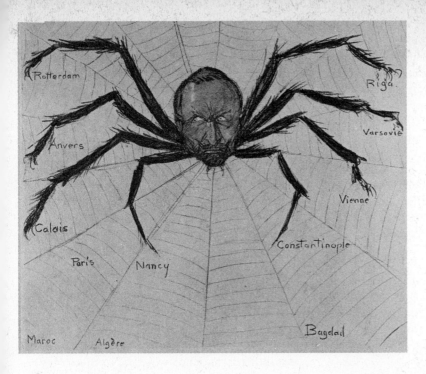

Labels on the web: Rotterdam, Riga, Anvers, Varsovie, Calais, Vienne, Paris, Nancy, Constantinople, Maroc, Algère, Bagdad

→ Dutch artist Louis Raemaekers depicted the German kaiser as a spider whose legs reached throughout Europe and whose predatory eye is cast as far away as Baghdad, Algeria, and Morocco.

closer tie between the two. By 1900, Berlin and London may have competed in economic and imperialistic terms, but they were far from any major strife in any either area.

The two countries could not, however, come together in an alliance. Even though important figures on both sides could see the advantages of an alliance, strong forces worked against this development. German and British interests did not match sufficiently to permit equal gain from an alliance. The kaiser's numerous bellicose statements and clumsy actions, such as his meddling in British colonial affairs with his telegram to South African President Paul Kruger in 1896, offended many British leaders. Germany's expanding influence in the Middle East and the Balkans worried the British as did Germany's tremendous economic progress.

Most threatening for London was Germany's plan to build a fleet that would compete with Britain's. In 1900, Germany initiated a huge naval program providing for, within a 20-year timetable, a fleet strong enough to keep Britain from interfering with German international goals. The British believed that the German program was aimed directly at them. For the island nation, the supremacy of the Royal Navy was a life-or-death matter. Since food and raw materi-

als had to come by sea, it was crucial that the navy be able to protect British shipping.

Challenged by Germany, Britain looked elsewhere for allies. In 1904 officials from London and Paris began to settle their outstanding differences and proclaimed the *Entente Cordiale* ("friendly understanding") setting aside a tradition of hostility dating back to the fourteenth century. The entente and an alliance with Japan in 1902 ended Britain's policy of diplomatic isolation and brought it into the combination that would be pitted against Germany's Triple Alliance. In 1907 London settled its problems with Russia, thereby establishing the Triple Entente. The British made no definite military commitments in the agreements with France and Russia. Theoretically they retained freedom of action, but they were now part of the alliance system.

The Moroccan Crises

In the decade before the First World War Europe experienced a series of crises on its peripheries, none of which vitally threatened the great powers' survival. However, because of the alliance systems, these incidents increased tensions and brought Europe ever closer to war.

The first serious test came in 1905 over Morocco. France sought control of this territory in order to establish a continuous line of dependencies from the Atlantic across the North African coast to Tunisia. Carefully timing their moves, the Germans arranged for the kaiser to visit the Moroccan port of Tangier, where he declared that all powers must respect the independence of the country. The French were forced to give up their immediate plans for taking over Morocco and agree to Germany's suggestion that an international conference be called at Algeciras (1906) to discuss the matter.

At this meeting the Germans hoped for a split between the British and French. This did not occur. On the contrary, all but one of the nations in attendance—even Italy—supported France rather than Germany. Only Austria-Hungary remained on the kaiser's side. The conference agreed that Morocco should still enjoy its sovereignty, but that France and Spain should be given certain rights to police the area.

In 1911 a second Moroccan crisis escalated tensions. When France sent an army into the disputed territory, ostensibly to maintain order, Germany responded by sending the gunboat *Panther* to the Moroccan port of Agadir. Great Britain came out with a blunt warning that all of its power was at the disposal of France in this affair. A diplomatic bargain was finally struck in which France got a free hand in Morocco and Germany gained a small area in Equatorial Africa. The two rival alliance systems managed to avoid war over Morocco. Feelings were soothed when the imperial powers compensated each other with pieces of the African landscape.

The Balkan Crises

The two rival alliances came to blows over the Balkans, where the interests of Austria-Hungary and Russia directly collided. In that complex area, the forces of local nationalism drew the great powers into a military showdown.

Austria and Russia had long kept a wary eye on each other's policies in southeastern Europe. During the nineteenth century each country had had an obsessive interest in the Balkan holdings of the Ottoman Empire. Neither side could afford for the other to gain too great an advantage in the area. Throughout the last part of the nineteenth century the two had occasionally disagreed over

issues involving Macedonia, railroads, and boundary revisions. In 1908 a crisis erupted that threatened to draw Europe into war. The issue that increased hostility was the Dual Monarchy's annexation of Bosnia and Herzegovina.

The Austro-Hungarian monarchy had administered the two areas since the 1878 Congress of Berlin, so the annexation actually changed very little. But the Slavs perceived the annexation as humiliating to them and their "protector," Russia. The fact that the Russians, through an ill-considered plan, had initiated the train of events that led to the annexation made the whole affair doubly frustrating for the Slavs.

A tsarist diplomat Count Izvolskii had initiated discussions whereby the Russians would approve the annexation in return for increased Black Sea rights for the Russians. Bosnia and Herzegovina were annexed, but the Russians never got their part of the bargain. Serbia was outraged by the incorporation of more Slavs into the Habsburg domain and expected its Slavic, Orthodox protector, Russia, to do something about it. The Russians had been badly bruised in their war with Japan and the Revolution of 1905. Aside from making threatening noises, they could do little, especially in the face of Germany's support for Austria-Hungary.

Austro-Hungarian interests in the Balkans were primarily concerned with defense and keeping Serbia under control. The Dual Monarchy was experiencing serious domestic strains as the multinational empire limped along under the terms of the renegotiated *Ausgleich*. Austro-Hungarian pretensions to great power status increasingly outdistanced its ability to play that role.

Germany's motives in the Balkans were largely strategic in the long term and diplomatic in the short term. The Germans envisioned a Berlin-based political and economic zone stretching from the Baltic Sea to the Persian Gulf. Berlin could not afford to alienate its Austrian ally through lukewarm support.

After 1908 tensions remained high in the Balkans. The Austrians looked to increase their advantage, knowing they had the full support of Germany. Serbia searched for revenge, while Russia found itself backed into a corner. The Russians in the future would be forced to act strongly and encourage aggressive policies on the part of their Balkan allies or lose forever their position of prestige. The 1908 crisis changed relatively few of the major features of the competition for influence in the Balkans, except to limit further the major powers' options.

In 1912 Serbia and its neighbors, especially Greece and Bulgaria, formed an alliance with the objective of expelling Turkey from Europe. The First Balkan War began later in the year and came to a quick end with the defeat of the Turks. Each of the Balkan allies had its own particular goals in mind in fighting the Ottomans. When the great powers stepped in to maintain the balance, problems arose.

Serbia had fought for a seaport and thought it had gained one with the defeat of the Turks. However, the Italians and Austrians blocked Serbia's access to the Adriatic by overseeing the creation of Albania in the Treaty of London of 1913. Denied their goals, the Serbs turned on their former ally, the Bulgarians, and demanded a part of

their spoils from the first war. Bulgaria refused and, emboldened by its successes in the first war, attacked its former allies, starting the Second Balkan War. The Serbs were in turn joined by the Romanians and the Turks. The Bulgarians were no match for the rest of the Balkans and signed a peace that turned over most of the territory that they had earlier gained. The Turks retained only a precarious toehold in Europe, the small pocket from Adrianople to Constantinople.

Had the great powers found a way to place a fence around the Balkans and allow the squabbling nations to fight their miniwars in isolation, the two Balkan wars of 1912 and 1913 would have had little significance. As it was, however, they added to the prevailing state of tension. The two competing alliances effectively tied their policies to the narrow constraints of the Balkans. In effect, the tail wagged the dog, as the

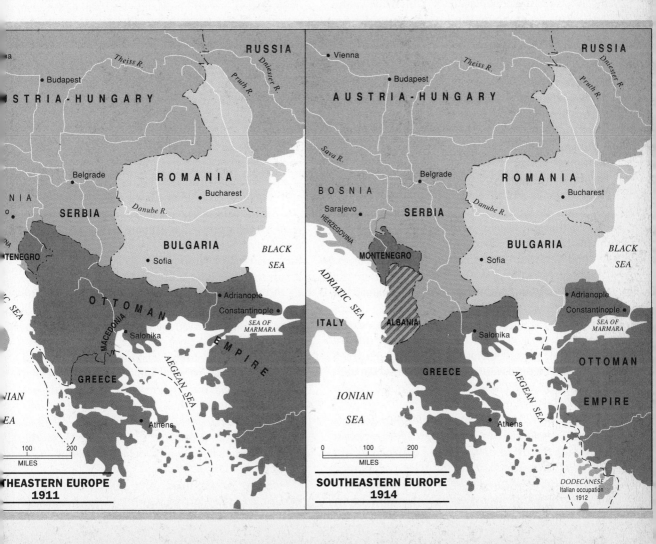

SOUTHEASTERN EUROPE 1911

SOUTHEASTERN EUROPE 1914

alliances reacted to every flareup in the turbulent peninsula.

By the end of 1913 no permanent solution had been found to the Balkan problems. Austria was more fearful than ever of Serbia's expansionist desires. Serbian ambitions had grown larger since its territory had doubled as a result of the recent wars. The Serbian prime minister declared: "The first round is won: now we must prepare the second against Austria." Russia's dreams of Balkan grandeur had not been blocked but only interrupted. The rest of Europe lay divided.

Assassination at Sarajevo

The spark that set off World War I was struck on June 28, 1914 with the assassination of the heir to the Austrian throne, Archduke Francis Ferdinand. The archduke and his wife were visiting the Bosnian town of Sarajevo, which his realm had recently annexed. While they were driving through the narrow streets in their huge touring car, a 19-year-old Bosnian student named Gavrilo Princip, one of seven youthful terrorists along the route, shot them.

Princip had been inspired by propaganda advocating the creation of a greater Serbia and assisted by Serbian officers serving in a secret organization. The direct participation of the Serbian government was never proved; even so, the Belgrade authorities were likely to have been involved, at least indirectly.

The legal details of the case were lost in Vienna's rush to put an end to the problem of Serbia. Count Leopold von Berchtold, the foreign minister, believed that the assassination in Bosnia justified crushing the anti-Austrian propaganda and terrorism coming from the Serbs. The kaiser felt that everything possible must be done to prevent Germany's only reliable ally from being weakened, and so he assured the Austrians of his full support. Berchtold received a blank check from Germany. Vienna wanted a quick, local Austro-Serbian war, and Germany favored quick action to forestall Russian intervention.

On July 23 the Austro-Hungarian foreign ministry presented an ultimatum to the Serbs. Expecting the list of demands to be turned down, Berchtold demanded unconditional acceptance within 48 hours. On July 25 the Austro-Hungarian government announced that Serbia's reply, which was conciliatory, was not satisfactory. The

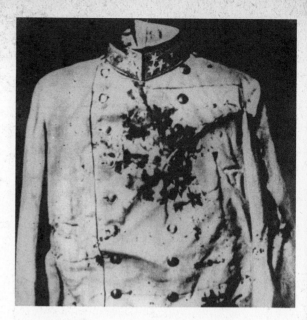

→ Archduke Francis Ferdinand was wearing this coat when he was assassinated at Sarajevo. The bloodstains left by the bullet wounds are clearly evident.

Austrian authorities immediately mobilized their armed forces.

The Alliances' Inevitable War

The Germans, having second thoughts, urged their ally to negotiate with Russia, which was anxiously following developments. Russia realized that if the Austrians succeeded in humbling the Serbs, Russia's position in the Balkans would suffer irreparably. The French, in the meantime, assured the Russians of their full cooperation and urged full support for Serbia. The British unsuccessfully advised negotiation.

Europe had reached a point of no return: the Austrians had committed themselves to the task of removing a serious opponent, and the Russians could not permit this removal to happen. Neither side would back down, and each had allies ready to come to its aid. Fearful that Serbia would escape from his clutches, Berchtold succeeded on July 27—thanks in part to deception—in convincing the Habsburg emperor that war was the only way out. On the following day the Austro-Hungarian empire declared war against Serbia.

As the possibilities of a general European war loomed, Berlin sent several frantic telegrams to Vienna. The German ambassador was instructed to tell Berchtold that "as an ally we must refuse to be drawn into a world conflagration because Austria does not respect our advice."[1] Had the Germans spoken to their ally in such tones a month earlier, war might have been avoided. But Austria's belligerence moved the Russians to act. The tsar ordered mobilization on July 30.

Germany was caught in a dilemma that Bismarck would never have allowed. Surrounded by potential enemies, the Germans had to move decisively or face defeat. The Russian mobilization threatened them, because in the event of war on the eastern front, there would also be war on the western front. The best plan for Berlin, one that had been worked out since 1905, seemed to be to launch a lightning attack against France, which could mobilize faster than Russia, crush France, and then return to meet Russia, which would be slower to mobilize. To allow Russian mobilization to proceed without action would jeopardize this plan. In the wake of the crisis, the Germans set into effect their long-planned strategy to gain European dominance.

On July 31 Germany sent ultimata to Russia and France, demanding cessation of mobilization from the former and a pledge of neutrality from the latter. Failing to receive satisfactory replies, Germany declared war on Russia on August 1 and on France two days later. On August 2, the German ambassador in Brussels delivered an ultimatum to the Belgian government announcing his country's intention to send troops through Belgium, in violation of the 1839 Neutrality Treaty. The Belgian cabinet refused to grant permission and appealed to the Triple Entente for help.

A majority of the British cabinet did not want war, but with the news of the German ultimatum to Belgium, the tide turned. Sir Edward Grey, the British foreign secretary, sent an ultimatum to Germany demanding that Belgian neutrality be respected. Germany refused, and on August 4 Great Britain declared war.

Because Germany and Austria-Hungary were not waging a defensive war, Italy declined to carry out its obligations under the Triple Alliance and for a time remained neutral. In the latter part of August, Japan joined the allies. Turkey, fearing Russia, threw in its lot with the Central Powers.

In the last days of peace, diplomats tried desperately to avert general war. Through confusion, fear, and loss of sleep, the nervous strain among them was almost unbearable. Many broke down and wept when it became apparent they had failed. Grey himself noted in his autobiography that one evening, just before the outbreak of the war, he watched the streetlights being lit from his office window and remarked: "The lamps are going out all over Europe; we shall not see them lit again in our lifetime."[2]

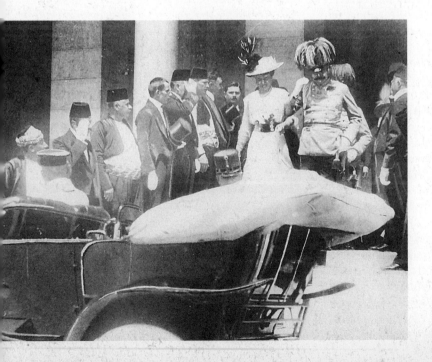

→ Archduke Francis Ferdinand and his wife, Sophie, leave the Senate House in Sarajevo on June 28, 1914. Five minutes after this photograph was taken, Serbian terrorist Gavrilo Princip assassinated them both, helping to set off World War I.

WORLD WAR I

Although the terrible struggle that racked the world from 1914 to 1918 was fought mainly in Europe, it is rightly called the First World War. In the sixteenth and seventeenth centuries European powers had competed across the globe; however, never had so many fighters and such enormous resources been brought together in a single conflict. Altogether 27 nations became belligerents, ranging the globe from Japan to Canada and from Argentina to South Africa to Australia.

The Central Powers—Germany, Austria-Hungary, Bulgaria, and Turkey—mobilized 21 million men. The Allies eventually called 40 million men to arms, including 12 million Russians. The two sides were more equally matched than the numbers would indicate, however. Since the Russian divisions were often poorly equipped and ineffectively used, the Allies' apparent advantage was not so great as the numbers would indicate. In addition, in the German army the Central Powers boasted superb generalship and discipline. Another advantage was that the Central Powers fought from a central position and were able to transfer troops quickly and efficiently to various fronts.

The Allies had the advantages of greater resources of finance and raw materials. Britain maintained its naval dominance and could draw on its empire for support. In addition, because Germany was effectively blockaded, the United States, even though officially neutral for most of the war, served as a major source of supplies for the Allies.

The warring nations went into battle in a confident mood. Each side was sure of its strength and felt it had prepared carefully. Each nation's propaganda machine delivered reassuring messages of guaranteed victory. All expected that the war would soon be over, concluded in a few decisive battles. It was generally believed that the war would be over by Christmas.

The First Two Years of War

All of the general staffs had been refining their war plans for years. The Germans knew that Allied naval supremacy would cut them off from needed sources abroad. They realized that they were potentially surrounded and that they should strike a quick knockout blow to end the war. Following the plan devised by Chief of the General Staff Alfred von Schlieffen, the Germans aimed to push the Belgians aside and drive rapidly south into France. The plan then called for the German forces to wheel west of Paris, outflank the French forces, and drive them toward Alsace-Lorraine, where they would be met by another German army. Within six weeks, the French would be destroyed, caught between the western hammer and the eastern anvil. Meanwhile, a small German force would be holding the presumably slow-moving Russians on the eastern front, awaiting the arrival via the excellent German rail system of the victorious western forces. The plan nearly worked.

The Germans marched according to the plan until they got so close to Paris that they could see the top of the Eiffel Tower. They were hurled back by a bold French offensive through a gap that opened between their armies in the First Battle of the Marne, fought between September 5 and 12. With the assistance of a small British expeditionary force and Parisian taxi drivers who provided transportation, the French then marched north in a race with the Germans to reach and control the vital ports along the English Channel. After much desperate fighting, the enemies established battle positions that stabilized, creating the "western front." This solid line of opposing trenches, which stretched from the

→ The Queen's Lancers pass a detachment of French mounted troops during the advance from the Marne to the Aisne in September 1914. The Aisne Valley was the site of four major battles of World War I.

WORLD WAR I

- Triple Entente
- Central Powers
- Allies of Triple Entente
- Neutral Nations
- → Allied thrust
- → Central Powers' Thrust
- Battles:
- × Allied Victory
- ⊗ Central Powers' Victory

0 100 200
MILES

Channel to near Nancy, was the scene for a grisly new war of attrition.

The other part of the German scheme that did not go according to plan was the unexpected speed with which the Russians mobilized. They penetrated deeply into East Prussia and overran the Austrian province of Galicia. However, confused leadership resulted in two catastrophic Russian defeats in East Prussia, and Germany never again faced a serious threat on its eastern frontier.

By the end of 1914 all sides knew that they were trapped in a new type of war, one of horrible consequences. Single battles claimed hundreds of thousands of lives, and the toll during the first few months of the conflict ran as high as 1½ million dead and wounded.

In 1915 the British attempted a major campaign to force open the Dardanelles, closed by Turkey when it joined the Central Powers. This plan, attributed to Winston Churchill, then first

→ Soldiers manning a Vickers machine gun at the Somme in July 1916 wear gas masks as protection against phosgene. The new technology of World War I included increased use of the machine gun and poison gas.

lord of the admiralty, was designed to open up the sea route to Russia, which was badly in need of war supplies, and to take the pressure off the western front. After heroic and costly attacks, Allied Australian and New Zealand troops, known as Anzacs, were forced to withdraw from their landing positions on the Gallipoli peninsula in European Turkey.

Another major Allied setback in 1915 was the defeat of the Russian forces in Poland. More than 1.2 million Russians were killed and wounded, and the Germans took nearly 900,000 prisoners. Although Russia somehow remained in the war and fought well against the Dual Monarchy, it was no longer a concern for the Germans. These defeats generated rising criticism against the tsar's government, and Russian morale deteriorated.

Serbia was the next Allied victim. In September 1915, Bulgaria, still aching from its defeat in the Second Balkan War, entered the war on the side of the Central Powers. Surrounded by enemies, Serbia was helpless and resistance was quickly crushed. The Austrians had finally gained their goal of the previous summer, but, in the context of the continental tragedy, this achievement no longer seemed significant.

The Allies' only bright spot in 1915 was Italy's entry into their ranks. Italy had remained neutral in August 1914 when it had defected from the Triple Alliance, of which it had been at best a token member. Italy joined the Allies fol-lowing promises made in a secret treaty in London promising the Italians huge concessions of territory once victory had been attained.

Stalemate

The Allies' strategy on the western front was to restrict attacks in France to intermittent nibbling, thus saving manpower and at the same time concentrating on their naval blockade. Denied badly needed imports, it was assumed, the German war effort would be seriously weakened. Countering this tactic, the German high command launched a massive offensive against the strategic fortress of Verdun in the spring of 1916. This forced the Allies to throw hundreds of thousands of men into battle. The slaughter brought on by massed artillery and infantry charges between the trenches was horrible. The total loss of wounded and dead from this battle came to some 700,000 men.

To ease the pressure against Verdun, the British army began an offensive along the Somme River along the western front. The attackers' losses were catastrophic: 60 percent of the officers and 40 percent of the men became casualties the first day of the battle. Despite these awesome figures, which included the British firing 2 million shells at the first battle of the Somme, the attacks continued for three months without any substantial gains. Total German losses at the Somme were about 450,000, while the British and French lost about 600,000 men.

The only major naval engagement of the war, the Battle of Jutland (May 31–June 1, 1916), reaffirmed British control of the seas. The Germans maneuvered brilliantly and took risks. They could afford to gamble because defeat would in no way worsen their existing position. The British fleet, on the other hand, had to act cautiously and absorbed greater losses. However the Germans retreated to their base and remained there for the rest of the war.[3]

On the eastern front in 1916 the Russians continued their generally successful campaigns against the Austro-Hungarian forces. But the Germans were always there to save their allies from destruction. Romania, impressed by the Russian victories, finally joined the Allies and launched an attack on the Hungarians. After an initial success, the Romanians were soon knocked out of the war by a joint German-Bulgarian invasion.

Total War and the Home Front

At the close of 1916, after more than two years of fighting, neither side was close to victory. Instead, the war had turned into a dreary contest of stamina, a far cry from the glories promised by the propaganda of 1914. War was no longer fought between armies, it was fought between states and every component within the state participated.[4]

→ German soldiers, huddled in a trench, their guns at the ready, rest during a lull in battle during World War I.

On the home front, rationing was instituted to ensure sufficient supplies for soldiers at the front. As men went off to fight, women took over their jobs in the workplace. Intensive propaganda campaigns encouraged civilians to buy more bonds and make more weapons. Nations

The Battle of Verdun

The initial euphoria accompanying World War I soon dissolved in the face of disasters such as the Battle of Verdun.

There are slopes on Hill 304 where the level of the ground is raised several meters by mounds of German corpses. Sometimes it happens that the third German wave uses the dead of the second wave as ramparts and shelters. It was behind ramparts of the dead left by the first five attacks, on May 24th, that we saw the Boches take shelter while they organized their next rush.

We make prisoners among these dead during our counterattacks. They are men who have received no hurt, but have been knocked down by the falling of the human wall of their killed and wounded neighbors. They say very little. They are for the most part dazed with fear and alcohol, and it is several days before they recover.

From *Source Records of the Great War,* vol. 4, edited by Charles F. Horne (New York: National Alumni, 1923).

Battle of the Somme

The "glories of war" were exposed for what they were—pain and suffering. These diary extracts show what war was like.

Diary of Private Tom Easton

A beautiful summer morning, though we'd had a bit of rain earlier. The skylarks were just singing away. Then the grand mine went up, it shook the earth for nearly a minute, and we had to wait for the fallout. The whistles blew and we stepped off one yard apart going straight forward. We were under orders not to stop or look or help the wounded. Carry on if you're fit, it was.

Men began to fall one by one. One officer said we were OK, all the machine-guns were firing over our heads. This was so until we passed our own front line and started to cross No Man's Land. Then trench machine-guns began the slaughter from the La Boiselle salient [German positions]. Men fell on every side screaming. Those who were unwounded dare not attend to them, we must press on regardless. Hundreds lay on the German barbed wire which was not all destroyed and their bodies formed a bridge for others to pass over and into the German front line.

There were few Germans, mainly in machine-gun posts. These were bombed out, and there were fewer still of us, but we consolidated the lines we had taken by preparing firing positions on the rear of the trenches gained, and fighting went on all morning and gradually died down as men and munitions on both sides became exhausted.

When we got to the German trenches we'd lost all our officers. They were all dead, there was no question of wounded. About 25 of us made it there.

Yes, as we made our way over the latter stages of the charge, men dropped all around like ninepins. Apart from machine-guns, the German artillery was also very active, great sheets of earth rose up before one. Every man had to fend for himself as we still had to face the Germans in their trenches when we got there.

I kept shouting for my MOTHER to guide me, strange as it may seem. Mother help me. Not the Virgin Mother but my own maternal Mother, for I was then only 20 years of age.

Diary of Captain Reginald Leetham

I got to my position and looked over the top. The first thing I saw in the space of a tennis court in front of me was the bodies of 100 dead or severely wounded men lying there in our own wire.

The dead were stretched out on one side [of the trench] one on top of the other six high. To do one's duty was continually climbing over corpses in every position. . . . Of the hundred of corpses I saw I only saw one pretty one—a handsome boy called Schnyder of the Berkshires who lay on our firestep shot through the heart. There he lay with a sandbag over his face: I uncovered it as I knew he was an officer. I wish his mother could have seen him—one of the few whose faces had not been mutilated.

Diary of Subaltern Edward G. D. Liveing

There was the freshness and splendor of a summer morning over everything.

A hare jumped up and rushed towards me through the dry yellowish grass, its eyes bulging with fear.

Suddenly I cursed. I had been scalded in the left hip. A shell, I thought, had blown up in a water logged crump hole and sprayed me with boiling water. Letting go of my rifle, I dropped forward full length on the ground. My hip began to smart unpleasantly, and I felt a curious warmth stealing down my left leg. I thought it was the boiling water that had scalded me. Certainly my breeches looked as if they were saturated with water. I did not know they were saturated with blood.

From Michael Kernan, "Day of Slaughter on the Somme," *The Washington Post*, June 27, 1976. © 1976 by the Washington Post. Reprinted by permission.

unleashed a barrage of propaganda inciting total hatred of the enemy, belief in the righteousness of the cause, and unquestioned support for the war effort.

Civil liberties suffered, and in some cases distinguished citizens were thrown into prison for opposing the war effort. In Britain, for example, the philosopher and mathematician Bertrand Russell was imprisoned for a short time for his pacifistic views. Governments took over control of their national economies and gambled everything on a victory in which the loser would pay all the expenses incurred in the war. The various states outlawed strikes and rigidly controlled currencies and foreign trade.

At the beginning of the war, all was flag-waving and enthusiasm. The international socialist movement, whose policy it was to promote international proletarian unity, fell victim to the rabid patriotism that infected the Continent. Workers of one country were encouraged to go out and kill workers of the enemy country in the name of the state. There was much idealism, sense of sacrifice, and love of country. At first there was no understanding of the horror, death, and disaster that comes with modern, industrialized war. British poet Rupert Brooke caught the spirit in his poem "The Soldier":

If I should die, think only this of me:
That there's some corner of a foreign field
That is forever England. There shall be
In that rich earth a richer dust concealed;
A dust whom England bore, shaped, made aware,
Gave, once, her flowers to love, her ways to roam,
A body of England's breathing English air,
Washed by the rivers, blest by suns of home.[5]

But this early idealism, this romantic conception of death in battle, gradually changed to one of war weariness and total futility. This growing mood is best seen in the poetry of the young British officer and poet Wilfrid Owen, himself a victim on the western front:

What passing-bells for those who die as cattle?
Only the monstrous anger of the guns. . . .
No mockeries for them; no prayers nor bells,
Nor any voice of mourning save the choirs,—
The shrill, demented choirs of wailing shells;
And bugles calling for them from sad shires.[6]

By the end of 1916 a deep yearning for peace dominated Europe. Sensing this mood, leaders on both sides put forth peace feelers. But these half-hearted overtures achieved nothing. Propaganda was used effectively to continue the war and support for it. The populations of the warring states were made to believe that their crusade was somehow divinely inspired. In reality, the Dual Monarchy and France fought for survival; Russia, German, and Italy all fought to improve their respective positions in Europe; while Britain fought for Belgium and a renewed balance of power on the Continent.

Allied Fatigue and American Entry

In 1917 British and French military strength reached its highest point, only to fall precipitously. Allied commanders were hopeful that the long-planned breakthrough might be accomplished, but a large-scale French attack was beaten back, with huge losses. Some French regiments mutinied rather than return to the inferno of "no-man's land" between the trenches. The British sacrificed hundreds of thousands of men without any decisive results in several massive offensives. The Allies also launched unsuccessful campaigns in Italy. Aided by the Germans, the Austrians smashed the Italian front at the battle of Caporetto (1917), an event vividly described by Ernest Hemingway in *A Farewell to Arms*. Italian resistance finally hardened, and collapse was barely averted.

The growing effectiveness of the German submarine menace deepened Allied frustration. By 1917 Allied shipping losses had reached dangerous proportions. In three months 470 British ships fell victim to torpedoes. Britain had no more than six weeks' supply of food on hand, and the supply situation became critical for the Allies. As it turned out, the very weapon that seemed to doom their cause, the submarine, was the source of the Allies' salvation: Germany's decision to use unrestricted submarine warfare brought the United States openly into the war.

The Americans had declared their neutrality in 1914 when President Woodrow Wilson announced that the American people "must be impartial in thought as well as in action." The events of the next two years showed that this would not be the case. American sentiment was overwhelmingly with the Allies from the first. France's help to the colonies in the American Revolution was warmly recalled. Britain and America were closely tied by language, literature, and democratic institutions. Because Britain cut off communications between Germany and the United States, British propaganda and management of the war news dominated public opinion. Another factor predisposing the United States to the Allied cause was Germany's violation of international law in the invasion of Belgium. This buttressed the widely held view created by the kaiser's saber-rattling speeches that the Germans were undemocratic, unpredictable, and unstable.

These attitudes were reinforced by the fact that the United States had made a substantial investment in the Allied war effort. As the war progressed it became apparent that the British blockade would permit American trade to be carried on only with the Allies. Before long, American factories and farmers were producing weapons and food solely for Great Britain and France. Industry expanded and began to enjoy a prosperity dependent on continued Allied pur-

→ The carnage left by war is evident as these soldiers wade through a battlefield heaped with dead bodies.

→ German troops advance through the smoke and fire of battle in the 1918 spring offensive on the Western Front. The body of a fallen French soldier lies in the foreground on the edge of a shell hole.

chases. Between 1914 and 1916 American exports to the Allies quadrupled. Allied bonds totaling about $1.5 billion were sold in the United States in 1915 and 1916. It was quite apparent to the Germans that there was little neutrality on the economic front in the United States.

The immediate cause of the U.S. entry into the war on the Allied side was the German submarine campaign. Blockaded by the British, Germany decided to retaliate by halting all shipping to the Allies. Its submarine campaign began in February 1915, and one of the first victims was the luxury liner *Lusitania*, torpedoed with the loss of more than 1000 lives, including 100 Americans. This tragedy aroused public opinion in the United States. In the fall of 1916 Wilson, campaigning with the slogan "he kept us out of war," was reelected to the presidency. Discovery of German plots to involve Mexico in the war against the United States and more submarine sinkings finally drove Wilson to ask Congress to declare war against Germany on April 6, 1917.

Submarine warfare and a wide range of other causes brought the president to the point of entering the war. Once in the conflict, however, he was intent on making the American sacrifice one "to make the world safe for democracy." Wilson's lofty principles caused a great surge of idealism among Americans.

Germany's Last Drive

The United States mobilized its tremendous resources of men and materiel more rapidly than

the Germans had believed possible when they made their calculated risk to increase submarine warfare. Nonetheless the Central Powers moved to try to gain a decisive victory before U.S. aid could help the Allies.

The fruitless offensives of 1917 had bled the British army white, and the French had barely recovered from their mutinies. The eastern front collapsed with the February/March revolution in Russia. Eight months later, Lenin and the Bolsheviks took power in Russia and began to negotiate for peace. By the Treaty of Brest-Litovsk early in 1918, Russia made peace with Germany, giving up 1.3 million square miles of territory and 62 million people.[7]

Freed from the necessity of fighting on the east, the Germans unleashed a series of major offensives against the west in the spring of 1918. During one of these attacks, a brigade of American marines symbolized the importance of U.S. support when they stopped a German charge at Chateau-Thierry. The Germans made a final effort to knock out the French in July 1918. It was called the *Friedensturm*, the peace offensive. The Germans made substantial gains, but did not score the decisive breakthrough. By this time the German momentum was slowing down, and more than a million American "doughboys" had landed in France. The final German offensive was thrown back after a slight advance.

With the aid of U.S. troops, Marshal Ferdinand Foch, the supreme Allied commander, began a counterattack. The badly beaten and continually harassed German troops fell back in rapid retreat. By the end of October, German forces had been driven out of France and Allied armies were advancing into Belgium. The war of fixed positions separated by "no man's land" was over. The Allies had smashed the trench defenses and were now in open country.

Already on October 1 the German high command urged the kaiser to sue for peace, and three days later the German chancellor sent a note to President Wilson seeking an end to hostilities. Wilson responded that peace was not possible as long as Germany was ruled by an autocratic regime. The German chancellor tried to keep the monarchy by instituting certain liberal reforms, but it was too late. Revolution broke out in many parts of Germany. The kaiser abdicated and a republic was proclaimed.

While Germany was staggering under the continual pounding of Foch's armies, the German allies were suffering even greater misfortunes. Bulgaria surrendered on September 30 and Turkey a month later. Austria stopped its fighting with Italy on November 3. Nine days later the Habsburg empire collapsed when Emperor Charles I fled Vienna to seek sanctuary in Switzerland.

At five o'clock on the morning of November 11, 1918, in a dining car in the Compiegne Forest, the German delegates signed the peace terms presented by Marshal Foch. At eleven o'clock the same day hostilities were halted. Everywhere except in Germany, the news was received with an outburst of joy. The world was once more at peace, confronted now with the task of binding up its wounds and removing the scars of combat. Delegates from the Allied nations were soon to meet in Paris, where the peace conference was to be held.

THE ALLIED PEACE SETTLEMENT

In November 1918 the Allies stood triumphant, after the costliest war in history. But the Germans could also feel well pleased in 1918. They had fought well, avoided being overrun, and escaped being occupied by the Allies. They could acknowledge they had lost the war but hoped that U.S. President Wilson would help them.

In February 1918 Wilson had stated that "there shall be no annexations, no contributions, no punitive damages," and on July 4 he affirmed that every question must be settled "upon the basis of the free acceptance of that settlement by the people immediately concerned."[8] As events transpired, however, the losers were refused seats at the peace conference and were the recipients of a dictated settlement.

Idealism and Realities

The destructive nature of World War I made a fair peace settlement impossible. The war had been fought on a winner-take-all basis, and now it was time for the Central Powers to pay. At the peace conference, the winning side was dominated by a French realist, a British politician, and an American idealist. The French representative was the aged French premier Georges Clemenceau, representing Britain was the British prime minister David Lloyd George, and the U.S. representative was President Woodrow Wilson. The three were joined by the Italian prime minister Vittorio Orlando, who attended to make sure his country gained adequate compensation for its large sacrifices. These four men made most of the key decisions, even though most of the interested nations and factions in the world were represented in Paris, except for the Soviet Union.

Clemenceau had played a colorful and important role in French politics for half a century. He had fought continuously for his political beliefs, opposing corruption, racism, and antidemocratic forces. He wanted to ensure French security in the future by pursuing restitution, reparations, and guarantees. Precise programs, not idealistic statements, would protect France.

The two English-speaking members of the big three represented the extremes in dealing with the Germans. Lloyd George had been reelected in December on a program of "squeezing the German lemon until the pips are squeaked." He wanted to destroy Berlin's naval, commercial, and colonial position and to ensure his own political future at home. In January 1918 U.S. President Wilson had issued to Congress the Fourteen Points describing his plan for peace. Wilson wanted to break the world out of its tradition of armed anarchy and establish a framework

→ The "Big Four" at the Versailles Peace Conference were, left to right, British prime minister Lloyd George, Italian prime minister Vittorio Orlando, French premier Georges Clemenceau, and President Woodrow Wilson of the United States. Representatives from Germany were excluded from the negotiating tables. The Big Four became the Big Three when Orlando withdrew abruptly because the conference refused to give Italy all it demanded.

John Maynard Keynes on Clemenceau

John Maynard Keynes caught the spirit of the peacemakers at Versailles in his work *The Economic Consequences of the Peace*. His portrait of Clemenceau is especially revealing.

He felt about France what Pericles felt of Athens—unique value in her, nothing else mattering; but his theory of politics was Bismarck's. He had one illusion—France; and one disillusion—mankind, including Frenchmen, and his colleagues not least. His principles for the peace can be expressed simply. In the first place, he was a foremost believer in the view of German psychology that the German understands and can understand nothing but intimidation, that he is without generosity or remorse in negotiation, that there is no advantage he will not take of you, and no extent to which he will not demean himself for profit, that he is without honor, pride, or mercy. Therefore you must never negotiate with a German or conciliate him; you must dictate to him. On no other terms will he respect you, or will you prevent him from cheating you. But it is doubtful how far he thought these characteristics peculiar to Germany, or whether his candid view of some other nations was fundamentally different. His philosophy had, therefore, no place for "sentimentality" in international relations. Nations are real things, of whom you love one and feel for the rest indifference—or hatred. The glory of the nation you love is a desirable end,—but generally to be obtained at your neighbor's expense. The politics of power are inevitable, and there is nothing very new to learn about this war or the end it was fought for; England had destroyed, as in each preceding century, a trade rival; a mighty chapter had been closed in the secular struggle between the glories of Germany and of France.

Prudence required some measure of lip service to the "ideals" of foolish Americans and hypocritical Englishmen; but it would be stupid to believe that there is much room in the world, as it really is, for such affairs as the League of Nations, or any sense in the principle of self-determination except as an ingenious formula for rearranging the balance of power in one's own interest.

From John Maynard Keynes, *The Economic Consequences of the Peace* (New York: Harcourt Brace Jovanovich, 1920).

for peace that would favor America's traditions of democracy and trade. At the peace conference he communicated his beliefs with a coldness and an imperiousness that masked his shy and sensitive nature and offended his colleagues.

The World War had not been a "war to end all wars" or a "war to make the world safe for democracy," as Wilson had portrayed it. The United States had hardly been neutral in its loans and shipments of supplies to the Allies before 1917. In fact, during the war, the financial and political center of balance for the world had crossed the ocean. The Americans made a rather abrupt shift from debtor to creditor status. The United States had entered the war late and had profited from it, and Wilson could afford to wear a rather more idealistic mantle.

The Europeans had paid for the war with the blood of their young and the coin of their realms.[9] The Allies now looked forward to a healthy return on their investment. The extent of that harvest had long been mapped out in secret treaties, copies of which the Bolsheviks released for the world to see.

Open Covenants, Secret Treaties

Wilson wanted to use his Fourteen Points as the base for a lasting peace. He wanted to place morality and justice ahead of power and revenge as considerations in international affairs. The first five points were general in nature and guaranteed: "open covenants openly arrived at," freedom of the seas in war and peace alike, removal of all economic barriers and establishment of an equality of trade among all nations, reductions in national armaments, and readjustment of all colonial claims, giving the interests of the population concerned equal weight with the claim of the government whose title was to be determined. The next eight points dealt with specific issues involving the evacuation and restoration of Allied territory, self-determination for minority nationalities, and the redrawing of European boundaries along national lines.

The fourteenth point contained the germ of the League of Nations, a general association of all nations, whose purpose was to guarantee political independence and territorial integrity to great and small states alike. When Wilson arrived in Europe, the crowds on the streets and the victorious and the defeated nations alike greeted him as a messiah. His program had received great publicity, and its general, optimistic nature had earned him great praise.

The victorious Allies came to Paris to gain the concrete rewards promised them in the various secret treaties. Under these pacts, which would not come to public knowledge until the beginning of 1919, the Allies had promised the Italians concessions that would turn the Adriatic into an Italian sea, the Russians the right to take over the Straits and Constantinople, the Romanians the right to take over large amounts of Austro-Hungarian territory, and the Japanese the right to keep the German territory of Kiaochow in China. In addition, the British and French divided what was formerly Ottoman-controlled Iraq and Syria into their respective spheres of influence. An international administrative organization would govern Palestine. In 1917 Great Britain pledged its support of "the establishment in Palestine of a national home for the Jewish people."

Wilson refused to consider these agreements, which many of the victors regarded as IOUs now due to be paid in return for their role in the war; but the contracting parties in the treaties would not easily set aside their deals to satisfy Wilson's ideals. Even before formal talks—negotiations that would be unprecedented in their complexity—began, the Allies were split. Lloyd George and Clemenceau discovered early that Wilson had his price, and that was the League of Nations. They played on his desire for this organization to water down most of the 13 other points. They were also aware that Wilson's party had suffered a crushing defeat in the 1918 elections and that strong factions in the United States were drumming up opposition to his program.

The League of Nations

When the diplomats began their first full meetings, the first issue was the formation of the League of Nations. Wilson insisted that the first work of the conference must be to provide for a league of nations as part of the peace treaty. After much negotiation, the covenant was approved by the full conference in April 1919. In order to gain support for the League, however, Wilson had to compromise on other matters. His Fourteen Points were partially repudiated, but he believed

→ When Wilson arrived in Europe in December 1918, cheering crowds hailed him as the "peacemaker from America." This photograph is from a parade in Paris.

that an imperfect treaty incorporating the League was better than a perfect one without it.

The Covenant of the League of Nations specified its aims "to guarantee international cooperation and to achieve international peace and security." To achieve this goal, Article X, the key section of the document, provided that

> *The Members of the League undertake to respect and preserve against external aggression the territorial integrity and existing political independence of all Members of the League. In case of any such aggression or in case of any threat or danger of such aggression, the Council shall advise upon the means by which this obligation shall be fulfilled.*[10]

The League of Nations was the first systematic and thorough attempt to create an organization designed to prevent war and promote peace. It was a valiant effort to curb the abuses of the state system while maintaining the individual sovereignty of each member of the community of nations.

The League's main organs were the Council, the Assembly, and the Secretariat. Dominated by the great powers, the Council was the most im-

portant body. It dealt with most of the emergencies arising in international affairs. The Assembly served as a platform from which all League members could express their views. It could make recommendations to the Council on specific issues, but all important decisions required the unanimous consent of its members, and every nation in the Assembly had one vote.

The Secretariat, which had 15 departments, represented the bureaucracy of the League. Numbering about 700, the personnel of the Secretariat constituted the first example in history of an international civil service whose loyalty was pledged to no single nation but to the interests of the world community. All treaties made by members of the League had to be registered with the Secretariat. It handled routine administrative matters relating to such League concerns as disarmament, health problems, the administration of former German colonies, and the protection of oppressed minorities.

Two other important bodies created by the Covenant of the League were the Permanent Court of International Justice and the International Labor Organization (ILO). The first was commonly referred to as the World Court. Its main purpose was to "interpret any disputed point in international law and determine when treaty obligations had been violated." It could also give advisory opinions to the Council or Assembly when asked for them. By 1937 41 nations had agreed to place before the World Court most basic international disputes to which they were a party. The ILO was established to "secure and maintain fair and humane conditions of labor for men, women, and children." The organization consisted of three divisions: a general conference, a governing body, and the International Labor Office.

Redrawing German Boundaries

After establishing the League, the diplomats got down to the business of dealing with Germany. France reclaimed Alsace-Lorraine, and plebiscites gave part of the former German empire to Denmark and Belgium. The French wanted to build a buffer state made up of former German territory west of the Rhine to be dominated by France. The Americans and the British proposed a compromise to Clemenceau, which he accepted. The territory in question would be occupied by Allied troops for a period of from 5 to 15 years, and a zone extending 50 kilometers east of the Rhine was to be demilitarized.

In addition, the French claimed the Saar basin, a rich coal area. Although they did not take outright control of the area, which reverted to the League administration, they did gain ownership of the mines in compensation for the destruction of their own installations in northern France. It was agreed that after 15 years a plebiscite would be held in the area. Finally Wilson and Lloyd George agreed that the United States and Great Britain by treaty would guarantee France against aggression.

To the east, the conference created the Polish Corridor, which separated East Prussia from the rest of Germany, in order to give the newly created state of Poland access to the sea. This creation raised grave problems, as it included territory in which there were not only Polish majorities but also large numbers of Germans. The land in question had been taken from Poland by Prussia in the eighteenth century. A section of Silesia was also ceded to Poland, but Danzig, a German city,

was placed under League jurisdiction. All in all, Germany lost 25,000 square miles inhabited by 6 million people, a fact seized upon by German nationalist leaders in the 1920s.

The Mandate System and Reparations

A curious mixture of idealism and revenge determined the allocation of the German colonies and certain territories belonging to Turkey. Because outright annexation would look too much like unvarnished imperialism, it was suggested that the colonies be turned over to the League, which in turn would give them to certain of its members to administer. The colonies were to be known as mandates, and precautions were taken to ensure that they would be administered for the well-being and development of the inhabitants. Once a year the mandatory powers were to present a detailed account of their administration of the territories of the League. The mandate system was a step forward in colonial administration, but Germany nevertheless was deprived of all colonies, with the excuse that it could not rule them justly or efficiently.

As the Treaty of Versailles took shape, the central concept was that Germany had been responsible for the war. Article 231 of the treaty stated explicitly:

> The Allied and Associated Governments affirm and Germany accepts the responsibility of Germany and her allies for causing all the loss and damage to which the Allied and Associated Governments and their nationals have been subjected as a consequence of the war imposed upon them by the aggression of Germany and her Allies.[11]

Britain and France demanded that Germany pay the total cost of the war, including pensions. The United States protested this demand, and eventually a compromise emerged in which, with the exception of Belgium, Germany had to pay only war damages, including those suffered by civilians, and the cost of pensions. These payments, called reparations (implying repair) were exacted on the ground that Germany should bear the responsibility for the war.

Although the Allies agreed that Germany should pay reparations, they could not agree on how much should be paid. Some demands ran as high as $200 billion. Finally, it was decided that a committee should fix the amount; in the meantime Germany was to begin making payments. By the time the committee report appeared in May 1921, the payments totaled nearly $2 billion. The final bill came to $32.5 billion, to be paid off by Germany by 1963.

The Allies required Germany, as part of "in kind" reparations payments, to hand over most of its merchant fleet, construct one million tons of new shipping for the Allies, and deliver vast amounts of coal, equipment, and machinery to them. The conference permitted Germany a standing army of only 100,000 men, a greatly reduced fleet, and no military aircraft. Munitions plants were also to be closely supervised.

The treaty also called for the kaiser to be tried for a "supreme offense against international morality and the sanctity of treaties," thus setting a precedent for the Nuremberg tribunals after World War II. Nothing came of this demand, however, as the kaiser remained in his Dutch haven.

THE PEACE SETTLEMENT IN EUROPE

Newly Created States
Ceded Territories

Dictated Treaties

Before coming to Paris in April 1919 to receive the Treaty of Versailles, the German delegation was given no official information about its terms. Even though the German foreign minister denied that "Germany and its people were alone guilty,"[12] he had no alternative but to sign. The continued blockade created great hardships in Germany, and the Allies threatened an invasion if the Germans did not accept the peace. The treaty was signed on June 28, the fifth anniversary of the assassination of the Archduke Francis Ferdinand in the Hall of Mirrors at Versailles, the same room where the German empire had been proclaimed. As one American wrote, "The affair was elaborately staged and made as humiliating to the enemy as it well could be."[13]

The Allies imposed equally harsh treaties on Germany's supporters. The Treaty of St. Germaine (1919) with Austria recognized the nationalist movements of the Czechs, Poles, and South Slavs. These groups had already formed states and reduced the remnants of the former Dual Monarchy into the separate states of Austria and Hungary. Austria became a landlocked country of 32,000 square miles and 6 million people. It was forbidden to seek *Anschluss*—union with Germany. Italy acquired sections of Austria, South Tyrol, Trentino (with its 250,000 Austrian Germans), and the northeastern coast of the Adriatic, with its large numbers of Slavs.

To complete their control of the Adriatic, the Italians wanted a slice of the Dalmatian coast and the port of Fiume. Fiume, however, was the natural port for the newly created state of Yugoslavia, and it had not been promised to the Italians in 1915. Wilson declared the Italian claim to be a contradiction of the principle of self-determination, and the ensuing controversy almost wrecked the peace conference. The issue was not settled until 1920, when Italy renounced its claim to Dalmatia and Fiume became an independent state. Four years later it was ceded to Italy.

By the Treaty of Sèvres (1920), the Ottoman Empire was placed on the operating table of power politics and divided among Greece, Britain, and France. An upheaval in August 1920 in Constantinople led to the emergence of the Nationalists under Mustapha Kemal, who refused to accept the treaty. Not until July 1923 did Turkey's postwar status become clear in the milder Treaty of Lausanne, which guaranteed Turkish control of Anatolia.

Hungary (Treaty of Trianon, 1920) and Bulgaria (Treaty of Neuilly, 1919) did not fare as well as Turkey in dealing with the Allies. The Hungarians lost territory to Czechoslovakia, Yugoslavia, and Romania. Bulgaria lost access to the Aegean Sea and territory populated by nearly one million people, had to pay a huge indemnity, and underwent demilitarization.

Those eastern European states that profited from the settlements proved to be useful allies for France in the first 15 years of the interwar period. Those that suffered were easy prey for the Nazis in the 1930s.

Evaluating the Peacemakers

The treaties ending the First World War have received heavy criticism from diplomatic historians, especially when compared with the work of the Congress of Vienna. The peace that emerged brought only weariness, new disagreements, and inflation.

There was a complete disregard of Russia. Lenin's government, in its weak position, indicated a willingness to deal with the West on the issue of prewar debts and border conflicts, if the West would extend financial aid and withdraw its expeditionary forces. The anti-Bolshevik forces in Paris did not take the offer seriously.[14] By missing this opportunity the Allies, in the view of a major American observer, took a course that had tremendous consequences for "the long-term future of both the Russian and the American people and indeed of mankind generally."[15]

Many commentators have laid the genesis of the Second World War just one generation later at the feet of the Paris peacemakers. The opportunism of Orlando and the chauvinism and revenge-seeking nature of both Clemenceau and Lloyd George appear shortsighted. Other critics point that the United States's reversion to isolationism doomed the work of the conference. Furthermore, never were there any broad plans for European economic recovery.

Considering the difficult conditions under which it was negotiated, the peace settlement was as good as could be expected. The delegates were the prisoners of their own constituents, who had themselves been heavily influenced by

→ Enemies in combat, Canadian and German soldiers help one another through the mud during the capture of Passchendaele, a small commune in Flanders that saw heavy fighting in October and November 1917.

nomic growth, military buildup, ambitious foreign policy, and inability to control its Austro-Hungarian ally helped bring the normally competitive European economic arena to a crisis in the summer of 1914. By violating Belgian neutrality and declaring war on Russia and France, Germany stood clearly as the aggressor in the First World War, a fact for which it was severely punished in the Treaty of Versailles.

When the victorious Allies gathered at Paris in 1919 to settle the peace, they did not have the luxury of time, distance, and power the leaders at the Congress of Vienna had enjoyed in 1815. The 1919 peacemakers had endured the most destructive war in history. In this total war, psychological methods were used to motivate all the people of each of the states to hate the enemy, during and after the war. In these conditions, the treaty settled at Versailles produced a mere break in the hostilities. Some observers have referred to the period from 1914 to 1945 as the "New Thirty Years' War."

With all that the Europeans shared, World War I was a conflict that need never have been fought. The Europeans threw away the advantages they had gained since 1815 and set in motion a series of disasters from which they did not recover until the 1960s.

wartime propaganda. In addition, the diplomats had to deal with the nationalistic pressures and territorial conflicts of the newly formed eastern European nations. Given the costs of the war and the hopes for the peace, it is not surprising that the treaties left a legacy of disappointment for those who won and bitterness for those who lost. Symbolic of the obstacles faced by the statesmen was the fact that while they worked to return order, the globe reeled under the blows of a Spanish influenza outbreak that, when the costs were added up, was shown to have killed twice as many as had died in the war. The influenza outbreak was both a tragic conclusion to the war years and a sign for the future.

CONCLUSION

For more than four years, the science, wealth, and power of Europe had been concentrated on the business of destruction. Germany's rapid eco-

→ Suggestions for Reading

The standard account on the causes of the war is F. Fischer, *Germany's Aims in the First World War* (Norton, 1968). Classic views on the war are to be found in W. L. Langer, *European Alliances and Alignments, 1871–1890* (Vintage, 1931) and *The Diplomacy of Imperialism, 1890–1902* (Knopf, 1935) and S. B. Fay, *The Origins of the World War* (Macmillan, 1928). Bernadotte Schmidt, *Triple Alliance and Triple Entente* (Fertig, Holt, 1934) is a good introduction. Mark Ferro examines the broader social and psychological aspects of the origins of World War I, especially the role of manipulated patriotism in *The Great War: 1914–1918* (Routledge & Kegan Paul, 1973). See also R. Albrecht-Carrié, *A Diplomatic History of Europe Since the Congress of Vienna* (Harper, 1973). A good overview of the war's origins is L. Lafore's *The Long Fuse: An Interpretation of the Origins of World War I* (Lippincott, 1971).

Specific topics are dealt with by Oron J. Hale, *The Great Illusion, 1900–1914* (Torchbooks, 1971); V. Dedijer, *The Road to Sarajevo* (Simon & Schuster, 1966); Colin Simpson, *The Lusitania* (Harper, 1976); A. Moorehead, *Gallipoli: Account of the 1915 Campaign* (Harper, 1956); A. Horne, *The Price of Glory: Verdun 1916* (St. Martin's, 1979); E. Coffman, *The War to End All Wars: The American Mili-*

tary Experience in World War I (Oxford, 1968); G. Ritter, *The Schlieffen Plan* (Praeger, 1958); and G. Feldman, *Army Industry, and Labor in Germany, 1914–1918* (Princeton, 1966).

Alexander Solzhenitsyn's *August 1914* (Bantam, 1974) is a fine piece of literature describing Russia's entry into the war. Barbara Tuchman's *The Guns of August* (many eds.) (Dell, 1964) is a fine history that is beautifully written. Paul Fussell captures the brutal nature and impact of the war in *The Great War and Modern Memory* (Oxford, 1977).

See A. S. Link, *Wilson the Diplomatist* (Hopkins, 1957) regarding the U.S. president's participation at Paris. Charles L. Mee, Jr., captures the aura of Paris during the negotiations in *The End of Order, Versailles, 1919* (Dutton, 1980). Harold Nicolson's beautifully written *Peacemaking, 1919* (Houghton Mifflin, 1939) is a fine firsthand account, as is J. M. Keynes, *The Economic Consequences of the Peace* (Macmillan, 1924). The diplomatic maneuvers behind the creation of the post-Ottoman levant is David Fromkin's *A Peace to End all Peace: Creating the Modern Middle East: 1914–1922* (Holt, 1989).

→ Notes

1. Quoted by C. J. H. Hayes, *A Political and Cultural History of Modern Europe*, II (New York: The Macmillan Co., 1939), p. 572.
2. Viscount Grey of Fallodon, *Twenty-Five Years*, II (New York: Frederick A. Stokes Co., 1925), p. 20.
3. *The New Cambridge Modern History*, 2nd ed., XII (Cambridge: Cambridge University Press, 1968), p. 191.
4. Quoted in F. P. Chambers, *The War Behind the War, 1914–1918* (New York: Harcourt Brace Jovanovich) p. 473.
5. "The Soldier," in *The Collected Poems of Rupert Brooke* (Canada: Dodd, Mead, & Co., 1915).
6. "Anthem for a Doomed Youth," in *Wilfred Owen: The Collected Poems of Wilfred Owen*. Copyright © 1963 by Chatto & Windus, Ltd., 1946). Reprinted by permission of New Directions Publishing Corporation and Chatto & Windus on behalf of the estate of Wilfred Owen.
7. D. W. Treadgold, *Twentieth Century Russia* (Chicago: Rand McNally & Co., 1959), p. 154.
8. Quoted in L. M. Hacker and B. B. Kendrick, *The United States Since 1865* (New York: F. S. Crofts and Co., 1939), p. 520.
9. A. J. Ryder, *Twentieth Century Germany: From Bismarck to Brandt* (New York: Columbia University Press, 1973), pp. 132–141.
10. Quoted in F. P. Walters, *A History of the League of Nations*, I (London: Oxford University Press, 1952), p. 48.
11. Quoted in R. J. Sontag, *European Diplomatic History, 1871–1932* (New York: Century Co., 1933), p. 275.
12. Quoted in E. Achorn, *European Civilization and Politics Since 1815* (New York: Harcourt Brace Jovanovich, 1938), p. 470.
13. Quoted in Sontag, *European Diplomatic History, 1871–1932*, p. 392.
14. Louis Fischer, *The Soviets in World Affairs* (New York: Vintage Books, 1960), p. 116.
15. George F. Kennan, *The Decision to Intervene* (Princeton: Princeton University Press, 1958), p. 471.

CHAPTER 30

EUROPEAN DEMOCRACIES 1919–1939

Democracies in 1919
Remaining Democracies in 1939

0   200   400
MILES

NORWAY · SWEDEN · FINLAND · ESTONIA · LATVIA · LITHUANIA

NORTH SEA · DENMARK

IRELAND · GREAT BRITAIN · NETH. · GERMANY · POLAND

ATLANTIC OCEAN · BELG. · LUX. · CZECHOSLOVAKIA

FRANCE · SWITZ. · AUSTRIA · HUNGARY

YUGOSLAVIA

PORTUGAL · SPAIN · CORSICA (Fr.) · SARDINIA (It.) · ITALY · ALBANIA · GREECE

MEDITERRANEAN SEA · SICILY (It.)

AFRICA

→ The Americans and the British handed the task of maintaining stability in war-weakened Europe to the French in 1919. Obsessed with gaining revenge against Germany and wanting to isolate the Soviet Union, Paris by 1929 proved to be unequal to the task. France would soon retreat behind the Maginot line.

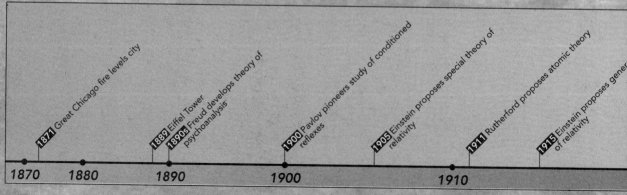

1871 Great Chicago fire levels city
1889 Eiffel Tower
1890s Freud develops theory of psychoanalysis
1900 Pavlov pioneers study of conditioned reflexes
1905 Einstein proposes special theory of relativity
1911 Rutherford proposes atomic theory
1915 Einstein proposes general of relativity

1870   1880   1890   1900   1910

The Economic and Political Collapse of the Democracies, 1918–1939

CHAPTER OUTLINE

Economic Disasters

Politics in the European Democracies

Democracy Overseas

The Western Tradition in Transition

MAP

European Democracies, 1919–1939

DOCUMENTS

Alex de Jonge on Inflation in Weimar Germany

Friedrich A. Hayek, The Decline of Liberalism

José Ortega y Gasset, The Rise of the Masses

W orld War I, the war that was to make the world "safe for democracy," left a legacy of physical damage, economic disruption, and doubt that endangered the hard-won liberal victories of the nineteenth century. The horrible costs of the war made the triumph a hollow one for the European victors, and after the initial taste for revenge had been satisfied, revulsion for war became widespread. The economic dislocation caused by inflation and depression sapped the strength of the middle classes, the traditional supporters of democracy. The certainty and belief in progress that had helped fuel Europe's dominance in the nineteenth century was replaced by doubt and cynicism.[1]

ECONOMIC DISASTERS

One of the most serious problems facing the survivors of World War I was the confused and desperate situation of the European economy. Much of the direct and indirect cost of the war had been covered by borrowing, and now the bills had come due in a world unable to pay them. The last-

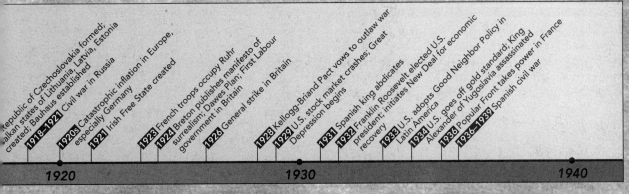

Republic of Czechoslovakia formed; Balkan states of Lithuania, Latvia, Estonia created; Bauhaus established

1918–1921 Civil war in Russia

1920s Catastrophic inflation in Europe, especially Germany

1921 Irish Free State created

1923 French troops occupy Ruhr

1924 Breton publishes manifesto of surrealism; Dawes Plan; First Labour government in Britain

1926 General strike in Britain

1928 Kellogg-Briand Pact vows to outlaw war

1929 U.S. stock market crashes; Great Depression begins

1931 Spanish king abdicates

1932 Franklin Roosevelt elected U.S. president; initiates New Deal for economic recovery

1933 U.S. adopts Good Neighbor Policy in Latin America

1934 U.S. goes off gold standard; King Alexander of Yugoslavia assassinated

1936 Popular Front takes power in France

1936–1939 Spanish civil war

1920   1930   1940

ing results of the war touched many areas. The conflict altered world trading patterns, reduced shipping, and weakened Europe's former economic dominance. The various peace treaties multiplied the number of European boundaries, which soon became obstacles to the flow of goods, especially in the successor states of the Habsburg monarchy and in Poland. Rail and communications lines had to be reconfigured to reflect the interest of newly created states.

The Costs of the War

It is impossible to give a true accounting of the costs of any war, because there is no way to calculate the contributions that might have been made by those killed in battle. From 2 to 3 million Russians died, and more perished in the 1918–1921 civil war. Among the other major participants, almost 2 million Germans, over 1.5 million French, close to a million English, a half-million Italians, 1.2 million from Austria-Hungary, and 325,000 from Turkey died in battle. These figures do not count the wounded whose lives may have been shortened as a result of their injuries. Put another way, the young paid the highest price; it is estimated that Germany and France each lost over 15 percent of their young men.

Estimates of the financial drain of the war range between $250 billion and $300 billion, citing the dollar at its early 1920s level. These figures do not bring home the depth of the war's impact on trade, shipping, and monetary stability. Belgium, for example, lost over 300,000 houses and thousands of factories, and 15,000 square miles of northeastern France were in ruins.

No balance sheet or set of figures can measure the psychological expense of the conflict. How does one calculate the cost of taking away from their jobs and their homes 75 million men who were mobilized? How can the mental carnage inflicted on the participants be measured?

Political institutions felt the effects of the war in different ways. The German, Habsburg, Russian, and Ottoman empires crumbled and disappeared from the historical stage. Replacing them were uncertain republics or dictatorships. Those colonial empires that remained were weakened, and indigenous nationalist movements made substantial progress.

The roots of the economic problems that plagued Europe after the war—agricultural overproduction, bureaucratic regulations, and protectionism—could be seen before 1914. Compounding these factors were the traditional challenges encountered in shifting from a wartime to a peacetime economy—especially that of demobilizing millions of soldiers and bringing them back into the labor market.

The Debt Problem

During the war a radical change had taken place in Europe's economic relationship with the United States. In 1914 the United States had been a debtor nation, mostly to Europe, for the amount of $3.75 billion. The war totally reversed this situation. The United States lent billions of dollars and sold tons of supplies to the Allies. British blockades kept the United States from being able to deal with the Germans, precluding further profits, but by 1919 Europeans owed the United States more than $10 billion. This tremendous debt posed what economists call a transfer problem. The international obligations could be paid only by the actual transfer of gold or by the sale of goods.

Complicating the picture, Allied powers in Europe had also lent each other funds, with the British acting as the chief banker, lending more than £1.7 billion. When their credit dried up, they turned to the United States for financial help. Even though Britain owed huge sums to U.S. financiers, it remained a net creditor of $4 billion because of money owed it by European debtors. France, on the other hand, stood as a net debtor of $3.5 billion. In addition to its own war debts, the French government suffered greatly when the Bolsheviks renounced repayment of the tsarist debt amounting to some 12 billion francs—one-quarter of France's foreign holdings.

Some of the Allies argued that the inter-Allied debts were political, that all of them had, in effect, been poured into a common pool for victory. These people wondered how France's contribution in the lives of its young men could be figured into the equation in terms of francs, dollars, or pounds. They proposed that, with victory, all debts should be canceled. The United States, on the other hand, which had gone to Paris with a conciliatory spirit toward Germany

PASSING THE BUCK.

→ A British cartoonist's view of the debt and reparations problems following World War I. Germany's inability to pay reparations meant that the Allies were unable to pay their inter-Allied war debts.

in the treaty negotiations, changed its tune when dollars and cents were involved. This attitude was best expressed in a remark attributed to Calvin Coolidge, who expected full repayment, when he said: "They hired the money, didn't they?" Beneath the extremes of these positions were the understandable motives of getting out of paying a huge debt or gaining from the payment of debts owed.

The additional problem of reparations complicated Germany's debt problem. Although reparations constituted an enormous drain on the economy, they were far more significant as a political factor. The Weimar leaders resorted to producing vast amounts of currency. In the first three years after the war, the German government, in a policy of deliberate inflation, spent much more than its income. This policy was masked by "floating debts . . . in other words, by the printing press."[2] The situation became so serious in the summer of 1922 that Great Britain proposed collecting no more from its debtors—Allied and German alike—than the United States collected from Britain itself. Such statesmanship

was prompted by the fact that London had gained what it wanted from the peace settlement: Germany's navy was destroyed, Germany's merchant ships were transferred as reparations, and Germany's empire was gone. No more could be squeezed out.

Britain saw that Germany would not be able to meet its reparations payments. Without those payments, the victors would not be able to make their own payments on the inter-Allied debts, especially debts owed to the United States. Although the United States insisted that there was no connection between the inter-Allied debts and German reparations, negotiations were carried on, and debt payment plans were set up with 13 nations. No reductions were made in principal, but in every case the interest rate was radically decreased. Still, the total amount owed came to more than $22 billion.

The German government's calculated inflationary policies contributed far more to the economic disaster that occurred in 1923 than did reparations. Between May and September 1921 the value of the German mark fell 80 percent. A year and a half later, after Germany defaulted on some payments, French troops, supported by Belgian and Italian contingents, marched into the rich industrial district of the Ruhr, undeterred by American and British objections. This shortsighted French move contributed nothing to the solution of Europe's problems and indeed played into the hands of radical German politicians.

Encouraged by the Berlin government, German workers defied the French army and went on strike, many ending up in jail. The French toyed for a while with the idea of establishing a separate state in the Rhineland to act as a buffer between Germany and France. Chaotic conditions in the Ruhr encouraged the catastrophic inflation of the German currency to make up for the loss of exports and to support the striking workers. The French, in return, gained very little benefit from the occupation.

Inflation and Stabilization

All European nations encountered a rocky path as they attempted to gain equilibrium after the war. Britain had minimal price increases and returned to prewar levels within two years after the signing of the Versailles treaty. On the continent, price and monetary stability came less easily. Only Czechoslovakia seemed to have its economic affairs well in hand.

France did not stabilize its currency until 1926, when the franc was worth 50 to the dollar (as contrasted with 5 to the dollar in 1914). In Austria prices rose to 14,000 times their prewar level until stability of sorts came in 1922. Hungary's prices went to 23,000 times prewar level, but this increase is dwarfed by Poland's (2.5 million times prewar level) and Russia's (4 billion times prewar level).

But Germany served as the laboratory of the horrible impact of inflation on society. Germany's prices went up a trillion times (a thousand billion) what they were in 1914. The German mark had been worth 4 to the dollar in prewar times. At its weakest point in November 1923, after the French occupation of the Ruhr, the German mark reached the exchange rate of 4.2 trillion to the dollar. During the worst part of the inflation, the Reichsbank had 150 firms using 2000 presses running day and night to print Reichnotes. To get out of their dilemma, the Germans made an effective transition to a more stable currency by simply forgetting the old one.[3]

Millions of middle-class Germans, small property owners who were the hoped-for base of the new Weimar Republic, found themselves caught in the wage-price squeeze. Prices for the necessities of life rose far faster than did income or savings. As mothers wheeled baby carriages full of money to bakeries to buy bread, fathers watched a lifetime of savings dwindle to insignificance. Pensioners on fixed incomes suffered doubly under this crisis. The bourgeoisie, the historical basis for liberal politics throughout Europe, suffered blows more devastating than those of war, since inflation stole not only the value of their labor, but the worth of their savings and insurance.

Where the middle classes and liberal traditions were strong, democracy could weather the storm. But in central Europe where they were not—especially in Germany, where the inflation was worst—the cause of future totalitarianism received an immense boost. Alan Bullock, a biographer of Adolf Hitler, wrote that "the result of inflation was to undermine the foundations of German society in a way which neither the war

→ Inflation in Germany during the 1920s grew so drastic that the German mark became nearly worthless. It was cheaper, for example, to start fires with marks than to use them to purchase kindling.

nor the revolution of 1918, nor the Treaty of Versailles had ever done."[4]

Temporary Improvements

After 1923 the liberal application of U.S. funds brought some calm to the economic storm. Business was more difficult to conduct because protectionism became more and more the dominant trait of international trade. *Autarky*, the goal of gaining total economic self-sufficiency and freedom from reliance on any other nation, increasingly became the unstated policy of many governments.

Nonetheless, production soon reached 1913 levels, currencies began to stabilize by mid-decade, and the French finally recalled their troops from the Ruhr. Most significantly, in September 1924, a commission under the leadership of U.S. banker Charles Dawes formulated a more

Alex de Jonge on Inflation in Weimar Germany

Alex de Jonge captured the truly devastating impact of inflation in Weimar Germany.

Hyperinflation created social chaos on an extraordinary scale. As soon as one was paid, one rushed off to the shops and bought absolutely anything in exchange for paper about to become worthless. If a woman had the misfortune to have a husband working away from home and sending money through the post, the money was virtually without value by the time it arrived. Workers were paid once, then twice, then five times a week with an ever-depreciating currency.

By November 1923 real wages were down 25 percent compared with 1913, and envelopes were not big enough to accommodate all the stamps needed to mail them; the excess stamps were stuck to separate sheets affixed to the letter. Normal commercial transactions became virtually impossible. One luckless author received a sizable advance on a work only to find that within a week it was just enough to pay the postage on the manuscript. By late 1923 it was not unusual to find 100,000 mark notes in the gutter, tossed there by contemptuous beggars at a time when $50 could buy a row of houses in Berlin's smartest street.

A Berlin couple who were about to celebrate their golden wedding received an official letter advising them that the mayor, in accordance with Prussian custom, would call and present them with a donation of money.

Next morning the mayor, accompanied by several aldermen in picturesque robes, arrived at the aged couple's house, and solemnly handed over in the name of the Prussian State 1,000,000,000,000 marks or one half-penny.

From Alex de Jonge, *The Weimar Chronicle, Prelude to Hitler* (New York: New American Library, 1978).

---

liberal reparations policy in order to get the entire repayment cycle back into motion. Dawes's plan, replaced in 1929 by the Young plan (named for its principal formulator, U.S. businessman Owen Young), reduced installments and extended them over a longer period. A loan of $200 million, mostly from the United States, was floated to aid German recovery. The Berlin government resumed payments to the Allies, and the Allies paid their debt installments to the United States—which in effect received its own money back again.

Prosperity of a sort returned to Europe. As long as the circular flow of cash from the United States to Germany to the Allies to the United States continued, the international monetary system functioned. The moment the cycle broke down, the world economy headed for the rocks of depression. One economic historian has written:

> In 1924–31 Germany drew some one thousand million pounds from abroad and the irony was that Germany, in fact, received far more in loans, including loans to enable her to pay interest on earlier loans than she paid out in reparations, thus gaining in the circular flow and re-equipping her industries and her public utilities with American funds in the processes in the 1920s before repudiating her debts in the 1930s.[5]

The system broke down in 1928 and 1929 when U.S. and British creditors needed their capital for investments in their own countries. Extensions on loans, readily granted a year earlier, were refused. Even before the U.S. stock market crash on October 29, 1929, disaster was on the horizon.

Few people in America could admit such a possibility during the decade, however. The United States had become the commercial center of the world, and its policies were central to the world's financial health. The United States still had an internal market in the 1920s with a seemingly inexhaustible appetite for new products such as radios, refrigerators, electrical appliances, and automobiles. This expansion, based on consumer goods and supported by a seemingly limitless supply of natural resources, gave the impression of solid and endless growth.

Tragically, the contradictions of the postwar economic structure were making themselves felt.

The cornerstones of pre-1914 prosperity—multilateral trade, the gold standard, and interchangeable currencies—were crumbling. The policies of autarky, with high tariff barriers to protect home products against foreign competition, worked against international economic health. Ironically, the United States led the way toward higher tariffs, and other nations quickly retaliated. American foreign trade seriously declined, and the volume of world trade decreased.

There were other danger signals. Europe suffered a population decline. There were 22 million fewer people in the 1920s in the western part of the continent than had been expected.[6] The decrease in internal markets affected trade, as did the higher external barriers. Around the globe, the agricultural sector suffered from declining prices during the 1920s. At the same time that farmers received less for their products, they had to pay more to live—a condition that afflicted peasants in Europe and Asia and farmers and ranchers in the United States.

In the hopes of reaching a wider market, farmers around the world borrowed money to expand production at the beginning of the decade. Temporarily, the food surplus benefited consumers, but across the world agricultural interests suffered from overproduction. Tariff barriers prevented foodstuffs from circulating to the countries where hunger existed. By the end of the decade, people in Asia were starving, while wheat farmers in Whitman County, Washington, dumped their grain into the Snake River and coffee growers in Brazil saw their product burned to fuel steam locomotives. Many farmers went bankrupt as they could not keep up with payments on these debts. The countryside preceded the cities into the economic tragedy.[7]

The Great Crash

Because of America's central position in the world economy, any development, positive or negative, on Wall Street reverberated around the globe. The United States, with roughly 3 percent of the world's population, produced 46 percent of the globe's industrial output. The country was ill-equipped to use its new-found power. Its financial life in the 1920s was dominated by the activities of daring and sometimes unscrupulous speculators who made the arena of high finance a precarious and exciting world of its own. The businessmen creating this world were not pursuing long-term stability. Their blind rush for profit led to America's crash, which in turn sparked a world disaster.[8]

Even before the stock market crash, Wall Street had been showing signs of distress such as capital shortfalls, excessively large inventories, and agricultural bankruptcies. But nothing prepared financiers for the disaster that struck on October 29, 1929—Black Thursday. By noon, Wall Street was caught in a momentum of chaotic fear. The end of the trading session halted the initial hemorrhage of stock values, but the damage was done.

John Kenneth Galbraith has written: "On the whole, the great stock market crash can be much more readily explained than the depression that followed it."[9] Overspeculation, loose controls, dishonest investors, and a loss of confidence in the "ever-upward" market trend can be identified as causes for the crash. Further causes can be traced to the inequitable distribution of wealth, with the farmers and workers left out—while the top 3 percent grew incredibly rich and irresponsible. Industrial overexpansion was fueled by speculators buying stock on the margin, with insufficient cash backing for the investments. In addition, the government's hands-off policies permitted massive abuses to take place unchecked.

The international impact of the crash can be explained by the involvement in the U.S. market of investors and bankers from a number of countries, the interdependent world economic structure, the peculiar Allied debt and reparations structure, the growing agricultural crisis, and the inadequate banking systems of the world.

Some economic historians believe that the cycle of highs and lows hit a particularly vicious low point in 1929. Crashes had occurred before, but never with such widespread repercussions over such a long period of time. In the United States, stock prices declined one-third overall within a few weeks, wiping out fortunes, shattering confidence in business, and destroying consumer demand. The disaster spread worldwide as American interests demanded payment on foreign loans and imports decreased. The Kredit-

Anstalt of Vienna did not have enough money to fill demands for funds from French banks and failed in 1931. This set in motion a dominolike banking crisis throughout Europe. Forecasts by Washington politicians and New York financiers that the worst was over and that the world economy was fundamentally sound after a "technical readjustment" convinced nobody. There would be no easy recovery.

The World Depression

By 1932 the value of industrial shares had fallen close to 60 percent on the New York and Berlin markets. Unemployment doubled in Germany, and 25 percent of the labor force was out of work in the United States. The middle classes, which had invested in the stock market, saw their investments and savings wiped out. In nation after nation, industry declined, prices fell, banks collapsed, and economies stagnated. In the western democracies the depression heightened the feelings of uneasiness that had existed since 1918. In other countries, the tendency to seek authoritarian solutions became even more pronounced. Throughout the world people feared a future marked by lowered standards of living, unemployment, and hunger.

The middle classes on the continent, which had suffered from inflation during the 1920s, became caught in a whiplash effect during the depression. Adherence to old liberal principles collapsed in the face of economic insecurity, and state control of the economies increased. Governments raised tariffs to restrict imports and used command economies, an expedient usually reserved for wartime. As conditions deteriorated, fear caused most governments to look no farther than their own boundaries. Under the competing systems of autarky, each nation tried to increase exports and decrease imports.

After almost a century of free trade, modified by a comparatively few protective duties levied during and after World War I, Great Britain finally enacted a high tariff in 1932 with provisions to protect members of its empire. In the United States the Hawley-Smoot Act of 1930 increased the value-added duty to 50 percent on a wide variety of agricultural and manufactured imports.

Another technique to increase exports at the expense of others was to depreciate a nation's currency—reduce the value of its money. When Japan depreciated the yen, for example, a U.S. dollar or British pound could buy more Japanese goods. In effect, lowering the yen reduced the price of Japanese exports. In most cases, however, devaluation brought only a temporary trade advantage. Other nations could play the same game, as the United States did in 1934 when it went off the gold standard and reduced the amount of gold backing for the dollar by 40 percent.

The debt problem that grew out of the war worsened during the depression. In 1931, U.S. President Herbert Hoover gained a one-year moratorium on all intergovernmental debts. The next year at the Lausanne Conference, German reparations payments were practically canceled in the hope that the United States would make corresponding concessions in reducing war debts. The Americans, for a variety of domestic financial and political reasons, refused to concede that there was a logical connection between reparations and war debts. As the depression deepened, the debtors could not continue their payments. France refused outright in 1932; Germany after 1933 completely stopped paying reparations; Britain and four other nations made token payments for a time and then stopped entirely in 1934. Only Finland continued to meet its schedule of payments.

Individual families had as many, or more, problems in paying their bills as did the governments of the world. Factories closed down and laid off their workers. Harvests rotted in the fields as the price of wheat fell to its lowest price in 300 years and other agricultural commodities suffered similar price declines. The lives of the cacao grower in the African Gold Coast, the coffee grower in Brazil, and the plantation worker in the Dutch East Indies were as affected as those of the factory worker in Pittsburgh, Lille, or Frankfurt.

The 1929 crash occurred in an economic framework still suffering from the dislocations of World War I. It began a downturn in the world economy that would not end until the world armed for another global conflict. Whether the depression ended because of World War II or whether the world would have eventually come out of the low part of the cycle is a question that will always be debated. The weaknesses in American stock market operations were by and large addressed in a series of reforms.

From the major banks to the soup lines in villages, the depression had profound implications for politics. The combination of inflation and depression threatened representative government. Unemployed and starving masses were tempted to turn to dictators who promised jobs and bread.

→ Germans line up for bread and soup during the Great Depression. Similar scenes were common in many other countries, including the United States.

The hardships of economic stability, even in those countries where the democratic tradition was strongest, led to a massive increase in state participation in the daily life of the individual.

POLITICS IN THE EUROPEAN DEMOCRACIES

During the interwar period, belief in the genius of big business and free-market capitalism received a death blow in most quarters, as business itself had to turn more and more to the powers of the state to survive. After 1918, parliamentary government, the foundation of all that the liberals of the nineteenth century had worked for, came under attack everywhere.

For the most part, only in the Scandinavian countries—Norway, Sweden, and Denmark—did representative government operate smoothly throughout the interwar period. Economic prosperity was the general rule here throughout the 1920s, and during the depression these countries suffered less than did Britain, France, or the United States. Switzerland, the Netherlands, and Belgium also maintained relatively high standards of living and kept their governments on the democratic road. But in the 20 years after peace came to Europe, Britain, France, and most of the other democracies exhibited lethargy and short-sightedness in the face of crisis.

Britain, 1919–1939

The 1920s were not a tranquil decade for Great Britain. The country endured a number of social and political crises tied to the bitter labor disputes and unemployment that disrupted the nation. Neither Liberals nor Conservatives could do much to alter the flow of events immediately after the war. From 1919 to 1922 David Lloyd George led a coalition, but it broke apart, leading to the division and decline of the Liberals. From May 1923 to January 1924 Stanley Baldwin led an unsuccessful Conservative government.

Ramsay MacDonald formed the first Labour government and became the first socialist prime minister. For ten months he and his party pursued a program to introduce socialism slowly and within the democratic framework. His move

Friedrich A. Hayek, The Decline of Liberalism

Friedrich A. Hayek described the malaise affecting liberal Europe in the interwar period. His judgment is deeply controversial.

The crucial point of which our people are still so little aware is, however, not merely the magnitude of the changes which have taken place during the last generation but the fact that they mean a complete change in the direction of the evolution of our ideas and social order. For at least twenty-five years before the specter of totalitarianism became a real threat, we had progressively been moving away from the basic ideas on which Western civilization has been built. That this movement on which we have entered with such high hopes and ambitions should have brought us face to face with the totalitarian horror has come as a profound shock to this generation, which still refuses to connect the two facts. Yet this development merely confirms the warnings of the fathers of the liberal philosophy which we still profess.

We have progressively abandoned that freedom in economic affairs without which personal and political freedom has never existed in the past. Although we had been warned by some of the greatest political thinkers of the nineteenth century, by De Tocqueville and Lord Acton, that socialism means slavery, we have steadily moved in the direction of socialism. And now that we have seen a new form of slavery arise before our eyes, we have so completely forgotten the warning that it scarcely occurs to us that the two things may be connected.

From Friedrich A. Hayek, *The Road to Serfdom* (Chicago: University of Chicago Press, 1944).

→ During the general strike of 1926 in England, armored cars equipped with machine guns patrolled London to suppress riots.

to recognize the Soviet Union was controversial. When the London *Times* published the so-called Zinoviev letter, a document in which the Communist Third International supposedly laid out the program for revolution in Britain, the public backlash defeated the Labour government in the October 1924 elections.

For the next five years the Conservatives under Baldwin held power. After renouncing the treaties the Labour cabinet had made with Russia, the Conservatives set out on a generally unsuccessful and stormy tenure. Britain returned its currency to the gold standard in 1925, a policy that led indirectly to an increase in labor unrest. The government struggled through a coal strike and a general strike in which more than 2.5 million of the nation's more than 6 million workers walked out. Baldwin reduced taxes on business, but this did little to remedy the deflationary effect of a return to the gold standard.

In May 1929 Labour under MacDonald won another victory. Once again the Labourites resumed relations with the Soviet Union and attempted their measured socialist program. The effects of the depression, however, condemned MacDonald and his government to failure. In two

years, exports and imports declined 35 percent and close to 3 million unemployed people roamed the streets. Labour could do little to address the basic causes of the disaster; in fact, no single party could. When MacDonald's government fell in 1931, it was replaced by a national coalition government dominated by the Conservatives. The coalition government initiated a recovery program featuring a balanced budget, limited social spending, and encouragement of private enterprise. By 1933, a substantial measure of prosperity had been regained, and productivity had increased by 23 percent over the 1929 level.

To achieve this comeback, some of what remained of laissez-faire policy was discarded. The government regulated the currency, levied high tariffs, gave farmers subsidies, and imposed a heavy burden of taxation. The taxes went to expanded educational and health facilities, better accident and unemployment insurance, and more adequate pensions as a prelude to post–World War II legislation that attempted to ensure security from "the cradle to the grave." As for the rich, they had a large portion of their income taxed away, and what might be left at death was decimated by inheritance taxes. It was ruefully declared that the rich could hardly afford to live, much less to die.

During the 20 years between the wars, there was an absence of forward-looking programs by the political parties. The parties seemed unable to measure up to the demands of a difficult new age. To many people, unemployed and maintained on a government pittance, the interwar period was aptly symbolized by a popular play of the time, *Love on the Dole*.

Interwar France

France suffered from World War I the most of any of the democracies; loss of lives as a proportion of the population and direct property damage were enormous. More than two out of every ten young Frenchmen died. Years later, the nation, which had not experienced as rapid a population growth in the nineteenth century as other European states, still felt the war's heavy losses.

Victory did not address any of France's basic political problems. The French labored under much the same political stalemate and social stagnation after 1918 as it had before 1914. The economic impact of the war and the social disruptions that occurred during and after the conflict exacerbated these conditions. A dangerous inflation plagued France and undermined its rather shallow prosperity. The multiparty system hampered the parliamentary structure of the Third Republic and the governments formed from shaky coalitions. The exhausted country lacked vitality and a sense of national purpose after gaining revenge against the Germans.

After 1919, the British wished to withdraw from Europe to look after their imperial interests, and the United States withdrew into isolationism. Working from a dispirited domestic base, France had to bear the burden of overseeing international affairs on the continent. Overall, with the exception of the counterproductive occupation of the Ruhr, the French carried their duties well in the 1920s. In the next decade, however, France retreated into the so-called Maginot mentality, after the construction of the Maginot line, a supposedly impenetrable line of fortresses to the east.

The depression struck France later than other countries, but in some ways the damage was greater. French leadership was no more astute than that of the other democracies before and during the depression. France managed to maintain a false prosperity from the 1920s for a while, partially because of its large gold holdings, but by the early 1930s it suffered much the same fate as the other countries. Tourism dried up, contributing to the already rising unemployment rate and budget deficits. In the face of these problems, the French carried the additional financial burden of rearming to face the renewed German threat.

Ministry after ministry took power, then collapsed a few months later. Citizens became impatient with the government, especially when the press exposed corruption in high places. One of the more shocking scandals was that surrounding the schemes of Alexander Stavisky, a rogue who had bribed officials and cheated French investors out of some 600 million francs. When the ministry in power in December 1933 refused to authorize an investigation after Stavisky's assumed suicide, thousands of angry citizens took to the streets of Paris in protest. In February 1934, mobs tried to storm the Chamber of Deputies.

The outcome of this affair was a new government, the National Union, a rightist coalition that endured strikes and avoided civil war for the next two years. France was becalmed. The leftists were unable to reorganize their forces quickly to gain control, and the rightist failed to deal with either domestic or foreign problems. In the spring of 1936 the leftist Popular Front took power.

This coalition, under the leadership of Léon Blum (1872–1950), won a national election and set in motion a program to bring socialist reforms to France's struggling economy. Blum's government tried to reduce the domination of the traditional ruling elite over the finances of the country on the one hand and on the other, work with the Communists to block the growing fascist influences. The cooperation with the Communists caused serious problems, including the usual one of how to work with the Moscow-dominated party without being captured by it. Many French voters refused to support the Popular Front from fear that it might commit France to fight against Germany for the benefit of the Soviet Union.

In foreign affairs the Popular Front worked closely with Great Britain and supported the work of the League of Nations. It also attempted to appease Germany, though it remained hostile to Italy. During the Spanish civil war (1936–1939), Blum's government, along with the British, declared neutrality in the face of fascist aggression, fearing a civil war.

In this atmosphere of social, economic, and international turmoil, Blum was unable to govern successfully. Further, an epidemic of sit-down strikes involving some 300,000 workers embarrassed the government. Gradually, laws introducing a 40-hour work week, higher wages, collective bargaining, and paid vacations were enacted to satisfy many of labor's demands. In addition, the government extended its control over the Bank of France and instituted a public works program. Blum navigated as best he could, favoring the worker against monopoly and big business while avoiding the totalitarian extremes of fascism and communism. After only a year in office, however, he was forced to resign. The unfavorable trade balance, huge public debt, and unbalanced budget brought down the Popular Front government. France swung back to the right with a government that ended the 40-hour week and put down strikes.

The National Union and the Popular Front mirrored the widening split between the upper and lower classes. The workers believed that the Popular Front's reforms had been sabotaged and that a France ruled by a wealthy clique deserved little or no allegiance. On the other hand, some business owners and financiers were horrified at the prospect of communism and openly admired Hitler's fascism. Soviet and German propagandists subtly encouraged the widening of the gulf.

While the French quarreled and France's economic strength declined, Germany—regimented and feverishly working—outstripped France in the manufacture of armaments. There were no leaders to bring France together, and the ingredients for the easy and tragic fall of the country in the spring of 1940 were in place.

Eastern Europe

With the exception of Finland and Czechoslovakia, democratic governments fared poorly in eastern Europe in the interwar period. By 1939, most of the states retained only the false front of parliamentary forms. Real power was exercised by varying combinations of secret police, official censors, armed forces, and corrupt politicians.

Most of these countries had an unhappy legacy of oppression by powerful neighbors, minority problems, economic weakness, and backward peasant societies. Poland, the Baltic States, Finland, Czechoslovakia, Yugoslavia, and Albania had not existed as states before 1913. Hungary, Bulgaria, and Austria had been on the losing side in World War I and paid dearly for that alliance in the treaties ending the war. Romania, which had been among the victors, gained large amounts of land and also a number of non-Romanian minorities.

For the first decade after the war, the small countries of eastern Europe had the opportunity to develop without undue external influence or interference. However, the exclusivist, aggressive, perhaps paranoid nationalism that dominated each nation thwarted any possibility of regional cooperation. The peace treaties had settled few of the problems plaguing the area and instead constructed a series of arbitrary political boundaries that brought far more conflict than accord. The countries in the region all sought autarkist solutions to their economic problems by erecting huge tariff barriers, which only served to emphasize the states' weaknesses.

Czechoslovakia. With its combination of a strong middle class, accumulation of capital, technology base, and high literacy rate, Czecho-slovakia possessed the greatest possibility among the eastern European states for successful democratic government. Four hundred years of Austrian domination had not crushed Czech national spirit. After the collapse of the Dual Monarchy in November 1918, the Czechs joined with the Slovaks, who had been under Hungarian domination for a thousand years, to establish a republic.

The new state possessed a literate and well-trained citizenry and a solid economic base, and managed to avoid the roller coaster ride of inflation in the immediate postwar period. The country was an island of prosperity, boasting solid financial institutions, advanced industry, and a small-farm–based agricultural sector. As in the other eastern European successor states, there were serious minority problems. But of all the new states Czechoslovakia extended the most liberal policies toward minorities. By the time of the depression, Czechoslovakia showed every indication of growing into a mature democratic country. The depression, however, heavily affected the country's export trade and hit especially hard in the textile industry, which was centered in the German-populated Sudetenland. By 1935 the economic blows had made the area ripe for Nazi agitation and infiltration.

Poland. Aside from Czechoslovakia, Poland had the best chance of the successor states to

→ Stalin's collectivization campaign involved confiscating privately owned land and livestock and "liquidating as a class" the *kulaks*, the better-off but hardly wealthy peasants. Many *kulaks*, protesting the policy, burned their crops and slaughtered their animals rather than see them taken by the state. Here, party agents, on Stalin's orders, drive the *kulaks* from a Ukrainian village in 1929.

form a democratic government. The Poles, however, had to overcome several problems: a border conflict with the Soviet Union, the dilemma of the Polish Corridor to Danzig, minority issues, and the fact that Poland had been partitioned for over a century. When the country was reunited after the war, the Poles chose to imitate the constitutional system of the French Third Republic. The multiplicity of parties, a weak executive, and the resultant succession of governments led to political paralysis until 1926, when Marshal Josef Pilsudski (1867–1935) led a military revolt against the Warsaw government.

For the next nine years Pilsudski imposed his generally positive, benevolent rule on the country. After his death in 1935, a group of colonels ruled Poland, and they permitted the formation of several proto-fascist organizations. By the time the Poles turned back toward a more liberal government in 1938, it was too late. For three years, they had played up to the Nazis and now they stood isolated before Hitler's advance.

The Baltic and Balkan States. Problems of geography plagued the Balkan states of Latvia, Lithuania, and Estonia, which came into existence in 1918. The democratic governments of these countries endured much political and economic strife before they eventually gave way to dictatorial forms of government to defend themselves against the Nazis.

The Balkan states of Yugoslavia, Albania, and Greece were buffeted by the ambitions of Italian imperialism, economic upheaval, and political corruption. Disintegration seemed a real possibility for Yugoslavia in the 1920s, but the conglomerate state stubbornly attempted to hold together the six major ethnic groups within its boundaries. King Alexander established himself as dictator in 1929 and ruled until 1934, when he was assassinated by Croatian separatists. Thereafter, the rising Nazi state drew parts of economically depressed Yugoslavia into its orbit, deeply splitting the country. By the end of the 1930s, both Greece and Albania were ruled by dictators.

Romania, another of the Balkan states, gained greatly from the First World War, doubling its area and its population. Although the state had great economic potential, the government was unable to impose a stable rule during the interwar period. Severe problems with minorities and peasants, and foreign control of the economy foiled the attempts of moderate politicians to rule, until by the 1930s fascist groups wielded a large amount of influence. In 1938 King Carol tried unsuccessfully to counter the pro-Nazi forces in Romania. Two years later the country lost one-third of its territory and population to the Bulgarians, Russians, and Hungarians, and Carol fled to Spain.

The Iberian Peninsula. During the interwar period, economic problems, aristocratic privilege, and peasant misery worked against successful democratic or parliamentary government in the Iberian peninsula. After the end of World War I, Portugal endured ten years of political indecision until Antonio de Oliveira Salazar (1889–1970), a professor of economics, became minister of finance in 1928. After helping straighten out some of the country's financial problems, Salazar became Portugal's premier and virtual dictator. He maintained Portugal's close ties with Britain while lending assistance to right-wing elements in Spain.

None of the political parties could deal adequately with Spain's problems in the 1920s. Revolts and strikes plagued the country until 1931, when the king abdicated and left the country. At the end of the year, a new liberal constitution was adopted, and a republic was proclaimed. The new constitution was extremely liberal, but it had the support of neither the left nor the right. Mob violence and the threat of military coups continually harassed the republic.

By 1936 the peasants and workers were beginning to take matters into their own hands, while the military in turn pursued its own political ends. In July, the army made its move and attacked the republican government. Even without Generalissimo Francisco Franco, there would have been a civil war in Spain. It would have come from the country's purely indigenous social antagonisms.[10]

DEMOCRACY OVERSEAS

The United States emerged from World War I as the strongest country in the world. But while other states looked to Washington to play its proper role in the world, the U.S. government turned

José Ortega y Gasset, The Rise of the Masses

In *Revolt of the Masses* the Spanish philosopher and writer José Ortega y Gasset captured the fear of the tyranny of the majority.

There is one fact which, whether for good or ill, is of utmost importance in the public life of Europe at the present moment. This fact is the accession of the masses to complete social power. As the masses, by definition, neither should nor can direct their own personal existence, and still less rule society in general, this fact means that actually Europe is suffering from the greatest crisis that can afflict peoples, nations, and civilisation. Such a crisis has occurred more than once in history. Its characteristics and its consequences are well known. So also its name. It is called the rebellion of the masses. . . .

There exist, then, in society, operations, activities, and functions of the most diverse order, which are of their very nature special, and which consequently cannot be properly carried out without special gifts. For example: certain pleasures of an artistic and refined character, or again the functions of government and of political judgment in public affairs. Previously these special activities were exercised by qualified minorities, or at least by those who claimed such qualification. The mass asserted no right to intervene in them; they realised that if they wished to intervene they would necessarily have to acquire those special qualities and cease being mere mass. They recognised their place in a healthy dynamic social system. . . .

The characteristic of the hour is that the commonplace mind, knowing itself to be commonplace, has the assurance to proclaim the rights of the commonplace and to impose them wherever it will. As they say in the United States: "to be different is to be indecent." The mass crushes beneath it everything that is different, everything that is excellent, individual, qualified and select. Anybody who is not like everybody, who does not think like everybody, runs the risk of being eliminated. And it is clear, of course, that this "everybody" is not "everybody." "Everybody" was normally the complex unity of the mass and the divergent, specialised minorities. Nowadays, "everybody" is the mass alone. Here we have the formidable fact of our times, described without any concealment of the brutality of its features.

From José Ortega y Gasset, *The Revolt of the Masses* (New York: W. W. Norton, 1932). Reprinted by permission.

---

inward, away from the international scene. Americans shelved Wilson's wartime idealism, ignored the League of Nations, and returned to isolationism.

The United States in the 1920s

During the 1920s, three Republican presidents—Warren G. Harding, Calvin Coolidge, and Herbert Hoover—profited from the well-being of the country and presided over a generally carefree time. Although refusing to join the League of Nations, the United States did participate in the Washington Naval Conference in 1921–1922 to limit the race in warship construction, the Dawes and Young plans for economic stabilization, and the Kellogg-Briand pact (1928) to outlaw war.

Harding's domestic policies were marked by protectionist economics, probusiness legislation, and scandal. After Harding died suddenly in 1923, the widespread corruption of his administration was exposed. His vice-president, Coolidge, easily weathered the storm and after his 1924 election advocated high tariffs, tax reduction, and a hands-off policy on federal regulation of business. Only nagging problems in the agricultural sphere detracted from the dazzling prosperity and honest government that marked his administration.

In the 1928 presidential elections, Herbert Hoover—a successful mining engineer who had directed Belgian relief during the war, had been present at the Versailles negotiations, and had overseen the Russian relief plan in the early 1920s—overwhelmed the governor of New York,

Alfred E. Smith, the first Catholic to be nominated for president. When Hoover took office in 1929, he had the support of a Republican Congress and a nation enjoying unbounded industrial prosperity. It would be his incredibly bad luck to have to deal with and be given the blame for the worst depression the United States has ever experienced.

By 1932 Americans felt the tragic blows of the Great Depression—25 percent unemployment, 30,000 business failures, numerous bank collapses, and a huge number of foreclosed mortgages. Hoover tried unprecedented measures to prop up faltering businesses with government money, devise new strategies to deal with the farm problem, and build confidence among the shaken citizenry. Yet he failed to shift the tide of the depression. Indeed, some observers note that the only force that brought an end to the crisis was the arrival of the Second World War.

In the 1932 elections, Franklin D. Roosevelt, only the third Democrat elected to the presidency since 1860, defeated Hoover by assembling a coalition of labor, intellectuals, minorities, and farmers—a coalition the Democratic party could count on for nearly a half-century. The country had reached a crisis point by the time Roosevelt was inaugurated in 1933 and quick action had to be taken in the face of a wave of bank closings.

Under Roosevelt's leadership the New Deal, a sweeping, pragmatic, often hit-or-miss program, was developed to cope with the emergency. The New Deal's three objectives were relief, recovery, and reform. Millions of dollars flowed from the federal treasury to feed the hungry, create jobs for the unemployed through public works, and provide for the sick and elderly through such reforms as the Social Security Act. In addition, Roosevelt's administration substantially reformed the banking and investment industries, greatly increased the rights of labor unions, invested in massive public power and conservation projects, and supported families who were in danger of losing their homes or who simply needed homes.

The Democrats' programs created much controversy among those who believed that they went too far toward creating a socialistic government and those who believed that they did not go far enough toward attacking the depression. Hated or loved, Roosevelt was in control, and the

→ Photographer Dorothea Lange used her camera to record the devastating human effects of the Great Depression as in this photograph of a former Missouri farmer forced to eke out a living as a migratory farm laborer in California.

strength and leadership he provided were unparalleled in the interwar democracies.

Interwar Latin America

The huge wartime demand for Latin American mineral and agricultural products resulted in an economic boom which, with a minor contraction, continued on into the 1920s. However, the area's crucial weakness remained—its economic dependence on only a few products. Among Latin America's 20 republics, Brazil based its prosperity on coffee, Cuba depended on sugar, Venezuela on oil, Bolivia on tin, Mexico on oil and silver, Argentina on wheat and meat, and the various Central American countries on bananas.

Another problem was that of land distribution. On many large estates, conditions resembled medieval serfdom. Because the Catholic church was a great landowner, certain churchmen combined with the landed interests to oppose land reforms.

During the 1920s, Mexico spearheaded the movement for social reform in Latin America. A series of governments, each claiming to be faithful to the spirit of the 1910 revolt, sought to gain more control over the vast oil properties run by foreign investors. The government solved the agrarian problem at the expense of the large landowners. These changes were accompanied by a wave of anticlericalism. Under these attacks, the Catholic church lost much property, saw many churches destroyed, and had to work through an underground priesthood for a time.

Mexico exerted a strong influence over other Latin American countries. Between 1919 and 1929 seven nations adopted new, liberal constitutions. In addition, there were growing demands for better economic and social opportunities, a breakdown of the barriers that divided the few extremely rich from the many abysmally poor, and improvement in health, education, and the status of women. Above all there was an increasing desire for more stable conditions.

Because of their dependence on raw material exports, the Latin American countries suffered a serious economic crisis during the depression. Largely as a result of the disaster, six South American countries had revolutions in 1930.

During the 1930s the "colossus of the north," the United States, attempted to improve its relations with Latin America and to stimulate trade. The Good Neighbor Policy, originated in Hoover's administration and begun in 1933, asserted that "no state has the right to intervene in the internal or external affairs of another." Less pious, but more effective, was the $560 million worth of inter-American trade that the new policy encouraged.

Rivalries among industrialized nations for the Latin American market became very intense during the 1930s. Nazi Germany concluded many barter agreements with Latin American customers and at the same time penetrated the countries politically by organizing German immigrants into pro-Nazi groups, supporting fascist politicians, and developing powerful propaganda networks. When war came, however, most of Latin America lined up with the democracies.

The British Empire

Demands for home rule grew during the interwar period in the British Empire, especially in India, Ceylon, Burma, and Egypt. An ominous trend was the growing antagonism between the Arab inhabitants of mandated Palestine and the Jewish Zionist immigrants. Yet these issues would not come to a crisis until after the Second World War.

Happier developments could be seen in the attainment of home rule by the Irish Free State (the southern part of Ireland) in 1921 and Britain's recognition in the Statute of Westminister (1931) of a new national status for the dominions (Canada, Australia, New Zealand, and South Africa). Collectively, the four states were then known as the British Commonwealth of Nations and would be held together henceforth only by loyalty to the crown and by common language,

→ Riding with Franklin Roosevelt to the Capitol after FDR's victory in the 1932 presidential election, former President Herbert Hoover remained silent and aloof beside the effervescent newly elected president.

legal principles, traditions, and economic interests. Democratic traditions in the dominions did not succumb to the pressures of the depression, even though they were painfully susceptible to the effects of the world slump.

THE WESTERN TRADITION IN TRANSITION

In the first two decades of the twentieth century, science made great strides, and such figures as Max Planck, Albert Einstein, Ivan Pavlov, and Sigmund Freud enlarged understanding of the universe and the individual. Even before the war, which had dealt a death blow to the nineteenth-century legacy of optimism, these physicists and psychologists pointed out that the old foundations and beliefs on which the European world rested had to be rethought. They and others like them opened new scientific vistas, and after 1918 their work began to have a much wider impact.

In the interwar period, artists too served as observant witnesses and penetrating critics of the difficult age in which they lived. After 1918, questioning of the accepted values and traditions of Western civilization increased.

Science and Society

The British physicist Ernest Rutherford advanced the theory in 1911 that each atom has a central particle, or nucleus, which is positively charged. Rutherford's argument repudiated the belief that the atom was indivisible. On the continent, discoveries with even greater consequences were being made. German physicist Max Planck (1858–1947) studied radiant heat, which comes from the sun and is identical in nature with light. He found that the energy emitted from a vibrating electron proceeds not in a steady wave, as was traditionally believed, but discontinuously in the form of calculable "energy packages." To such a package, Planck gave the name *quantum*, hence the term *quantum theory*. This jolt to traditional physics was to prove invaluable in the rapidly growing study of atomic physics.

The scientific giant of the first half of the twentieth century, Albert Einstein (1879–1955),

supported Planck's findings. In 1905 Einstein contended that light is propagated through space in the form of particles, which he called photons. Moreover, the energy contained in any particle of matter, such as the photon, is equal to the mass of that body multiplied by the square of the velocity of light (approximately 186,300 miles per second). This theory, expressed in the equation $E = mc^2$, provided the answer to many mysteries of physics. For example, questions such as how radioactive substances such as radium and uranium are able to eject particles at enormous velocities and to go on doing so for millions of years could be examined in a new light. The magnitude of energy contained in the nuclei of atoms could be revealed. Above all, $E = mc^2$ showed that mass and energy are equatable. In 1905, Einstein formulated his special theory of relativity, which set out a radically new approach to explain the concepts of time, space, and velocity.

Ten years later, Einstein proposed his general theory, in which he incorporated gravitation into relativity. He showed that gravitation is identical to acceleration and that light rays would be deflected in passing through a gravitational field—a prediction confirmed by observation of an eclipse in 1919 and by various experiments carried out in the American space programs in the 1960s and 1970s and the Hubble Telescope in 1994. The theory of relativity has been subsequently confirmed in other ways as well. The conversion of mass into energy was dramatically demonstrated in the atomic bomb, which obtains its energy by the annihilation of part of the matter of which it is composed.

Einstein's theories upset the Newtonian views of the universe. Einstein's universe is not Newton's three-dimensional figure of length, breadth, and thickness. It is, instead, a four-dimensional space-time continuum in which time itself varies with velocity. Such a cosmic model calls for the use of non-Euclidean geometry. Einstein's theory changed scientists' attitude toward the structure and mechanics of the universe. On a broader scale, his relativistic implications have penetrated philosophical, moral, and esthetic concepts of the twentieth century.

Planck and Einstein investigated the infinite extent of the external universe, with a massive impact on the state of knowledge. At the same time, the equally infinite extent of that universe known as the mind also began to be studied in greater depth than ever before.

The Russian scientist Ivan Pavlov (1849–1936) gave the study of psychology a new impetus. In 1900 he carried out a series of experiments in which food was given to a dog at the same time that a bell was rung. After a time, the dog identified the sound of the bell with food. Henceforth, the sound of the bell alone conditioned the dog to salivate, just as if food had been presented. Pavlov demonstrated the influence of physical stimuli on an involuntary process.

The psychology of "conditioned reflexes," based on Pavlov's work, achieved a wide popularity especially in the United States, as the basis for behaviorism, which considered the human as analogous to a machine responding mechanically to stimuli. Behaviorism stressed experimentation and observational techniques and did much to create relatively valid intelligence and aptitude tests. It also served to strengthen the materialist philosophies of the period.

Probably the most famous and controversial name associated with psychology is that of Sigmund Freud (1856–1939). Placing far greater stress than any predecessor on the role of the unconscious, Freud pioneered the theory and methods of psychoanalysis. This theory is based on the idea that human beings are born with unconscious drives that from the very beginning seek some sort of outlet or expression. Young children often express their drives in ways that violate social conventions for proper behavior. Parents typically forbid these behaviors and punish children for performing them. As a result, many innate drives are repressed—that is, pushed out of conscious awareness. Repressed drives, however, continue to demand some kind of expression. Freud believed that many repressed drives were sublimated, or channeled into some kind of tolerated or even highly praised behavior.

Freud was particularly interested in psychological disorders, and he treated emotional disturbances by encouraging patients to bring back to the surface deeply repressed drives and memories. By making them aware of their unconscious feelings, Freud hoped that patients would understand themselves better and be able to respond more effectively to the problems they faced. Freud used the techniques of free association and dream interpretation to explore how uncon-

→ Sigmund Freud. Freud's theory of psychoanalysis gave people a new way of understanding and interpreting human behavior and new methods for treating mental disorders.

scious feelings might be related to patients' symptoms. He believed that many of his patients' symptoms resulted from repressed sexual and aggressive drives. Freud's theories have not only had tremendous influence in the science of psychology, they have also had a profound impact on our culture as a whole.

The Testimony of Artists

Even before the war, many of Europe's writers, artists, and musicians had begun to question the generally held faith in European progress. The barbarism and tragedy of the war and its aftermath merely confirmed their perceptions. A whole generation of artists and thinkers cast doubts on their society and the worth of individuals caught in civilization's web. The war had shown to many the fallacies of the old order.

→ Franz Kafka. In his visionary and symbolic works, Kafka explored the existential dilemma of the contemporary world—the anxiety individuals experience as they struggle to find meaning in a meaningless world.

Some artists sought release in drugs, oriental religions, or bohemian lifestyles. Other found comfort in ideas drawn from Einstein's relativity theory, which held that nothing was "fixed" in the universe, or in Freud's notions of the overwhelming power of the unconscious.

Among writers, Franz Kafka (1883–1924) perhaps best captured the nightmarish world of the twentieth century. In works such as *The Metamorphosis* and *The Trial*, he portrayed a ritualistic society in which a well-organized insanity prevails. Rational, well-meaning individuals run a constant maze from which there is no exit, only more structures. Many sensitive artists and writers cast serious doubt on the Renaissance notion that "man is the measure of all things." The Western world had gone very far off course, and the best that could be hoped for was survival.

Historians worked under the profound influence of Oswald Spengler's *Decline of the West*. The book, finished one year before the defeat of the Central Powers, was more widely quoted than read. In it, the German historian traced the life span of cultures—from birth through maturity to death—and identified the symptoms of the West's demise. Other writers expressed a similar fascination with the death of their civilization, but perhaps more significant was that people in the West knew Spengler's name, just as earlier they had known the names of Freud, Einstein, and Darwin and their general messages.

Since before 1914, a number of composers had been rebelling strongly against lyrical romanticism and engaged in striking experimentation. Breaking with the "major-minor" system of tonality, which had been the musical tradition since the Renaissance, some of them used several different keys simultaneously, a device known as polytonality. Outstanding among such composers was Igor Stravinsky (1882–1971), who was less concerned with melody than with achieving effects by means of polytonality, dissonant harmonies, and percussive rhythms. Other composers, such as the Austrian-born Arnold Schoenberg (1874–1951), experimented with atonality, the absence of any fixed key. Schoenberg developed the 12-tone system, an approach in which compositions depart from all tonality and harmonic progressions, while at the same time stressing extreme dissonances. Stravinsky's and Schoenberg's music may strike the first-time listener as harsh and unpleasant, yet it must be acknowledged that these experiments with polytonality and atonality had validity for a time in which the old absolute values were crumbling, a time of clashing dissonance.

Artists all over the world took up abstract, nonrepresentational painting. (For a number of examples, see Portfolio Eight following p. 928.) During the interwar period Pablo Picasso (1881–1973) modified his cubist style and became a public figure through paintings such as *Guernica*, a mural that captures vividly the human horrors of the destruction of a small town in Spain by fascist air forces during that country's civil war. Henri Matisse (1869–1954) continued to exercise a major influence on young painters through his abstract works. Less significant but a useful example of artistic response to the times was the Dada school, which viewed World War I as proof that rationality did not exist and that, therefore, neither did artistic standards. Salvador Dali (1904–1989) perhaps indicated his convictions about the artistic establishment and the society it represented when he gave a lecture on art while wearing a diver's helmet.[11]

A more lasting movement that came out of the 1920s was surrealism. The proponents of this approach saw the subconscious mind as the vehicle that could free people from the shackles of modern society and lead them to total creative freedom. They felt an affinity with "primitive art" and its close associations with magical and mythological themes. They exalted the irrational, the violent and the absurd in human experience. French writer André Breton (1896–1966) wrote a manifesto of surrealism in 1924, but the movement had its greatest impact in the visual arts, in the works of such artists as Dali, Georgio de Chirico (1888–1978), and René Magritte (1898–1967).

Sculpture and Architecture

These two most substantial forms of art went through radical changes during the generation before and after the war. Auguste Rodin (1840–1917) has been called the father of modern sculpture. The realistic honesty and vitality of his work made him the object of stormy controversy during his career. He shared the impressionist painters' dislike of finality in art and preferred to let the viewers' imagination play on his work. Rodin's technique of "rough" finish can best be seen in his bronze works, which feature a glittering surface of light and shadow and convey a feeling of immediacy and incompleteness that emphasizes their spontaneous character.

While Rodin was making major contributions in sculpture, architects in Europe were taking advantage of new materials and technologies developed through industrialization to make major improvements in construction. With new resources and methods, architects were able to span greater distances and enclose greater areas than had hitherto been possible.

The Great Chicago fire of 1871 may have leveled much of the city, but it had the beneficial effect of permitting new building on a large scale. A new form of structure emerged—the steel-skeleton skyscraper, which enabled builders to erect much taller structures. Before, high buildings had required immensely thick masonry walls or buttresses. Now a metal frame allowed the weight of the structure to be distributed on

→ René Magritte, *Man with a Newspaper*, 1928. In his works, the Belgian surrealist combines precise images of ordinary reality with the mysterious and unexpected to suggest a reality beyond that which is apparent.

an entirely different principle. Also, the metal frame permitted a far more extensive use of glass than ever before.

Outstanding among the pioneers in this new approach was American architect Louis Sullivan (1856–1924), who did most of his important work in Chicago. Like others, Sullivan saw the value of the skyscraper in providing a large amount of useful space on a small plot of expensive land. He rejected all attempts to disguise the skeleton of the skyscraper behind a false front and boldly proclaimed it by a clean sweep of line. Sullivan had a far-reaching influence on the approach of choosing function over form.

In Europe, the French engineer Alexandre Gustave Eiffel (1832–1923) planned and erected

→ Louis Sullivan, Carson Pirie Scott & Co. Building, Chicago (1899–1904). Sullivan influenced the development of the skyscraper, the dominant architectural form of the twentieth century.

a 984-foot tower for the Paris International Exposition in 1889. Delicately formed from an iron framework, the tower rests on four masonry piers on a base 330 feet square.

In the decade prior to World War I, an "international" style of architecture, which broke sharply with tradition, developed in Germany. This style, which stressed the use of different techniques from the machine age, was particularly well suited to early twentieth-century industrialization. In 1914 one of the outstanding leaders of this movement, Walter Gropius (1888–1969) designed an exhibition hall in Cologne that emphasized horizontal lines, used glass, exposed staircases, and did not hide its functionalism. Even at the end of the twentieth century this hall is still regarded as contemporary. Proponents of this new movement in architecture established a highly influential school of functional art and architecture, the *Bauhaus*, in 1918.

One of Louis Sullivan's pupils, Frank Lloyd Wright (1869–1959), originated revolutionary designs for houses. One feature of Wright's structures was the interweaving of interiors and exteriors through the use of terraces and cantilevered roofs

(see Portfolio Seven following p. 768). He felt that a building should look appropriate on its site; it should "grow out of the land." His "prairie houses," with their long, low lines, were designed to blend in with the flat land of the Midwest. Much of what is today taken for granted in domestic architecture stems directly from Wright's experiments at the beginning of the century.

Mass Culture

While the creative geniuses of high culture responded in their own ways to the era, purveyors of mass culture made amazing strides to please and entertain a widening audience. Movies became the most popular, most universal art form of the twentieth century. Movie newsreels brought home to millions the immediacy of the rise of Adolf Hitler, the drama of Franklin D. Roosevelt, and the home run power of Babe Ruth.

From the theaters of Main Street, U.S.A., to the private projection rooms of the Kremlin, artists such as Charlie Chaplin became universal favorites. Chaplin's favorite character, the Little Tramp, was an archetypal figure that communicated across all cultures. The tramp's struggle for food and shelter was universal, as was his appeal for freedom and dignity. Despite the odds, he always struggled against the forces of inhumanity, whether the soulless mechanization of the assembly line, as brilliantly shown in *Modern Times* (1935) or jackboot tyranny, as in *The Great Dictator* (1940), where the ranting "Furore" is ironically juxtaposed with the little Jewish barber who pleads for decency and predicts that "so long as men die, liberty will never perish."

Technology touched the common people in many ways and vastly expanded mass culture. Henry Ford's Model T made cars widely accessible and opened up the world to those who cared to drive. In cities, virtually every home had electricity, which powered bright lights, refrigeration, and other conveniences. Radio brought music, drama, and news into millions of living rooms. Politicians quickly learned the usefulness of the new medium; Stanley Baldwin in Britain, Franklin D. Roosevelt in the United States, and Adolf Hitler in Germany became masters at projecting their personalities and their ideas over the airwaves. The three great networks in the United States and organizations such as the

→ Charlie Chaplin as the little tramp in "The Gold Rush," 1925. Chaplin used the new popular art form of the movies as a vehicle for both social commentary and humor. His little tramp character became a folk hero whose antics were touched with pathos yet who remained incorrigibly optimistic that one day things would get better.

British Broadcasting Corporation (BBC) in Europe got their start during these years.

The combination of increased leisure time, greater mobility, and improved communications led to the development of the modern "star" system in sports and entertainment. As times became more difficult and while front-page news was grim, Americans, Germans, and French citizens could find some diversion in reading about their boxers—Jack Dempsey, Max Schmeling, and Georges Carpentier. In the United States golfers and baseball stars became better known and better paid than presidents.

Through radio and phonograph records the mass audience discovered jazz, formerly the special preserve of black musicians and their audiences. Louis Armstrong and his trumpet and Paul Whiteman and his band became known worldwide. At the same time, Rosa Ponselle, Arturo

Toscanini, and other figures from the opera and concert world became celebrities known to millions more than could ever have seen them perform in person.

Mass culture, with its movie stars, athletic heroes, and musical favorites, provided a diversion for many, even if it drew criticism from the elite. While intellectuals struggled to comprehend and express the changes occurring around them, mass culture provided release and relief from the stresses of the interwar period.

CONCLUSION

The democracies won World War I, and they dictated the peace at Paris, but the peace did not bring them the fruits of victory they so ardently desired. In the West, the vanguard of progress since the Middle Ages had been the middle classes. This group, originally small property owners, pursued private enterprise in an urban setting and favored an economy based on minimal governmental interference and free markets. After the war, the economic disasters of inflation and the depression depleted the middle classes' economic strength and weakened the democracies.

Other basic institutions and assumptions also came under attack. The total mobilization for victory during the war laid the foundations for increased state dominance over society. By the end of the 1930s, Bismarck's welfare state had been copied in almost every country in the West. The family's obligation to care for its own members soon passed to the society and the state. Whether in the identification card of the French citizen or the social security number of the United States, every adult came to find a tentacle of the state reaching out to him or her to insure, support, and protect, while at the same time taxing and restricting.

→ Suggestions for Reading

E. H. Carr, *The Twenty Years' Crisis* (Torchbooks, 1964) and A. J. P. Taylor, *From Sarajevo to Potsdam* (Harcourt Brace Jovanovich, 1966) give compelling and eloquent coverage of the malaise of the democracies in the interwar period. The problems of peacemaking and the aftermath of Versailles are discussed by J. M. Keynes, *The Economic Consequences of the Peace* (Macmillan, 1921) and F. P. Walters, *A History of the League of Nations* (Oxford Univ., 1952).

Harold Nicolson's thoughtful *Peacemaking* (Houghton Mifflin, 1939) is an essential introduction to the era.

The economic situation is well treated in David Landes, *The Unbound Prometheus* (Cambridge Univ., 1969) and Sidney Pollard, *European Economic Integration, 1815–1870* (Harcourt Brace Jovanovich, 1974). See Fritz Ringer, ed., *The German Inflation of 1923* (Oxford Univ., 1969) and Gustav Stolper, et al., *The German Economy 1870 to the Present* (Harcourt Brace Jovanovich, 1967) for the view from Berlin.

J. K. Galbraith's *The Great Crash 1929* (Houghton Mifflin, 1965) is wise and beautifully written. C. P. Kindelberger, *The World in Depression* (Univ. of California, 1975) covers the global perspective of the 1930s. C. Maier surveys the social and political consequences of the difficult interwar period in *Recasting Bourgeois Europe* (Princeton Univ., 1975).

Two first-rate biographies of interwar British leaders are David Marquand, *Ramsay MacDonald* (Jonathan Cape, 1977) and Keith Midlemas, *Baldwin, A Biography* (Macmillan, 1970). J. Stevenson and C. Cook provide a good survey of British life between the wars in *Social Conditions in Britain Between the Wars* (Penguin, 1977). For developments in France between the wars, see John T. Marcus, *French Socialism in the Crisis Years, 1933–1936* (Praeger, 1963) and Peter Larmour, *The French Radical Party in the 1930s* (Stanford Univ., 1964).

→ Notes

1. E. H. Carr, *The Twenty Years' Crisis* (New York: Harper & Row, 1964), p. 224.
2. A. J. Ryder, *Twentieth Century Germany: From Bismarck to Brandt* (New York: Columbia University Press, 1973), p. 216.
3. David S. Landes, *The Unbound Prometheus* (Cambridge: Cambridge University Press, 1969), pp. 361–362; Gustav Stolper, Karl Hauser, and Knut Borchardt, *The German Economy: 1870 to the Present*, trans. Toni Stolper (New York: Harcourt Brace Jovanovich, 1967), p. 83.
4. Alan Bullock, *Hitler, A Study in Tyranny* (New York: Torchbooks, 1964), p. 91.
5. Sidney Pollard, *European Economic Integration, 1815–1970* (New York: Harcourt Brace Jovanovich, 1974), p. 138.
6. Landes, *The Unbound Prometheus*, p. 365.
7. Pollard, *European Economic Integration, 1815–1970*, pp. 140–142.
8. William R. Keylor, *The Twentieth Century World* (Oxford: Oxford University Press, 1984), p. 133.
9. John Kenneth Galbraith, *The Great Crash 1929* (Boston: Houghton Mifflin Co., 1961), p. 173.
10. Brian Crozier, *Franco* (London: Eyre & Spottiswoode, 1967), p. 13.
11. A. J. P. Taylor, *From Sarajevo to Potsdam* (New York: Harcourt Brace Jovanovich, 1965), p. 116.

CHAPTER 31

TOTALITARIAN REGIMES IN EUROPE IN THE 1930s

- Communist Regimes
- Fascist Regimes
- Authoritarian Regimes

0   200
MILES

→ A mere 20 years after Woodrow Wilson proclaimed his desire to make the world safe for democracy, totalitarian and authoritarian political regimes dominated Europe. By July 1940, only England remained to carry the flag of democracy.

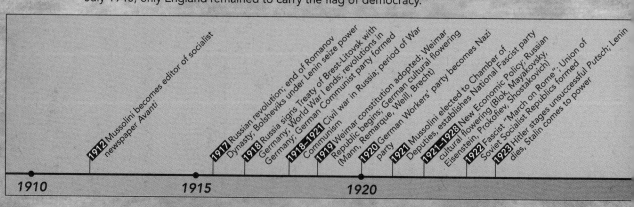

1912 Mussolini becomes editor of socialist newspaper *Avanti*

1917 Russian revolution; end of Romanov Dynasty; Bolsheviks under Lenin seize power

1918 Russia signs Treaty of Brest-Litovsk with Germany; World War I ends; revolutions in Germany; German Communist party formed

1918–1921 Civil war in Russia, period of War Communism

1919 Weimar constitution adopted; Weimar Republic begins; German cultural flowering (Mann, Remarque, Weill, Brecht)

1920 German Workers' party becomes Nazi party

1921 Mussolini elected to Chamber of Deputies; establishes National Fascist party

1921–1928 New Economic Policy; Russian cultural flowering (Blok, Mayakovsky, Eisenstein, Prokofiev, Shostakovich)

1922 Fascist "March on Rome"; Union of Soviet Socialist Republics formed

1923 Hitler stages unsuccessful Putsch; Lenin dies; Stalin comes to power

1910   1915   1920

The Quest for Total Power

Russia, Italy, and Germany

World War I and its aftershocks prepared the way for authoritarian rule in Europe. By 1939, dictators ruled Russia, Italy, and Germany. Using modern technology, they tried to form a new kind of state, described as *totalitarian* by Benito Mussolini in 1925.

Totalitarian regimes, such as those led by Joseph Stalin and Adolf Hitler, are at an opposite pole from democratic governments, which respect laws, representative assemblies, and civil and human rights. Totalitarianism exalts the leader of the state, who uses law and society for the regime's goals. It invades and controls all areas of an individual's life, using propaganda to manipulate the masses. It orchestrates elections to achieve the "democratic fiction" of popular support. When totalitarian rule is perfected, society is atomized so there is no obstacle between the might of the leader and the individual.[1]

The costs of war and the incompetence of dual power destroyed the Provisional Government in Russia. The disappointments of the peace and unsettled economic conditions undermined the Italian government and the German Weimar Republic. Even before the war and the economic upheaval, the political climate in these

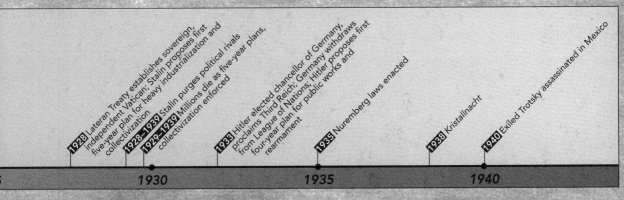

1928 Lateran Treaty establishes sovereign, independent Vatican; Stalin proposes first five-year plan for heavy industrialization and collectivization

1928–1939 Stalin purges political rivals

1929–1939 Millions die as five-year plans, collectivization enforced

1933 Hitler elected chancellor of Germany, proclaims Third Reich; Germany withdraws from League of Nations; Hitler proposes first four-year plan for public works and rearmament

1935 Nuremberg laws enacted

1938 Kristallnacht

1940 Exiled Trotsky assassinated in Mexico

1930   1935   1940

countries had not been conducive to the development of liberal government. The postwar conditions combined with the exhaustion of the democracies led to the authoritarian alternative.

THE RUSSIAN REVOLUTION, 1917–1939

The enormous costs of the war set the stage for the February/March 1917 revolution. Nicholas and his subjects entered the war in August 1914 in a buoyant and patriotic mood.[2] It took only two months to dampen their initial optimism and to expose the army's weakness and the government's corruption. By the middle of 1915 drastic losses (more than 2 million in that year alone) and food and fuel shortages lowered morale. Strikes increased among the factory workers during 1916, and the peasants, whose sons were dying in large numbers and whose desire for land reform was being ignored, became discontented.

The tsar and his government did little. Nicholas came more under the influence of his wife, Alexandra. She, in turn, had fallen under the control of the "holy man" Rasputin, the man who seemed to be able to stop the bleeding of the tsar's hemophiliac son. Rasputin scandalized Petrograd by his influence over Alexandra and by his well-known seductions—he believed that "great sins made possible great repentances"[3] and in pursuit of that goal became one of history's notable sexual athletes.

When Nicholas took the symbolic act of assuming command of his armies in the field—a move that did nothing to help the Russian forces—Alexandra and Rasputin's authority increased. The two capriciously dismissed capable generals and officials, making the government and army even less efficient. In December 1916 a group of Russian nobles tried to kill Rasputin by luring him to an apartment and poisoning him. When the massive amounts of poison had no effect, they shot him and then threw him into the Neva River. According to the autopsy, he finally died by drowning.

Alexandra's and Rasputin's roles in the capital reflected the sad state of the tsarist government in 1917. Under the pressure of war, the Russian economic and political structures dissolved. The tsarina and her associate did not cause the outbreak of the revolution. Rather, "the complex revolutionary situation of 1917 was the accumulated deposit of Russian history, detonated by the explosion of war."[4]

The February/March Revolutions of 1917

While politicians, ideologists, and generals acted out their parts in the drama, a spontaneous event

→ Tsar Nicholas and Tsarina Alexandra are surrounded by their daughters (left to right) Marya, Tatiana, Olga, and Anatasia. The young tsarovitch sits below his parents. Nicholas and his entire family were executed by the Bolsheviks in July 1918.

→ Convinced of the Russian monk's supernatural powers because of his apparent ability to relieve her son's hemophilia, Tsarina Alexandra came more and more under the influence of the mysterious Rasputin. The name Rasputin, which he acquired during his youth, means appropriately "the Debauchee."

Three events occurred between March 12 and March 15 that marked the end of the old regime. On March 12 the Duma declared the formation of a provisional committee (renamed the Provisional Government on March 15) to serve as a caretaker administration until a Constituent Assembly could be elected to write a constitution for the future Russian republic. On the same day Marxist socialists in Petrograd formed the Soviet (council) of Workers' Deputies (renamed three days later the Soviet of Workers' and Soldiers' Deputies). Nicholas abdicated on March 15 to his brother Michael, who turned down the throne the next day in favor of the Provisional Government. After more than three centuries in power, the Romanov dynasty ceased to rule.

For the next six months, Russia proceeded under a system Leon Trotsky, the great Marxist theoretician and revolutionary, described as dual power—the Provisional Government and the Soviet. The moderates and liberals in the Provisional Government quickly produced a program of civil rights and liberties that gave Russia a springtime of freedom in 1917 the likes of which the country had never known before and would not experience again for 70 years. From the first, however, the Provisional Government was hampered by its temporary nature: it refused to take permanent action on major issues until the constituent assembly, elected by all Russians, could convene.

The Soviet was dominated by the Menshevik wing of the Russian Social Democratic party. The Mensheviks believed, in accord with Marx's teachings, that a liberal, bourgeois revolution had to run its course. Even though they had greater popular support than the Provisional Government, they refused to take power until what they deemed to be the historically proper moment as defined by Marx's theories. After the fall of the tsar, power passed to those who could not rule or would not rule.

From the first, the dual power system functioned in a contradictory and ineffective way. On March 14 the Soviet issued its first law, Order No. 1, which placed the running of the army on a democratic basis, through a committee structure. Soldiers were to obey only those orders that agreed with the official position of the Soviet, which wanted peace. At the same time, the Provisional Government insisted on carrying out the

from below sparked the 1917 Russian revolution. In the first part of March (late February in the Julian calendar in use in Russia at the time; all dates will be given in the new style), a strike broke out in a Petrograd (formerly St. Petersburg) factory. By March 8 sympathy strikes had virtually paralyzed the city. At the same time, a bread shortage occurred, which brought more people into the streets. Scattered fighting broke out between the strikers and protesters on one side and the police on the other.

The tsar ordered the strikers back to work and dismissed the Duma (parliament) on March 11. His orders touched off the revolutionary crisis. The Duma refused to go home and the strikers defied the government and held mass meetings. The next day the army and police openly sided with the workers.

→ Soldiers gathered in Petrograd's Admiralty Square in April 1917. The banners (reading left to right) proclaim: "Long Wave the Democratic Republic," "Land and Freedom," and "Let Us Reject the Old World."

war, in hopes of gaining the Bosporous, Constantinople, and the Dardanelles.

As the months wore on, the position of moderates in both parts of the system weakened, and all the parties involved became discredited. The Provisional Government put off calling the constituent assembly and thereby deferred any possibility of finding solutions to the problems facing Russia. It continued to pursue the war to "honor its commitments" and to gain the prizes promised in the secret treaties. The Mensheviks refused to take control, reasoning that the liberal, bourgeois phase of history had not run its course in Russia. The masses who suffered from economic hardships or fought and died on the front lines could find little consolation in either branch of dual power.

By July, the liberals and moderates had given up the reins of power. Alexander Kerensky (1881–1970), who was further to the left and who had been the only real revolutionary in the original cabinet, became the head of the Provisional Government. He was in an impossible situation. Leftists accused the Provisional Government of heartlessly pursuing the war, while rightists condemned it for tolerating too many leftists. In the meantime the Soviet extended its organization throughout Russia by setting up local affiliates. Through the summer, however, the Soviets lacked the forceful leadership to take control of the country.

Lenin's Opportunity, October/November 1917

In 1917 Lenin returned to Russia from exile in Switzerland, intent on giving the revolution the leadership it lacked. He had spelled out his tactics and ideas in the previous decade, and his disciples in Russia, the Bolsheviks, had built up a core of supporters in the factories and the army. As late as December 1916 he had stated that the revolution would not occur within his lifetime. Four months later, working through Swiss contacts and with German assistance, he returned to Russia. The Germans gave him transportation and financial support in the hope that he would cause widespread chaos, forcing Russia to withdraw from the war.

From the moment he stepped off the train at the Finland station in Petrograd on the evening of April 16, Lenin tried to control the revolution. He proposed immediately stopping the war against Germany and starting one against "social oppressors." He called for giving all power to the Soviets and nationalizing all land. He also pushed for calling all Social Democrats, of whatever persuasion, communists. Lenin badly misjudged his audience, and the Mensheviks and Social Revolutionaries rejected his program.

During the summer and fall of 1917 the Provisional Government and the Soviet continued their misgovernment. Kerensky tried to rule through a series of coalitions in which the political balance continually shifted to the left. By the middle of July, after a moderately successful offensive against the Austrians, soldiers began to desert in large numbers rather than face a useless death. The Russian front, along with the army, disintegrated. In the capital, the Mensheviks continued their refusal to take power through the Soviet: the historical time was not right. As if to match the ineptness of dual power, the Bolsheviks made an ill-conceived attempt to take power. The move backfired, and Lenin was forced to flee in disguise to Finland.

After surviving the Bolshevik crisis, Kerensky faced a new threat from the right when General Lavr Kornilov tried to "help" the government by sending his troops to the capital. Kerensky and the Soviet interpreted this action as a right-wing counterrevolutionary move and mobilized to head it off. Kornilov's ill-advised maneuver failed and, ironically, he weakened the people he wanted to help.

Between March and October 1917, the force of the revolution ground to bits all of Russia's structures and parties, from monarchist to Menshevik. The economic system fell apart as the rhythms of planting and commerce were disrupted by the uproar. To the people caught in this chaos, the moderates' political dreams, the Mensheviks' revolutionary timing, and the Bolsheviks' schemes for the seizure of power were all totally irrelevant.

The actual revolution took place far away from the politicians and "great men." The army withered away as mass desertions and the execution of officers became commonplace. In the countryside the peasants began carrying out land reform on their own, expelling landowners and killing those who would not leave. In the cities,

The Program of the Provisional Government

The freedom enjoyed by Russia from March to November 1917 was the greatest ever experienced in that country. A major reason for the freedom was the program of the Provisional Government.

Citizens, the Provisional Executive Committee of the members of the Duma, with the aid and support of the garrison of the capital and its inhabitants, has triumphed over the dark forces of the Old Regime to such an extent as to enable it to organize a more stable executive power.

The cabinet will be guided in its actions by the following principles:

1. An immediate general amnesty for all political and religious offenses, including terrorist acts, military revolts, agrarian offenses, etc.
2. Freedom of speech and press; freedom to form labor unions and to strike. These political liberties should be extended to the army in so far as war conditions permit.
3. The abolition of all social, religious and national restrictions.
4. Immediate preparation for the calling of a Constituent Assembly, elected by universal and secret vote, which shall determine the form of government and draw up the Constitution for the country.

5. In place of the police, to organize a national militia with elective officers, and subject to the local self-governing body.
6. Elections to be carried out on the basis of universal, direct, equal, and secret suffrage.
7. The troops that have taken part in the revolutionary movement shall not be disarmed or removed from Petrograd.
8. On duty and in war service, strict military discipline should be maintained, but when off duty, soldiers should have the same public rights as are enjoyed by other citizens.

The Provisional Government wishes to add that it has no intention of taking advantage of the existence of war conditions to delay the realization of the above-mentioned measures of reform.

From *Documents of Russian History, 1914–1917*, ed. F. A. Golder, trans. E. Aronsberg (New York: Appleton-Century-Crofts, 1927).

workers began to take over factories. The Russian empire broke apart from internal conflicts, the continued pressure of war, and the rising spirits of the nationalities who had been oppressed for centuries.

Only the Bolsheviks seemed to have an answer to Russia's crisis; even their slogans, such as "Peace, Land, and Bread," reflected what was already happening. Furthermore, they had the discipline and adaptability to take advantage of events. The Mensheviks clung to brittle intellectual formulas, while the Provisional Government continued to dream of Russian control of the Bosporous and Constantinople. Lenin and his colleagues took advantage of the Kornilov debacle and the failure of dual power to form their own revolution.

By October 1917 the Bolsheviks had discarded their slogan of "All Power to the Soviets." Frankly, Lenin, the unchallenged Bolshevik leader, no longer needed these local organizations. After much hesitation, he decided to move on November 6 (October 24 in the Russian calendar). The Bolshevik Military Revolutionary Committee led by Leon Trotsky and supported by the Communist-dominated crew of the battleship *Aurora* took control of the communications and police centers in Petrograd. With the exception of sporadic fighting around the Winter Palace, Trotsky's military forces had little trouble. They arrested those members of the Provisional Government who could be found. Kerensky escaped from the capital in a car flying the U.S. flag.

Lenin then found himself leading a party of more than 200,000 people (an increase from 23,600 in February), which claimed control of a state of more than 170 million people. It was not his individual genius or his plans but rather his discipline and opportunism that enabled him to gain power. He endured the mistakes of April and July to take power. He did not make the revolution, but he did pick up the pieces and profit from the changes brought about by the breakdown of the tsarist government under the pressure of war.

Power, Allied Intervention, Civil War

The Bolsheviks assumed power over a war-weakened, revolution-ravaged state that was in terrible condition. Lenin's takeover split the Soviet itself when the Mensheviks and the Social Revo-lutionaries refused to participate. Lenin had a bare majority at the Soviet's first postrevolutionary meeting. In the free elections held in December to form a constituent assembly, the Bolsheviks received just one-fourth of the votes.

Yet such details as democratic representation did not stop Lenin. He proceeded to rule Russia. The Bolsheviks immediately put through decrees to declare peace and settle the land question. In the meantime, his cadres imposed their control over Moscow and the other cities in the country.

Lenin then began to lay the foundations for the single-party dictatorship that characterized Russia until 1989. When the Constituent Assembly convened in Petrograd on January 18, 1918, and proved that it would not be a tool for Lenin, the Bolsheviks closed it down at bayonet point the next day. By dissolving the Constituent Assembly, Lenin crushed all remnants of the briefly flowering democracy. This decisive step sealed the fate of the Mensheviks and most other opposition leftist parties. Not for 71 years would there be contested elections, open criticism of the central power, and the possibility of a potential democratic opposition.

Lenin had to make peace with Germany and, after two months of negotiations, concluded the Treaty of Brest-Litovsk. This agreement drastically reduced the territory under Russian control and made the centers of government much more exposed to attack. In reality, Lenin sacrificed territory over which he had no control and took his country out of a war it could not fight.

In the late spring the revolutionary government came under attack from the White forces and the Allies. The Whites, a powerful but fragmented group of anti-Bolsheviks, began a civil war that would claim as many casualties in three years as the country had lost in World War I. The Allied Powers sent several expeditionary armies to Russia for the stated purpose of controlling material they had sent the former tsarist army. In reality, they helped the Whites. The Allies, still at war with Germany, feared that the Bolsheviks were in a conspiracy with the Germans, especially after the terms of the Brest-Litovsk treaty became known. They also hoped that if Lenin could be overthrown, the Whites might reopen fighting against the Central Powers. By the fall of 1918, the Bolsheviks were besieged.

From its new capital at Moscow, the Red (Bolshevik) government took all means to defend the revolution. Lenin's forces reimposed the death penalty (it had been abolished by the Provisional Government) and unleashed a ghastly reign of terror. The Red Army and the Cheka (secret police) systematically destroyed the enemies of the revolution as well as those who were only lukewarm in their support of the new regime. Prison camps and repressive terror harsher than any since Ivan IV dominated life in the Russian state. In July 1918, the former tsar and his family, under house arrest since the outbreak of the revolution, were herded into the cellar of the house in which they were being held, and were executed.

After the Central Powers surrendered in November 1918, Allied intervention in Russia ceased, and the Bolsheviks concentrated their energies against the Whites. Trotsky turned the Red Army into a disciplined, centralized force. The disorganized and dispersed White opposition, whose units ranged from Siberia to the Caucasus to Europe, could not match the Red forces. Taking advantage of their shorter supply lines, ideological unity, and dislike of Allied intervention, the Bolsheviks put an end to White resistance by 1920. The Whites were united on few issues besides their hatred of the Bolsheviks. After their defeat, nearly a million of them scattered across the globe, eternal émigrés grieving the loss of their country and their dreams.

Theory, Reality, and the State

Lenin had no hesitation about revising Marx's doctrines to fit Russian conditions. He had long opposed all democratic parliamentary procedures, especially the concept of an officially recognized opposition party. He advocated instead a revolutionary "dictatorship of the proletariat" under Bolshevik leadership. The new order would rule in accord with "democratic centralism," in which the vanguard party would anticipate the best interests of the masses and rule for them.

Lenin altered certain aspects of the Marxist concept of the historical process. He accepted the view that the proletarian-socialist revolution must be preceded by a bourgeois-democratic revolution. He interpreted the March 1917 events as the first democratic revolution and his own coup d'état in November as the second, or proletarian-socialist, revolution. This approach drastically shortened the historical process by which the bourgeois stage was to run its course. Lenin justified dissolving the Constituent Assembly on the grounds that a higher form of democratic principle had now been achieved, making the constituent assembly superfluous. The November revolution had vested all power in the Russian republic in the people themselves, as expressed in their revolutionary committees, or soviets.

Many orthodox Marxists believed that the state would "wither away" once the dictatorship of the proletariat had eliminated the bourgeoisie. Once in power, however, Lenin found that he had to create a far stronger, more efficient state to govern Russia. The Bolsheviks, as the ultimate democratic centralists, ruled with an iron hand and prepared the way for the totalitarianism of Joseph Stalin.

The state acted in many spheres. In policies reminiscent of Robespierre's tenure during the French Revolution, the new government attacked the church, changed the calendar (adopting the Gregorian and rejecting the Julian system), and simplified the alphabet. The Cheka enforced ideological unity with a level of terror that set the standard for later Soviet secret police organiza-

→ This photograph of Lenin with Stalin was taken in 1922, shortly after Stalin had been appointed general secretary of the Central Committee of the Communist Party.

tions. The individual came to be ground down by the all-encompassing power of the state.

In the first six years after Lenin seized power, there were three major developments relating to the Communist party, the name adopted by the Bolsheviks in 1918. First, all other parties were suppressed. Second, the function of the party was changed from that of carrying out the revolution to that of governing the country. Third, within the party itself, a small elite group called the Politburo, which set policy, consolidated power in its hands. Among the members of the first Politburo were Lenin, Trotsky, and Stalin. The second major organ of the party was the Secretariat for the Central Committee, which oversaw the implementation of policy into practice.

The state itself came to be known as the Russian Socialist Federated Soviet Republic (RSFSR). As the Moscow-based communist government extended its authority after the civil war, the jurisdiction of the RSFSR grew. In 1922, the Union of Soviet Socialist Republics (USSR) was formed, consisting of the four constituent socialist republics: the RSFSR, the Ukraine, White Russia (Belorussia), and Transcaucasia.

The communists had established the first constitution for their government in 1918, but events and growth soon led to the need for a new one, which was adopted in 1924. It set up a system based on a succession of soviets in villages, factories, and cities. This pyramid of soviets in each constituent republic culminated in the All-Union Congress of Soviets at the apex of the federal government. But, while it appeared that the congress exercised sovereign power, this body was actually governed by the Communist party, which was controlled in turn by the Politburo.

So great did the authority of the Communist party become over the formation and administration of policy that before Lenin's death in early 1924 it could be said without exaggeration that party and state were one. Consequently, whoever controlled the party controlled the state, and in the new Soviet state the key person would be Joseph Stalin.

War Communism and the NEP

Lenin's ability as a politician can be seen in his flexibility between 1917 and 1924. From 1918 to 1921 he tried to apply undiluted Marxist principles to eliminate private ownership of land; nationalize banks, railways, and shipping; and restrict the money economy. This policy, known as War Communism, was widely unpopular. The peasants who had just attained their centuries-long goal of controlling their own land did not like the prospects of collectivization and the surrender of their surplus grain to the state. Many workers did not want to be forced to work in factories. Former managers showed little enthusiasm for running enterprises for the state's benefit.

In the early months of 1920 the new government faced its most dangerous crisis to date. Six years of war and civil strife had left Russia exhausted. Industrial production was 13 percent of what it had been in 1914. Crop failures, poor management, and transportation breakdowns contributed to the disaster. Famine brought more than 20 million people to the brink of starvation. The government was forced to ask for help, and organizations such as Herbert Hoover's American project to bring relief to Russia helped the country through the crisis, but not before about 5 million people died.

Internal chaos plus controversy with Poland over disputed borders further plagued Lenin's government. From 1918 to 1921 other areas of the former Russian empire—Finland, Estonia, Latvia, Lithuania, and Bessarabia—chose to go their own way. In February 1921 sailors at Kronstadt, formerly supporters of the regime, rebelled against the Bolsheviks and were massacred by the Red Army. Lenin said that the revolt "illuminated reality like a flash of lightning,"[5] and chose to make an ideological retreat.

War Communism was a total failure. Lenin decided that it was necessary to take "one step backwards in order to go two steps forward." He explained that Russia had tried to do too much too soon in attempting to change everything at once. He also noted that there had not been a firestorm of complementary communist revolutions sweeping the globe. The outbreaks in Germany and Hungary had been brutally squashed. Russia stood alone. Compromise was necessary to survive, and besides altering his diplomatic front abroad, he recommended a return to certain practices of capitalism, the so-called new Economic Policy, or NEP.

This retreat from War Communism lasted from 1921 to 1928 and allowed the Russian state to get on its feet. Peasants were relieved from the wholesale appropriation of grain. After paying a fixed tax, they were permitted to sell their surplus produce in the open market. Private management could once again run firms and factories employing fewer than 20 employees. Workers in state industries received a graduated wage scale. Foreign commerce and technology were actively sought. These compromises proved to be highly beneficial, and the Soviet economy revived.

Ideological purists criticized the policy and pointed out that the *kulaks,* as those ambitious peasants who accumulated property were called, and private businesses profited greatly. Lenin's concessions and compromises gave the communists time to regroup and recover, and the Russian people gained much-needed breathing space. Lenin emphasized the absolute necessity for the party to "control the commanding heights of the economy." The state continued to manage banking, transportation, heavy industry, and public utilities.

The NEP was Lenin's last major contribution. In broken health since he survived an assassin's bullet in 1918, he worked as much as he could until his death in January 1924. In his 54 years Lenin deeply changed the world's history. He bequeathed to the globe its first Marxist state and provided the base from which his variant of Marxism could spread. He changed the tone and tactics of Marxism, stripping it of much that was humane and tolerant. His defenders argue that such steps were needed to apply a theory intended for industrialized society to an agrarian state. His critics argue that his methods and ideas were merely the reflection of his own ego. His tomb in Moscow's Red Square, in which his embalmed body was placed on display, became a shrine for thousands of followers to come to pay homage to the creator of the Soviet state. Ironically, this secular, atheistic man who led a spartan existence was made by Stalin into a cult figure at the center of a new religion.

Trotsky Versus Stalin

A weakness of all dictatorships is that there is no well-defined mechanism to pass power from one leader to the next. Lenin was the one person in the party who possessed unchallenged authority and whose decrees were binding. After his death, Leon Trotsky and Joseph Stalin, rivals with conflicting policies and personalities, fought for power.

Leon Trotsky (1879–1940), born Lev Davidovich Bronstein, was a star in the political arena. He was a magnificent, charismatic orator, an energetic and magnetic leader in all areas, and a first-rate intellectual and theoretician. He turned to Marxism as a teenager and, like Lenin, had been exiled to Siberia for his revolutionary activities. He participated in the major events of Russian Social Democracy. Trotsky was a member of the *Iskra* group, had been present in London in 1903 for the Bolshevik-Menshevik split, played a key role in the 1905 Russian revolution, and was an essential figure in the 1917 revolutions and the Civil War. He had an ego and arrogance that contrasted with the shrewd and cunning nature of his less colorful, but more calculating rival.

Joseph Stalin (1879–1953), born in Georgia as Joseph Vissarionovich Dzhugashvili, labored for the revolution in obscurity. Where Trotsky was a star, Stalin worked behind the scenes. Trotsky was a crowd-pleasing orator; Stalin, when he spoke in his second language, Russian—Georgian was his first—was not an inspiring speaker. Admitted to a seminary to be trained for the priesthood, the young Stalin was later expelled for radical opinions. In the years before the revolutions, Stalin served the Bolsheviks by robbery to gain funds for the party's organization and propaganda activities. In all ways he faithfully supported Lenin, unlike Trotsky, who had not been a uniformly obedient disciple. Stalin was exiled east of the Urals a number of times before he returned to Petrograd in 1917 to play an active role in the events of that year. He knew his own strengths and weaknesses. He also formed his opinion of Trotsky rather early on, characterizing him in 1907 as being "beautifully useless."[6]

After the 1917 revolutions Stalin did much of the less glamorous organizational work of the party; he was also responsible for dealing with the various nationalities. While others in the Politburo dealt with ideological questions or fought the civil war, Stalin built up his own network of associates and gained control of the bureaucracy. In 1922, *Pravda,* the official party newspaper, carried a brief announcement that the Central Committee had confirmed Stalin as general secretary of the secretariat, a position that became the most powerful in the Soviet Union.

→ Following Lenin's death, the struggle for power in the Soviet Union pitted Stalin against Leon Trotsky. Losing to Stalin, Trotsky was exiled from the Soviet Union in 1929 and assassinated in Mexico in 1940, presumably on Stalin's order.

After Lenin's death, Stalin moved to construct a new secular religion for the Soviet Union. Leninism formed in 1924 and remained powerful for more than 60 years. The mark of faith came to be unquestioning loyalty to Lenin. (The city of Petrograd, for example, was renamed Leningrad.) Stalin became Lenin's St. Peter, even though Lenin had criticized both Trotsky and Stalin in his so-called last will and testament, which, although written in 1922, was not widely published until the 1950s.

In the competition with Trotsky, Stalin won because he was the better organizer and the more skillful manipulator of people. Staying in the background, the modest "helper," Stalin played the game of divide and conquer as members of the Politburo fought among themselves. By 1926 party members realized that Stalin had consolidated his position and had the full support of the party apparatus. By the end of that year, Trotsky and other opponents were removed from the Politburo. By 1929, Stalin was referred to as the "Lenin of today." Stalin's supporters occupied the key posts in both government and party, and he became the chairman of the Politburo. By 1940 he had eliminated all of the old Bolsheviks, including Trotsky, who was exiled and finally struck down by an assassin's ice axe in Mexico, on Stalin's orders.

More than just an opportunist or a superbureaucrat, Stalin too had ideological views on the future of the country. Trotsky and others had believed along with Lenin that the USSR could not survive indefinitely as a socialist island in a capitalist ocean. It was the duty, they held, of Russian communists to push for revolution elsewhere. Stalin, less a theorist than a political realist, viewed the idea of a world revolution as premature. He correctly noted that Marxism had made little headway outside the USSR, despite the existence of what, from the Marxist standpoint, were advantageous conditions for revolution in Germany and Italy. Stalin called for a new policy—"building up socialism in a single state." (Lenin had once hinted at that alternative in 1921.) He put an end to the NEP, and began taking "two steps forward"—with results that were both brutal and far-reaching.

Economics and Totalitarianism

Russia had begun industrialization at a late date, and from the 1890s on was continuously aware of its backwardness. The drastic destruction of World War I and civil war reversed much of the progress that had been made, and by the late 1920s Stalin was deeply concerned with the country's economic weakness. He ordered a radical overhaul of the entire country and society to make 50 years' progress in 10.

The NEP was scrapped in 1928 and Stalin imposed a series of five-year plans calling for heavy industrialization and collectivization of agriculture. Long working hours and a six-day work week were instituted in an attempt to revolutionize Russia's economic structure. For the first time in history, a government truly controlled all significant economic activity through a central planning apparatus.

In the struggle to achieve its goals, the USSR went through what one scholar has called the "totalitarian breakthrough," in which there was "an all-out effort to destroy the basic institutions of the old order and to construct at least the framework of the new."[7] To drive the entire population along, Stalin strengthened his secret police so they could force the nation through what would be a decade of convulsive internal struggle. By 1939 Stalin had consolidated his personal dictatorship, at the cost of between 10 and 20 million lives.

War on the Peasants

Stalin wanted to transform the peasants into a rural proletariat, raising food on state and collective farms, not on their own plots. He had little doctrinal help from Marx, who had not considered that the revolution he forecast could take place in a peasant-dominated society. Marx left little guidance about what to do with the peasants, beyond mention of collectivized agriculture. He had assumed that capitalism would convert peasants into day laborers before the socialist revolution took place; hence farming would continue, except now the state would own the farms.

Lenin's War Communism programs had failed, yet Stalin went back to them as he drew up his guidelines to transform agriculture. The major problem he faced was to convince the peasants to surrender their private lands, which they had finally got in 1917, to the state and collective farms.

Under Stalin's program, the state farms (sovkhoz) would be owned outright by the government, which would pay the workers' wages. The collective farms (kolkhoz) would be created from land taken from the kulaks—that hazily defined group of farmers who owned implements or employed others—and from the peasants who would voluntarily accept the government's decree to merge their own holdings. Kolkhoz members would work the land under the management of a board of directors. At the end of the year, each farm's net earnings would be totaled in cash and in kind, and the members would be paid on the basis of the amount and skill of their labor.

The theoretical advantages of large-scale mechanized farming over small-scale peasant agriculture were obvious. In addition, the government intended the reforms to permit the more efficient political education of the peasants. Further, the new programs would liquidate the kulaks, successful capitalist farmers who owned more property than their neighbors and who represented a disturbing element on the socialist landscape.

In actual practice, Stalin's collectivization program was a disaster. The vast majority of the peasants disagreed violently with Stalin's program. They did not want to give up their land. When the peasants did not flock to the government's banners, Stalin ordered harsher methods. When the class war between the poor peasants and the kulaks did not take place, he sent the secret police and the army to the villages. The transition to collectivization was carried out under some of the most barbarous and brutal measures ever enacted by a government against its own people.

In the butchery that followed, millions of people, especially in the Ukraine, died either from direct attack, from starvation, or in work camps. By a decree of February 1930, the state forced about one million kulaks off their land and took their possessions. Many peasants opposed these measures, slaughtering their herds and destroying their crops rather than hand them over to the state. In 1933 the number of horses was less than half of the number there had been in 1928, and there were 40 percent fewer cattle and half as many sheep and goats.

In some sections the peasants rebelled en masse, and thousands were executed by firing squads. Villages that failed to capitulate were surrounded by army units that opened fire with machine guns. Official policy resulted in dislocation, destruction of animals and crops, and famine that claimed millions of lives. After nine years of war on the peasants, 90 percent of the land and 100 million peasants were in the collective and state farms.

At the time, the atrocities accompanying Stalin's programs were largely overlooked or unknown in the West. Not until World War II was a casualty figure given, and then only casually when Stalin mentioned to British Prime Minister Winston Churchill a loss of life totaling around 10 million people. By the end of the 1980s Soviet authorities began to reveal the full extent of the massive suffering inflicted on the Soviet peasantry.

Все в колхоз!
для
жизни
для
юнних борцов.

→ Russian children
the propaganda
campaign for co[l]
of agriculture. T[
reads, "Everybo[dy]
Collective Farm."
py faces belie t[
resulting from t[
vization program[
millions died e[
slaughter or starv[
program was enfo[

The Five-Year Plans

Stalin introduced the system of central planning in 1928. He and his advisers assumed that by centralizing all aspects of the allocation of resources and removing market forces from the economy they could ensure a swift buildup of capital goods and heavy industries. The five-year plans, which began in 1929, restricted the manufacture of consumer goods and abolished capitalism in the forms permitted under the NEP. Citizens were allowed to own certain types of private property, houses, furniture, clothes, and personal effects. They could not own property that could be used to make profits by hiring workers. The state was to be the only employer.

The first five-year plan called for a 250 percent increase in overall industrial productivity. The state and police turned their entire effort to this goal. Even in the chaos that occurred—when buildings were erected for no machines and machines were shipped to where there were no buildings—growth did take place.

Whether the statistics the party cited to prove that the plan had been achieved in four and one-half years were accurate—and they have been vigorously challenged—Soviet industry and society were totally transformed. The costs were disastrous, but Stalin portrayed Russia as being in a form of war with the world, and without strength, he pointed out, Russia would be crushed.

The second five-year plan began in 1933 and sought to resolve some of the mistakes of the first. The government placed greater emphasis on improving the quality of industrial products and on making more consumer goods. The third plan, begun in 1938, emphasized national defense. State strategies called for industrial plants to be shifted east of the Urals, and efforts were made to develop new sources of oil and other important commodities. Gigantism was the key, as the world's largest tractor factory was built in Chelyabinsk, the greatest power station in Dnepropetrovsk, and the largest automobile plant in Gorki.

The plans achieved remarkable results. In 1932 Soviet authorities claimed an increase in industrial output of 334 percent over 1914 levels; 1937 output was 180 percent over that of 1932.

But the high volume of production was often tied to mediocre quality, and the achievements were gained only with an enormous cost in human life and suffering. At first the burdensome cost of importing heavy machinery, tools, equipment, and finished steel from abroad forced a subsistence scale of living on the people. These purchases were paid for by the sale of food and raw material in the world's markets at a time when the prices for such goods had drastically fallen.

In the rush to industrialize, basic aspects of Marxism were set aside. The dictatorship *of* the proletariat increasingly became the dictatorship *over* the proletariat. Another ideological casualty was the basic concept of economic egalitarianism. In 1931 Stalin declared that equality of wages was "alien and detrimental to Soviet production" and a "petit-bourgeois deviation." So much propaganda was used to implant this twist that the masses came to accept the doctrine of inequality of wages as a fundamental communist principle. Piecework in industry became more prevalent, and bonuses and incentives were used to speed up production. It is ironic that capitalist practices were used to stimulate the growth of the communist economy. Stalin and Russia had deviated far from the Marxist maxim of "from each according to his ability, to each according to his need." Until the 1950s centralized planning enabled Russia to build a powerful industrial base and survive Hitler's assault. However, in the

Stalin and State Terror

Stalin's totalitarianism brought the development of state terror to unparalleled heights. Nadezhda Mandelstam described the nature of the terror.

When I used to read about the French Revolution as a child, I often wondered whether it was possible to survive during a reign of terror. I now know beyond doubt that it is impossible. Anybody who breathes the air of terror is doomed, even if nominally he manages to save his life. Everybody is a victim—not only those who die, but also all the killers, ideologists, accomplices and sycophants who close their eyes and wash their hands—even if they are secretly consumed with remorse at night. Every section of the population has been through the terrible sickness caused by terror, and none has so far recovered, or become fit again for normal civic life. It is an illness that is passed on to the next generation, so that the sons pay for the sins of the fathers and perhaps only the grandchildren begin to get over it—or at least it takes on a different form with them.

The principles and aims of mass terror have nothing in common with ordinary police work or with security. The only purpose of terror is intimidation. To plunge the whole country into a state of chronic fear, the number of victims must be raised to astronomical levels, and on every floor of every building there must always be several apartments from which the tenants have suddenly been taken away. The remaining inhabitants will be model citizens for the rest of their lives—this will be true for every street and every city through which the broom has swept. The only essential thing for those who rule by terror is not to overlook the new generations growing up without faith in their elders, and to keep on repeating the process in systematic fashion. Stalin ruled for a long time and saw to it that the waves of terror recurred from time to time, always on an even greater scale than before. But the champions of terror invariably leave one thing out of account— namely, that they can't kill everyone, and among their cowed, half-demented subjects there are always witnesses who survive to tell the tale.

Reprinted with the permission of Atheneum Publishers, an imprint of Macmillan Publishing Company from *Hope Against Hope: A Memoir* by Nadezhda Mandelstam, translated from the Russian by Max Hayward. Copyright © 1970 by Atheneum Publishers.

→ The Magnitogorsk Steel Works, built on Mount Magnitnaya on the upper Ural River, was one of Stalin's major gigantic industrial projects. The mill, which was constructed between 1929 and 1931, produced the Soviet Union's cheapest steel, which was then supplied to thousands of the nation's industrial centers.

past four decades, as the Soviet economy has had to become more flexible, the system has proven to be counterproductive.

The Great Purges

During the 1930s Stalin consolidated his hold over the Communist party and created the political system that would last until the ascent to power of Mikhail Gorbachev. Stalin established an all-powerful, personal totalitarian rule by doing away with all of his rivals, real and potential, in the purges. He also took the opportunity to remove all scientific, cultural, and educational figures who did not fit in with his plans for the future. By the end of the decade, Russians marched to Stalin's tune, or they did not march.

The long arm of the secret police gathered in thousands of Soviet citizens to face the kangaroo court and the firing squad. All six original members of the 1920 Politburo who survived Lenin were purged by Stalin. Old Bolsheviks who had been loyal comrades of Lenin, high officers of the Red Army, directors of industry, and rank-and-file party members were liquidated. Millions more were sent to forced labor camps. It has been estimated that between 5 and 6 percent of the population spent time in the pretrial prisons of the secret police.

Party discipline prevented party members from turning against Stalin, who controlled the party. The world watched a series of show trials in which loyal communists confessed to an amazing array of charges, generally tied after 1934 to the assassination of Sergei Kirov, Leningrad party chief and one of Stalin's chief aides. Western journalists reported news of the trials to the world, while the drugged, tortured, and intimidated defendants confessed to crimes they had not committed. By 1939, 70 percent of the members of the central committee elected in 1934 had been purged. Among officers in the armed forces, the purges claimed 3 of 5 army marshals, 14 of 16 army commanders, 8 of 8 admirals, 60 of 67 corps commanders, 136 of 199 divisional commanders, 221 of 397 brigade commanders, and roughly one-half of the remaining officers, or some 35,000 men. A large portion of the leadership of the USSR was destroyed.

In a sense, the purges culminated in Mexico with Trotsky's assassination in 1940. The lessons of the purges were chilling and effective. The way to succeed, to survive, was to be a dependable member of the apparatus—an *apparatchik*.

Changes in Soviet Society

In the 20 years after 1917, all aspects of Soviet society came under the purview of the party. The atomization of society, a prime characteristic of totalitarian government, did not permit such secret, self-contained, and mutually trusting groups as the family to exist at ease. The party dealt in contradictory terms with various aspects of social life, but by and large the government worked to weaken the importance of the family. Initially after the revolution, divorces required no court proceedings, abortions were legalized, women were encouraged to take jobs outside the home, and communist nurseries were set up to care for children while their mothers worked. Pressure on the family continued under Stalin, but in different ways. Children were encouraged to report to the authorities "antirevolutionary" statements made by their parents.

The party did work to upgrade medical care, improve the treatment of the nationalities—at least initially—and extend educational opportunities. But even here political goals outweighed humanitarian objectives. Education existed primarily to indoctrinate pupils with Communist precepts and values. Religious persecution was widespread. The church lost most of its power in education, and religious training was prohibited, except in the home.

The constitution of 1936 declared, "All power in the USSR belongs to the workers of town and country as represented by the Soviet of workers' deputies." Ironically, this document did not mention the Soviet Union's official ideology of Marxism-Leninism and referred only once to the Communist party. On the surface, the 1936 constitution affirmed many basic rights, such as free speech, the secret ballot, and universal suffrage, but it was mere window-dressing with no effective application in reality. Secret ballots meant little in a one-party state, and the parliament of the people, the Supreme Soviet, had no power. The Communist party, with a membership of less than 1.5 percent of the total population, dictated the life of every individual.

In the first decade after the revolution, intellectuals and artists experienced much more freedom than they would in the 1930s. The party emphasized the tenets of social realism but permitted some innovation. The Bolsheviks initially tolerated and even encouraged writers of independent leanings. Even though a large number of artists and writers fled the country after the revolution, others, including the poets Alexander Blok (1880–1921) and Vladimir Mayakovsky (1893–1930), remained and continued to write. During the NEP, Russia's cultural life bloomed in many areas, especially the cinema, as can be seen in the works of the great director Sergei Eisenstein (1898–1948). In music, composers Sergei Prokofiev (1891–1953) and Dmitri Shostakovich (1906–1975) contributed works that added to the world's musical treasury.

Once Stalin gained control, he dictated that all art, science, and thought should serve the party's program and philosophy. Artists and thinkers were to become, in Stalin's words, "engineers of the mind." Art for art's sake was counterrevolutionary. Socialist realism in its narrowest sense was to be pursued. History became a means to prove the correctness of Stalin's policies.

Under Stalin's totalitarian rule, critics and censors tightened their control over artists and scholars. Artists and intellectuals found it safer to investigate, write, and perform according to the party line. Literary hacks and propagandists gained official favor, churning out what Western critics referred to as "tractor novels."

ITALY AND MUSSOLINI

After entering the war on the Allied side in 1915, Italy entered the peace negotiations with great expectations. The Italians had joined the Allies with the understanding that with victory they would gain a part of Albania, Trieste, Dalmatia, Trentino, and some territory in Asia Minor. They came away from Versailles with minor gains, not nearly enough to justify the deaths of 700,000 of their youth.

Postwar Italy suffered social and economic damage similar to that of the other combatants. Inflation—the lira fell to one-third of its prewar value—and disrupted trade patterns hampered recovery. These ailments exacerbated the domestic crises the country had been struggling with before the war. There were not enough jobs for the returning soldiers, and unemployed veterans were ripe targets for the growing extremist parties. In some cities residents refused to pay their rent in protest over poor living conditions. In the countryside, peasants took land from landlords. Everywhere food was in short supply.

In the four years after the armistice, five premiers came and went, either because of their own incompetence or because of the insolubility of the problems they faced. The situation favored the appearance of "a man on a white horse," a dictator. Such a man was a blacksmith's son named Mussolini, who bore the Christian name of Benito, in honor of the Mexican revolutionary hero Benito Juarez.

Benito Mussolini (1883–1945) grew up in and around left-wing political circles. Although he became editor of the influential socialist newspaper *Avanti* ("Forward") in 1912, he was far from consistent in his views and early on demonstrated his opportunism and pragmatism. When a majority of the Italian Socialist party called for neutrality in World War I, Mussolini came out for intervention. Party officials removed *Avanti* from his control and expelled him from the party. He then proceeded to put out his own paper, *Il Popolo d'Italia* ("The People of Italy"), in which he continued to call for Italian entry into the war on the Allied side.

To carry out his interventionist campaign, Mussolini organized formerly leftist groups into bands called *fasci*, a named derived from the Latin *fasces*, the bundle of rods bound around an ax, which was the symbol of authority in ancient Rome. When Italy entered the war, Mussolini volunteered for the army, saw active service at the

➤ Benito Mussolini, shown here speaking to a crowd in 1934, promised that a strong state could cure Italy's postwar ills, strengthen its economy, and rebuild national pride.

front, and was wounded. When he returned to civilian life, he reorganized the *fasci* into the *fasci di combattimento* ("fighting groups") to attract war veterans and try to gain control of Italy.

The Path to Power

In the 1919 elections, the freest until 1946, the Socialists capitalized on mass unemployment and hardship to become the strongest party. But the party lacked effective leadership and failed to take advantage of its position.

The extreme right-wing groups did not elect a single candidate to the Chamber of Deputies, but they pursued power in other ways. The fiery writer and nationalist leader Gabriele D'Annunzio (1863–1938) had occupied the disputed city of Fiume with his corps of followers, in direct violation of the mandates of the Paris peace conference. This defiance of international authority appealed to the fascist movement. D'Annunzio provided lessons for the observant Mussolini, who copied many of the writer's methods and programs.

The fascists gained the backing of landowning and industrial groups, who feared the victory of Marxist socialism in Italy. Mussolini's toughs beat up opponents, broke strikes, and disrupted opposition meetings in 1919 and 1920 while the government did nothing. Despite these activities, the extreme right-wing politicians still failed to dominate the 1921 elections. Only 35 fascists, Mussolini among them, gained seats in the Chamber of Deputies, while the Liberal and Democratic parties gained a plurality. Failing to succeed through the existing system, Mussolini established the National Fascist party in November.

The Liberal-Democratic government of 1922 proved to be as ineffective as its predecessors, and the Socialists continued to bicker among themselves. Mussolini's party, however, attracted thousands of disaffected middle-class people, cynical and opportunistic intellectuals, and workers. Frustration with the central government's incompetence, not fear of the left, fueled the fascist rise. One historian has noted, "It was not on political ideas that fascism thrived, but on the yearning for action and the opportunities it provided for satisfying this yearning."[8]

In August 1922 the trade unions called a general strike to protest the rise of fascism. Mussolini's forces smashed their efforts. In October, after a huge rally in Naples, 50,000 fascists swarmed into Rome and soon thereafter King Victor Emmanuel III invited Mussolini to form a new government. During the next month Mussolini assembled a cabinet composed of his party members and nationalists, and gained dictatorial powers to bring stability to the country. The fascists remained a distinct minority in Italy, but by gaining control of the central government they could place their members and allies in positions of power. The October "March on Rome" ushered in Mussolini's 20-year reign.

Building the Fascist State

The new Italian leader followed no strict ideology as he consolidated his dictatorial rule. He threw out all the democratic procedures of the postwar years and dissolved rival political parties. He and his colleagues ruthlessly crushed free expression and banished critics of their government to prison settlements off Italy's southern coast. They censored the press and set up tribunals for the defense of the state (not the citizens). Although he retained the shell of the old system, the fascist leader established a totally new state.

Mussolini controlled all real power through the Fascist Grand Council, whose members occupied the government's ministerial posts. At one time, he personally held no fewer than eight offices. All this activity and centralization of power provided a striking contrast to the lethargy of the four years immediately after the war. Encouraged by the popular support for his regime, Mussolini passed a series of laws in 1925 and 1926 under which the Italian cities lost their freely elected self-governments and all units of local and provincial government were welded into a unified structure controlled from Rome.

Once he had centralized Italian political life, Mussolini pursued the development of his ideology in a pragmatic manner. As one scholar noted, "If he had any principle or prejudice it was against the capitalists, the Church, and the monarchy; all of his life he abused the bourgeoisie."[9] But he would learn to work with all of those elements in his flexible pursuit of power. He once stated in an interview, "I am all for motion."[10] Movement, not consistency and science, marked his ideology.

Early in the 1920s Mussolini, a former atheist, began to tie the church into the structure of his new society. In 1928 he negotiated the Lateran Treaty with church representatives in order to settle the long-standing controversy between Rome and the Vatican. The new pact required compulsory religious instruction and recognized Catholicism as the state religion. Vatican City, a new state of 108 acres located within Rome itself, was declared to be fully sovereign and independent. In addition the state promised the Vatican $91 million. Mussolini gained a measure of approval from devout Italians and the Vatican's support for his fascist government.

Mussolini's economic system, which has come to be known as state capitalism, aimed to abolish

→ One of the most ominous acts of Mussolini's Fascist regime was the burning of books and other literature deemed "subversive."

class conflict through cooperation between labor and capital, by state force if necessary. In communist theory, labor is the basis of society. In fascism, labor and capital are both instruments of the state. The fascists constructed a corporate state, in which the country was divided into syndicates, or corporations—13 at first, later 22. Initially 6 of these came from labor and an equal number represented capital or management. The thirteenth group was established for the professions. Under state supervision, these bodies were to deal with labor disputes, guarantee adequate wage scales, control prices, and supervise working conditions. After 1926 strikes by workers and lockouts by employers were prohibited.

The pragmatic leader believed that private enterprise was the "most efficient method" of production: "The state intervenes in economic production only when private enterprise fails or is insufficient or when the political interests of the state are involved."[11] Mussolini liked to claim that his structure embodied a classless economic system that stood as one of fascism's greatest contributions to political theory.

Reflecting the practice of the time, the Italians sought economic self-sufficiency, especially in the areas of food supply, power resources, and foreign trade. Wheat production and hydroelectric-generating capacity both increased, but the drive for self-sufficiency was carried to an extreme and unprofitable degree. The state, in its quest for economic independence, launched many projects to provide for a home supply of products that could be obtained much more cheaply from other nations.

State and Struggle

Mussolini's ideology built in a haphazard way on the cult of the leader, or "great man." The Italian dictator asserted that "life for the Fascist is a continuous, ceaseless fight," and "struggle is at the origin of all things."[12] Aside from statements of this type and his economic theories, it is difficult to determine exactly what Mussolini intended fascism to be, beyond nationalistic, anticommunist, antidemocratic, expansionist, and statist. The lack of a theoretical base for his programs and policies did not concern Mussolini. He simply believed that his corporate state offered a solution to the basic social questions of the twentieth century.

In his speeches, Mussolini referred constantly to the legacy of the Roman empire. He encouraged a high birth rate, but noted that individuals were significant only insofar as they were part of the state. Children were indoctrinated "to believe, to obey, and to fight."

Beneath the talk of struggle and the trappings of grandeur was the reality of Italy. Mussolini was no Stalin or Hitler, and his fascism was a far milder form of totalitarianism than that seen in the USSR or Nazi Germany. The Italian people simply defused many of the potentially atrocious elements of fascist rule. There was no class destruction or genocide in Italy. The Italians, who had endured control by Goths, Normans, French, and Austrians before unification, were survivors.

As in the case of the other dictatorships, Mussolini's programs had some worthwhile features such as slum clearance, rural modernization, and campaigns against illiteracy and malaria. The trains *did* run on time, as Mussolini boasted, and the omnipresent Mafia was temporarily dispersed, with many of its more notable figures fleeing to the United States. But these positive achievements were more than outweighed by the ruinous drives into Ethiopia, excessive military spending, and special benefits to large landowners and industrialists. In 1930 real wages remained low in comparison to the rest of industrialized Europe.

The depression hit Italy later than other countries, but it lasted longer and its effects were devastating to Mussolini's economy. The 33 percent increase in 1929 gross national product over that of 1914 was soon wiped out, and the old problems of inadequate natural resources, unfavorable balance of trade, and expanding population made the country vulnerable to economic

Mussolini on Fascism

Benito Mussolini laid out his definition of fascism in the *Enciclopedia Italiana* in 1932.

The nation as the State is an ethical reality which exists and lives in so far as it develops. To arrest its development is to kill it. Therefore the State is not only the authority which governs and gives the form of laws and the value of spiritual life to the wills of individuals, but it is also a power that makes its will felt abroad, making it known and respected, in other words, demonstrating the fact of its universality in all the necessary directions of its development. . . . Thus it can be likened to the human will which knows no limits to its development and realizes itself in testing its own limitlessness.

The Fascist State, the highest and most powerful form of personality, is a force, but a spiritual force, which takes over all the forms of the moral and intellectual life of man. It cannot therefore confine itself simply to the functions of order and supervision as Liberalism desired.

It is not simply a mechanism which limits the sphere of the supposed liberties of the individual. It is the form, the inner standard and the discipline of the whole person; it saturates the will as well as the intelligence. Its principle, the central inspiration of the human personality living in the civil community, pierces into the depths and makes its home in the heart of the man of action as well as of the thinker, of the artist as well as of the scientist: it is the soul of the soul.

Fascism, in short, is not only the giver of laws and the founder of institutions, but the educator and promoter of spiritual life. It wants to remake, not the forms of human life, but its content, man, character, faith. And to this end it requires discipline and authority that can enter into the spirits of men and there govern unopposed. Its sign, therefore, is the Lictors' rods, the symbol of unity, of strength and justice.

disaster. In 1933 the number of unemployed reached one million and the public debt soared to an alarming level.

Despite a reorganization of the nation in 1934 into 22 government-controlled corporations, a massive public works program, and agricultural reforms, Italy continued to suffer. In the 1930s Italy's fate and future came to be closely tied to that of Germany.

THE GERMAN TRAGEDY

In the first week of November 1918, revolutions broke out all over Germany. Sailors stationed at Kiel rebelled; leftists in Munich revolted. The kaiser fled to Holland after the authority of his government crumbled. On November 9 the chancellor transferred his power to Friedrich Ebert, leader of the majority party, the Social Democrats, and the new leader announced the establishment of a republic.

Violence spread quickly. The Spartacists, led by Karl Liebknecht and Rosa Luxemburg, who formed the German Communist party at the end of 1918, wanted a complete social and political revolution. Ebert's Social Democrats favored a democratic system in which property rights would be maintained. At the beginning of 1919 the radical and moderate socialists clashed violently. Experiments in revolutionary government in Bavaria and Berlin horrified traditionalists and even the Social Democrats. In the spring a coalition of forces ranging from moderate socialists to right-wing bands of unemployed veterans crushed the leftists and murdered Liebknecht and Luxemburg.

By the end of the year, Germany had weathered the threat of a leftist revolution. Meanwhile, the moderate parties triumphed in elections to select a constitutional convention, with the Social Democrats winning the most votes. The constitution they wrote at Weimar, adopted in mid-1919, created some of the problems that would plague the new government.

The liberal document provided for a president, a chancellor who was responsible to the Reichstag, and national referenda. In addition, the constitution guaranteed the rights of labor, personal liberty, and compulsory education for everyone up to the age of 18. Once the new system was put into operation, its weaknesses were readily apparent. The multitude of parties permitted by the constitution condemned the government to function solely by shaky coalitions that often broke apart and forced the president to rule by emergency decree—thus bypassing legal constitutional procedures.

→ Rosa Luxemburg. A radical Marxist and one of the leaders of the Spartacist insurrection in Germany, she was arrested and was murdered while being taken to prison.

Failure of the Weimar Republic ⟶

The Weimar Republic faced overwhelming obstacles. First, the new republic had to live with the stigma of having accepted the Versailles treaty, with its infamous war guilt clause. The defeatist image, combined with opposition from both right- and left-wing extremists, plagued the Weimar moderates. The myth of betrayal in accepting the Versailles treaty helped Field Marshal Paul von Hindenburg, a stalwart Prussian and war hero, win election to the presidency in 1925. In 1927 he formally renounced the theory of war guilt, a politically popular move but one with little effect on the obligation to pay reparations. Although these payments did not noticeably affect the standard of living after 1925, they continued to be a visible sign of defeat—especially insofar as the money used to pay the victorious Allies had to come from foreign loans.

The Weimar government ruled during an economically chaotic period. The government caused inflation, wiped out savings, and destroyed much of the confidence of the middle class, shaking the resolve of the group on whom the fate of the republic rested. Even after 1923, when the economy took a turn for the better, perceptive observers noted that the new prosperity rested on shaky foundations.

During the five years before the depression, Germany rebuilt its industrial plant with the

→ George Grosz, *The Pillars of Society*. The satirical painting captures the artist's contempt for militarism, capitalism, the complacent bourgeoisie, and the corrupt society of the Weimar Republic.

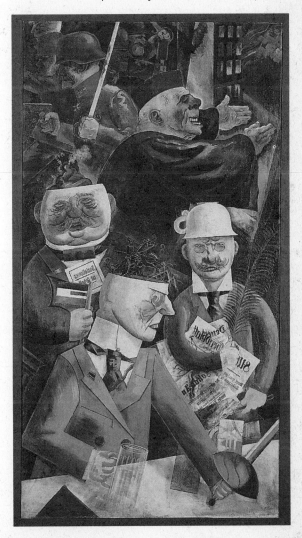

most up-to-date equipment and techniques available, becoming the second-ranking industrial nation in the world. Rebuilding, however, was financed largely with foreign loans, including some $800 million from the United States. In fact, the Germans borrowed almost twice as much money as they paid out. When the short-term loans came due, the economic bubble burst.

In addition to these economic difficulties, other problems plagued the Weimar government. Many people in Germany still idealized the authoritarian Prussian state. The German General Staff and its numerous and powerful supporters were not placed under effective civilian control. Disregarding the Versailles restrictions on military growth, Germany increased its armed forces in the 1920s in cooperation with the Soviet Union, the other European outcast. Probably more dangerous to the Weimar Republic's existence was that group of individuals described by Peter Gay as the *Vernunftrepublikaner*, "rational republicans from intellectual choice rather than passionate conviction." These intellectuals, politicians, and businessmen who should have been the strength of Weimar, "learned to live with the Republic but they never learned to love it and never believed in its future."[13]

The insecurity of the middle classes was the factor most responsible for the failure of the Weimar Republic. After the war and inflation, what professionals, white-collar workers, and skilled trades people feared most was being dragged down to the level of the masses. Right-wing orators played on such fears and warned that the Weimar Republic could not stop the growth of communism. After 1929, the insecurity and discontent of the middle classes crystallized around their children, who blamed their parents for the catastrophe of 1918 and the humiliations that followed. German youth, many of them unemployed after 1929, repudiated the Weimar Republic and sought a new savior for their country and themselves. In their rise to power, the Nazis skillfully exploited the fears and hopes of German middle-class youth.

Adolf Hitler

The man who was to "save the fatherland" came from outside its borders. Adolf Hitler (1889–1945) was born in Austria, the son of a minor customs official in the Austro-Hungarian monarchy. A mediocre student and something of a loner during his school days, he went to Vienna in 1908 hoping to become an architect or artist. When he failed to gain acceptance to the art institute, his hopes of pursuing a career in art came to an early end.

In the cosmopolitan capital of Vienna, surrounded by a rich diversity of nationalities and religions, Hitler, always the loner, formed his political philosophy. He avidly read pamphlets written by racists who advocated the leader concept and variations of social Darwinism. Hajo Holborn has written that it was on the basis of such "popular and often cranky and murky writings that Hitler formed his original racist and anti-Semitic ideas. [He] derived his ideology from few sources, all of them of a rather low type."[14] Anti-Semitism was a popular political platform, and the city's mayor openly espoused it. Hitler also dabbled in Pan-Germanism and Marxist socialism. The swirl of ideas and theories percolated in the brain of the impoverished young man and furnished him with the motivations and ambitions that drove him forward.

A year before World War I, Hitler moved to Munich, where he earned a meager living by selling his drawings. When the conflict erupted in 1914 he joined a German regiment and was sent to France, where he fought well and bravely. At the time of the armistice in 1918 he was in a hospital recovering from being blinded in a gas attack. He later said that news of Germany's defeat caused him to turn his face to the wall and weep bitterly.

Following his recovery, Hitler returned to Munich, where he was hired by city authorities to act as a special agent to investigate extremists. In the line of duty he checked on a small organization called the German Workers' party. Hitler became attracted to the group's fervently nationalistic doctrine and agreed with their antidemocratic, anticommunist, and anti-Semitic beliefs. He joined the party and soon dominated it.

In 1920, the party took the name National Socialist German Workers' Party, and the words *National Socialists (Nationalsozialistiche)* became abbreviated to *Nazi*. That same year the party founded a newspaper to spread its views; formed a

→ Hitler's ability to communicate effectively and persuasively with a majority of the German population was a major asset in his rise to power and popularity. Here he is shown speaking with young members of the Nazi party.

paramilitary organization from out-of-work veterans, the Storm Troops (SA); and adopted a symbol, the swastika set on a red background. The swastika has been used by many cultures to express the unending cycle of life. The red background symbolized the community of German blood.

More important than the party or its symbol was Hitler, who became widely known for his remarkable powers as a speaker. His ability to arouse and move mass audiences drew large crowds in Munich. Even those who hated all that he stood for were fascinated by his performances. In the early days he would hire a number of beer halls for his adherents and speed from one to the next delivering his emotion-filled message. He called for land reform, the nationalization of trusts, the abolition of all unearned incomes, expansion to include all German-speaking peoples in Europe, and the cancellation of the Versailles treaty. The points of his arguments were less important than the way he delivered them. As the ultimate demagogue he could package his concepts to fit whatever audience he addressed, and his popularity soared.

In November 1923, at the depth of Germany's crisis, Hitler staged his *Putsch*, or revolt, in Munich. Poorly planned and premature, the attempt failed. Hitler was sent to prison after his arrest and there, in comparatively luxurious conditions, he dictated his statement of principles in *Mein Kampf* ("My Struggle"). This work, far from a literary masterpiece, was both an autobiography and a long-winded exposition of Nazi philosophy and objectives.

In *Mein Kampf* Hitler wrote that history is fashioned by great races, of which the Aryan is the finest. The noblest Aryans, according to Hitler, are the Germans, who should rule the world. He charged that the Jews are the archcriminals of all time, that democracy is decadent, and communism is criminal. He stated that expansion into the Soviet Ukraine and the destruction of France are rightful courses for the Germans, who will use war and force, the proper instruments of the "strong," to achieve their goals. The book, which was initially dismissed as the ravings of a wild man, was widely read in the 1930s. Its sales made Hitler a wealthy man.

Hitler's Chance

Hitler's first attempt to take advantage of economic disaster failed, but he would not fail the second time. After 1930 the *Führer* ("leader") took advantage of the desperate conditions resulting from closed banks, 6 million unemployed, and people roaming the streets for food. Night after night police and military police battled mobs of rioting communists and Nazis. The depression was "the last ingredient in a complicated witches' brew" that led to Hitler's takeover.[15]

The depression brought on the collapse of the moderates' position in the Weimar government. In the 1930 elections the Nazis increased their number of seats in the Reichstag from 12 to 107. As conditions grew worse, the hungry and frightened as well as rich and powerful turned to Hitler. The latter groups feared the communists and saw the Führer as a useful shield against a proletarian revolution.

As the Nazi movement grew in popularity, Hitler's brilliant propaganda chief, Joseph Goebbels, used every communications device available to convert the masses to Nazism. He staged huge spectacles all over Germany in which thousands of Storm Troopers and the audiences themselves all became supporting players to the "star" of the drama, Adolf Hitler. Such controlled hysteria was more important than the message Hitler continued to repeat.

Despite Goebbels's work, Hitler lost the March 1932 presidential elections to the aged World War I hero Hindenburg. However, after a strong showing by the Nazis in the July Reichstag elections, Hindenburg, following the advice of his supporters and the business community, asked Hitler to join a coalition government. The Führer refused, demanding instead the equivalent of dictatorial power.

The stalemate led to the dissolution of the Reichstag in September, and for the next two months the government limped along, until a second general election was held. This costly campaign nearly emptied the Nazis' treasury. It was also politically costly in that they lost some of their seats in the Reichstag.

Some observers believed that the Nazis had passed the crest of their power. At this critical point, however, a clique of aristocratic nationalists and powerful industrialists, fearing a leftist revolution, offered Hitler the chancellorship. In January 1933 a mixed cabinet was created with Hitler at the head. Because he did not have a clear majority in the Reichstag, Hitler called another general election for March 5.

The Nazis used all the muscle at their disposal during this campaign. They monopolized the radio broadcasts and the press, and their Storm Troopers bullied and beat the voters. Many Germans became disgusted with the strong-arm methods, and the tide definitely swung against the Nazis. Hitler needed a dramatic incident to gain a clear majority in the election.

On the evening of February 27, a fire gutted the Reichstag building. The blaze had been set by a twenty-four-year-old Dutchman, Marinus van der Lubbe, as a statement against capitalism. Apparently acting alone, van der Lubbe gave the Nazis the issue they needed to mobilize their support. Goebbels's propaganda machine went into action to blame the fire on the international communist movement. Uncharacteristically, the propaganda minister overplayed the story, and most of the outside world came to believe that the Nazis themselves had set the fire.

Hitler may not have made much profit from the incident internationally, but he did use it to win the election. The Nazis captured 44 percent of the deputies, a result which—with the 8 percent controlled by the Nationalist party—gave them a bare majority. Quickly, Hitler's forces put through the Enabling Act, which gave the Führer the right to rule by decree for the next four years.

Every aspect of the Weimar government was overturned, legally. The Nazis crushed all opposition parties and put aside the Weimar constitution, a document that was never formally abolished. Germany for the first time became a unitary national, not a federal, state. After Hindenburg died in 1934, Hitler became both chancellor and president. As if to put the world on notice that a renewed German force was rising in central Europe, he withdrew Germany from the League of Nations in 1933. Two years later, he introduced conscription, in defiance of the Versailles treaty.

Hitler proclaimed his regime to be the Third Reich, succeeding the First Reich of Otto the Great, which had lasted from 962 until 1806, and Bismarck's Second Reich, which lasted from 1871 to 1918. Hitler quickly introduced aspects of his Nazi variant of fascism, which was much more pernicious than Mussolini's. Hitler's ideology united the diverse German peoples and expressed resentment against the rapid industrialization that had cut many of the people away from their traditional values. But it was primarily the racist elements of Aryan supremacy and hatred of the Jews that set Nazism apart.

War on the Jews

An essential part of the Nazi ideology was an absolute hatred of the Jews, an element of society the Nazis considered unfit to continue in the new world. After crushing all opposition, real and potential, Hitler began to destroy the Jews. When he took power, he ruled over 500,000 Jews and 66 million Germans. Since 1880 the number of Jews in the population had been declining and would have continued to do so through assimilation. Hitler, however, proclaimed that Jews were everywhere and pledged to destroy the Jewish plot to gain control of the world. He based his policy on his own contempt for the Jews, not on the demographic reality.

All Jewish officials in the government lost their jobs, Jews were forbidden to pursue their business and industrial activities, and Jewish businesses were boycotted. Non-Jews snatched up at bargain prices valuable properties formerly owned by Jews. Non-Jewish doctors and lawyers profited when Jewish professionals were forced from their practices. Hitler gained solid supporters among the business and professional classes as he pursued his racist policies. Germans willingly believed that the Jews deserved their fate as the price they had to pay for the Versailles treaty, for the harmful aspects of capitalism, and for internationalism. Half-hearted international protests failed to limit the anti-Semitic policies. Hitler had many fervent supporters both inside and outside Germany.

The Nazis built concentration camps immediately, but it was some time before these turned into death camps. In the meantime, the immediate pressures of government policies pushed many Jews into committing suicide. It has been estimated that in 1933 alone, 19,000 German citizens killed themselves and 16,000 more died from unexplained causes.

In 1935 the so-called Nuremberg laws came into force. Marriages between Aryans and non-Aryans were forbidden. Jews (defined as any person of one-fourth or more Jewish blood) lost their citizenship, and anti-Semitic signs were posted in all public places. (During the 1936

→ Nazi persecution of Jews sometimes included humiliation. Here, a Nazi officer stops a Jewish businessman and orders him to sweep the gutter.

Berlin Olympic games, these notices were taken down in order not to upset visitors.) Increasingly, there was public mention of the "inferior blood" of the Jews. As the state came to need more and more money for armaments, the Jews would be made to pay. This enterprise reached a climax on the evening of November 9, 1938, "the *Kristallnacht* or night of broken glass [when] above the loss of life and heavy property damage, a fine of a billion marks was imposed on the Jewish community in retaliation for the murder of a German diplomat in Paris."[16]

Attacked, deprived of their citizenship and economic opportunities, and barred from public service, the Jews of Germany, most of whom considered themselves to be good German citizens, bore the barbaric blows with remarkable resilience. Some, including a number of Germany's best scientific minds, were able to flee the country—a loss that may well have doomed Hitler's war effort. Most stayed. They, and the outside world that showed little concern, did not realize

→ The Nazi message to women proclaimed that "German girls must be strong, to bear more children for the armies, for death in the victorious battles of the Fatherland."

that Hitler's true goal was the "final solution," which would lead to the deaths of at least 6 million Jews throughout central and eastern Europe and the Soviet Union and 3 million others not "lucky" enough to be Aryan.

Nazi Propaganda and Education

Hitler and Goebbels controlled all of the media in the totalitarian Third Reich. A Reich culture cabinet was set up to instill a single pattern of thought in literature, the press, broadcasting, drama, music, art, and the cinema. Forbidden books, including works of some of Germany's most distinguished writers, were seized and destroyed in huge bonfires. The cultural vitality of the Weimar Republic, represented by the likes of Thomas Mann, Erich Maria Remarque, Kurt Weill, and Bertolt Brecht, was replaced by the sterile social realism of the Third Reich.

The state used mass popular education, integrated with the German Youth Movement, to drill and regiment boys and girls to be good Nazis. Boys learned above all else to be ready to fight and die for their Führer. The girls were prepared for their ultimate task, bearing and rearing the many babies to be needed by the Third Reich.

German universities, once renowned for their academic freedom, became agencies for propagating the racial myths of Nazism and for carrying out far-fetched experiments in human genetic engineering on selected concentration camp inmates. Only good Nazis could go to universities, and professors who did not cooperate with the regime were fired. As Jacob Bronowski wrote, "When Hitler arrived in 1933 the tradition of scholarship in Germany was destroyed, almost overnight."[17]

Religion became entrapped in the totalitarian mechanism. Since Nazism elevated the state above all else, a movement was started to subordinate religion to the Hitler regime. The organized churches originally backed the Nazis warmly, until it became apparent that they were to serve the larger aim of the Aryan cause. The Protestant churches suffered under the Nazi attempt to make them an arm of the state, and several dissident ministers were imprisoned. By the end of the decade, the Catholic church too came under subtle but constant attack.

Economic Policies

As in Italy, fascism in Germany revolved around a form of state capitalism. In theory and practice, Nazism retained capitalism and private property. The state, however, rigidly controlled both business and labor. The Nazis dissolved labor unions and enrolled workers and employers in a new organization, the Labor Front. As in Mussolini's corporate state, the right of the workers to strike or of management to call a lockout was denied. The Nazis took compulsory dues from the workers' wages to support Nazi organizations. As a sop, the state set up the "Strength Through Joy" movement, which provided sports events, musical festivals, plays, movies, and vacations at low cost.

The Nazis' ultimate goal was self-sufficiency —autarky—which they would try to reach through complete state control of the economy. They assumed, as did the fascists in Italy, that only the state could ensure the social harmony needed to attain the maximum productive potential for the state's benefit.

The government tried to solve the nation's very serious economic problems by confiscating valuable Jewish property, laying a huge tax load on the middle class, and increasing the national debt by one-third to provide work for the unemployed. To create jobs, the first four-year plan, established in 1933, undertook an extensive program of public works and rearmament. The unemployed were put to work on public projects (especially noteworthy was the system of super-highways, the *Autobahnen*), in munitions factories, and in the army.

Overlapping the first program, the second four-year plan was initiated in 1936. The objective of this plan was to set up an autarkist state. In pursuit of self-sufficiency, substitute commodities—frequently inferior in quality and more costly than similar goods available on the world market—were produced by German laboratories, factories, and mills. The gross national product increased by 68 percent by 1938, but the standard of living did not rise in proportion to the higher economic growth rate. At the beginning of World War II, German industry still produced insufficient munitions, even after Hitler took the Czech Skoda works. Germany's war economy did not hit its stride until 1942.

CONCLUSION

The Soviet Union, Italy, and Germany each had separate and distinct cultural, social, and politi-

cal roots that gave unique qualities to the authoritarian governments that developed in them. However, each of the states shared similar circumstances. Each faced economic upheavals, had weak traditions of middle-class dominance and liberal rule, and turned up ambitious individuals ready to take command. In the absence of dynamic democratic forces at home, these circumstances produced the interwar government structures of the totalitarian states.

To be sure, the communists and the fascists differed in theory: The fascists used capitalism while the communists opposed it; fascism emphasized nationalism while communism preached internationalism; fascism had a weak dogmatic basis while communism was based on Marx's scientific socialism; fascism made use of religion while communism attacked it. But by 1939 the common interests of the totalitarian states, whether fascist or communist, were much more important than theoretical differences. Although they may have been philosophically separate, in their domination of the individual the totalitarian states were remarkably similar.

In the face of economic chaos and hardship, communism promised a society of well-being and peace, in which each person could work at full potential. In the face of governments marked either by weakness or a desperate pragmatism, the certainty and effectiveness of the fascists was especially attractive.

The ultimate figure symbolizing totalitarian rule was Adolf Hitler. How an advanced "civilized" nation such as Germany could have thrown itself willingly under Hitler's control is one of history's great questions. Other nations had stronger authoritarian traditions, greater economic problems, and more extreme psychological strain. Some observers maintain that there could have been no Third Reich without this unparalleled demagogue, that in fact the reason Germany erupted as it did is due solely to the happenstance of his personality mixing with the disruptive elements of the postwar world.

✦ Suggestions for Reading

Attempts to analyze the new forms of government in the twentieth century have occupied H. Arendt in *The Origins of Totalitarianism* (Harcourt Brace Jovanovich, 1968); E.

Weber in *Varieties of Fascism* (Anvil, 1973), and C. J. Friedrich and Z. K. Brzezinski in *Totalitarianism, Dictatorship and Autocracy* (Praeger, 1966). Novelist A. Koestler has perhaps best captured the essence of the diminution of the individual in *Darkness at Noon* (Signet, 1961).

Michael Florinsky's analysis of the forces destroying the tsarist regime, *The End of the Russian Empire* (Collier, 1961) is still useful. Alexander Solzhenitsyn beautifully sketches the shifting moods of Russia on the entry into the war in *August 1914* (Bantam, 1974). The best overall survey of Russian history in this century is Donald W. Treadgold, *Twentieth Century Russia* (Houghton Mifflin, 1981). A thorough analysis of the infrastructure crisis that doomed the tsarist system is Lars T. Lih's *Bread and Authority in Russia, 1914–1921* (Univ. of California, 1990). The best study of the first of the 1917 revolutions is Tsuyoshi Hasegawa's *The February Revolution: Petrograd, 1917* (Univ. of Washington, 1981). Alec Nove, *The Soviet Economic System* (Allen & Unwin, 1977) is an essential study.

B. Wolfe's *Three Who Made a Revolution* (Delta, 1974) is a classic study of Lenin, Trotsky, and Stalin. Adam Ulam's *The Bolsheviks* (Macmillan, 1964) gives a clear discussion of the party's development, while S. Cohen in *Bukharin and the Bolshevik Revolution* (Random House, 1974) provides another perspective. J. L. H. Keep dissects the multifaceted and complex actions of the various elements in Petrograd in *The Russian Revolution: A Study in Mass Mobilization* (Norton, 1977). R. Daniels in *Red October* (Scribner's, 1969) gives scholarly depth to the journalistic enthusiasm of John Reed in *Ten Days That Shook the World* (Vintage, 1960).

The most detailed analysis of the Russian revolutions and their aftermath is the multivolumed work of E. H. Carr, *The Russian Revolution* (Pelican, 1966). A discussion of the revolutionary aftermath in the outlying areas appears in R. Pipes, *The Formation of the Soviet Union* (Atheneum, 1968). The civil war is nicely outlined in J. F. N. Bradley's *Civil War in Russia 1917–1920* (Batsford, 1975). George F. Kennan has written the best analysis of Western relations with the young Soviet regime in *Decision to Intervene* (Princeton Univ., 1958) and *Russia and the West Under Lenin and Stalin* (Mentor, 1961). Louis Fischer's *The Soviets in World Affairs* (Vintage, 1960) is a thorough discussion of East-West relations in the 1920s. Sheila Fitzpatrick's *The Russian Revolution 1917–1932* (Oxford Univ., 1982) is a first-rate analysis that establishes the themes undergirding the Stalinist society that emerged in the 1930s. Isaac Deutscher has written sharply drawn biographies of *Stalin* (Vintage, 1961) and *Trotsky*, 3 vols. (Vintage, 1965). Placed in the context of A. Rabinowitch's *The Bolsheviks Come to Power* (Norton, 1978), Deutscher's two works provide a compelling description of the generation after 1917. Robert C. Tucker has compiled the most complete set of analyses of the influence of this century's most powerful man in *Stalinism* (Norton, 1977).

Important social changes that occurred in the Soviet Union are discussed in H. Geiger, *The Family in Soviet Russia* (Harvard Univ., 1968). The relationship between Marxist ideals and the peasantry is discussed in David Mitrany, *Marx Against the Peasant* (Collier, 1961). Stalin's purges are thoroughly analyzed in Robert Conquest, *The Great Terror* (Penguin, 1971). Conquest details the campaign against the peasantry in *Harvest of Sorrow* (Oxford Univ., 1986) and the prison camp system in *Kolyma, the Arctic Death Camps* (Viking, 1978). The most passionate description of the labor camps is Alexander Solzhenitsyn's *The Gulag Archipelago*, 3 vols. (Harper & Row, 1973). R. Medvedev approaches the same subject from another perspective in *Let History Judge* (Random House, 1973). The response of some Western intellectuals to events in the Soviet Union is covered in David Caute, *The Fellow Travelers* (MacMillan, 1973).

Events in Italy have been concisely and clearly detailed by C. Seton-Watson in *Italy from Liberalism to Fascism: 1870–1925* (Methuen, 1967). A collection of Mussolini's ideas has been compiled in Benito Mussolini, *Fascism: Doctrine and Institution* (Fertig, 1968). A clear and concise study of Italy under Mussolini is Elizabeth Wiskemann, *Fascism in Italy: Its Development and Influence* (St. Martin's, 1969). A more detailed discussion of the Fascist advance can be found in A. Lyttelton, *The Seizure of Power: Fascism in Italy 1919–1929* (Scribner's, 1973).

Weimar Germany's brief time in the sun can be studied in A. J. Ryder, *Twentieth Century Germany: From Bismarck to Brandt* (Columbia Univ., 1973) and Erich Eyck, *History of the Weimar Republic*, 2 vols. (Atheneum, 1962). Peter Gay's *Weimar Culture* (Torchbooks, 1968) and *Freud, Jews, and Other Germans* (Oxford Univ., 1979) are penetrating studies of a turbulent time. Fritz Stern, *The Politics of Cultural Despair* (Univ. of California, 1974) and G. Mosse, *The Crisis of German Ideology* (Grosset and Dunlap, 1964) are essential to understand the mental underpinnings supporting the rise of Hitler. A. Dorpalen, *Hindenburg and the Weimar Republic* (Princeton Univ., 1964) examines the dilemma faced by liberals in the 1920s. J. P. Nettl, *Rosa Luxemburg*, 2 vols. (Oxford Univ, 1966) is a fine study of the socialists' dilemma in Germany.

Alan Bullock, *Hitler: A Study in Tyranny* (Torchbooks, 1964) remains the best biography. John Toland, *Adolf Hitler* (Ballantine, 1977) is more readable. William S. Allen, *Nazi Seizure of Power: The Experience of a Single Town 1930–1935* (New Viewpoints, 1969) makes Hitler's takeover more comprehensible. A. Schweitzer, *Big Business and the Third Reich* (Indiana Univ., 1977) details the collaboration between capitalism and fascism. A. Beyerchen, *Scientists Under Hitler* (Yale Univ., 1977) shows institutional responses to the Führer. K. D. Bracher gives a good structural analysis of fascism in operation in *The German Dictatorship* (Praeger, 1970). D. Schoenbaum discusses the social effects of the Nazis in *Hitler's Social Revolution: Class and Status in Nazi Germany* (Anchor, 1967).

→ Notes

1. Leonard Schapiro, "Totalitarianism," *Survey*, Autumn 1969.
2. Novelist Alexander Solzhenitsyn captures the mood in chapter 7 of *August 1914*, trans. Michael Glenny (New York: Bantam Books, 1974).
3. Sir Bernard Pares, "Rasputin and the Empress, Authors of the Russian Collapse," *Foreign Affairs*, VI, no. 1 (October 1927), p. 140.
4. *The New Cambridge Modern History*, XII (Cambridge: Cambridge University Press, 1960), p. 9.
5. J. N. Westwood, *Endurance and Endeavour: Russian History 1812–1986*, 3rd ed. (Oxford: Oxford University Press, 1987), p. 276.
6. Isaac Deutscher, *Stalin: A Political Biography* (New York: Vintage Books, 1961), p. 91.
7. Zbigniew Brzezinski, "The Nature of the Soviet System," in Donald W. Treadgold, ed., *The Development of the USSR* (Seattle: University of Washington Press, 1964), pp. 6–8.
8. Christopher Seton-Watson, *Italy from Liberalism to Fascism: 1870–1925* (London: Methuen, 1967), p. 518.
9. Elizabeth Wiskemann, *Fascism in Italy: Its Development and Influence* (New York: St. Martin's Press, 1969), p. 12.
10. Benito Mussolini, *Fascism: Doctrine and Institutions* (New York: Howard Fertig, 1968), p. 38.
11. Wiskemann, *Fascism in Italy*, p. 23.
12. Mussolini, *Fascism*, pp. 35, 38.
13. Peter Gay, *Weimar Culture* (New York: Torchbooks, 1968), p. 23.
14. Hajo Holborn, *Germany and Europe: Historical Essays* (New York: Anchor Books, 1971), pp. 221–224.
15. David S. Landes, *The Unbound Prometheus* (Cambridge: Cambridge University Press, 1969), p. 398.
16. A. J. Ryder, *Twentieth-Century Germany: From Bismarck to Brandt* (New York: Columbia University Press, 1973), p. 348.
17. J. Bronowski, *The Ascent of Man* (Boston: Little, Brown, 1973), p. 367.

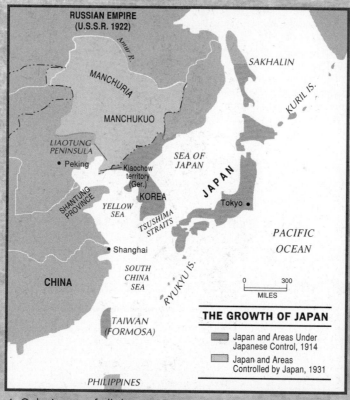

CHAPTER 32

THE GROWTH OF JAPAN

- Japan and Areas Under Japanese Control, 1914
- Japan and Areas Controlled by Japan, 1931

→ Only Japan, of all the non-European world, had been able to make the necessary adjustments to a modern industrial economy by 1900. After World War I, no country in East Asia could match its economic and political strength.

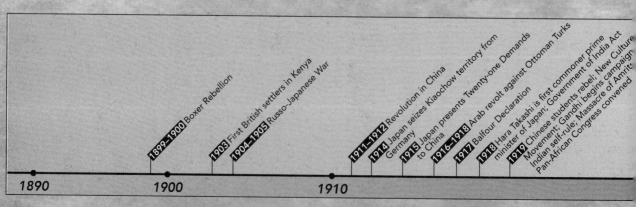

1899–1900 Boxer Rebellion

1903 First British settlers in Kenya

1904–1905 Russo-Japanese War

1911–1912 Revolution in China

1914 Japan seizes Kiaochow territory from Germany

1915 Japan presents Twenty-one Demands to China

1916–1918 Arab revolt against Ottoman Turks

1917 Balfour Declaration

1918 Hara Takashi is first commoner prime minister of Japan; Government of India Act

1919 Chinese students rebel; New Culture Movement; Gandhi begins campaign for Indian self-rule; Massacre of Amritsar; Pan-African Congress convened

1890   1900   1910

Asia and Africa, 1918–1939

CHAPTER OUTLINE

Japan

China: Revolution and Republic

Nationalism in Southeast Asia

India: The Drive for Independence

Changes in the Muslim World

Africa: From Colonialism to Nationalism

MAPS

The Growth of Japan

The Kuomintang Regime

Mandated Areas of the Middle East

The Mandate System in Africa, 1926

DOCUMENTS

Kita Ikki's Plan for Japan

Memorandum of the General Syrian Congress

Fifty years of aggressive expansion by the West had spread a veneer of Europeanization on much of the world. At the same time, the imperialists also exported Western social and political ideas to their colonies. The explosive concepts of nationalism and self-rule, tied to Western science and technology, revitalized the societies of Asia and Africa.

World War I and its aftershocks strengthened independence movements in Africa and Asia. Nationalist campaigns, present in embryonic form in most of the colonies before the war, grew rapidly in virtually all of the European possessions and mandates. Japan emerged as a world power, but by the late 1920s the impact of the depression and a population crisis threatened its weakly rooted democratic institutions. China endured revolution and civil strife as the areas of Southeast Asia pursued independence. India's independence movement strengthened under the leadership of Mohandas Gandhi. Across the Islamic world and Africa, indigenous peoples emerged from under the shadow of European domination, which was in full retreat by the end of the 1930s.

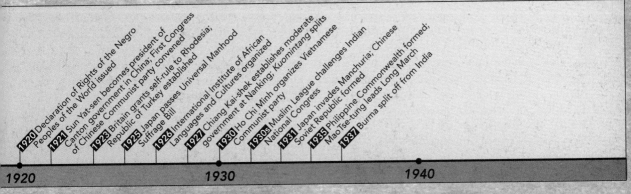

Timeline:

1920 Declaration of Rights of the Negro Peoples of the World issued

1921 Sun Yat-sen becomes president of Canton government in China; First Congress of Chinese Communist party convened

1923 Britain grants self-rule to Rhodesia; Republic of Turkey established

1925 Japan passes Universal Manhood Suffrage Bill

1926 International Institute of African Languages and Cultures organized

1927 Chiang Kai-shek establishes moderate government at Nanking; Kuomintang splits

1930 Ho Chi Minh organizes Vietnamese Communist party

1930s Muslim League challenges Indian National Congress

1931 Japan invades Manchuria; Chinese Soviet Republic formed

1935 Philippine Commonwealth formed; Mao Tse-tung leads Long March

1937 Burma split off from India

1920   1930   1940

JAPAN

Japan's victory over Russia in the 1904–1905 Russo-Japanese War served notice of the success of the Meiji era reforms. In two generations, the island nation had changed from a static, mostly agricultural nation into a modern, highly industrialized state. In the government, liberal statesmen tried to strengthen democratic practices. They faced serious problems. The rapidly increasing population strained the nation's limited size and resources. Ten years after World War I, economic pressures combined with a revival of militarism to launch the Japanese toward war and dictatorship.

Authoritarian Victory

From 1889 to 1918 an aristocratic oligarchy of elder statesmen called the *Genro* controlled the Japanese government. By the 1920s most of the patriarchs had passed away and the field of politics was open to new blood. Hara Takashi, the first commoner to hold the post of prime minister, was elected to the office in 1918.

Over the next 12 years, Japan seemed to be moving toward the establishment of a democratic, parliamentary government under its new political leaders. However, the liberals faced serious obstacles. There was no widespread tradition of democratic or parliamentary practices in Japan. Japanese society had concentrated wealth and power in the hands of a few families, while the traditional culture encouraged a militaristic system of values. The secret societies and the cult of Shintoism favored authoritarianism over liberalism.

Despite these obstacles, liberals in the Japanese parliament, the Diet, showed great promise and courage as they tried to lead the nation away from militant nationalism. They pressed for reforms at home while criticizing the imperialistic intervention of the Japanese army in Siberia during the Russian Civil War. Although the democratic cause suffered a serious setback in 1921 with the assassination of Prime Minister Hara, the liberals continued their work. Passage of the Universal Manhood Suffrage Bill in 1925 strengthened the liberal base. By 1930, after a reactionary interlude, Prime Minister Hamaguchi Yuko established the most liberal government Japan had ever had.

As was the case in Europe, as long as the economy remained strong, the liberals did well.

In the 1920s the Japanese built thousands of factories that turned out products enabling Japan to claim a major share of the world textile market and to flood the world with mass-produced, cheap, low-quality goods. Japanese industrialists were quick to adopt modern machine techniques and slow to raise wages. A few giant concerns working together controlled the greater part of the country's wealth.

Prosperity—and by implication the liberals' position—rested on fragile foundations. Japan lacked natural resources, and its population grew at a rapid rate. In 1920 there were more than 55 million inhabitants. Eleven years later there were 65 million people, crowded into a land area smaller than the state of California. By 1932 the average annual population increase was 1 million. The Japanese economy had to create 250,000 jobs yearly and find food to feed the growing population. Up to 1930 Japan paid its way by expanding exports. But between 1929 and 1931, the effects of the great depression cut export trade in half. Unemployment soared, leading to wage cuts and strikes. As in Germany on the eve of Adolf Hitler's rise to power, frustration became widespread among the younger generation.

In response to the economic crisis, Prime Minister Hamaguchi adopted measured fiscal reforms and a moderate foreign policy. The first approach failed to satisfy the workers and the second approach offended the militarists. Hamaguchi was shot in November 1930 and died the following spring. The assassin's bullets dealt a blow to Japanese liberalism from which it did not recover until after World War II.

A new group of ultranationalistic and militaristic leaders came to power, ruling not through a charismatic leader as in Germany and Italy but through a military clique. The members of the clique, who had nothing but contempt for democracy and peaceful policies, terrorized the civilian members of the government, plotted to shelve parliamentary government, and planned to use force on the mainland of China. Their goals were to gain resources for the economy, living space for the population, markets for Japanese goods, and cultural domination throughout Asia. They referred to their program as a "beneficial mission" and called it the "New Order in Asia." The military clique took its first step with the invasion of Manchuria in 1931, setting off the sequence of aggression that would lead to World War II.

Kita Ikki's Plan for Japan

While liberal Europe struggled with the burdens of victory, Japan experimented with a variety of governmental approaches. A radical social and economic concept was enunciated by Kita Ikki, who was executed in 1937.

Suspension of the Constitution: In order to establish a firm base for national reorganization, the Emperor, with the aid of the entire Japanese nation and by invoking his imperial prerogatives, shall suspend the Constitution for a period of three years, dissolve the two houses of the Diet, and place the entire country under martial law.

The true significance of the Emperor: We must make clear the fundamental principle that the Emperor is the sole representative of the people and the pillar of the state. . . .

Abolition of the peerage system: By abolishing the peerage system, we shall be able to remove the feudal aristocracy which constitutes a barrier between the Emperor and the people. In this way the spirit of the Meiji Restoration shall be proclaimed. . . .

The members of the Deliberative Council shall consist of men distinguished in various fields of activities, elected by each other or appointed by the Emperor.

Limitation on private property: No Japanese family shall possess property in excess of one million yen. A similar limitation shall apply to Japanese citizens holding property overseas. No one shall be permitted to make a gift of property to those related by blood or to others, or to transfer his property by other means with the intent of circumventing this limitation.

Nationalization of excess amount over limitation on private property: Any amount which exceeds the limitation on private property shall revert to the state without compensation. No one shall be permitted to resort to the protection of present laws in order to avoid remitting such excess amount. Anyone who violates these provisions shall be deemed a person thinking lightly of the example set by the Emperor and endangering the basis of national reorganization. As such, during the time martial law is in effect, he shall be charged with the crimes of endangering the person of the Emperor and engaging in internal revolt and shall be punished by death.

Limitation on private landholding: No Japanese family shall hold land in excess of 100,000 yen in current market value. . . .

Lands held in excess of the limitation on private landholding shall revert to the state. . . .

Distribution of profits to workers: One half of the net profits of private industries shall be distributed to workers employed in such industries. . . .

Continuation of the conscript system: The state, having rights to existence and development among the nations of the world, shall maintain the present conscript system in perpetuity. . . .

Positive right to start war: In addition to the right to self-defense, the state shall have the right to start a war on behalf of other nations and races unjustly oppressed by a third power. (As a matter of real concern today, the state shall have the right to start a war to aid the independence of India and preservation of China's integrity.)

As a result of its own development, the state shall also have the right to start a war against those nations who occupy large colonies illegally and ignore the heavenly way of the co-existence of all humanity. (As a matter of real concern today, the state shall have the right to start a war against those nations which occupy Australia and Far Eastern Siberia for the purpose of acquiring them.)

From David John Lu, *Sources of Japanese History,* Vol. 2. (New York: McGraw-Hill, 1974.) Reprinted by permission of the publisher.

SHANGH PORT TREATI

TR

JAPANESE GOV'T. PROMISES
WORLD COURT
L. OF N. COVENANT

KELLOGG PACT

NINE POWER TREATY

JAPAN

→ Japan's invasion of Manchuria in September 1931 violated a number of treaties, covenants, agreements, and promises that had been made after World War I in the hope of maintaining worldwide and lasting peace.

The Asian Great Power

Despite dramatic domestic institutional and social changes, Japan's goals in China remained remarkably consistent after the Meiji restoration. In 1914 the Japanese ordered the Germans to remove their warships from the Far East and to surrender Kiaochow territory in China to them. When the Germans refused to reply to this order, Japan declared war on Germany and seized the territory without consulting China. In 1915, Japan presented China with the Twenty-one Demands, a document whose frank statement of Japan's aims on the Asian continent startled the world.

The Chinese government, weakened by a half-century of decline and revolution, could do little but give in to the first 16 demands, reserving the final 5 for further consideration. By leaking news of the demands to the press, the Chinese attracted the attention of the United States. Washington kept China from falling totally under Japan's domination. Nevertheless, the Chinese had no choice but to recognize Japan's authority in Shantung province and extend Japanese land and rail concessions in southern Manchuria. In 1917 the Allies secretly agreed to support Japanese claims against China, in return for Japan's respecting the Open Door policy.

Japan's sphere of economic dominance expanded during the 1920s in Shantung, Manchuria, and south Mongolia. It also occupied the former German islands north of the equator. The Washington Conference of 1921 acknowledged the Japanese navy as the third most powerful in the world. The signatories (United States, Great Britain, France, Italy, Japan, Belgium, the Netherlands, Portugal, and China) of the Nine-Power Treaty, signed in Washington in 1922, agreed to respect the independence, sovereignty, territoriality, and administrative integrity of China and to respect the Open Door policy.

The United States and Britain, however, were alarmed by the growth of Japanese power. By 1931, Japanese investments in China were second only to those of Great Britain, constituting around 35 percent of all foreign investment in China. That same year, responding to population pressures and resource needs, the Japanese disregarded international treaties and opinions and invaded China.

CHINA: REVOLUTION AND REPUBLIC

During the nineteenth century China endured one of the darkest periods in its four thousand years. The old Confucianist, imperial government failed as China lost territory, suffered under the imposition of extraterritoriality, and witnessed its customs and tariffs come under foreign control. The 1898 reform movement and the Boxer Uprising of 1899–1900 were, in effect, two attempts to remove the Manchu dynasty. Thereafter, there were two approaches to change: the constitutionalist attempt to set up representative government and the revolutionary program to overthrow the dynasty.

Sun Yat-sen and Revolution

Sun Yat-sen (1867–1925) proved to be the key figure in the transition from the old to the new China. Born near Canton to a tenant farmer, he received a Western education in Hawaii. He converted to Christianity and in 1892 earned a diploma in medicine in Hong Kong. Soon, he became a leader in the Chinese nationalist movement, directing his energies toward the overthrow of the Manchus and the formation of a republic. For his activities, he was forced into exile in 1895 and thereafter traveled widely throughout the world seeking political and financial aid from Chinese living abroad. During that period he organized the movement that eventually became the *Kuomintang*, or Nationalist party.

In 1911 a revolt broke out in China over a foreign loan to finance railways. The outbreak spread like wildfire throughout the country. Yuan Shih-kai (1859–1916), an outstanding north Chinese military leader with modern ideas, persuaded the imperial clan that the Manchu dynasty was doomed. In 1912 the child emperor abdicated, and Yuan was asked to form a republican government. Although a few months earlier a revolutionary assembly in Nanking had elected Sun president of the new republic, he stepped aside in the interest of national unity and the Nanking assembly elected Yuan.

During the next 15 years China went through a period quite similar to the dynastic interregnums that had punctuated its previous history. Trouble broke out in 1913 when Yuan negotiated a large loan with bankers from Britain, France, Germany, and Russia that gave these powers substantial influence in the government of the republic. Resentment over this agreement led to a new rebellion, backed by Sun. Yuan still had control of the army and put down the revolt,

→ Statesman and revolutionary leader Sun Yat-sen, the organizer of the *Kuomintang*, is known as the father of modern China

forcing Sun to flee to Japan until 1917. Overestimating his strength, Yuan dismissed the parliament and proclaimed the restoration of the monarchy with himself as emperor. This act sparked another rebellion, and this time Yuan's prestige evaporated. In June 1916 the now discredited dictator died.

China then entered a period of political anarchy. Warlords heading armies based on local power centers marched across the country seeking control of Peking. Possession of the city apparently was seen as conferring legitimacy on its occupier. For a time, China was divided between two would-be governments, one in the north at Peking and the other in the south at Canton. The southern force was composed largely of those who had engineered the revolution of 1911–1912. The Canton government elected Sun president in 1921, and he remained there until his death in 1925, unable to unify the country.

Sun's genius was in making revolution, not in governing. His social ideology, however, provided some key elements for twentieth-century Chinese political theory. Sun's *Three Principles of the People*, developed from a series of lectures, became the political manual of the *Kuomintang*. The three principles are (1) nationalism, the liberation of China from foreign domination and the creation of a Chinese nation-state; (2) democracy, "government by the people and for the people"; and (3) livelihood, economic security for all the people.

In 1923, after failing to obtain aid from the West to overthrow the Peking government, Sun turned to the Soviet Union for advice and assistance. A military and political advisory group arrived, led by Michael Borodin. Under Borodin's guidance, the *Kuomintang* adopted many of the planks of the program subscribed to by the Soviet Communist party as well as the party's organizational structure.

Chiang Kai-shek "Unites" China

Sun's successor as leader of the *Kuomintang* was Chiang Kai-shek (1886–1975), the son of a minor landlord. Chiang studied at a military academy in Japan before becoming caught up with Sun's vision for a new China. He returned home to take an active part in the revolution. His obvious abilities and loyalty attracted Sun's attention, and in 1923 he was sent to Russia for a brief period of training. Before establishing himself as leader of the *Kuomintang*, he formed a united force and began to drive northward in 1926. Chiang's group encountered little opposition, and by the early spring of the following year they reached the Yangtze valley. However, dissension broke out between the radical and the conservative elements of the *Kuomintang*, and Chiang crushed the communists in his ranks when he occupied Shanghai. He went on to create a moderate government at Nanking, and before the end of 1927, public opinion had swung behind his regime.

Chiang continued to purge the leftist elements. The end of the *Kuomintang* alliance with the communists was written in blood, when a proletarian uprising in Canton was crushed, with the loss of 5000 lives. The Soviet advisers returned to Moscow and many radicals, including the widow of Sun Yat-sen, were driven into exile. The Chinese communists fled to the hills and mountains of China.

The 1927 split of the *Kuomintang* is a major event in modern Chinese history. Not only were Marxist radicals ousted, but many moderate liberals also came under attack. Chiang built his strength on the urban professional, banking, and merchant classes. His government depended for financial support on the foreign bankers of Shanghai. The regime took on a conservative, urban character, far removed from the huge mass of the Chinese people, the peasantry in the countryside.

→ Chiang Kai-shek, successor to Sun Yat-sen as leader of the *Kuomintang*, broke with the communists in 1927 and set up a new government at Nanking.

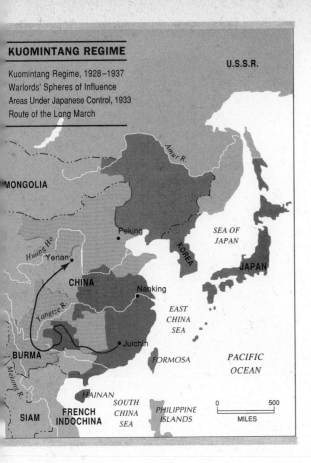

KUOMINTANG REGIME

Kuomintang Regime, 1928–1937
Warlords' Spheres of Influence
Areas Under Japanese Control, 1933
Route of the Long March

U.S.S.R.

MONGOLIA

Amur R.

SEA OF
JAPAN

Peking

KOREA

JAPAN

Huang Ho

Yenan

CHINA

Nanking

Yangtze R.

EAST
CHINA
SEA

Juichin

BURMA

Mekong R.

FORMOSA

PACIFIC
OCEAN

HAINAN

SIAM

FRENCH
INDOCHINA

SOUTH
CHINA
SEA

PHILIPPINE
ISLANDS

0   500

MILES

Chiang engineered substantial changes in Chinese urban life. More Chinese received education. Linguists championed the use of a new, more colloquial written language, while scholars labored for the adoption of Mandarin (a standardized version of the Peking dialect, used in government affairs) so that people from all parts of China could speak to one another. Social customs changed and Western dress and folkways appeared. Large cities installed telephones, electric lights, modern water systems, and movie palaces. Much of the import of Western conveniences was paid for by the foreign entrepreneurs who controlled most of Chinese industry. Despite numerous changes, civil war, a weak currency, and inadequate transportation kept China an underdeveloped nation with grinding poverty.

A fervent patriot, Chiang unfortunately had little appreciation for the social and economic problems of his nation. Bandits continued to tyrannize the people while famine in the northwest of the country claimed the lives of millions. Instead of responding to the plight of his nation, Chiang, a Christian whose faith incorporated much from Confucian principles, pursued the moral regeneration of his people through a combination of his religion and his culture—the New Life Movement which he established in the mid-1930s. He would have done better to appreciate the intellectual changes taking place and the social and economic hopes of the peasants.

The New Culture Movement and Chinese Communism

A Chinese intellectual revolution began at Peking University during World War I and spread from there to students all over the country. The first influential voice for this intellectual group was the magazine *New Youth*. This journal transmitted the ideas of students who had returned from universities in the United States and Europe on subjects ranging from Western science to liberalism to socialism. These students wanted to establish a new order and a new set of values to replace much of the old Confucian tradition.

The students became disillusioned with the West after the Versailles peace treaty, which gave Chinese Shantung to Japan. Virulent anti-Western sentiment fueled a violent student demonstration on May 4, 1919. A new ideological orientation began in the New Culture Movement.

With his government established at Nanking, Chiang, his armies, and his warlord allies again moved north and occupied Peking. China once again appeared to be united, but it was a unity more in appearance than in fact. While large areas of the country had been conquered by Chiang's forces, other regions came under the *Kuomintang* by agreement between Chiang and local warlords. In theory the warlords were subordinate to Chiang, but they maintained power in their spheres of influence.

Chinese foreign relations improved during the 1920s. The Nine-Power Treaty guaranteed China's territorial integrity, and China was a member of the League of Nations. The government regained the right to set its own tariffs in 1929, when ten foreign powers gave up or lost the right of extraterritoriality. Partially in response to this development foreign trade was seven times as great in 1929 as in 1894. In addition, while the liberals were in power in Japan, Tokyo was relatively conciliatory toward China.

Study groups were formed, especially at Peking University, where professors and students began to read Marx and Lenin and to apply their theories to conditions in China. Lenin's analysis of and attack on imperialism struck a responsive chord.

With some guidance from Russian Comintern agents, the First Congress of the Chinese Communist party was held in July 1921. A young student at Peking University named Mao Tse-tung was a delegate. About the same time, Chinese worker-students in France established the Young China Communist party in Paris. One of its leaders was Chou En-lai, later premier of Chinese People's Republic.

Mao Tse-tung (1893–1976) was born in Hunan province, a traditional center of Chinese revolutionary activity. In 1918 he went to Peking University, where he worked as library assistant under Li Ta-chao, the founder of an important Marxist study group and one of the founders of the Chinese Communist party. Mao began to emerge as a distinctive leader with a new program for revolution when he wrote a report for the Communist party in 1927 about the peasant movement in Hunan. In that document Mao expressed his belief that the revolution must base itself on peasant uprisings, a view that was condemned by the Central Committee of the Chinese Communist party, which closely adhered to the Russian policy of basing the revolution on the urban proletariat.

Mao led a Hunanese peasant uprising that became known as the Autumn Harvest Uprising. It was crushed, and in May 1928 Mao and other Communist leaders joined forces in the border region of Hunan and Kiangsi provinces. Acutely conscious of peasant needs, Mao organized the peasants in his region into a Chinese "soviet." Other Communist leaders did the same in other regions, and in 1931 delegates from the various local soviets in China met and proclaimed the birth of the Chinese Soviet Republic. Even though Chiang Kai-shek destroyed the Shanghai apparatus of the Communist party, Mao and his colleagues could still claim control of regions containing 9 million inhabitants.

Mao's success as a Communist leader stemmed from his observation that it was the Chinese peasant, not the urban worker, who could be made the agent of the revolution. In pursuit of this objective, Mao encouraged the

→ Mao Tse-tung has been called the "Stalin" of Chinese Communism.

establishment of farmers' cooperatives and equitable tax systems. He also redistributed land in the areas he controlled. Mao's achievements worried Chiang, who between 1931 and 1934 launched five military campaigns against the Communists—the last one using one million men and a German military staff. To avoid annihilation, the Communists made their famous Long March 2000 miles to the northwest. Only a remnant of the original force reached Yenan, in Shensi province, where in 1935 a new Communist stronghold was set up.

NATIONALISM IN SOUTHEAST ASIA

The drive for independence became stronger in Southeast Asia between the two world wars. Taking advantage of the war-weakened colonialists, local leaders adapted the ideologies of the day—whether Wilson's "self-determination of peoples" or socialism, or a combination of the two—to their campaigns for freedom. The example of

Japan's rise to the status of a great power showed that the West had no monopoly on harnessing technology and organization to national goals.

Populations grew dramatically in Southeast Asia during the interwar period. From 1930 to 1960 the number of people in Siam, Malaya, and the Philippines increased more than 100 percent; in Indonesia, Burma, and Indochina the number increased more than 50 percent. Population pressures naturally contributed to unrest.

Certain economic trends also characterized most of the region. The imperialist powers continued to exploit their colonies, ignoring the democratic rhetoric they had mouthed during the First World War. Europe's draining of the area's resources coupled with an irregular world market that crashed in 1929 led to increased hardship in much of the region. The Chinese played an increasingly important role as merchants and middlemen in the local economies. In Burma, Indians played the same role. European and Chinese capital investment encouraged a rapid growth in exports of minerals and forest products. In Siam, Indochina, and a few other countries rice production grew more rapidly than population, and as a result the economies became based on rice exports.

Throughout the area the elite became assimilated to European culture as more and more young people went to the "parent countries" to be educated. The masses, however, were barely touched by this process. The result was a growing cultural and social divide between the local leadership and the people at large. With the exception of the United States in the Philippines and Great Britain in Burma and Ceylon, none of the imperialist powers undertook to prepare their colonies for eventual self-government, since they had no intention of letting them go.

Indochina

French rule in Indochina was in some ways the least enlightened of all the colonial regimes in Southeast Asia. In 1941, for example, the colonial government had the highest proportion of Europeans in its service of any in the region—some 5,100 French officials to 27,000 Indochinese. Four-fifths of the population was illiterate, and of the more than 21 million people, only about 500,000 children received any higher education. French rule was characterized by politi-

cal oppression, severe economic exploitation, and a rigid and stagnant traditional culture.

Revolution seemed the answer to Vietnam's problems. During World War I over 100,000 Vietnamese laborers and soldiers were sent to France, where many of them came in contact with liberal and radical thinking, which they then brought home. The Vietnam Nationalist party, patterned organizationally and intellectually on the Chinese *Kuomintang*, was officially outlawed, and by the late 1920s resorted to terrorism as the only form of political expression open to it.

Communism rapidly became the major revolutionary ideology in the French colony. In 1920 a young Vietnamese calling himself Nguyen Ai Quoc ("Nguyen, the Patriot"), and later known to the world as Ho Chi Minh (1890–1969), participated actively in the formation of the Communist party in France. In 1930 he organized in Hong Kong what eventually became the Vietnamese (later Indochinese) Communist party. Commu-

→ Ho Chi Minh found in communist ideology a road to his ultimage goal: the liberation of his native Vietnam.

nist ideas and organization spread throughout Vietnam in the 1930s while the colonial government answered Vietnamese uprisings against French oppression with strong repressive measures. As a result, when World War II began, the Communist party was the major vehicle for the expression of Vietnamese nationalism.

The Philippines

The United States established its form of government in the Philippines on July 4, 1901, under William H. Taft as civil governor of the area. President McKinley declared that the primary aim was to prepare the Filipinos for self-government. The first elections were held in 1907 and by 1913 Filipinos dominated both houses of the legislature, while an American remained as governor-general. By 1935, when the Philippine Commonwealth was inaugurated with a new constitution and the promise of independence within ten years, the islands had developed a complex governmental structure and a sophisticated political life.

Economic developments, however, constricted Philippine independence at the same time that the islands were being prepared for self-rule. Before the outbreak of World War II, four-fifths of Philippine exports went to the United States and three-fifths of its imports came from America. As with most underdeveloped economies, the export trade was dominated by a very few primary products: hemp, sugar, coconuts, and tobacco. Independence, with its accompanying imposition of tariffs, would have been economically difficult. The United States had prevented the development of a colonial-type plantation economy by forbidding non-Filipinos to own plantation lands, but native landlordism was rampant, and the oppressed peasants launched a brief uprising in the mid-1930s.

Dutch East Indies

Unlike other Western imperial powers that loosened controls over their colonies, either through domestic weakness or planned decolonization, the Dutch increased their control in the East Indies. Stretched over 3100 miles of water, the numerous islands of Indonesia were integrated into a communications and political system by the Dutch. At the same time, the strict limits put on the power and advancement of native elites led to bitterness and resentment. Dutch imperialism strengthened Indonesian self-consciousness and nationalism.

A Communist party, organized in 1920, attempted unsuccessful uprisings in Java and Sumatra in late 1926 and early 1927. Police repression increased. In 1930 the Dutch attempted to crush the Nationalist party and arrested one of its leaders, Achmed Sukarno (1901–1970), the man who after World War II became the first president of independent Indonesia. The Dutch banned all discussions of any subject that might involve the concept of national independence. Even the name *Indonesia* was censored from official publications.

Siam/Thailand

In the interwar period, Siam, which changed its name to Thailand in 1939, continued to modernize. Educational improvements, economic growth, and increased political sophistication contrasted sharply, however, with the political and administrative domination of the country by the rather extensive royal family. In 1932 a French-trained law professor led a bloodless coup d'état, and a new constitution was promulgated with the agreement of the king, turning him into a reigning, not ruling, monarch. Since then the country has been ruled by an alliance of army and oligarchy.

Burma and Malaya

The Burmese independence movement modeled itself on the tactics practiced by the Indian National Congress, but Buddhism provided the focus for organizational activity. A Young Men's Buddhist Association, formed in 1906, organized a General Council of Burmese Associations in 1921. The General Council brought nationalism to the village level.

British promises to promote Indian self-government created a similar demand in Burma, and in 1937 Burma was administratively split off from India. A parliamentary system was begun with a Burmese prime minister under a British governor, who held responsibility for foreign relations, defense, and finance.

No strong nationalist movement developed in Malaya, perhaps because the large ethnic groups living there distrusted one another more than they felt the need to make common cause against the British. The Malays feared Chinese ethnic domination; eventually, the Chinese came to outnumber the Malays themselves. The Chinese were primarily interested in commerce and in developments in China. The Indians, for the most part workers on plantations and in mines, were loyal to India as their homeland.

INDIA: THE DRIVE FOR INDEPENDENCE

Before 1914, many observers had predicted that in the event of war, Great Britain would find India a serious liability. When hostilities began, however, nearly all anti-British activity in India ceased.

Gradual Steps Toward Self-Rule

By 1917 Indian nationalists expected immediate compensation for their loyalty in terms of more self-government. The British, however, pursued a policy stressing gradual development of self-government within the British Empire. To this end, in 1918, a British commission sent to India to study the question of self-government recommended a new constitution. The Government of India Act provided for a system of dual government in the provinces by which certain powers were reserved to the British while the provincial legislatures were granted other, generally lesser, powers.

To Indian nationalists, this act represented only a small step toward self-rule. Their frustrations led to the outbreak of a struggle with the British in 1919. In an ill-advised move the British passed the Rowlatt Act (1919), which allowed the police and other officials extraordinary powers in searching out subversive activity. Although the act was never enforced, it was deeply resented as a symbol of repression.

Disgruntled and disheartened by the Government of India Act and the violence that followed, many nationalists demanded sweeping changes. Britain, however, lacked a comprehensive plan to grant independence, and a large segment of British public opinion strongly opposed any suggestion of the breakup of the empire, such as Indian independence.

Gandhi and Civil Disobedience

The foremost nationalist leader in India was Mohandas K. Gandhi (1869–1948). Born of middle-class parents, Gandhi had been sent to London to study law; later he went to South Africa, where he built up a lucrative practice. During these years his standard of values changed completely. The new Gandhi repudiated wealth, practiced ascetic self-denial, condemned violence, and believed firmly that true happiness could be achieved only through service to others.

Gandhi began his career as a reformer and champion of his people in South Africa. The Indians there were subject to numerous legal restrictions that hampered their freedom of movement, prevented them from buying property, and imposed added taxes on them. Disdaining the use of violence, Gandhi believed that a just cause would triumph if its supporters attempted to convince those in power of injustices by practicing "civil disobedience." With Gandhi as their leader, the Indians in South Africa carried out various protests, including hunger strikes. They refused to work, held mass demonstrations, and marched into areas where their presence was forbidden by law. By the use of such passive resistance, or noncooperation, Gandhi forced the government to remove some restrictions.

When he returned to his native land shortly after the outbreak of World War I, Gandhi was welcomed as a hero. During the war he cooperated with the British government, but the disappointing concessions in the new constitution and the Rowlatt Act led him to announce his determination to force the British to give India self-rule.

Gandhi introduced his campaign in 1919. A mass strike was declared in which all work was to cease and the population was to pray and fast. Contrary to Gandhi's plan, however, riots took place. After Europeans were killed, soldiers came in to restore order. Although the British forbade public gatherings, a large body of unarmed Indians assembled at a temple in Amritsar. British troops broke up the meeting, killing hundreds in what has come to be known as the Massacre of Amritsar.

This incident put a temporary end to all hope of cooperation between Indians and Britons. Many British colonials supported the bloody suppression of the Amritsar demonstrators. Arrested in 1922, Gandhi seemed to welcome being placed on trial; he assured the British magistrate that the only alternative to permitting him to continue his opposition was to imprison him. Sentenced to six years imprisonment, Gandhi suffered a temporary eclipse.

Road to Reform

A promising road to conciliation opened in 1930 when a series of round-table conferences was arranged in London. A new scheme of government was hammered out, providing for a federal union, which would bring the British provinces and the states of the princes into a central government. In the provinces the dual government system was replaced by full autonomy, while in the federal government all powers were transferred to the Indians except defense and foreign affairs, which remained in the control of the British viceroy. From 1937, when this new Government of India Act came into operation, until 1939 the scheme of self-government worked smoothly. The possibility of federation, however, faded when the native princes refused to enter the central government.

The new system of government failed to satisfy the demands of the Indian nationalists, who continued to use demonstrations and articles in the popular press to push for complete independence. The chief element in the independence movement was the powerful Indian National Congress, which had become the organ of the militant nationalists. The membership of several million was predominantly Hindu but also included many Muslims and members of other religious groups. Soon after the First World War, the Congress had come under the leadership of Gandhi, whose personal following among the people was the chief source of the party's tremendous influence.

Gandhi transformed the Congress, which had been primarily a middle-class organization, into a mass movement that included the peasants. Gandhi had other goals besides freeing India. He sought to end all drinking of alcohol, raise the status of women, remove the stigma attached to the untouchables, and bring about cooperation between Hindus and Muslims. Permeating all of Gandhi's ideas and actions was his belief in nonviolence; he was convinced that injustices could be destroyed only through the forces of love, unselfishness, and patience.

In the 1930s Gandhi shared his leadership with Jawaharlal Nehru (1889–1964), who came

→ Mohandas Gandhi used the weapons of nonviolent protest and noncooperation in his struggle to win independence for India. An immensely popular and beloved leader, Gandhi was given the title Mahatma, or "Great Soul," by the people.

→ Jawaharlal Nehru, along with Gandhi a leader of Indian nationalism, served as prime minister of independent India.

from a Brahmin family of ancient lineage. In his youth Nehru had all of the advantages of wealth: English tutors, enrollment in the English public schools of Harrow and later Trinity College, Cambridge, where he obtained his B.A. in 1910. Two years later he was admitted to the bar. On his return to India, he showed little interest in the law and gradually became completely absorbed in his country's fight for freedom.

A devoted friend and disciple of Gandhi, Nehru could not agree with the older leader's mystical rejection of much of the modern world. At heart, Nehru was a rationalist, an agnostic, an ardent believer in science, and a foe of all supernaturalism. Above all, he was a blend of the cultures of both East and West, perhaps with the latter predominating. As he himself said: "I have become a queer mixture of the East and the West, out of place everywhere, at home nowhere.

Perhaps my thoughts and approach to life are more akin to what is called Western than Eastern, but India calls me."[1]

The Hindu-Muslim Clash

India is the classic example of a fragmented society. The major division in India was between the Hindus and Muslims, who were poles apart in culture and values. As Britain's imperial control over India began to show signs of ending, hostility between the two communities surfaced. Many Muslims believed that with independence they would become a powerless minority. Thus the conflict was a struggle for political survival.

In the early 1930s the Muslim League, a political party, began to challenge the claim of the Indian National Congress to represent all of India. The leader of the Muslim League, Muhammad Ali Jinnah (1876–1948), originally a member of the Congress and once dubbed by Indian nationalists the "ambassador of Hindu-Muslim unity," had become alienated by what he considered the Hindu domination of the Congress and its claim to be the sole agent of Indian nationalism.

The Muslim League began to advance the "two-nation" theory, and in 1933 a group of Muslim students at Cambridge University circulated a pamphlet for the establishment of a new state to be known as Pakistan. This leaflet was the opening act of a bloody drama. In 1939 the Muslim League emphatically denounced any scheme of self-government of India that would mean majority Hindu rule.

CHANGES IN THE MUSLIM WORLD

The Ottoman Empire had clung to a shaky dominance over the Muslim world of the Middle East and North Africa at the beginning of the nineteenth century. With the exception of Morocco, North Africa was nominally ruled by the Turkish sultan. By the end of the century, however, Europeans dominated North Africa, while the Middle East discontentedly remained under the sultan. World War I and its aftershocks fundamentally changed this situation.

The Arab Revolt

In 1913 an Arab Congress meeting in Paris demanded home rule and equality with the Turks in the Ottoman Empire. Because the Middle East was so important to Britain, the London government followed the Arab movement with great interest, especially after Turkey joined the Central Powers in the war. In the latter half of 1915, the British High Commissioner in Cairo carried on an extensive correspondence with Sherif Husein of Mecca (Husein ibn-Ali, 1856–1931), guardian of Islam's holy places. The British told Husein that in the event of an Arab revolt against the Turks, Great Britain would recognize Arab independence except in those regions of coastal Syria that were not wholly Arab—presumably excluding Palestine—and in those places that might be claimed by France.

In addition to the British alliance with the Arab nationalist movement, the desert warrior Abdul ibn-Saud (1880–1953), sultan of Nejd in south central Arabia, agreed to adopt a policy of benevolent neutrality toward Britain. The wooing of the Arabs blocked the Turkish attempt to rouse the Muslim Middle East by preaching *jihad,* or holy war, against the British.

The Arab revolt began in late 1916. Husein raised the standard of rebellion in Hejaz, proclaimed independence from the Turks, and captured Mecca. In the fighting that followed, the Arab forces were commanded by the third son of Sherif Husein, Emir Faisal (1885–1933), who was assisted by a charismatic English officer, Colonel T. E. Lawrence (1888–1935), later known as Lawrence of Arabia.

Under Lawrence, the Arabs played a decisive role in the last battle against the main Turkish forces in September 1918. When World War I ended, Syria was occupied by the victorious Allied forces; a small French force was located along the coast of Lebanon; Emir Faisal and his Arab forces were in the interior, grouped around Damascus; and the British controlled Palestine.

A Flawed Peace

With Turkey defeated, the Arab leaders sought the independence they thought the British had promised in their correspondence with Husein. When the peace conference met in Paris, it became painfully clear that the problem of political settlement in the Middle East was a jumble of conflicting promises and rivalries.

A number of important commitments had been made during World War I, beginning with Britain's pledge to Sherif Husein in 1915. Britain, France, and Russia signed the secret Sykes-Picot Agreement in 1916. Under this pact, Syria and Iraq were divided into four zones with London and Paris each controlling two, and Russia gained parts of Asiatic Turkey. Palestine was to be placed under an international administration. The most important commitment bearing on the postwar history of the Middle East was Britain's declaration to the Jewish Zionist organization in 1917.

Jewish hopes to create a national home in Palestine grew rapidly after 1900. In 1903 a sympathetic British government had offered Theodore Herzl, the creator of the Zionist idea of a Jewish state, land in East Africa for a Jewish settlement. This proposal, however, had not been accepted. Following Herzl's death in 1904, the leadership of the Zionist movement had been assumed by Dr. Chaim Weizmann (1874–1952), a Russian Jew who had become a British subject. An intimate intellectual friendship developed between Weizmann and the English statesman Arthur James Balfour (1848–1930), who came to support the Zionist program. Balfour held a deep admiration for Jewish religious and cultural contributions. He believed that "Christian religion and civilization owed to Judaism a great debt and [one] shamefully repaid."[2]

During the course of World War I, the British government, strongly influenced by Balfour, then foreign secretary, became convinced that its support of a Zionist program in Palestine would not only be a humanitarian gesture but would also serve British imperial interests in the Middle East. Thus in November 1917 Britain issued the Balfour Declaration:

> *His Majesty's Government views with favour the establishment in Palestine of a national home for the Jewish people, and will use their best endeavors to facilitate the achievements of that object, it being clearly understood that nothing shall be done which may prejudice the civil and religious rights of existing non-Jewish communities in Palestine or the rights and political status enjoyed by Jews in any other country.*

Zionists were disappointed that the declaration did not unequivocally state that Palestine should be *the* national home for the Jewish people. In 1918 Great Britain made several declarations recognizing Palestinian national aspirations, and an Anglo-French pronouncement pledged the establishment of national governments "deriving their authority from the initiative and free choice of the indigenous populations."

At the Paris Peace Conference Emir Faisal, aided by Lawrence, pleaded the cause of Arab independence, but in vain. Faisal was still ruler in Damascus, and in March 1920, while the statesmen in Paris argued, a congress of Syrian leaders met and resolved that he should be king of a united Syria, including Palestine and Lebanon. But in April the San Remo Conference decided to turn over all Arab territories formerly in the Ottoman Empire to the Allied powers to be administered as mandates. Syria and Lebanon were mandated to France; Iraq and Palestine to Britain.

Mandated Areas

The Arabs saw the mandate system as a poor substitute for independence and a flimsy disguise for imperialism. The great powers were caught up in their web of conflicting aims and promises. Apologists for Britain and France pointed out that Britain made promises to France during the war because the British could hardly deny the requests of their most important ally, which had close missionary and educational ties to Syria. In 1915 Britain made its ambiguous pledge to Husein because of its desperate need for Arab friendship. In the Balfour Declaration, Britain acted according to short-range interests—to swing the support of the world's Jewish community to the Allied cause and to maintain communications in the Middle East.

It should be kept in mind that British statesmen sincerely believed that a Jewish national home could be reconciled with Palestinian interests. They had no idea of the massive influx of Jewish immigration that would come in the 1930s. The fact remains, however, that the Allied statesmen during the war and at the peace conference were profoundly unaware of the intensity of Arab nationalism.

Against strong Arab opposition, France took control of both Syria and neighboring Lebanon, which it separated into two mandates. Its regime harshly suppressed political liberties but did construct new roads, public buildings, and irrigation works. The Lebanese situation was especially complex. While its population was predominantly Arab, it was divided by many religious groups. Among the Christians there were ten different sects, the Maronites being the largest. There were also various Muslim groups, including the ultra-orthodox Druze. Rivalries between these faiths plagued the life and politics of the country.

In Iraq, Arab rebellion immediately confronted British mandatory rule, and the British moved rapidly to try to satisfy Iraqi nationalism. In 1920 Faisal was recognized as king, with Britain retaining control of the finances and military control of the new state. Ten years later Iraq gained its full independence. By these concessions, Britain avoided the conflict that France experienced with Arab nationalism in Syria and Lebanon.

Arab-Jewish Conflict

Between the two world wars, Palestine was the most complex area in the Middle East. Britain tried to protect its imperial interests and at the same time reconcile them with Zionist and Palestinian nationalism. Almost as soon as the mandate was set up, the Palestinians rioted.

In 1919 the population of Palestine was estimated to be 700,000, of which 568,000 were Palestinians. Of the remaining about 58,000 were Jews and 74,000 were others, mainly Christians. Recognizing the concerns of the Arabs, the British sought to define the Balfour Declaration more precisely. While not repudiating Palestine as a national home for the Jews, the British government declared that it "would never impose upon [the Palestinians] a policy which that people had reason to think was contrary to their religious, their political, and their economic interests."[3]

Such pronouncements and the fact that Jewish immigration was not large made possible a period of peace and progress from 1922 to 1929. As the Zionists reclaimed land, set up collective farms, harnessed the Jordan River for power, and established many new factories, a veritable economic revolution took place. Unfortunately, this brought little benefit to the Palestinian majority. Tel-Aviv grew into a thriving modern city, an

Memorandum of the General Syrian Congress

World War I and its destruction of the old empires paved the way for the rise of Arab nationalism. The memorandum of the General Syrian Congress sounded themes that would be heard throughout the twentieth century:

We the undersigned members of the General Syrian Congress, meeting in Damascus on Wednesday, July 2nd, 1919, made up of representatives from the three Zones, viz., The Southern, Eastern, and Western, provided with credentials and authorizations by the inhabitants of our various districts, Moslems, Christians, and Jews, have agreed upon the following statement of the desires of the people of the country who have elected us.

1. We ask absolutely complete political independence for Syria.
2. We ask that the Government of this Syrian country should be a democratic civil constitutional Monarchy on broad decentralization principles, safeguarding the rights of minorities, and that the King be the Emir Feisal, who carried on a glorious struggle in the cause of our liberation and merited our full confidence and entire reliance.
3. Considering the fact that the Arabs inhabiting the Syrian area are not naturally less gifted than other more advanced races and that they are by no means less developed than the Bulgarians, Serbians, Greeks, and Roumanians at the beginning of their independence, we protest against Article 22 of the Covenant of the League of Nations, placing us among the nations in their middle stage of development which stand in need of a mandatory power.
4. In the event of the rejection of the Peace Conference of this just protest for certain considerations that we may not understand, we, relying on the declarations of President Wilson that his object in waging war was to put an end to the ambition of conquest and colonization, can only regard the mandate mentioned in the Covenant of the League of Nations as equivalent to the rendering of economical and technical assistance that does not prejudice our complete independence. And desiring that our country should not fall a prey to colonization and believing that the American Nation is farthest from any thought of colonization and has no political ambition in our country, we will seek the technical and economic assistance from the United States of America, provided that such assistance does not exceed 20 years.
5. In the event of America not finding herself in a position to accept our desire for assistance, we will seek this assistance from Great Britain, also provided that such does not prejudice our complete independence and unity of our country and that the duration of such assistance does not exceed that mentioned in the previous article.
6. We do not acknowledge any right claimed by the French Government in any part whatever of our Syrian country and refuse that she should assist us or have a hand in our country under any circumstances and in any place.
7. We oppose the pretensions of the Zionists to create a Jewish commonwealth in the southern part of Syria, known as Palestine, and oppose Zionist migration to any part of our country; for we do not acknowledge their title but consider them a grave peril to our people from the national, economical, and political points of view. Our Jewish compatriots shall enjoy our common rights and assume the common responsibilities.

From *Foreign Relations of the United States: Paris Peace Conference*, vol. 12 (Washington, D.C.: Government Printing Office, 1919), pp. 780–781.

excellent university was founded at Jerusalem, and Palestine became the center of a Hebrew renaissance.

The era of peace ended in 1929 when serious disorders broke out, mainly Palestinian attacks on Jews. Violence continued in the early 1930s as the Nazi persecution of the Jews brought about a steep rise in immigration to Palestine and threatened the Palestinians' predominant position in the area. In 1937 a British commission of inquiry recommended a tripartite division: Palestine would be divided into two independent states, one controlled by the Palestinians and one by the Jews, with Britain holding a third portion, a small mandated area containing Jerusalem and Bethlehem. This recommendation satisfied no one and was not accepted.

Throughout the 1930s the "Palestine question" provoked heated discussion in many parts of the world. Zionists argued that Jews had a historic right to the Holy Land, their original home. They stated that Palestine had been promised to them in the Balfour Declaration and that the promise had been legalized by the League of Nations. They also pointed out that Jewish colonization constituted a democratic and progressive influence in the Middle East and that Palestinian hostility was mainly the work of a few wealthy *effendis,* since the mass of Palestinians were profiting from the wealth being brought into the area.

The Palestinians responded that Palestine had been their country for more than a thousand years and declared that the Balfour Declaration did not bind them because they had not been consulted in its formulation. They further insisted that much of Zionist economic development was not healthy because it depended on massive subsidization of outside capital. Finally, they asked how any people could be expected to stand idly by and watch an alien immigrant group be transformed from a minority into a majority.

With the threat of war looming in 1939, Britain sought desperately to regain Arab good will and thereby strengthen its position in the Middle East. A white paper was issued declaring that it was Britain's aim to have as an ally an independent Palestine, to be established at the end of ten years, with guarantees for both Palestinian and Jewish populations. During this ten-year period land sales were to be restricted. After the admission of 50,000 Jews, with the possibility of another 25,000 refugees from Nazi Germany, no more immigration would take place without the consent of the Palestinians. War between the two groups erupted in 1938, but the greater conflict of World War II shelved the quarrel in Palestine. The controversy would break out again with dire consequences.

Saudi Arabia, Iran, and North Africa

The defeat of Turkey in 1918 left several rival states contending for supremacy in the Arabian peninsula. Following some hostilities, ibn-Saud welded all tribal groups into the new kingdom of Saudi Arabia. The discovery of vast oil reserves gave it enormous wealth.

Persia (or Iran, as it came to be known in the 1920s), a land Muslim in religion but not Arabic in culture, came under the rule of Riza Shah Pahlavi (1878–1944) following World War I. The new shah rapidly followed the path of modernization, especially in the military and in industry, and pursued an independent path. Iran became caught up in the events surrounding World War II, and in August 1941 Riza Shah Pahlavi was

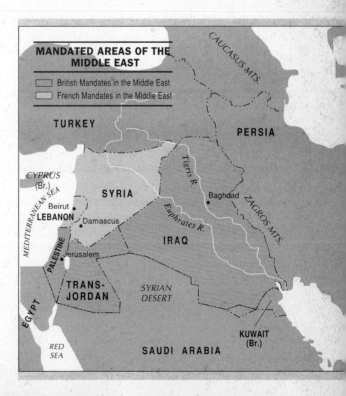

→ Riza Shah Pahlavi. As shah of Iran from 1925 to 1941, he modernized the country by strengthening its infrastructure.

forced out by the British and Russians and replaced by his more cooperative son, Mohamed Riza Pahlavi (1919–1980).

While the Muslims in the Asian part of the Islamic band of countries struggled for the right of self-determination, a parallel development was taking place in North Africa. After three years of disorder in Egypt, the British government announced that Egypt would no longer be a protectorate of Britain. It was to be a sovereign state. However, Britain remained responsible for defense of the country, protection of foreign interests, and the Suez Canal—an essential link in the British Empire's communications. Egypt grudgingly accepted this declaration, made its sultan a king, and proclaimed a constitution in 1923. Anglo-Egyptian relations remained unsettled, however, until 1936, when common fear of Mussolini's Italy brought the two nations together in a defense treaty.

In North Africa, economies prospered and living standards advanced under French colonial rule. Algeria had become politically integrated with France long before World War I. Tunisia, which prospered under French rule, had maintained its native ruler, the bey. Similarly, in the French Moroccan protectorate, the native sultan had been retained. Nevertheless, the storm signals of bitter nationalism appeared in North Africa, particularly in Morocco. A fundamental split existed between the privileged French Christian minority and the overwhelming Muslim majority.

Mustafa Kemal and the New Turkey

Forty years before the war, the Young Turks had sought to establish a modern secular state. In 1908 they began to implement their dreams. However, defeat in the war and the Arab revolt convinced some Turkish patriots that only the most drastic measures, such as the massacre of more than 700,000 Armenians in 1915, could save their country. In addition, they bitterly rejected the Treaty of Sèvres (1920). It was bad enough to lose their empire, but it was much worse to see their homeland—namely Anatolia—partitioned and the city of Smyrna (Izmir) invaded by the Greeks.

The patriots rallied around the military hero Mustafa Kemal (1880–1938), who had a brilliant record against the British imperial forces at Gallipoli in World War I. An important figure in the Young Turks movement, Kemal was a born leader, thoroughly Western in outlook and education. After the defeat of Turkey, he had been sent by the sultan to demobilize the Turkish troops in Asia Minor. Disregarding instructions, he reorganized the troops and successfully defied the Allies. A new government was set up in Ankara and Kemal was selected as president and commander in chief. The National Pact, a declaration of principles supported by Kemal, galvanized Turkish patriotism. This document upheld self-determination for all peoples, including the Turks, and proclaimed the abolition of the special rights previously enjoyed by foreigners in Turkey.

In 1921 Kemal's armies blocked Greek designs on Turkish land. The following year, the sultanate was abolished and a republic was established. The Allies agreed to a revision of the Treaty of Sèvres, and the Treaty of Lausanne, signed in 1923, returned to Turkey some Aegean islands and

As president of the Turkish republic from its beginning until his death in 1938, Mustafa Kemal instituted many civil and cultural reforms. In 1934 he was given the name Atatürk ("father of Turks").

territory adjoining Constantinople (Istanbul). The Turkish heartland, Anatolia, remained intact, and no reparations were demanded.

The new constitution was democratic in form, but in reality, Kemal was a dictator who tolerated no interference with his plans. In the new Turkey there was little of the cult of the superior race and no concentration camps or purges. There was just the rule of a single individual in a situation where rough, efficient power was seen to be superior to that of the more lengthy processes of parliamentary rule. Kemal saw his dictatorial rule as a necessary stage in raising his people to that level of education and social well-being that democratic government and parliamentary rule require. Under his rule the old institutions and customs of a backward state were transformed or replaced within a few years.

AFRICA: FROM COLONIALISM TO NATIONALISM

After 1890 the Europeans organized and consolidated their colonial possessions in sub-Saharan Africa. They mapped previously unknown areas, defined boundaries, and set up railroads and communications systems. The improvement of indigenous products such as rubber and palm oil, the introduction of new cash crops such as cotton and cocoa, and the importation of better breeds of cattle enriched the African economies. The colonialists placed forestry on a scientific basis, opened diamond, gold, and tin mines, and rapidly increased trade throughout Africa. European settlement also increased, especially in the highland areas.

The Europeans exported their systems of bureaucracy and tried to stamp out intertribal warfare, cannibalism, and dangerous secret societies. They opened educational facilities, primarily through the churches, and began the laborious task of transcribing the native tongues to become written languages. The colonial governments introduced clinics, hospitals, and sanitation campaigns to improve public health. Meanwhile, agricultural and veterinary officers taught the Africans methods of fighting erosion, securing better seed, using fertilizers, and managing their herds more efficiently.

In the two decades following World War I European culture and technology spread throughout Africa, affecting all parts of the continent in varying degrees. While in some isolated bush areas tribes lived in Neolithic isolation, in the new cities many Africans led lives almost wholly European, at least in externals. Under colonial rule, Africans had to obey the laws and regulations of white administrators as well as those of their tribal councils and chiefs. To pay for better roads, public buildings, health and agricultural departments, taxes now had to be paid in cash, forcing many Africans to seek employment outside of their tribal areas in the towns and mines, through menial domestic or governmental service, or on plantations. Habits of living changed, new styles of dress were adopted, and new farming methods designed to produce cash crops were introduced. The desire to buy imported goods grew.

Contacts with European modes of life rapidly undermined old faiths, customs, tribal loyalties, and social institutions—a process known as detribalization. The Africans belonged neither to their old tribal world nor to the white world. No longer bound by tribal laws, they were uneasy about the courts and the law of the Europeans. While accepting Christian doctrine, they retained

→ After World War I, a new wave of liberal thinking and the League of Nations mandate system produced new efforts to improve the standard of living (measured by European standards) for Africans by building hospitals, libraries, and schools. The schools, like that shown here in the Congo, were run by Europeans and taught European, rather than African, history and culture.

their belief in the powers of tribal deities. No matter what the benefits of imperial rule might have been, it was paternal at its best and exploitative at its worst. Perhaps it was necessary and perhaps desirable that Africa be brought into the mainstream of the modern world, but it was a profoundly disruptive experience.

Colonial Rule

While colonial systems of administration varied, few Africans were allowed to participate in the important aspects of colonial government. In British and French colonies, a modicum of training in self-government was available to a small minority. In British Nigeria, one of the most advanced colonies in terms of political participation, the Legislative Council of 46 members in 1922 included 10 Africans, 4 of whom were elected. These were the first elected Africans in the legislatures of British tropical Africa.

The colonial policies of Portugal and Belgium between 1914 and 1939 differed from those of Britain and France in important ways. Belgium had virtually no colonial policy in the Congo, a territory more than three times the size of Texas with vast mineral wealth. Belgian officials ran a day-to-day, efficient economic system with little thought of ultimate objectives. Race relations were relatively harmonious, and the color bar was generally mild. The main emphasis was placed on the material improvement of the Africans and the development of valuable exports. Excellent medical services were provided together with the best system of elementary education in tropical Africa. There was, however, little secondary training, and university education was nonexistent. White settlement was not encouraged and the few thousand nonofficials who worked in the Congo were denied any voice in its political affairs. During the two decades after 1919, Belgium prided itself on the success of this paternal rule. It had created a population of artisans, mechanics, medical assistants, and clerks devoid of any dangerous thoughts of self-government.

The territories of Angola and Mozambique were constitutionally part of Portugal, so any ideas of separation and self-determination were unthinkable. The most backward in Africa, these territories stagnated in part because of Portugal's poverty and an exploitative administration. In early years, the territories were poorly staffed and badly governed. Their officials were described as "spending their time collecting taxes and mistresses."[4]

In theory, Portugal's objective was to develop an integrated society. Once Africans became assimilated, they would become Portuguese citizens with full voting rights. To become assimilated, they had to become Christian (Roman Catholic), practice monogamy, and learn to speak and write Portuguese. Above all, they had to learn "the dignity of labor." While this colonial system often referred to its "civilizing mission" in Africa, reality and practice fell far short. In Mozambique, for example, out of a population of 6 million, only some 5,000 had become legally assimilated. The white population grew slowly, in the 1930s numbering only about 30,000 in Angola and some 18,000 in Mozambique. Many of the immigrants were poor and untrained, and a considerable number "went native"—ending up in African bush villages. The most admirable feature was the absence of any color bar. The most deplorable aspect of Portuguese colonial rule was its extensive use of forced labor, frequently accompanied by cruel punishments, for the benefit of private business.

Mandate Administration

As a result of growing liberal sentiments and opposition to imperialism, all territories conquered by the Allies in World War I were declared to be mandates. Article XXII of the League of Nations Covenant stated that the "well-being and development" of backward colonial lands was a "sacred trust of civilization." In essence, the mandate system was a compromise between annexation of the spoils of war by the victors (although the mandatory powers were never accorded any sovereign rights over the mandates) and establishment of an international trusteeship. Parts of the Cameroons, Togoland, and German East Africa (Tanganyika) were to be administered by Great Britain. The remaining portions of the Cameroons and Togoland became French-administered mandates. Belgium received the mandate of Rwanda-Burundi (also a part of German East Africa), while the former German colony of Southwest Africa was allotted to the Union of South Africa.

The Permanent Mandates Commission inspected the annual reports the mandatory governments submitted. While the commission had no effective power to improve unsatisfactory conditions in a mandate, it could place the matter before the eyes of the world. On numerous occasions the mandatory powers accepted the criticisms and heeded the suggestions and criticisms of the commission.

Judgments of the mandate system, a radically new concept in colonial administration, have differed widely. To many critics, international supervision was a unique invasion of national sovereignty. To others, the Permanent Mandate Commission did not have enough power, especially the right to send its own observers into the mandated areas.

"New Britains" Kenya and Rhodesia

Few Europeans lived in the French and British colonies of West Africa, and even they did not think of themselves as permanent settlers. Most returned home for retirement to escape the inhospitable climate. Such was not the case in British East and Central Africa, however, where Kenya and Rhodesia experienced the last thrust of European colonialism.

Although located on the equator, Kenya's highland area, which ranges from 6000 to 9000 feet above sea level, has a cool and bracing climate. With the British government's encouragement, the first settlers arrived in 1903, securing rich farmland in the interior. They attempted to make Kenya a white country, although the

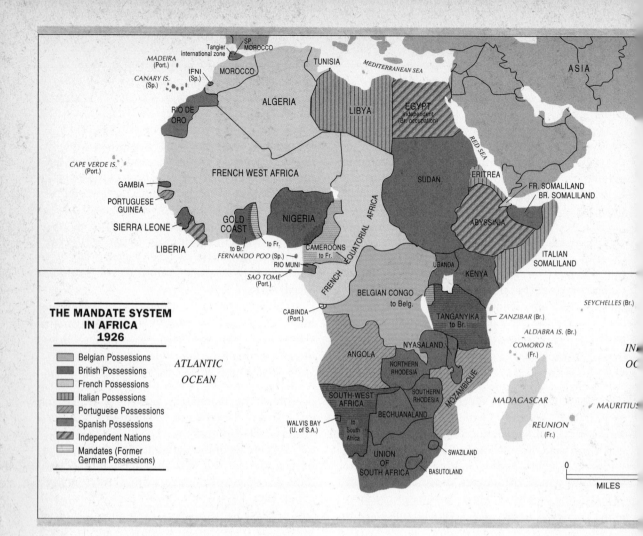

THE MANDATE SYSTEM
IN AFRICA
1926

Belgian Possessions
British Possessions
French Possessions
Italian Possessions
Portuguese Possessions
Spanish Possessions
Independent Nations
Mandates (Former German Possessions)

majority of the population was African. That was the goal of Lord Delamere, the leader of the white settlers, who wrote:

> In East Africa, England has possessed herself of a miniature new dominion, a little New Zealand tucked away between deserts and tropics and lakes, where yet another cutting from the British parent stock could be planted and would grow and flourish.[5]

Nairobi, the capital, became a modern city. New methods of agriculture and stock raising were introduced, which were later to form the basis of prosperity for a new black African nation. White settlement lagged, however, and by 1939 there were only 18,000 Europeans as compared with 3 million Africans. The rapid development of black nationalism in the 1930s made it obvious that Kenya would ultimately obtain self-government, not for the white settlers but for the Africans.

To the south, in central Africa, another attempt to establish a British outpost was in the making. With the support of Cecil Rhodes, white immigrants began entering the region known as Rhodesia in the 1890s. The country had rich mineral and agricultural resources, and its white population increased more rapidly than in Kenya. Britain granted self-government to the area in 1923, subject to British retention of certain powers relating to the rights of the African majority.

By 1931 the population of Rhodesia consisted of 50,000 whites and 1 million Africans. The European community, whose numbers were growing slowly, controlled the country's best land

and resources as well as its government. As the country developed economically and race relations remained calm, Europeans in the late 1930s were optimistic about their dominant role. The stormy days of the 1970s, with their militant rise of African nationalism, lay ahead.

White Exploitation in the Union of South Africa

South Africa was the most explosive area in the interwar period. Here African discontent was the deepest and the breakdown of traditional ways of life was the most widespread. Within the white population, the Dutch (called Boers) were rivals of the British settlers. Since 1902 when Britain defeated the two Boer republics, there had been tension between victors and vanquished.

United in 1909, the country had become a self-governing dominion in the British Commonwealth. But this union did not bring cooperation between the two dominant white groups, beyond enshrining segregation in law, in a series of enactments between 1910 and 1913. In 1914 one Boer faction staged an unsuccessful rebellion against South Africa's participation in "England's war." Partnership between Boers and Britons continued to be strained into the 1930s. Even though the Boers gained official recognition of their language, Afrikaans (developed mainly from seventeenth-century Dutch), they continued to insist on their own flag and national anthem.

Constantly they discussed secession from the Commonwealth.

Although the rift between Britons and Boers was serious, even more dangerous was the increasing numerical gap between all Europeans on the one hand and the native population on the other. After World War I, the Europeans began to eye the statistics nervously. There were 5.5 million Africans in the Union and 1.8 million whites—just under 50 percent of them of British stock. In addition, there were 200,000 Asians and 600,000 "coloured." Fearful of being overwhelmed by sheer numbers, many whites became convinced that the blacks had to be kept separate from the European community socially and politically, and that all political control must remain in the hands of the Europeans.

Segregation and the color bar continued to spread rapidly in the 1920s and 1930s. Africans were restricted to their tribal reserves. Only those who obtained special permission could work on farms owned by Europeans or in the cities, and in urban areas they were obliged to live in squalid, segregated "locations." If found without their passes and identity cards, they were subject to arrest and fine or imprisonment. Native labor unions were discouraged and strikes forbidden. In addition, governmental regulations of the white labor unions excluded Africans from certain skilled trades.

Uneducated Europeans, the so-called poor whites, found it hard to make a living, compet-

→ In the rich gold mines of South Africa, whites held relatively high-paying, skilled jobs while native workers received miserable wages for the grueling tasks they performed, like drilling veins in the cramped tunnels of the mines.

ing, as they did, with the black majority, which would work for pathetically low wages for limited jobs. To support the "poor whites" the white government passed laws allocating to them certain jobs with inflated wages on the railroads and in city services. Special subsidies, drawn from taxes on the entire population, paid for these jobs. This discriminatory practice resulted in huge wage disparities, the average wage for Europeans being just under $4 a day, while that for the African was just over $3 a week. Africans were also excluded from politics. They could not vote or hold office in any influential elective body or parliament outside their own tribal reserves.

The pressures of increasing population in the reserves forced Africans to seek their livelihood outside. By 1936 more than 1 million Africans worked in white urban areas; another 2 million worked on European farms. About 3.5 million remained on the tribal reserves, which were neglected or impoverished. African unrest manifested itself in the increasing crime rate in the cities, in the formation of underground organizations, and in efforts to work for political rights. In the back alleys and cellars of Johannesburg and other cities, young Africans ran mimeograph machines, turning out handbills and papers advertising their grievances.

In spite of the political and social unrest, the country experienced substantial economic progress, as did much of sub-Saharan Africa, where by the early 1930s outside investments totaled nearly $5 billion. In South Africa agricultural production soared, together with mining products such as gold and diamonds. Africans, however, had little share in this economic progress.

Pan-Africanism and African Nationalism

All over Africa, opposition to imperialism grew throughout the war years. The fact that Europeans were killing one another on the battlefields did much to weaken white prestige. At the Paris Peace Conference, Wilson's ideology with its message of self-determination found a ready response among African intellectuals. Black leaders in the United States demanded greater recognition of rights for blacks, especially in Africa, and argued that the peace conference should help form an internationalized, free Africa. Dr. W. E. B. Du Bois (1868–1963), one of the organizers of the National Association for the Advancement of Colored People (NAACP) and editor of the influential newspaper *Crisis*, proposed the nucleus for a state of some 20 million people, guided by an international organization.

In 1919 Du Bois and other black leaders from the United States traveled to Paris to present their ideas in person to the delegates at the

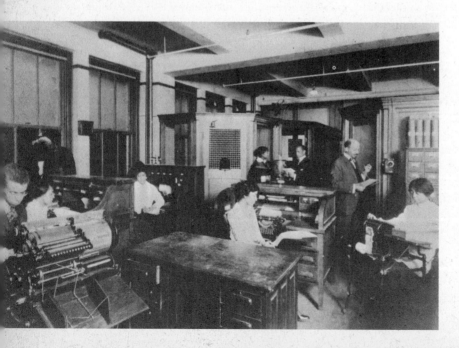

→ W. E. B. Du Bois, shown here (standing at far right) in the editorial offices of the *Crisis*, was the pioneer advocate of the Pan-African movement.

peace conference. While there, Du Bois was instrumental in convening a Pan-African Congress with representatives from 15 countries. The gathering urged that the former German colonies be placed under an international agency, rather than under the rule of one of the victorious colonial powers, such as Britain.

Complementing the sentiments expressed at the Pan-African Congress were the ideals of black nationalism. In a convention held in New York in 1920, the members issued the Declaration of Rights of the Negro Peoples of the World. This document protested race discrimination in the United States and the "inhuman, unchristian, and uncivilized treatment" of Africans in the colonial empires. Frustrated by the patronizing attitudes of Christian missionaries, many Africans founded their own churches, based on the doctrine of the "fatherhood of God and the brotherhood of man regardless of color or creed."[6]

Africans in most colonies formed nationalist groups, but they were largely ineffectual. The most important center for nationalist aspirations was in London, where a group of Nigerian students organized. African rights groups existed in South Africa, but the white government there was already perfecting its method of police repression that was to be so effective throughout the twentieth century.

Closely connected with Pan-Africanism and black nationalism was the movement among black intellectuals to recover and rediscover the African past. Relatively little was known about the religious systems, tribal organization, and agriculture of sub-Saharan Africa. Students of social anthropology, a new branch of the social sciences, took field trips to Africa as the interest in African life and culture spread among anthropologists, missionaries, and learned societies. New discoveries made it clear that Africa's comparative backwardness was due in large part to disease and isolation. The International Institute of African Languages and Cultures was organized in 1926. It was claimed with some justification that this project opened up a new era of international cooperation in the service of Africa. New departments in African studies were set up in various universities, and a small number of Africanists began to be trained in the United States.

Perhaps the most significant consequence of colonialism was the emergence of a small nucleus of African intellectuals, who took advantage of scattered educational opportunities and rare chances for study abroad, mainly in Britain, France, and the United States. The most prominent among this group of indigenous African leaders included Jomo Kenyatta (c. 1894–1978) of Kenya, Leopold Sedar Senghor (b. 1906) of Senegal, Kwame Nkrumah (1909–1972) of the Gold Coast (Ghana), and Benjamin Azikwe from Nigeria. It was largely from their ranks that the future leaders of independent Africa were recruited.

CONCLUSION

Between the two world wars, imperialism went on the defensive before the rise of nationalism in the non-Western world. In the opening decades of the twentieth century, Japan made amazing progress in industrialization and attempted to introduce a democratic system of government. By 1919 the island nation had become one of the world's leading powers. Its spectacular rise to power was accompanied by serious demographic and resource problems that endangered the weakly rooted democratic forces.

Although China was not, strictly speaking, part of the colonial world, in many ways this vast land was under the indirect influence of the great powers. Chinese Nationalists, under the leadership of Sun Yat-sen, overthrew the Manchu Dynasty and established a republic. After years of confusion and conflict among rival factions, Chiang Kai-shek consolidated power in the *Kuomintang* regime. A nascent Chinese Communist movement, under Mao Tse-tung, survived the efforts of the Chinese Nationalists to destroy it.

The strongest nationalist movement was that in India, under the leadership of Mohandas Gandhi. He preached a message of nonviolence and civil disobedience to force Britain to grant a substantial measure of self-government to the Indians. In the lands formerly controlled by the Ottomans, Arab nationalists bitterly contested European control in the mandated areas. Outbreaks of violence occurred in Palestine, where the Arabs resented the British attempt to set up a national home for the Jews.

In Africa, black nationalists sought to replace colonial rule with self-government and to bring about the cultural resurgence of a people whose way of life was slowly disintegrating in the face of Western imperialism. The Pan-African movement did not affect the masses of the people in most areas; only in the troubled multiracial society of South Africa was there widespread unrest among Africans.

→ Suggestions for Reading

For an overview, see P. Welty, *The Asians: Their Heritage and Their Destiny* (Lippincott, 1973). Thorough coverage of Japan is provided in E. O. Reischauer, *Japan: The Story of a Nation* (Knopf, 1974) and Takashi Fuktake, *The Japanese Social Structure: Its Evolution in the Modern Century* (Univ. of Tokyo, 1982). For a detailed description of how the military extremists undermined parliamentary government in Japan, see Richard Storry, *The Double Patriots: A Story of Japanese Nationalism* (Greenwood, 1973). Economic pressures in internal Japan are discussed in James Morley, ed., *Dilemmas of Growth in Prewar Japan* (Princeton Univ., 1971).

J. K. Fairbank and K. C. Liu, *The Cambridge History of China*, XII, "Republican China 1912–1949" (Cambridge Univ., 1983) is the essential starting point for pre-Mao China. For a solid analysis of the four decades of revolution in China see Lucien Bianco, *Origins of the Chinese Revolution* (Stanford Univ., 1971). See also Edward Friedman's study on Sun Yat-sen, *Backward Toward Revolution* (Univ. of California, 1974). Stuart Schram, ed. *Mao Tse-tung Unrehearsed* (Penguin, 1974) is a good selection of the Chairman's thoughts. D. G. E. Hall, *A History of Southeast Asia* (St. Martin's, 1968) and H. J. Berda and J. A. Larkin, *The World of Southeast Asia* (Harper & Row, 1967) provide good general coverage of the area.

For invaluable studies of the architects of Indian nationalism see K. Kripalani, *Gandhi: A Life* (Verry, 1968); E. Thomson, *Rabindranath Tagore* (Greenwood, 1975); and M. C. Rau, *Jawaharlal Nehru* (Interculture, 1975). See also B. R. Nanda, *Gokhale, Gandhi, and the Nehrus: Studies in Indian Nationalism* (St. Martin's, 1975).

See S. N. Fisher, *The Middle East: A History* (Knopf, 1968) for a comprehensive outline of forces and events. A short history of the Jewish people is Abba Eban, *My Country* (Random House, 1972). See also B. Halpern, *The Idea of the Jewish State* (Harvard Univ., 1969). An analysis of Arab changes is presented in M. Halpern, *The Politics of Social Charge in the Middle East and North Africa* (Princeton Univ., 1967). On the impact of Westernization in Turkey see Bernard Lewis, *The Emergence of Modern Turkey* (Oxford Univ., 1968). See also studies by S. H. Longrigg: *Syria and Lebanon under French Mandate* (Octagon, 1972) and *Iraq, 1900 to 1950* (Verry, 1972). Ann M. Lesch's *Arab Politics in Palestine* (Cornell Univ., 1979) traces the rise of Arab nationalism in Palestine. A clear summary of developments in the Middle East is M. E. Yapp, *The Near East Since the First World War* (Longman, 1991).

An astute observer surveying Africa as it was before World War II is John Hatch, *Africa Emergent* (Regnery, 1974). See also C. G. Segre, *Fourth Shore: The Italian Colonization of Libya* (Univ. of Chicago, 1975); Michael Crowder, *West Africa Under Colonial Rule* (Northwestern Univ., 1968); and W. Cartey and M. Kilson, eds., *The Africa Reader I, Colonial Africa* (Vintage, 1970). Robin Hallett gives a solid survey in *Africa Since 1875* (Univ. of Michigan, 1974).

→ Notes

1. J. Nehru, *Toward Freedom* (New York: John Day, 1942), p. 353.
2. Quoted in Blanche E. C. Dugdale, *Arthur James Balfour* (New York: G. P. Putnam's Sons, 1937), p. 325.
3. Quoted in Hans Kohn, *Nationalism and Imperialism in the Hither East* (London: G. Routledge and Sons, 1932), pp. 132–133.
4. Robin Hallett, *Africa Since 1875* (Ann Arbor: University of Michigan Press, 1974), p. 51.
5. Quoted in T. Walter Wallbank, "British East Africa—A Case Study in Modern Imperialism," *World Affairs Interpreter*, Autumn 1983, p. 293.
6. Robert I. Rotberg, *A Political History of Tropical Africa* (New York: Harcourt Brace Jovanovich, 1965), p. 341.

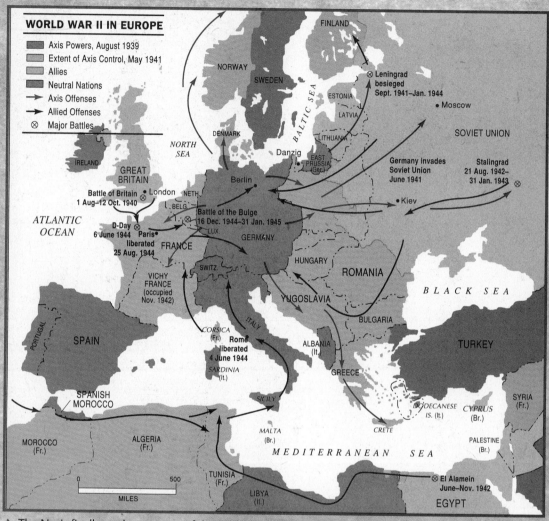

CHAPTER 33

WORLD WAR II IN EUROPE

- ■ Axis Powers, August 1939
- ■ Extent of Axis Control, May 1941
- ■ Allies
- ■ Neutral Nations
- → Axis Offenses
- → Allied Offenses
- ⊗ Major Battles

FINLAND

NORWAY

SWEDEN

Leningrad besieged
Sept. 1941–Jan. 1944

ESTONIA

LATVIA

• Moscow

LITHUANIA

SOVIET UNION

NORTH SEA

DENMARK

Danzig

EAST PRUSSIA (Ger.)

Germany invades Soviet Union June 1941

Stalingrad
21 Aug. 1942–
31 Jan. 1943 ⊗

IRELAND

GREAT BRITAIN

Berlin

• Kiev

Battle of Britain ⊗
1 Aug.–12 Oct. 1940

• London

NETH.

ATLANTIC OCEAN

BELG.

Battle of the Bulge
16 Dec. 1944–31 Jan. 1945

D-Day ⊗
6 June 1944

Paris•
liberated
25 Aug. 1944

FRANCE

LUX.

GERMANY

HUNGARY

ROMANIA

BLACK SEA

VICHY FRANCE (occupied Nov. 1942)

SWITZ.

YUGOSLAVIA

BULGARIA

TURKEY

SPAIN

PORTUGAL

CORSICA (Fr.)

Rome
liberated
4 June 1944

ITALY

ALBANIA (It.)

GREECE

SARDINIA (It.)

SPANISH MOROCCO

SICILY

DODECANESE IS. (It.)

CYPRUS (Br.)

SYRIA (Fr.)

CRETE

PALESTINE (Br.)

MOROCCO (Fr.)

ALGERIA (Fr.)

MALTA (Br.)

MEDITERRANEAN SEA

0   500
MILES

TUNISIA (Fr.)

LIBYA (It.)

El Alamein ⊗
June–Nov. 1942

EGYPT

BALTIC SEA

→ The Nazis finally made a success of the Schlieffen Plan in 1940. Aided by the Molotov-Ribbentrop Pact of the previous August, the Germans ripped through the Low Countries and France. The Maginot line proved totally useless in World War II.

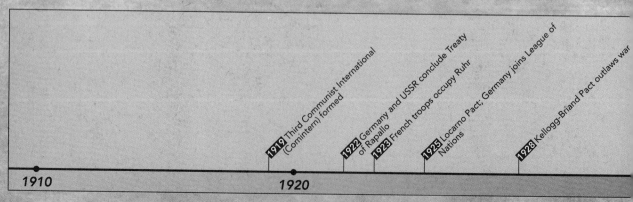

1919 Third Communist International (Comintern) formed

1922 Germany and USSR conclude Treaty of Rapallo

1923 French troops occupy Ruhr

1925 Locarno Pact; Germany joins League of Nations

1928 Kellogg-Briand Pact outlaws war

1910   1920

Diplomatic Failure and World War II, 1920–1945

In the first decade after World War I, statesmen with global vision made serious attempts to control conflict through international organizations and treaties limiting arms and outlawing war. In the 1930s, however, the competition among states resumed its traditionally violent course. Ambitious dictators made war in Asia, Africa, and Europe, while representatives from the democracies tried to reason with them.

From 1939 to 1945 the Second World War, with its new and horrible technologies, ravaged the globe. Large bombers took the war to civilians hundreds of miles behind what used to be known as the front lines. Hitler made use of industrial technology to try to destroy an entire people. Only a massive counterattack by the Allied powers, capped by the use of the atomic bomb in Japan, brought an end to the fighting.

THE TROUBLED CALM: THE 1920S

The aftershocks of the First World War overwhelmed the interwar period. The horror, expense, and exhaustion of the tragedy dominated the losers and winners alike. The better part of a

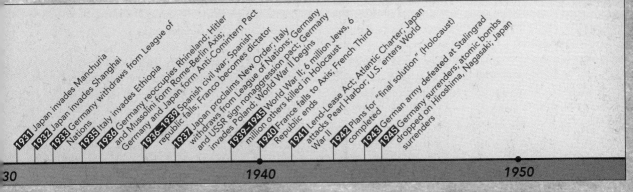

1931 Japan invades Manchuria

1932 Japan invades Shanghai

1933 Germany withdraws from League of Nations

1935 Italy invades Ethiopia

1936 Germany reoccupies Rhineland; Hitler and Mussolini form Rome-Berlin Axis; Germany and Japan form Anti-Comintern Pact

1936–1939 Spanish civil war; Spanish republic falls, Franco becomes dictator

1937 Japan proclaims New Order; Italy withdraws from League of Nations; Germany and USSR sign nonaggression pact; Germany invades Poland; World War II begins

1939–1945 World War II; 6 million Jews, 6 million others killed in Holocaust

1940 France falls to Axis; French Third Republic ends

1941 Lend-Lease Act; Atlantic Charter; Japan attacks Pearl Harbor; U.S. enters World War II

1942 Plans for "final solution" (Holocaust) completed

1943 German army defeated at Stalingrad

1945 Germany surrenders; atomic bombs dropped on Hiroshima, Nagasaki; Japan surrenders

30   1940   1950

young generation had died. Political leadership fell either to the old who had gained authority before 1914 or to the untried young. It was in this uncertain environment that the League of Nations began its work.

The League of Nations

The League's record from 1919 to 1929 was one neither of dismal failure nor of complete triumph. Such threats to peace as disputes between Sweden and Finland and between Britain and Turkey were resolved. When a major power defied the League, however, as in the case of Italy's quarrel with Greece over Corfu, the organization could do nothing. The refusal of the United States, the world's strongest democracy, to join weakened the League's peacekeeping possibilities.

Through no fault of the League's, little progress was made in the field of disarmament. On one occasion, perhaps because of its relative weakness, Russia proposed complete disarmament. The British delegates, among others, were suspicious of Russia's sincerity in wanting to surround the world in a "loving embrace."[1] The member-states' firmly rooted feelings of mutual distrust and fear of losing sovereignty hurt the League's ability to keep the peace.

However, the League had a distinguished list of accomplishments in other areas. It supervised the exchange and repatriation of prisoners of war and saved thousands of refugees from starvation. It helped Austria, Bulgaria, and Hungary to secure badly needed loans. The League also provided valuable service in administering the region of the Saar Basin and the Free City of Danzig. It investigated the existence of slavery in certain parts of the world, sought to control traffic in dangerous drugs, and stood ready to offer assistance when disasters brought suffering and destruction.

In the intellectual and cultural realm the League published books and periodicals dealing with national and international problems of all kinds and from its own radio station broadcast important information, particularly in the field of health. Unfortunately, the League's excellent record in these areas has been obscured by its failure to maintain a lasting peace.

→ The Senate's refusal to ratify the Treaty of Versailles meant that the United States would not join the League of Nations.

France Seeks Security

Because the United States chose to play a limited role in international affairs and Great Britain returned to its traditional focus on the empire and Commonwealth, France assumed the leadership of postwar Europe. In 1919 the French pursued a very simple, but difficult, foreign policy goal—absolute security. Since the Napoleonic grandeur a century earlier, the French had seen their power and authority diminish while German economic and military strength had increased. Twice in 50 years Germany had invaded France, with terrible results.

France spent much of the postwar decade trying to guarantee its own safety by keeping Germany weak. In the first five years after the armistice the French wanted to impose maximum financial penalties on the Germans. In 1923, assisted by the Belgians, they occupied the

Ruhr region in a move that had immense short- and long-range implications. Some historians have seen in this act the first step toward World War II because it hardened the German desire for revenge. Even though the Dawes Plan eased the situation, the French attitude divided the former Allies and provided ammunition to German ultranationalists.

The rift between the French and Germans was papered over in Locarno, Switzerland, in 1925. In the Locarno Pact, Germany, Great Britain, France, and Italy agreed to guarantee the existing frontiers along the Rhine, to establish a demilitarized zone 50 kilometers deep along the east bank of the Rhine, and to refrain from attacking one another. The problems along France's eastern frontier would be dealt with by international guarantee (although the British dominions stated their disagreement) and U.S. money. Germany received, and accepted, an invitation to join the League of Nations, a symbolic act that seemed to indicate its return to the international community. Still, the Locarno Pact addressed only the western frontier of Germany and left unresolved the controversial issues of the territories of the newly formed and contentious nations of eastern Europe. Another well-meaning but ultimately ineffectual agreement was the Kellogg-Briand Pact (1928), developed by U.S. Secretary of State Frank Kellogg and French Foreign Minister Aristide Briand. This pact, which was eventually signed by 62 nations, outlawed war as an instrument of national policy, but omitted provisions to enforce the agreement.

The Paris government had little faith in the Covenant of the League of Nations as a guarantee of France's survival. The French instead depended more and more on their own diplomats. They tried to construct a wall of allies along Germany's eastern frontier that would simultaneously surround the Germans and isolate the Soviet Union. While Germany was weak and dependent on Western loans, France could stand as the strongest diplomatic power on the continent. But even in the 1920s, France lacked the strength to serve as the leader of Europe. When Germany and Italy began to flex their muscles in the 1930s, France—even with British help—faced fascist aggression from a position of weakness.

Soviet and German Cooperation

The Soviet Union and Germany, the two diplomatic outcasts of the 1920s, quickly forged a working relationship that was useful to both of them. The USSR had isolated itself by signing the Treaty of Brest-Litovsk, nationalizing foreign property, and repudiating foreign debts as well as by its communist ideology. Probably the greatest barrier was the ideological one, as expressed through the activities of the Third Communist International, or Comintern. That body, organized in 1919, was dedicated to the overthrow of capitalism throughout the world.

In the 1920s the Comintern spread communist propaganda, established communist parties, and infiltrated labor unions and other working class groups throughout the world. Even after Lenin had given up hope for an immediate world revolution and started to normalize relations with the West, the Comintern encouraged radicals who had broken off from moderate socialist groups to organize communist parties. Communists of all countries became members of the Comintern, meeting in congresses held in Moscow and setting up committees to coordinate their activities. Communist parties were different from other national political groups because they owed their allegiance to an international organization rather than to the nations in which they resided.

By 1922 the Soviet Union was pursuing a two-pronged foreign policy. One approach used the communist parties abroad to achieve ideological goals, as in China, where the communists were active until defeated by Chiang Kai-shek in 1927. The other approach worked through normal international channels for traditional economic and diplomatic goals, generally in Europe.

From the time Lenin left Switzerland to return to Petrograd, the Soviet Union enjoyed a mutually advantageous relationship with Germany. At the beginning of the 1920s the two nations carried on secret agreements allowing for joint military training enterprises. Their first major open diplomatic contact came at Rapallo, Italy, in 1922, where they renounced the concept of reparations. In the Rapallo pact, the Germans and Russians agreed to cooperate in a number of areas. Germany was extremely bitter about the treatment it had received at Versailles; the

→ An illustration from the French satirical magazine *Le Rire* shows Italian King Victor Emmanuel III greeting Georgi Vasilievich Chicherin, the Soviet commissar for foreign affairs, at Genoa in 1922. Chicherin negotiated the Treaty of Rapallo with Germany, the pact which renounced the war indemnities resulting from the peace settlements at Versailles following World War I and pledged Germany and the Soviet Union to cooperation in a number of areas, including military training.

Soviets had faced Allied intervention during the civil war. It naturally followed that a main feature of the foreign policies of both countries would be either to ignore the Versailles settlement or to escape from its consequences. Both countries shared the ambition to dominate Poland, against whom the USSR had fought at the beginning of the decade.

Although, as Lenin perceptively noted, Russia wanted revolution while Germany sought revenge, the two nations cooperated closely until 1934. Then, after a five-year gap, they cooperated again in the Nazi-Soviet nonaggression pact.

The Weimar government under Gustav Stresemann wanted to rearm but was forbidden to do so by the Versailles treaty. Stresemann backed

the cooperation between his government and the Soviet Union to build up German military might. Berlin supplied technical aid to the USSR while German pilots and specialists went on maneuver in Russia. Even after the proclamation of the so-called spirit of Locarno, the two nations worked with each other. In 1926 the Rapallo pact was renewed for another five years.

THE EPOCH OF THE AGGRESSORS

The world found little peace or stability after the First World War. Economic and social discontent buttressed by widespread disillusionment with the peace treaties posed grave problems for the victorious Allies. Almost as weak as the defeated powers, the Allies had to take on the responsibility for maintaining the peace. The awful toll taken by World War I convinced the democracies that never again should humanity have to endure such a tragedy. From the point of view of the new aggressors, however, this attitude reflected weakness and cowardice—and opportunity.

Japan Invades Manchuria

The first challenge to the fragile peace occurred in September 1931, when Japan moved into the traditional Chinese buffer zone of Manchuria. In occupying this region, Tokyo pursued centuries-old goals made more urgent by present-day pressures of resource scarcity and overpopulation. The Japanese invasion of Manchuria was the first step on the road to World War II.

Unable to cope with the invader, the Chinese appealed to the League of Nations, which appointed a committee of inquiry in 1933. The committee's report condemned the aggression, but at the same time tried not to provoke Japan. The outcome was that the League neither put an end to the aggression nor kept Japan as a member—two years later Tokyo withdrew from the organization.

When the Chinese resorted to an effective nationwide boycott of Japanese goods, the invaders attacked Shanghai in 1932 and began to push deeper into northern China. To slow down the invasion and give themselves a chance in the inevitable struggle, the Chinese agreed to a truce

Erich Maria Remarque, *The Road Back*

Erich Maria Remarque, who wrote so eloquently of the horrors of war in *All Quiet on the Western Front*, compellingly expressed the despair and frustration of German veterans in *The Road Back*. He captures the mood that helped Hitler gain power.

Demonstrations in the streets have been called for this afternoon. Prices have been soaring everywhere for months past, and the poverty is greater even than it was during the war. Wages are insufficient to buy the bare necessities of life, and even though one may have the money it is often impossible to buy anything with it. But ever more and more gin palaces and dance halls go up, and ever more and more blatant is the profiteering and swindling.

Scattered groups of workers on strike march through the streets. Now and again there is a disturbance. A rumour is going about that troops have been concentrated at the barracks. But there is no sign of it as yet.

Here and there one hears cries and counter-cries. Somebody is haranguing at a street corner. Then suddenly everywhere is silence.

A procession of men in the faded uniforms of the front-line trenches is moving slowly toward us.

It was formed up by sections, marching in fours. Big white placards are carried before: *Where is the Fatherland's gratitude?—The War Cripples are starving.*

It was no good to go on assuming that a common basis for all the different groups and classes in Germany could be found. The break between them became daily wider and more irreparable. The plebiscite of the Right "against the Young Plan and the war-guilt lie" proved just as unsuccessful as those arranged in former years by the Left, but the poison of the defamatory agitation remained in the body of the community, and we watched its effects with anxiety.

In my own family the political antagonism was growing past endurance. In October Fritz had finished his apprenticeship in an old-established export house, at the precise moment when the firm went bankrupt—a minor incident compared with such events as the breakdown of the Frankfurt General Insurance Company and the Civil Servants' Bank or the enforced reorganization and amalgamation of the Deutsche Bank and the Disconto-Gesellschaft, which all happened in the course of the year and dangerously damaged the whole economic life of Germany. Yet for my brother the bankruptcy of his firm overshadowed all other happenings, since it meant that he lost his job. His three years' training was in vain—there was not a single export firm which was not forced to dismiss as many of its employees as possible.

"Yes, that's just it—millions! If it isn't my fault, whose fault is it? I tell you—your friends, the French, the English, the Americans, all those damnable nations who inflict on us one dishonorable penalty after the other—they are to blame for all this. Before the war the whole world bought German goods. My firm exported to Africa, to the German colonies. Hundreds of thousands we turned over every year. But they have robbed us of our colonies, of all our foreign markets. They have stolen the coal mines in the Saar and in Upper Silesia, they squeeze millions of marks out of our bleeding country. We'll never rise again unless we free ourselves by another war."

"Don't be foolish, Fritz. Things are bad in the whole world."

"I don't care about the world, I care only about Germany, which you and your pacifists have delivered into the hands of our enemies. I despise you, you are not worthy to call yourself a German."

→ Japanese soldiers, concealed on a camouflaged armored train, fire on the Chinese at Tsitsihar during Japan's invasion of Manchuria in 1931. The invasion was the first step in Japan's undeclared war against China, during which a number of Chinese cities including Peking and Shanghai fell to Japanese forces. More than 20 million Chinese died during the war, many of them civilians killed in the relentless aerial bomb attacks. Atrocities committed by Japanese troops against Chinese civilians outraged the rest of the world.

in May 1933 that recognized Tokyo's conquests in Manchuria and northern China.

Despite virtual civil war between Chiang Kai-shek's nationalist forces and the communist movement led by Mao Tse-tung, China strengthened its position in the face of the Japanese threat. Following Soviet directions, Mao stated that the first objective of all China should be wholehearted resistance against foreign imperialists. A united front between Chiang and Mao was difficult, but in December 1936–January 1937 the communists and nationalists put aside their conflicts, proclaimed a truce, and established a united front against the Japanese. Neither of the parties in the front trusted the other, but both feared the Japanese more.

In 1937 the Japanese, with no official declaration of hostility, renewed their advance and began what would be an eight-year period of war. After advancing rapidly up the Yangtze River to Nanking, where they committed atrocities, Tokyo's forces captured Peking and proclaimed the "New Order" in eastern Asia. The New Order's objectives were to destroy Chiang Kai-shek's regime, expel Western interests from east Asia, and establish a self-sufficient economic bloc, to include Japan, Manchuria, and China.

The outbreak of war in Europe in 1939 gave Japan a golden opportunity to expand the New Order in China and into the Asian colonies of the Western powers. The Japanese took the island of Hainan in 1939 and, after the fall of France in June 1940, built naval and air bases in Indochina. From there they put pressure on the Dutch East Indies and the British outposts at Hong Kong and Singapore.

None of the three great powers that might have halted the Japanese advance in the 1930s did anything. Britain was in the depths of an economic crisis, France was suffering from political and economic paralysis, and the United States was totally absorbed in fighting the depression.

Italy Attacks Ethiopia

While Japan pursued old goals in new ways, Italy set out to claim a prize it had failed to take in 1896—Ethiopia, the only important independent state left in Africa. Late in 1934 fighting broke out between the Ethiopians and the Italians, and in the following year, Mussolini's forces invaded the country. Emperor Haile Selassie made a dramatic appearance before the League to appeal for help.

The League tried to arrange for arbitration. Unconvinced by the shameless Italian argument that Ethiopia, not Italy, was the aggressor, the League voted to prohibit shipment of certain goods to Italy and to deny it credit. But the effect of the sanctions was minor because oil—without which no modern army can fight—was not included in the list of prohibited articles. France and Britain gave only lukewarm support to the sanctions because they did not want to alienate Italy. The United States, which had not joined the League, and Germany, which had left it by that time, largely ignored the prohibitions. Only outraged public opinion, moved by newspaper photographs showing barefooted Ethiopians fighting the modern Italian army, drove the governments to even the pretense of action.

Using bombs, mustard gas, and tanks the Italians advanced swiftly into Ethiopia and crushed Haile Selassie's valiant but poorly armed soldiers. Meanwhile, the German reoccupation of the Rhineland in March helped shift international attention away from the conflict in Africa. The whole, sorry story ended in July 1936 when sanctions were removed. Haile Selassie, an emperor without a country, went to live in Britain, the first of several royal exiles who would be forced from their countries in the next decade.

The Rhineland and the Axis

Soon after taking power, Hitler carried out the revisions the Germans wanted in the Versailles treaty. He also won his country's support by seeking revenge against the Allies. As George F. Kennan noted at the time, "The man is acting in the best traditions of German nationalism, and his conception of his own mission is perhaps clearer than that of his predecessors because it is uncomplicated by any sense of responsibility to European culture as a whole."[2] During his first two years in power Hitler paid lip service to peace while increasing the tempo of rearmament. In March 1935 he negated the disarmament clauses of the Versailles treaty, and a year later reoccupied the Rhineland.

The move, which Hitler described as producing the most nerve-wracking moments of his life, sent German troops marching boldly into the Rhineland in defiance of the Versailles treaty and the Locarno agreements. The Germans could not have resisted had the British and French moved in response. London did nothing and Paris mobilized 150,000 troops behind the Maginot line—but did no more. Hitler later confessed that had the French advanced against him, "We would have had to withdraw with our tails between our legs, for the military resources at our disposal would have been totally inadequate for even a moderate resistance."[3]

The League's weak response to the Japanese invasion of China and the Italian attack on Ethiopia combined with the feeble British and French reaction to German reoccupation of the Rhineland encouraged the aggressors and served as a prelude to the formation of the Axis alliance. Until Hitler gained power, Germany had been without close allies. After the Ethiopian crisis and the League sanctions, Italy and Germany began to work more closely together. In 1936 they formalized the friendship in the Rome-Berlin Axis, and one year later, Mussolini followed Hitler's lead by withdrawing from the League of Nations.

Japan, the third major member of the Axis, joined forces with Germany in 1936 in the Anti-Comintern pact. A year later, Italy also joined in that agreement, which effectively ringed the Soviet Union. Relations between Moscow and Berlin had cooled after 1934, and the Soviet Union now became the object of anticommunist rhetoric. Many right-wing leaders in the West hoped that the "Red menace" would be taken care of by the Führer and his allies.

All in all, 1936 was a banner year for Hitler. He had gained allies, pleased his own people by remilitarizing the Rhineland, learned the weakness of the democratic powers and the League, and gained international prestige from his successful staging of the Olympic games. Finally, he found a successful device to distract potential opponents' attention in the Spanish Civil War.

The Spanish Tragedy

By 1936 the Spanish republic was disintegrating. It had brought neither prosperity nor stability to Spain. Reactionary forces had tried to gain control of the government while left-wing groups had resorted to terrorism. The liberal approach had failed, and in the summer of 1936 the army revolted against the legal government in Madrid.

General Francisco Franco (1892–1975) commanded the insurgents, who included in their ranks most of the regular army troops. Mussolini strongly backed Franco, and the rightist forces expected a quick victory. However, many groups stood by the republic, and they put up a strong resistance against the insurgents, stopping them at the outskirts of Madrid.

By the end of 1936 each side had gained the backing of a complicated alliance of forces. Franco had the support of the Italians—who sent large numbers of planes, troops, and weapons—and the Germans, who tested their latest military technology against the republicans. The republic gained the support of the Soviet Union—which sent arms, "advisers," and other supplies—and large numbers of disorganized but idealistic antifascist fighters, including a number from Britain and the United States.

The insurgents capitalized on the Soviet support for the republic, and Franco pronounced his cause to be strictly an anticommunist crusade—a cunning oversimplification that would not have any validity except "for a few months (in 1938) the communists were in firm control of a remnant of republican Spain," until Stalin decided to pull out his support.[4] While Spain bled, suffering more than 700,000 deaths, outside forces took advantage of the tragic situation for their own selfish purposes.

The democratic powers—Great Britain, France, and the United States—attempted to stay officially out of the conflict. Britain did not want to risk a continental war. France suffered from internal divisions that made its leaders fear that their country, too, might have a civil war. The United States declared its official neutrality. Instead of permitting arms to be sent to the recognized, legally constituted republican government, which had the right under international law to purchase weapons for self-defense, Great Britain and France set up a nonintervention system by which the nations of Europe agreed not to send arms to either side. Only the democracies adhered to this arrangement, which was meant to limit the scope of the conflict. The various dictators continued to send support to their respective sides.

Madrid fell in March 1939, and the Spanish republic was no more. Franco, at the head of the new state, gained absolute power, which he held until his death. The Spanish civil war was a national catastrophe that left permanent scars on a proud and gallant people.

Appeasement and Weakness

In 1937, Neville Chamberlain (1869–1940) became prime minister of Great Britain. Years before he took office, the British had tried to build a detente with the Germans backed by "an efficient bomber air force." Chamberlain tried a new strategy: a defense policy based on a fighter air force and centered solely on protecting Britain. He wanted to make "more positive overtures to

✦ Members of the Condor Legion raise their arms in the Nazi salute as they pass the reviewing stand during a victory parade in Madrid shortly after the fall of the last Republican stronghold in Spain, marking the end of the Spanish Civil War. The civil war in Spain served as a rehearsal for the wider struggle ahead as Germany and Italy came together to support Franco's insurrectionists against the republicans, who received aid in the form of technicians and political advisers from the Soviet Union.

➜ After the fall of Barcelona in 1939, which marked the end of the Spanish Republic, thousands of Spanish refugees streamed to the French frontier to escape the fascists.

Germany to appease her grievances and reach a settlement on the basis not of fear by deterrence but of mutual interests and separate spheres of influence." Chamberlain's name came to symbolize the policy of appeasement, "the policy of meeting German demands and grievances without asking firm reciprocal advantages; asking instead only for future 'mutual understandings.'"[5]

Chamberlain took the direction of foreign policy on his own shoulders in his attempt to explore every possibility for reaching an understanding with the dictators. He dedicated himself to an effort to ease international tensions despite snubs from those he wished to placate and warnings from his military and foreign policy advisers. He based his policy on the most humane of motives—peace—and on the most civilized of assumptions—that Hitler could be reasonable and fair minded. By showing good faith—by withdrawing from any possibility of being able to wage war on the continent—Chamberlain froze himself into a position of having to avoid war at any cost. His policies were strongly supported in Great Britain and throughout most of the British Commonwealth.

France had shown that it would not move militarily without British backing, and under Chamberlain the entente with France was put on the back burner, a development that hurt French resolve. The democratic world became uneasily aware of its growing weakness in comparison with the dictators. As the European balance of power shifted, the small states began to draw away from the impotent League of Nations.

The Axis's prestige blossomed. Some nations tried to make deals with Germany and Italy, while others, including the Scandinavian countries and Holland, withdrew into the shelter of neutrality and "innocent isolation." In eastern Europe semifascist regimes came to be the order of the day, as the states in that unhappy region, with the exception of Czechoslovakia, lined up to get in Germany's good graces. In 1934 Poland had signed a nonaggression pact with Germany.

Belgium gave up its alliance with France. In eastern Europe, only Czechoslovakia remained loyal to Paris.

Hitler became increasingly aware of the opportunity presented by Britain's "peace at any price" policy and the decline of the French alliance system. On November 5, 1937, in a meeting at the Reich Chancellery in Berlin that lasted for more than four hours, Hitler laid out his plans and ideas for the future. According to the notes of the meeting taken by Colonel Hossbach, the Führer gave a statement that was to be regarded "in the event of his death, as his last will and testament."

"The aim of German policy," Hitler noted, "was to make secure and to preserve the racial community and to enlarge it. It was therefore a question of space. Germany's future was wholly conditional upon the need for space." The answer to that question was "force," which was to be applied in the next six years, because after 1943 German technological and military superiority would be lost. Hossbach noted that "the Führer believed that almost certainly Britain, and probably France as well, had already tacitly written off the Czechs."[6]

Historians still debate the importance of the Chancellery meeting. Hitler's message was not favorably received by the military staff present, since they knew full well that Germany was in no shape to fight. Yet the significance of the message can be found in the wholesale changes in personnel Hitler introduced at the end of 1937 and in the contrast it affords to the views of Chamberlain. The prime minister wanted peace at any price. The Führer wanted space at any price.

Toward Austria and the Sudetenland

When Hitler announced the military reoccupation of the Rhineland in the spring of 1936 he stated, "We have no territorial demands to make in Europe." He lied. By 1938, with the German army growing in strength and the air force becoming a powerful unit, the Führer began to implement one of his foreign policy goals—placing the German-speaking peoples under one Reich. The first step on that path was to unite Austria and Germany in the Anschluss (literally, "a joining").

In 1934 the Nazis had badly bungled an attempt to annex Austria. Two years later, softening-up operations began again, and by 1938 intense pressure had been levied against Austrian chancellor Kurt von Schuschnigg to cooperate with Berlin. After a stormy meeting with Hitler in February, Schuschnigg restated his country's desire to be independent, although concessions would be made to Germany. He called for a plebiscite in March to prove his point. Outraged at this independent action, Hitler ordered Schuschnigg to resign and to cancel the vote. Both actions were taken, but Hitler sent his forces into Austria anyway.

By March 13, 1938, a new chancellor, approved by Hitler, announced the union of Austria and Germany. After a month in which all opposition was silenced, Hitler held his own plebiscite and gained a majority of 99.75 percent in favor of union. The democratic powers did not intervene to help Austria. "Indeed, Neville Henderson (the British ambassador to Berlin) had indicated only too clearly that Britain would welcome alteration in Austria's status, if it were done peaceably."[7]

Following his success in Austria, Hitler moved on to his next objective, the annexation of the Sudetenland. This area along the western border of Czechoslovakia was populated mainly by German textile workers who had suffered economically during the depression. The Sudetenland was also the site of the extremely well-fortified Czech defenses. In September 1938 the Führer bluntly informed Chamberlain that he was determined to gain self-determination for the Sudeten Germans. He charged, falsely, that the Czechs had mistreated the German minorities. In fact, among the eastern European states Czechoslovakia had the best record in dealing with minority nationalities. But in this affair, Great Britain and France consistently overlooked both the record of the Prague government and the Czech statesmen themselves.

Chamberlain persuaded French premier Edouard Daladier that the sacrifice of Czechoslovakia would save the peace. When the French joined the British to press the Czechs to accept the Nazi demands, the Prague government had little choice but to agree. Chamberlain informed Hitler of the Czech willingness to compromise, only to find that the German demands had

The Hossbach Memorandum

Two years before the outbreak of World War II, Adolf Hitler recapitulated his goals in a secret meeting. Colonel Friedrich Hossbach took down Hitler's comments.

The aim of German policy was to make secure and to preserve the racial community and to enlarge it. It was therefore a question of space.

The German racial community comprised over 85 million people and, because of their number and the narrow limits of habitable space in Europe, constituted a tightly packed racial core such as was not to be met in any other country and such as implied the right to a greater living space than in the case of other peoples. . . .

Germany's future was therefore wholly conditional upon the solving of the need for space, and such a solution could be sought, of course, only for a foreseeable period of about one to three generations. . . .

The question for Germany ran: where could she achieve the greatest gain at the lowest cost. . . .

Case 1: Period 1943–1945

After this date only a change for the worse, from our point of view, could be expected.

The equipment of the army, navy, and Luftwaffe, as well as the formation of the officer corps, was nearly completed. Equipment and armament were modern; in further delay there lay the danger of their obsolescence. In particular, the secrecy of "special weapons" could not be preserved forever. The recruiting of reserves was limited to current age groups; further drafts from older untrained age groups were no longer available.

Our relative strength would decrease in relation to the rearmament which would by then have been carried out by the rest of the world. If we did not act by 1943–45, any year could, in consequence of a lack of reserves, produce the food crisis, to cope with which the necessary foreign exchange was not available, and this must be regarded as a "waning point of the regime." Besides, the world was expecting our attack and was increasing its counter-measures from year to year. It was while the rest of the world was still preparing its defenses that we were obliged to take the offensive. . . .

Case 2

If internal strife in France should develop into such a domestic crisis as to absorb the French Army completely and render it incapable of use for war against Germany, then the time for action against the Czechs had come.

Case 3

If France is so embroiled by a war with another state that she cannot "proceed" against Germany.

For the improvement of our politico-military position our first objective, in the event of our being embroiled in war, must be to overthrow Czechoslovakia and Austria simultaneously in order to remove the threat to our flank in any possible operation against the West. In a conflict with France it was hardly to be regarded as likely that the Czechs would declare war on us on the very same day as France. The desire to join in the war would, however, increase among the Czechs in proportion to any weakening on our part and then her participation could clearly take the form of an attack toward Silesia, toward the north or toward the west. . . .

The Fuehrer saw case 3 coming definitely nearer; it might emerge from the present tensions in the Mediterranean, and he was resolved to take advantage of it whenever it happened, even as early as 1938.

From *Auswärtiges Amt: Documents on German Foreign Policy,* Series D (Washington, D.C.: Government Printing Office, 1949), vol. 1. pp. 29–49, passim.

increased considerably. Angered by the Führer's duplicity, Chamberlain refused to accept the new terms, which included Czech evacuation of some areas and the cession of large amounts of material and agricultural goods.

Munich and Democratic Betrayal

The crisis over Czechoslovakia would be the last major international issue decided only by European powers. Symbolically it would be viewed as a failure that would affect diplomatic decisions for generations to come. On September 28, 1938, Chamberlain received a note from Hitler inviting him to attend a conference at Munich. The following day, Chamberlain flew to Germany to meet with Hitler, Mussolini, and Daladier at Nazi headquarters. They worked for 13 hours on the details of the surrender of the Sudetenland. No Czech representative was pre-

sent, nor were the Russians—outspoken allies of the Czechs—consulted.

The conference accepted all of Hitler's demands and, in addition, rewarded Poland and Hungary with slices of unfortunate Czechoslovakia. The tragedy for the Czechs brought relief for millions of Europeans, half-crazed with fear of war. But thoughtful individuals pondered whether this settlement would be followed by another crisis. Winston Churchill, who was then in political eclipse in Britain, solemnly warned: "And do not suppose that this is the end. This is only the beginning of the reckoning."[8]

The mounting fears of French and British statesmen were confirmed in 1939. Deprived of its military perimeter, the Czech government stood unprotected against the Nazi pressure that came in March. Hitler summoned Czech president Emil Hacha to Berlin. Subjected to all kinds of threats during an all-night session, Hacha

→ At the Munich Conference in September 1938, British Prime Minister Neville Chamberlain (left) and French Premier Edouard Daladier (next to him) capitulated to Hitler's demands regarding Czechoslovakia. Italian dictator Benito Mussolini stands to the right of Hitler.

PARTITION OF CHOSLOVAKIA

Czechoslovakia oundary, 1937

ESTONIA

LITHUANIA

EAST PRUSSIA

Vistula R.

Warsaw

GERMANY

Oder R.

POLAND

To Germany Oct. 1938

Teschen To Poland Oct. 1938

ORE MTS.

SUDETENLAND

Prague

Krakow

BOHEMIAN FOREST

PROTECTORATE OF BOHEMIA-MORAVIA

SLOVAKIA

To Hungary Nov. 1938

CARPATHIAN MTS.

Vienna

CARPATHO-UKRAINE

ALPS

AUSTRIA To Germany Mar. 1938

Budapest

HUNGARY

ROMANIA

LY

Danube R.

200

YUGOSLAVIA

and along the Rhine, President Franklin D. Roosevelt and the State Department worked quietly to alert the American people to the dangers of the world situation. In October 1937 Roosevelt pointed out that "the peace, the freedom, and the security of 90 percent of the population of the world is being jeopardized by the remaining 10 percent who are threatening a breakdown of all international order and law." The president's call, in this so-called quarantine speech, for "positive endeavors to preserve peace brought forth a hostile reaction from the press and public."[9] Two years later Roosevelt told political leaders that the Germans and Italians could win the next war. His warnings went unheeded, as a significant portion of the American public hoped that the Nazis could do away with the communists in Russia.

The Nazi-Soviet Pact

The final step on the road to World War II was Germany's attack on Poland. The Treaty of Versailles had turned over West Prussia to Poland as a Polish corridor to the sea. While 90 percent of the corridor's population was Polish, the Baltic city of Danzig—a free city under a League of Nations high commissioner—was nearly all German. Late in March 1939 Hitler proposed to Poland that Danzig be ceded to Germany and that the Nazis be allowed to occupy the narrow strip of land connecting Germany with East Prussia. Chamberlain, with French concurrence, warned the Nazis that "in the event of any action that clearly threatens Polish independence," the British, will "at once lend the Polish government all support in their power." This was an essentially symbolic gesture, since Poland's geography made any useful Western aid impossible.

In the months that followed the Allied warnings, France and Britain competed with Germany for an alliance with Russia. Stalin had closely observed the actions of the democratic powers since Hitler's rise to power. He was aware of the hope expressed in some Western conservative circles that Hitler might effectively put an end to the Soviet regime. Further, he pledged to stay out of a war between "imperialists." He had to make a closely reasoned choice between the two sets of suitors competing for Soviet partnership.

finally capitulated and signed a document placing his country under the "protection" of Germany. His signature was a mere formality, however, for German troops were already crossing the Czech frontier. Not to be outdone, Mussolini took Albania the following month. The two dictators then celebrated by signing a military alliance, the so-called Pact of Steel.

In response to the taking of Czechoslovakia and violation of the Munich pledges, Britain ended its appeasement policy and for the first time in its history authorized a peacetime draft. In Paris, Daladier gained special emergency powers to push forward national defense.

In the United States, isolationism reigned supreme. Between 1935 and 1937, in response to feelings of revulsion stemming from World War I, the U.S. Congress passed neutrality acts that made it unlawful for any nation at war to obtain munitions from the United States. At the same time, in response to events in Ethiopia, Spain,

Chamberlain and Daladier had ignored Moscow at Munich, and generally British relations with the communists were quite cool. Now, with the Polish question of paramount importance, the French and British approaches struck Stalin as being opportunistic. In May, Vyacheslav Molotov became the Soviet foreign minister. While Molotov negotiated publicly with the British and French, who sent negotiators not empowered to make agreements, he was also in secret contact with the highest levels of the Third Reich.

For centuries, Germany and Russia had shared a concern with the fate of Poland. They had been able to reach agreement at Poland's expense in the eighteenth and nineteenth centuries. From late 1938 on, Moscow and Berlin pondered yet another division of the country. Negotiations between the two proceeded intensely from June through August 1939. While top-ranking German and Soviet diplomats flew between the two capitals, the lower-ranking mission sent to Moscow by Britain traveled leisurely by boat.

By 1939 Stalin had to choose wisely between the Western democracies with their spotty record of defending their friends and Nazi Germany, which could offer him concrete advantages in eastern Europe. On August 21, to the world's great amazement, the Soviet Union and Germany signed a nonaggression pact.

In retrospect, it is not at all surprising that Stalin chose to work with the Nazis. Through this agreement, Stalin gave Hitler a free hand in Poland and the assurance of not having to fight a two-front war. After the British and French guarantees to the Poles in March, Hitler knew that his attack on Poland would precipitate a general European war. The Führer had prepared plans that called for the invasion to begin in August 1939, and with the nonaggression pact, Hitler could attack without fear of Moscow's intervention. Furthermore, he did not believe that Britain and France would dare oppose him.

The nonaggression pact gave Russia time to build up its strength while the imperialists weakened themselves in war. In addition, through secret agreements, Russia would gain Finland, Estonia, Latvia, eastern Poland, and Bessarabia. Germany would get everything to the West, including Lithuania. In addition, the Nazis got guarantees of valuable raw materials and grain from the Soviets. Ideological differences could be set aside for such a mutually profitable pact.

WORLD WAR II

When Nazi forces crossed the Polish border early on the morning of September 1, 1939, they started World War II, the conflict that killed more people more efficiently than any previous war. In all areas, the latest scientific and technological advances were placed in the service of war. New techniques and attitudes revolutionized the field of intelligence. Scientists made major advances in both codemaking and codebreaking. Intelligence-gathering no longer depended on the old cloak-and-dagger stealing of messages and secrets. Now high-altitude aerial reconnaissance aircraft, radar, the first computers, and radio intercepts allowed enemies to find out each others' plans. Among the major advances on the Allied side were the breaking of the Japanese code and the discovery of the German code mechanism. Less than a decade before the war an American statesman had noted that "gentlemen do not read other gentlemen's mail." In the new style of warfare, information meant victory, and the cultured assumptions of an earlier age had to be discarded.

A New Way of War

Tactics and weaponry changed greatly between the two world wars. Tanks and planes had been used in World War I, but the concept of the *Blitzkrieg*, massive mobile mechanized movements and saturation bombings behind the lines, made the weapons far more lethal. The trench warfare of the First World War and the concept of fixed, fortified positions such as the Maginot line proved to be useless.

Mobility was the key—even more so than superior numbers of men and weapons. Better communications, provided by improved radio systems, increased mobility. To strike quickly, in great force, and then to exploit the advantage proved to be the main characteristics of the German successes in 1939 and 1940. The Germans broke through enemy lines by using a large number of tanks, followed by the infantry. Rarely,

→ A German motorized detachment rides through a Polish town badly damaged by *Luftwaffe* bombs. Poland was unable to withstand Hitler's *Blitzkrieg* of a combined air and ground attack and fell to the Germans within a month.

ing bombs such as the V-1, rockets such as the V-2 used by the Germans. Aircraft carriers and amphibious forces played an important part in the war in the Pacific. The Japanese used carriers in their attack on Pearl Harbor and the Americans used amphibious forces in "island hopping" across the Pacific.

As in World War I, however, military success lay in the ability of the states to mobilize their populations and resources. During World War II, states came to control all aspects of life. But the final, deciding factor was the ability of the individual soldier, following the directions of such brilliant commanders as Rommel or Eisenhower, to apply all of these resources.

In the end, all of these factors were overwhelmed by the ultimate scientific and technological accomplishment, the atomic bomb. Ironically, although created to protect state interests, this ultimate weapon could destroy civilization.

Blitzkrieg and Sitzkrieg

After staging an "incident" on the morning of September 1, 1939, Nazi troops crossed the Polish frontier without a declaration of war. At the same time the *Luftwaffe* began to bomb Polish cities. On the morning of September 3 Chamberlain sent an ultimatum to Germany demanding that the invasion be halted. The time limit was given as 11 A.M. the same day. At 11:15 Chamberlain announced in a radio broadcast that Britain was now at war. France also soon declared war. After 21 years, Europe was once again immersed in war.

The world now had the chance to see the awesome speed and power of Nazi arms. The Polish forces collapsed, crushed between the German advance from the west and, two weeks later, the Russian invasion from the east. By the end of the month, after a brave but hopeless resistance, the Poles once again saw their country partitioned between the Germans and the Russians.

Britain and France did not try to breach Germany's western defensive line—the Siegfried line along the Rhine. With their blockade and mastery of the seas, they hoped to defeat Hitler by attrition. During the winter of 1939–1940 there was little fighting along the Franco-German frontier. The lull in action came to be referred to as the phony war, or *Sitzkrieg*.

since Napoleon, had speed and concentrated force been used so effectively.

Complementing increased mobility on the ground was the expanded use of air power, which could spread devastating firepower across continents. The new forms of war, however, sparked the inventive genius of the scientists as each technological advance elicited a response—long-range German bombers brought the need for improved radar; improved propeller-driven aircraft set off the development of jet-powered airplanes. No matter how sophisticated the aerial technology became, however, the war proved that, with the exception of nuclear weapons, air power alone could not bring an enemy to its knees.

Other innovations appeared during the war—paratroopers, advanced landing crafts, fly-

Russia took advantage of the lull to attack Finland in November. This campaign revealed to Moscow's embarrassment the Finns' toughness and the Soviet Union's military unpreparedness in the wake of the purges. After an unexpectedly difficult four-month-long campaign, the immense Soviet Union forced tiny Finland to cede substantial amounts of territory.

"Blood, Toil, Tears, and Sweat"

In the spring of 1940 the Nazi high command launched its attack on western Europe. In its scope, complexity, and accomplishments it was one of the most successful military campaigns ever carried out. In April, Nazi forces invaded Norway and Denmark. The Norwegians fought back fiercely for three weeks before being vanquished, while Denmark was taken in even less time. In the second week of May the German armies overran neutral Holland, Belgium, and Luxembourg. The next week they went into northern France and to the English Channel. In the process they trapped an Anglo-French army of nearly 400,000 on the beach at Dunkirk.

The reversals in Norway and the Low Countries and the military crisis in France led to Chamberlain's resignation. Winston Churchill (1874–1965) became prime minister of Great Britain. Churchill had uneven success in both his political and military careers. In the 1930s his warnings against Hitler and Mussolini had been largely ignored. He was viewed as a "might-have-been; a potentially great man flawed by flashiness, irresponsibility, unreliability, and inconsistency."[10] Yet in 1940, at the age of 66, Churchill offered qualities of leadership equal to the nation's peril. For the next five years he was the voice and symbol of a defiant and indomitable Britain.

Faced with the prospect of the destruction of the British army at Dunkirk, Churchill refused to be publicly dismayed. Appearing before Parliament as the new prime minister he announced, "I have nothing to offer but blood, toil, tears, and sweat." He prepared his people for a long and desperate conflict, knowing full well that only the Channel, a thin screen of fighter aircraft, and an untried device called radar protected Britain. Churchill's example inspired his people. Hitler had found his match in the area of charismatic leadership.

Hitler hesitated to squash the forces trapped at Dunkirk, thereby allowing time for hundreds of small craft protected by the Royal Air Force to evacuate across the Channel 335,000 soldiers, including more than 100,000 French troops. At first, military leaders had hoped that they might be able to save 30,000 of the trapped men; now they had 11 times that number. An army had been saved, even though it had lost all of its heavy equipment.

After Dunkirk, the fall of France was inevitable. Eager to be in on the kill, Mussolini declared war on France on June 10. Designated as an open city by the French to spare its destruction, Paris fell on June 14. As the German advance continued, the members of the French government who wanted to continue resistance were voted down. Marshal Philippe Pétain (1856–1951), the 84-year-old hero of Verdun in the First World War, became premier. He immediately asked Hitler for an armistice, and in the same dining car in which the French had imposed armistice terms on the Germans in 1918, the Nazis and French on June 22, 1940, signed another peace agreement. The Germans had gained revenge for their shame in 1918.

France was split into two zones, occupied and unoccupied. In unoccupied France, Pétain's government at Vichy was supposedly free from interference, but in reality it became a puppet of the Nazis. The Third Republic, created in 1871 from the debris of defeat suffered at Germany's hands, now came to an end because of a new blow from the same country.

A remarkable patriot, Brigadier-General Charles de Gaulle (1890–1970), fled to London and organized the Free French Government, which adopted as its symbol the red cross of Lorraine, flown by Joan of Arc in her fight to liberate France five centuries earlier. De Gaulle worked to keep alive the idea of France as a great power and continued to aid the Allied cause in his sometimes quixotic way throughout the war.

Only Britain remained in opposition to Hitler, and the odds against the British seemed overwhelming. The Nazis planned a cross-Channel assault, while in Buckingham Palace, the Queen, the present Queen mother, took pistol lessons, saying, "I shall not go down like the others."[11] Britain possessed an army that left its best equipment at Dunkirk, radar, and fast fighter aircraft flown by brave pilots. Churchill had his eloquence to inspire his people:

We shall go on to the end. . . . [W]e shall defend our island, whatever the cost may be, we shall fight on the beaches, we shall fight on the landing grounds, we shall fight in the fields and in the streets, we shall fight in the hills; we shall never surrender.[12]

The Germans sent an average of 200 bombers over London every night for nearly two months in the summer and fall of 1940. They suffered heavy losses to the Royal Air Force, which profited from a combination of superior aircraft, pilots, radar sightings, and visual detection. Yet, all through the fall and winter of 1940–1941 Britain continued to be racked by terrible raids. Night bombing destroyed block after block of British cities. Evacuating their children and old people to the north, going to work by day and sleeping in air raid shelters and underground stations at night, Britain's people stood firm—proof that bombing civilians would not break their will.

→ The Nazi air attacks on London in the Battle of Britain caused widespread devastation but failed to bring the city to a halt or destroy the morale of its people.

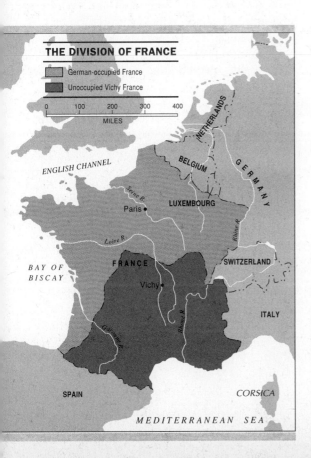

THE DIVISION OF FRANCE

German-occupied France

Unoccupied Vichy France

0 100 200 300 400
MILES

NETHERLANDS
BELGIUM
GERMANY
LUXEMBOURG
ENGLISH CHANNEL
Seine R.
Paris
Loire R.
Rhine R.
SWITZERLAND
BAY OF BISCAY
FRANCE
Vichy
ITALY
Garonne R.
Rhône R.
SPAIN
CORSICA
MEDITERRANEAN SEA

Mastery of Europe

During the fall and winter of 1940–1941 Hitler strengthened his position in the Balkans, but not without some difficulty. By March 1941 Hungary, Bulgaria, and Romania had joined the Axis. Hitler had to control the Hungarians and Bulgarians, who were pursuing ancient ambitions for Romanian land. In the process Romania lost a third of its population and territory to its two neighbors. The Romanians emerged, however, as helpful allies for the Germans.

Mussolini, eager to gain some glory for his forces, invaded neutral Greece in October 1940. This thrust proved to be a costly failure when in December the Greeks successfully counterattacked. The Italians met other defeats in North Africa and Ethiopia, which the British recaptured.

Partially in an attempt to pull Mussolini out of a humiliating position, the Germans in the first four months of 1941 overran Yugoslavia and Greece. Two months of intense aerial and infantry attacks were needed to defeat the Yugoslavs and Greeks, forcing Hitler to spend considerable amounts of men and resources. But, by the end of that time, the Führer had secured his right flank prior to his invasion of Russia.

The results of these forays into the Balkans may have been positive for the Axis in the short run. But by going into the Balkans, Hitler delayed his attack on Russia by six to eight weeks. This delay plus inadequate intelligence and bad planning may have cost him victory on the Russian front. In addition, the Germans and the Italians controlled only the major cities of Yugoslavia. Large bands of resistance fighters and partisans roamed the area, among them communist forces led by Joseph Tito. Hitler had to leave behind German troops formerly committed to the Russian invasion and replace them with lesser Bulgarian and Hungarian forces.

By the spring of 1941 nearly all of Europe had come under German control. Only Portugal, Switzerland, Sweden, Ireland, and Turkey remained neutral. While ostensibly neutral, Spain under Franco was pro-Nazi. Britain, though still dangerous, could do little to interfere on the con-

tinent. The United States became more disturbed over the Nazi successes, but not enough to take action.

War with Russia

Hitler and Stalin had signed the nonaggression pact for their own specific, short-term advantages. From the first there was tension and mistrust between the two, and neither side had any illusions about a long-lasting friendship. Stalin had hoped for a much more difficult war in the west among the "imperialists" and had not expected that Hitler would so quickly be the master of Europe.

As early as July 1940 Hitler resolved to attack Russia in an operation code-named Barbarossa. In the fall of the year he decided not to invade Britain, but instead to pursue his original goal of obtaining living space. During 1941 British and American intelligence experts told Stalin of Hitler's intentions to attack, but the Soviet dictator clung to his obligations under the nonaggression pact. Even while the Nazis were invading Russia in June 1941, shipments of Soviet grain were headed to Germany.

Operation Barbarossa required far more effort and resources than were expended later against the British and Americans in North

→ German troops at the Kharkov front in Russia pass a burning farmhouse. The same factors that had halted Napoleon and his army more than a hundred years earlier—bitter cold and inadequate protection against it—helped stop the German advance. Russia paid a heavy price for stopping the Germans, losing nearly 10 percent of its population in the war.

Africa. Along a battlefront 1800 miles long, 9 million men became locked in struggle. At the outset, the Nazi panzer units were unstoppable, as they killed or captured enormous numbers of Russian troops. In October Hitler's army neared the center of Moscow (a monument today between the city's Sheremetevo Airport and the Kremlin marks the farthest advance of the German army). A month earlier, the Nazis had besieged Leningrad, beginning a two-year struggle in which over one million civilians died. Russia appeared to be on the verge of collapse.

When winter came earlier, and more severely than usual, the Nazi offensive broke down. Weapons froze, troops were inadequately clothed, and heavy snows blocked the roads. The German attack halted and in the spring of 1942 the Russian army recovered some territory. One reason the Russians could bounce back was the success of the five-year plans in relocating industry behind the Urals. Another reason was the sheer bravery and tenacity of the Soviet people. Also, the United States and Britain had begun sending lend-lease supplies to Russia.

The United States Enters the War

Following the collapse of France and during the Battle of Britain, the American people had begun to understand the dangerous implications of an Axis victory. After Dunkirk, the United States sent arms to Britain, set forth on a rearmament program, and introduced the peacetime draft. The Lend-Lease Act of 1941 empowered the president to make arms available to any country whose defense was thought to be vital to the U.S. national interest. Despite ideological differences, America sent more than $11 billion worth of munitions to Russia.

To define the moral purpose and principles of the struggle, Roosevelt and Churchill drafted the Atlantic Charter in August 1941. Meeting "somewhere in the Atlantic," the two pledged that "after the final destruction of Nazi tyranny," they hoped to see a peace in which "men in all the lands may live out their lives in freedom from fear and want." If the United States had not yet declared itself at war in the fall of 1941, it was certainly not neutral.

One event on December 7, 1941, brought the full energies of the American people into the war against the dictators—the Japanese attack on Pearl Harbor. Even though Hitler was seen as the most important enemy, it was Japan's expansionist policy that brought the United States into the war.

Confronted with Tokyo's ambitions for the New Order in Asia and widely published accounts of Japanese atrocities, the United States had failed to renew trade treaties, frozen Japanese funds, and refused to sell Japan war materiel. Despite these measures Japan decided to continue its expansion. In October 1941 General Hideki Tojo (1884–1948), a militarist, became premier of Japan. On Sunday, December 7, while special "peace" envoys from Tokyo were negotiating in Washington, ostensibly to restore harmony in Japanese-American relations, Japanese planes launched from aircraft carriers attacked the American bases at Pearl Harbor, Hawaii. The stunningly successful attack wiped out many American aircraft on the ground and crippled one-half of the United States Pacific fleet.

On the following day the United States declared war on Japan, as did Britain. The British dominions, the refugee governments of Europe, and many Latin American nations soon followed the Americans and British. Four days later, Germany declared war on the United States. On January 2, 1942, the 26 nations that stood against Germany, Italy, and Japan solemnly pledged themselves to uphold the principles of the Atlantic Charter and declared themselves united for the duration of the war.

The Apogee of the Axis

After Pearl Harbor, Japanese power expanded over the Pacific and into Southeast Asia. Tokyo conquered Hong Kong, Singapore, the Dutch East Indies, Malaya, Burma, and Indochina. The Philippines fell when an American force surrendered at Bataan. The Chinese, however, from their remote inland fortress capital of Chungking, still managed to hold off the Japanese.

The summer of 1942 was an agonizing period for the nations allied against the Axis. A new German offensive pushed deeper into Russia, threatening the important city of Stalingrad. The forces of the gifted German general Rommel menaced Egypt and inflicted a decisive defeat on the British army in Libya. All over the globe the Axis powers were in the ascendancy. But their advantage was to be short-lived.

→ The magazine of the destroyer U. S. S. *Shaw* explodes during the Japanese attack on Pearl Harbor, Hawaii, in December 1941.

Japanese expansion in the Pacific was halted by two major American naval victories, the Coral Sea in May and Midway in June. In the first the Americans sank more than 100,000 tons of Japanese shipping and stopped the Japanese advance toward Australia. In the second the Americans turned back the advance toward Hawaii by devastating the Japanese carrier force. In both cases the American forces benefited by having broken the Japanese code and intercepting key messages. After these spectacular victories, U.S. marines began the tortuous rooting out of the Japanese at Guadalcanal and driving them back, island by island.

In November 1942 British and American troops landed in North Africa and the British defeated Axis troops at El Alamein in Egypt. By May 1943 all Axis troops in North Africa had been destroyed or captured. In July 1943 the Allied forces invaded and captured Sicily. On the twenty-fifth of that month, the whole edifice of Italian fascism collapsed, as Mussolini was stripped of his office and held captive. (He was rescued by Nazi agents in September.) In the meantime, the Allies began their slow and bitter advance up the Italian boot. The new Italian government signed an armistice in September 1943, months before Rome was taken in June 1944. German resistance in northern Italy continued until the end of the war.

The Russian Turning Point

As important as the victories in the Pacific, North Africa, and Italy were, the decisive campaign took place in Russia. Hitler threw the bulk of his men and resources against the Soviet troops in the hope of knocking them out of the war and of gaining badly needed resources and food supplies. Hitler's strategy and operations along the Russian front constituted one mistake after another.

The Nazis lost a great opportunity to further the disintegration of the Soviet Union in 1941, because they treated the peoples they encountered as *Untermenschen*, or subhumans. Often the Nazis, far from encountering resistance, would be treated as liberators by the villages they entered and given the traditional gifts of bread and salt. Often peasants dissolved the unpopular collective farms in the hope that private owner-

Portfolio Eight

The Modern World

↬ Pablo Picasso, *Girl Before a Mirror* (1932). Although Picasso is considered a founder of cubism, the range of his works extends over most of the significant trends in twentieth-century art. With its clearly defined shapes and boldly curved outlines, *Girl Before a Mirror* is an example of what has been described as curvilinear cubism.

→ The most famous surrealist painter was Salvador Dali, who sought to express the subjective world of dreams through disturbing and bizarre images like those in *The Persistence of Memory* (1931), left. The paintings of Marc Chagall, a forerunner of surrealism, also have a dreamlike quality, but the images are light and whimsical, as in *The Poet Reclining* (1915), below. The poet in the picture is Chagall himself who painted the work during the honeymoon of his intensely happy marriage to Bella.

↘ The first major movement in painting to develop after World War II was abstract expressionism, sometimes called action painting because the activity of painting seems as important as the finished product. One of the leaders of abstract expressionism was Willem de Kooning, whose best-known works are his woman paintings, a series of female nudes, such as *Woman IV* (1952–1953), executed in broad, violent brush strokes on large canvases.

→ The act of painting is as important in color-field painting as it is in abstract expressionism, although the technique is quite different. Morris Louis, for example, applied extremely thin acrylic paint to absorbent, unstretched canvas, allowing the paint to sink in and stain the fabric rather than lie on top of the surface. The technique produces shapes of rich, although subdued, colors and soft, fuzzy edges. A characteristic example is *Point of Tranquility* (1959–1960).

→ The realistic portrayal of real objects and images reaches an extreme in photo, or super, realism, in which images are first photographed, then translated into meticulously realistic paintings. The result is a painting of a photograph, executed in a completely detached, impersonal, and objective manner. The devotion to detail and complete accuracy characteristic of photo realism are evident in the works of Richard Estes, such as *Drugstore* (1970).

→ Pop art, a movement of the 1960s, emphasizes the materialism of contemporary industrialized society by focusing on the realistic presentation of commonplace items of popular culture, such as soup cans, comic strips, and diners. Andy Warhol used images of advertising in his paintings, producing facsimiles of familiar products, such as *Campbell's Soup* (1965), above left. Roy Lichtenstein is noted for his use of comic-strip techniques, flat surfaces, hard edges, and bright colors. In *Stepping Out* (1978), above right, the female companion of the dapper young man is reminiscent of surrealist images of the 1920s. Pop art sculptor George Segal frequently uses white plaster casts of the human figure set in realistic environments. His works, such as *The Diner* (1964–1966), right, with their mood of loneliness, have been compared to Edward Hopper's paintings.

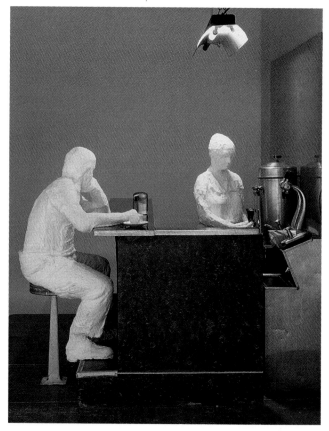

→ Among the artistic influences on British sculptor Henry Moore were primitive and archaic art, such as the Mexican pre-Columbian sculptures of Toltec culture and the monoliths of Stonehenge in England. Moore, who believed the human body to be the basic subject of sculpture, chose to emphasize monumentality and strength over detail. In *Reclining Figure* (1938), made from green hornton stone and extending to a length of about 54 inches, the design of the figure is in complete harmony with the striations of the stone.

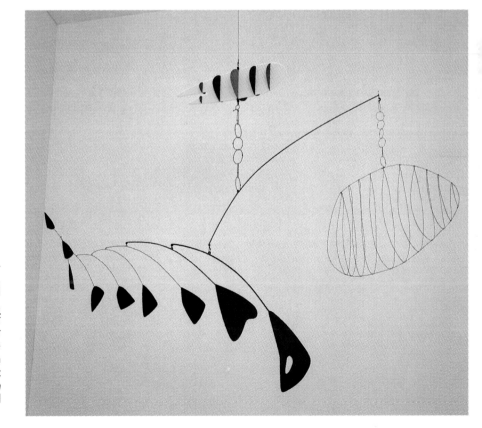

The American Alexander Calder pioneered in the construction of kinetic, or mobile, sculpture in which physical motion is an essential part of the piece. Calder's mobiles are constructions of sheet metal and wire hinged together and so delicately balanced that the slightest breath of air sets the pieces in graceful motion. One of the largest hanging mobiles, *Lobster Trap and Fish Tail* (1939), is more than 8½ feet high and over 9½ feet in diameter.

→ Frida Kahlo, *Self-Portrait with Monkey* (1945). Mexican artist Frida Kahlo combines Mexican folk art motifs and European surrealist elements of absurd juxtapositions and dreamlike settings in her often biographical and psychologically complex works. Living in chronic pain as the result of a childhood bout with polio and a near-fatal streetcar accident during her adolescence led Kahlo to a preoccupation with her own body in much of her art. Her bohemian lifestyle, including two stormy marriages to fellow Mexican artist Diego Rivera, also exerted an influence on her distinctive painting style.

→ Computer-generated imagery emerges from the combination of science, technology, and art. The use of computers in artmaking ranges from producing finished images to generating ideas or models for works ultimately produced in another medium.

ship would be restored. The separatist Ukrainians looked forward to German support for reinstituting their state. The Nazi occupation negated all of these potential advantages. The Nazis carried their mobile killing operations of genocide with them, conscripted Slavs for slave labor in Germany, and generally mistreated the population in areas that they occupied.

Hitler's campaign gave Stalin the opportunity to wrap himself in the flag of Russian patriotism. He replaced the ideological standards with those of nationalism and orthodoxy. He even went so far as to announce the end of the Comintern in 1943, an act more symbolic than real. For the first and perhaps the only time, the Communist party and the Soviet people were truly united in a joint enterprise.

The long (September 14, 1942, to February 2, 1943) and bloody battle between the Germans and the Russians was focused on the strategic,

industrial city of Stalingrad on the Volga River. Hitler had fanatically sought to take the city, which under the constant pounding of artillery had little of importance left in it. His generals advised him to stop the attempt and retreat to a more defensible line. Hitler refused, and the German Sixth Army of 270,000 men was surrounded and finally captured in February 1943. A German soldier trapped at Stalingrad wrote in a letter:

> Around me everything is collapsing, a whole army is dying, day and night are on fire, and four men busy themselves with daily reports on temperatures and cloud ceilings. I don't know much about war. No human being has died by my hand. I haven't even fired live ammunition from my pistol. But I know this much: the other side would never show such a lack of understanding for its men.[13]

Along the long front 500,000 German and affiliated troops were killed or taken prisoner. By the ·

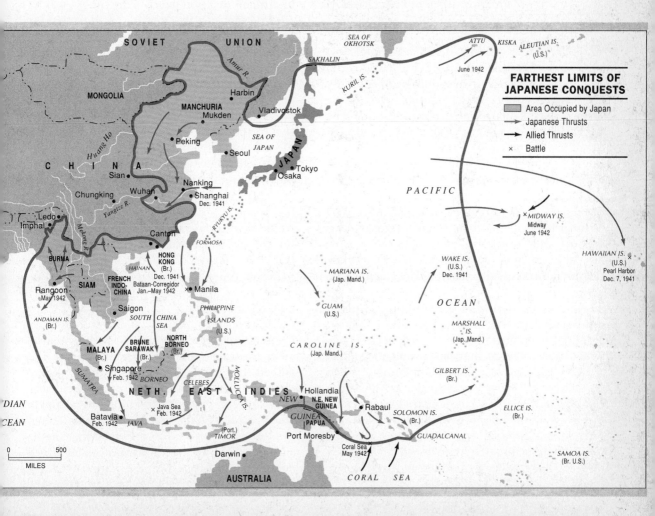

→ The British victory over the Axis troops at El Alamein, Egypt, in 1942 helped turn the tide of the war in favor of the Allies.

autumn of 1943 an army of 2.5 million Germans faced a Soviet force of 5.5 million.

The initiative had definitely passed to the Allies in the European theater. The Germans lost their air dominance and the American industrial machine was cranking up to full production. By the beginning of 1944 the Germans were being pushed out of the Soviet Union, and in August Soviet troops accepted the surrender of Romania. Bulgaria was next to be "liberated" by the Soviet Union, while the Allies continued doggedly fighting their way north in Italy. But whereas the western Allies were—in their fashion—fighting the war to its military end, Stalin placed the postwar political objectives in the forefront of his advance into Europe.

An example of the Soviet use of military tactics to gain political goals could be seen in the action around Warsaw in August–September 1944, when the Red Army deferred the capture of the Polish capital to allow the Nazis to destroy potential opponents. The Polish resistance, which was centered in Warsaw and in contact with the exile government in London, had noted the arrival of Soviet forces in Warsaw's eastern suburbs. When the Nazis prepared to evacuate the city, the resistance rose up to claim control of the capital. Since these were noncommunist Poles, Stalin's forces refused to advance to the city, choosing instead to withdraw back across the Vistula.

During the next five months, the Soviets refused to permit the British and the Americans, who wanted to airdrop supplies to the resistance, to land and refuel in the Ukraine. Because the flight to Warsaw from London was too far to make in a round trip, the Allies could not supply the resistance. The Nazis stopped their retreat, returned to Warsaw, and totally destroyed the resistance. Russian forces then advanced and took the capital in January. Poland was now deprived of many of its potential postwar, noncommunist leaders. When the Soviets advanced, they brought with them their own properly prepared Polish forces, both military and political, to control the country.

Axis Collapse

Following months of intense planning and days of difficult decision making, the Allies on June 6, 1944, launched a vast armada of ships that landed half a million men on the beaches of Normandy. The Allied armies broke through the German defenses and liberated Paris at the end of August and Brussels at the beginning of September. The combined forces wheeled toward Germany. After fending off a major German offensive in the Battle of the Bulge in December, the Allies were ready to march on Germany.

It took four more months for the Allies from the west and the Russians from the east to crush the Third Reich. By May 1, the Battle of Berlin had reached a decisive point, and the Russians were about to take the city. By contrast with the First World War, German civilians suffered greatly in the Second. The Allies gained total command of the skies and for every ton of bombs that fell on English cities, more than 300 tons fell on German settlements.

With victory in sight, Stalin, Roosevelt, and Churchill met at Yalta in the Crimea in February 1945 to discuss the peace arrangements. They agreed the Soviet Union should have a preponderant influence in eastern Europe, decided that Germany should be divided into four occupation zones, discussed the makeup and functioning of the United Nations, and confirmed that the Russians would enter the war against Japan after the defeat of Germany, which they did—two days after the atomic bomb was dropped on Hiroshima.

→ This panoramic view of the D-Day invasion shows the land, sea, and air craft preparing for the conquest. The waters are filled with ships as reinforcements and supplies pour ashore; balloon barrages float overhead to protect the ships from low-flying enemy aircraft, while long lines of trucks transport troops and supplies inland.

Yalta was the high point of the alliance. After this conference, relations between the Western powers and the Soviets rapidly deteriorated.

The European Axis leaders did not live to see defeat. Mussolini was seized by antifascist partisan fighters and shot to death, and his mutilated body and that of his mistress were hung by the heels in a public square in Milan on April 28, 1945. Hitler committed suicide two days later. His body and that of his mistress, Eva Braun, whom he had just married, were soaked in gasoline and set afire.

President Roosevelt also did not live to see the end of the war. He died suddenly on April 12, 1945, less than a month before the German armies capitulated. The final surrender in Europe took place in Berlin on May 8, 1945, named by the newly installed president, Harry Truman, as V-E Day, Victory in Europe Day.

The Unspeakable Holocaust

As the Allied armies liberated Europe and marched through Germany and Poland they came on sites that testified to the depths to which human beings can sink—the Nazi death camps. Nazi Propaganda Minister Joseph Goebbels wrote in his diary on March 14, 1945, that "it's necessary to exterminate these Jews like rats, once and for all. In Germany, thank God, we've taken care of that. I hope the world will follow this example."[14]

He was only too accurate in saying that Germany had "already taken care of that." In Belsen, Buchenwald, Dachau, Auschwitz, and other permanent camps and in mobile killing operations that moved with the armies, Hitler's forces sought to "purify the German race" and to "remove the lesser breeds as a source of biological infection." Working under the efficient efforts of the Gestapo, led by Chief Heinrich Himmler, and with the aid of hardworking Deputy Chief Reinhard Heydrich, the Nazis set out to gain the "final solution" of the Jewish question.

Although preparations had been under way for ten years, the completed plan for the final solution came in 1942. More than 3 million men, women, and children were put to death at Auschwitz, where more than 2000 people at a time could be gassed in half an hour; the operation could be repeated four times a day. The able-bodied worked until they could work no more, and then they were gassed. Millions more died

➢ A guant Roosevelt, looking already close to death, sits between Churchill and Stalin at the Yalta Conference. The discussions at the conference, especially those concerning the establishment of new governments in liberated countries, exposed the mounting tensions that would divide the Allies after the war.

from starvation, on diets that averaged from 600 to 700 calories a day. Torture, medical experimentation, and executions all claimed a large toll. The victims' eyeglasses were collected, their hair shaved off, their gold fillings were removed, and their bodies were either burned or buried.

Thus the captured Jews and assorted *Untermenschen* served a "biological necessity" by being destroyed and made an economic contribution on the way. The Nazis did not act alone: they were aided by anti-Semitic citizens in Poland, Romania, France, Hungary, and the Soviet Union. Few of the more than 3 million Polish Jews survived the war, and similar devastation occurred among the Romanian Jewry.

With the exception of a few human beasts, all of this was done with bureaucratic efficiency, coldness, discipline, and professionalism. Himmler believed that his new variety of knights must make "this people disappear from the face of the earth." Had this been done in a fit of insanity and madness by savages, it perhaps could be comprehended. But that it was done by educated bureaucrats and responsible officials from a civilized nation made the act all the more chilling and incredible.

Between 1939 and 1945 the Jewish population in Nazi-occupied Europe decreased from 9,739,200 to 3,505,800. Six million were killed directly in Nazi gas chambers or in executions. In addition, another 6 million people—Slavs, Gypsies, homosexuals, and others—also fell victim to direct Nazi slaughter.[15]

The Atomic Bomb

While the Allied armies finished off the Germans, the Americans from the summer of 1943 advanced toward Japan, capturing on the way the islands of Tarawa, Kwajalein, and Saipan after bloody struggles on sandy beaches. In October 1944, with their victory in the battle of Leyte Gulf, the greatest naval engagement in history, the Allies ended the threat of the Japanese fleet.

The final phase of the war against Japan began to unfold. The Allies took Iwo Jima and Okinawa, only a few hundred miles from Japan. From these bases waves of American bombers rained destruction on Japanese cities. In the China-Burma-India theater, the Chinese with U.S. aid made inroads on areas previously captured by Japan.

But the decisive developments took place across the Pacific in New Mexico, where by 1945 U.S. scientists, with the help of scientists who had fled central Europe to escape Hitler, invent-

→ This photograph is mute testimony to the unspeakable horror of the Holocaust. The picture is of a mass grave of political prisoners who were interred in the Nazi concentration camp at Belsen, Germany, and who died before the Allies could liberate them.

The Nazi Death Camps

Henry Friedlander gave a dispassionate description of the functioning of the Nazi death camps.

The largest killing operation took place in Auschwitz, a regular concentration camp. There Auschwitz Commandant Rudolf Hoess improved the method used by Christian Wirth, substituting crystallized prussic acid—known by the trade name Zyklon B—for carbon monoxide. In September, 1941, an experimental gassing, killing about 250 ill prisoners and about 600 Russian POWs, proved the value of Zyklon B. In January, 1942, systematic killing operations, using Zyklon B, commenced with the arrival of Jewish transports from Upper Silesia. These were soon followed without interruption by transports of Jews from all occupied countries of Europe.

The Auschwitz killing center was the most modern of its kind. The SS built the camp at Birkenau, also known as Auschwitz II. There, they murdered their victims in newly constructed gas chambers, and burned their bodies in crematoria constructed for this purpose. A postwar court described the killing process:

Prussic acid fumes developed as soon as Zyklon B pellets seeped through the opening into the gas chamber and came into contact with the air. Within a few minutes, these fumes agonizingly asphyxiated the human beings in the gas chamber. During these minutes horrible scenes took place. The people who now realized that they were to die an agonizing death screamed and raged and beat their fists against the locked doors and against the walls. Since the gas spread from the floor of the gas chamber upward, small and weak people were the first to die. The others, in their death agony, climbed on top of the dead bodies on the floor, in order to get a little more air before they too painfully choked to death.

From Henry Friedlander, "The Nazi Camps," in *Genocide: Critical Issues of the Holocaust,* ed. Alex Grobman and David Landes (Los Angeles: The Simon Wiesenthal Center, 1983), pp. 222–231.

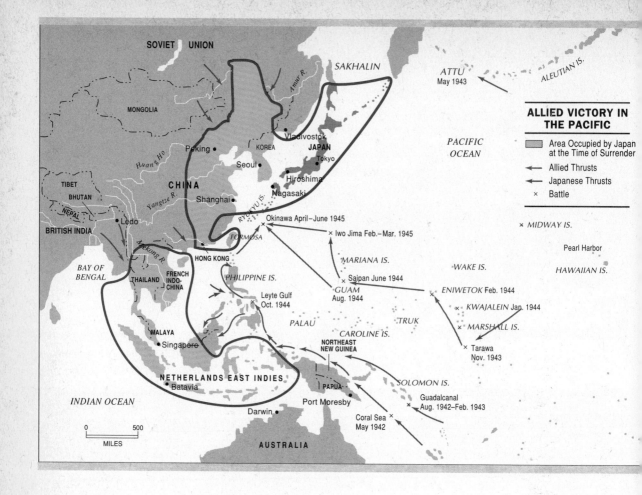

MILES

ALLIED VICTORY IN THE PACIFIC

- ☐ Area Occupied by Japan at the Time of Surrender
- ← Allied Thrusts
- ← Japanese Thrusts
- × Battle

ed a new and terrible weapon—the atomic bomb. Based on figures from the island-hopping campaigns, the projected casualty rate for the taking of the main island of Japan ran into the hundreds of thousands.

When the Japanese refused to surrender, an American bomber on August 6 dropped the atomic bomb on the city of Hiroshima. As the mushroom-shaped cloud rose over the city, only charred ruins were left behind. An expanse of approximately 3 square miles, 60 percent of the city, was pulverized. The Japanese government estimated the bomb killed 60,000 people, wounded 100,000, and left 200,000 homeless. Three days later, a second bomb was dropped on the city of Nagasaki, with similar results.

The Japanese finally sued for peace. The surrender ceremony took place aboard the battleship *Missouri* on September 2, 1945, almost six years to the day after Hitler plunged the world into the Second World War.

CONCLUSION

When the war was finally over, the living counted the dead. The Germans lost 4.2 million military and civilian dead, while the Western Allies lost 1.5 million. The Soviet Union suffered the greatest losses: close to 25 million citizens. Yugoslavia had the greatest per capita casualty rate—one in every ten. In Asia, the census for 1950 showed a loss of some 55 million people, even after a five-year period of recuperation.[16] A meaningful financial accounting for the six years of bloodshed is not possible.

The world went through this carnage to put an end to German, Italian, and Japanese aggres-

The Bombing of Hiroshima

Nuclear weapons totally changed the nature and possibilities of warfare. The U.S. Strategic Bombing Survey gave a detached version of what happened at Hiroshima.

At about 0815 there was a blinding flash. Some described it as brighter than the sun, others likened it to a magnesium flash. Following the flash there was a blast of heat and wind. The large majority of people within 3,000 feet of ground zero were killed immediately. Within a radius of about 7,000 feet almost every Japanese house collapsed. Beyond this range and up to 15,000–20,000 feet many of them collapsed and others received serious structural damage. Persons in the open were burned on exposed surfaces, and within 3,000–5,000 feet many were burned to death while others received severe burns through their clothes. In many instances clothing burst into spontaneous flame and had to be beaten out. Thousands of people were pinned beneath collapsed buildings or injured by flying debris. Flying glass particularly produced many nonlethal injuries and the distances at which they occurred are discussed in the following chapter, but the foregoing presentation was necessary for one to appreciate the state of the population immediately after the bomb exploded.

Shortly after the blast fires began to spring up over the city. Those who were able made a mass exodus from the city into the outlying hills. There was no organized activity. The people appeared stunned by the catastrophe and rushed about as jungle animals suddenly released from a cage. Some few apparently attempted to help others from the wreckage, particularly members of their family or friends. Others assisted those who were unable to walk alone. However, many of the injured were left trapped beneath collapsed buildings as people fled by them in the streets. Pandemonium reigned as the uninjured and slightly injured fled the city in fearful panic.

From "The Effects of Atomic Bombs on Health and Medical Services in Hiroshima and Nagasaki," in *The United States Strategic Bombing Survey* (Washington, D.C.: U.S. Government Printing Office, 1948).

---

sion, which came frighteningly close to succeeding in its goal of world dominance. By contrast with the First World War, which has spawned many historiographical controversies concerning its causes, there is no doubt that the key figure in the Second World War was Adolf Hitler. He was the essential link, the man whose policies and ideas welded together the dictators.

Unlike the Japanese and the Italians, whose global influence was limited by either geographical or internal problems, Hitler could build on Germany's industrial might and central location to forge a force for world conquest. Historians vary sharply on his goals and motivations. Some see him as a politician playing the traditional game of European power politics in a most skillful way, while others view him as a single-minded fanatic pursuing the plans for conquest laid out in *Mein Kampf*. Between these two extremes are the scholars who believe that the Führer had deeply thought-out, long-term goals but pursued them haphazardly, as opportunities presented themselves.

Hitler struck the spark that set off the worldwide conflagration. Aiding and abetting his ambitions was the obsessive desire of the democracies for peace. By 1939, the lesson had been learned that appeasement does not guarantee peace, nor does it take two equally belligerent sides to make a war.

→ Suggestions for Reading

Two helpful introductions to the 1919–1945 period are Laurence Lafore, *The End of Glory* (Lippincott, 1970) and Joachim Remak, *The Origins of the Second World War* (Prentice-Hall, 1976).

The diplomacy leading up to and conducted during the war has received extensive study. Hans Gatzke, ed., *Euro-*

pean Diplomacy Between the Two Wars, 1919–1939 (Quadrangle, 1972) gives definition to some of the major problems involved in this period. His Stresemann and the Rearmament of Germany (Norton, 1969) emphasizes an interwar continuity. Jon Jacobson discusses a pivotal four years in Locarno Diplomacy: Germany and the West 1925–1929 (Princeton Univ., 1972). Gerhard Weinhard gives a penetrating analysis in The Foreign Policy of Hitler's Germany: Diplomatic Revolution in Europe 1933–1936 (Univ. of Chicago, 1970). Equally essential is Weinhard's follow-up study, The Foreign Policy of Hitler's Germany 1937–1939 (Univ. of Chicago, 1980). In The Nazi Dictatorship (Arnold, 1985), Ian Kershaw makes the case that Hitler's ideology, from the first, could eventuate only in war. Still one of the best studies of Soviet foreign policy is George Kennan's Russia and the West Under Lenin and Stalin (Mentor, 1961). W.L. Langer and S.E. Gleason discuss important aspects of U.S. foreign policy in The Challenge to Isolation (Harper & Row, 1952). Herbert Feis's Churchill, Roosevelt, Stalin (Princeton Univ., 1967) is a classic. René Albrecht-Carrié traces France's travail in France, Europe, and the Two World Wars (Harper & Row, 1961). George Kennan's Memoirs, Vol. I (Bantam, 1969) offers perceptive contemporary observations. Other fine studies on interwar affairs are Etienne Mantoux, The Carthaginian Peace (Ayer, 1978) and Sally Marks, International Relations in Europe: 1918–1939 (St. Martin's, 1976). Robert Young's In Command of France: French Foreign Policy and Military Planning, 1933–1940 (Harvard Univ., 1978) gives needed perspective on France's dilemma.

One of the most discussed aspects of the interwar period is appeasement and the Munich Conference. Keith Middlemas, The Strategy of Appeasement (Quadrangle, 1972) gives a balanced survey of this very controversial issue. Francis L. Loewenheim, ed., Peace or Appeasement (Houghton Mifflin, 1965) provides a selection of documents, including the Hossbach Memorandum. Keith Eubank's study, Munich (Univ. of Oklahoma, 1963) is a good summary.

The Spanish Civil War has also received much scholarly attention. John Coverdale discusses one aspect of the conflict in Italian Intervention in the Spanish Civil War (Princeton Univ., 1975). Gabriel Jackson, The Spanish Republic and the Civil War 1931–1939 (Princeton Univ., 1965), Stanley G. Payne, Spanish Revolution (Norton, 1970), and Hugh Thomas, The Spanish Civil War (Harper & Row, 1977) are all first-rate studies. George Orwell, Homage to Catalonia (Harcourt Brace Jovanovich, 1938) remains an invaluable contemporary description of the tragedy of the Spanish republic.

The war from the German perspective has to take into consideration the Führer himself, and Robert G. Waite's The Psychopathic God: Adolf Hitler (Mentor, 1983) offers fascinating insights into his personality. Harold C. Deutsch's Hitler and His Germans: The Crisis of January–June 1938 (Univ. of Minnesota, 1974) provides good insights into German planning and policies. David

Irving, Hitler's War is a first-rate survey (Viking, 1977). Albert Speer gives an insider's point of view in Inside the Third Reich (Macmillan, 1970). Alexander Dallin's German Rule in Russia 1941–1945 (St. Martin's, 1957) discusses occupation policies and problems. Albert Seaton's The Russo-German War 1941–1945 (Praeger, 1970) is especially strong in its analysis of Soviet strategy.

The diplomacy surrounding Poland is well covered in Anna Cienciala, Poland and the Western Powers 1938–1939 (Univ. of Toronto, 1968). John A. Armstrong, Soviet Partisans in World War II (Univ. of Wisconsin, 1964) is a deft analysis of a subtle theater of action. George Bruce gives thorough coverage of the 1944 Polish tragedies in Warsaw Uprising 1 August–2 October (Hart-Davis, 1972). Harrison Salisbury, The Nine Hundred Days: The Siege of Leningrad (Harper & Row, 1975) is a heartbreaking story of heroism. The tragic story of repatriated Soviet citizens is told in Nikolai Tolstoy, Victims of Yalta (Hodder & Stoughton, 1978).

Three good books on the Pacific theater are Christopher Thorne, Allies of a Kind: The United States, Britain, and the War Against Japan (Oxford Univ., 1978); Gordon W. Prange, At Dawn We Slept: The Untold Story of Pearl Harbor (McGraw-Hill, 1981); and Yoshiburo Ienaga, The Pacific War, 1937–1945 (Pantheon Univ., 1978), which views the war from Japan's perspective.

Other aspects of the war are covered in Anthony Adamthwaite, France and the Coming of the Second World War 1936–1939 (Frank Cass, 1977), Maurice Cowling, The Impact of Hitler: British Politics and British Foreign Policy 1933–1940 (Univ. of Chicago, 1977), Henri Michel, The Shadow War, European Resistance 1939–1945 (Harper & Row, 1972), Leila J. Rupp, Mobilizing Women for War, 1939–1945 (Princeton Univ., 1977), and Len Deighton, Fighter: The True Story of the Battle of Britain (Jonathan Cape, 1977). Three books dealing with intelligence activities are F.W. Winterbotham, The Ultra Secret (Dell, 1979), William Stevenson, A Man Called Intrepid (Ballantine, 1976), and R.V. Jones, The Wizard War: British Scientific Intelligence 1939–1945 (Coward, McCann, 1978).

The Nazis' genocide policies have been analyzed by Raul Hilberg, The Destruction of the European Jews (Quadrangle, 1961); Karl A. Schleunes, The Twisted Road to Auschwitz: Nazi Policy Toward German Jews 1933–1939 (Univ. of Illinois, 1970); and Lucy S. Dawidowicz, ed., A Holocaust Reader (Behrman House, 1976). See also Dawidowicz's The War Against the Jews: 1933–1945 (Bantam, 1976). Telford Taylor's memoir, The Anatomy of the Nuremberg Trials (Knopf, 1994) is a thorough and compelling discussion of these unprecedented hearings.

Just about all major participants who survived the war—on all sides—have produced memoirs. The classics among them are Churchill's The Second World War, 6 vols. (Bantam) and Charles De Gaulle, Mémoires (Plon).

→ Notes

1. Quoted in A. G. Mazour, *Russia Past and Present* (New York: Van Nostrand Reinhold, 1951), p. 576.

2. George F. Kennan, *Memoirs* (New York: Bantam Books, 1969), p. 122.

3. Quoted in John Toland, *Adolf Hitler* (New York: Ballantine Books, 1977), pp. 522–529.

4. Donald W. Treadgold, *Twentieth Century Russia* (Chicago: Rand McNally, 1959), pp. 324–325.

5. Keith Middlemas, *The Strategy of Appeasement* (Chicago: Quadrangle Books, 1972), pp. 1–8.

6. The minutes of the conference in Reich Chancellory, as extracted and quoted in Francis L. Loewenheim, *Peace or Appeasement* (Boston: Houghton Mifflin, 1965), pp. 2–4.

7. Middlemas, *The Strategy of Appeasement*, p. 177.

8. W. S. Churchill, *Blood, Sweat and Tears* (New York: G. P. Putnam's Sons, 1941), p. 66.

9. F. D. Roosevelt, "Address at Chicago, October 5, 1937," in *The Literature of the United States*, II, W. Blair, T. Hornberger, and R. Stewart, eds. (Chicago: Scott, Foresman, 1955), pp. 831–832.

10. S. E. Ayling, *Portraits of Power* (New York: Barnes & Noble, 1963), p. 159.

11. Nigel Nicolson, ed., *Harold Nicolson, The War Years 1939–1945*, Volume II of *Diaries and Letters* (New York: Atheneum, 1967), p. 100.

12. Churchill, *Blood, Sweat and Tears*, p. 297.

13. *Last Letters from Stalingrad*, trans. Franz Schneider and Charles Gullas (New York: Signet Books, 1965), p. 20.

14. Quoted in John Vinocur, "Goebbels, in Published 1945 Diary Blames Goring for Nazis' Collapse," *New York Times*, January 3, 1978.

15. See Raul Hilberg, *The Destruction of the European Jews* (Chicago: Quadrangle Books, 1961), passim; and Maurice Crouzet, "L'Epoque Contemporaine," *Histoire Générale des Civilisations*, VII (Paris: Presses Universitaires de France, 1957), pp. 358–359.

16. Simon Kuznets, *Postwar Economic Growth: Four Lectures* (Cambridge: Harvard Univ. Press, 1964), pp. 72–76, as cited in David Landes, *The Unbound Prometheus* (Cambridge: Cambridge Univ. Press, 1969), p. 487.

CHAPTER 34

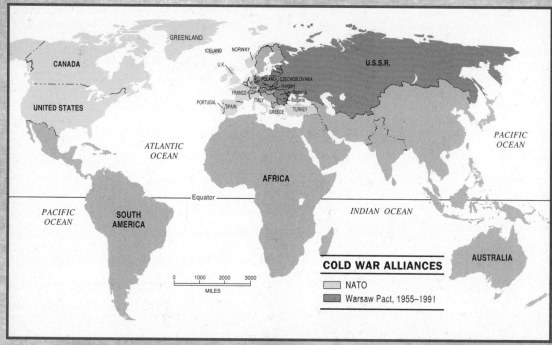

COLD WAR ALLIANCES
- NATO
- Warsaw Pact, 1955–1991

→ After 1945 maps showing balance of power alignments had not a European center but a center based on the North Polar region, the shortest access route for nuclear missiles between Moscow and Washington. There were only two states of consequence in the nuclear age: the United States and the USSR.

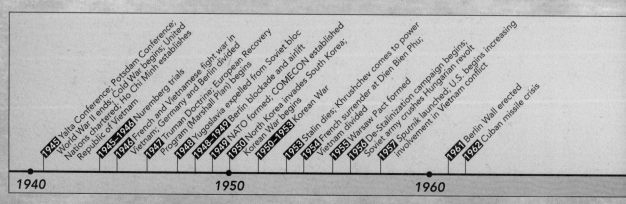

- **1945** Yalta Conference; Potsdam Conference; World War II ends; Cold War begins; United Nations chartered; Ho Chi Minh establishes Republic of Vietnam
- **1945–1946** Nuremberg trials
- **1946** French and Vietnamese fight war in Vietnam; Germany and Berlin divided
- **1947** Truman Doctrine; European Recovery Program (Marshall Plan) begins
- **1948** Yugoslavia expelled from Soviet bloc
- **1948–1949** Berlin blockade and airlift
- **1949** NATO formed, COMECON established
- **1950** North Korea invades South Korea; Korean War begins
- **1950–1953** Korean War
- **1953** Stalin dies; Khrushchev comes to power
- **1954** French surrender at Dien Bien Phu; Vietnam divided
- **1955** Warsaw Pact formed
- **1956** De-Stalinization campaign begins; Soviet army crushes Hungarian revolt
- **1957** Sputnik launched; U.S. begins increasing involvement in Vietnam conflict
- **1961** Berlin Wall erected
- **1962** Cuban missile crisis

1940   1950   1960

938

The Cold War, Russia, and Eastern Europe, 1945–1995

CHAPTER OUTLINE

The Elusive Peace

The Cold War: Part I, 1945–1953

The Cold War: Part II, 1953–1962

The Cold War: Part III, 1962–1985

The End of the Cold War

Eastern Europe

MAPS

Cold War Alliances

The Division of Germany

The Vietnam War

Successor Republics of the Former Soviet Union

The Breakup of Yugoslavia

DOCUMENTS

The Truman Doctrine

Nikita Khrushchev, Address to the Twentieth Party Congress

The devastating power of nuclear weapons ensured that the United States and the Soviet Union never directly fought each other during the nearly half-century of international tension after World War II known as the Cold War. However, "proxy wars" fought by their clients—and their own occasional intervention—killed millions in Asia, Africa, and Latin America. Ironically Europe, the stage for the previous two world wars, became caught in the stalemate between the two superpowers and enjoyed its longest time of peace in recorded history.

From the first, the West's economy was more productive than that of the Soviet bloc. Despite this, the Warsaw Pact achieved military parity with the West by the mid-1970s. The next round of weapons technology competition contributed to the Soviet bloc's economic exhaustion, which led to the end of the Cold War by 1990. Cooperation increasingly characterized the relations between Moscow and Washington as the exhausted superpowers looked to a new era in which they would try to keep their dominant roles in a rapidly changing world.

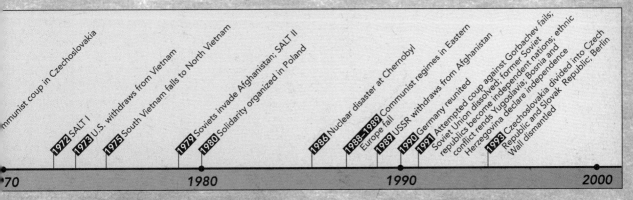

Timeline: Communist coup in Czechoslovakia · 1972 SALT I · 1973 U.S. withdraws from Vietnam · 1975 South Vietnam falls to North Vietnam · 1979 Soviets invade Afghanistan; SALT II · 1980 Solidarity organized in Poland · 1986 Nuclear disaster at Chernobyl · 1988–1989 Communist regimes in Eastern Europe fall · 1989 USSR withdraws from Afghanistan · 1990 Germany reunited · 1991 Attempted coup against Gorbachev fails; Soviet Union dissolved; former Soviet republics become independent nations; ethnic conflict rends Yugoslavia; Bosnia and Herzegovina declare independence · 1993 Czechoslovakia divided into Czech Republic and Slovak Republic; Berlin Wall dismantled

'70 · 1980 · 1990 · 2000

THE ELUSIVE PEACE

After World War II, many of the living had reason to envy the dead. Fire bombs and nuclear weapons had depopulated and irradiated parts of Japan. One-fourth of Germany's cities were in rubble, as were much of Italy and central Europe. The war claimed 10 percent of Yugoslavia's population. In China, after 15 years of fighting, survivors faced hunger, disease, civil war, and revolution. Twenty-five million people died in the Soviet Union, and the country lost one-third of its national wealth. Although casualty rates in Britain and France were lower than in World War I, both countries paid dearly in lives and in the ruin that took one-fourth of their national wealth.

Postwar Problems

Europe faced two immediate problems: dealing with Nazi collaborators and resettling millions of labor slaves. In countries that had been occupied by the Germans, victorious resistance groups began to take vigilante justice against those who had worked with the invaders. Across Europe they executed thousands of collaborators. In France alone 800 were sent to their deaths. After the war and into the 1990s, courts sentenced thousands more to prison terms. Eight million foreign labor slaves who had been used by the Nazis remained to be resettled. By the end of 1945, five million of them had been sent home, including many Soviet citizens who were forced to return. Some of them chose suicide rather than return to Stalin's rule.

In Germany, the Allies then began to carry out a selective process of denazification. Some former Nazis were sent to prison while thousands received the benefits of large-scale declarations of amnesty. Many ex-Nazis were employed by the scientific and intelligence services of each of the Allies. Symbolically, the most important denazification act came at the 1945–1946 trials of war criminals held at Nuremberg. An international panel of jurists conducted the proceedings and condemned 12 leading Nazis to be hanged and sent 7 to prison for crimes against humanity. The panel acquitted 3 high officials. Critics condemned the trials as an act of vengeance, "a political act by the victors against the vanquished." The prosecution stated, however, the Nazi crimes were so terrible that "civilization cannot tolerate their being ignored because it cannot survive their being repeated."[1]

> After World War II, the bombed-out cities of Europe seemed almost beyond hope. In 1947 Churchill described the Continent as "a rubble heap, a charnel house, a breeding ground of pestilence and hate." This photo is of Berlin's business district as it appeared in 1945. This section of the city received heavy shelling during the Allied bombing of Berlin.

Following the Yalta agreement, the Allies established four occupation zones in Germany—French, British, American, and Russian. They divided the capital, Berlin, located in the Soviet sector, into four parts. The Russians promised free access from the western zones to Berlin. Growing hostility between the Soviet Union and the United States by the end of the war blocked a comprehensive peace settlement for Germany.

At the Potsdam Conference in the summer of 1945 the Allies set up a council of ministers to draft peace treaties with Berlin's allies. After two years of difficult negotiations, treaties were signed with Italy, Romania, Bulgaria, Hungary, and Finland. In 1951, an accord between the Western powers and the Japanese reestablished Japan as a sovereign state. Austria's position remained in flux until 1955, when a peace treaty was signed and occupation forces were withdrawn.

Not until the signing of the Helsinki Accords in 1975 was a postwar status for Europe acknowledged, and that agreement did not have the force of a binding legal treaty. The diplomatic issues spawned by World War II finally were put to rest in a series of treaties signed by all European parties in the summer of 1990, following the reunification of Germany and the collapse of the Soviet bloc.

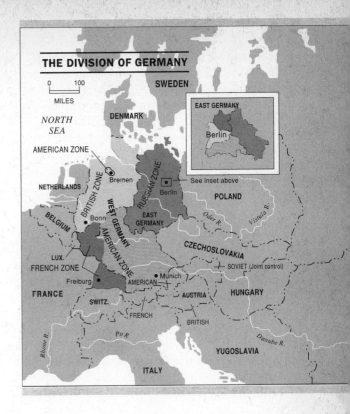

THE DIVISION OF GERMANY

The United Nations

On only one issue, the establishment of an international peacekeeping organization, could the powers agree after the war. Great Britain and the United States laid the foundations for the United Nations in 1941 when they proposed "the establishment of a wider and permanent system of general security" so "that men in all lands may live out their lives in freedom from fear and want." Subsequent meetings in Moscow and Yalta led representatives of 50 governments meeting in San Francisco from April to June 1945 to draft the Charter of the United Nations.

To pursue its goals of peace and an improved standard of living for the world, the UN would work through six organizations: the Security Council, to maintain peace and order; the General Assembly, to function as a form of town meeting of the world; the Economic and Social Council, to improve living standards and extend human rights; the Trusteeship Council, to ad-

vance the interests of the colonial peoples; the International Court of Justice, to resolve disputes between nations; and the Secretariat, headed by the secretary-general, to serve the needs of the other organizations. Much of the responsibility for improving the economic and social conditions of the world's people was entrusted to a dozen specialized agencies, such as the International Labor Organization; the Food and Agricultural Organization; the World Health Organization; and the UN Educational, Scientific, and Cultural Organization.

The greatest controversy at San Francisco arose over the right of veto in the Security Council. The smaller countries held that it was unjust for the big powers to be able to block the wishes of the majority. But the Big Five—the United States, the Soviet Union, China, France, and Great Britain—affirmed that singly and collectively they had special interests and responsibilities in maintaining world peace and security. The UN Charter, therefore, provided that the Security Council should consist of 11 members, 5 permanent members representing the great powers and 6 elected by the General Assembly for a term of two years. These numbers would be increased as the membership of the UN grew. On purely procedural matters a majority of 7 votes was sufficient; on matters of substance, all permanent members had to agree.

The UN proved to be more effective than the League of Nations. The UN, like the League, lacks the sovereign power of its member states. However, as was shown in the Korean conflict in the 1950s, the Gulf War in 1991, and subsequent peacekeeping and humanitarian activities in Asia, Europe, and Africa, it has become more wide-reaching in its impact. In 1946 it had 51 members; in 1995, membership stood at 184. Over the years the UN's usefulness has repeatedly been demonstrated despite the difficulties of the Cold War, the strains of massive decolonization, and four Arab-Israeli wars—not to mention an interminable series of smaller crises. As was the case with the League, the UN cannot coerce the great powers when any of them decides a major national interest is involved.

THE COLD WAR: PART I, 1945–1953

The Soviets and Americans differed in their views on economics, politics, social organization, religion, and the role of the individual. The Nazi threat produced a temporary unity between the two systems, but by 1943 tension increased over Soviet frustration with the slowness of its allies to open the second front, discontent with being shut out of participation in the Italian campaign, and unhappiness with the amount of U.S. financial assistance.

The Western allies were suspicious of Soviet secrecy. London and Washington gave detailed data on strategy and weapons to Moscow, but got little information from the Soviets. Over $12 billion in Lend-Lease aid was sent to the Soviet Union, but its extent and value were not publicly acknowledged for four decades in the Soviet Union.[2]

After the breakdown of wartime cooperation, the Cold War began. From 1945 to 1953 the struggle was centered in Europe and focused on Joseph Stalin's attempts to consolidate his hegemony in Eastern Europe.

Postwar Stalinism

Despite the immense destruction it had suffered, the USSR emerged after the war as one of the world's two superpowers. Stalin took seriously his role in building communism and pursuing world revolution. He used the secret police to rid Soviet society of any Western contamination. To achieve military equality with the United States, he launched the fourth Five-Year Plan in 1946, pushing growth in heavy industry and military goods. To increase Soviet output, he imposed double shifts on many workers.

Stalin harshly rewarded the Soviet people for their sacrifices in World War II with a return to the iron repression of the 1930s. In the city of Leningrad (now known by its original name of St. Petersburg), which had lost one million people, streets had been renamed in honor of the war dead. Stalin's *apparatchiki* ripped down these spontaneous tributes and restored the old, officially approved names.

Huge new factories producing an estimated 80 percent of industrial output sprang up east of a line from Leningrad to Moscow to Stalingrad (now Volgograd). The state lured workers to the new sites with salary increases and other benefits, but much of the need for workers was filled by mass deportation of people to labor camps. Those whose loyalty to Stalin was in the least suspect were sent to a network of camps spread from Siberia to central Asia to the Arctic region. "The economic demand for cheap labour [dictated] the supply of the guilty."[3] Thousands died in the camps from overwork, inadequate food, and the bitter cold.

To rebuild the devastated farming regions Stalin returned to his collectivization policies. Smaller farms became parts of larger units, and the ultimate goal remained to make peasants into members of the rural proletariat, working in "industrialized agriculture." After 1950 the effort was stepped up, but at the cost of discontent and low productivity.

The dictator continued to place his supporters in all important offices, combining "the supreme command of the party with the supreme administration of the state."[4] He made entry into the party more difficult and purged many people who had slipped in through the relaxed membership standards during wartime. The party became a haven for the managerial elite rather than the ideologically pure. The 1946 Supreme Soviet elections illustrated Stalin's political control. The voters were given only one choice for each office. Officials reported that 99.7 percent of the citizens voted; of this total fewer than 1 percent crossed out the name of a candidate.

In the early 1950s Stalin lashed out more ruthlessly and unpredictably than ever before, as he came to suspect everyone. His half-million strong security police squashed any sign of dissent, criticism, or free expression. He ordered genocidal attacks on entire peoples such as the Crimean Tatars. After Stalin removed and later executed the director of national economic planning, there were indications that Stalin was preparing a major purge that would go beyond "elite self-renewal."

In January 1953, the police announced that a "doctors' plot" had been uncovered and charged a group of physicians serving high military and governmental officials with planning to undermine their patients' health. Seven of the nine accused were Jewish, and in some quarters it was feared that an anti-Zionist campaign was in the making. The purge did not occur because on March 5, 1953, Stalin died after a painful illness.

Thus passed one of the most powerful men in world history. He had taken Lenin's revolution and preserved it in Russia while exporting it to the world. In a quarter-century he remade his society, withstood Hitler's strongest attacks, and emerged from the Second World War as leader of one of the two superpowers. He built the Soviet economic and political systems, which lasted until 1987 and cultivated a group of bureaucratic survivors— the *apparatchiki*—who ran the country until the advent of Mikhail Gorbachev. In doing all of this, he killed more of his people than Hitler had.

The Cold War in Eastern Europe to 1953

After the February 1945 Yalta Conference it soon became clear that Stalin had his view of the composition of postwar eastern Europe, and Roosevelt and Churchill had theirs. As early as April 1, 1945, Roosevelt sent a telegram to Stalin protesting the violation of Yalta pledges. A month later Churchill sent a long message of protest to Stalin in which he concluded:

> There is not much comfort in looking into a future where you and the countries you dominate . . . are all on one side, and those who rally to the English speaking nations . . . are on the other. Their quarrel would tear the world to pieces.[5]

From 1945 to 1948 Stalin expanded his control over the region carefully, working through his allies' domination of the various coalition governments. He had a number of advantages. Most of the local elites had either been killed during the war or were condemned for collaborating with the Nazis. The communist parties, most of which were underground during the interwar period, had gained public support by leading the resistance to the Nazis after June 1941. Further, the Red Army remained in place to intimidate Eastern Europe.

The communists occupied the most powerful positions in the coalition governments; opposition parties gained largely symbolic posts. The communists soon used intimidation and outright force. The Czechs remained free longer than the other Eastern European states. In the 1946 elections the communists had received only 38 percent of the vote, and they were losing support. In the spring of 1948 the Soviets forced Czechoslovakia to submit to communist control. By the end of 1948, when the Americans had totally withdrawn from Europe, the governments in Warsaw, East Berlin, Prague, Budapest, Bucharest, Sofia, and Tirana operated as satellites orbiting the political center of Moscow.

Stalin used the Soviet bloc as a 400-mile-deep buffer against capitalist invasion and as a source to help the USSR rebuild. He blocked any political, economic, or cultural contact with the West. Once his allies gained control, he ordered a purge of the local parties, based on those in the Soviet Union in the 1930s. The main target for the purge was the national communists, those who were seen as being more loyal to their own nation than to Moscow or Stalin. Overall, the purge removed one in every four party members. Many of those eliminated had been loyal communists since the beginning of the century.

Meanwhile, in the three years after 1945, the four-power agreement on the governing of Germany soon broke apart. In the fall of 1946, Britain and America merged their zones into one economic unit, which came to be known as Bizonia. The French joined the union in 1948. Germany was now split into two parts, one administered by the Western allies and the other by the

Russians, and would remain divided until the line between the two powers—dubbed the Iron Curtain by Churchill—disappeared in 1990.

The Marshall Plan and Containment

The Soviets did not return their armies to a peacetime status after 1945. They and their allies challenged the West in Greece, Turkey, and Iran. Britain was too weak to play its former role in the region. The Americans, as they would subsequently do throughout the globe, filled the gap left by the British and French. President Harry Truman responded to Soviet pressure by announcing that the United States would support any country threatened by communist aggression. Soon after proclamation of the Truman Doctrine in 1947, the United States sent economic and military aid to Greece and Turkey, a move traditionally held to mark the American entry into the Cold War.

The United States' wartime goodwill toward the Soviet Union turned quickly to paranoid fear of international communism. The Americans, comfortable with their nuclear monopoly, had looked forward to a peaceful postwar world. They were angered by Soviet actions in the United Nations, Eastern Europe, and China, and by the growth of communist parties in western Europe. Conservatives attacked the Yalta agreement as a "sellout" and launched a new "Red Scare" campaign. A French observer noted the rapid change in attitude by pointing out that "a whole nation, optimistic and naive, placed its trust in a comrade in arms."[6] Now that comrade was the enemy.

The American diplomat George F. Kennan explained that the correct stance to take toward Stalin's policies was one of containment. In an article entitled "The Sources of Soviet Conduct," written under the byline of "Mr. X" in the July 1947 issue of *Foreign Affairs*, Kennan proposed a "realistic understanding of the profound and

The Truman Doctrine

Once the Americans recovered from their post-1945 euphoria, President Truman spelled out his response to perceived Soviet aggression.

The peoples of a number of countries of the world have recently had totalitarian regimes forced upon them against their will. The Government of the United States has made frequent protests against coercion and intimidation, in violation of the Yalta agreement, in Poland, Rumania, and Bulgaria. I must also state that in a number of other countries there have been similar developments.

At the present moment in world history nearly every nation must choose between alternative ways of life. The choice is too often not a free one.

One way of life is based upon the will of the majority, and is distinguished by free institutions, representative government, free elections, guaranties of individual liberty, freedom of speech and religion, and freedom from political oppression.

The second way of life is based upon the will of a minority forcibly imposed upon the major-

ity. It relies upon terror and oppression, a controlled press and radio, fixed elections, and the suppression of personal freedoms.

I believe that it must be the policy of the United States to support free peoples who are resisting attempted subjugation by armed minorities or by outside pressures.

I believe that we must assist free peoples to work out their own destinies in their own way.

I believe that our help should be primarily through economic and financial aid, which is essential to economic stability and orderly political processes.

From U.S. Congress, *Congressional Record*, 80th Congress, 1st Session (Washington, D.C.: U.S. Government Printing Office, 1947), vol. 93, p. 1981; and U.S. Congress, Senate Committee on Foreign Relations, *A Decade of American Foreign Policy: Basic Documents. 1941–1949* (Washington, D.C.: U.S. Government Printing Office, 1950), pp. 1270–1271.

→ To try to force the Western powers out of Berlin, in July 1948 the Russians imposed a blockade on the city. In response, the allies organized an airlift to fly in supplies to the city and its beleaguered citizens. In May 1949, the Soviets lifted the blockade.

deep-rooted difference between the United States and the Soviet Union" and the exercise of "a long-term, patient but firm and vigilant containment of Russian expansive tendencies."[7] This advice shaped U.S. policy throughout Europe.

The policy of containment was first used in Yugoslavia, where a split between Joseph Broz Tito (1891–1980) and Stalin marked the first breach in the Soviet advance. The Yugoslavs initiated the ideological break known as national communism. Supported financially by the West, the Yugoslavs were able to survive Stalin's attacks.

The broad economic and political arms of containment came into play. Secretary of State George C. Marshall proposed a plan of economic aid to help Europe solve its postwar financial problems. Western European nations eagerly accepted the Marshall Plan, while the Soviet Union rejected American aid for itself and its bloc. Congress authorized the plan, known as the European Recovery Program, and within four years the industrial output of the recipients climbed to 64 percent over 1947 levels and 41 percent over prewar levels. The European Recovery Act stabilized conditions in western Europe and prevented the communists from taking advantage of postwar problems.

Rival Systems

In July 1948, after opposing a Western series of currency and economic reforms in Germany, the Soviets blocked all land and water transport to Berlin from the West. For the next ten months the allies supplied West Berlin by air. They made over 277,000 flights to bring 2.3 million tons of food and other vital materials to the besieged city. Rather than risk war over the city, with the threat of American nuclear weapons, the Russians removed their blockade in May 1949. In the same month the Federal Republic of Germany came into existence, made up of the three Western allied zones. Almost immediately, the Soviet Union established the German Democratic Republic in East Germany. Germany would remain divided for the next 41 years.

In the spring of 1949 Washington established the North Atlantic Treaty Organization (NATO), an alliance for mutual assistance. The initial members were Great Britain, France, Belgium, Luxembourg, the Netherlands, Norway, Denmark, Portugal, Italy, Iceland, the United States, and Canada. Greece and Turkey joined in 1952, followed by West Germany in 1955. In 1955 also the Soviets created the Warsaw Pact, which formalized the existing unified military command

A U.S. Army Howitzer fires on Communist troops in night action during the Korean War. The Cold War erupted into heated conflict in 1950 when North Korean troops invaded South Korea. A cease-fire agreement was reached in 1951 but sporadic fighting continued until an armistice was signed in July 1953. The Korean conflict escalated tensions between the Cold War rivals and sped up the mounting weapons and nuclear arms race between the superpowers.

in Soviet-dominated Eastern Europe. Warsaw Pact members included, in addition to the Soviet Union, Albania, Bulgaria, Romania, Czechoslovakia, Hungary, Poland, and East Germany. The alliance lasted until 1991.

The tension between the rival systems finally snapped in Korea. After Japan's surrender, Korea had been divided at the 38th parallel into American and Soviet zones of occupation. When the occupying troops left, they were replaced by two hostile forces, each claiming jurisdiction over the entire country. On June 25, 1950, North Korean troops crossed the 38th parallel into South Korea. Washington immediately called for a special meeting of the UN Security Council, whose members demanded a cease-fire and withdrawal of the invaders. The Soviet delegate was boycotting the Council at the time and was not present to veto the action.

When North Korea ignored the UN's demand, the Security Council sent troops to help the South Korean government. Three years of costly fighting followed, in what the UN termed a "police action." United Nations forces led by the United States, which suffered over 140,000 casualties, repelled the invaders, who were supported by the USSR and the Chinese People's Republic. An armistice was signed in July 1953, after Stalin's death in March and the U.S. threat to use nuclear weapons against China.[8] The border between the two parts of the country was established near the 38th parallel, and South Korea's independence was maintained. The peninsula remained a crisis point into the mid-1990s.

By 1953 the first phase of the Cold War was over. Both the Soviet Union and the United States possessed terrifying arsenals of nuclear weapons, both competed in all aspects of the Cold War, and both constantly probed for weaknesses in the other's defenses. Varied forms of controlled conflict characterized the next four decades of relations between Moscow and Washington.

THE COLD WAR: PART II, 1953–1962

Stalin's death introduced a period of collective leadership in the Soviet Union. The transition from an all-powerful despot to a clique of competing *apparatchiki* brought a change to the nature and scope of Soviet foreign policy for the two years after 1953. Nikita S. Khrushchev dominated global events after 1955, as the Cold War spread throughout Asia, Africa, and Latin America. The introduction of intercontinental ballistic missiles (ICBMs) brought a chilling immediacy to the formation and conduct of foreign affairs.

Khrushchev: The "Uncultured" Man

A committee made up of Lavrenti Beria (secret police), Georgi Malenkov (chief Stalin aide), and Vyacheslav Molotov (foreign affairs) succeeded Stalin. The new rulers issued orders after his death urging the people to guard against enemies and prevent "any kind of disorder and panic." They placed Stalin's embalmed body in the tomb next to Lenin and then relaxed his policies. They dropped the doctors' plot charges, eased censorship, reduced terror, and released many from prison and the labor camps.

Within three years, the initial triumvirate had disappeared, elbowed aside by Nikita Sergeyevich Khrushchev (1894–1971). Khrushchev was a self-made man who rose by his wits and ability. Born of peasant parents, he was a shepherd at seven and later a miner and factory worker. He joined the Communist party and quickly rose through its ranks. Like so many of his colleagues, he came to power in the 1930s by taking the jobs of people killed by Stalin, and ascended to the Politburo by 1939. By July 1953 he was the first secretary of the party; by 1955 he led the country.

Educated Russians viewed Khrushchev as uncultured and uncouth. He delighted in shocking people by his blunt and frequently profane remarks. His crude behavior disguised a subtle, supple, and penetrating mind, which got rapidly to the center of a problem.

One of Khrushchev's main goals was to reform agriculture. He proposed increasing incentives for the peasants and enlarging the area under production in Soviet Siberia and central Asia—the virgin lands. Between 1953 and 1958 production rose by 50 percent. Thereafter farming in the virgin lands proved to be economically wasteful and environmentally disastrous. This, combined with other setbacks, ultimately undermined Khrushchev's position.

De-Stalinization

Khrushchev's greatest contribution to the history of the USSR was to launch the de-Stalinization campaign. In February 1956 at the Twentieth Party Congress he gave a speech entitled the "Crimes of the Stalin Era." He attacked his former patron as a bloodthirsty tyrant and revealed many of the cruelties of the purges and the mistakes of World War II. He carefully heaped full responsibility on the dead dictator for the excesses of the past 25 years, removing the blame from the *apparatchiki* such as himself whom Stalin had placed in power. Khrushchev blamed Stalin's crimes on the dictator's "cult of the personality." The speech hit like a bombshell and shocked every level of Soviet society. In 1961 Stalin's body was removed from the Lenin mausoleum and placed in a grave by the Kremlin wall. His name disappeared from streets and cities; the "hero city" of Stalingrad was renamed Volgograd. Yet, the governing structure Stalin had built was carefully preserved, and his protégés remained in

→ Stalin's chief supporters surround the bier at his funeral, March 6, 1953. Left to right, they are Vyacheslav Molotov, Kliment Voroshilov, Lavrenti Beria, Georgi Malenkov, Nikolai Bulganin, Nikita Khrushchev, Lazar Kaganovich, and Anastas Mikoyan. Khrushchev was the victor in the power struggle to succeed Stalin.

place until Mikhail Gorbachev came to power in 1985.

Khrushchev's speech echoed throughout the communist world, helping to spark uprisings in Poland and Hungary and to widen the gulf between China and the Soviet Union. Chinese-Soviet relations soured drastically after 1956 and by 1960 Khrushchev had pulled all Soviet technicians and assistance out of China. During the next decade, the split grew still wider as Mao proclaimed himself to be Khrushchev's equal in ideological affairs.

Khrushchev survived an attempt to oust him from power in the summer of 1957, and from then until 1962, he dominated both Soviet and international affairs. During his rule, the standard of living in Russia gradually improved. Soviet scientists made remarkable strides, launching the first earth satellite, *Sputnik*, in the fall of 1957, and building a powerful fleet of ICBMs. Khrushchev also relaxed, until 1959, the tensions of the Cold War and pursued "peaceful coexistence." From 1959 to 1962, however, he pursued aggressive policies in Asia, Africa, and Latin America that brought the world to the brink of nuclear war.

"Peaceful Coexistence"

After Stalin's death in March 1953 the USSR endured a three-year period of transition, and its foreign policy shifted from military probing to a more sophisticated approach. When Khrushchev gained control in 1955, he imposed his point of view that nuclear war would be suicidal for all concerned. He returned to the Leninist doctrine of peaceful coexistence and renounced the idea that open war between the socialist and capitalist worlds was inevitable. Peaceful coexistence ushered in momentarily better relations between Moscow and Washington and led to a summit meeting in Geneva in 1955 and Khrushchev's visit to the United States in 1959. Violence increased in Asia, Latin America, Africa, and the Middle East, however, where the rival systems competed for influence.

Two Soviet technological triumphs in 1957 escalated the tensions between the United States and the USSR. Moscow's scientists put the first artificial satellite into orbit and began to produce ICBMs. These advances enabled the Soviet Union to deliver a nuclear weapon to U.S. territory in 25

minutes. Despite the surface relaxation of relations between Washington and Moscow, the Cold War became more dangerous.

Berlin, which had long been a thorn in the Soviet side, became the main flash point for war between the two powers. West Berlin's wealth and freedom stood in sharp contrast to the drab, repressive picture presented by East Berlin. Thousands of East Germany's technical and intellectual elite easily escaped through Berlin. The Soviets, who had tried to drive the West from Berlin in the 1948 blockade, demanded the withdrawal of all Western forces and recognition of Berlin as a "Free City." They presumably wanted to bring the whole metropolis under communist control. The Allies, strengthened in part by the major advances in U.S. rocket power, refused to give in to this demand.

A series of events from 1960 to 1962 brought the superpowers closer to the brink of nuclear war. A summit convened in Paris in 1960 broke up angrily with the shooting down of an American U-2 reconnaissance plane over the USSR. Khrushchev took the opportunity to denounce the West and marshal his forces for a series of provocative moves. He demanded the resignation of UN Secretary-General Dag Hammarskjold who, he believed, opposed the Soviet-backed side in the Congolese civil war (see p. 1020). The failure of the U.S. Bay of Pigs campaign, an attempt to land forces of Cuban exiles to overthrow Premier Fidel Castro, gave Khrushchev another trump card to play.

In the spring of 1961, with John F. Kennedy, a young and inexperienced president, in office, Moscow stepped up all of its pressures around the world. The Soviets again demanded the withdrawal of the Allies from West Berlin. Once again, citing postwar agreements, the West refused to back down. This time, the East Germans, acting under Soviet supervision, erected a wall between the two halves of the city, thereby blocking the escape route formerly used by thousands. Tensions also rose in Laos and Vietnam. To a generation of leaders in the United States, students of the lessons of "appeasement" in Munich a quarter-century earlier and of the success of containment, it seemed evident that force had to be met with force.

In October 1962 the world came as close as it ever has to full-scale nuclear war. Three years earlier, Fidel Castro had led a successful revolution against the right-wing Cuban dictator Ful-

Nikita Khrushchev, Address to the Twentieth Party Congress

After a quarter-century of Stalinist rule, the USSR badly needed a policy change. Khrushchev justified the change on the grounds that Stalin had departed from Leninist norms and pursued the "cult of the personality."

When we analyze the practice of Stalin in regard to the direction of the party and of the country, when we pause to consider everything which Stalin perpetrated, we must be convinced that Lenin's fears were justified. The negative characteristics of Stalin, which, in Lenin's time, were only incipient, transformed themselves during the last years into a grave abuse of power by Stalin, which caused untold harm to our party.

We have to consider seriously and analyze correctly this matter in order that we may preclude any possibility of a repetition in any form whatever of what took place during the life of Stalin, who absolutely did not tolerate collegiality in leadership and in work, and who practiced brutal violence, not only toward everything which opposed him, but also toward that which seemed to his capricious and despotic character, contrary to his concepts.

Stalin acted not through persuasion, explanation, and patient cooperation with people, but by imposing his concepts and demanding absolute submission to his opinion. Whoever opposed this concept or tried to prove his viewpoint, and the correctness of his position—was doomed to removal from the leading collective and to subsequent moral and physical annihilation. This was especially true during the period following the 17th party congress, when many prominent party leaders and rank-and-file party workers, honest and dedicated to the cause of communism, fell victim to Stalin's despotism. . . .

. . . Lenin's traits—patient work with people; stubborn and painstaking education of them; the ability to induce people to follow him without using compulsion, but rather through the ideological influence on them of the whole collective—were entirely foreign to Stalin. [Stalin] discarded the Leninist method of convincing and educating; he abandoned the method of ideological struggle for that of administrative violence, mass repressions, and terror. He acted on an increasingly larger scale and more stubbornly through punitive organs, at the same time often violating all existing norms of morality and of Soviet laws. . . .

During Lenin's life party congresses were convened regularly; always when a radical turn in the development of the party and the country took place Lenin considered it absolutely necessary that the party discuss at length all the basic matters pertaining to internal and foreign policy and to questions bearing on the development of party and government. . . .

Were our party's holy Leninist principles observed after the death of Vladimir Ilyich?

Whereas during the first few years after Lenin's death party congresses and central committee plenums took place more or less regularly; later, when Stalin began increasingly to abuse his power, these principles were brutally violated. This was especially evident during the last 15 years of his life. Was it a normal situation when 13 years elapsed between the 18th and 19th party congresses, years during which our party and our country had experienced so many important events? These events demanded categorically that the party should have passed resolutions pertaining to the country's defense during the patriotic war and to peacetime construction after the war. Even after the end of the war a congress was not convened for over 7 years. . . .

In practice Stalin ignored the norms of party life and trampled on the Leninist principle of collective party leadership.

From U.S. Congress, *Congressional Record*, 84th Congress, 2nd Session, 1956, CII, pp. 9389–9403, passim.

gencio Batista. Castro immediately began to transform the island into a communist state. After the failure of the American effort to overthrow him at the Bay of Pigs, the Soviets began to install missiles in Cuba.

To the United States, these missiles were a dangerous threat to the Cold War balance of power. Kennedy ordered what was, in effect, a naval blockade around Cuba and demanded that Moscow withdraw the offensive weapons. After a few days of "eyeball-to-eyeball" crisis in which one incident might have triggered direct military action between Moscow and Washington, Khrushchev ordered the missiles removed, after having received assurances that the United States would respect Cuba's territory and other concessions.

After drawing the world to the brink of catastrophe in the Cuban missile crisis in October 1962, Khrushchev pulled back from the final step that would have resulted in nuclear war. His blunders in Cuba and failures in agricultural policies led finally to his removal from power. While on vacation in October 1964 he received news from his colleagues that he had been "released from state duties" and that he had to return to Moscow. The fallen leader became a pensioned "un-person" under a mild form of house arrest in a comfortable compound outside Moscow. He remained largely isolated from the public, writing his memoirs until his death in 1971.

The Vietnam War: 1950–1975

A misreading of the "containment" doctrine drew the United States into a quagmire in Indochina that would change Americans' views toward their role in the world and their government. After World War II France was forced to grant a measure of autonomy to Cambodia and Laos, its former colonial possessions in Southeast Asia. The status of Vietnam posed a greater problem. In 1945 a nationalist and procommunist movement led by Ho Chi Minh had established the independent Republic of Vietnam, usually referred to as the Vietminh regime.

Negotiations between the Vietminh and the French led nowhere, and war broke out in December 1946. The cruel and violent struggle, anticolonial as well as ideological, lasted for nearly eight years. In May 1950 the United States began sending substantial financial and military support to the French. The end came dramatical-

ly in 1954 when the French, despite U.S. assistance, surrendered their isolated outpost at Dien Bien Phu, along with 10,000 troops.

In a conference at Geneva later that year a truce line was established at the 17th parallel, to be regarded as a temporary boundary pending nationwide elections. These elections were never held, and instead a new group proclaimed the Republic of South Vietnam, based in Saigon, south of the truce line. Meanwhile, the division between the Vietminh regime in Hanoi and the Saigon government increased. Along with the movement of hundreds of thousands of Roman Catholic Vietnamese refugees from the north came a powerful infiltration of communist military personnel and materiel from Hanoi.

The United States shipped large numbers of men and weapons to Saigon in an attempt to create a South Vietnamese state capable of holding its own against the Vietminh and their allies in

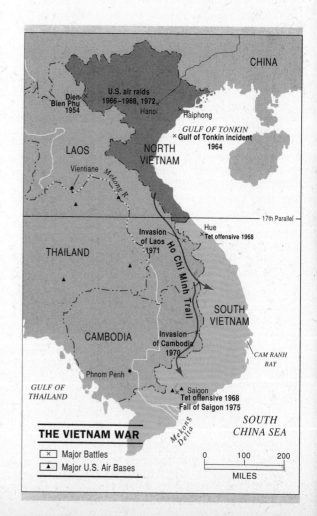

THE VIETNAM WAR
☒ Major Battles
▲ Major U.S. Air Bases

South Vietnam. The military activity on both sides violated the Geneva agreements, but it could be argued that since none of the governments had signed them, they simply were not binding. Washington also sponsored the establishment of the Southeast Asia Treaty Organization (SEATO) to stop the spread of communism into Cambodia, Laos, and South Vietnam.

At first the Americans gave full support to Ngo Dinh Diem, the leading figure of the noncommunist south. He rejected Ho Chi Minh's requests to hold elections throughout all Vietnam under the Geneva agreements because he feared that his government would lose. He also refused to carry out comprehensive land reforms desired by Washington, choosing instead to rely for support on the landlords and the urban middle classes.

At the same time, the communists, thwarted in their aim to unite North and South by an election, began guerrilla operations against Diem's government. This so-called Second Vietnamese War began in 1957. Many peasants, disillusioned by Diem's failure to carry out land reform, tacitly or actively supported the communist guerrilla effort. In December, the National Liberation Front (NLF)—popularly known as the Viet Cong—was established in the south and gained full support from Hanoi.

Diem, in the face of a rising crisis, became even more autocratic and less inclined to make reforms, perhaps reflecting Washington's shift in policy from President Eisenhower's emphasis on "nation building" to Kennedy's strategy of "counterinsurgency." The NLF threatened to take over the entire government by force, and a coup and Diem's assassination did little to improve the situation. Following a series of short-lived, essentially military governments, Nguyen van Thieu became president of South Vietnam in 1967.

The Americanization of the War

In 1960 there were only 800 U.S. military advisers in the country. Four years later, this figure had risen to 23,000. In August 1964 Washington accused North Vietnam of attacking United States destroyers in the Gulf of Tonkin. Following President Lyndon B. Johnson's request, Congress adopted—by a Senate vote of 88 to 2 and a House vote of 416 to 0—a joint resolution approving "all necessary measures . . . to prevent further aggression" and authorized the president to assist South Vietnam in its defense, using military force if required.

Thereafter, the war in all of its aspects became increasingly Americanized. By 1968 there

→ A marine helicopter drops off U.S. troops in Vietnam in 1965. In 1963, there were 16,000 U.S. combat troops in Vietnam; five years later, the number had increased to 500,000. More than 58,000 Americans were killed in action in Vietnam, making the Vietnam conflict the United States' fourth deadliest war—after the Civil War and World Wars I and II.

were more than 500,000 U.S. troops in the country. In 1965 the United States started an intensive air campaign against North Vietnam. The aerial campaign failed to intimidate the North Vietnamese and became a subject of bitter controversy in the United States.

Many Americans began to question the U.S. role in Vietnam. Their doubts were sharpened in the early spring of 1968 when the Viet Cong launched the Tet offensive against the Saigon forces and the Americans. Widely covered by television and print journalists, the offensive turned into a military disaster for the NLF and Hanoi, but the images of death and destruction communicated a notion of helplessness to the American people. The U.S. military victory became a political defeat for President Johnson.

As the number of Americans killed in Vietnam grew, the antiwar movement spread from a few score campus radicals to include moderate politicians, suburbanites, and mainstream clergy. The financial costs of the war were enormous, helping fuel an inflation that continued through the 1970s. The political cost for Lyndon Johnson was equally high, forcing him to step down after one term.

During the final months of Johnson's administration peace talks began in Paris with all interested parties represented. The Nixon administration continued the talks through three years of frustrating negotiations until, in January 1973, the Paris accord was signed. It provided for a cease-fire, the withdrawal of U.S. troops, and the release of all prisoners of war.

Pending elections to be arranged later, Nguyen van Thieu's South Vietnamese government was to remain in power. An international commission was to be established to investigate cease-fire violations. The Paris Accord contained no provision for the withdrawal of North Vietnamese forces. Once the Americans withdrew, the North Vietnamese continued their advance, and the commission was predictably ineffectual. In early 1975, the Hanoi forces, soon to be the fifth strongest military in the world, began a massive offensive. Deprived of U.S. support, the southern forces fell apart once the northern frontiers were overrun. Saigon, now named Ho Chi Minh City, was captured in late April. Many South Vietnamese fled their homeland and some 140,000 gained sanctuary in the United States.

For the United States the legacy of the Vietnam conflict was 58,000 killed, a financial outlay of at least $146 billion, a society bitterly split, and a host of veterans who were rebuked or ignored. It took 10 years for the United States to come to terms with the war. The legacy for Vietnam was a 20-year delay in the Vietminh takeover and incalculable human and material losses. By 1994 the country had barely begun to recover economically.

➔ After the United States withdrew its troops from Vietnam in 1973, many South Vietnamese fled the country. Here, a mother and her children struggle across a river to escape the aerial bombardment of their village.

Repercussions of the U.S. Failure

The United States had expanded the fighting into neutral Cambodia in the spring of 1970, invading it with the goal of cutting North Vietnamese supply lines and driving the Hanoi army from its sanctuaries there. Following the North Vietnamese victory in 1975, communists took control of Cambodia and Laos. The ruthless and brutal Khmer Rouge regime created a reign of terror in Cambodia, which was renamed Kampuchea. In Phnom Penh, the capital, nearly all the inhabitants—more than 2 million people—were driven into the countryside, regardless of age or infirmity. People in other cities suffered the same fate; many died from sickness or starvation. A new social system of farm units with labor brigades and communal kitchens was set up. The slightest sign of disobedience resulted in death.

The leader of the Chinese-supported Khmer Rouge regime was Pol Pot. His followers murdered thousands of innocent peasants along with "anyone who had been associated with the cities, with foreigners, or with intellectual, business, or technical activities."[9] The regime's goal seems to have been a self-sufficient agricultural society in which most people would have food and shelter but no pay. It is estimated that between 1975 and 1980 between 2 and 3 million Cambodians died—"shot, beaten to death, starved, brutalized. Few people in modern times have been subjugated to such barbarism."[10] The Pol Pot regime was overthrown when Vietnamese armies invaded the country. The Cambodians now suffered the ravages of war in addition to continued, indiscriminate killings and massacres.

While China supported Pol Pot, the Soviet Union supported the Vietnamese invaders and a Cambodian faction opposed to Pol Pot. Early in 1979 Chinese armies invaded Vietnam, destroying several of its northern towns, but failed to draw Vietnamese armies out of Cambodia. After this brief sortie, the Chinese forces withdrew, and the world gained an appreciation of the military strength of the Vietnamese regime.

Although the situation in Laos was not so chaotic, there also the Vietnamese regime imposed some regimentation and abuse of the Laotians, some of whom were sent to "reeducation camps." Many professional people fled the country, and soon the lack of food and the deplorable health conditions made Laos's standard of living nearly the lowest in the world.

Until the early 1990s, much of Indochina was a confused mass of fleeing refugees. Unwilling to accept communist rule, thousands took to the sea in rickety boats. Many Chinese living in Vietnam were mistreated by the new regime and retreated across the border to China. Great numbers of refugees fled from Laos and Cambodia to Thailand, Malaysia, Indonesia, and Hong Kong. In addition, thousands of "boat people" drowned at sea in their leaky craft, were attacked by pirates in the South China Sea, or died of thirst and starvation when refused permission to land.

Finally, by the mid-1990s, comparative stability returned to the region. Normal diplomatic and trade relations were restored between the U.S. and Vietnam. In Cambodia, a massive UN operation stabilized the country and permitted an election in 1993 that included all parties. By 1994, the Khmer Rouge, because of their continued military activities, were expelled from participation in the Phnom Penh government. It would take more time for the Indochinese peninsula to recover from the ravages of a half-century of war.

THE COLD WAR: PART III, 1962–1985

Following Khrushchev's "retirement," a classic *apparatchik*, Leonid Brezhnev (1906–1982), dominated the next stage of Cold War and Soviet history. Working with Aleksei Kosygin (1904–1980), he constructed an alliance with the military to deliver support that would enable the USSR to gain military parity with the Americans. This diversion of resources into military spending did little to help the larger economy, which suffered a serious decline at the end of the 1980s. Brezhnev and his colleagues profited from the U.S. involvement in Vietnam to make diplomatic gains—despite the entry of China on the international stage as a major power. Ironically, the invasion of Afghanistan in 1979 led the Soviets into a dilemma that was almost a mirror image of the tragedy the U.S. experienced in Vietnam. As the Vietnam war turned out to be a major turning point for the Americans, the Afghanistan adventure propelled the USSR toward its eventual decline and fall.

The Last of Stalin's Protégés

From 1964 to 1974, Brezhnev and Kosygin split power, Brezhnev acting as General Secretary and Kosygin as premier, overseeing sporadic reform attempts. Brezhnev later became president of the country under terms of the 1977 constitution. Serious health problems limited his effectiveness in the last years of his tenure until his death in 1982.

Politics remained based on Stalin's foundations, as modified by Khrushchev. The central planners continued to emphasize industrial growth and slowly increase the supply of consumer goods. In foreign policy, the new team pursued peaceful coexistence at the same time that they greatly strengthened the Soviet armed forces. Brezhnev worked closely with military leaders to ensure that they had everything needed to gain equality with the United States in missiles, air, land, and sea forces. During the 18 years of his rule, the Soviet Union built a powerful, global navy to support its foreign policies.

While the USSR gained military parity with the West, its civilian economy ground to a halt. The long-standing agricultural crisis grew worse. The Soviets spent huge amounts to import grain from abroad to cope with food shortages at home. Especially maddening to the Soviet leaders was the extraordinary amount of crops that rotted in the fields or en route to market. Private plots worked by peasants after hours for their own profit, which accounted for only 3 percent of sown land, provided 30 percent of all the table food in the Soviet Union.

The party leaders struggled to deal with low per capita output, poor quality, technological backwardness, transport breakdowns, and widespread corruption. Over the next 20 years, despite numerous reform attempts, the Soviet economy stagnated. The military sector absorbed most economic and technological improvements. Living standards slowly improved, but at a terrific cost. The Soviet Union exacerbated its economic problems by allowing political and ideological considerations to take precedence over productive efficiency.[11]

Brezhnev was succeeded by Iuri Andropov (1914–1984), a railway worker's son who worked his way up the ranks to become Soviet ambassador to Hungary from 1954 to 1957. After putting down the 1956 revolution in Hungary, Andropov returned to Moscow to take a number of increasingly important party and political jobs. In 1967 he became chief of the KGB, the organization which combined the powers and responsibilities of the U.S. FBI and CIA but without the legal restraints affecting those two groups. He remained in that post for the next 15 years. Andropov entered the Politburo in 1973 and, seven months before Brezhnev's death, became the secretary of the Central Committee. He rose to the top position in the Soviet Union the day after Brezhnev's death.

Andropov's jobs put him at the crossroads of all information. He knew the disastrous condition of the USSR's infrastructure. He brought a large number of people from the provinces to work in high party positions in Moscow and set out immediately to increase output, fight corruption, and strengthen the military. He started campaigns to fight alcoholism and cheating and fired people who did not perform up to his standards. However, his own health problems caught up with him, and from the summer of 1983 until his announced death in February 1984, Andropov was out of public view.

The last of the Stalin protégés was Konstantin Chernenko (1912–1985), who succeeded Andropov to the posts of first secretary and president. Chernenko had ridden Brezhnev's coattails since the 1950s but had been soundly defeated by Andropov for the top job in 1982. His age and poor health signified that he would be a transition figure between the old guard and a new generation. The strain of leadership almost immediately broke Chernenko's fragile health, and even before his death in March 1985, wholesale changes were taking place in the highest levels of the Soviet government.

Diplomacy and Arms Control Agreements

After 1962 the Soviet Union and the United States did not approach the brink of nuclear conflict. Close consultations between the two superpowers, even during proxy wars, helped head off danger. The "hot line" in its increasingly sophisticated forms kept the Kremlin and the White House in minute-by-minute contact and helped avoid possible nuclear holocausts in the dangerous Vietnamese and Middle Eastern situations. In addition, the USSR saw its options narrow after 1972 with the emergence of China as an independent player in the international game.

The Cuban crisis convinced leaders in Moscow and Washington of the need to reduce the peril of nuclear war and ushered in a continuing process of tortuous and complex negotiations dealing with all aspects of the risk of nuclear war. An immediate result of these talks was a limited nuclear test ban treaty negotiated in 1963 and signed on August 5 of that year by Great Britain, the Soviet Union, and the United States. The treaty outlawed the testing of nuclear devices in outer space, the atmosphere, or under water. Over 100 states signed the agreement, although France, China, and India refused to become signatories. The Latin American Nuclear-Free Zone Treaty was signed in 1968, and treaties and conventions dealing with the nonproliferation of nuclear weapons (1970, expanded 1978) followed.

In 1971 agreements were reached further reducing the risk of nuclear war and updating the "hot line." In 1975 a convention dealing with biological weapons and agreements concerning the threat of catastrophic war were signed. In addition, the Mutual Balanced Force Reduction Talks (MBFR) began between NATO and the Warsaw Pact to limit conventional forces. These dragged on into the 1990s, when they were finally concluded with the dissolution of the Warsaw Pact.

The two most important treaties were the Strategic Arms Limitation Talks (SALT I and SALT II). In these negotiations the two superpowers acknowledged, in effect, an equivalence of kill power that led to the capacity for "mutual assured destruction" (MAD). After two years of complicated talks, SALT I was signed by President Richard Nixon and General Secretary Leonid Brezhnev in Moscow in the spring of 1972. SALT I limited the number of ICBMs that each side could deploy for five years and restricted the construction of antiballistic missile systems to two sites in each country to maintain MAD.

Technological advances soon made the limits of SALT I obsolete, as both sides developed the ability to deploy multiple independently targeted reentry vehicles (MIRVs), which vastly expanded the kill power of each missile. At a meeting in Vladivostok in November 1974, U.S. President Gerald Ford and Brezhnev established guidelines to deal with the addition of MIRVs that led to the SALT II agreement. Even though considerations such as the Soviet invasion of Afghanistan and domestic politics in each country precluded the formal adoption of SALT II, the attempt to maintain parity continued. Each side charged the other at times with violating the understanding implicit in SALT II, which was eventually signed by President Jimmy Carter and Brezhnev in Vienna in 1979.

Throughout the 1980s Moscow and Washington both adhered to the general framework of SALT II, while maneuvering for strategic superiority. The arms control talks were complex, difficult, and subject to frustration as neither side could permit the other to gain the strategic advantage. So, while negotiations continued in the Strategic Arms Reduction Talks (START) in 1982, so too did full-scale weapons research and espionage. In the first half of the 1980s the USSR upset the balance of force in Europe by placing SS-20 missiles in the territory of its Eastern European allies. The START talks were broken off, and the Americans responded by deploying Pershing II and ground-launched cruise missiles, a strategic necessity given NATO's military inferiority in conventional weapons. After Mikhail Gorbachev became Soviet leader, arms talks on all levels resumed.

The USSR's "Quagmire": Afghanistan

Despite close general cooperation on the nuclear weapons talk, Cold War tensions escalated on another front in 1979 when the Soviet Union invaded Afghanistan. Armed coups and assassination had characterized the postwar political history of Afghanistan. After 1945 the Soviet Union extended its influence in the area, the site of the "Great Game" between tsarist Russia and Great Britain in the nineteenth century.

In 1978 Moscow increased its influence in Kabul by signing a "friendship treaty" with the Afghans. This agreement had little impact outside the capital; neither did postwar efforts by Kabul leaders to introduce changes based either on Western or Marxist models reach very far. The strongly conservative Muslim tribes opposed and

→ Soviet armored vehicles and trucks arrive in Kabul in January 1980 during the Soviet occupation of Afghanistan. The Afghan resistance, using weapons supplied by the United States, proved equal to the Soviet invaders, who withdrew without victory in 1989.

continue to oppose modernization in almost any form. Finally, in the late 1970s, civil war erupted.

By 1979 it appeared that the government of President Hafizullah Amin, which received support from the USSR, would be toppled by the rebellion. Earlier the Soviets had sent in 5000 military and civilian advisers to assist him. Moscow had made such a large investment that it could not tolerate the loss of its client state. In late December, thousands of Soviet troops crossed the border, captured the airport, and stormed the presidential palace in Kabul. They killed their erstwhile ally Amin and installed Babrak Kamal.

Kamal announced that Soviet troops had been invited in to save Afghanistan from imperialist plots fomented by the United States. Few nations accepted this explanation. But coming as it did during the U.S. dilemma in Iran (see p.1014), the invasion gave the USSR the chance to dominate this strategic region with little risk of armed opposition. In the next year the USSR gained control of Afghan cities, while an assortment of tribal guerrilla forces roamed the countryside. The Soviet advance sputtered to a stop during the next few years.

Moscow had gotten itself caught in a destructive quagmire that paralleled in many ways the American's experience in Vietnam. The Afghan resistance, lavishly supported by the United States, stalemated the Soviets and their puppets. The one advantage the USSR had in the battlefield, air power, was negated by the Afghan's effective use of the American-supplied Stinger anti-aircraft missile. As the decade wore on, Afghanistan became for the USSR what Vietnam had been for the United States: a costly, demoralizing, divisive conflict. Similarly, the cost to the Afghan peoples was immense. Millions were uprooted, villages were destroyed, and many areas were littered with mines and booby traps. Finally in 1989 the Soviet Union withdrew its forces. The civil war continued into the 1990s, and Afghanistan returned to its tradition of tribal competition. The difference was that now the firepower available to the combatants was immensely more powerful.

THE END OF THE COLD WAR

After Konstantin Chernenko's death, a new generation of Soviet leaders came to the fore, led by Mikhail Gorbachev. No less devoted to Marxism-Leninism than the former generation, the new leadership—many of whom had been placed in positions of influence by Andropov—more openly attacked the economic and social problems facing the USSR. Moscow continued to claim that the Soviet bloc would equal the West in technology by 2000, but to all observers it was apparent that the centrally planned system simply failed to be competitive in the new global economy. A by-product of the need to introduce new domestic policies was the collateral obligation to withdraw from the global competition that characterized the Cold War.

The Gorbachev Revolution: The Domestic Phase

Mikhail Gorbachev (b. 1931) moved rapidly to take power by implementing a platform based on *glasnost* (openness) and *perestroika* (restructuring) to try to bring new life to the Soviet system. *Glasnost* was Gorbachev's way of motivating the Soviet people to be more creative and work harder. *Perestroika* attempted to remove the structural blocks to modernization. These two themes launched the final act in the de-Stalinization campaign begun by Khrushchev in 1956.

Gorbachev tried to mobilize the support of the cultural and scientific elite by encouraging them to participate in political life. He brought physicist Andrei Sakharov back from internal exile and permitted publication of the works of exiled author Aleksandr Solzhenitsyn, who returned to his native land in 1994. The party relinquished much of its control over culture for the first time since the 1920s. Stalin's total dictatorship over form, content, and esthetics in the arts—his insistence that artists, writers, and musicians be "engineers of the soul"—had died with him. However, the party maintained its hold on all aspects of culture and the mass media. *Glasnost* to a large degree brought back to Russia creative freedom that had been absent since the 1917 revolution.

For the first time the party acknowledged mistakes, such as the Chernobyl nuclear disaster in April 1986. Past tragedies—especially those of the 1930s—that had long been common knowledge were now openly discussed. Gorbachev permitted unprecedented criticism of party and political leaders by the press and television. He sponsored broad reforms in Soviet society, imposing the strongest antialcoholism campaign in history and making the force of the drive felt at the highest levels.

One of the unexpected results of *glasnost* was a revival of separatist movements in the various Soviet republics. People in Estonia, Lithuania, Latvia, Armenia, Azerbaijan, the Ukraine, Moldova, Kazakhstan, and Georgia declared the supremacy of their laws, institutions, and programs over those of the central government and claimed ownership of resources found within their borders.

→ Mikhail Gorbachev and his wife Raisa greet a crowd of admirers in 1988. Gorbachev, who came to power in 1985, ushered in a new era of *perestroika* ("economic restructuring") and *glasnost* ("openness") in the Soviet Union. When Gorbachev's policies failed to revive the USSR's stagnant economy but did spark ethnic separatist uprisings in various Soviet republics, admiration for his regime gave way to criticism.

Gorbachev originally sought to use *perestroika* to fine-tune the traditional central planning apparatus and party and state procedures, but the total failure of the Stalinist system demanded a more wide-ranging program. By 1990 the depth and severity of the Soviet Union's problems drove Gorbachev to attempt to impose a market economy, reduce the role of the "vanguard party," and alter the governmental structure. The broader scope of *perestroika* sought foreign capital, markets, and technology in order to make the USSR competitive. Gorbachev attempted to rebuild most aspects of the Soviet economic structure, such as its banking system.

Until the summer of 1991, Gorbachev was the undisputed master of the party and the state, putting down rivals with great skill and using public opinion and free elections to neutralize opponents, while building a new power base. After being named president in October 1988, he set out to reform that most secret and powerful of all Soviet institutions, the KGB, urging its new leaders to imitate the structure of the U.S. CIA.

Until 1989 the Supreme Soviet was a carefully preselected, rubber-stamp body. Real power was concentrated in the Council of Ministers, headed by a prime minister. After the elections of March and April 1989 many powerful officials were voted down, even though they had run unopposed. The Congress of People's Deputies, which was to meet annually and be reelected every five years, replaced the old Supreme Soviet. From the ranks of the Congress came a new Supreme Soviet. Unlike the old Supreme Soviet, which never saw a *no* vote, the Congress and the new Supreme Soviet were outspoken and controversial bodies, even with the guaranteed positions for communist leaders.

The Communist party posed a special problem for Gorbachev, a dedicated Leninist. He criticized the cumbersome and unresponsive functioning of the organization with its theoretical capstone, the Party Congress, which typically met once every five years and elected the 450-strong (300 voting, 150 nonvoting) Central Committee. The Committee, in turn, typically met at least once every six months to consider policies and elect the highest party body, the Politburo, with its 12 voting and 8 nonvoting members. From his post as General Secretary, Gorbachev could see that the party and its special commissions would not solve the basic problems of the country.

The party had become corrupt and reactionary, concerned more with its privileges than its responsibilities. It was so inflexible that Gorbachev had to diminish its role after the July 1990 party congress. Thereafter, no major political figure sat on the Politburo, with the exception of the Soviet president. The party became subordinate to the state, losing its leading role. Millions gave up their party memberships after 1989, many of them going to work in city and republic governments where there was greater opportunity.

Gorbachev invoked *glasnost* and *perestroika* to jump-start the moribund economy. Although gross domestic product figures continued to indicate that the Soviet economy was the second-largest in the world, the reality was that the infrastructure was made up of outmoded technologies, inefficient factories, a dispirited and underemployed work force, and environmental disasters. Unlike the Chinese, who had in 1978 started their economic reforms in the countryside so as to ensure an adequate supply of food, Gorbachev relied on a more Leninist, democratic centralist approach—and failed miserably. He attacked the Stalinist central planning system with all of its layers of managers and bureaucratic elites that were devoted to fulfilling the plan, not to taking risks to improve profit. Economists spoke openly of letting market forces set prices. Universities stopped the compulsory study of the works of Marx and began, instead, to feature the rhetoric of American neoconservatives and nineteenth-century English liberals. Gorbachev himself spoke of the fact that the welfare and happiness of the individual would be best served by economic individualism, the free operation of the market, and not the governmentally triggered "group think" of Stalinist days.

Admirable though these sentiments might have been, the *apparatchiki* that still remained in place sabotaged many of the reform efforts. Gorbachev tried to deal with the USSR's systemic problems by firing large numbers of government, industry, military, and party officials, replacing them with younger, more aggressive people who could better implement his program. Unfortunately, he faced challenges that demanded more than just a limited change in personnel, and the longer he pursued his program, the smaller his constituency became.

Nagging economic problems and resistance from the *apparatchiki* blocked Gorbachev's plans for reforms and forced him to make continual adjustments in order to hold power. In September 1990, he abandoned a bold plan to bring a market economy to the Soviet Union within 500 days, dashing the hopes of progressives. For the next ten months his former liberal advisers and supporters either resigned or were dismissed from their positions.

As economic and social conditions deteriorated, Gorbachev increased concessions to party and bureaucratic hardliners, buying time to hold power and pursue his foreign policy objectives. In the spring hundreds of thousands of people marched in the streets of Moscow protesting the hardliners and Gorbachev's attempts to mollify them. In the Baltic Republics, Georgia, the Ukraine, and Moldova, separatist pressures increased. The economic system continued to decline, and standards of living plummeted along with productivity.

Domestic problems grew more severe during the summer of 1991. Agriculture faced an estimated grain shortfall of 77 million metric tons in the 1991 harvest, assuming the crop could even be brought in from the field. The tailspin in which the economy found itself continued to intensify. Economists who had predicted an 11 percent decline in Soviet gross national product for 1991 were revising those figures to forecast an even greater decline. Boris Yeltsin (b. 1931), who had been popularly elected president of the Russian Republic in the spring, became an increasingly powerful figure, as rudimentary public opinion polls gave Gorbachev a 7 percent approval rating.

In response to these crises, Gorbachev and Soviet Republic officials negotiated the Union Treaty, which was to reallocate both authority and resources in the Soviet Union between the USSR government and the various republics. To be signed on August 20, it would have sharply reduced the authority of both the central power of the Soviet Union and the party.

On August 19, while Gorbachev was on vacation in the Crimea, an eight-man State Emergency Committee made up of leaders of the KGB, the military, the interior department, and other offices of the central government—all appointed by Gorbachev—launched an attempt to take power. Gorbachev's vice president announced that his leader was ill and that a state of emergency was to be imposed for six months.

The attempted coup was immediately denounced by Yeltsin, who barricaded himself inside the offices of the Russian parliament building

→ On August 19, 1991, president of the Russian Republic Boris Yeltsin stands atop an armored carrier in Moscow to read a statement urging people to resist the attempted hardline coup.

in Moscow and instructed all army and KGB units not to obey the coup leaders' orders. The next day, 50,000 people turned out in Moscow to face down tanks sent by the central government. Larger groups mobilized in Leningrad and Kishinev. Several units of KGB and army forces refused to obey the central command's orders, and the coup began to unravel. By August 21, the crisis was over, and Yeltsin had emerged as the man of the hour.

When Gorbachev returned, he immediately attempted to govern and to follow his old Leninist convictions. He soon found that he, compared to Yeltsin, had little standing, especially after Gorbachev reiterated his belief that the party was the proper vehicle to carry out reform. Even as the coup leaders languished under arrest—or committed suicide—Gorbachev continued to defend the party. Finally, six days after the attempted coup, the reality of the situation became clear. Gorbachev resigned as leader of the Soviet Communist party and recommended dissolution of the Central Committee. Yeltsin claimed control of party archives and KGB records, and across the Soviet Union in a vast revolution the Communist party—after 74 years of almost total power—was cut off from all its vanguard roles in running the country. In addition, the party had to surrender its wealth and property to the parliaments of the various republics. Gorbachev remained as president of the Soviet Union, at least until popular elections could be held.

But the Soviet Union itself would last only four more months. The Baltic republics of Lithuania, Latvia, and Estonia gained diplomatic recognition; and Ukraine, Moldova, Belarus, and Georgia declared independence. The USSR ended its 69 years of existence on December 21, 1991. It was replaced by the Commonwealth of Independent States.

Where Peter the Great had overwhelmed his opposition with sheer power, and Stalin had sent his secret police, Gorbachev used *glasnost* and limited force to respond to his growing number of opponents. Ironically, it was the very people he chose who brought him down, and his defense of the party and the concepts he embraced that kept him down. His greatest gift to the Soviet people was that through *glasnost*, he had removed fear.

But the overwhelming problems of a nonfunctional infrastructure remained.

The Gorbachev Contribution to the End of the Cold War

Although Gorbachev's policies largely failed to solve the domestic crises, he made major contributions in the foreign policy arena. In acknowledgment of his accomplishments, he received the Nobel Peace Prize in 1990.

He renounced the Brezhnev doctrine permitting Soviet armed intervention into socialist states. By doing so he allowed the Soviet bloc and its Warsaw Pact military strength to disintegrate, thereby opening the way for the revolutionary events of 1989 in Eastern Europe. He pulled Soviet troops out of Afghanistan in 1989 and worked to bring peace to several hot spots in Africa, including Angola. Most remarkably, he chose not to obstruct the reunification of Germany. He joined in the UN resolutions condemning Iraq's takeover of Kuwait in 1990 and cooperated in the alliance's military defeat of Saddam Hussein's forces in 1991.

In arms control Gorbachev brought the process to a logical conclusion. In November 1985 he met with President Ronald Reagan in Geneva to continue the discussion of arms control issues. The two leaders agreed to further consultation, but in the interim, both argued forcefully over alleged Soviet violations of the SALT agreements and the U.S. Strategic Defense Initiative (SDI). The SDI was, on paper, a space-deployed system employing the most advanced technologies against nuclear missiles. American negotiators argued that SDI was an attempt to change the nature of arms control from assured destruction to assured defense. The Soviets saw SDI as a technological quantum leap that would upset the weapons parity between the two powers. American domestic opposition and Soviet flexibility defused the SDI issue, and the two powers were able to sign the Intermediate Nuclear Forces (INF) agreement in Washington in 1987. The INF accord set up the destruction of all intermediate and shorter range missiles within three years.[12] Further, the treaty would be monitored by on-site verification, with Soviet and U.S. experts confirming the fulfillment of the treaty's provisions in each other's country.

By the end of the 1980s new talks on strategic long-range weapons were resumed, as were negotiations to shut down plutonium production plants. The MBFR (Mutual Balanced Force Reductions) talks, which accomplished more in two months than had negotiations over the past ten years, became moot with the disappearance of the Warsaw Pact as a military force. Clearly, the combination of economic pressures, especially serious in the USSR, and mutual interest brought the superpowers into close accord to control weapons that could destroy the planet. The need to survive and prosper brought the superpowers together on the nuclear weapons issue.

The end of the Cold War removed from the world the nightmare of bipolar nuclear annihilation. The signing of the Strategic Arms Reduction Treaty (START) in July 1991 marked the first step in cutting down the large stockpiles of nuclear warheads on each side. In 1994, Moscow and Washington formally altered the targeting software in their missiles, removing each other's

SUCCESSOR REPUBLICS OF THE FORMER SOVIET UNION

strategic areas from the target list. The two also pledged to work together to fight nuclear proliferation.

Unfortunately, the genie appeared to be out of the nuclear bottle, and even great power agreement could not stop proliferation. Some analysts asserted that by 1996 there would be more than 20 countries with the ability to build and deliver nuclear weapons. In addition, terrible new chemical and biological weapons threatened humanity. Perversely, some commentators had begun to look back on the Cold War with some nostalgia, as a time when there was dependable order.

The Yeltsin Years

After August 1991, Boris Yeltsin emerged as the most important Russian politician. As had other leaders at the end of a revolution, he found that a change in government did not remove the terrible problems facing Russia: inflation, budget deficits, minorities problems within and without the Russian boundaries, privatization, and setting up the new infrastructure for international trade and commerce. After five years, demographic figures graphically indicated that Russia was not solving its problems. By 1993, the average life expectancy for the Russian male had dropped to 59 years—13 years fewer than that for men in the United States and equal to the life span of men in India. In addition, the birth rate plummeted. Another of the demographic crises facing Russia was an infant mortality rate that rose from 17.4 per thousand in 1990 to 19.1 per thousand in 1993.

Almost immediately Yeltsin had to deal with opposition from the *apparatchiki*-laden Congress of People's Deputies, elected under the old Soviet model. The Congress consistently blocked Yeltsin's attempts to implement a series of market-oriented economic reforms, such as liberalizing prices on most nonfood goods. In addition, Yeltsin faced problems from deputies who accused him of caving in to Western pressures in both domestic and foreign policies. Yeltsin retained his personal popularity, as could be seen in his victory in the April 1993 referendum on his economic policies and leadership; however, this had little effect on the Congress of People's Deputies, which continued to block the president.

Yeltsin's contest with the parliament reached a stalemate in September 1993. When the Congress of People's Deputies threatened to take much of his authority away, he responded by dissolving the Congress and calling for new elections in December. He then sent troops to surround the Parliamentary building—the Russian White House—and told deputies that they would have to leave the building by October 4. These actions provoked widespread criticism throughout Russia, as leaders of 62 out of 89 regional councils called for Yeltsin to remove the troops.

On October 3, forces opposing Yeltsin took the office of the mayor of Moscow and attacked the state television center. To an audience watching these events live on television, it was remarkable that only 62 people died in the fighting. The next day Yeltsin sent tanks and artillery against the Russian White House and battered the resisters into submission.

Yeltsin's forces and the new constitution barely carried the day in the December elections, winning enough seats to prevent the opposition from having enough votes in the parliament to impeach the president. However, extremists such as Vladimir Zhirinovsky, a nationalist and virulent anti-Semite, attracted the votes of many moderate Russians who resented the conditions that four years of reform had brought them. Zhirinovsky momentarily gained worldwide attention, which he promptly used to espouse the regaining of Russia's boundaries, including reclaiming Alaska.

To maintain power in the face of the extremist coalition—which seemingly was held together only by its opposition to Yeltsin—the president took a centrist course, advocating a rebirth of the Great Russian state, damping down essential programs to produce a privatized economy, and distancing himself from the West in foreign affairs—especially the extension of early NATO membership to the former East European states and Western intervention in the former Yugoslavia.

Russia's economy during the Yeltsin years proved unable to make the comparatively rapid change to a market system, as had the economies of Poland, the Czech Republic, and Hungary. The ethnic and social diversity of the continent-sized state made impossible a "cold turkey" transition to the market system. As a result, in the three years after Yeltsin took power, the state tried to meet its problems by printing more money, leading to an inflation in which the worth of the ruble declined from $1.00 = 300 rubles in 1992 to $1.00 = over 5000 rubles in 1995. Standards of living for many continued to decline, while the few spectacularly wealthy attained a level of living comparable to that of tsarist-era nobles. Inflation and a deepening deficit together kept economic development limited. Still, the West knew that Yeltsin must be kept afloat, and that loans made for peace were not nearly as expensive as money spent for war. They had to support Yeltsin, whose vulnerability was further accentuated in February 1994 when his enemies from the 1991 August coup attempt and the 1993 October uprising were freed by parliament.

By the beginning of 1995 inflation had slowed down and over 15,000 businesses had made the transition to a market-based system. Privately held firms employed more than three-fourths of Russian factory workers. On the positive side Russia had undergone a revolution in many ways more profound and widespread than that in 1917 with a minimum amount of violence. On the negative side, widespread criminal activities and mounting resentment of the economic and social changes provided fertile ground for the enemies of reform.

In the successor states, economic and political developments ranged from the tragic in the Caucasian republics to the corrupt and inefficient in Ukraine. Kiev had nuclear weapons, untapped economic potential, and a disastrously corrupt and inept government. In July 1994, the Western powers offered to loan Ukraine $4 billion and to aid in the rebuilding or replacing of the Chernobyl plant.

Countries such as Moldova took heroic measures to introduce the discipline and quality needed to compete in the international market. However, they faced political, supply, and transportation problems plus the Russian 14th army, which was a continual threat. On the other hand, only the imposition of Russian arms brought a tenuous peace to the Caucasus. Armenians and Azeris battled over control of Nagorno-Karabakh; Georgians and Abkhazians and roving bands of independent mercenaries fought over long-disputed lands.

The Russians felt susceptible to military actions from their former allies—the so-called near

→ Confrontation between Russian president Boris Yeltsin and the Russian parliament reached a climax in September–October 1993. On the morning of October 5, 1993, army troops stormed the Russian White House, where Yeltsin's opponents had barricaded themselves. By mid-afternoon, the resistance crumbled and many of the anti-Yeltsin forces surrendered.

abroad—where independent armed forces used some of the most advanced weaponry from the former Soviet army. In the 15 newly independent states of the former Soviet republics, significant minority problems continue. Russia itself can claim 81 percent ethnic Russians, but the figures for Ukraine are 22 percent; Kazakhstan, 37 percent; Latvia, 34 percent; and Estonia, 31 percent. It is as much concern for their fellow Russians as for purely defensive reasons that there were more than 120,000 Russian soldiers outside Russia at the beginning of 1995. The Russians wanted to look after their own people, while fearing the numerous private armies, some of them stocked with powerful weapons that became available in the wake of the decline of the USSR.

Another crisis facing Russia was the environmental pollution left by the former Soviet defense plants and heavy industry. The residue of nuclear accidents—Chelyabinsk in 1957, Chernobyl in 1985, Tomsk in April 1993, and a bacteriological warfare plant in Sverdlovsk (Yekaterinburg) in 1979—has contributed in some regions to a precipitous decline in living standards and life-expectancy rates. Throughout the former Soviet bloc the nuclear power industry, powered by outmoded and potentially dangerous reactors, remained a disaster waiting to happen.

The American position, mirroring its previous policy of personalizing its foreign policy toward Russia, was to depend on Yeltsin. Of some $68 billion promised in aid from the West in 1992 and 1993, only $20 billion actually arrived. Part of the reason for this failure could be found in bureaucratic inertia and corruption on the Western side and in a lack of infrastructure for any effective use of this aid, except for direct cash transfers for the new elite. Even with the full extent of aid, the legacy of the Soviet centrally planned economy presented problems that might be insoluble. The question remained whether the Russians could develop the political skills of consensus-building and compromise needed to make the changes required to keep Russia from sliding back to another authoritarian model, as it had so often in the past after a time of change. As cynics remarked, "Russia had to move on from its historic questions: What's to be done? Who is to blame?"

EASTERN EUROPE

After consolidating political control over Eastern Europe by 1948, Moscow attempted to organize its allies through the trade organization COMECON. The USSR set up COMECON in 1949 as a response to the Marshall Plan and other Western projects to promote economic growth. In its first decade the organization served Soviet postwar recovery needs. Moscow worked a reverse system of mercantilism on the region, exporting raw materials at high prices and buying back finished goods at low cost. Eastern Europe suffered greatly under this system, and nowhere could the contrast between the capitalist and communist systems be seen more dramatically than in Berlin.

In the 1960s and 1970s the Soviet bloc states began to profit from buying cheap energy supplies from the USSR in return for which they could send goods they could not market to the West. Their standard of living began to improve along with their economic growth rates. However, by the end of the 1970s, COMECON faced a serious crisis. The region fell behind the rest of the world economically because of the rigidity of the centrally planned system used in the bloc economies and the restrictive bilateral nature of COMECON. Everything had to go through Moscow. Prague and Budapest, for instance, could not work directly to achieve production or trade efficiency. COMECON countries faced far more barriers than did the Common Market countries. Further, each country's currency was nonconvertible; it could be spent only within that country.

Aggravating the situation for the Eastern Europeans was the fact that as the world energy prices fell in the latter part of the 1980s, they were trapped into paying premium prices for Soviet oil and gas. Several Eastern European states borrowed heavily from the West and invested the proceeds unwisely. Far more damaging that these purely fiscal concerns were the environmental disasters spawned by the Soviet-model centrally planned economies. Eastern Europe, as well as the former USSR, was one of the most devastatingly polluted areas in the world. Fifty years of Soviet domination were a terrible burden for the peoples of Eastern Europe.

East Germany

After 1945 Eastern Europe reflected the changes that took place in the USSR. Nowhere was this more evident than in East Germany from 1945 to 1990. Following the organization of the eastern zone of Germany into the German Democratic Republic, communist authorities broke up large private farms and expanded heavy industry. Thousands of discontented East Germans fled each week to West Germany through Berlin. In June 1953, severe food shortages coupled with new decrees establishing longer working hours touched off a workers' revolt, which was quickly put down. The westward flow of refugees continued, however, until 1961, when the Berlin Wall was constructed.

The wall stopped the exodus of people, and East Germany stabilized. For the next 28 years the country had the highest density of armed men per square mile in the Soviet bloc and the communist world's highest economic growth rate. The country's athletes and businesses did well in world competition, and slowly and subtly under Erich Honecker and a new generation of *apparatchiki*, the German Democratic Republic improved relations with West Germany.

Gorbachev's program of liberalization threatened Honecker and his colleagues. After 1987 East German authorities stopped the circulation of Soviet periodicals that carried stories considered to be too liberal. At the same time, analysts noted the slowing economic growth rate of East Germany and the fact that the standard of living in West Germany was far higher. Old facilities, old managers, and old ideas eroded the economy of East Germany.

In September 1989, East Germans looking for a better life again fled by the thousands to the West, this time through Hungary and Czechoslovakia. This exodus, followed by Gorbachev's visit to Berlin in October, helped precipitate a crisis bringing hundreds of thousands of protesters to the streets of Berlin. Honecker was removed in October and on November 9 the Berlin Wall was breached. Once that symbolic act took place, both East and West Germans began to call for a unified Germany. Press exposés revealed the corruption and scandals among the communist elite. In the East German elections of March 1990 pro-Western parties won an overwhelming triumph. By October 1990 Germany was reunited, with the first free all-German elections since Hitler took power.[13] Berlin was once again the capital of all Germany. Once the thrill of reunification had passed, Germans faced the difficult task of making the two parts of their country into one efficient unit. By 1995 they had made significant progress toward true economic and social unification.

Poland

In Poland, as in Yugoslavia, communism acquired a national character after a slow, subtle

→ As the existence of the Berlin Wall was the most visible reminder of the reality of the Cold War, the destruction of the Wall in November 1989 became the most powerful image of the war's end. Here a demonstrator pounds away at the Wall as East German border guards standing atop the Brandenburg Gate look on impassively.

struggle that broke open in the fall of 1956—following Khrushchev's "Crimes of the Stalin Era" speech. Polish leader Wladyslaw Gomulka set out on a difficult path to satisfy both Moscow and Warsaw—Soviet power and Polish nationalism. Gomulka governed skillfully through the 1960s until 1970, when he fell victim to the pressures caused by economic discontent on one hand and an increasingly corrupt party structure on the other.

Demonstrations and strikes broke out around the country, and some, such as those at the Baltic port city Gdansk, were bloodily repressed. Gomulka was replaced by Edward

Gierek, who throughout the 1970s walked the same narrow line as Gomulka between satisfying Moscow and Poland. Gierek borrowed extensively from the West and made several ill-advised economic decisions. By 1980 Poland was laboring to pay the interest on a foreign debt of $28 billion, and in the summer of 1980 the delicate compromise created by Gomulka and Gierek fell apart in a series of strikes caused by increases in food prices.

A nationwide labor movement, *Solidarnosc,* or Solidarity, came into being. By October, around 10 million Poles from all segments of society had joined this movement, which stood for reform, equality, and workers' rights. In many ways, Solidarity's programs were protests against the Leninist concept of the party. It was Solidarity's proletarian base that made it so appealing to the world and so threatening to the other Marxist-Leninist leaders of the Soviet bloc. Unfortunately, the problems that had brought down Gierek remained. A year of Solidarity-dominated government brought no solutions, only continued frustration.

Conflict with the government, now headed by General Wojciech Jaruzelski, appeared inevitable. Solidarity's leader, Lech Walesa—an out-of-work electrician who had been fired for earlier attempts to organize a trade union in Gdansk—showed an instinctive genius for dealing effectively with every element of the Polish spectrum and the Soviet Union. He attempted to maintain a moderate position.

When Walesa's backers pushed him to call for a national vote to establish a noncommunist government, the Jaruzelski government responded with force, partially to maintain itself, partially to avoid Soviet intervention. Jaruzelski declared martial law, and security forces rounded up Solidarity leaders. Outward shows of protest were squelched within two weeks.

Through the 1980s, Communist party morale dipped as membership fell 20 percent. Although banned, Solidarity retained the genuine affection of the Poles and the support of the Roman Catholic Church, headed by Pope John Paul II, the former Polish Cardinal Wojtyla. To the embarrassment of the Polish state, Lech Walesa received the Nobel Peace prize in 1983. The economic situation deteriorated as inflation rates increased, the standard of living plummeted, and

→ Under the dynamic leadership of Lech Walesa, Solidarity, the Polish workers' union, grew into a nationwide social movement. In this photo from 1981, Solidarity members carry Walesa on their shoulders to celebrate a Polish Supreme Court decision upholding the workers' right to stage protest strikes throughout Poland.

foreign debt soared to $40 billion. The party could not solve the problems it faced and, in desperation, turned to Solidarity—which had been outlawed for eight years—in 1989. The June 1989 elections resulted in an overwhelming victory for the union, and in July it took its place in the Polish parliament, the *Sejm,* as the first opposition party to win free elections in Eastern Europe since 1948. Solidarity won 99 out of 100 seats in the upper house and 161 seats (35 percent) in the lower house—all that was allotted to it in a preparatory round table.

In January 1990, Poland decided to adopt a market economy. Even with substantial financial support from the West, the country faced rising unemployment and recession. The strains produced by the shift to a market economy tested even the Solidarity movement, which split into two wings: one led by Mazowiecki Tadeusz; who briefly became prime minister in 1990, and one led by Lech Walesa, who eventually emerged to become the president of Poland.

Despite political roadblocks, Poland made amazing success toward privatization and market reforms. Even when Poland's former Communists, now called Social Democrats, took power in 1993, they did not reverse course. Poland stands as one of the success stories in the former Soviet bloc, with economic growth of 4 percent in 1993, the activity of its stock market, and successful transition from a centrally planned to a market economy.

Czechoslovakia

After the fall of the democratic government in 1948, the Czechoslovak Communist party, the most Stalinist of the European parties, imposed harsh control for 20 years. However, in the spring of 1968, the country's liberal traditions came into the open. Under the influence of Marxist moderates, a new form of communism—"socialism with a human face"—was put into effect by the Slovak leader Alexander Dubcek. As in Yugoslavia under Tito, the Czechoslovaks chose not to rebel against Moscow, but rather to adapt communism to their own conditions, but in August 1968 the Soviet Union and four Soviet bloc allies invaded Prague with more than 500,000 troops. Within 20 hours, the liberal regime, which advocated policies strikingly similar to those to be supported by Gorbachev 20 years later, was overthrown. The Soviets captured Dubcek and took him to Moscow to confront Brezhnev.

The Soviets took their action against Czechoslovakia under the so-called Brezhnev Doctrine, under which communist states were obliged to aid their fraternal colleagues against "aggression," even when the fraternal colleague does not ask for aid, in order to safeguard the communal gains of the socialist movement. The Soviet-led forces crushed the Czechoslovak reforms to "protect the progress of socialism." Like that of East Germany, the Czech economy by the late 1980s was hampered by outmoded technology, timid leadership, and obsession with discredited ideology. The country suffered greatly from polluted air and acid rain, and the population suffered under a declining standard of living.

The wave of change from Moscow caught the Czech party out of place. Dissidents, including president-to-be Vaclav Havel, who in January 1989 had been thrown in jail for human rights protests, found themselves running the country by December. Events in East Germany precipitated the October 1989 events in Prague, when a prodemocracy meeting by over 10,000 demonstrators was savagely broken up. Protests in November met similar results. Still the Czechoslovaks were not deterred. In the "Velvet Revolution" of November 1989, some 200,000 demonstrators in Prague demanded free elections and the resignation of the communist leaders. Dubcek came out of internal exile, and in December Havel became president, a result confirmed in the June 1990 elections. As in the other Eastern European states, however, the high spirits of the 1989 revolution were soon replaced by the sober realities of repairing the effects of two generations of communist rule.

By 1992 serious political and Slovak separatist demands were threatening the existence of Czechoslovakia, then called the Czech and Slo-

→ Playwright Vaclav Havel, who was soon to become president of Czechoslovakia, hugs former Czech leader Alexander Dubcek following the "Velvet Revolution" of November 1989 in which the entire communist government of Czechoslovakia resigned.

vak Federated Republic. The two regions finally split into the Czech Republic and the Slovak Republic on January 1, 1993. The Czech Republic suffered little from the ending of the 65-year-old country. The Slovaks, on the other hand, suffered from economic decline and political instability under the rule of the former communist hard-liner Vladimir Meciar. At the beginning of 1994 unemployment in Slovakia was over 15 percent as compared to the rate of 3.5 percent among the Czechs.

Hungary

After the Stalin purges, the Hungarian Communist party became increasingly inept, until October 1956 when discontent with Soviet dominance erupted into revolution. For a week, a popular government existed, and Russian troops withdrew from Budapest. When the new government announced its intentions to leave the Warsaw Pact and be neutral, Soviet forces returned and crushed the rebellion. More than 200,000 refugees fled to the West.

Over the next 30 years, Janos Kadar (1912–1989) oversaw an initially bloody repression of the revolution and the execution of Hungarian premier Imre Nagy. Later Kadar led a subtle pursuit of a Hungarian variant of communism. In the process, the Hungarians gained a higher standard of living than the Soviets, an active intellectual life, and a range of economic reforms. In the mid-1980s, however, the Hungarian economic system, which encouraged more private initiative and decentralization, experienced difficulties. Hungary's foreign debt increased and inflation rose. Gorbachev encouraged the Hungarians to pursue their reforms, sometimes at the discomfort of Kadar, who was gently moved from power in 1987.

In 1989 the Hungarians dismantled the barriers, fences, and minefields between themselves and the Austrians. Hungary imposed the first income tax and value added tax in Eastern Europe, allowed 100 percent foreign ownership of Hungarian firms, opened a stock market, and set up institutions to teach Western management methods to Hungarian businessmen.

By March 1990 Hungary had installed a multiparty system and was holding free elections, which led to the election of a right-of-center government led by Joszef Antall and the overwhelming repudiation of the communists. However, the next four years proved to be frustrating to the Hungarians. Substantial Western investment came into Hungary, but at the same time, the degree of suffering among the poorer population in the country increased.

Tragically, in an area where, thanks to the Holocaust, there is no longer any significant concentration of Jews, anti-Semitism reemerged as a powerful political force. Anti-Gypsy feelings also intensified. These attitudes reflected the general lack of satisfaction with the right-of-center government elected in 1990. The 1994 elections resulted in a victory for the Communist Social Democrats, who promised to maintain the free market reforms while extending social justice.

Bulgaria, Romania, and Albania

Bulgaria. Bulgaria proved to be a loyal ally of Moscow after 1945, and its standard of living greatly improved. The Bulgarian economy averaged a growth rate of close to 3 percent a year and became increasingly diversified. Todor Zhivkov skillfully followed the Soviet lead and showed flexibility in responding to the early Gorbachev programs, especially the agricultural reforms. Until the autumn of 1989 the party appeared to be conservative and nationalist, as shown in its campaign against the country's Turkish minority (nearly 8 percent of the population) to deprive them of their heritage.

The wave of freedom hit Bulgaria at the end of 1989. Zhivkov was ousted in a party-led coup and replaced by Peter Mladenov. It seemed in the free elections in May 1990 that Mladenov and his allies would be the only party group to make the transition and maintain power in Eastern Europe. But even he was thrown out in July when his role as orchestrator of the Zhivkov Palace coup was noticed, and the noncommunist philosopher Zhelyu Zhelev became president.

Romania. After the 1960s Romania under Nicolae Ceausescu was the most independent of the Warsaw Pact countries in foreign policy. Domestically, the country labored under one of the most hard-line and corrupt regimes in the bloc, whose economic policies of self-sufficiency plunged the standard of living to unprecedented depths. Ceausescu achieved his goal to become free of foreign debts by the summer of 1989, but at a cruel cost in human suffering.

Ceausescu, accused by critics of desiring to achieve "socialism in one family," developed the "cult of the personality" to new heights. While imposing severe economic hardship on the nation, he built grandiose monuments to himself. Protected by his omnipresent secret police, the *Securitate*, he seemed to be totally secure. But the 1989 wave of democracy spread even to Romania, which was the only country to experience widespread violence during that revolutionary year. Ceausescu was captured and on Christmas day he and his wife were executed, thus bringing an end to their dreadful regime.

The Romanian pattern of political corruption continued, and Ion Iliescu manipulated the elections of May 1990 to keep power. The National Salvation Front made shameless use, later in the summer, of miners and former *Securitate* officials to terrorize its critics. An uneasy equilibrium was attained, but little progress was made to heal the devastating wounds inflicted by the Ceausescu regime. Under Iliescu, the Leninist heritage remained strongest in Romania of all of the former bloc states, leading to the retention of an authoritarianism that had a chilling effect on the pluralistic tendencies in the region.

Albania. Albania under Enver Hoxha (d. 1985) worked closely with the Soviet Union until 1956. After Khrushchev's denunciation of Stalin, the country switched its allegiance to the Chinese until 1978. For the next decade Albania—the poorest, most backward country in Europe—went its own way. Slowly, the Albanians entered into trade, diplomatic, and sports relations with other nations. Even Albania felt the pressure of change in the summer of 1990, when people desperate to escape the country flooded foreign embassies. In early 1991 some 40,000 Albanians fled to Italy and Greece. Democratic elections were held in March in this last of the Stalinist states to enter the post–Cold War world. But even here, the Albanians marched to their own tune as the communists carried two-thirds of the vote. Two years later the Democratic party won an overwhelming victory. Albania remained the poorest, most backward country in Europe.

Yugoslavia—and After

One of Stalin's major failures after 1945 was in his dealings with Marshal Joseph Broz Tito of Yugoslavia. Tito had been a loyal communist and a good Stalinist in the 1930s. During the war he was an effective resistance leader, surviving attacks from Germans, Italians, and various right-wing factions in Yugoslavia. He had been in close contact with the Western allies and after the war began to receive substantial assistance from them. Tito led the liberation of Yugoslavia from the Nazis and kept the country out of Moscow's orbit.

Stalin noted Tito's independence and from 1946 on sought measures to oppose him. Ethnically divided Yugoslavia overcame its internal divisions and a 10 percent casualty rate during the war to unite behind Tito. The Yugoslav leader's national backing, geographical distance from the Soviet Union, and support from the West enabled him to stand firm against increasing Soviet meddling in his country.

Tito became the first national communist—that is, a firm believer in Marxism who sought to apply the ideology within the context of his nation's objective conditions. This position placed him directly against Stalin, who believed that communists the world over must work for the greater glory and support of the Soviet Union. Tito believed that the setting in which ideology was found had to be taken into consideration, pointing out that Lenin had to adapt Marxist doctrine to conditions in Russia. Stalin insisted that Moscow's orders and examples must be slavishly followed. In 1948 Tito and Yugoslavia were expelled from the Soviet bloc. Successfully withstanding Stalin's pressures, including assassination attempts, Tito emerged as a key figure in the development of world communism.

After 1948 the six republics containing ten ethnic groups that formed Yugoslavia survived the pressures of national diversity, the political stresses of the bipolar world, and serious economic difficulties. Many observers doubted that the country could survive Tito's death in 1980. However, Yugoslavia remained tenuously united under its unique system of annually rotating the head of state despite an 80 percent inflation rate and a 30 percent decline in the standard of living.

The ethnic strife among Serbs and Croats and the Albanians of Kossovo finally destroyed

THE BREAKUP OF YUGOSLAVIA

mony. The Bosnian Serbs, inheriting the bulk of the old Yugoslav armed forces' supplies and weapons and backed by their brothers in Belgrade, gained 70 percent of Bosnia-Herzegovina, and in the process became international pariahs. They carried on genocidal attacks on the Bosnians—who labored under an arms embargo imposed by the West.

The Western allies made noises of protest and even got the Russians to share in the token condemnations of the Serbs, but the only tangible Western aid for the Bosnians came from the U.S. airlift, which in its first year made more sorties over the region and dumped more supplies in the general region than did the U.S. Air Force supplying Berlin in 1948. NATO forces also launched air strikes and periodically bluffed the Serbs into pulling back from the Muslim enclaves such as Sarajevo and Gorazde. Truces and peace plans came and went and there was no solution, while the West hoped that the economic sanctions against Serbia would finally yield some results.

the unity of the multinational state in 1991. Armed conflict broke out in the summer, as the Slovenes and Croats sought successfully to break away from the Serbian-dominated coalition. Bosnia and Herzegovina declared their independence in December 1991.

Serbs, Croats, and Bosnian Muslims fought in a continually shifting multiple-front war to claim what each side saw as its legitimate patri-

CONCLUSION

In 1989 the Soviet bloc disintegrated in a revolutionary change not seen since 1848. However, after the fractured shells of the old *apparatchik*-ridden governments fell, the new states—like

➔ Bosnian Serb soldiers dash through the ruins of a mobile amusement park in Brcko, a town in northeastern Bosnia destroyed in the fighting for control of the corridor connecting northern Bosnia and Serbia. Ethnic warfare continues to kill millions as peace plans are rejected and cease-fire agreements violated.

those that emerged after the 1848 revolutions—faced all the accumulated problems of the past. Initially, with the exception of the Romanians and the Serbs, the former Soviet bloc renounced communists.

By the end of 1994, after five years of difficult economic and social transition from the centrally planned systems to market-dominated economies, the communists staged a comeback in Hungary, Lithuania, Ukraine, and other parts of the former Soviet Union. As in the interwar period, the Czechs appeared to be the exception to the rule. The democratic reformers, for a number of reasons, failed to gain success. But these communists were a different breed from the Marxist-Leninist-Stalinist variety dominating that part of Europe for a half-century, just as the complex diplomatic patterns of the 1990s are so different from those of the Cold War.

✦ Suggestions for Reading

Lynn E. Davis, *The Cold War Begins* (Princeton Univ., 1974) is a thorough account of the origins of the conflict. Perhaps the best overview on the historiographical conflict is Louis J. Halle, *The Cold War as History* (HarperCollins, 1994). Various points of view on American-Soviet relations can be found in Walter La Feber, *America, Russia, and the Cold War* (Wiley, 1976); P. Hammond, *Cold War and Détente: The American Foreign Policy Process Since 1945* (Harcourt Brace Jovanovich, 1975); and L. Wittner, *Cold War America: From Hiroshima to Watergate* (Praeger, 1974). Other studies of note on the Cold War are J.C. Donovan, *The Cold Warriors: A Policy Making Elite* (Heath, 1974); and H.S. Dinerstein, *Soviet Foreign Policy Since the Missile Crisis* (Johns Hopkins Univ., 1976). The selection of articles edited by Charles S. Maier, *The Origins of the Cold War and Contemporary Europe* (Franklin Watts, 1978) is a good survey of the opportunities and dangers presented the continent by the Moscow-Washington conflict. Adam Ulam gives a good survey of Moscow's policies in *Expansion and Coexistence: Soviet Foreign Policy 1917–1973* (Holt, 1974). A penetrating study of the major figures in U.S. foreign policy formation is W. Isaacson and E. Thomas, *The Wise Men* (Touchstone, 1988). Robbin F. Laird and Erik P. Hoffman, eds., *Soviet Foreign Policy in a Changing World* (Aldine, 1986) is a solid collection of articles on the dilemmas facing the Soviets. Peter Zwick, *Soviet Foreign Relations: Process and Policy* (Prentice-Hall, 1990) spells out the factors shaping Moscow's policies. The Committee on Foreign Affairs analysis of *Soviet Diplomacy and Negotiating Behavior—1979–1988: New Tests for U. S. Diplomacy* (Government Printing Office, 1988) gives good insights into Washington's understanding of Soviet diplomacy. Michael R. Beschloss, *The Crisis Years:*

Kennedy and Khrushchev 1960–1963 (HarperCollins, 1994) is a well-written work based on recently released documents. The Soviet world at the beginning of the 1990s still labored under the impact of Stalin's policies and accomplishments; R.C. Tucker, ed., presents the panorama of Stalin's life and policies in *Stalinism: Essays in Historical Interpretation* (Norton, 1977).

On the Vietnam War, see Stanley Karnow, *Vietnam: A History* (Penguin, 1984). Thomas Powers, *The War at Home* (Grossman, 1973) and Paul Kattenberg, *The Vietnamese Trauma in American Foreign Policy* (Transaction, 1980) deal with the anti–Vietnam War movement. For personal assessments see J. Buttinger, *Vietnam: The Unforgettable Tragedy* (Horizon, 1976); A. M. Schlesinger, Jr., *The Bitter Heritage: Vietnam and American Democracy* (Premier, 1972); F. Fitzgerald, *Fire in the Lake* (Vintage, 1973); and George C. Herring, *America's Longest War: The United States and Vietnam, 1950–1975* (Wiley, 1979). The best summary of the tragedy in the Indochina peninsula is Marilyn Young, *The Vietnam Wars: 1945–1990* (HarperCollins, 1994).

M. Djilas, *Conversations with Stalin* (Harcourt Brace Jovanovich, 1962) gives a vivid, first-hand account of Stalin's personality. Khrushchev's tenure is competently covered in E. Crankshaw, *Khrushchev, a Career* (Viking, 1966) and in Khrushchev's own words in *Khrushchev Remembers* (Ballantine, 1976). Hedrick Smith, *The New Russians* (Random House, 1990) is an outstanding update of his classic introduction to the "way things really work." Martin McCauley, ed., presents an all-encompassing study of Khrushchev's time in power in *Khrushchev and Khrushchevism* (MacMillan, 1987). Impressionistic and important is Roy Medvedev's *Khrushchev* (Doubleday, 1983). Elizabeth Valkenier discusses the problems of overextension in *The Soviet Union and the Third World: An Economic Bind* (Praeger, 1983). The Brezhnev years are examined by Archie Brown and Michael Kaser, eds., in *The Soviet Union Since the Fall of Khrushchev* (Free Press, 1976). Gail Lapidus examines the difficult lot of women in *Women, Work and Family in the Soviet Union* (M.E. Sharpe, 1982). Frederick Starr's splendid *Red and Hot: The Fate of Jazz in the Soviet Union, 1917–1980* (Oxford, 1983) gives a unique insight into cultural vitality in the "totalitarian" Soviet Union. A work anticipating the current crisis of the USSR is Paul Dibb, *The Soviet Union: The Incomplete Super Power* (Illinois, 1986). Martin Ebon gives essential background to the key figure in Soviet political change in *The Andropov File* (McGraw-Hill, 1983). Marshall Goldman's perceptive *Gorbachev's Challenge: Economic Reform in the Age of High Technology* (Norton, 1987) anticipates the Soviet crisis of the 1990s. A good primer on the "balance of terror" is Ray Perkins, Jr., *The ABCs of the Soviet-American Nuclear Arms Race* (Brooks/Cole, 1991). Stephen White, *Gorbachev and After* (Cambridge Univ., 1991) gives a solid account of the denouement of the Gorbachev revolution.

Eastern European developments through the 1960s can be studied in the surveys by Hugh Seton-Watson, *The East European Revolution* (Praeger, 1961); Ivan Volgyes, *Politics* in *Eastern Europe* (Dorsey, 1986); and Z. Brzezinski, *The Soviet Bloc: Unity and Conflict* (Harvard Univ., 1971). F. Fejto, *History of the People's Democracies* (Pelican, 1973) is a solid survey of post-1945 Eastern Europe. Dennis Rusinow, *The Yugoslav Experiment, 1948–1974* (Univ. of California, 1977) gives a view of the multinational state to the mid-1970s. Jorg K. Hoensch, *A History of Modern Hungary: 1867–1986* (Longman, 1988) is an objective survey. Easily the best coverage of the collapse of communism in Eastern Europe is Gale Stokes, *The Walls Came Tumbling Down* (Oxford Univ., 1993).

The Czech crisis of 1968—and after—is well covered in G. Golan, *Reform Rule in Czechoslovakia* (Cambridge Univ., 1971). Norman Davies, *Heart of Europe: A Short History of Poland* (Oxford Univ., 1987) gives the best short survey of recent events in that country in Chapters 1 and 7. Joseph Rothschild, *Return to Diversity: A Political History of East Central Europe* (Oxford Univ., 1989) is a first-rate analysis of the last half-century in the former bloc countries.

→ Notes

1. Max Radin, "Justice at Nuremberg," *Foreign Affairs*, April 1946, p. 371.
2. A useful guide to the historiography of the Cold War can be found in J. L. Black, *Origins, Evolution, and Nature of the Cold War: An Annotated Bibliographic Guide* (Santa Barbara, CA: ABC-Clio, 1986).
3. J. P. Nettl, *The Soviet Achievement* (New York: Harcourt Brace Jovanovich, 1967), p. 198.
4. Leonard Schapiro, *The Communist Party of the Soviet Union* (London: Methuen, 1963). pp. 534–535.
5. Winston Churchill, *Triumph and Tragedy* (Boston: Houghton Mifflin, 1953), p. 497.
6. Raymond Aron, "The Foundations of the Cold War," in *The Twentieth Century*, Norman F. Cantor and Michael S. Werthman, eds. (New York: Thomas Y. Crowell, 1967), p. 157.
7. David Rees, *The Age of Containment* (New York: St. Martin's Press, 1967), p. 23.
8. Joseph L. Nogee and John Spanier, *Peace Impossible— War Unlikely, the Cold War Between the United States and the Soviet Union* (Glenview, IL: Scott, Foresman/ Little, Brown, 1988), p. 67.
9. Sheldon W. Simon, "Cambodia: Barbarism in a Small State Under Siege," *Current History*, December 1978, p. 197.
10. Robert A. Scalapino, "Asia at the End of the 1970s," *Foreign Affairs*, 1980, no. 3, p. 720.
11. Alec Nove, *The Soviet Economic System* (London: George Allen & Unwin, 1977), p. 320.
12. Alvin Z. Rubinstein, *Soviet Foreign Policy Since World War II*, 3rd ed. (Glenview, IL: Scott, Foresman, 1988), p. 266.
13. Gale Stokes, *The Walls Came Tumbling Down* (New York: Oxford University Press, 1993), pp. 60–65.

CHAPTER 35

EUROPE 1996

Member of the European Union

0   200   400   600
MILES

NORTH SEA

BALTIC SEA

ATLANTIC OCEAN

MEDITERRANEAN SEA

FINLAND
NORWAY
SWEDEN
ESTONIA
RUSSIA
LATVIA
LITHUANIA
RUS.
BELARUS
IRELAND
DEN.
GREAT BRITAIN
NETH.
BEL.
GERMANY
POLAND
UKRAINE
LUX.
CZECH REP.
SLVK.
FRANCE
SWITZ.
AUSTRIA
HUNGARY
MOL.
SLOV.
CRO.
ROMANIA
B. & H.
ITALY
YUGO.
BULGARIA
PORT.
SPAIN
MAC.
ALB.
TURKEY
GREECE

→ European nations regained a dominant role in global economics in the European Union. It is anticipated that by the end of the twentieth century several countries in northern and eastern Europe would join the EU.

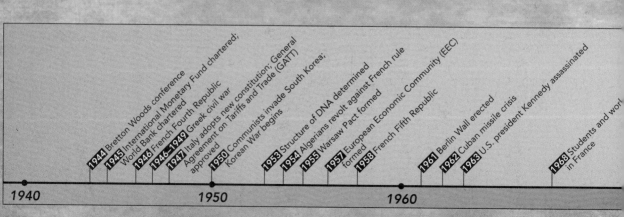

1944 Bretton Woods conference
1945 International Monetary Fund chartered; World Bank chartered
1946 French Fourth Republic
1946–1949 Greek civil war
1947 Italy adopts new constitution; General Agreement on Tariffs and Trade (GATT) approved
1950 Communists invade South Korea; Korean War begins
1953 Structure of DNA determined
1954 Algerians revolt against French rule
1955 Warsaw Pact formed
1957 European Economic Community (EEC) formed
1958 French Fifth Republic
1961 Berlin Wall erected
1962 Cuban missile crisis
1963 U.S. president Kennedy assassinated
1968 Students and worl in France

1940   1950   1960

The Developed World: Economic Challenges and Political Evolution

CHAPTER OUTLINE

In the first five hundred years of the nation-state system, the primary factor in international relations was military power. Until the 1940s the state that could deliver the most force usually dominated the others. The development of nuclear weapons changed the nature of international relations.

The Cold War came to an end not as the result of a surprise nuclear attack, but because the USSR's social and economic infrastructure crumbled and the United States was undergoing considerable social and economic stress. A nation-state's power came to be defined by its ability to compete effectively in the world's economic—rather than political or military—arena.

THE MODERN GLOBAL ECONOMY

Even before the defeat of the Axis in World War II, the Allies made plans to avoid the horrendous economic crisis that had followed the First World War. Forty-four nations met in July 1944 at the New Hampshire resort town of Bretton Woods to

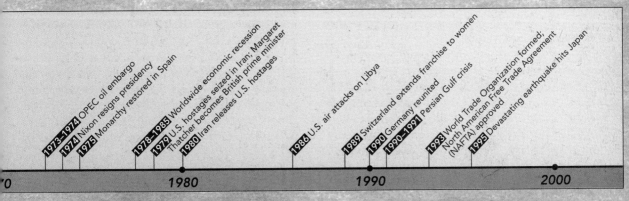

1973–1974 OPEC oil embargo
1974 Nixon resigns presidency
1975 Monarchy restored in Spain
1978–1985 Worldwide economic recession
1979 U.S. hostages seized in Iran; Margaret Thatcher becomes British prime minister
1980 Iran releases U.S. hostages
1986 U.S. air attacks on Libya
1989 Switzerland extends franchise to women
1990 Germany reunited
1990–1991 Persian Gulf crisis
1993 World Trade Organization formed; North American Free Trade Agreement (NAFTA) approved
1995 Devastating earthquake hits Japan

'70   1980   1990   2000

put the peacetime world economy on a solid footing. Recalling the protectionist lessons of the 1930s, the financial leaders devised plans to ensure a free flow of international trade and capital. Later the Marshall Plan for Europe and the Dodge Plan for Japan provided capital to support reconstruction of the war-torn areas.

A New International Framework

The Bretton Woods conference created the International Monetary Fund (IMF), chartered in 1945, to restore the money system that had collapsed in previous decades when countries abandoned the gold standard and resorted to protectionist devices such as currency devaluation. The conference intended that the IMF would oversee a system of fixed exchange rates, founded on the dollar, which could be easily exchanged for gold at the rate of $35.00 an ounce. The IMF was based on a foundation of currencies paid in by the member states. These deposits served as a world savings account from which a member state could take short-term loans to handle debt payments without having to resort to the disruptive tactics of manipulating exchange rates or devaluation. The standard for the exchange rates among the various currencies was that in existence as of the first day of the Bretton Woods conference. Member countries could not change their currency's values without approval of the IMF. Although the system faced some problems based on the weaknesses of many of the member states' economies after the war, the IMF supported a generation of monetary stability that allowed businesses to pursue their plans with confidence in a stable market.

The conference also established the International Bank for Reconstruction and Development—the World Bank, chartered in December 1945. In its first ten years, the World Bank focused mostly on the rebuilding of Europe. Over the next three decades, the World Bank devoted most of its resources to aiding states undergoing development or rebuilding.

A key development in reforming the world economy was the establishment in 1947 of the General Agreement on Tariffs and Trade (GATT), under U.S. leadership. Having absorbed the lessons of the protectionist and autarchic 1930s, the allies put together an international institution to set up rules for business worldwide that would give nations the confidence to break down old barriers that blocked free trade. GATT operated through a series of meetings between nations to remove protectionist restrictions. The assurance a nation received for entering the GATT framework was the most-favored-nation-clause, which guaranteed that any trade advantage worked out on a nation-to-nation agreement would be automatically shared by all members of GATT.

Buttressing the activities of these international institutions was the economic and strategic self-interest of the world's most powerful nation, the United States. The Marshall Plan supplied most of the capital the western European states needed for reconstruction. The Marshall Plan funds came with strict conditions: the recipients had to promise to balance their budgets, free prices, fight inflation, establish a stable currency, and eliminate protectionist trade measures. The Dodge Plan played the same role in Japanese recovery that the Marshall Plan played in Europe.[1]

The developed world achieved its present status of wealth and productivity thanks largely to the far-sighted—and self-interested—American investments in the Marshall Plan and the Dodge Plan and to the structure provided by the Bretton Woods Conference, GATT, and other institutions. Trade grew at a phenomenal annual rate of 7 percent—adjusted for inflation in the first quarter-century after the war. Even during difficult times, such as the OPEC (Organization of Petroleum Exporting Countries) oil embargo and the banking crisis of the 1980s, the postwar international financial structures have proven to be dynamic and creative.

Stalin and his successors, until Gorbachev, chose not to participate in the new world economic structure. While the individual economies of the non–Soviet bloc countries prospered within the new structure, the economies of the Soviet bloc states stagnated. By the 1980s the economic gap between the two sides forced Moscow and its allies in COMECON to seek admission to the IMF and to GATT. It was apparent that the global political economy was the most important factor in world relations. Nations such as the Soviet Union, which allowed ideological considerations to determine economic policy, did so with disastrous results.

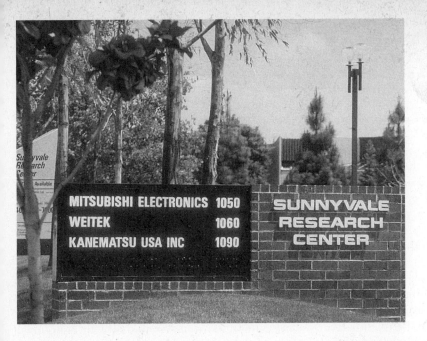

→ California's Silicon Valley, a narrow valley in northern California stretching from Palo Alto to San Jose, prospered from the technological revolution and the developing global economy, becoming a center for the growing computer industry during the 1970s. Both domestic and foreign companies populate the Valley; here the research facilities for a U.S.- and a Japanese-owned firm stand side-by-side.

Technological Revolutions

Propelling the developed world's economic growth was the exceedingly fruitful work of its scientists and engineers. Atomic energy continued to present its Janus-like face of unlimited energy and great danger—as seen in the disastrous meltdown at Chernobyl in 1985. Advances in biology and biochemistry produced a similar mixed picture. In 1953 James D. Watson and Francis H.C. Crick revealed a model of the structure of the DNA (deoxyribonucleic acid) molecule, the fundamental genetic building block. Research stemming from their work brought new insights into processes of heredity and led to the possibility of shaping the future of numerous species—from tomatoes that last longer on the supermarket shelf to shaping human beings to order. Like the problems raised by nuclear power, this capability posed profound social and ethical issues.

The potential for automation in industry was vastly enhanced by the development of the silicon chip. This was a complex miniature electric circuit etched onto a tiny wafer of silicon crystal. One type of chip, the microprocessor, could serve as the "brain" of a computer. Besides being able to carry out computing functions in a very small space, no larger than a thumbnail, it was much cheaper than earlier technology and much more

reliable. Microtechnology markedly affected corporate structure and organization, as well as the nature and extent of work. Communications systems have become more sophisticated, inventories can be more effectively monitored, and financial operations have been simplified. These new systems have led to the increased use of robotics in assembly lines, cheaper and more effective than humans in carrying out repetitive work.

By the mid-1990s all parts of the world were industrializing. There were major petrochemical complexes in the Middle East, automated steel mills in India, computer factories in Brazil, and sophisticated hydroelectric installations in Africa. All around the Pacific rim, nations big and small experienced technological transformation. A vast network of highways, pipelines, railways, shipping and air lanes, fiber optic cables, and communications satellites united the world. All of these served the needs of multinational firms and publicly owned enterprises.

Technology in turn transformed agriculture and diet. Food canning and refrigeration, together with the bulk transport of grains, permitted the shipping of perishable goods to all parts of the world. Food production was increased by plant genetics, new managerial methods, and large-scale agribusinesses—with machines steadily reducing the number of workers doing menial labor. New business methods and technology made the world a smaller and more profitable place. However, the nations of the world were more interdependent than ever before.

Uncertain Times

After 1945 the world experienced unprecedented economic growth and change. But business forms and conditions changed. President Richard Nixon's decision in 1971 to end the policy of the dollar's convertibility into gold dealt a blow to the Bretton Woods framework and opened the way for currency speculation on an unprecedented scale. Multinational firms, headquartered in one country but with operations throughout the world, spread rapidly. Countries whose economies depended on the export of raw materials began to band together in an attempt to affect the price of their goods. The oil embargo of the 1970s imposed by the Organization of Petroleum Exporting Countries dealt a serious blow to international stability.

Even more serious was the debt crisis of the 1980s. Banks in the United States, Europe, and Japan made substantial loans to countries in eastern Europe, Latin America, and Africa—whose total debt by the end of the decade topped $1.3 trillion. Brazil's debt was nearly $100 billion; Mexico's was close to $90 billion. To ensure their survival, nations such as Brazil, Hungary, and Poland allowed World Bank personnel to impose regulations on domestic economic policy in return for loans, an unprecedented sacrifice of national sovereignty to an international body. Nonetheless, nonpayment by the debtor nations threatened to topple the world's banking structure. The crisis pressed the IMF to the limit. Debts continued to be rescheduled, but the largest debtors showed an ever-declining ability to pay.[2]

This situation plus the world recession of 1978 to 1985 had different effects on different parts of the globe. Unemployment soared across the world, especially in the less developed countries, which were also plagued with soaring population rates. In the United States the recession contributed to huge trade deficits and federal budget deficits. The United States was the first nation to recover from the recession, largely at the expense of generating a huge national debt and borrowing heavily from foreigners. A creditor since 1917, the United States now became a debtor nation.

By the late 1980s the United States lost its financial dominance to the Japanese, who themselves would later be challenged by the "Four Tigers" of South Korea, Taiwan, Hong Kong, and Singapore. New technologies and cheaper labor overseas produced high-quality items that cost less than U.S. manufactured goods. Competition was especially severe for the Americans in the advanced technology and automobile markets.

The resulting foreign trade deficits increased the desire for protectionist legislation in the 1980s, especially in the United States. Many congressional members argued that Japanese trade restrictions and subsidies harmed U.S. agricultural and technological exports while American markets remained relatively open to foreign imports. The GATT mechanism was pushed to the breaking point. In 1989 the United States invoked Section 301 of the Trade Act of 1974 to levy sanctions against India, Brazil, and Japan for unfair trade practices.

Given the turbulence of the previous half-century, however, the foundation established at Bretton Woods allowed the world to avoid the inflation and depression that marked the 1920s and 1930s. The long-running Uruguay Round of the GATT talks in which the United States worked with 115 other states to update the GATT rules ended successfully in December 1993. This led to the establishment of the World Trade Organization (WTO), a streamlined approach to continuing the fight against trade barriers that had been successfully waged by GATT since World War II.

THE UNITED STATES SINCE 1945

The United States emerged from World II with its landscape unscathed and its economy the most powerful in the world. This wealth enabled the United States over the next 30 years to assume vast global responsibilities such as those involved with the Marshall Plan, the expansion of a broad range of public services demanded by the expanded welfare state, and maintenance of a global military presence. Until 1981 both Democratic and Republic administrations based their policies firmly on the legacy of Franklin D. Roosevelt's New Deal. Those who opposed the Roosevelt programs suffered decisive defeats. In the 1980s and after, both Republican and Democratic presidents questioned basic aspects of the New Deal, as leaders had to deal with the fact that there were simply not enough resources to meet the demands of an economically challenged population.

Postwar Leadership

In addition to his foreign policy accomplishments after 1945, Harry Truman, who served as president from 1945 to 1953, continued to crusade for the rights of the "common man" and against the "fat cats" as he extended the New Deal. Republican Dwight David Eisenhower, the former supreme commander of Allied forces in Europe, was twice elected to the presidency with overwhelming victories. He continued, with somewhat less enthusiasm, to oversee the growth of federal programs.

Eisenhower's successor, the Democrat John F. Kennedy, was elected president in 1961 and promised a "New Frontier" spirit for America. While working actively for programs to aid the poor and minorities, he was unable to deal effectively with Congress. He captured the nation's idealism, especially with the Peace Corps, but his assassination in November 1963 cut short his presidency.

The Crisis of the Presidency

Kennedy's vice-president, Lyndon B. Johnson picked up the burden of the slain chief executive and completed a series of major domestic reforms. Johnson could claim credit for the Civil Rights Act of 1964, the war on poverty, Medicare, important environmental legislation, and the creation of the Department of Housing and Urban Development. However, major problems such as environmental pollution, decay of the urban "inner cores," and minority discontent—the crisis of rising expectations—remained unsolved.

In foreign affairs, the increasingly unpopular Vietnam conflict (see pp. 951–952) plagued Johnson's presidency. The war alone cost more than $30 billion annually, and that plus the expensive domestic programs fueled the inflation of the 1970s. Congress was slow to provide the massive funds needed to improve conditions for minorities and the inner cities and at the same time carry on the Vietnam War. In response, a powerful protest movement developed and many average Americans found themselves in deep and serious opposition to their government's policies. The political turmoil led in 1968 to the assassination of civil rights leader Dr. Martin Luther King, Jr., and of Senator Robert F. Kennedy, brother of the former president, who was close to gaining the Democratic presidential nomination before being shot in Los Angeles.

The fragmentation of the liberal opposition led to the 1968 election—by a razor-thin margin—of Richard M. Nixon, Eisenhower's vice-president who had himself been narrowly defeated by John F. Kennedy in 1960. Nixon, reelected by a landslide in 1972, shifted toward a more pragmatic philosophy of government. To fight inflation, caused in part by the costs of the Vietnam War and social programs, the administration imposed a wage-price freeze from August to November 1971 and wage-price controls from November 1971 to January 1973. These measures helped reduce the rate of inflation from 5

→ The motto "The Buck Stops Here," displayed on Harry Truman's desk, reflected his belief in the authority of the president. Uninformed about confidential government policy when he assumed the presidency in April 1945, Truman presided over the military victories over Germany and Japan ending World War II. Truman contended with two major events following his election in 1948: the Korean War and the right-wing challenge of McCarthyism.

→ In August 1961 the first Peace Corps volunteers to leave the United States arrived in Ghana where they were to spend two years teaching in Ghana's secondary schools. Peace Corps volunteers provide educational, health care, and agricultural services to help developing countries meet their basic needs.

to about 3 percent. But when the administration returned to a free-market policy by the end of April 1974, prices began to rise. An oil embargo imposed by Arab nations opposed to American support of Israel contributed to the rise in inflation rates to 12 percent and a 6 percent unemployment rate.

The Nixon administration concentrated on foreign affairs during this time, especially those relating to ending the war in Vietnam, keeping peace in the Middle East, opening relations with China, and maintaining détente with the Soviet Union. In each area Nixon and his chief advisor, Henry Kissinger, compiled a substantial record of success. However, this record was overshadowed by scandal.

Nixon's vice-president, Spiro Agnew, resigned his office under the weight of charges of bribery, extortion, and kickbacks dating from his time as governor of Maryland. Nixon himself resigned the presidency in the wake of the Watergate scandal. Men connected with Nixon's 1972 reelection campaign were arrested and charged with the break-in at the Democratic campaign headquarters in the Watergate Hotel in Washington. On the grounds of presidential confidentiality, Nixon withheld information concerning these activities from a special prosecutor, a grand jury, and the public. After lengthy televised hearings and the conviction of his closest associates, Nixon lost the confidence of most of the nation. In May 1974 the Judiciary Committee of the

House of Representatives began impeachment proceedings and in July the committee voted to recommend an impeachment trial in the Senate. Repudiated and disgraced, Nixon resigned in August. His appointed successor, Gerald R. Ford, who had also been appointed to the office of vice-president on Agnew's resignation, granted Nixon a full pardon.

The Limited Presidency

Economic problems, including high inflation, high unemployment, and a falling dollar, continued to plague the nation. In 1976 Ford ran against the relatively unknown Jimmy Carter, former governor of Georgia. Carter campaigned on promises to restore trust in government, extend social programs, and improve economic conditions. Carter won the close election, becoming the first president from the Deep South since the Civil War.

Carter inherited the same problems as his predecessors and incurred some new ones. To deal with the crisis in the Middle East he brought together at the presidential retreat of Camp David the leaders of Egypt and Israel. He continued to pursue limitations on nuclear arms, but for many his greatest accomplishment was that he made human rights considerations an operative part of American foreign policy. Domestically Carter attempted to enact an extremely ambitious program of social and economic benefits while maintaining sufficient military strength.

Henry Kissinger, *White House Years*

Henry Kissinger, who served as Secretary of State under Presidents Nixon and Ford, advocated a balance-of-power approach to foreign relations and a policy of détente with the Soviet Union.

In my view, Vietnam was not the cause of our difficulties but a symptom. We were in a period of painful adjustment to a profound transformation of global politics; we were being forced to come to grips with the tension between our history and our new necessities. For two centuries America's participation in the world seemed to oscillate between overinvolvement and withdrawal, between expecting too much of our power and being ashamed of it, between optimistic exuberance and frustration with the ambiguities of an imperfect world. I was convinced that the deepest cause of our national unease was the realization—as yet dimly perceived—that we were becoming like other nations in the need to recognize that our power, while vast, had limits. Our resources were no longer infinite in relation to our problems; instead we had to set priorities, both intellectual and material. In the Fifties and Sixties we had attempted ultimate solutions to specific problems; now our challenge was to shape a world and an American role to which we were permanently committed, which could no longer be sustained by the illusion that our exertions had a terminal point. . . .

But in our deliberations at the Pierre Hotel the President-elect and I distilled a number of basic principles that were to characterize our approach to US-Soviet relations as long as we were in office:

The principle of concreteness. We would insist that any negotiations between the United States and the Soviet Union deal with specific causes of tensions rather than general atmospherics. Summit meetings, if they were to be meaningful, had to be well prepared and reflect negotiations that had already made major progress in diplomatic channels. We would take seriously the ideological commitment of Soviet leaders; we would not delude ourselves about the incompatible interests between our two countries in many areas. We would not pretend that good personal relations or sentimental rhetoric would end the tensions of the postwar period. But we were prepared to explore areas of common concern and to make precise agreements based on strict reciprocity.

The principle of restraint. Reasonable relations between the superpowers could not survive the constant attempt to pursue unilateral advantages and exploit areas of crisis. We were determined to resist Soviet adventures; at the same time we were prepared to negotiate about a genuine easing of tensions. We would not hold still for a détente designed to lull potential victims; we were prepared for a détente based on mutual restraint. We would pursue a carrot-and-stick approach, ready to impose penalties for adventurism, willing to expand relations in the context of responsible behavior.

The principle of linkage. We insisted that progress in superpower relations, to be real, had to be made on a broad front. Events in different parts of the world, in our view, were related to each other; even more so, Soviet conduct in different parts of the world. We proceeded from the premise that to separate issues into distinct compartments would encourage the Soviet leaders to believe that they could use cooperation in one area as a safety valve while striving for unilateral advantages elsewhere. . . .

We would have to learn to reconcile ourselves to imperfect choices, partial fulfillment, the unsatisfying tasks of balance and maneuver, given confidence by our moral values but recognizing that they could be achieved only in stages and over a long period of time.

It was a hard lesson to convey to a people who rarely read about the balance of power without seeing the adjective "outdated" precede it.

↣ An embattled Richard Nixon raises his arms in a victory salute after resigning the presidency on August 9, 1974.

Not surprisingly, spending increased despite the goal of a balanced budget.

Rising fuel prices and declining per capita output exacerbated economic difficulties. American helplessness and frustration grew when Iranian militants captured 53 hostages during a takeover of the U.S. embassy in Teheran. The combination of economic problems, the foreign policy crisis surrounding the Soviet invasion of Afghanistan, and the hostage dilemma led to Carter's defeat in November 1980 by former actor and governor of California Ronald Reagan. In a final blow to Carter, the hostages held in Iran were released just as Reagan took the oath of office in January 1981.

Reagan won the presidency with an overwhelming victory, and he promised to set about reversing a half-century of increasing federal involvement in American life by making drastic cuts in federal programs. These cuts were part of his "New Federalism" program to reduce the budget, which also included proposals to cut personal tax rates by 25 percent and to make huge reductions in taxes paid by businesses. The administration also planned to substantially increase military spending. The assumption underlying the policy was that the budget cuts and tax cuts would simultaneously cure inflation and bring about economic growth.

However, the tax cuts were not matched by reduced federal spending. The percentage of gross national product (GNP) spent by government increased during Reagan's first term. By the time he left office in 1988, the federal deficit had soared to unprecedented heights. Inflation rates fell significantly, but interest rates remained high.

The economic problems posed little obstacle to Reagan in the 1984 election, in which he took 49 states. Not even his most bitter critic could deny the effect of his will and personality on the office of president. Observers looked back to Franklin D. Roosevelt to find Reagan's equal as a communicator and master of the legislative process. Reagan won major tax and budget victories in the Democrat-controlled House of Representatives and gained backing in the Senate for such controversial diplomatic initiatives as the sale of sophisticated equipment to Saudi Arabia and the INF treaty. He survived an assassination attempt in March 1981, and this, plus his considerable charm, gave him an aura of authority and respect—despite a sometimes shocking lack of mastery of the details of his own programs—that no president since Eisenhower had enjoyed.

Reagan faced a number of foreign policy challenges as a result of the rapid changes occurring during the latter part of the Cold War. He sent contingents of Marines to Lebanon in 1982 to act as part of an international peacekeeping force in that fragmented country. A bombing in October 1983 killed 241 Marines. This atrocity forced Reagan to withdraw U.S. troops from the area. Relations with Israel cooled when Israeli forces bombed an Iraqi nuclear facility, annexed the Golan heights, and invaded Lebanon. The aggressive policies of Libyan leader Muammar el-Kadaffi led to conflicts with the United States, which included U.S. air attacks on Libya in the spring of 1986. In another controversial move, Reagan sent U.S. naval forces to the Persian Gulf when the Iran-Iraq war threatened to disrupt international oil shipments.

Festering social and economic problems in Latin America erupted into revolutionary movements in El Salvador and Nicaragua. The Reagan administration sent in military advisers and millions of dollars to support those factions it considered to be democratic. When Congress withdrew support for efforts to support the Contra rebels against the Sandinista government of Nicaragua, officials in the Reagan administration conspired to carry out illegal maneuvers to gain financial support, including the shipping of weapons to supposed moderates in Iran. The "Iran-Contra" controversy cast a pall over the last two years of the Reagan administration and led to felony convictions of high-ranking Reagan aides.

The Republicans maintained their hold on the White House with the election of George Bush in 1988. The new president failed to continue the momentum Reagan had established to extend American influence favorably to affect the development of democracy and the market in the Soviet Union after 1988. Bush instead drew back, choosing to be "prudent" and to consult closely with allies and opponents alike to maintain stability during the massive changes occurring in Eastern Europe and the Soviet Union during 1989. Bush's major success in foreign policy was his successful leadership of the anti-Iraq coalition during the Persian Gulf War. Deftly working through the United Nations and mobilizing a broad coalition, Bush effectively stymied the Iraq government diplomatically and then sent U.S. troops to lead the UN coalition forces in a powerful bombing campaign against Iraq. A 100-hour ground offensive ultimately drove Saddam Hussein's Iraqi forces out of Kuwait. However, for most of Bush's term, the administration responded to foreign events more often with slogans such as the "New World Order" rather than with carefully thought-out policies.

Bush's administration faced worsening economic problems: the growing budget deficit, productivity declines, balance of trade problems, the failure of many savings and loan institutions, and the fear of recession. Makeshift solutions to foreign opportunities, the deficit crisis, and other pressing domestic problems contributed to the president's decline in public opinion polls, with the exception of a momentary improvement in his standing during the Persian Gulf crisis of 1990–1991.

Nagging economic problems helped ensure the 1992 victory for Bill Clinton of Arkansas, whose campaign revolved around the working rule to his staff, "It's the Economy, Stupid." In his first two years the former Arkansas governor attempted to take the Democratic party to a

→ Health-care reform was a major component of President Bill Clinton's platform. Riders of the president's "Health Security Express" gathered at a rally on Capitol Hill in August 1994. The next month Clinton announced the details of his reform package. Defeat of the plan was a major setback for the president.

more centrist position, responding to the conditions in the bond market more than his assumed constituency of labor, the poor, and the disaffected. Despite successes such as gaining U.S. acceptance of the North American Free Trade Alliance (NAFTA), the nagging cloud of earlier personal improprieties and inadequate staff work gave the Clinton administration a troubled image of muddling inefficiency in both domestic and foreign affairs that contributed to the Republican Party's overwhelming victory in the 1994 elections, giving the Republicans control of both houses of Congress.

JAPAN: FROM DEFEAT TO DOMINANCE

On August 28, 1945, 19 days after the atomic bomb was dropped at Nagasaki, an advance party of 150 Americans, the lead group of a substantial army of occupation, landed on Japan. Supreme Commander General Douglas MacArthur soon arrived to preside over Japan's transition from one military authority to another. The Japanese had successfully recast their infrastructure during the Meiji Restoration. They would make another massive—and successful—adjustment after 1945.

Postwar Japan

The terms of armistice took all territory outside the four main islands away from Japan and imposed complete demilitarization on the Japanese. Key wartime military leaders were placed on trial, and Japanese Premier General Hideki Tojo and six of his colleagues were executed. Other militarist governmental and business leaders were blocked from postwar activities. For a while, industries were dismantled for reparations, but this practice was soon stopped.

In return, the allies gave aid under the Dodge Plan to rebuild the shattered economy, while insisting on democratic institutions in the government and society. The new education system was based on the American pattern of decentralized public schools, with textbooks rewritten to delete militant nationalism. A land reform policy intended to reduce tenancy and absentee landlordism was introduced. Unions gained the right of collective bargaining, and their membership grew rapidly. American authorities tried with limited success to reduce the great concentration of wealth in the hands of monopolistic industries, the *zaibatsu*.

A new constitution, drafted in consultation with the occupation government, came into effect in May 1947. It set up a democratic, two-house parliamentary-cabinet system in which the majority party selected the prime minister. Sovereignty rested in the people; the emperor, forced to renounce his divinity, was referred to as "the symbol of state." No limitations were placed on voting because of income or sex. War was renounced as a sovereign right and the maintenance of "land, sea, and air forces, as well as other war potential" was forbidden.

As a result of the Cold War in Europe and the communist invasion of South Korea in 1950, Japan became the United States' principal ally in the Pacific. Despite Soviet opposition and without the participation of the USSR, a peace treaty was signed in 1951 and went into effect the next year, giving Japan full sovereignty. A security pact between Japan and the United States allowed Americans to station troops in Japan.

Political and Social Change

Until 1994 conservatives have consistently, except for two brief periods, controlled the Japanese government. In 1955 two conservative parties merged to form the Liberal Democratic party, which was friendly to the West, favored modest rearmament, and backed the alliance with the United States. Based on professional civil servants and business interests, it was sufficiently strong to endure periodic charges of corruption for the next 38 years. The Socialist party, the major opposition, demanded nationalization of industry, opposed the 1947 security pact, and favored neutrality in foreign affairs. The small Communist party was vocal but weak.

The new system was flexible enough to absorb the radical transformation Japan has experienced in the past half-century, although charges of corruption brought the political system to near-paralysis in the mid-1990s. In 1994 alone there were three prime ministers, including a Socialist. After a half-century reformers seemed ready to shake off the legacy of the Liberal Democratic party and attack problems in the economy, politics, and society.

Rapid urbanization posed the greatest social challenges. Rural areas lost population while city populations—and consequent environmental problems—skyrocketed. With more than 11 million people, Tokyo became the largest urban area in the world. Three great concentrations of industry and population clustered around Tokyo, Osaka, and Nagoya occupied only 1 percent of the country's land area but contained over one-fourth of the country's population.

In the cities traditional values and attitudes changed. Parental authority and family ties weakened as young married couples, forsaking the traditional three-generation household, set up their own homes. The stresses and strains of urbanization were reflected in student riots and

→ The influence of both the West and the media in modern Japan is reflected in this photo of the large group of Japanese teenage Elvis impersonators.

in the appearance, for the first time in Japanese history, of juvenile delinquency. Western influence—seen in fashions, television, sports, and beauty contests and heard in rock music—clashed with the traditional culture. The harmony that characterized industrial concerns disappeared, and guaranteed life-time employment

came increasingly under challenge. Corporate paternalism had to be discarded to satisfy the demands of efficiency. Slowly but surely the communalism that had dominated Japanese life weakened under the impact of economic and cultural individualism.

Perhaps the greatest changes were those affecting women. Before World War II there was little opportunity for Japanese women outside the family. After 1945 they gained the right to own property, sue for divorce, and pursue educational opportunities. By the end of the 1980s, women constituted nearly 50 percent of the nation's work force, and more than 30 percent of women high school graduates attended post-secondary institutions.

Economic Dominance

Japan faced serious obstacles in its path to economic development. It had to import much of the food for its growing population (125 million by 1995) and most of the raw materials for its industries. The Korean War gave Japan an initial boost, as American forces spent lavishly. In 1950 the GNP was $10 billion. The 1973 oil embargo and subsequent price increases of more than 400 percent by all of the OPEC producers severely affected Japan. Inflation skyrocketed, economic growth plunged, and for a while the balance of

→ Male and female officials of a computer firm in Japan discuss a technical question. Japan passed an equal opportunity law in 1985, widening access to the paid work force for many Japanese women. Although many women have taken jobs outside the home, their upward progress has been limited as the Japanese tradition of male dominance continues to be strong.

trade was negative. Japan's business managers made the necessary adjustments for recovery.

By the end of the 1970s the Japanese built half the world's tonnage in shipping and had become the world's biggest producer of motorcycles, bicycles, transistor radios, and sewing machines. The Japanese soon outpaced the United States in automobile production and drove the American domestic television industry virtually out of business. After the October 1987 stock market slide, Tokyo became the world financial center, dominating banking.

In the late 1980s the Japanese began to watch uneasily as South Korea, Taiwan, Hong Kong, and Singapore, using the Japanese formula of a strong and disciplined work force and efficient use of new technology, became effective competitors in the world market. South Korea especially launched a direct challenge to Japan in high-technology and automotive markets. By the 1990s, however, the Japanese continued to boast one of the world's strongest economies. Japan's per capita GNP was nearly $30,000—compared to the U.S. per capita GNP of $20,800. By 1993, Japan's GNP had risen to $3,705 billion.

THE WESTERN EUROPEAN STATES

The most significant development in postwar Europe was the progress toward economic integration. The desire for cooperation came from the lessons learned during World War II, taught by visionaries such as the French statesmen Jean Monnet and Robert Schumann. In 1950 Monnet and Schumann put forth a program to create the European Coal and Steel Community to coordinate the supply of those two essential industrial commodities in West Germany, France, Italy, Belgium, the Netherlands, and Luxembourg. Five years later, the European Atomic Energy Community was created.

The same six nations that participated in these supranational organizations in 1957 established the European Economic Community (EEC), the Common Market. The organization's goal was to build "the enduring foundations for the closer union between European peoples." To that end it reduced tariffs among its members and created a great free trade union that became the fastest-growing area in the Western world.

Jean Monnet on European Unity

Jean Monnet was a pioneer in building the foundations for a unified Europe. In a 1953 speech, he expressed his hopes in a future—to be attained in 1992.

Mr. President, Ladies and Gentlemen, on behalf of my colleagues of the High Authority and myself, I wish to say how very pleased we are to have this meeting to-day with the members of the Common Assembly and the members of the Consultative Assembly. The co-operation between the Council of Europe and the European Coal and Steel Community has now definitely entered a concrete phase. . . .

In respect of coal and steel, the community has set up a huge European market of more than 150 million consumers, i.e., equal in number to the population of the United States of America. Under the terms of the Treaty, customs duties and quota restrictions have been abolished between Germany, Belgium, France, Italy, Luxembourg and the Netherlands; the

principal discriminations in respect of transport have been done away with. . . . [T]he road along which the six countries of the Community have set out is the right road, but we must continue to seek even more zealously ways and means of achieving a more complete understanding with the other countries of Europe. When they have seen and understood, as we have done, what this new and living Europe means for them, they will, one of these days, I hope, themselves join in.

From the Joint Meeting of the Members of the Consultative Assembly of the Council of Europe and of the Members of the Common Assembly of the European Community of Coal and Steel, *Official Report of the Debate*, Strasbourg, 22 June 1953.

From EEC headquarters in Brussels, a staff of some thousands of experts administered the organization's affairs. In the 1950s the income of its members doubled. While the U.S. economy grew at a rate of 3.8 percent, that of France expanded by 7.1 percent, Italy by 8.4 percent, and West Germany by 9.6 percent. During the rest of the decade trade nearly doubled among EEC members. Their factories and power plants hummed with activity, their work force augmented by more than 10.5 million workers who migrated, many with their families, from southern Europe.

Lagging far behind these advances, Britain became a member of the Common Market in 1973; Ireland and Denmark also joined in that year. The admission of Spain and Portugal in 1986 brought the number to 12. While the member nations jealously guarded their sovereignty, they made substantial strides toward total economic integration. Various advances have been made toward adopting a common passport, setting a basic work week and holiday policy for all workers, and equalizing welfare benefits.

Europe became a single market at the end of 1992, by an act similar to that created by the 1707 Act of Union between England and Scotland, the Constitution of the United States, and the north German *Zollverein* in the first part of the nineteenth century. Reaching the goal of "Europe 1992" was not easy. Serious controversies over agricultural policy, banking policies, and tax differences had to be overcome. The European leaders worked hard to reassure the rest of the world that their 12-nation market would not be protectionist, while they put together the more than 300 directives that would form the laws for the commercial union.

The program of the 12 nations involved the opening up of their union's boundaries so that there would be no restriction to the movement of goods and people and the establishment of the "social dimension" to define the "rights of ordinary people in the great market and to help the poorer among them." There was also a more difficult drive toward economic and monetary unity, including a single European currency and central bank. Economic union also included single standards on electricity, pressures, safety, and health.

The momentum toward political unity slowed somewhat during the 1990s. Obstacles

born of a thousand years of nationalism remained. Unresolved issues included a state's favoring its own industries in the purchase of supplies and equipment, protection of particular industries by sovereign states, and the value-added tax.[3]

The political changes of the late 1980s brought the EEC challenges of expansion. By 1995 the members of the European Free Trade Association—Finland, Austria, Iceland, and Sweden—had gained membership within the EEC. Norway voted not to join. The former Soviet bloc states and Switzerland, Turkey, Malta, and Cyprus want to establish a relationship with the "Twelve." Given the problems involved in integrating the poorer nations of Europe, especially Greece, the European Community's leadership was hesitant to extend full membership to the former Soviet bloc states.

In response to the Common Market's successes, other trade zones were established: NAFTA, which included Canada, Mexico, and the United States; and the Asia Pacific Economic Cooperation (APEC), which included the Pacific rim states of Australia, Brunei, Canada, China, Hong Kong, Indonesia, Japan, South Korea, Malaysia, New Zealand, Philippines, Singapore, Taiwan, and the United States.

Great Britain

Great Britain emerged from World War II at the height of its prestige in the twentieth century, but the glow of victory and the glory earned by its sacrifices served only to conceal Britain's dismal condition. The country was in a state of near-bankruptcy. As a result of the war, its investments had drastically declined and huge bills had been run up for the support of British armies overseas. In addition, the increase in welfare benefits drained the economy.

After 1945 the London government could not reinstate the delicately balanced formula under which Britain had paid for the massive imports of food and raw material through exports and income from foreign investments, banking, and insurance. The British people, who had paid dearly to defeat the Axis powers, did not produce the necessary export surplus to restore Britain's wealth. Over the next 40 years they would watch their vanquished enemies become wealthy while they struggled with aging industrial facilities and extremely costly welfare programs.

Since 1945 the Conservatives have dominated politics, with interludes of Labour rule. The Conservatives oppose nationalization of industry, encourage private enterprise, and favor a reduced social welfare program. Labour supports nationalization of industry and a thorough welfare state. Neither party has been able to find a wholesale cure for the serious ailments afflicting the country.

After the wartime coalition government of Conservatives and Labour, the country held its first peacetime regular election in July 1945, and to the amazement of many, Labourite Clement Attlee defeated wartime leader Winston Churchill. Attlee was a low-key, hardworking, honest politician who came from a comfortable middle-class background. In foreign affairs the Labour government continued to work closely with the United States, while in domestic policy it set out to improve basic living standards while converting to a peacetime economic base. Within two years most major industrial and financial functions had been nationalized. In Britain's "mixed economy," 80 percent remained employed by private enterprise. The Labour party suffered, as it would for the next 40 years, from factionalism between its left wing, which was inclined to be anti-American and pro-Russian, and the mainstream. Weakened by this split, Labour lost the general election in 1951, and the Conservatives began a 13-year dominance.

Churchill returned as prime minister until 1955, when he resigned and was succeeded by Anthony Eden. Eden resigned in January 1957 following the Suez crisis, and Harold Macmillan took the party's leadership until July 1963. During the 1950s economic conditions slowly improved until 1959, when they rapidly deteriorated. Britain went deeply in the red in its balance of payments. By the end of 1960 the economic outlook was grim. The next year the government applied for membership in the Common Market, in the belief that a closer trading association with the Continent would reverse their terrible economic condition. The issue of membership in the EEC split both the Conservative and Labour parties. Further, during the negotiations with the EEC, French president Charles de Gaulle moved successfully to block British membership.

The long period of Conservative rule ended in 1964 with the election of a small Labour majority headed by Harold Wilson, who had previously been the youngest cabinet minister in 150 years. Under his leadership Labour made important advances in education, slum clearance, and housing. But the old economic problems remained to plague the government. In 1967 Wilson was forced to devalue the pound. Labour's lackluster performance in the late 1960s led to a victory in the 1970 election for the Conservatives under the leadership of Edward Heath. Heath's only significant achievement was bringing his country into the Common Market. Labor unrest in 1973 and the Arab oil embargo dealt crippling blows to the British economy, and Heath's bland leadership could not save his party from defeat in the 1974 elections. Labour returned once again, led by Wilson, who commanded a narrow majority. Continued industrial unrest, declining production, and alarming inflation led to major changes.

In 1975 Wilson resigned, to be succeeded by James Callaghan, a pragmatic moderate. He warned that "we are still not earning the standard of living we are enjoying. We are only keeping up our standards by borrowing, and this cannot go on indefinitely."[4] During 1976, Britain had to borrow $5.3 billion from ten other countries. Massive cuts were proposed for social services and the armed forces. Many unions denounced this action, but it seemed imperative to all responsible leaders. Callaghan's inability to deal with what one authority called "the most serious challenge in [Britain's] recent history as a liberal democracy" led to yet another change in the spring of 1979.

Margaret Thatcher led her Conservative forces to victory by proposing radical changes in Britain's economic and social programs. Thatcher's success in carrying out her programs gave her overwhelming victories in 1983 and again in 1987. She demanded—and received—sacrifices from her own people, a more favorable treatment from the Common Market, and firm backing from the United States. She built a solid political base against a disorganized Labour opposition. From there she proceeded to change the nature of the Conservative party and to attempt to reform British society, until she was removed by her party in 1990 and replaced by John Major,

→ The first woman to head a major British party (the Conservative party) and the first woman to be prime minister of Great Britain, Margaret Thatcher held that post for 1½ years.

who barely kept power in the 1992 elections. Major never enjoyed the standing or the success of Thatcher.

Slow economic growth and unemployment have been constant problems since 1945. Britain continued to try to find the difficult balance between making an industrial comeback without seriously sacrificing its extensive welfare services. Another serious dilemma was the stark contrast between the rich southeastern part of the country and the permanently depressed areas of the Midlands, Scotland, and Wales. The Irish problem remained, with violent incidents occurring almost daily in Northern Ireland. Racial problems generated by English resentment over the influx of "coloured" peoples from the Commonwealth defied easy solution.

France: Grandeur and Reality

While most of France agreed to do the "rational" thing and capitulate to the Nazis in June 1940, Charles de Gaulle urged the government to move to North Africa and continue the struggle. During the war he personified France as a great power, rather than a humiliated Nazi victim. In a famous broadcast to the French people from his exile in London de Gaulle declared:

> Whatever happens, the flame of French resistance must not and shall not die. . . . Must we abandon all hope? Is our defeat final and irremediable? To those questions I answer—No![5]

After the liberation of Paris in August 1944, de Gaulle was proclaimed provisional president and for 14 months was a virtual dictator by consent. Elections held in October 1945 confirmed that the people wanted a new constitution. Sharp differences, however, developed between de Gaulle and members of the government. The general resigned in January 1946, occupying himself with the writing of his memoirs. In the fall of that year, the Fourth Republic was established. Unfortunately, the old confusing patterns of the Third Republic were repeated. Too many parties and too much bickering precluded any significant action. The Fourth Republic had a mixed record during its dozen years of existence.

The Fourth Republic collapsed over the issue of Algeria. Revolt against the French colonial government there began in 1954 and for the next eight years drained French resources. The French population in Algeria, more than a million, insisted that Algeria be kept French. Army leaders supported them. Plots to overthrow the government in Paris were started. Faced with the prospects of a civil war, the ineffectual French government, which had been referred to as a "regime of mediocrity and chloroform," resigned in 1958, naming de Gaulle as president. His new government was granted full power for six months.

De Gaulle had been awaiting his nation's "call" in his country home. Eager to reenter the political arena, he returned to Paris and oversaw the drafting of a new constitution, this for the Fifth French Republic. The new code was overwhelmingly approved by referendum in September 1958. De Gaulle was named president for seven years and proceeded to make this office the most important in the government. In both the Third and Fourth Republics the legislature had been dominant, but now the president and cabinet held supreme power. During a crisis the executive could assume nearly total power. De Gaulle once commented, "The assemblies debate, the ministers govern, the constituent council thinks, the president of the Republic decides."

De Gaulle ended the Algerian war and shrugged off assassination plots and armed revolts. Then he set forth on his foremost objective—to make France a great power, to give it grandeur. He noted in his *Memoirs* that "France cannot be France without greatness." For the next seven years he worked to make France the dominant power in Europe, a third force free of either U.S. or Soviet domination. To this end he persisted in making France an independent nuclear power. In 1966 he withdrew French military forces from active participation in NATO, although France remained a consultative member of the alliance. Above all, de Gaulle was opposed to membership in any supranational agency. For this reason, while he tolerated the Common Market, he blocked any attempts to transform it into a political union. Even though he wielded great influence internationally, at home his position weakened.

A serious upheaval of university students and workers' strikes in 1968 further diminished de Gaulle's authority. A national referendum had been called to reorganize the government on a regional basis. De Gaulle unnecessarily made it a vote of confidence. When the referendum failed, he resigned his office and retired to his country estate, where he died 18 months later. His successor was Georges Pompidou, an able administrator who gave evidence of vision in his leadership. When Pompidou died prematurely in 1974, the country elected Valéry Giscard d'Estaing as president. A resistance hero and brilliant student, he had entered government service and become a high-ranking civil servant by the age of 26. The new president initiated a series of important reforms relating to urban growth, real estate, and divorce. He also favored a voting age of 18.

Despite the generally high level of leadership in France, the country was also afflicted by the international economic difficulties relating to the energy crisis and American financial problems after 1973. Problems of inflation and housing shortages helped the rise to power of the Communist and Socialist parties, whose active participation in the wartime resistance had increased their popularity. There was a real possibility that a combined political program by the two parties might lead to a Marxist domination of the government. The March 1978 election, however, proved the alliance to be a weak one. Nevertheless the strength of the left was evident and continued to grow in the face of economic problems and discontent with Giscard's personal rule. In May 1981, socialist leader François Mitterand was elected president, and 20 years of right-of-center government came to an end.

In June the Socialist party gained a majority in the National Assembly, and Mitterand set out to reverse two centuries of French tradition by decentralizing the governmental apparatus installed by Napoleon. In addition, he pursued a program to nationalize some of France's largest business and banking enterprises. Mitterand's "honeymoon" did not last long, as the parties to his right began to practice stalling tactics in the Assembly to block his programs. The communists, on the other hand, who had lost badly in the 1981 elections, received four relatively insignificant seats in the cabinet, in return for which they promised cooperation with the new government.

Mitterand has had to deal with the economic problems of slow industrial growth, inflation, and unemployment, and he found these to be as resistant to solution as did Giscard. By the end of 1985 the economy began to improve. The president lost his majority in elections in March 1986 but regained it in 1988. Since then he has continued his policy of close cooperation with the United States and moderate domestic government.

West Germany: Recovery to Reunification

The most dramatic postwar European transformation has been that of West Germany. Recovering from the death, disaster, and destruction of World War II, the Bonn government accomplished political and economic miracles. When the Soviet bloc disintegrated in 1989, the Bonn government moved rapidly to extend economic aid and work for reunification. By October 1990, unification had been accomplished, justifying the dreams of postwar Germany's most important leader, Konrad Adenauer, who led his country from the status of despised outcast to that of valued Western ally.

Born in 1876, Adenauer entered politics in 1906 as a member of the city council of Cologne. In 1917 he became mayor of the city, holding office until 1933, when the Nazis dismissed him. During Hitler's regime he was imprisoned twice, but lived mostly in retirement at home, cultivating his rose garden. After 1945 he entered German national politics, becoming leader of the new Christian Democratic party. With the approval of the allied occupation authorities, German representatives drafted a constitution for the German Federal Republic, which was ratified in 1949. Adenauer, at the age of 73, became chancellor of West Germany.

In the new democratic government, the presidency was made weak, while the real executive, the chancellor, was given specific authority to determine "the fundamental policies of the government." The chancellor was responsible to the Bundestag, a popularly elected legislative body. One of the weaknesses of the Weimar Republic had been the existence of many small parties, leading to unstable multiparty coalitions. In the new government, to be recognized a party had to win at least 5 percent of the total election votes.

Adenauer assumed power when Germany was still an outcast and its economy was in ruins. His one driving obsession was to get his people to work. Taking advantage of the tensions of the Cold War, he succeeded admirably. Under the force of his autocratic and sometimes domineering leadership, the Germans rebuilt their destroyed cities and factories using some $3 billion in Marshall Plan assistance. As early as 1955 West German national production exceeded prewar figures, with only 53 percent of former German territory. Providing the initial economic guidance for this recovery was Adenauer's minister of economics Dr. Ludwig Erhard, a professional economist and a firm believer in laissez-faire economics. Germany's economic growth was accompanied by little inflation, practically no unemployment, and few labor problems.

Adenauer's achievements in foreign affairs were as remarkable as his leadership in domestic affairs. The German Federal Republic gained full sovereignty in 1955. At that same time, West Germany was admitted into the NATO alliance. Adenauer decided to align closely with the West and cultivated close ties with the United States. In 1963 he signed a treaty of friendship with France, ending a century-long period of hostility. Adenauer expressed his attitude toward foreign affairs when he said, "Today I regard myself primarily as a European and only in second place as a German." It was natural that he brought his nation into Europe's new institutions: the European Coal and Steel Community and the Common Market. Adenauer's great frustration in foreign affairs was his failure to achieve the reunification of West and East Germany.

In 1963, after 14 years in office, Adenauer retired and was succeeded by Ludwig Erhard as chancellor, who was in turn succeeded by Kurt Kiesinger. The big change in German politics occurred in 1969 with the victory of the Social Democratic party. This moderate, nondoctrinaire socialist party was led by Willy Brandt, who became chancellor. A foe of the Nazis, Brandt had fled to Norway, where he became a member of the resistance after Hitler's conquest. After the war he returned to Germany and became prominent in the Social Democratic party. In 1957 he became mayor of West Berlin, then in 1966 foreign minister in Bonn. Brandt was very active in setting West Germany's foreign policy. He was instrumental in getting Britain into the Common Market, and he tried to improve relations with eastern Europe and the Soviet Union through *Ostpolitik*, a policy of cooperation with Warsaw Pact nations. In journeys to both Moscow and Warsaw in 1970 he negotiated a treaty with the USSR renouncing the use of force and an agreement with Poland recognizing its western border along the Oder and Neisse rivers. A treaty was also signed with East Germany for improving contacts and reducing tensions. These negotiations and others paved the way for the entry of the two Germanies into the United Nations.

Brandt's concentration on foreign affairs led to the appearance of neglect of domestic issues such as inflation and rising unemployment. Important segments of German public opinion attacked him on the policy of *Ostpolitik*. Finally a spy scandal rocked the government, and Brandt resigned in the spring of 1974. Helmut Schmidt, who succeeded him, paid closer attention to domestic affairs.

Under Schmidt's leadership Germany continued its strong economic growth in the wake of the oil embargo. German workers did not suffer the unemployment problems of other countries because of the practice of firing and sending home foreign workers when job cutbacks were needed. Germany's economy in the 1980s was not immune to issues such as foreign trade fluctuations and oil imports. Still, Schmidt, as head of the most powerful western European nation, had the prestige and record to ensure his victory in the 1980 elections.

In the late 1970s Schmidt had asked the United States to counter the Soviet placement of SS-20 intermediate range missiles by placing intermediate range ballistic missiles in Europe, thereby setting off controversial debate that did not end until 1983. Schmidt faced both the disapproval of antinuclear demonstrators who did not want the missiles and the displeasure of conservatives in his country and the United States over German economic ties with the Soviet Union. In the autumn of 1982 political power passed again to the Christian Democratic Party, now led by Helmut Kohl.

Into the mid-1990s Kohl's party proved to be a staunch supporter of the United States, in particular of its program to place U.S. intermediate range missiles in Europe. In the face of strident Soviet protests, Kohl guided a bill through the West German parliament in November 1983 to deploy the missiles. After that success, and a strong victory in 1987, Kohl—despite his reputation as a plodding politician—came to play a strong role in European affairs and in relations with the Soviet Union. In the course of his tenure, Kohl changed with the times to deal with environmental issues brought forcefully to the public forum by the Green party. He masterfully took advantage of the breakdown of the German Democratic Republic in 1989 to claim the issue of reunification for himself and his party. By the end of 1994, Kohl had confounded those who had contempt for his intellect and those who thought him politically naive. He overcame all the opposition for election, and his three-party coalition once again enabled him to remain chancellor.

Italy: Political Instability, Economic Growth

Following the end of Mussolini's regime, Italy voted by a narrow margin to end the monarchy. A new constitution, adopted in 1947, provided for a premier and a ministry responsible to the legislature. The Christian Democratic party—strongly Catholic, pro-Western, and anticommunist—was the leading middle-of-the-road group. Its spokesman and leader was Alcide de Gasperi, whose ministry governed the country from 1947 to 1953. Like Adenauer, de Gasperi was a strong adherent of democracy and supported European unity. Italy joined NATO in 1949 and became a member of the Common Market in 1957.

Within little more than a decade the Italian economy changed from predominantly agricultural to industrial. For a time, in the late 1950s and early 1960s, industry advanced faster in Italy than in any other part of Europe. In 1960 the output of manufacturing tripled pre-1939 levels, and in 1961 steel production exceeded one million tons. By the end of the 1980s Italy ranked among the world's leaders in high-tech industry, fashion, design, and banking. Most economic development occurred in northern Italy around the thriving cities of Turin, Milan, and Bologna.

Southern Italy has not progressed as rapidly. Too many people, too few schools, inadequate roads, landlordism, and inefficient, fragmented farms worked by poor peasants are among the problems besetting the area. The government has offered help in the form of subsidies, tax concessions, and programs for flood control and better highways, but southern Italy remains a challenge and an urgent problem.

While the Italian economy was a source of optimism, politics was another story. After de Gasperi's retirement in 1953, politics became increasingly characterized by a series of cabinet crises, shaky coalitions, and government turnovers. Between the end of World War II and the mid-1990s there had been over 50 governments.

In the 1970s, labor unrest, unemployment, and inflation posed problems that politicians could not deal with, even in coalitions in which the Communist party joined with other factions. For a while terrorism dominated political life. In 1978 the anarchist Red Brigade kidnapped one of Italy's most prominent public figures, former premier Aldo Moro, and assassinated him nearly two months later, leaving his body in a car parked equidistant between the Christian Democratic and Communist party headquarters in Rome. Terrorists spread chaos among business and political leaders. Finally, during the 1980s the government, dominated by Bettino Craxi and Ciriaco de Mita, improved conditions. The terrorist networks were broken and law enforcement agencies began to attack the Mafia organization in southern Italy and Sicily.

Widespread corruption and inefficiency in the Christian Democratic–dominated system were exposed in a series of trials that reached to the highest levels of Italian society and government in the 1990s. Exposure of the nationwide network of corruption in 1992 sent some of the most powerful Italian leaders to jail, where some committed suicide. The revulsion provoked by the widespread corruption led in 1993 to a reform of the political system from that of a Senate based on a proportional system of representation to a scheme in which power went to the group claiming the majority of votes. In 1994 a national election to form the new parliament resulted in victory for the charismatic television businessman, soccer team owner, and right-winger Silvio Berlusconi. Berlusconi's *"Forza Italia"* ("Let's Go, Italy") coalition included openly fascist politicians. Predictably, within six months, Berlusconi's government itself was embroiled in crisis.

Portugal, Spain, and Greece

In the western and eastern peninsulas of Europe, politics since 1945 has been marked by dictatorships and radicalism, but parliamentary forces have clung tenaciously to power. Portugal, Spain, and Greece have all experienced severe economic problems and traditions of instability.

Portugal. Portugal was an incredibly corrupt monarchy until 1910. The country then became a republic, but its record of internal turmoil continued. Between 1910 and 1930 there were 21 uprisings and 43 cabinets. Toward the end of that period the army ousted the politicians and took control of the government. In 1932 the generals called on Antonio de Oliveira Salazar to run the country. This former economics professor, a fer-

vent and austere Catholic, shunned social life and was content to live on a very small salary. He devoted all of his time to running an authoritarian government. The press was censored and education—in a country in which two-thirds of the population was illiterate—was neglected. Some economic improvement did take place, but the people, who were frozen out of politics, remained poor. In 1955 a five-year program to stimulate the economy was launched, but its gains were cancelled by population increases and the huge costs resulting from colonial wars in Portugal's African holdings.

Salazar retired in 1968 because of ill health, and six years later a group of junior army officers overthrew the government. Serious divisions appeared between the moderate liberal factions and the communists. In the summer of 1976, however, elections confirmed the victory of the moderate socialists. A new constitution was enacted, establishing a democratic system. The government faced difficult economic problems. Six hundred thousand refugees from Portuguese Africa had to be absorbed, adding to the high unemployment and runaway inflation. After the 1974 revolution, workers had seized many businesses, large farms, and hotels. In most instances, private ownership had to be restored under efficient management. During the 1980s political and economic stability returned to the country, led in the latter part of the decade by Mario Soares, ruling through a socialist coalition. Compared with the rest of Europe, Portugal remained poor, with over 12 percent inflation and only 85 percent literacy, but in terms of the Iberian peninsula, much progress had been made.

Spain. In the four decades after the Second World War, Spain passed from the Franco dictatorship to a rapidly industrializing, modern European state. Franco ruled over an almost ruined country after taking control in 1939. Many of Spain's most talented and productive people had fled, and 700,000 people had died in the civil war. So horrible was the conflict and so great the losses that Franco gained a grudging toleration from the majority of the exhausted population. Those who did not cooperate faced his secret police.

Cold War tensions eased Spain's reentry into the community of nations in the 1950s. The United States resumed diplomatic relations and Spain became a member of the UN in 1955. The following year the Pact of Madrid provided naval and air bases for the Americans, in return for which Spain received more than $2 billion a year in aid. In the 1960s and 1970s the widespread poverty and backwardness that had long characterized Spain began to diminish. Inspired by the Portuguese revolution of 1974, workers and students began to demonstrate and show their unrest. In the summer of 1975 Franco died. He had named Prince Juan Carlos as his successor, thereby indicating his wish that the monarchy be restored.

The young king was crowned in November 1975, and in his speech of acceptance he promised to represent all Spaniards, recognizing that the people were asking for "profound improvements." In 1976, the reformed government announced amnesty for political prisoners, freedom of assembly, and more rights for labor unions. An orderly general election took place in the spring of 1977. Post-Franco Spain began its parliamentary-monarchy phase with impressive stability. Underneath, deep ideological divisions remained, which decreased over time. The major crisis came in February 1981 when radical elements of the army invaded the parliament building to attempt a coup. It immediately became apparent that there was no support for the coup either in the military or among the public at large, and the attempt was brushed aside.

In May 1982 Spain joined NATO—still a controversial decision—and later that year elected Felipe Gonzales of the Socialist party to run the country. Gonzales brought Spain into the Common Market and worked hard to diversify the country's economy. He strengthened his position in the 1986 elections and by 1990 was governing a country attractive to investors in high-tech industries.

Greece. Greece, since its modern creation in 1821, has rarely enjoyed political stability. From that year until 1945 there were 15 different types of government with 176 premiers, who obviously averaged less than one year in office. Inefficiency in government, economic backwardness, and political crises have continued to plague Greece since 1945. In the Greek civil war (1946–1949) pro-Western forces, who controlled only the

→ Spanish Prime Minister Felipe Gonzales signs the treaty admitting Spain and Portugal to membership in the European Common Market in June 1985.

major cities, turned back a powerful communist surge for power and reestablished the monarchy. Greek politicians ignored the complex economic issues affecting the peasants, preferring instead to attempt to regain control of various islands and territories controlled by Greeks in the long-distant past. In the spring of 1967 a group of army colonels seized power. A dictatorship was established that jailed many political figures and harshly punished any criticism of its rule. Many Greeks fled into exile. The military junta made a serious miscalculation in 1974 when it connived to increase Greek authority on Cypress, a move that led to a Turkish invasion of the island. This mistake led to the junta's downfall.

Thereafter the Greeks created a republic, complete with a new constitution. They applied for membership in the Common Market in 1975 and were admitted in 1981. In its application, the government stated that its desire to join the European Community was "based on our earnest desire to consolidate democracy in Greece within the broader democratic institutions of the European Community to which Greece belongs." Since that time, Greek leaders have maintained their democratic traditions. In November 1981 the Socialist party led by Andreas Papandreou gained power and held it through 1989. He led his party back to power four years later. Papandreou ran on pledges to evict U.S. forces from Greek bases and to move Greek foreign policy away from Western orientation. In the middle of the decade, Papandreou followed traditional Greek irredentist tendencies to mobilize the nation by actively opposing Macedonia—the former republic of Yugoslavia and now independent state—on political, economic, and historic grounds.

Yet the Greeks remained active participants in NATO and the Common Market. Like Portugal, Greece is, by European standards, a poor country with a stagnant economy and an inflation rate of 18 percent. In the 1989 elections, these factors plus scandals surrounding Papandreou's personal life led to the defeat of the Socialists and the forming of an unlikely coalition made up of the Communist and Conservative parties, which enjoyed a short tenure in power.

SHARED CONCERNS: WOMEN'S STATUS AND THE ENVIRONMENT

The achievement of a high level of economic success brought with it a number of new concerns for the developed world. Principal among them are women's struggle for equality and environmental pollution.

Women's Status. In 1989 Switzerland extended the franchise to women, the last of the Western nations to allow women the right to vote. This struggle still goes on throughout much of the developing world. In the developed world women gained legal and political equality at varying rates, although progress once gained was neither continuous nor consistent, as could be seen in the failure to pass the Equal Rights Amendment in the United States. Even in countries where women had gained citizenship rights, they remained subject to wage and job discrimination and to commercial exploitation as sex objects. In the United States, at the beginning of the 1990s, the labor force was more than one-half female. However, the average woman earned only about 70 percent as much as the average man.

The Environment. The world's financial and political leaders have become increasingly aware of the spread of pollution and the deterioration of the environment. The UN Conference on the Human Environment held in Stockholm in 1972 produced no serious negotiations but did sound the call that environmental problems know no national boundaries. This led to the creation of

→ Young Iranian women, surrounded and protected by young men, march in a women's rights demonstration in Tehran. The spread of religious fundamentalism has in some cases eroded the struggle for women's rights. In some countries women must keep their head covered, a requirement sometimes viewed as a sign of women's subservience to men, although others regard wearing the veil as a symbol of commitment to one's religious beliefs.

Simone de Beauvoir, *The Second Sex*

A profound, far-reaching postwar movement was the struggle undertaken to improve the status of women. In *The Second Sex*, an analysis of women's secondary status in society, de Beauvoir likened women's status to that of other oppressed groups. The work has become a classic of feminist literature.

The parallel drawn . . . between women and the proletariat is valid in that neither ever formed a minority or a separate collective unit of mankind. And instead of a single historical event it is in both cases a historical development that explains their status as a class and accounts for the membership of *particular individuals* in that class. But proletarians have not always existed, whereas there have always been women. They are women in virtue of their anatomy and physiology. Throughout history they have always been subordinated to men, and hence their dependency is not the result of a historical event or a social change—it was not something that *occurred*.

From Simone de Beauvoir, *The Second Sex*, trans. H.M. Parshley (New York: Alfred A. Knopf, 1952).

---

the UN Environmental Program (UNEP), based in Nairobi, Kenya. Unfortunately inadequate funding and jurisdictional disputes prevented UNEP from living up to its expectations. However, in the 1970s and 1980s a series of conventions relating to the environment were signed, including agreements dealing with pollution from ships, prevention of marine pollution from land-based sources, transboundary air pollution, conservation of migratory species, protection of the Mediterranean Sea from land-based pollution, various regional pollution agreements, and protection of the ozone layer.

In the 1990s it became apparent that vastly more efficient fishing fleets were exhausting the oceans' capacity to replenish their fish. In addition, pollution destroyed traditionally rich fishing grounds such as those in the Black Sea, threatening one of the basic food sources for the globe's rapidly expanding population. In the United States, the Environmental Quality Index compiled by *National Wildlife* showed overall declines in the condition of wildlife, air quality, water quality, forests, and the soil.

It was difficult enough to deal with the rate at which modern industry and technology generated by-products that destroyed the environment and the equivalent pace of the planet's forests. But discovery of massive environmental problems in the former Soviet bloc, especially Central Asia, and the abysmal conditions in which the centrally planned economies had left Eastern

→ Garbage, much of it nonbiodegradable plastic, pollutes a canal in Kao-hsiung, Taiwan's leading port. Environmental damage has been one of the tragic consequences of rapid and unchecked industrialization.

Europe and Russia overwhelmed planners and reformers.[6] The developed world has yet to work out the conflict between economic development and environmental safety for itself, let alone the peoples of the former Soviet Union and the developing world.

CONCLUSION

By the mid-1990s, the United States, Japan, and the western European states competed for global economic dominance. The United States struggled to deal with its economic problems and to make its pluralistic system work. Japan seemingly reached its peak by 1990 and thereafter had to deal with the residue of political, social, and economic problems generated during its rapid rise to power. If Europe could work out the old problems of political and cultural particularism, it seemed that the economic union held the promise that in the twenty-first century, as in the nineteenth, economic dominance would return to the Europeans.

→ Suggestions for Reading

The Marshall Plan and its impact are well covered in Stanley Hoffman and Charles Maier, *The Marshall Plan: A Retrospective* (Westview Press, 1984) and Michael J. Hogan, *The Marshall Plan: America, Britain, and the Reconstruction of Western Europe* (Cambridge Univ., 1987), which treats the U.S. initiative as a consistent part of an American vision to regain capitalist momentum.

Post-1945 events in the United States are discussed in Jim Heath, *Decade of Disillusionment: The Kennedy-Johnson Years* (Univ. of Indiana, 1984). Allen J. Matusow, *The Unraveling of America: A History of Liberalism in the 1960s* (Harper & Row, 1984) traces the political results of that shocking decade. At the end of the 1980s, Joseph S. Nye, Jr., wrote a magisterial analysis of the changing nature of the United States' role in *Bound to Lead: The Changing Nature of American Power* (Basic Books, 1989). Most of the postwar presidents have produced their memoirs. Probably the best and most enjoyable are Truman's *Memoirs* (Doubleday, 1955–1956). See also Lyndon B. Johnson, *The Vantage Point* (Holt, Rinehart and Winston, 1971) and Dwight D. Eisenhower, *The White House Years* (Doubleday, 1963). See also Doris Kearns, *Lyndon Johnson and the American Dream* (Harper & Row, 1976).

Edwin O. Reischauer, *Japan: The Story of a Nation* (Knopf, 1974) provides the best general coverage. See also Reischauer's *The Japanese* (Harvard Univ., 1977). K. Kawai, *Japan's American Interlude* (Univ. of Chicago, 1960) discusses occupation policies and their impact. R.P. Dore

traces one major problem in *Land Reform in Japan* (Univ. of California, 1958). John K. Fairbank et al. discuss the challenges of change in *East Asia: Tradition and Transformation* (Boston, 1973).

The resurgence of Western Europe is dealt with in J. Robert Wegs, *Europe Since 1945* (St. Martin's, 1991). Michael Emerson et al., *The Economics of 1992: The E.C. Commission's Assessment of the Economic Effects of Completing the Internal Market* (Oxford Univ., 1988) is a wise assessment of the challenges and promises of the united Europe. See also Neil McInnes, *The Communist Parties of Western Europe* (Oxford Univ., 1979) and T. Geiger, *The Fortunes of the West: The Future of the Atlantic Nations* (Univ. of Indiana, 1973).

Good accounts of the various western European countries are David McKie and Chris Cook, eds., *The Decade of Disillusionment: Britain in the 1960s* (St. Martin's, 1973); C.J.A. Bartlett, *A History of Postwar Britain* (Longman, 1977); John Darby, *Conflict in Northern Ireland* (Barnes and Noble, 1976); George Dangerfield, *The Damnable Question* (Little, Brown, 1976); Henry Ashly Turner, Jr., *The Two Germanies Since 1945* (Yale Univ., 1987); P.A. Allum, *Italy: Republic Without Government* (Norton, 1974); Roy C. Macridis, *French Politics in Transition* (Winthrop, 1975). Max Gallo, *Spain Under Franco* (Dutton, 1974) and Paul Preston, ed., *Spain in Crisis* (Barnes and Noble, 1976) study the evolution of that country under Franco. Neil Bruce, *Portugal: The Last Empire* (Halstad, 1975) presents the background of the 1974 revolution.

For pioneering works of environmental concern, see Barbara Ward and René Dubos, *Only One Earth: The Care and Maintenance of a Small Planet* (Penguin, 1973) and Barbara Ward, *The Home of Man* (Norton, 1976). On the profound transformation in women's roles in the twentieth century, see Simone de Beauvoir, *The Second Sex* (Vintage, 1974) and Betty Friedan, *The Feminine Mystique* (Dell, 1977). For a worldwide survey, see Kathleen Newland, *The Sisterhood of Man* (Norton, 1979).

→ Notes

1. *The Economist*, Vol. 332, No. 7871, July 9, 1994, pp. 69–75.
2. For a good summary of international economics and politics at the end of the 1980s see Walter S. Jones, *The Logic of International Relations* (Glenview IL; Scott, Foresman, 1988), chapters 12–14.
3. Nicholas Colchester, "Europe's Internal Market, A Survey," *The Economist*, July 8–14, 1989, after p. 48, insert, pp. 1–52.
4. Michael R. Hodges, "Britain Tomorrow: Business as Usual," *Current History*, March 1975, p. 138.
5. Charles de Gaulle, *The Call to Honor* (New York: Viking Press, 1955), p. 33.
6. See Murray Feshbach and Alfred Friendly, Jr., *Ecocide in the USSR* (New York: Basic Books, 1992).

CHAPTER 36

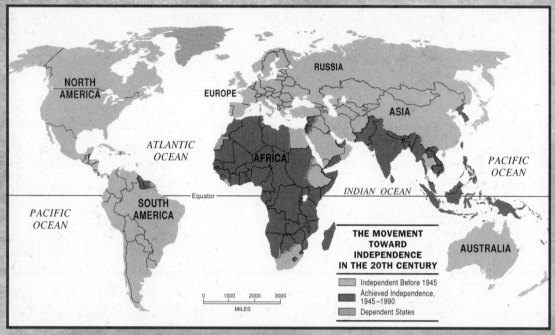

THE MOVEMENT
TOWARD
INDEPENDENCE
IN THE 20TH CENTURY

Independent Before 1945
Achieved Independence,
1945–1990
Dependent States

→ Even before the end of the Cold War, the global map was undergoing territorial redefinition in the wake of decolonization. The new nations faced the challenges of mastering new technologies while dealing with massive population and economic problems.

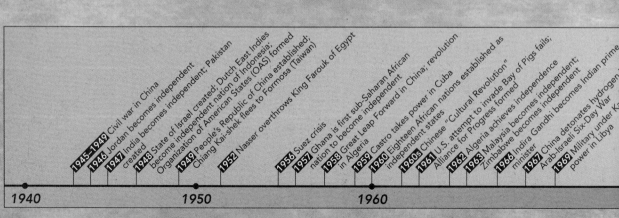

1945–1949 Civil war in China
1946 Jordan becomes independent
1947 India becomes independent; Pakistan created
1948 State of Israel created; Dutch East Indies become independent nation of Indonesia; Organization of American States (OAS) formed
1949 People's Republic of China established; Chiang Kai-shek flees to Formosa (Taiwan)
1952 Nasser overthrows King Farouk of Egypt
1956 Suez crisis
1957 Ghana is first sub-Saharan African nation to become independent
1958 Great Leap Forward in China; revolution in Algeria
1959 Castro takes power in Cuba
1960 Eighteen African nations established as independent states
1960s Chinese "Cultural Revolution"
1961 U.S. attempt to invade Bay of Pigs fails; Alliance for Progress formed
1962 Algeria achieves independence
1963 Zimbabwe becomes independent
1965 Malaysia becomes independent; Indira Gandhi becomes Indian prime minister
1967 China detonates hydrogen ; Arab-Israeli Six-Day War
1969 Military under Ka power in Libya

1940   1950   1960

998

The Developing World: The Struggle for Survival

Chapter Outline

The developing world comprises three categories of nation-states: the more than 80 new countries in Asia and Africa created after 1945 when the old European empires disappeared, the nations of Latin America, and ancient classical civilizations such as those in China, Indochina, and the Subcontinent. The developing world served as an arena for competition between Moscow and Washington during the Cold War and was buffeted by the economic upheavals of the past half-century.

In the mid-1990s, the vast majority of the nations of the developing world remained trapped by poverty, overpopulation, and the indifference of the developed world. Less than 8 percent of the world's population lived in areas where the per capita GNP exceeded $3000. Two-thirds of the world's population lived in areas classified as developing, producing less than one-sixth of the world's output. Various factors accounted for this widespread backwardness: dependence on a single export crop, the dominance of a peasant subsistence economy, lack of capital, lack of education, rising fuel prices, inflation, and overpopulation.

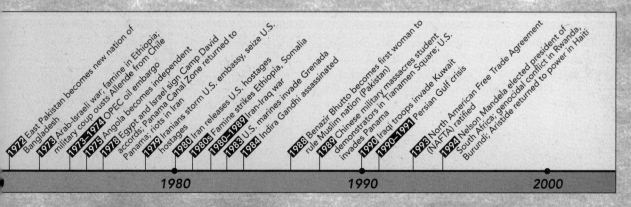

- **1972** East Pakistan becomes new nation of Bangladesh
- **1973** Arab-Israeli war; famine in Ethiopia; military coup ousts Allende from Chile
- **1973–1974** OPEC oil embargo
- **1975** Angola becomes independent
- **1978** Egypt and Israel sign Camp David accords; Panama Canal Zone returned to Panama; riots in Iran
- **1979** Iranians storm U.S. embassy, seize U.S. hostages
- **1980** Iran releases U.S. hostages
- **1980s** Famine strikes Ethiopia, Somalia
- **1980–1989** Iran-Iraq war
- **1983** U.S. marines invade Grenada
- **1984** Indira Gandhi assassinated
- **1988** Benazir Bhutto becomes first woman to rule Muslim nation (Pakistan)
- **1989** Chinese military massacres student demonstrators in Tianamen Square; U.S. invades Panama
- **1990** Iraqi troops invade Kuwait
- **1990–1991** Persian Gulf crisis
- **1993** North American Free Trade Agreement (NAFTA) ratified
- **1994** Nelson Mandela elected president of South Africa; genocidal conflict in Rwanda; Burundi; Aristide returned to power in Haiti

1980   1990   2000

CHINESE REVOLUTIONS

Between 1927 and 1937 Chiang Kai-shek's Nationalist Chinese *(Kuomintang)* government initiated useful reforms in the cities, which, had it not been for Japanese aggression in China, might have expanded to include the rest of the country. Unfortunately for Chiang, the Nationalists after 1937 lost many of their strongest supporters and most of their prosperous area to Japanese control. By the end of World War II, after eight years of combat, Chiang's Chinese Nationalist government was a defeated and worn-out regime. In contrast, the communists after the war enjoyed great popularity, control of an area with 90 million people, and a disciplined and loyal army of 500,000.

Civil War in China

Following the victory over Japan, U.S. troops, cooperating with Chinese Nationalist forces, recaptured land taken by the Japanese. The Americans helped move Chinese troops to strategic areas such as Manchuria. At the same time, the Soviet Union reclaimed areas formerly controlled by the tsars. During this time Chiang tried unsuccessfully to negotiate a settlement with Mao Zedong (Mao Tse-tung). In October 1945 heavy fighting broke out between the Chinese Nationalist and communist forces.

For the next three years the United States tried to end the conflict. In December 1945 President Truman defined American policy toward China. The United States regarded the Nationalist regime as the legal government of China, but since it was a one-party system, it was necessary that full opportunity be given to other groups to participate in a representative government. To that end, Truman urged an end to the fighting.

U.S. Army Chief of Staff General George C. Marshall went to China to implement Truman's policy and to act as friendly mediator. Marshall, newly appointed as American secretary of state, returned home in January 1947, his mission a failure. In his final report, he blasted extremists on both sides for failing to make peace.

The Communist Victory

Chiang's army—poorly equipped, miserably paid, and suffering low morale—began to disintegrate.

The communists captured city after city, frequently facing only token resistance. Economic problems added to Chiang's military dilemma. The Nationalists had been unable to rebuild the economy after 1945, and inflation soared. The U.S. dollar came to be worth 93,000 Chinese dollars on the black market. Serious riots broke out, and in Shanghai thousands of workers went on strike.

By the end of 1947 the Nationalist forces went into retreat, and in 1948 the Nationalist presence in Manchuria collapsed. The complete defeat of Chiang's armies occurred in 1949 when the "People's Liberation Army" captured the major cities in China. Mao proclaimed the establishment of his government on October 1, 1949, and by the middle of 1950 Mao ruled all of mainland China. Chiang's Nationalists sought refuge on Formosa.

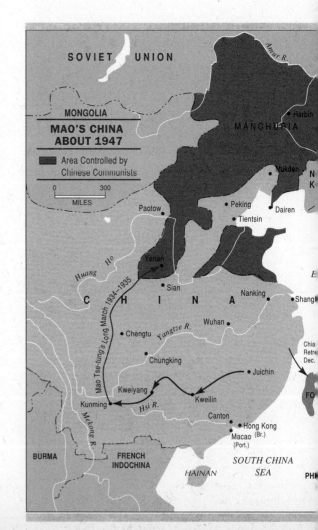

Mao and his forces imposed a tightly centralized administration extending to Manchuria, Inner Mongolia, and Chinese Turkestan. In 1950 his armies moved into Tibet. The Beijing government continued to seek to regain the traditional holdings of the "Central Kingdom," especially those lands gained by Russia during the nineteenth century. Such a policy caused serious problems not only for the Soviet Union but also for Vietnam, Burma, and India.

Mao's policy attracted a large following, calling as it did for a mild program of reform, including the confiscation of large farms, state control of large businesses, protection of small private concerns, rapid industrialization under state control, and increased benefits to labor such as social insurance. The government that eventually appeared, however, was far more fierce and totalitarian.

Right-wing Americans, influenced by the demagoguery of Senator Joseph McCarthy, charged that liberals and "fellow travelers" (those who espoused social aims similar to the communists') lost China.[1] U.S. American military aid to China during World War II totaled $845 million; from 1945 to 1949 it came to slightly more than $2 billion. It is extremely doubtful whether additional American military aid to China would have changed the final outcome of the civil war. The bulk of the Nationalist forces had lost the will to fight. Large quantities of American arms sent to Chiang's army were turned over to the communists by apathetic Nationalist leaders.

Mao's Government

After 1949, Mao used his version of Marxism to change the whole order of society from its traditional patterns. Tolerating no opposition, he concentrated all power in the Communist party, which was led by the People's Central Committee. This group held all major civil and military positions. The day-to-day work of the central committee fell to a smaller politburo, headed by Mao, the chairman of the republic.

The new government brought both inflation and corruption under control, and then began to apply the Soviet model of the 1930s to China. Since more than 70 percent of farmland was owned by 10 percent of the rich landlords, the government proceeded to confiscate large holdings and redistribute them, temporarily, to land-

→ Celebrating the first anniversary of Mao's government in 1950, Chinese workers march through the streets of Beijing carrying giant placards depicting their leader.

less peasants. Late in 1953 the party stripped the large landowners and even prosperous peasants of their holdings, executing an estimated 2 to 5 million of them in the process. The party then established huge farm collectives. Within three years, nearly all peasants had become members of rural collectives in which, although individual land ownership was retained in theory, all labor, farm equipment, and land were pooled.

A Soviet-style five-year plan for economic development in industry was initiated in 1953. The Chinese made impressive advances in heavy industry, and the success of the first plan led to the second five-year plan, the so-called Great Leap Forward. The Chinese built on their own experience, rejecting parts of the Soviet model. They launched the Great Leap Forward with a huge propaganda campaign and galvanized millions of urban and rural workers into a frenzied effort to increase tremendously the production of steel, electricity, and coal. Thousands of small, backyard furnaces sprang up to produce steel. The Chinese boldly predicted that they would surpass British industrial capacity in 15 years.

In the countryside Mao installed the People's Communes. The state created some 26,000 of these units, each averaging 5,000 households, or

Mao Zedong on Communism in China

Mao Zedong adapted Marxism to China. After paying tribute to the Soviet Union in 1949, he stated his goals for the future.

Communists the world over are wiser than the bourgeoisie, they understand the laws governing the existence and development of things, they understand dialectics and they can see farther. The bourgeoisie does not welcome this truth because it does not want to be overthrown.

As everyone knows, our Party passed through these twenty-eight years not in peace but amid hardships, for we had to fight enemies, both foreign and domestic, both inside and outside the Party. We thank Marx, Engels, Lenin and Stalin for giving us a weapon. This weapon is not a machine-gun, but Marxism-Leninism. . . .

The Russians made the October Revolution and created the world's first socialist state. Under the leadership of Lenin and Stalin, the revolutionary energy of the great proletariat and labouring people of Russia, hitherto latent and unseen by foreigners, suddenly erupted like a volcano, and the Chinese and all mankind began to see the Russians in a new light. Then, and only then, did the Chinese enter an entirely new era in their thinking and their life. They found Marxism-Leninism, the universally applicable truth, and the face of China began to change. . . .

There are bourgeois republics in foreign lands, but China cannot have a bourgeois republic because she is a country suffering under imperialist oppression. The only way is through a people's republic led by the working class. . . .

Twenty-four years have passed since Sun Yat-sen's death, and the Chinese revolution, led by the Communist Party of China, has made tremendous advances both in theory and practice and has radically changed the face of China. Up to now the principal and fundamental experience the Chinese people have gained is twofold:

1. Internally, arouse the masses of the people. That is, unite the working class, the peasantry, the urban petty bourgeoisie and the national bourgeoisie, form a domestic united front under the leadership of the working class, and advance from this to the establishment of a state which is a people's democratic dictatorship under the leadership of the working class and based on the alliance of workers and peasants.

2. Externally, unite in a common struggle with those nations of the world which treat us as equals and unite with the peoples of all countries. That is, ally ourselves with the Soviet Union, with the People's Democracies and with the proletariat and the broad masses of the people in all other countries, and form an international united front.

To sum up our experience and concentrate it into one point, it is: the people's democratic dictatorship under the leadership of the working class (through the Communist Party) and based upon the alliance of workers and peasants. This dictatorship must unite as one with the international revolutionary forces. This is our formula, our principal experience, our main programme. . . .

The Communist Party of the Soviet Union is our best teacher and we must learn from it. The situation both at home and abroad is in our favor, we can rely fully on the weapon of the people's democratic dictatorship, unite the people throughout the country, the reactionaries excepted, and advance steadily to our goal.

From Mao Tse-tung, Speech "In Commemoration of the 28th Anniversary of the Communist Party of China, June 30, 1949," in *Selected Works*, vol. 5 (New York: International Publishers, n.d.), pp. 411–423.

about 25,000 people. The heads of the communes collected taxes and ran schools, child-care centers, dormitories, communal kitchens, and even cemeteries in this massive attempt at social experimentation. Mao tried to convert peasants into a rural proletariat paid in wages. Until the late 1970s, all land, dwellings, and livestock reverted to the effective ownership of the communes. During the two decades in which the People's Communes functioned, they helped produce improvements in medical care and literacy.

The Great Leap Forward ultimately proved to be disastrous for China. Central planners erred in allocating resources and capital, and farm production fell. The steel and iron produced in the backyard furnaces turned out to be unusable. At the same time the Great Leap was failing, the Soviet Union withdrew its technological and financial support. From 1959 to 1961 Chinese industry lacked essential raw materials and millions of people went without adequate food. Between 1960 and 1962 the combination of bad weather and chaos bequeathed by the failure of the Great Leap Forward resulted in malnutrition and the premature death of between 16 and 30 million people.

Faced with this crisis, the government radically changed its economic policy. In the communes social experimentation and centralized control were relaxed. Working conditions were improved and private plots in which peasants were allowed to keep or sell the crops and animals they raised were used as incentives to increase agricultural production. Between 1961 and 1964 industry also recovered, and the discovery of petroleum provided new energy sources. China made advances in light industry, especially in consumer goods and cotton production. Signs of technological progress included the detonation of a nuclear device in 1964 and a hydrogen bomb in 1967.

The Cultural Revolution and After

By the early 1960s an ideological schism widened between Mao and some of his long-time comrades. Moderates advocated gradual social change and economic development, while radicals sought to carry on immediately with the drastic restructuring of Chinese society. Mao be-

lieved, or so it seemed, that many in the party had lost their revolutionary zeal.

In the mid-1960s Mao mobilized the Red Guards, a radical student militia. They attacked the moderates and forced Maoist orthodoxy on party members and populace alike. In all areas, from surgery to nuclear physics and beyond, Mao's words were law. Application of the wisdom of Chairman Mao, as contained in the "little red book," *The Thoughts of Chairman Mao*, was to lead to miraculous achievements. Placing political purity above economic growth, the Red Guards hampered production and research. Their rallies and demonstrations disrupted the entire educational system.

The effects of this "Cultural Revolution" were dire. By 1967 industrial production had plummeted and basic education and research had ceased; some areas of the country were approaching anarchy. Into this void stepped the People's Liberation Army (PLA), which was the most important element in Chinese politics until 1985. The PLA brought the Red Guards under

→ In this photograph from the Cultural Revolution period, members of the Red Guard display for public humiliation several Chinese students wearing dunce caps. The Guard denounced the students as leaders of "antirevolutionary" groups.

control, restored order, and put an end to the excesses of the Cultural Revolution.

Mao's long-time associate, Premier Chou Enlai (1898–1976) restored the country's industrial productivity. The return to political stability was more difficult, but Chou managed to hold the country together while rival factions intrigued for power. Chou removed China from the diplomatic isolation in which it had resided since 1958. He responded to a diplomatic initiative made by the Nixon administration in 1971 and moved closer to the United States, motivated perhaps by the armed border clashes with the USSR that occurred along the Amur River. In addition, China sought to develop its industrial capacity through the use of foreign technology and to bring in foreign currency through both an expanded banking system based in the British crown colony of Hong Kong and the development of a tourist industry.

China Since 1976

After Chou's—and Mao's—death in 1976, jockeying for control continued with varying intensity. Leading the more militant faction, the so-called Gang of Four, was Mao's widow, Jiang Xing (Chiang Ching), who was overthrown, disgraced, and brought to a televised show trial in 1980. Her demise paved the way for the advent of a more moderate, pragmatic group of officials led by Deng Xiaoping (Teng Hsiao-Ping).

Deng was a political survivor, whose roots in the party went back to the 1920s. He endured political exile and the Cultural Revolution to introduce his variant of reform Marxism, in which the party kept control of the "commanding heights" of the economy. Aided by his liberal chief lieutenants, Hu Yaobang and Zhao Ziyang, Deng introduced a pragmatic series of economic reforms.

The first major move to introduce a more market-oriented economy came in the countryside in 1978. The party allowed greater personal profit for the peasants, and this resulted in a vast increase in productivity. China had a grain surplus in six of the next seven years. With an increased food supply and a contented peasantry, Deng in 1985 encouraged the introduction of the free market economy in the cities, with the goal of gaining similar economic gains there. To foster the rapid transformation of the underdeveloped country, Deng permitted the entry of Western experts and technology. Western, especially American, influence grew in the cities in China during the 1980s, along with foreign trade and the influx of foreigners.

The government continued to keep the cost of medicine low and supplemented wages with accident insurance, medical coverage, day-care centers, and maternity benefits. The standard of living in China improved, but the removal of price controls on food and other staple items led to inflation. Even with economic progress, the standard of living in China remained far below the standards in industrialized countries.

The educational system changed drastically under the communists. In the 1930s only 20 percent of the people had been literate. By the end of the 1980s, the figure had risen to 75 percent. Across China, a crash program of schooling was initiated, and "spare-time" schools with work/study programs for those unable to attend school full-time were established. Thousands of Chinese students emigrated abroad to study, including some 40,000 to the United States.

Deng Xiaoping had worked for the economic liberalization of his country but failed to sponsor similar reform on the political front. Students were the first to express discontent with inflation and corruption in China. In the spring of 1989, students across China demonstrated in honor of the liberal politician Hu Yaobang, who had died in March. The demonstrators went on to criticize Deng's government. The protest reached a climax in May and June when thousands of demonstrators calling for democracy occupied the ceremonial center of modern China, Tiananmen Square in Beijing.

The party split over how to deal with the protesters and their supporters, sometimes numbering a million strong. Zhao advocated accommodation but hard-line Prime Minister Li Peng called for a crackdown. While the debate went on within the party, the students erected a tall replica of the Statue of Liberty to symbolize their demands for democracy and an end to corruption. By the end of May the students had won the enthusiastic support of the workers and citizens of Beijing, Shanghai, and Chengdu. Finally, in June the party had decided what to do about the protesters. The People's Liberation Army, using tanks and machine

→ A Beijing citizen faces down a convoy of tanks rolling down the Avenue of Eternal Peace during the pro-democracy demonstrations in Tiananmen Square in June 1989.

guns, cleared the Square and the surrounding area of the student demonstrators. Over 3000 people were killed in the massacre.

By 1990, it was apparent that China would not retreat into another period of diplomatic isolation. Deng Xiaoping had integrated his country too firmly into the world economy for that. Chinese leaders worked skillfully to maintain their commercial relations and to regain two traditionally Chinese areas to help their struggling economy.

The leaders in Beijing had already worked out an agreement with the British in which the rich crown colony of Hong Kong would come under Chinese authority in 1997. Beijing saw a major potential source of economic strength across the Straits of Formosa in Taiwan, where Chiang and the remnant of his forces had fled in 1949. For the next quarter-century, the United States recognized the Taipei government as the legitimate government of China. By 1992 Taiwan's GNP had reached $210.5 billion, and its 21 million people had an average annual per capita income of close to $9300. Mainland China, in contrast, had an estimated GNP of $600 billion, and a per capita income of $560 for its 1.15 billion people.

During the 1990s China's export trade expanded dramatically, and foreign economic interests increased their activities in China. Economic ties between the Chinese and the United States grew to such an extent that President Clinton was forced to overlook human rights abuses when he renewed most favored nation trading status to China in 1994. Inflationary pressures resulting from rapid economic growth threatened to create major social problems for the Chinese communist leadership. At the same time, the Chinese continued to construct enterprise zones along the coast in which the most modern technology was used by Chinese businesses working closely with world banking and commercial interests for joint profits.

At the same time the presence of the Communist Party remained, ever stronger, counting around 52 million members in 1992, even though fewer than 10 percent of those applying for party membership were admitted. Observers speculated that after the passing of Deng Xiaoping (he was 89 in 1994) a power struggle might ensue within the party, leading to a fragmentation of the country into modern variants of warlordism. But should China make the leadership transition successfully, it is poised to become a true world power in the twenty-first century.

On China's periphery, the "Four Tigers" of South Korea, Taiwan, Hong Kong—which will revert to China in 1997—and Singapore continued their phenomenal growth. Not only had they successfully competed with Japan in a wide range of high-tech products and automobiles, they were erecting financial institutions that challenged Japanese banks and investment firms. The "Tigers" knew that they could not rest complacently on their laurels. China's increasingly aggressive commercial sector and the entry of Indonesia, Malaysia, and India as competitors promised to make the Pacific rim the most active arena for business for the final decade of the twentieth century.

SOUTHEAST ASIA

One of the first indications that the whole structure of imperialism would quickly collapse came in the late 1940s when Indonesian nationalists demanded a complete break with the Netherlands. An ugly war ensued, and finally in 1948, through UN mediation, the Dutch East Indies became the nation of Indonesia. The biggest and potentially richest nation in Southeast Asia,

Indonesia has enjoyed little tranquillity since it gained independence.

The state is 88 percent Muslim but encompasses a mixture of many cultures in its 3000 islands, ranging from Stone Age people to urban professionals and intellectuals. Complicating the situation is the prominence of the Chinese minority, which dominates. There have been anti-Chinese riots and plots in various islands against the central government in Java.

For the first 15 years after independence, Indonesia experienced declining exports, inflation, and food shortages. Its population increased while its economy declined. The main responsibility for this situation belonged to Indonesia's flamboyant president Achmed Sukarno (1901–1970). He contracted huge Russian loans for arms, fought a costly guerrilla campaign against Malaysia, confiscated foreign businesses, and wasted money on expensive, flashy enterprises.

Muslim students in Indonesia triggered the events that led to Sukarno's downfall. At the beginning of 1966 they launched attacks on Indonesians they believed to have communist connections. An estimated 300,000 to 500,000 were killed. The army's chief of staff, General T.N.J. Suharto became effective head of state, and in March 1968 became president officially.

Initially, Suharto installed a more Western-oriented government and in return received substantial American aid for the country, but over the next 25 years Suharto's military regime engaged in several violent incidents. In 1971 and again in 1974 there were serious racial outbursts during which thousands of students went on rampages, looting and damaging Chinese shops and homes. The Indonesians invaded East Timor, the Portuguese half of the island, in 1975 and initiated a savage occupation that led to the death of over 200,000 people. During the 1970s some 30,000 political dissidents were imprisoned, while rampant corruption dominated government, the civil service, and business. Enormous wealth remained concentrated in the hands of a very few individuals.

Created out of former British holdings, the Federation of Malaysia was admitted into the British Commonwealth in 1957. In 1963 it became independent and immediately faced Sukarno-sponsored guerrilla attacks. As in Indonesia, a major problem in Malaysia was the country's racial mix and the resulting hostilities. The majority of the population is Malay and Muslim, but the mainly Buddhist Chinese hold the majority of the wealth, and what they do not control is owned largely by the small Hindu Indian minority. In the late 1960s and early 1970s Malays attacked the other two groups.

One of the richest areas in Southeast Asia after the war was Singapore, a city-state roughly three times the size of Washington, D.C. Singapore withdrew from the Federation of Malaysia in August 1965 and after that was dominated by the People's Action Party, run by Lee Kuan Yew. Taking advantage of its superb location at the Straits of Malacca, Singapore became one of the richest places in the world. At the end of the 1980s its 2.5 million people generated a GNP of more than $29 billion. What Lee Kuan Yew did not provide in terms of unfettered civil rights—

including prohibitions on the sale of chewing gum—he more than made up for in the efficiency and stability of his rule. His successor, Goh Chok Tong, who came to power in 1990, has continued and built on Lee Kuan Yew's policies.

THE SUBCONTINENT

In the Indian subcontinent, the western thrust of the Japanese armies induced the British government to make substantial concessions to Indian Nationalist leaders. In 1942 Britain offered India independence within or without the British Commonwealth following the war. Tragically, during and immediately after the war, antagonism between the Muslim and Hindu populations in India became acute. Britain, represented by Lord Mountbatten, eased tensions by persuading both groups that partition of the country was inevitable. The coming of independence in 1947 shattered the fragile economic and geographic unity of the subcontinent.

Pakistan was an artificial creation separated into two parts by about 1000 miles of intervening Indian territory. India itself was not a single nation but a mixture of racial, linguistic, and cultural groups. Once the British left, there was no longer an external force to bind together the ancient and conflicting cultural and regional loyalties. The immediate aftermath of the partition was a rash of bloody riots between Hindus and Muslims. One of the victims of this violence was Mahatma Gandhi, who because of his tolerance toward Muslims was assassinated by a Hindu.

India: The Largest Democracy

In the long list of states newly independent after 1945, few have retained genuine liberal regimes. Until 1975, the only outstanding example was India, the world's largest democratically governed state. After independence, India's parliament functioned with little friction. This success was due to Jawaharlal Nehru (1889–1964), the country's first prime minister and an ardent devotee of democratic government. Nehru sought to maintain close relations with both the Soviet Union and China, often to the discomfort of the United States. However, a border conflict that led to major military action between India and China in the first part of the 1960s drained India's economic growth.

Nehru's daughter, Indira Gandhi (1917–1984), was elected prime minister in 1966. Her popularity reached a peak with the defeat of Pakistan in the 1971 war that led to the creation of the country of Bangladesh. Within two years, however, India's mildly socialist economy was battered by serious crop failures, food riots, strikes, and student unrest. In June 1975 Gandhi announced a state of emergency and assumed dictatorial powers. She jailed 10,000 of her critics, imposed a rigid press censorship, and suspended fundamental civil rights.

With all opposition muzzled, the people were exhorted to "work more and talk less." After a year, the new order claimed numerous gains, advances in productivity, a drop in inflation, curbs in the black market, and more widespread birth control measures to alleviate India's population pressures. Although Gandhi declared that her drastic measures were only temporary, some critics observed that she was trying to move "from dictatorship to dynasty." Early in 1977, there was some relaxation of authoritarianism.

In that same year, the government released many political prisoners and announced that national elections would be held. In the elections Gandhi lost her seat in parliament and resigned her post as prime minister. A new government, led by aged politicians, tried with little success to solve India's problems. Caste tensions were on the rise, there was widespread violence, strikes increased, and student demonstrations closed universities. Still, all the old economic problems remained. More than half of the population was illiterate and lived below the poverty level.

Disenchanted with the incompetent rule of bickering politicians, the Indian voters returned Gandhi to power in the 1980 elections. She promised the country strong leadership, but with no more "excesses." For the next four years she pursued a neutral course, reflecting the geopolitical position in which India found itself. India's alliance with Russia served as a defensive shield against both Pakistan and China. The Soviet invasion of Afghanistan raised some disturbing questions, but Gandhi refrained from criticizing the action.

In October 1984 Gandhi was assassinated by Sikh bodyguards who were connected to the Sikh separatist movement. She was succeeded by her son Rajiv Gandhi, a former pilot and political novice who soon showed a surprising degree of confidence and competence in governing the world's largest democracy of more than 800 million citizens. Continuing his mother's basic policies, he consolidated his political position. Still, the country's widespread poverty and vast diversity—especially the continuing Sikh separatist movement and the long-standing Kashmir border dispute with Pakistan—posed great challenges that Rajiv Gandhi could not overcome. He was defeated in elections at the end of 1989 and replaced by V.P. Singh of the National Front party, who similarly could not find solutions to India's overwhelming problems. The world's largest democracy balanced tenuously between sectarian fragmentation and unity in the elections of 1991, when Rajiv Gandhi was assassinated in May.

During the first half of the 1990s Indian leaders abandoned many of the socialist foundations of their economic structure and introduced many aspects of the capitalist, market economy. Analysts had pointed out during the 1980s that India possessed the largest essentially untapped middle-class market in the world. With the entry of market forces into the country, the Indian economy began to improve. The countryside had gained self-sufficiency in the 1970s and 1980s. Now it was the turn of the cities and the business community to become major players in the international economy.

In 1995 P.V. Narasimha Rao was the only prime minister not in the bloodline of the Nehru-Gandhi dynasty to have lasted through the first half of a parliamentary term. Working with his finance minister, Manmohan Singh, and enjoying the total support of the business community, he continued to pursue market reforms. India's economy has continued to grow rapidly under the changes in the central government in the 1990s.

Pakistan

After its creation in 1947, Pakistan was plagued by feuds between its eastern and western wings. Shortly after independence the prime minister

→ In retaliation for government suppression of a Sikh uprising and the storming of the Golden Temple at Amritsar, the most sacred Sikh shrine, Sikh bodyguards assassinated Indira Gandhi, Indian prime minister, in 1984. She was succeeded by her son Rajiv, who was himself assassinated in 1991 while he was campaigning to regain the position he had lost in the elections of 1989.

was assassinated; a number of short-lived governments followed, accompanied by intermittent rioting and states of emergency.

In 1958 General Mohammad Ayub Khan (1907–1974) gained power. His regime gave Pakistan reasonable stability and some relief from corrupt politicians. Under his tutelage, the country made economic progress. Ten years later, however, pent-up dissatisfaction against corruption in the government led to a new military dictatorship under General Yahya Khan. Regionalism continued to be a major problem. While Pakistan's population was predominantly Muslim, its two main provinces differed widely in race, economic interest, and language—in addition to the problem of geographic separation. East Pakistan complained continually of being exploited by more prosperous West Pakistan, and these complaints escalated into riots and threats of secession.

Troops sent into the eastern region in 1971 set off a reign of terror. The influx of refugees into India created an intolerable burden, and in December the Indian army invaded East Pakistan, defeating the central government's forces. India encouraged the region to break away, and in 1972 East Pakistan became the new state of Bangladesh. Bangladesh, covering an area not much larger than the state of Arkansas, was an instantaneous economic disaster with twice the population density of Japan and nothing approaching the Japanese economic productivity. The Bangladesh population in 1990 was 121 million, while the per capita GNP was a mere $155.

A civilian government was reestablished in Pakistan, led by Zulkifar Ali Bhutto (1928–1979), who governed under a democratic constitution. Throughout the 1970s, Pakistan's economic problems persisted, along with its domestic instability. Bhutto, overthrown in 1977 by General Mohammad Zia al Haq, was executed in 1979. The new military dictator, who faced widespread opposition, invoked martial law and postponed elections indefinitely. Like his predecessors, he had to contend with both Indian hostility and potential Soviet intervention. Pakistan retained its traditional alignment with China, while India kept close ties with Moscow.

In 1979, events in Iran and Afghanistan posed particular threats to Pakistan. Thirty-six Islamic foreign ministers meeting in Pakistan condemned the Soviet aggression against the Afghan people. In 1981, however, a substantial American aid agreement was negotiated, providing for $3.2 billion in arms over a period of six years. Pakistan, thereafter, served as the American support base for the Afghan resistance.

The Developing World: The Struggle for Survival   **1009**

Benazir Bhutto, who in 1988 became the first woman to lead a Muslim nation when she was elected prime minister of Pakistan, stands amid a crowd of her supporters before debarking on a cross-country campaign trip in 1992. In the October 1993 elections Bhutto and her Pakistan People's Party defeated the incumbent prime minister Nawaz Sharif and the Pakistani Moslem League.

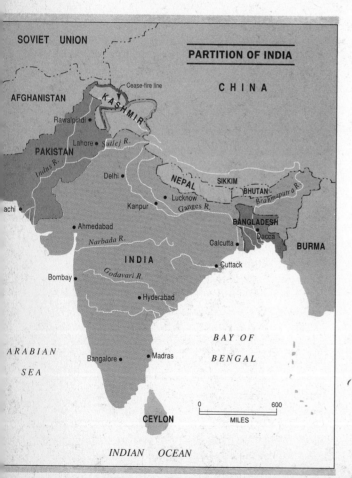

PARTITION OF INDIA

In 1988 Zia al Haq was assassinated and succeeded by Bhutto's daughter Benazir, the first woman elected to govern a Muslim nation. She lasted 20 months, until, under pressure from the army, she was dismissed under accusations of incompetence and corruption, only to return again in the mid-1990s. Even with the relatively moderate Benazir Bhutto, relations between India and Pakistan remained tense, especially over the issue of Kashmir.

THE MIDDLE EAST

Decolonization in the Middle East began with British recognition of the independence of Jordan in 1946 and the end of the British mandate in Palestine in 1948. In the meantime, the arrival of European Jews seeking refuge in the area after the war, Zionist terrorist activities, and great power political pressure led to the creation of the state of Israel in May 1948. This touched off a bitter conflict between the new state and the Arab world that was intensified by the perennial statelessness of the more than one million Palestinian Arab refugees represented by the Palestine Liberation Organization. Complicating this volatile situation were the Islamic fundamentalist revival, Iraqi aggression, and the overall great power competition between the Soviet Union and the United States.

At the end of World War II, Arab leaders joined forces to form the Arab League. Set up to advance common Arab interests and, in part, to counter Israel, it was used to further the pan-Arab ambitions of Egypt, a republic since 1953. The dominant figure in the Arab world was Colonel Gamal Abdel Nasser (1918–1970), leader of the Egyptian military junta that had over-thrown King Farouk in 1952. From his base in Cairo, Nasser offered guidance and assistance to liberation movements in Sudan, Tunisia, Morocco, and Algeria. From that first step toward throwing off the West, the region has seen the remarkable emergence of Islamic fundamentalism in the West Bank and Gaza, Lebanon, Jordan, Iran, Algeria—where foreign workers and westernized professionals were being assassinated—Egypt, Sudan, and Somalia.

The Arab-Israeli Conflict

Conscious of their hostile surroundings, the Israelis took steps to become militarily, economi-cally, and politically strong. The success of their efforts became quite evident in 1956 when, as al-lies of the British and French, they overwhelmed the Egyptians in a war for control of the Suez Canal. International pressure applied by the United States, the USSR, and the United Nations forced the Israelis to withdraw from their territo-rial gains.

The conclusion of this crisis brought only a temporary reprieve from hostilities. In the next decade the issues of oil, Palestinian rights, the existence of the state of Israel, and free access to the Suez Canal monopolized the attention of for-eign offices within the region, as well as in Moscow and Washington. As it became apparent that there were no simple solutions to the Middle Eastern problems, the Arabs sought to solve them in 1967 by mobilizing their forces. They requested the withdrawal of the UN peacekeep-ing forces and blockaded the Gulf of Aqaba, Israel's access to the Red Sea. War broke out on June 5. Within 72 hours Israel completely over-whelmed and humiliated the combined Arab forces. When a cease-fire was arranged five days later, Israel occupied the Sinai peninsula, includ-ing the east bank of the Suez Canal, old

Jerusalem, and border areas inside manding tactically important heights no lasting solution to the conflict, ho in 1973 the threat of war reappeared.

As in 1967, the opening of this hostility was preceded by a period of sion, characterized by attacks by Arab gu and regular army detachments into Leba. The Soviet Union was a major supplier of arm and technicians to the Arabs. The United States committed itself to the existence of Israel, invest-ing billions of dollars a year in foreign aid. Real-izing the danger of a Russo-American confronta-tion in the Middle East should a new round of war explode, Britain, France, the United States, and the USSR explored ways to bring the con-tending parties to agreement.

The issues discussed were the possibility of some return of captured Arab territory, the inter-nationalization of Jerusalem, and a solution to the refugee problem. The Israelis, however, in-sisted on the Arabs' unequivocal recognition of Israel as a sovereign state with the right to exist. Acceptance of a cease-fire in the summer of 1970 gave some hope for a settlement, but the situa-tion deteriorated a few months later when Israel charged Egypt with cease-fire violations and Nasser suddenly died.

On October 6, 1973, war broke out again when the Egyptians and Syrians launched a coor-dinated attack on Israel. For the first few days the Arabs held the initiative, but Israeli forces coun-terattacked, crossing the Suez Canal into Egypt and driving to within 25 miles of Damascus, the capital of Syria. In some of the most concentrated armored combat since World War II, 1800 tanks and 200 aircraft were destroyed.

During the fighting, the United States orga-nized a large airlift of arms to Israel, and the Russians responded with troop movements. Soviet and American leaders averted a possible showdown through consultations, and the dan-ger passed when the UN arranged a cease-fire. In January 1974 Egypt and Israel signed a final pact, providing for mutual troop withdrawals, the occupation of the east bank of the canal by Egypt, a UN buffer zone, and the return of pris-oners. Fighting continued between Israel and Syria in the strategic Golan Heights area. U.S. Secretary of State Henry Kissinger led the efforts for a cease-fire on that front in May 1974. This

.nent provided for the return by Israel of captured Syrian territory, a UN zone, and return of prisoners.

The 1973 war and its spin-offs were costly or the world. Israel spent $5 billion and suffered 5000 casualties, plus an ever-increasing rate of inflation generated by war expenses. Arab casualties were more than five times the Israeli losses. But where the Israelis came to a sober realization of their population and financial limitations, the Arabs came out of the second war with improved morale. After the 1967 war, Arab radicals, especially those in the Popular Front for the Liberation of Palestine, pushed the oil-producing countries to use the "oil weapon"—cutting or drastically reducing the export of petroleum—against Israel and its allies. Such a policy adopted after the 1973 war spread devastation throughout the economy of the industrial world.

In one of the few instances of effective cooperation by the states of the developing world, the OPEC-led embargo of the industrialized world harshly affected Japan and the western Europeans, who respectively received 82 and 72 percent of their oil from the Middle East. The United States, which imported only 11 percent of its oil supplies from the Arabs, suffered substantial disruption in its economic activity. By March 1974 when the embargo was lifted, Arab oil production was 15 percent lower than in October.

Egyptian-Israeli Détente

In September 1975 Egypt and Israel reached a second pact in which additional territory in the Sinai peninsula was returned to Egypt and both sides agreed not to resort to force. The United States agreed to provide up to 200 civilian technicians to maintain a precautionary warning system between the two sides. Washington also committed additional arms and financial aid to Israel.

In late November 1977 President Anwar Sadat (1918–1981) initiated a dramatic shift in regional affairs when he flew to Jerusalem to conduct peace talks with Israeli leaders. Sadat, born of a peasant family, had excelled in school and entered the Royal Military Academy. He had worked with other officers to rid Egypt of British

domination and in the coup to expel King Farouk. He was a loyal follower of Nasser and succeeded him as president in 1970. He demonstrated his ability to make controversial decisions in 1972 when he ordered the 18,000-member corps of Soviet military and technical advisers out of his country. Sadat faced serious problems at home brought on by a faltering economy and a rapidly increasing population. These problems had led to severe riots, sparked by runaway inflation. Still, Sadat recognized that Egypt's most compelling need was for peace and recovery. Nothing he did was more courageous than making the trip to Jerusalem in 1977.

The United States strongly supported Sadat's venture and U.S. President Jimmy Carter invited Sadat and Israeli Prime Minister Menachem Begin to meet at Camp David outside Washington in September 1978. After intense negotiations, the three leaders produced a framework for a permanent peace treaty. Israel agreed to return all the Sinai to Egypt, but no definite agreement was reached on the status of the West Bank, where the one million displaced Palestinian Arabs lived. It was agreed, however, that negotiations should begin to set up an elected self-governing authority of Palestinians and to end the Israeli military government. Following this step, there would be a transitional period of five years during which negotiations would take place on the final status of the West Bank, an issue that remained in conflict at the end of the 1980s. Sadat and Begin received the Nobel Peace Prize in 1978.

The formal peace treaty signed in March 1979 ended the state of war between Egypt and Israel and began the process of returning all of the Sinai to Egypt. It also opened the Suez canal to Israeli ships. In 1980 the two nations opened their borders to each other, exchanged ambassadors, and began air service between the countries.

The Iranian Revolution

Iran, which had served as an area of competition between the British and the Russians since the nineteenth century, became a bone of contention between the United States and the Soviet Union after World War II. As the result of an agreement

→ Israeli Prime Minister Menachem Begin embraces U.S. President Jimmy Carter as Egyptian President Anwar Sadat looks on and applauds. Carter invited Begin and Sadat to a summit meeting at Camp David in September 1978 to work out a peace agreement between Israel and Egypt.

between the British and the Russians in 1941, Shah Mohammad Reza Pahlavi (1919–1980) gained the Iranian throne. After the war he asked foreign troops to withdraw from his country, but following the slow return of the Soviet army to its borders, aggressive activities of the Iranian Communist party (Tudeh), and an assassination attempt on the Shah's life, Iran firmly tied itself to the West.

In 1953, Iranian premier Mohammad Mosaddeq advocated nationalization of Iran's oil fields and a comparatively radical tax program, and forced the Shah to flee the country. A CIA-supported military coup overthrew Mosaddeq in 1954 and restored the Shah to power. For the next 25 years, Iran rested firmly within the orbit of the United States, a valuable source of oil and an independent military force in a vitally strategic region.

The Shah attempted a rapid modernization of his country, but the so-called White Revolution threatened the integrity of the Iranian cultural fabric. The presence of over 100,000 foreigners, including 47,000 Americans, alienated orthodox Muslims, who perceived the Shah as attacking the Muslim political and economic base. Opposition to the Shah's rule spread widely, from militant communists to Shi'ite clergy to discontented nationalities. In addition, inflation alienated some of the business classes and the laborers.

To stem this growing opposition, the Shah set off a reign of terror. After seven years, the storm broke in January 1978 when large numbers of students demonstrated against the absolute monarchy. Many were killed and wounded by the Shah's troops. Strikes and demonstrations paralyzed the country. The army and secret police proved helpless in the face of the national revolt. In January 1979 the Shah fled the country, seeking asylum first in the United States, then Panama, and finally in Egypt, where he died in 1980.

The diffuse and widespread revolution found its focus in the aged Ayatollah Ruhollah Khomeini, a Shi'ite holy man who had been in exile since 1963. From Iraq and then from Paris he had carried on an incessant propaganda effort against the "godless and materialistic" rule of the Shah. Khomeini was intensely opposed to Western culture and once in power set to work to purge Iran of its "wickedness." Western music on radio and television was banned, as were "provocative" bathing suits, liquor, and a broad range of other items. The Ayatollah stamped out secular Western political forms and instituted instead a theocratic state based on the Koran.

The Ayatollah viewed the United States as the "Great Satan" and encouraged Iranians to

→ Pro-Iranian Lebanese Muslims raise their hands in salute to Ayatollah Khomeini during a symbolic funeral held in Beirut to honor the deceased Iranian spiritual leader.

express anti-American sentiments. In November 1979 a mob of young Iranians stormed and seized the U.S. embassy and took 53 hostages, whom they held for over a year. Finally, the financial drain of the war with Iraq—begun when Iraqi leader Saddam Hussein attacked Iranian airfields and oil refineries in September 1980—forced the Iranians to release the hostages in return for the United States' release of Iranian assets frozen in response to the hostage taking.

The Iran-Iraq war lasted for the rest of the decade until an armistice in 1989—brought on by exhaustion. It had been a war of attrition in which both sides suffered enormous losses. The Iranians employed all of their resources, including 12- and 13-year-old children, in attacks against the well-ensconced but smaller Iraqi army. The Iraqis on their side violated the accepted rules of combat by using chemical weapons

and poison gas. Khomeini died in June 1989, but his Islamic Republic lived on under the rule of Hashemi Rafsanjani, who was reelected in 1993.

A Tragic Stage

Few areas better illustrate the tragedy of the Middle East during the past half-century than Beirut. Once the most beautiful and civilized city in the Middle East, it was a center for prosperity and a crossroads of cultures and religions. In the 1970s it became an arena in which all of the competing factions of the Middle East played out their ambitions.

The Palestine Liberation Organization (PLO) led by Yasir Arafat from its headquarters in Lebanon stepped up demands for Israeli withdrawal from the West Bank of the Jordan River and the Gaza Strip, both captured by Israel during the 1967 war. The PLO wanted an independent Palestinian state and in pursuit of that goal launched terrorist raids from its bases in southern Lebanon and encouraged riots to harass Israeli authorities. In response, beginning in 1978, Israel made repeated incursions into Lebanese territory to strike back at the PLO bases.

Civil war added to Lebanon's troubles. This small and racially mixed nation, its area slightly less than that of Connecticut, is divided between Christian and Muslim factions. Before the influx of the Palestinians, the Christians held a slight majority, and the various factions maintained a delicately adjusted political balance. The influx of Palestinians in 1975 shattered that balance. The Christians, at first supported by the Syrians, and the Muslims with their Palestinian allies fought until the October 1976 cease-fire. The cost was 25,000 dead, thousands more wounded, and sections of the city gutted. The country's once flourishing economy was at a standstill.

In the summer of 1981 PLO forces fired rockets into Israel, which responded with massive air attacks on Palestinian strongholds in Beirut. Hundreds of civilians were killed. In the summer of 1982 the Israelis invaded Beirut, surrounding Muslim-held west Beirut. The PLO evacuated Beirut in September, under the direction of a French, Italian, and United States multinational contingent. After the multinational force departed, the newly elected president, the Phalange Christian Bashir Gemayel and 26 of his colleagues were killed by a bomb. In apparent response, Christian militiamen, allies of the Israelis, massacred hundreds of Palestinian men, women, and children in two refugee camps.

In the succeeding decade the skeletal outlines of bombed buildings, shadowy videotapes of hostages, and pictures of young and old darting through streets to avoid gunfire gave the world an image of the total futility of violence. Beirut's tough citizens remained hopeful that, perhaps finally, an equilibrium could once again be found in the Middle East. By 1995 the city had finally begun to recover.

Toward a New Balance

During the 1980s the four key elements in the Middle East were Egypt, Israel, the United States, and Iraq. In 1990, an event occurred that cut across the traditional antipathies and its resolution gave a small opening for U.S. and Soviet diplomats to try to nudge the region onto a new path.

During the first part of the 1980s Egypt remained an outcast among Arab countries because of its détente with Israel. In October 1981, a small group of Islamic militants assassinated Sadat while he was reviewing a military parade. Shortly before his death, he had ordered a crackdown on the Muslim brotherhood, which opposed his reconciliation with Israel and Egypt's increasingly secular nature.

Sadat's successor, Hosni Mubarak, pledged to continue Sadat's commitments and welcomed the support and friendship of the United States. During the 1980s Mubarak improved Egypt's relations with other moderate Arab states as he struggled with his country's overwhelming economic problems, brought on by a mushrooming population along the Nile Valley and Delta. Mubarak solidified his position and maintained Sadat's foreign policies.

Huge outlays for defense drove Israel's inflation rate to average over 50 percent in the last part of the 1980s. The Israelis came to depend more and more on aid from the United States, whose annual announced subsidies exceeded $4 billion a year. Adding to Israel's concern was a shift in American public opinion as extreme Arab provocations in the Intifada—Palestinian active and passive resistance to Israeli policies—drew harsh Israeli police responses, which American television almost uniformly cast in a bad light.

While committed to Israel's security, the United States, especially during the administration of President George Bush, increased its interests in aiding friendly Arab states who opposed what they saw as Israeli aggression. This was particularly the case with Saudi Arabia, the main supplier of American oil imports. It was this concern that led the United States to sell the Saudis large quantities of sophisticated weapons and to send the U.S. Navy to keep the Persian Gulf oil shipment lanes open during the latter stages of the Iran-Iraq war.

Iraq, a country with immense oil and agricultural potential, had squandered much of its wealth on military strength. Under Saddam Hussein, the Iraqis had developed extensive capabilities in chemical and bacteriological warfare. Their nuclear facilities, destroyed by the Israelis in 1980, were rebuilt. Iraq had launched a war against Iranian airfields and oil refineries in September 1980, and over the next nine years, more than a million people died in fighting that saw the use of poison gas and chemical weapons. In August 1990, Iraqi troops invaded and overran the oil-rich sheikdom of Kuwait in one day. This aggressive act, plus the implied threat to Saudi Arabia of Saddam Hussein's million-man army, produced an immediate response. The fear that Iraq, if it took the Saudi oil fields, would control one-third of the global oil reserves moved the UN Security Council to impose a series of strict sanctions on Baghdad. In the post–Cold War world, the Soviet Union, a former patron of Saddam Hussein, lined up in opposition to the Iraqi dictator.

For the next six months the UN, led by a coalition assembled by the United States, increased diplomatic pressure on Saddam Hussein by increasing sanctions and embargoes on his country. Hussein received the support of the Palestinians, the young throughout much of the Arab world, and Jordan.

When sanctions and embargoes failed to move Iraq to withdraw from Kuwait, the American-led 26-nation coalition (including Egypt,

→ U.S. soldiers, part of the UN coalition forces sent to the Middle East to force Iraq to withdraw from Kuwait, keep watch from their sandbag-surrounded bunker in the Saudi desert. After Iraq invaded Kuwait in 1990, King Fahd of Saudi Arabia invited the coalition troops to deploy on Saudi soil to defend Kuwait and repel the invaders.

Saudi Arabia, Syria, Turkey, France, Italy, and the United Kingdom) began heavy bombardment of Iraq beginning in January 1991. A month later, the allies launched a land offensive that in 100 hours evicted Iraq from Kuwait and left the coalition in possession of one-fifth of Iraq.

The successful smashing of Iraq's forces by the coalition opened the possibility that the Middle East might be able to break out of its entrenched hostilities. Fervent diplomatic activity throughout the major capitals of the world prepared the way for conferences that could

bring a lasting peace to the region. A major step in that direction took place in September 1993 when PLO leader Yasir Arafat and Israeli leader Shimon Peres met in Washington to sign an agreement to turn certain lands over to the Palestinians in return for guarantees of peace for Israel. Secret negotiations overseen by the Norwegian foreign minister had brought the bitter enemies together.

The PLO, isolated from much of its financial support because of its backing Iraq, and challenged by the rise of Islamic fundamentalists,

→ Encouraged by U.S. President Bill Clinton, Israeli Prime Minister Yitzhak Rabin (left) and PLO Chairman Yasir Arafat shake hands after the signing of a peace accord in September 1993. The agreement pledged the signatories to strive to achieve a "just, lasting and comprehensive peace settlement."

saw this as perhaps a last chance to maintain a position in the Middle East. Israel saw an opportunity to construct a peace that would fragment its opponents while finally addressing the problems of a homeless people.

The agreement set up a five-year-long framework of limited autonomy for the Palestinians in Jericho and the Gaza strip and continuing negotiations for a permanent settlement. By June 1994 the Israelis had withdrawn from areas specified by the treaty, turning the region over to a Palestinian police organization. In addition, Jordan and Israel exchanged diplomatic recognition during 1994.

AFRICA

In Africa, the European powers approached decolonization in a variety of ways. The British devised programs to provide financial and technical aid to prepare their colonies for independence within the Commonwealth. France also gave loans and grants, but the French wanted to create a postcolonial political and economic structure dominated by Paris. Belgium showed no understanding of the need to prepare the Congo for the future and continued its paternalistic approach. Portugal had neither the resources nor the will to prepare its colonies for the future.

In the first decade after World War II, however, it was apparent that independence would come to Africa faster than anyone had anticipated. While on a visit to British Africa in 1960, Prime Minister Harold Macmillan declared: "The wind of change is blowing through this continent, and whether we like it or not, this growth of national consciousness is a political fact and our national policies must take account of it."[2] Africans rightly think of 1960 as their year. Eighteen new nations emerged, the most important being Nigeria and the Congo. Unfortunately, over the next 30 years, many places in Africa experienced severe decline in standards of living.

By the mid-1990s Africa was deep in debt. Zambia, for example, in 1994 owed foreign lenders about $900 per citizen, a figure more than twice the average annual wage per person. Foreign debt in sub-Saharan Africa, the world's poorest region, doubled in the 1980s. "In 1965 Ghanaians were less poor . . . than South Koreans . . . [and] Nigerians were better off than Indonesians. . . . [In 1994,] the total wealth of Africa with twice the population of the United States is little more than that of Belgium."[3]

The Challenges of State-Making

France had enacted various reforms to keep its African territories as autonomous republics within a French community. (Guinea, however, had elected to become completely independent in 1958.) This compromise did not satisfy African hopes. In 1960 all 13 African republics within the French community proclaimed their independence. While the dream of a great French imperial structure had ended, France did retain a unique status in its former colonies. Its culture persisted in Africa, and France maintained its financial and technical dominance.

In 1945 there had been 4 independent African nations; by the end of the 1980s over 50 sovereign states could be identified. But independence did not bring a golden age. The optimism that accompanied the gaining of sovereign status did not last. State-building in the late twentieth century was a difficult process.

Each of the new states had to bear the heavy costs of creating a trained corps of bureaucrats, diplomats, and soldiers. All of the new states worked to build stable democratic governments led by just and strong executives. They wanted to work through responsible and freely elected legislatures and enjoy the benefits of incorruptible courts. But all of them, especially Kenya, which had emerged from revolutionary struggle, faced serious challenges.

The most pressing problem was how to build and maintain national unity among distinct and sometimes antagonistic religious, cultural, and ethnic groups. In most cases, the new African states were not the product of a long historical process such as took place in Europe, where small feudal principalities were hammered into homogeneous nation-states. Most African boundaries were arbitrary creations of the imperialists and had little relation to the people who lived there. Nigeria, for example, the result of British arms and the imagination of British geographers, encompassed many diverse and hostile ethnic and tribal segments. Throughout sub-Saharan

Frantz Fanon, *The Wretched of the Earth*

Frantz Fanon in 1963 noted the growing inequality between the industrialized and the nonindustrialized worlds as seen in a colonial town.

The colonial world is a world cut in two. The dividing line, the frontiers are shown by barracks and police stations. In the colonies it is the policeman and the soldier who are the official, instituted go-betweens, the spokesmen of the settler and his rule of oppression. . . .

It is obvious here that the agents of government speak the language of pure force. The intermediary does not lighten the oppression, nor seek to hide the domination; he shows them up and puts them into practice with the clear conscience of an upholder of the peace; yet he is the bringer of violence into the home and into the mind of the native. . . .

The settlers' town is a strongly-built town, all made of stone and steel. It is a brightly-lit town; the streets are covered with asphalt, and the garbage-cans swallow all the leavings, unseen, unknown and hardly thought about. The settler's feet are never visible, except perhaps in the sea; but there you're never close enough to see them. His feet are protected by strong shoes although the streets of his town are clean and even, with no holes or stones. The settler's town is a well-fed town, an easy-going town; its belly is always full of good things. The settler's town is a town of white people, of foreigners.

The town belonging to the colonised people, or at least the native town, the negro village, the medina, the reservation, is a place of ill fame, peopled by men of evil repute. They are born there, it matters little where or how; they die there, it matters not where, nor how. It is a world without spaciousness; men live there on top of each other, and their huts are built one on top of the other. The native town is a hungry town, starved of bread, of meat, of shoes, of coal, of light. The native town is a crouching village, a town on its knees, a town wallowing in the mire. It is a town of niggers and dirty arabs. The look that the native turns on the settler's town is a look of lust, a look of envy; it expresses his dreams of possession—all manner of possession: to sit at the settler's table, to sleep in the settler's bed, with his wife if possible. The colonised man is an envious man. And this the settler knows very well; when their glances meet he ascertains bitterly, always on the defensive "They want to take our place." It is true, for there is no native who does not dream at least once a day of setting himself up in the settler's place.

This world divided into compartments, this world cut in two is inhabited by two different species. The originality of the colonial context is that economic reality, inequality and the immense difference of ways of life never come to mask the human realities. When you examine at close quarters the colonial context, it is evident that what parcels out the world is to begin with the fact of belonging to or not belonging to a given race, a given species. . . .

It is not enough for the settler to delimit physically, that is to say with the help of the army and the police force, the place of the native. As if to show the totalitarian character of colonial exploitation the settler paints the native as a sort of quintessence of evil. Native society is not simply described as a society lacking in values. It is not enough for the colonist to affirm that those values have disappeared from, or still better never existed in, the colonial world. The native is declared insensible to ethics; he represents not only the absence of values, but also the negation of values. . . .

The Church in the colonies is the white people's Church, the foreigner's Church. She does not call the native to God's ways but to the ways of the white man, of the master, of the oppressor. And as we know, in this matter many are called but few chosen.

From Frantz Fanon, *The Wretched of the Earth*, trans. Constance Farrington. Copyright © 1963 by Presence Africaine. Used by permission of Grove Weidenfeld.

Africa, tribal fragmentation continues to work against the development of nationalism, as was tragically seen in the Hutu-Tutsi conflict and accompanying genocidal activities in Rwanda and Burundi in 1994.

These difficulties plus the economic problems, some produced by unwise investments in prestige-enhancing but economically wasteful enterprises, hampered the attainment of stable democratic governments. Between 1960 and 1967, 27 newly independent states experienced forceful takeovers. In four months in 1967 there were four military coups. In 1980 a dozen revolts took place, five of which successfully toppled the governments in power. Imitating some communist states, many of the leaders, including moderates such as Daniel Arap Moi of Kenya, discarded the two-party system in favor of a single-party government, while insisting that their political systems were essentially democratic. In fact, in some countries, the one-party states did provide stability and progress. But this was not always the case; for example in Uganda between 1971 and 1979 thousands of people were killed and the country's economy went to ruin as the capricious and uneducated General Idi Amin pursued a quirky and unpredictable rule.

North Africa

France's two protectorates in North Africa—Tunisia and Morocco—gained independence in a relatively peaceful way in 1956. In sharp contrast stands the transfer of autonomy to Algeria. France had invested millions of dollars in the development of this territory, and by 1960 French immigrants constituted about one-tenth of the population. The French dominated Algeria's industry, agriculture, and government, while the Muslim majority remained hopelessly poor.

Although Algeria was an integral part of France and sent representatives to Paris, resentment against foreign control grew among the non-French majority. Following a mounting campaign of violence, revolution broke out in 1958. After four years of savage conflict, whose repercussions brought down the French Fourth Republic, Charles de Gaulle paved the way for Algeria's independence in 1962. Seventy percent of the Europeans left the scarred and battered

country, emigrating to France. Well over 200,000 people had been killed and the number seriously wounded was even higher.

Since its independence, Algeria has played an important diplomatic role in the world, serving as a crossroads in the Arab world. The economy has become more diversified, with petroleum and agricultural exports. By 1990 Algeria's per capita GNP reached $2400. However, the country's domestic tranquillity was shattered by the activities of Islamic fundamentalists who, after having achieved electoral victories in 1992—which were thrown out—resorted to a widespread assassination campaign against Algerian and foreign professionals and journalists.

Libya made the transition from Italian colony to independent nation with help from the United Nations. The military led by Colonel Mu'ammar el-Kaddafi took power from the monarchy in 1969, and eight years later the country became known as the Socialist People's Libyan Arab Jamahiriya. Since that time the quixotic leader has pursued, generally unsuccessfully, military adventures against Egypt (1977), Uganda (1979), and Chad (1980). He has also supported international terrorism, drawing the anger of the United States, which on three occasions in the 1980s shot down attacking Libyan jets in the Mediterranean and bombed Tripoli once. Revenues from the country's rich oilfields help finance Kaddafi's ventures and contribute to a per capita GNP of more than $5600 for the roughly 4 million Libyans.

Middle Africa

Ghana was the first nation south of the Sahara to gain independence. In 1957 Kwame Nkrumah, its prime minister, was the idol of African nationalists, and his newly freed nation was the symbol of liberalism and democracy in Africa. But almost immediately, Nkrumah began to muzzle the press and imprison the opposition. He quickly developed into an outright dictator while at the same time embarking on ruinous economic policies such as showy projects and a large military establishment. Nkrumah's controlled press called him the Great Redeemer and His Messianic Majesty, while his economy slid downhill under the impact of incompetence and corruption.

→ Jomo Kenyatta (center), flanked by his wife Njina and Chief Justice Sir John Ainley, is sworn in as president of the newly independent Republic of Kenya, December 12, 1964.

In 1966 a group of army officers seized control of the government. Eager to speed economic recovery and restore some semblance of political freedom, the army leaders permitted the return to parliamentary institutions in 1969. Ghana thus became the first African country to return to multiparty government after being a one-party state. During the 1970s another military junta carried off a coup, but by the end of the decade, civilian rule returned again. In 1981 the military under Flight Lieutenant Jerry Rawlings once again took control and remained in control throughout the 1980s.

In contrast, the independent nation of Kenya gained stability and a sound economy under the sole political party, the Kenya African National Union, founded by the statesman Jomo Kenyatta. The state was able to mediate between the Kikuyu and Luo tribes and make its capital at Nairobi into a showplace for the continent. Kenya's history is not uniformly positive, however, since in 1972 Kenyatta expelled the East Indians, who had dominated trade.

Events were not so fortunate in Zaire (formerly the Belgian Congo), a huge dependency as large as western Europe but lacking any ethnic or economic unity. In 1959 the Belgians, in the face of general unrest and serious rioting, promised independence. When self-government came the next year, civil war broke out among some of the 70 major groups. At the request of the Congolese government, UN forces intervened to restore order, which they did by 1964. By the

mid-1970s a new regime under (Joseph) Mobutu Sese Seko succeeded in establishing the central government's uneasy authority over the tribal groups. The large, resource-rich country suffered from ineffective rule and terrible poverty among the general population. By the end of the 1980s the per capita GNP was only $172.

When it gained independence in 1960, Nigeria offered the most promise among the new African states of a prosperous and stable future. It had several thousand well-trained civil servants, more than 500 doctors, an equal number of lawyers, and a substantial body of engineers and other professionals. It made rapid progress toward modernization, endowed as it was with a variety of important natural resources, especially oil. Unlike the Belgian Congo, it had some 40 years of training in self-government. Its constitution was the result of a decade of constitutional experiments and discussion with British officials.

Nigeria, however, was similar to the Congo in its tribal and ethnic complexity. It had more than 200 tribes and a dozen important languages. Yet it appeared to have the forces of unity to overcome any fragmenting tendencies in its state structure. Nigeria was held up to be democracy's best hope in Africa; unfortunately this hope was not realized.

Between 1962 and 1966 a series of crises—disputed elections, corruption, and crime waves—threatened to tear the new nation apart. After witnessing these events, the Ibo tribal region proclaimed its independence as the state

1020 Civilization Past & Present

of Biafra. The Hausa and Yoruba encircled the Ibo and crowded them into a small area without sufficient food or supplies. Thousands, especially children, died of starvation. In 1970 the Ibo surrendered and reconciled with the other tribes.

After 13 years of military rule, civilian government was restored in 1979, along with a new constitution patterned after that of the United States. Designed to prevent a return of the ethnic-regional feuds that had wrecked the first republic, the new constitution created a federal system providing for the allocation of powers between a central and 19 state governments. However, Nigeria returned to military rule in 1983 and all political parties were banned, and it has thus remained, despite pledges from the military leadership to return the country to civilian rule.

The Eastern Horn of Africa, consisting of the Somali Republic and Ethiopia, became geopolitically significant after 1945 because of its proximity to the sea lanes of the Red Sea and the Persian Gulf. The British liberated Ethiopia from the Italians in 1941 and permitted Emperor Haile Selassie to return. While not an unenlightened ruler, he was unable to adapt to postwar conditions.

The crisis that led to his expulsion began with a famine in 1973 that killed 100,000 people. Strikes, student unrest, scandal among the royal family, and mismanagement all combined to bring success to the coup attempt that removed Selassie. The new rulers were bitterly divided among moderates and radicals, and following two years of quarrels, the radicals gained control. Their governing council immediately set to work to abolish the country's traditional feudal system, transforming Ethiopia into a socialist state with a one-party system of a Stalinist type: collective farms, censorship, government control of all productive property, imprisonment, and mass execution of at least 10,000 opponents.

The council then turned to the problems in the Ethiopian provinces of Ogaden, adjacent to Somalia, and Eritrea on the Red Sea. Somalia took possession of Ogaden in 1977 but the next year the Ethiopians signed a treaty with the Soviet Union that gave them $1 billion in aid, 17,000 Cuban troops, and modern weapons. The Ethiopians launched a counteroffensive and pushed the Somalis back. In the late 1970s the Ethiopians turned their attention on the Eritrean rebels and were able to expel them from some of their urban strongholds.

Overwhelming all of the political and diplomatic maneuvering was the series of massive famines that rocked the area during the 1980s. The government of Mengistu Haile-Mariam, who ruled until May 1991, either through intent or incompetence allowed thousands of Ethiopians to die, despite the massive outpouring of aid from churches, charitable organizations, and rock musicians.

In Somalia, clan warfare and famine reduced that country by the end of 1992 into a land of poverty and death. Televised pictures of dead and dying infants moved the United States to action in December 1992 when a Marine detachment landed at Mogadishu to try to bring order between the competing clans and to permit the various humanitarian organizations to distribute food. Although the situation stabilized somewhat, the clans retained their followers and strength. By the spring of 1993 the U.S. Marines had become a factor in, rather than an arbitrator over domestic politics. The clan leaders patched together a détente the following year, and the Somali people had the opportunity to put in a crop and harvest it.

Southern Africa

Many significant events rocked the southern part of the continent. In 1974 the revolt of the Portuguese army in Lisbon ended nearly half a century of dictatorial rule. The military junta concluded 13 years of costly revolt by black nationalists in Portugal's African territories—Angola, Mozambique, and Guinea-Bissau. The last two gained independence with little difficulty. Freedom for Angola was complicated by the presence of a half-million European inhabitants. Following the granting of independence in 1975, bloody strife among three rival nationalist groups broke out. Fighting continued until 1989 among the groups, which drew support from Cuba, the Soviet Union, and South Africa.

Zimbabwe, formerly Rhodesia, shares a border with Mozambique. In the first part of the 1960s this colony contained some 250,000 whites and more than 5 million Africans. In 1963 the white minority-controlled colony declared its independence from Great Britain, which had insisted that such action could not be agreed to without the prior grant of full political rights to the African majority. Neither a crippling trade embargo imposed by Britain nor economic sanctions levied by the UN could force compromise. In 1970 the final ties with Britain were severed and Zimbabwe assumed the status of a republic.

During the 1970s violence increased as forces crossed over Mozambique and Zambia, while South African troops joined local forces in search-and-destroy missions against the guerrillas. By the end of the decade, the 250,000 Europeans voted to accept black-majority rule. Black factions led by Robert Mugabe boycotted the elections held in April 1979, and new elections were held in 1980. Mugabe, a Marxist, won and ruled Zimbabwe through the decade.

The country recovered quickly from the conflicts of the 1970s that left 25,000 dead and many more wounded, and produced massive unemployment and food shortages. Mugabe proved to be a skilled leader, keeping the white infrastructure in place and producing a per capita GNP of $540 by 1986. Tourism picked up and economic obstacles began to disappear. The de facto one-party state appeared to be one of the more stable and progressive on the continent.

Conditions in South Africa remained tense in the post-1945 period. With its booming cities, rapidly growing industries, and rich mining enterprises, South Africa was a thoroughly modern state, except for its racial policies. The Republic of South Africa, with a population that was 70 percent black, 18 percent European, and the remainder "coloured," had to deal with the rising discontent of the African majority and with the censure of its racial policies of apartheid by the world community.

The South African government tried a program of territorial segregation, setting up ten distinct and partially self-governing African states known as Bantustans, which were aided by substantial economic grants. First to be established was Transkei, with its Bantu population of 3.5 million people. This program did not satisfy the African populations, and strikes and political protests against apartheid continued through the 1980s. The government continued the program, granting partial independence to Transkei in 1976 and establishing two additional Bantustans three years later. The states, or Homelands, were generally poor and underdeveloped, forcing a constant exodus of blacks to find employment in white urban areas. Those who could not find work and housing and meet other requirements

were classed as illegal immigrants and shipped back to their Homelands.

In 1978, Prime Minister P.W. Botha, who retained that position until 1989, declared that the country "must adapt or die." Advocating a new program of race relations, he urged a lessening of race discrimination in the areas of loans and mortgage opportunities, jobs, working conditions, and wage disparities. In 1980 a new plan of government was announced. A President's Council was to be created, consisting of a white-nominated majority, coloured and East Indian members, and one Chinese representative. This body was to advise on constitutional proposals. This was the first time some political representation was given to non-Europeans. The plan denied Africans any such rights except in their tribal Homeland.

Botha oversaw some relaxation of apartheid: races began to mix freely in public places, areas reserved "for whites only" were reduced, and new

black unions were legalized. In effect apartheid remained intact. Ultra-right wingers forced the prime minister to pull back, and the frustrations of the non-Europeans increased, fueled by the gain of independence in Angola and Zimbabwe. Militancy increased. When a new constitution was adopted in 1983, providing for a strong executive presidency and a three-part parliamentary body—whites, coloured, and Asians—blacks remained unrepresented and without rights except in their tribal Homelands. Only the white part of the parliament had any power.

F.W. DeKlerk, who replaced Botha in September 1989, moved to try to defuse the seemingly inevitable bloodshed between the races. In the face of death threats launched by extreme right-wing, proto-Nazi white parties, he opened negotiations with the African National Congress. He made the symbolically important step of releasing Nelson Mandela, ANC founder and symbolic leader of many South African blacks, from almost three decades of imprisonment and began serious negotiations to pave the way for a multiracial political structure. In response, the ANC suspended its 29-year declaration of war against the South African government. DeKlerk's white opponents accused him of capitulation.

Observers noted that by the year 2000, whites would number a bare 13 percent of the population. South African industry would depend largely on black labor and expertise. Apartheid would be an unworkable anomaly in a black, hostile continent, a situation brought increasingly to world attention in 1985 and 1986 when the scale of violence steadily increased. Without wide-ranging reforms, long-term prospects looked bleak.

DeKlerk and Mandela, an unlikely combination, began the process of dismantling apartheid and preparing the way for the writing of a new constitution. Once that was accomplished, they began preparations for elections to be held in the spring of 1994. Predictably, the extreme right-wing white organizations advocated violence and obstructionism, while Zulu leaders worked against what they saw as the overwhelming position of the ANC. Almost miraculously, elections of April 1994 proceeded with few problems. Nelson Mandela was elected president of South Africa, with DeKlerk as one of his vice presidents. A crisis that a decade earlier seemed soluble only through tragic civil war had been resolved democratically.

→ A most dramatic end to the policy of apartheid in South Africa was the election of African National Congress leader Nelson Mandela to the presidency in May 1994. Here the newly elected president and Second Deputy President F. W. DeKlerk join hands in triumph as they greet the crowd following their inauguration on May 10.

Another controversial area is Namibia. A German colony until 1919, the area was known as Southwest Africa and administered as a mandate under the supervision of the League of Nations. Following World War II, South Africa refused to transfer its jurisdiction to the United Nations, which formally ended South Africa's mandate in 1966. South Africa held onto control this huge area—half the size of Alaska—which is inhabited by a million blacks and 100,000 whites. Namibia contained valuable mineral deposits, but more importantly to South Africa, it served as a buffer against potentially unfriendly black nations to the north. While South Africa reached an agreement with a coalition of blacks and whites for a form of self-rule, it refused to recognize the militant Southwest African Peoples' Organization (SWAPO), which was based in Angola and supplied by the Soviets. In the early 1980s a UN-sponsored plan for an election was blocked by the South Africans, who sent troops in to attack the guerrillas, killing hundreds and also killing Soviet advisers. In the mid-1990s, the Namibia crisis still resisted solution.

LATIN AMERICA: REFORM OR REVOLT

After World War II, Latin America shared many of the problems experienced by the developing countries of the world outside Europe. Formerly competitive economies such as those of Argentina, Mexico, and Brazil had fallen far behind rapidly advancing areas such as South Korea, Taiwan, and Singapore. Whether in countries of primarily European stock (Argentina, Uruguay, and Chile), dualistic Indian-Spanish societies (Peru, Bolivia, Ecuador, and Mexico), melting pot societies such as Brazil and Venezuela, or single-crop economies such as those of Central America, Latin America faced serious problems at the end of the century.

The Perils of the Postwar Era

The period since 1945 witnessed much political instability and social unrest in the region. For example, the only countries with continuously elected governments after 1950 have been those dominated by a single major party. Between 1950 and 1966 14 governments were forcefully overthrown and dictatorial rule was imposed on more than half the Latin American population. The political instability and the seeds of social upheaval spring from appalling socioeconomic disparities. Despite the region's great natural resources, the average citizen of Latin America is desperately poor. Shantytowns on the edges of large cities house thousands amid filth, disease, hunger, and crime. Life expectancy for Latin American males is around 55 years—15 years less than in North America. Agricultural productivity is inefficient and low. The population increases by about 3 percent yearly. By 1990 the region's population topped 500 million, most living in cities. Educational and health services are insufficient and literacy rates remain low.

Since 1948 the countries south of the Rio Grande have been aligned with the United States in the Organization of American States (OAS). Dominated by the United States, the OAS has sought to prevent communists from acquiring control in Latin American countries by well-meaning, if incomplete, social and economic aid. In 1959, Fidel Castro rapidly transformed Cuba into a communist country; afterwards his attempts to export his revolution were countered by an OAS boycott.

In Castro's Cuba, educational and health standards rose appreciably, as did living conditions among the peasants who constituted the great majority of the population. The professional and middle classes, however, suffered losses in both living standards and personal liberties, and many hundreds of thousands fled to the United States. Cuba exported sugar to other communist countries in exchange for major economic subsidies from the Soviet Union. In 1975 16 members of the OAS voted to end the embargo and the United States intimated a desire for détente. This last possibility was made remote with the intervention of thousands of Cuban troops and advisers in Angola and other African countries.

By the mid-1990s global political changes isolated Castro. Cuba's role overseas ended with peace talks in Africa. The Soviet Union could no longer afford the luxury of propping up Castro's failing economy, and Russia virtually ignored him. His version of Marxism-Leninism was shared only in North Korea. Castro's rule in Cuba sharpened U.S. interest in the area south of its border. After the failure of the American invasion attempt at the Bay of Pigs in 1961, President John F. Kennedy initiated the Alliance for Progress, with Latin American cooperation.

The United States pledged $20 billion, to be matched by the other members of the alliance. After 20 years, the alliance had done little to change basic conditions. Oligarchic rule, paternalism, and incompetence hindered economic and political reform. By the mid-1990s, Brazil suffered from a high inflation rate while Mexico remained deeply in debt, paying the interest on foreign loans with difficulty. Rapidly increasing inflation also hampered economic growth. In Brazil there was substantial indication that a large percentage of the foreign loans were not being invested in needed industrialization and regional integration, but were instead being funneled to Swiss banks by top-ranking bureaucrats.

The Yankee Factor

A key element in Latin America is the relationship between the United States and its neighbors. American economic involvement in Latin America has remained massive. American companies continue to employ about 2 million people, pay 25 percent of the region's taxes, and produce one-third of its exports. Softening the imperialist presence are the activities of humanitarian efforts from the Rockefeller Foundation and churches, and federal programs of educational, agricultural, and social improvements. In response to the development of the European Union and the possibility of a unified Asian market, the United States pushed for the creation of the North American Free Trade Association, which was put into effect when Canada, Mexico, and the United States ratified the agreement in 1993. This marked one of the great successes of Mexican President Carlos Salinas and his Institutional Ruling Party (PRI). In 1994, when the PRI appeared well on its way toward yet another victory, its designated candidate, Luis Donaldo Colosio, was assassinated.

At the same time, the U.S. Central Intelligence Agency used large sums to support the opponents of Chilean President Salvador Allende, an avowed pro-Soviet Marxist. In his hasty efforts to nationalize industry, both domestic and foreign-owned, and to redistribute land holdings, Allende had antagonized many of his own people. His regime came to a bloody end in a 1973 coup. Military leaders ousted the president, who died—perhaps by his own hand—during the fighting. The new repressive regime, under General Auguste Pinochet, imposed a harsh rule and acted aggressively to curb all opposition, which had been growing since the early 1980s. Pinochet stepped down in 1990 and was replaced by the moderate Patricio Aylwin.

One long-standing source of discord between the United States and Latin America was removed in 1978 when the United Senate approved the treaty that returned the Panama Canal Zone to the Republic of Panama, while safeguarding American interests in the area. This agreement, negotiated over a period of 14 years under four American presidents, was a sign to some that the United States was eager to improve relations with its neighbors. The American military invasion of Panama in December 1989, however, indicated that there were some excesses the United States would not tolerate. Allegations that Panamanian President Manuel Noriega cooperated in drug-running and overturned democratic elections moved U.S. President Bush to order the preemptive strike to oust Noriega.

In the last decade the countries of Latin America dealt differently with the economic, social, and political challenges they faced. Many remained under military rule. Others, such as Nicaragua, carried out successful socialist revolutions, but faced the powerful overt and covert opposition of the United States. Democratic elections in the spring of 1990 led to the defeat of the Sandinista party in Nicaragua, but economic and social problems remained to plague the new government. Tiny El Salvador struggled through a bloody civil war, in which death squads from both right and left brought terror to the countryside. Brazil made tentative economic progress before a series of poor policy decisions darkened that country's future. Out-of-control inflation destroyed Argentina's economy, though elected officials were able to restore normal democratic politics. Mexico was stable under a single-party domination but faced a population rate that outstripped its economic progress. Colombia found its basic sovereignty undermined by drug lords, both foreign and domestic.

In the Caribbean, the British successfully ushered in independence in the West Indies—Jamaica, Tobago, Trinidad, and Barbados. The Caribbean island of Grenada fell to a leftist government, before U.S. President Ronald Reagan sent U.S. Marines to the island to overthrow the regime in 1983. Unrest continued in Haiti, the poorest country in the Western Hemisphere. President for Life Jean Claude Duvalier, "Baby Doc," was forced out of office and fled the country in February 1986. In February 1991, Jean-Bertrand Aristide, a Catholic priest, was elected president. Seven months later the army kicked him out. In response, the UN laid an oil and arms embargo on the country, which led to a compromise under which Aristide would be allowed back in the country. When the compromise collapsed, a wave of reprisals and random murders swept the country and led to the frantic exodus of thousands of Haitians on fragile craft to avoid punishment. By autumn 1994, after the coup leaders refused to give in to international demands for Aristide's return, the United States

and its Caribbean allies forced the coup leaders out and placed Aristedes back in power.

With the end of the Cold War, the United States began to take a longer-term, more economically focused view of Latin America. Enhanced perceptions of stability moved Washington to policies that may well prove to be mutually beneficial to North and South.

CONCLUSION

In the last half of the twentieth century the developing world has emerged as the major theater of action for the next century. In these countries are the world's fastest-growing populations, its most essential resources, and the most politically explosive situations. All these countries, from richest to poorest, have been affected by decolonization, the Cold War and its conclusion, and the technological revolution. All of them were brought into the modern age by forceful contact with the Europeans, but in the next century they will have to choose their own paths. All face major economic and demographic crises that find expression in political instability.

China, the most powerful country in the developing world, participated in Cold War episodes from Korea to Vietnam and fought its own ideological battles before entering a period of rapid modernization after 1978. In the rest of Asia and in Africa, nations freed themselves from the yoke of European dominance, but independence unleashed powerful ethnic and religious antagonisms, most of which remain unresolved. After the British withdrew from the Subcontinent, India and Pakistan entered a half-century of sometimes peaceful, sometimes armed competition. Great power intervention in the Middle East and in Africa exacerbated an already difficult situation and led to increased bloodshed.

More than Cold War tensions, economic upheavals have affected the Latin American states. The region's accumulation of massive debts and its dependence on the export of oil or agricultural products left it at the mercy of the North Atlantic powers. This economic domination provided a rich opportunity for revolutionaries in Cuba and Nicaragua, who fought against the obvious exploitation of the population.

→ Suggestions for Reading

John K. Fairbank et al. discuss the challenges of change in *East Asia: Tradition and Transformation* (Boston, 1973).

Stuart Schram, *Mao Tse-tung* (Penguin, 1966) is good for the formative stages of the leader's life. R.H. Soloman, *Mao's Revolution and the Chinese Political Culture* (Univ. of California, 1971) ties political change to social transformation. Edward F. Rice gives a good summation of Mao's theories in *Mao's Way* (Univ. of California, 1975). Roderick Mac Farquar, *Origins of the Cultural Revolution* (Oxford Univ., 1983) is first-rate. Changes in the countryside are considered in Jan Myrdal, *Report from a Chinese Village* (Signet, 1969), which discusses political change from a rural perspective. Thomas Raski gives an overall view of economic modernization in *China's Transition to Industrialism* (Univ. of Michigan, 1980). See also I.K.Y. Hsu, *China Without Mao: The Search for the New Order* (Oxford Univ., 1982). Bruce D. Porter, *The USSR in Third World Conflicts: Soviet Arms and Diplomacy in Local Wars, 1945–1980* (Cambridge Univ., 1984) presents analyses of various episodes of Soviet participation in Third World crises and the changing nature of Moscow's involvements. Franz Ansprenger gives a helpful account of decolonization in *The Dissolution of the Colonial Empires* (Routledge, 1989).

For studies of Southeast Asia see Michael Leifer, *The Foreign Relations of the New States* (Longman, 1979); R.N. Kearney, *Politics and Modernization in South and Southeast Asia* (Halstead, 1974); and Robert Shaplan, *A Turning Wheel: The Long Revolution in Asia* (Random House, 1979). On Indonesia, see W.T. Neill, *Twentieth Century Indonesia* (Columbia Univ., 1973) and A.M. Taylor, *Indonesian Independence and the United Nations* (Greenwood, 1975).

Some valuable surveys of modern India include W. Norman Brown, *The United States and India, Pakistan, and Bangladesh* (Harvard Univ., 1972) and Stanley Wolpert, *A New History of India* (Oxford Univ., 1982). A solid biography of Indira Gandhi is Z. Masani, *Indira Gandhi* (Crowell, 1976). An informative guide to Indian politics is Richard L. Park and Bruce Bueno de Mesquita, *India's Political System* (Prentice-Hall, 1979).

The Middle East's complexity is dealt with in M. Halpern, *The Politics of Social Change in the Middle East and North Africa* (Princeton Univ., 1967) and W.R. Polk, *The Elusive Peace: The Middle East in the Twentieth Century* (St. Martin's, 1980). M.E. Yapp's survey of the region, *The Near East Since the First World War* (Longman, 1991) is the best overview of this century's complex events. On the Arab point of view see W.R. Polk, *The United States and the Arab World* (Harvard Univ., 1975). Two insightful books on Iran are R.K. Ramazani, *The Persian Gulf: Iran's Role* (Univ. of Virginia, 1972) and Sepehr Zabih, *Iran's Revolutionary Upheaval* (Alchemy Books, 1979).

David Pryce-Jones writes of the Arab victims in *The Face of Defeat: Palestinian Refugees and Guerrillas* (Holt, Rinehart and Winston, 1973). Soviet participation in the area is spelled out in Jon D. Glassman, *Arms for Arabs: The Soviet Union and War in the Middle East* (Johns Hopkins Univ., 1976). Two phases of Arab-Israeli war are studied in R. and W. Churchill, *The Six Day War* (Houghton Mifflin, 1967) and Chaim Herzog, *The War of Atonement, October 1973* (Little, Brown, 1975). See also H.M. Sachar, *A History of Israel* (Knopf, 1976) and W. Laqueur, *A History of Zionism* (MacMillan, 1968). Daniel Yergin's *The Prize* (Touchstone Press, 1991) is a beautifully written and acutely analytical study of the impact of oil on politics and diplomacy in the world.

The difficulties of transition from white-dominated to black-dominated African states can be seen in the collection gathered on the former Rhodesia in George M. Daniels, ed., *Drums of War* (Third Press, 1974). See also Henry Wiseman and A.M. Taylor, *Rhodesia to Zimbabwe: The Politics of Transition* (Pergamon Press, 1981). A study of Ethiopia on the eve of Haile Selassie's fall is Patrick Gilkes, *The Dying Lion* (St. Martin's, 1975). Leonard Thompson and Jeffrey Butler, *Change in Contemporary South Africa* (Univ. of California, 1975) is a superior collection of interpretive essays. L.H. Gann and Peter Duignan, *Africa South of the Sahara: The Challenge to Western Security* (Stanford Univ., 1981) details this region's strategic importance to the West. See also Gwendolyn Carter and Patrick O'Meara, *Southern Africa: The Continuing Crisis* (Univ. of Indiana, 1979). A solid collection of essays dealing with the global economic response to South Africa's racial policies is Robert E. Edgar, ed., *Sanctioning Apartheid* (Africa World Press). Leroy Vail's *The Creation of Tribalism in Southern Africa* (Univ. of California, 1989) is an innovative look at the mobilization of ethnic identity to political ends in Southern Africa since 1918. John Seiler's *Southern Africa Since the Portuguese Coup* (Westview Press, 1980) discusses some of the most contentious regions of the continent. For a fine overall view of politics since independence, see Basil Davidson, *Let Freedom Come: Africa in Modern History* (Little, Brown, 1978).

The following works help illuminate the complex developments in Latin America: Julio Cotler and Richard Fagen, eds., *Latin America and the United States: The Changing Political Realities* (Stanford Univ., 1974); R.J. Shafer, *A History of Latin America* (Heath, 1978); and Irwin Isenburg, ed., *South America: Problems and Prospects* (Wilson, 1975). See also R.E. Poppino, *Brazil: The Land and the People* (Oxford Univ., 1973) and J.N. Goodsell, *Fidel Castro's Personal Revolution in Cuba* (Knopf, 1973).

→ Notes

1. Richard Rovere, *Senator Joe McCarthy* (London: Methuen, 1959), p. 24.
2. From a speech by British Prime Minister Harold Macmillan's, 3 February 1960, as printed in *Vital Speeches*, 1 March 1960.
3. *The Economist*, March 5, 1994, p. 21.

Epilogue

TOWARD THE THIRD MILLENNIUM

This edition of *Civilization Past & Present* leads into the second thousandth anniversary of the birth of Christ and hence to the arrival of the "third millennium." In the Bible, the *millennium* related to the prophecy in the Book of Revelations of Christ's thousand-year reign on earth and looked forward to an era of happiness and benign government. Associated with any such era is the concept of an ideal society, a *utopia*. In previous chapters, we have referred to some of them: Plato's *Republic*, Thomas More's *Utopia*, and Francis Bacon's *New Atlantis*.

In contrast to these earlier works about societies where everything is fundamentally good, twentieth-century literature includes a number of *dystopias*, where things are basically bad. Among them are Aldous Huxley's *Brave New World*, George Orwell's *1984*, and Jacques Ellul's *Technological Society*.

What are we to make of this? Is our society fundamentally good and getting better, or bad and getting worse? We hear talk about a new world order, but few believe that it will usher in any golden age. Yet if we cannot live in a utopia, our challenge is to make sure that our actions, however well-intentioned, do not produce a dystopia.

"I am like a man standing between two worlds: I look both forward and backward." So spoke the Italian poet and father of humanism, Francesco Petrarch, who has been described as "the hinge of the door" between two very different societies: the Middle Ages with its emphasis on faith and collective values, and the Renaissance with its secular concerns and emphasis on individual values. Is it possible that we too are in the midst of a societal shift, one that will become increasingly apparent as we move into the twenty-first century? To determine whether we are at another "hinge of the door," let us emulate Petrarch by looking both backward at our recent past and then forward as we prepare for the third millennium.

THE TWENTIETH CENTURY IN RETROSPECT

As we come to the close of the twentieth century, we have the opportunity to look back at its evolution, the description of which occupies nearly a quarter of the pages of the eighth edition of *Civilization Past & Present*. The twentieth century has been probably the most tumultuous and creative—certainly the most populous—period in recorded history. Perhaps its unique characteristic has been to create what was described by the American statesman Wendell Willkie in the 1940s as "One World" and later by Marshall McLuhan as the "global village." This century has seen the globalization of communication networks, air routes, weather systems, scientific and medical discoveries, trade and commerce, travel and tourism, sports and other entertainment, and a host of computerized technologies. Sadly, it has also known warfare and carnage on a global scale, as well as the despoliation of our planetary environment.

Along with *global*, our language makes increasing use of a number of related terms that give a distinctive quality to our times: terms such as *systemic, holistic, interconnected*, and *interacting*. Whereas in the past, preeminence was accorded such concepts as nationalism and independence, in today's increasingly integrated world, we find an unprecedented emphasis on internationalism and interdependence, as demonstrated everywhere by the activities of transnational corporations and intergovernmental agencies.

Scientific and Technological Change

Scientific and technological advances have revolutionized our understanding of the world's basic structure and processes. Some of the major scientific breakthroughs occurred early in this century with Planck's quantum mechanics, Einstein's relativity theory, and Heisenberg's uncertainty principle, while later decades saw the development of systems and chaos theories. Advances in biology, especially in molecular biology, have opened the way to genetic engineering in plants and animals and the treatment of various human diseases.

Atomic fission created the nuclear age by releasing vast new energy sources for civilian and military purposes. But this has proved to be a two-edged sword. On the one hand, nuclear power gives promise of a seemingly endless source of energy that might be employed, for example, to desalinize ocean waters on a massive scale for irrigating deserts. On the other hand, atomic bombs destroyed urban populations in Hiroshima and Nagasaki, while a nuclear reactor explosion wreaked havoc in Chernobyl and beyond. A continuing problem is the safe disposal of ever-growing amounts of spent radioactive nuclear fuel.

A quantum leap in the technological evolution of humanity occurred with the invention of heavier-than-air machines to move into the third, or vertical, dimension, thereby ushering in the space age. The invention of computer technology has led us forward into the information age in which an incredible amount of data can be disseminated at the speed of light.

Political Change

Our century has been marked by tensions and competition in two areas: nationalism and ideology. World War I was largely a struggle between competing national ambitions; World War II witnessed a struggle to the death among liberal democracy, fascism, and communism. In its aftermath we have again seen nationalist struggles breaking out in Europe, Asia, and Africa.

Probably the most far-reaching political change since 1945 has been the dismantling of colonial empires and their replacement by large numbers of new nation-states in Asia, Africa, and the Middle East. All too often their respective roads to independence and economic viability proved rocky, thereby threatening global stability. Their problems underscored a potentially dangerous threat to all societies, namely, an increas-

ing disparity in living standards between the rich industrial countries and the impoverished developing countries.

Economic Change

Throughout this century, in times of peace and war alike, national economies continued to expand. Industrialization triumphed in the North (so-called because most of the advanced economies are situated north of the equator). Notable, too, has been the creation of a truly global economic market, spearheaded by the North's transnational corporations. Their penetration into the South (that is, the world's developing countries) has in turn stimulated the governments of East Asia to establish market economies geared to emulate the North's industrial processes and manufacture of consumer goods on a massive scale. East Asia, led by China, has now become the world's fastest growing economic region.

However, in attempting to modernize their economies, many countries in Africa and Latin America embarked on ambitious programs largely financed by borrowing from the North's financial institutions. As a result, the South now faces a debt crisis. Meanwhile, the failure of state-controlled economies in the former Soviet Union and other socialist countries in eastern Europe led to abrupt, wholesale shifts to market economies that caused widespread economic suffering and social unrest.

After decades of unprecedented growth, the North's economies have been confronted by major problems. Postwar expansion enabled governments to embark on publicly funded programs that have created the welfare state. In the 1990s, recession and skyrocketing public debts brought into question the affordability and even the value of retaining the welfare state.

Social Change

The greatest population explosion in history has occurred in our century. Concurrent with this demographic explosion has been the mass migration to cities on every continent. Urban dynamics in this and other countries found expression also in two major social movements: universal free public education and universal suffrage. Increasing dependence on specialized skills and scientific knowledge translated into a fundamental need for effective systems of education. The expansion of educational opportunities for women, especially at the postsecondary level, was part of the drive toward gender parity in society.

The urban explosion and way of life were certain to strengthen a globally oriented type of society, given the continuous communication exchanges among all cities. The city is also the prime locality of what has been called mass society. Here, too, we encounter widespread socioeconomic tensions. In addition, the dynamics of social change gave voice in the 1960s to the counter culture phenomenon: rebellion, particularly among the young, against traditional values and the materialism of the acquisitive society. Our century has indeed produced a volatile global society.

Society will be challenged in the coming decades on a number of fronts. Peoples' right of privacy must be protected from intrusion by governments and corporations using sophisticated information technologies to store, and exploit, highly personalized data. They need also to be safeguarded against the ideological intolerance of extremist groups, as well as the phenomenon of "political correctness" whereby pressure is applied by groups insisting that views not in agreement with their own doctrines must be condemned out of hand. American citizens, too, will have to take resolute action against the rampant use of drugs which currently saps the resources and moral fiber of all segments of society. Closely related to the drug epidemic is another ubiquitous problem: the pervasiveness and increase of crime. This country has both the highest per capita possession of weapons in the world and far greater homicide rates than Europe or Canada. Why? Crimes have also included massive bombings—by Middle East terrorists at the New York World Trade Center and by domestic terrorists at the Oklahoma City federal building in 1995. Yet these acts by vicious and profoundly hostile political subcultures also initiated a positive reactions: They brought Americans together from all regions in the face of tragedy and imbued them with a heightened resolve to safeguard and enhance America's democratic traditions.

THE TWENTY-FIRST CENTURY IN PROSPECT

From our present experiences, we can extrapolate in order to project foreseeable issues of fundamental importance for the twenty-first century. The basic issues we have examined throughout the pages of *Civilization Past & Present* will simultaneously affect global society and the future prospects of American society. They extrapolate logically from the experiences and behavior of the twentieth century and, in turn, are intermixed with both promises and perils. In this Epilogue, we set forth these issues in the form of challenges—challenges confronting all people in greater or less degree.

Sustaining the Natural Environment

All species depend for survival on the planet's resources, derived from its waters, soil, and air. Hence, it is logical that ecologists and philosophers alike are now discussing whether we humans own the earth and its resources or have the right only to act as its stewards. According to the Haida Indians, "We do not inherit the earth from our fathers; we borrow it from our children." Poets and painters describe its beauty by word and brush; societies are organized on its land; governments seek to control specific parcels of territory and adjacent waters; economists devise means to account for its wealth; from time immemorial men and women have labored to sustain themselves by the harvests of the soil and seas. Technologists, meanwhile, have invented ever more effective means to obtain and use the earth's resources.

As a consequence of these activities, our species' relationship to its environment has shifted from simple adaptation to progressively more powerful usage and exploitation. Today we see about us the consequences of this exploitation, while tomorrow will confront us with prospects and problems that will challenge humankind's ingenuity to preserve the planet and its myriad inhabitants. In the decades ahead, we shall have to cope with at least the following environmental issues:

1. The ecological pressures caused by the continuing population explosion

2. Demographic pressures that will accelerate the diminution of nonrenewable resources, such as minerals and fossil fuels, and the destruction of many renewable resources
3. Gases released by the use of refrigerants and aerosols that have resulted in the depletion of the atmosphere's ozone layer
4. Global warming resulting from the unchecked emission of greenhouse gases, such as carbon dioxide, methane, and chlorofluorocarbons
5. Increasing pollution of the lower atmosphere from smog and other harmful substances
6. Economic burdens inherited from environmental problems: water pollution, depletion of groundwater; the proliferation of hazardous wastes and toxic chemicals, acid rain, and desertification

Balancing Population and Resources

Each of these two global issues poses massive problems by itself. But when we treat them in terms of their interconnections with the natural environment as well as with each other, they pose probably the greatest threat to planetary existence as we know it today.

Population change results primarily from two interrelated components: mortality and fertility. The major cause for the spectacular jump in modern population has been the rapid fall in death rates because of medical advances and increased life expectancy. Birth rates have not declined proportionately or evenly among the world's regions: In the next century the North's population will reach steady state, but the South's growth will continue, becoming about nine times that of the North's population by the year 2050.

Population control will have to depend in large measure on ethical and moral considerations. And on political will. The international population conference held in Cairo in 1994 showed how difficult it will be to mobilize sufficient political consensus to make a substantial difference in reducing global population growth.

Can the growing human population continue to feed itself? Here the experts are divided. The optimists, comprising economists and some agricultural scientists, argue that the earth can produce more than enough food for the expected population in 2050 because of technological innovation and continued investment of human capital. The pessimists, led by environmentalists, regard the situation as a catastrophe in the making. A third position is that both are extremist: The real problem lies in the maldistribution of resources and wealth, and this will continue to be the case until the developing countries of the South have greater access to resources and have greater freedom of economic initiative.

Growing global population also means increased consumption of both renewable and nonrenewable resources. This pressure applies alike to the planet's waters, forests, minerals, and energy resources. Pollution can be expected to become even more of a major health problem in all industrializing regions, notably China and other Third World countries. Amazonia and regions elsewhere in the world will continue to suffer heavily from deforestation. Maritime nations will be confronted with the problem of renewing fish stocks in areas already overharvested. Resource scarcities will increase in Third World societies. To reverse this situation will require creative social response and innovation, at once economic, social, technical, and political. Within a global perspective, we have to concern ourselves with the consequences of the increasing mutual vulnerability of the rich North and the impoverished South.

Developments in Science and Technology

The twentieth century has seen spectacular discoveries in science. With the continued acceleration and globalization of knowledge, we can expect to find scientific breakthroughs to be no less impressive and innovative in the coming century.

Science will not only greatly increase our knowledge of how the world is structured and acts but also will strongly affect our understanding of the "why" of existence, that is, our religious, philosophical, and moral beliefs. Applied science, such as in biology, can be expected to make further massive strides in genetic engineering in plants and animals, to accelerate our medical knowledge and techniques, and to pose important ethical questions resulting from an unprecedented capability to alter our species' genetic makeup.

As events in the twentieth century proved, while technology may be in itself morally neutral—as in the release of atomic energy—its uses almost invariably have either beneficial or detrimental effects for society. As we move into the twenty-first century, we find that technology is becoming fully global in dimensions and dynamics alike.

Technology increasingly dictates the structure and behavior of national and transnational business, security systems, information outlets and networks, as well as the curricula of schools and colleges. Technological innovation both creates new jobs and destroys old ones and hence requires continuous technical and cultural retooling of workers and professionals. In the twenty-first century these retooling processes are almost certain to accelerate as the technological order does its dynamic utmost to create a global village.

Tomorrow's communication world has already been anticipated by the Internet. This has been described as "a vast international network of networks that enables computers of all kinds to share services and communicate directly, as if they were part of one giant, seamless, global computing machine."[1] It has been called "the nearest thing to a working prototype of the information superhighway," linking together large commercial computer-communications services as well as tens of thousands of smaller university, government, and corporate networks. By 1994 the Internet reached some 25 million computer users and was doubling every year. A characteristic of the Internet is its "bottom-up" nature: It is the offspring of individuals and groups wanting "to create something for themselves and, more often than not, to share their creation with the rest of the Internet community."[2] Within this democratic spirit a cyberspace has been created "where everyone's words look the same, national boundaries and social distinctions become less important"—in short, the Internet is creating a "one-worldness" in which "people can get more closely connected based on common interests, mutual objectives, mutual need."[3]

Another specialized branch of technology that is certain to increase by leaps and bounds in the next century is automation and robotics. Automation has certain obvious advantages: Burdensome and repetitious manual tasks can be relegated to machines that perform them with a speed and precision human hands can never match. And automation can step up production and industrial output spectacularly. As postindustrial societies evolve in the coming century, it will become commonplace to have entire factories automated, with perhaps only a few supervising engineers on hand.

The Global Economy

Capitalism triumphed over state-controlled socialism in the twentieth century; in the twenty-first century we can expect to see the completed conversion of national economies to the market system. At the forefront of this conversion are the North's transnational corporations, making use of state-of-the-art industrial technology and managerial techniques. Japan leads the way in automating its industries. Automation of the manufacturing process signifies a new industrial revolution throughout the world and with it a massive challenge to the employment of work forces at the preautomation rate.

When the North's richest countries convened in Naples in 1994, they had some 35 million unemployed workers. They put this unemployment problem at the top of their agenda but failed to find a solution. Even in the South, with its low labor cost economies, the increasingly automated plants established by transnational corporations are having adverse consequences for employment. In March 1994, the International Labour Organization reported that 30 percent of the world's labor were either unemployed or underemployed—the worst situation since the Great Depression. Some 700 million people were unable to meet even minimum living standards. In the coming century, people throughout the world will have to cope with continuing large-scale unemployment, perhaps at an unprecedented level and much of it permanent.

Meanwhile, economies have to contend with the phenomenon described as the "revolution of rising expectations." Societies in the North long believed that every new generation would be richer, healthier, and better educated than its predecessors. These rising expectations are now shared by societies in the South. But they depend on a continuous increase in the use of the planet's resources, a high level of employment, and assured growth of a consumer type of society. Environmentalists warn that the present rate of resource consumption cannot continue indefinitely and that we should already be cutting back.

This warning strikes at the heart of the free enterprise system as we know it today. The concept of growth has always been considered essential to the structure and behavior of this system, which historically has made spectacular gains in producing goods and services and in raising living standards. But this growth ethos always assumes that abundant physical resources and energy can continue to satisfy all future requirements, whatever the scale. The twenty-first century will test this basic assumption as never before.

The testing will take place while the economic system undergoes a dynamic transformation. As the South's economies rapidly industrialize to catch up with the North—and in so doing increasingly drain the planet's reservoir of resources—the North's economies will shift progressively to a postindustrial stage of high-tech production and services, a stage that expects to do more with less consumption of physical resources while raising living standards still higher. Nevertheless, the overall consumption of global resources will continue to grow dramatically.

There is another kind of growth with which all economies will have to grapple in the next century: government debts. Already in the 1990s the size of the South's debts to the North's governments and banks had reached crisis proportions. Interest payments amounted to some $100 billion a year. They have become twice as large as the balance-of-trade account for the South as a whole, and almost seven times the size of trade balances for the net debtor countries. The debt crisis does not affect only the South. The inability of its economies to buy Northern goods and to pay interest to Northern banks results in turn in the loss of jobs in the North.

Each of the world's richest economies has acquired an unprecedented debt load. Here we encounter a paradoxical situation: Despite all the economic growth in the twentieth century, the next century will see countries saddled with national debts that have been increasing faster than the rate of GNP growth. Can this global debt crisis be reversed, and are we prepared to

shoulder the attending heavy political and social costs?

Within the North's economies, too, economic development has been occurring with widespread social implications for the future. Income inequality has widened, resulting in a growing divide between the rich and poor. In the United States, the gap between rich and poor has become so wide that the Organization for Economic Cooperation and Development warned that inequalities, particularly in health and education, threaten the country's long-term economy. In 1992, the wealthiest 20 percent of Americans received 14 times more after-tax income than did the bottom 20 percent. Meanwhile, for years the middle class has been falling behind in real income. Following the congressional elections in 1994, President Clinton called for a $60 billion tax cut; the Republicans called for double that amount. These tax cuts were bound to increase the federal debt unless entitlement programs were sharply reduced. Any such spending cuts would fall mainly on the poor, exacerbating an income gap already among the worst in the North. Numerous parts of the world are now experiencing ethnic and racial tensions and political fragmentation. In the United States and other rich societies, a rising danger for tomorrow lies not in political but in social fragmentation.

Nationalism and Internationalism

We can divide political structures into two broad categories: those that are national in size and behavior and those that are international, that is, transnational in scope and purposes. We find more entities in both categories than ever before in history. Given the strength of each, we will be confronted with an ongoing challenge: Can they be reconciled so as to coexist and strengthen each other, or will they act at cross-purposes and exacerbate, rather than solve, future global political issues, which may well involve war-and-peace decisions?

Several chapters in *Civilization Past & Present* have examined nationalism as a historical phenomenon. Nationalism, which constitutes loyalty to a group with common ties of language, race, culture, religion, or historical tradition, has been one of the most powerful forces in the development of the modern world. In 1993 there were 191 nation-states, of which 184 were members of the United Nations—more than three and a half times the number when the organization was created in 1945.

The nation-state system came into being with the Peace of Westphalia in 1648; it conferred on nation-states the attributes of sovereignty: national government; internationally recognized boundaries; and the right to have their own currency, armed forces, and to engage in diplomatic relations with one another. A primary claim under sovereignty is the unfettered right to act as the state wished within its own borders. But in an increasingly interdependent global society, how long can sovereignty be regarded as unfettered?

Nationalism has enriched global civilization by providing and sustaining many different patterns of national culture, thereby giving special meaning to the lives of members of national groups. On occasion it has provided the essential spirit that enabled people to withstand aggression—as in the case of the defenders of Leningrad against Hitler, and Londoners during the blitz in 1940. Conversely, nationalism has its negative and violent aspects. Pride in belonging to a particular political entity has often been accompanied by feelings of superiority over other groups. This characteristic has sometimes led directly to racism, a form of biological nationalism as expressed by Nazism's Aryan superiority and that led to the Holocaust and its gas chambers.

Nationalism has historically been associated with the development of Western societies and their creation of the nation-state system, but since World War II especially, it has been at the heart of decolonization and the creation of new countries in Asia and Africa. It has been a strong driving force in the ideological reconstruction of states in eastern Europe and in the reemergence of independent countries from republics of the former Soviet Union.

Historically, nationalism has taken two forms, described in a recent study by Michael Ignatieff as *civic* and *ethnic*.[4] The first type of nationalism regards the nation as composed of citizens possessing rights in common and sharing political values, practices, and institutions. In contrast, ethnic nationalism claims "that an individual's deepest attachments are inherited, not chosen. It is the national community that defines the individual, not the individuals who define the national community."[5] This psychology of belonging can be stronger than that of civic nationalism, but when it fails to create social cohesion, ethnic regimes all too often try to maintain unity by force rather than consent.

In this century, many federal states have tried to keep a balance between civic and ethnic forms of nationalism. The mid-1990s saw the brutal triumph of "ethnic cleansing" in the emergence of microstates that have replaced Yugoslavia, while what has been described as "tribal cleansing" cost a million dead in Rwanda. In the absence of an enforceable new world order, we see alarming indications that the nation-state system could be wrenched apart by ethnic civil wars. Given the demographic pressures of the next century, accompanied by increasing competition for limited resources, such conflicts could wreak tremendous havoc.

Paradoxically, the proliferation of new nation-states—and hence the fragmentation of the global political landscape—has been taking place at a time when, as never before in history, the forces of global integration are cutting across national boundaries. We see these forces creating free trade agreements among the United States, Canada, and Mexico in North America; a common market and political union embracing a dozen or more states in Europe; and new forms of transnational cooperation emerging in Asia.

The traditional nation-state players on the global stage have been joined, and progressively challenged, by other prominent actors: transnational corporations, intergovernmental organizations, and nongovernmental organizations, all of whose numbers have been increasing rapidly. The global networks of transnational corporations can determine the decisions of national governments, as shown in the passage of NAFTA and other international agreements. The proliferation of intergovernmental and nongovernmental organizations has been no less significant. These organizations cover every aspect of human activity on a global scale, and with the transnational corporations are busily creating for the next century a vast network of communication on an electronic superhighway.

What will this shift toward a global village do to our political systems and traditional beliefs and loyalties? Will nationalism and internationalism prove mutually exclusive? Will the nation-state as we now know it have to be radically altered because the unregulated sovereignty that it has practiced can no longer be tolerated in a world of nuclear arms and critical environmental, resource, and demographic problems? Or can nationalism and internationalism coexist in ways that are mutually beneficial, that is, within a new reciprocating relationship, summed up in the phrase, "Think globally, act locally"?

In the post–Cold War era, marked by long-standing national rivalries, intense ethnic and religious turmoil, poverty, and deep economic inequities, no one country can be expected to assume the role of global policeman. For this reason, governments have turned to the United Nations to take a stronger role in securing international peace. But to be effective, that organization in turn will have to be strengthened. Its member governments will have to make the UN's peacekeeping machinery more effective. The enforcement capacity of the UN Charter was largely ignored during the Cold War. The Charter envisaged the gradual conversion of the existing military setup into a worldwide system of collective security. "Such a system would be a giant step forward from the belated and improvised efforts to which the United Nations has so far been limited. . . . Governments, if they want the United Nations to be respected and taken seriously, will also have to respect its decisions, and make decisions that can if necessary be enforced. Such changes in attitude would be the best practical test of a commitment to a 'new world order.'"[6]

Social Changes and Challenges

At the international level, we will have to recognize that in an interdependent world peoples everywhere must be treated as social equals. Global acceptance of nondiscrimination could become critical as population/resource problems build up and regions in the South cry out for help. Realistic responses on the North's part will require not only aid and rehabilitation assistance to poorer societies at critical times, but also willingness by the richer economies to share a larger proportion of their own resources for the South's long-term development. Given the growing mutual vulnerability of the two great segments of the planet's peoples, such cooperation will be indispensable in the next century to make them mutually viable.

A related factor affecting North and South alike will be the massive movement of peoples. This has been constant throughout history, but its scale now is made unique by the speed of the process combined with the density of existing settlements. "Migration, both from within countries and across borders, is mounting."[7] Among the many millions of migrants are refugees fleeing from political conflicts and civil wars and seeking asylum beyond their national borders. These migration flows will pose mounting social and ethical questions for Northern societies when developing their immigration policies.

At the national level, we can expect that social change in the coming century will be marked by a continuation of the "liberation" movements that have become prominent in recent decades. They are characterized by "rights" that their proponents insist must be recognized as fundamental. The first deals with racial and ethnic minority rights; the second broad movement relates to women's rights. Female emancipation continues to be a long and difficult struggle for hundreds of millions of women in the South. Suffrage was won in this century by women in the North, but their attempts to gain commensurate economic and social rights continue to be protracted, with their gains too often begrudgingly yielded and circumscribed. "Coming out of the closet" is a familiar phrase associated with a third broad movement: the right of homosexuals to disclose their sexual preference without being ostracized or denied rights to full economic and social parity.

Related to these broad social changes will be the need to advance the role of education on a global scale. After decades of international efforts to eradicate illiteracy, over a billion adults still cannot read or write, and over 100 million children of primary school age are not able to attend school every year.[8] These problems exist primarily in the South where in the last 30 years the educational gap with the North has increased. A close correlation exists between national levels of education, the status of women, and fertility rates. When education is widely available to women, the average family size drops sharply, birth rates decline to socially manageable proportions, and health and living standards improve.[9]

In the developed countries of the North, the dynamics of widespread technological change will call for the continuing educational upgrading of the work force, with technical and professional programs geared to both training and retraining. In other words, education in the next century is likely to be regarded as a lifelong process for all citizens—not only because of the demands of economies to remain competitive in the global economy, but also because of the need for altering and enriching our understanding of why and how the world community is changing and what the privileges and accompanying responsibilities of world citizenry entail.

A historic change is occurring in the accumulation of knowledge and the ability of our educational system to assimilate information and deliver it effectively. Until modern times, humanity suffered from an overall paucity of knowledge whose acquisition emphasized much rote learning at school. Today, in sharp contrast, we have a plethora of information bombarding us from all directions and have ready access for retrieving it from data banks. In fact, we seem to be suffering progressively from information overload, and we run the risk as societies of becoming too complex and dysfunctional.

Are today's students controlled by the dictates of the computer and data bank, or are they being empowered to use the new technology creatively to solve problems and set meaningful goals? There is much experimentation these days in educational theory and pedagogy as educators recognize that fundamental change will be essential if our schools are to cope with tomorrow's many challenges.

Making the Human Condition Humane

Taken together, these changes and challenges in the next century pose what could be the most personally focused of questions: What will become of the character and quality of the human condition in the coming century?

Our age has been described as the century of the individual in a mass society. This is an age of mass thought and tastes in which economies of scale produce mass conformity. What happens to the individual in an age of bigness—big business, big labor, big government, big institutions? Will he or she be free to make fundamental personal choices and be autonomous, or instead become progressively manipulated to assume the role of automaton? The dystopia depicted in Huxley's *Brave New World* used as a tool to secure conformity a reliance on subliminal advertising, while Orwell's *1984* extirpated all humanitarian values and choices and recruited the latest technology to ensure mass acceptance of the beliefs and behavior dictated by "Big Brother," the apocryphal leader of a privileged elite.

The English philosopher Bertrand Russell has pointed out that humans engage concurrently in three types of conflict: with their physical environment, with their fellow humans, and with themselves. Because of our collective failure to resolve the first two types of conflict, many of us feel that we are being controlled by impersonal forces over which we have scant control as individuals. Possession of physical comforts does not allay our fears and frustrations but often strengthens feelings of guilt that compare our relative affluence with the plight of the less fortunate.

Paradoxically, the North's rich industrial societies have the world's highest living standards coupled with its highest incidence of suicide. This paradox of material plenty mated to psychological insecurity leads many to turn to medical technology to ease their tensions. One solution offered is tranquilizers, but then addiction to drugs threatens to get out of hand, a phenomenon that saps the physical and mental resources of all segments of the population. Closely related to the incidence of drugs is the problem of the pervasiveness and increasing incidence of crime. The U.S. Congress in 1994 passed a $30 billion crime bill designed to restrict gun sales, build more prisons, enact tougher laws, and recruit additional police. Will such deterrent measures control violence, or are there deeper issues that must also be addressed—poverty, homelessness, racial and ethnic discrimination—before our society can hope to be healed?

Despite these stark realities, it may also be true that Americans are too anxious about their anxieties. No creative age in history has been devoid of tensions and dangers. Indeed, these appear to be essential in providing the adrenaline that sparks the stimulus to seek out new worlds. Surely, they are no less required to provide the moral courage to right old wrongs and to confront individuals with the test of their own worth.

In the past, religious, political, and educational elites felt responsible for providing guidelines to enable society as a whole to remain integrated. Among them the intellectuals' task was to apply the processes of reason to both physical and social phenomena. However, in a century that has experienced so much of the violent and irrational in human behavior, the best educated among us sometimes seem to be paralyzed by a lack of belief in the continuing need of their traditional roles. Yet it will be no less true tomorrow than in an earlier and technologically primitive time that "Where there is no vision, the people perish."

Nowhere is the challenge to traditional values as fiercely contested as over the two issues of population control and abortion. With global population likely to reach 10 billion by 2050, ecologists and other scientists warn of a possible catastrophe. What shall we do? Ultimately the dilemma is a moral one and, as such, poses a challenge both to collective societal initiatives and to the individual's choice of conduct. If we have to decide how many human lives are "good" for the planet and its environment, then how do we balance this overall collective necessity with the fundamental question of the inherent worth, or sanctity, of an individual life?

THE CONTINUING RELEVANCE OF HISTORY

Shortly before he died in 1852, the Duke of Wellington, victor over Napoleon at Waterloo and possibly the most famous English public figure in the first half of the nineteenth century, feared that the years ahead would usher in a period of darkness and despair for his country. Yet despite the Iron Duke's jeremiad, the subsequent decades saw the British Empire reach its zenith. This example should serve as a warning to those who undertake to predict the shape of things to come, and especially to all prophets of gloom and doom.

Studying the Future

Throughout history, human striving and aspirations have been essential elements of problem solving. As we move into the twenty-first century, what is new is not the existence of problems but humankind's more acute awareness of them and of an impending need to solve them. What is also unique for our times is that these major problems and the challenges they present are truly global in dimension. If the challenges are great, so too are the numbers of people in every society who are deeply concerned about humankind's future prospects. In itself, this awareness bodes well for a creative collective response.

Lest we become complacent, we must ask ourselves: How much lead time do we have to make and then implement critical decisions for a global-scale civilization that is changing at accelerating speed? The most intelligent planning can be thwarted by sociocultural inertia, that is, by an inherent resistance to basic changes. A large, complex society can be likened to a supertanker whose size and momentum prevent it from coming to a stop for many miles. To pursue this analogy, those concerned about the future have no intention of trying to halt society in its tracks. Even if that were possible, a sudden stoppage could prove catastrophic. Rather they seek to alert society to be ready to change course. This requires not only the charting of alternative routes but also ensuring that all concerned are fully alerted to the need for a change of direction and will, in turn, accept the new destination. The critical factors here are awareness and timing, because setting a new course cannot wait for the storm that could engulf us if unprepared. We must develop contingency plans well in advance and be ready to act on them.

The Relevance of History: Three Views

With our society in the midst of accelerating change and intellectual turbulence, we may well ask what relevance knowledge of the past has for an age undergoing global transformation. Three American historians have presented timely but different views.

According to David Donald of Harvard University, undergraduates want "an understanding of how the American past relates to present and future." Americans once enjoyed an abundance of land and resources that enabled them to develop distinctive ways of coping with social problems. But that age of abundance has ended. "The people of plenty have become the people of paucity." If we save what is left of our natural resources, we choke our economy; if we use it, we impoverish our posterity. "Consequently, the 'lessons' taught by the American past are today not merely irrelevant but dangerous. We can no longer answer demands for equalizing the rewards of our society by cooking up a bigger pie." So what can a historian tell undergraduates that might help them in this new age? "Perhaps my useful function would be to disenthrall them from the spell of history, to help them see the irrelevance of the past, to assist them in understanding what Lincoln meant in saying, 'The dogmas of the quiet past are inadequate to the stormy present.'"[10]

In reply, Edward Keenan, also of Harvard, argues that relevance is contingent on context and mode of thought. To him, the question is not *whether* but *how* history is relevant. Focusing on Donald's interpretation of American history, Keenan suggests that by placing it in a broader context, we can derive a different meaning from the facts in question. Other nations have also depleted their resources and found themselves with problems far greater than those of the United States. What is "dangerous" is not so much the lessons of the past as the risk of being drawn by present preoccupations into a one-sided, materialistic view of that past. The "most crucial resources are human resources, those embodied in a highly trained, inventive, and responsive citizenry. Such resources we still have, even in our present travail, in an abundance that is the child of our abundance."[11]

For her part, Blanche Cook of City University of New York argues that the fact that "the age of simple abundance for a small class is coming to an end is no cause for despair. . . . History is about time and change and people." The West never did possess unlimited resources of its own; it controlled resource-rich territories that are now sovereign. We have now to recognize their independence. "Such change demands accommodation. For our survival we must seek a world order based on the recognition of planetary scarcity and mutual need. That is progress." People alone are capable of progress, because they can control their own destinies. We live in revolutionary times, and "revolution is a process, not an event." Historians "must avoid the temptation to become antiquarians. During World War II, the great French historian Marc Bloch, a victim

of the Holocaust, wrote of the difference: 'Antiquarians revere buildings and institutions. They romanticize the past. Historians are citizens of the present who love life.'"[12]

"Telling the Truth About History"

In recent years, the traditional values of American society have been subjected to intense scrutiny and criticism. Long-venerated certainties are now being challenged, coupled with broad skepticism of the claims of academic disciplines, including history, to provide objective knowledge and truth. Critics contend that all knowledge is laden with values and ideological bias, and to some the American past is basically a mythology camouflaging power wielded by white, male, capitalist elites.

Three historians have analyzed the causes of this state of affairs and offer a prescription for its cure.[13] They begin by pointing to the role of eighteenth-century science as the "heroic" model to combat superstition and tyranny and that promised a neutral, value-free, objective view of reality. Physics' success led to its emulation by other disciplines, including history. In the 1830s, Leopold von Ranke emphasized mastery of "facts" to record "exactly what happened." This became the motto for a scientific and objective type of history.

Later historians, however, showed that these "facts" were not neutral or objective, but reflected biases of gender, class, and race.[14] Charles Beard demonstrated the role of economic interests in making the U.S. Constitution, while social historians in the 1960s revealed the extent to which minorities—Jews, blacks, Catholics, women, and the poor—had been marginalized or ignored in traditional works. Meanwhile, social historians of science showed that scientific research was hardly neutral or value free. Literary theorists analyzed the rhetoric and narrative style employed in historical writing and concluded that it was no more authoritative than novels or poetry.

What has evolved is a new form of criticism attacking the foundations of science and history. Challenging convictions about the objectivity of knowledge and the stability of language, postmodernism renders problematic all belief in progress. According to the postmodernist thesis, it is impossible in historical writing to distinguish between cause and effect or to sort out text from context; yesterday's objectivity and certainty have been replaced by subjectivity and relativism. Postmodernism will continue to exert a profound impact on the study and writing of history. But the three historians cited above contend forcefully that historians can write intelligible and just accounts of history by approaching it in terms of practical realism. Views of the past are constructed by the historian, but it is possible to establish correspondences between that past and the historian's account of it. "One representation of the past is not as good as another, for the documents and material remains are there to be consulted and checked by fellow-historians; the experiment can be replicated and errors exposed. It is therefore not difficult to discriminate between competing accounts of past reality."[15]

Talk about the future of history pivots around the question of how best to deploy the passion to know. Focusing that passion is the investigators' belief that the past can reveal an aspect of what it is to be human. The desire to touch the past is a yearning to master time, to anchor oneself in worldliness, to occupy fully one's own historical context by studying its antecedents. Given the immediacy of human passion, the present is always implicated in the study of the past. Lived experience alters the questions historians ask, foreclosing some research agendas while inspiring new ones. This sensitivity of historians to the lived moment is particularly visible at times of deep and significant historical change such as the world is witnessing now.[16]

If we are indeed moving toward a new type of civilization—one progressively multicultural and transnational—we shall have to present humankind's historical experiences from a planetary perspective. In the convergence of once-compartmentalized political, economic, and social structures, we have to learn to think in new ways. The planet's peoples can no longer be regarded as a collection of disconnected entities but as interconnected segments of a planetary societal system. As part of our conceptual reorientation, we will need to study humanity's historic encounters and experiences within a global matrix—in other words, world history for a world community.

Acquiring this new perspective will not be easy, especially given the diverse problems confronting the residents of the next century. But problems and people's determination to solve

them have always been part of what it means to be human. We can be certain that as the problems we now foresee are solved, others will take their place. Yet it is by responding creatively to these challenges that humankind has been able to realize its extraordinary potential. Ruminating on this historic process, an outstanding philosopher of modern times, Alfred North Whitehead, has written:

One main factor in the upward trend of animal life has been the power of wandering. . . . Animals wander into new conditions. They have to adapt themselves or die. Mankind has wandered from the trees to the plains, from the plains to the seacoast, from climate to climate, from continent to continent, and from habit of life to habit of life. When man ceases to wander, he will cease to ascend in the scale of being. Physical wandering is still important, but greater still is the power of man's spiritual adventures. . . .

The very benefit of wandering is that it is dangerous. . . . The future will disclose dangers . . . pessimism over the future of the world comes from a confusion between civilization and security. In the immediate future there will be less security than in the immediate past, less stability. . . . But, on the whole, the great ages have been unstable ages.[17]

History's role can be likened to Janus, the Roman god who had two opposite faces. History enables us to view and appreciate the past as past and, in turn, to visualize the past and present as prologue to the future. Past and present conjoin to alert us to the need not only to engage in new forms of planning for the years ahead, but no less to be willing to rethink our existing social goals and value systems. The historical evolution of humanity is open-ended: Far from being immutable, its beliefs, values, and goals are continuously changing. Here the historical record becomes invaluable because it can provide us with what we will continue to require: as long and accurate a perspective as possible in order to make realistic analyses of contemporary problems that are global in scope and to take appropriate kinds of action to safeguard our planetary inheritance and improve our quality of life.

Viewed from this perspective, our Epilogue becomes a Prologue to a new stage of human "wandering," of encountering new dangers, yet buoyed by the prospect of attaining a more humane societal order. Our Paleolithic ancestors inhabited a single, socially undifferentiated planet. Since then, their descendants have spiraled through stages of progressive control of the environment and increasing complexity of economic activity, social organization, and political decision making until today we find ourselves still inhabiting a single but now highly differentiated and interrelated planet. One species as ever, occupying innumerable ecological and cultural niches within a shared global ecosystem. A new chapter in our irreversible history is being written. The story line is still far from clear, and the plot will have its full share of surprises. But it is certain to prove interesting. . . .

Notes

1. Philip Elmer-Dewitt, "Battle for the Soul of the Internet," *Time*, July 25, 1994, p. 42.
2. Gregory B. Newby, *Directory of Directories on the Internet: A Guide to Information Services* (Westport, London: Meckler, 1994), p. 2.
3. Barbara Kantrowitz and Adam Rogers, "The Birth of the Internet," *Newsweek*, August 8, 1994, p. 58.
4. Michael Ignatieff, *Blood and Belonging: Journeys into the New Nationalism* (New York: Penguin Books, 1994).
5. Ignatieff, *Blood and Belonging*, pp. 7–8.
6. Brian Urquhart, former Undersecretary General of the United Nations, "Learning from the Gulf," *The New York Review of Books*, March 7, 1991, pp. 34–37.
7. United Nations, Department of Economic and Social Development, *Report on the World Social Situation 1993* (New York: United Nations, 1993), p. 3.
8. UNDP, *Human Development Report 1992* (New York: Oxford University Press, 1992), p. 2.
9. Paul Kennedy, *Preparing for the Twenty-first Century* (New York: HarperCollins, 1993), pp. 339–343.
10. David H. Donald, "Our Irrelevant History," *The New York Times*, September 8, 1977.
11. Edward L. Keenan, "One Harvard Historian to Another," *The New York Times*, September 26, 1977.
12. Blanche Wissen Cook, "A Response," American Historical Association *Newsletter*, December 1977.
13. Joyce Appleby, Lynn Hunt, and Margaret Jacob, *Telling the Truth About History* (New York: W. W. Norton, 1994).
14. See *Theory and Practice in Historical Study: A Report of the Committee on Historiography*, Bulletin 54, Social Science Research Council, New York, 1946.
15. Keith Thomas, "Coming to Terms with the Death of Certainty," Book Review of *Telling the Truth About History*, in the *Guardian Weekly*, September 18, 1994.
16. Appleby et al., *Telling the Truth About History*, p. 271.
17. Alfred North Whitehead, *Science and the Modern World* (New York: New American Library, 1953), pp. 207–208.

Credits

Color Photographs

Portfolio One following p. 64
1   Alex Greely/Alpha/FPG
2   (BOTH) Copyright the British Museum
3   Erich Lessing/Art Resource, New York
4   (L) Copyright the British Museum
4   (R) Robert Frerck/Odyssey Productions, Chicago
5   Hirmer Fotoarchiv, Munich
6   (T) Robert Frerck/Odyssey Productions, Chicago
6   (C) Scala/Art Resource, New York
6   (B) Robert Frerck/Odyssey Productions, Chicago
7   Scala/Art Resource, New York
8   Giovanni Paolo Pannini, *The Interior of the Pantheon, Rome*, c.1734/1735, Samuel H. Kress Collection, © 1994 Board of Trustees National Gallery of Art, Washington, D.C.

Portfolio Two following p. 192
1   Gian Berto Vanni/Art Resource, New York
2   (T) Courtesy of The Cultural Relics Bureau, Beijing and The Metropolitan Museum of Art
2   (B) Copyright the British Museum
3   Chinese and Japanese Special Fund, Courtesy, Museum of Fine Arts, Boston
4   Eugene Fuller Memorial Collection/Seattle Art Museum
5   SuperStock, Inc.
6   Robert Frerck/Odyssey Productions, Chicago
7   (T) Copyright the British Museum
7   (B) Ife Museum
8   (T) St. Louis Art Museum, Gift of Morton D. May
8   (BL&BR) Lee Boltin

Portfolio Three following p. 320
1   (L) The Board of Trinity College, Dublin
1   (R) Copyright the British Museum
2   Pierpont Morgan Library
3   Scala/Art Resource, New York
4   (T) Scala/Art Resource, New York
4   (B) Erich Lessing/Art Resource, New York
5   (T) Scala/Art Resource, New York
5   (B) Scala/Art Resource, New York
6   Scala/Art Resource, New York
7   (T) English Heritage as Trustees of Iveagh Bequest, Kenwood
7   (B) Saskia/Art Resource, New York
8   The Metropolitan Museum of Art, Gift of Henry G. Marquand, 1889. Marquand Collection (89.15.21)

Portfolio Four following p. 448
1   (T) (45.9) Freer Gallery of Art, The Smithsonian Institution, Washington, D.C.

1   (B) Four By Five/SuperStock, Inc.
2   (T) *Prunis Vase (Meiping) with Blossoming Lotus: Fahug Ware.* Porcelain with polychrome glazes, H.37.5 cm. China, Jiangxi Province, Jingdezhen kilns, late 15th century, Ming dynasty. The Cleveland Museum of Art, 1994, Bequest of John L.Severance, 42.716.
2   (B) Tokyo National Museum
3   (T&B) Lee Boltin
4   Map Division/New York Public Library, Astor, Lenox and Tilden Foundations
5   The British Library
6   (T) Werner Forman/Art Resource, New York
6   (B) Wieckmann Collection, Ulm Museum
7   Pierpont Morgan Library/Art Resource
8   (T) Andre Gamet/Rapho/Photo Researchers
8   (B) The Metropolitan Museum of Art, Rogers Fund, 1928 (28.195.2)

Portfolio Five following p. 544
1   Giraudon/Art Resource, New York
2   Bridgemann/Art Resource, New York
3   (TL) Giraudon/Art Resource, New York
3   (TR) Sir Joshua Reynolds, *Lady Elizabeth Delmé and Her Children*, 1777–1779, Andrew W. Mellon Collection, © 1994 Board of Trustees, National Gallery of Art, Washington, D.C.
3   (B) Erich Lessing/Art Resource, New York
4   Erich Lessing/Art Resource, New York
5   (T) Fridmar Damm/Leo de Wys
5   (B) The Metropolitan Museum of Art, Wolfe Fund, 1931. Catharine Lorillard Wolfe Collection (31.45)
6   Steve Vidler/Leo de Wys
7   Scala/Art Resource, New York
8   (T) The Metropolitan Museum of Art, Bequest of Mary Stillman Harkness, 1950 (50.145.8)
8   (B) Giraudon/Art Resource, New York

Portfolio Six following p. 672
1   The Metropolitan Museum of Art, Gift of Harry Payne Bingham, 1940 (40.175)
2   Claude Monet, French, 1840–1926, *Water Lilies*, oil on canvas, 1906, 87.6 × 92.7 cm., Mr. and Mrs. Martin A. Ryerson Collection, 1933.1157. The Art Institute of Chicago. All Rights Reserved.
3   (TL) Mary Cassatt, American, 1844–1926, *The Bath*, oil on canvas, 1891/92, 39-1/2 × 26 in., Robert A. Waller Fund, 1910.2. The Art Institute of Chicago. All Rights Reserved.
3   (TR) Pierre August Renoir, French, 1841–1919, *Two Sisters on the Terrace*, oil on canvas, 1881, 100.5 × 81 cm., Mr. and Mrs. Lewis Larned Coburn Memorial Collection, 1933.455. The Art Institute of Chicago. All Rights Reserved.
3   (B) The Metropolitan Museum of Art, Bequest of Mrs. H. O. Havemeyer, 1929. The H. O. Havemeyer Collection (29.100.128)

4 Erich Lessing/Art Resource, New York
5 (T) Erich Lessing/Art Resource, New York
5 (B) Guildhall Art Gallery, London
6 (T) Giraudon/Art Resource, New York
6 (B) Vincent Van Gogh, *The Starry Night*. New York. (1889). Oil on canvas, 29 × 36-1/4″. The Museum of Modern Art, New York. Acquired through the Lillie P. Bliss Bequest. Photograph © 1995 The Museum of Modern Art, New York.
7 Philadelphia Museum of Art, George W. Elkins Collection
8 Musée D'Orsay, Paris

Portfolio Seven following p. 768
1 Samuel Finley Breese Morse ((1791–1872) *Gallery of the Louvre*, 1831-33, oil on canvas, 73-3/4 × 108 in. (187.3 × 274.3 cm) Terra Foundation for the Arts, Daniel J. Terra Collection, 1992.51. Photograph © 1994 Terra Museum of American Art, Chicago
2 (T) St. Louis Art Museum
2 (B) New York Public Library, Astor, Lenox and Tilden Foundations
4 (T) South Australian Museum
4 (B) Robert Frerck/Odyssey Productions, Chicago
5 (T) Musée de l'Homme, Paris
5 (B) Werner Forman/Art Resource, New York
6 (T) The British Library
6 (B) Laurie Platt Winfrey, Inc.
7 Mariners' Museum, Newport News, Virginia, Carl H. Boehringer Collection
8 Eisei Bunko, Tokyo

Portfolio Eight following p. 928
1 Pablo Picasso. *Girl Before a Mirror* Boisgeloup, March 1932. Oil on canvas, 64 × 51-1/4″. The Museum of Modern Art, New York. Gift of Mrs. Simon Guggenheim. Photograph © 1995 The Museum of Modern Art, New York. © 1996 Artists Rights Society, Inc./SPADEM, Paris
2 (T) Salvador Dali. *The Persistence of Memory* (Persistence de la mémoire). 1931. Oil on canvas, 9-1/2 × 13″. The Museum of Modern Art, New York. Given anonymously. Photograph © 1995 The Museum of Modern Art, New York.
2 (B) Tate Gallery, London/Art Resource, © 1996 Artists Rights Society, Inc. ADAGP, Paris
3 The Nelson-Atkins Museum of Art, Kansas City, Missouri, Gift of William Inge 56-128
4 Hirshhorn Museum and Sculpture Garden, Smithsonian Institute, Gift of Joseph H. Hirshhorn, 1966. Photo: Lee Stalsworth
5 The Cleveland Museum of Art
6 (TL) Andy Warhol. *Campbell's Soup*. (1965). Oil silkscreened on canvas 36-1/8 × 24″. The Museum of Modern Art, New York. Philip Johnson fund. Photograph © 1995 The Museum of Modern Art, New York.
6 (TR) Roy Lichtenstein. The Metropolitan Museum of Art, Purchase, Lila Acheson Wallace, Gift, Arthur Hoppock Hearn Fund, Arthur Lejwa Fund in honor of Jean Arp, the Bernhill Fund, Joseph H. Hazen Foundation, Inc., Samuel I. Newhouse Foundation, Inc., Walter Bareiss, Marie Bannon McHenry, Louise Smith and Stephen C. Swid Gifts, 1980. (1980.420)
6 (B) Collection Walker Art Center, Minneapolis, Gift of the T. B. Walker Foundation, 1966.
7 (T) Tate Gallery, London/Art Resource
7 (B) Alexander Calder, *Lobster Trap and Fish Tail* (1939). Hanging mobile: painted steel wire and sheet aluminum, about 8′ 6″ high × 9′ 6″ diameter. Collection, The Museum of Modern Art, New York. Commissioned by the Advisory Committee for the stairwell of the Museum.
8 (T) Schalkwisk/Art Resource
8 (B) © 1987 Siggraph

Black and White Photographs
9 Naturhistorisches Museum, Vienna
10 Ministry of Works, England
14 Hirmer Fotoarchiv, Munich
17 Giraudon/Art Resource, New York
19 Courtesy, Museum of Fine Arts, Boston
21 Ace Williams/Black Star
23 The Metropolitan Museum of Art, Museum Excavations, 1926–1929 and Rogers Fund, 1930 (30.3.31)
24 Hirmer Fotoarchiv, Munich
25 The Metropolitan Museum of Art, Carnarvon Collection, Gift of Edward S. Harkness, 1926 (26.7.1394)
26 Agyptisches Museum, Berlin/Staatliche Museen Preussischer Kulturbesitz
27 Agyptisches Museum, Berlin/Staatliche Museen Preussischer Kulturbesitz
30 P.35076/N.22200/Oriental Institute, The University of Chicago
31 Erich Lessing/Art Resource, New York
36 P.20949/N.23522/Oriental Institute, The University of Chicago
43 (T) Hirmer Fotoarchiv, Munich
43 (B) Hirmer Fotoarchiv, Munich
44 Hirmer Fotoarchiv, Munich
45 National Museum, Athens
50 Copyright the British Museum
52 Hirmer Fotoarchiv, Munich
53 Scala/Art Resource, New York
55 TAP Service/Acropolis Museum, Athens
59 Copyright the British Museum
65 (L) Hirmer Fotoarchiv, Munich
65 (C) Hirmer Fotoarchiv, Munich
65 (R) Hirmer Fotoarchiv, Munich
66 Scala/Art Resource, New York
77 Alinari/Art Resource, New York
80 Giraudon/Art Resource, New York
88 Roger-Viollet
89 (T) Copyright the British Museum
89 (B) Alinari/Art Resource, New York
91 National Trust/Art Resource, New York
94 The Metropolitan Museum of Art, Rogers Fund, 1903 (03.14.13)
96 Archives Photographiques, Paris
97 Alinari/Art Resource, New York
108 Pakistan National Museum
112 National Museum, Naples
119 (T) Brown Brothers
119 (B) Seattle Art Museum, Eugene Fuller Memorial Collection
121 Academia Sinica, Taipei
122 East Asian Library, Columbia University
123 Freer Gallery of Art, The Smithsonian Institution, Washington, D.C.
130 Seth Joel/Laurie Platt Winfrey, Inc.
133 AP/Wide World
143 Hebrew University, Jerusalem. Photo: Helene Bieberkraut
147 Hirmer Fotoarchiv, Munich
150 Alinari/Art Resource, New York

435 ACL, Brussels
438 The Huntington Library and Art Gallery, San Marino, CA.
439 A. H. Robbins Co.
446 AP/Wide World
453 Giraudon/Art Resource, New York
454 By courtesy of the Victoria & Albert Museum
459 Ewing Galloway
460 DeBry, VOYAGES 1606
461 Korean Cultural Center
465 Orion Press, Tokyo
466 The Art Institute of Chicago. All Rights Reserved.
469 Bob Landback/Black Star
474 Schloss Charlottenburg, Berlin
480 Service Photographique de la Reunion des Musées Nationaux
486 Rijksmuseum Foundation, Amsterdam
489 Danish Royal Collection of Rosenborg Castle, Copenhagen
491 Library of Congress
494 Giraudon/Art Resource, New York
503 (T) Verlag Gundermann
506 City of Bristol Museum and Art Gallery
508 Reproduced from the original in Bedfordshire Record Office
513 (T) The Metropolitan Museum of Art, Gift of Mr. and Mrs. Herbert N. Straus, 1928
513 (B) Bettmann Archive
515 Alinari/Art Resource, New York
518 SOVFOTO
520 The Rhode Island Historical Society
522 Nationalgalerie, Berlin/Staatliche Museen Preussischer Kulturbesitz
523 Courtesy of Hillwood Museum, Washington, D.C.
525 Austrian National Library, Vienna
534 Universitätsbibliothek, Basel
537 Jacques Louis David/Bulloz
539 Copyright the British Museum
540 Marburg/Art Resource, New York
541 Barenreiter-Verlag
546 Collection of Lord Harrowby, Sandon Hall, Stafford, England
552 National Portrait Gallery, London
554 From Clark, An Album of Methodist History, Abingdon Press
563 The British Library
568 Library of Congress
570 Independence National Historical Park Collection/Eastern National Parks and Monuments Association
575 Bulloz
576 Bulloz
578 (T) Bulloz
578 (B) Bulloz
580 Bulloz
581 Spencer Collection/New York Public Library, Astor, Lenox and Tilden Foundations
582 ACL, Brussels
596 Library of Congress
597 The Metropolitan Museum of Art
601 Mary Evans Picture Library
603 Hulton Deutsch Collection Ltd.
604 The British Library
606 National Maritime Museum, Greenwich, England
612 Courtesy, Museum of Fine Arts, Boston
613 Milt & Joan Mann/Cameramann International, Ltd.
615 The Minneapolis Institute of Arts

620 Giraudon/Art Resource, New York
623 Service Photographique de la Reunion des Musées Nationaux
626 Prints Division/New York Public Library, Astor, Lenox and Tilden Foundations
628 Organization of American States
632 John Freeman/FOTOMAS INDEX
634 The British Library
635 Library of Congress
636 Copyright the British Museum
639 (T) Ewing Galloway
639 (B) Mansell Collection
644 Copyright the British Museum
648 Mary Evans Picture Library
649 Science Museum, London
652 From Gustav Doré and Blanchard Jerrold, London: A Pilgrimage, Grant & Co., London, 1872
654 Rheinisches Bildarchiv, Cologne
655 From the Collections of Henry Ford Museum & Greenfield Village
656 Mansell Collection
657 Mansell Collection
663 Culver Pictures
665 Culver Pictures
666 National Library of Medicine, Bethesda, Maryland
667 AP/Wide World
668 Bettmann Archive
669 Roger-Viollet
671 UPI/Bettmann
674 John Freeman/FOTOMAS INDEX
675 Bibliothèque Nationale, Paris
676 The Metropolitan Museum of Art, Rogers Fund, 1921 (21.36.138)
677 National Portrait Gallery, London
678 Bettmann Archive
680 Pablo Picasso, Three Musicians, 1921. (summer). Oil on canvas, 6′ 7″ × 7′ 3-3/4″. The Museum of Modern Art, New York. Mrs. Simon Guggenheim Fund.
681 Mary Evans Picture Library
686 Bibliothèque Nationale, Paris
687 Bettmann Archive
689 Bibliothèque Nationale, Paris
690 L'Illustration, September 30, 1848
692 Copyright the British Museum
693 Roger-Viollet
694 Alinari/Art Resource, New York
697 Historisches Bildarchiv, Bad Berneck
699 Staatliche Museen Preussischer Kulturbesitz
701 State Historical Museum, Moscow
703 Weidenfeld & Nicolson Ltd.
711 The Museum of London
715 Bibliothèque Nationale, Paris
717 Historical Pictures/Stock Montage, Inc.
719 SOVFOTO
720 Copyright the British Museum
730 Library of Congress
731 (T) Australian News & Information Bureau
731 (B) Museo Nacional Historia Castillo de Chapultepec
734 Library of Congress
736 Tasmanian Museum
737 National Archives of Canada
742 Hampton University Museum, Hampton, Virginia
743 (T) Baker Library, Harvard Business School
743 (B) Library of Congress
746 Library of Congress
748 Instituto Nacional de Bellas Artes

Index ➤

Caravaggio [kah-rah-*vahd*-joh], Michelangelo da, 409

Caribs, 438, 440

Carlsbad Decrees, 688

Carmelites, 381–382

Carnot [kar-*noh*], Lazare, 581

Carol (Romanian king), 838

Carolingians [kar-uh-*lihn*-jee-uhnz], 275–276, 283, 299, 301–305, 307

Carolowitz, peace of, 601

Carpentier [kar-pon-tee-*ay*], Georges, 847

Carriera, Rosalba, 540

Carter, Jimmy, 955, 980, 982, 1012–1013

Carthage [*kahr*-thij], 76, 81–82, 84, 98–99, 235

Carthusians, 286

Cartwright, Edmund, 644

Cartwright, John, 573

Cartwright, Thomas, 394

Carver, George Washington, 742–743

Cassatt, Mary, 679

Cassiodorus, 283

Caste system, 110–111, 206

Castiglione, Baldassare [bahl-dahs-*sah*-ray kah-steel-*yoh*-nay], 337, 348

Castile [kah-*steel*], 320–321, 389, 417

Castlereagh [kassl-*ray*], Lord, 636, 638

Castro, Fidel, 948, 950, 1024

Catal Hüyük [*shah*-tahl hoo-yook] excavation, 7, 9

Catalonia, 389

Cateau-Cambrésis [kah-*toh* kahn-bray-*see*], treaty of, 391–393

Cathedrals, 280–281

Catherine I, 491

Catherine II, 491, 496, 523–524, 544, 698, 721

Catherine of Aragon, 370

Catholic Emancipation Act, 702, 709

Catholicism, 141, 148, 168, 267, 345, 359–382, 387–402, 426–428, 430–431, 439, 478, 484, 487, 533–534, 562–563, 566, 622, 630, 702, 709–710, 712, 731, 737–738

Catholic Reformation, 359–360, 378, 380–382, 387–402

Cato [*kay*-toh] the Elder, 80

Catullus [kuh-*tull*-us], 98

Caudillos [kor-*dee*-yos], 746–748

Cavendish, Henry, 536

Cave paintings, 6

Cavour, Camillo Benso di [kah-*mee*-loh dee kah-*voor*], 685, 693–695

Ceausescu, Nicolae [nee-koh-*lie* chow-*shehs*-koo], 968–969

Cellini [cheh-*lee*-nee], Benvenuto, 346–347

Celts [kelts], 268–269, 283

Central Intelligence Agency (CIA), 954, 958

Central Powers, 806–814

Ceruti [seh-*roo*-tee], Giacomo, 515

Cervantes [suhr-*vahn*-tays], Miguel de, 352–353

Cetshwayo, 759

Ceuta [*soo*-tah], 418

Ceylon [see-*lahn*], 117, 135, 436, 486, 780

Cézanne [say-*zahn*], Paul, 679–680

Chabray, Louison, 576

Chad, 1019

Chaeronea [ker-oh-*nee*-ah], battle of, 56

Chaldean empire, 29, 32–33, 35–36

Chamberlain, Houston Stewart, 670

Chamberlain, Neville, 916–918, 920–924

Champa, 468

Champagne, 272

Champlain, Samuel de, 437

Chams, 466

Chandernagore, 483

Chandragupta, Maurya [mow-ree-uh chun-druh-*goop*-tuh], 115–116

Changamire, 434, 598

Ch'ang-an, 129–130, 209, 211, 219

Chaplin, Charlie, 846–847

Chardin [shar-*dan*], Jean, 539

Charlemagne [*shahr*-leh-mayn], 161, 192, 275–276, 279, 301–305

Charles I (Austrian emperor), 814

Charles I (English king), 404–406, 439

Charles II (English king), 486–487, 493, 562, 599

Charles II (Spanish king), 484

Charles V (Holy Roman emperor), 345, 359, 362–363, 365–366, 369–370, 388–389, 422, 427, 435, 447, 450, 479

Charles VII (French king), 318

Charles VIII (French king), 344

Charles IX (French king), 392

Charles X (French king), 686

Charles XI (Swedish king), 483–484

Charles XII (Swedish king), 492

Charles Albert (Sardinian king), 691

Charles the Bald, 305

Charles the Bold, 319

Charles Frederick of Baden, 525

Chartism, 703

Château-Thierry [sha-*toh* tier-ree], battle of, 813

Chatelet [sha-teh-*lay*], Emile du, 536, 543

Chaucer, Geoffrey [*jef*-ree *chaw*-suhr], 279–280

Cheka, 857–858

Chekhov, Anton, 679

Chernenko, Konstantin, 954, 956

Cherokees, 573

Chernobyl reactor meltdown, 957, 963–964, 977, E-2

Chesterfield, Lord, 516, 565

Chia-ch'ing [jee-*ah*-ching], 612

Chiang Kai-shek [jee-*ahng* kye-*shek*], 886–888, 911, 1000, 1005

Chicago, 845

Chichen Itza [chih-chen et-*sah*], 255–256

Chicherin, Georgi Vasilievich, 912

Chichimecs [chee-chee-mex], 255–256, 429

Ch'ien-lung [jee-*ehn* luhng], 609–610, 612, 782

Chile [*chil*-ee, *chee*-lay], 259, 423, 429, 628, 731, 746, 750, 1024–1025

Chimu [*chee*-moo] kingdom, 259–260

China, 5, 105–106, 120, 134–137, 156, 215, 217, 220–221, 416, 420, 460–462, 468–469, 605, 745, 793, 798, 816, 927

Ch'in dynasty, 127–130
Ch'ing dynasty, 782–783
Chou dynasty, 122–127
Communist Revolution, 1000–1001
early twentieth century, 882, 884–888, 911–912, 914, 940
Han dynasty, 130–134, 207
late twentieth century, 941, 946, 948, 953, 955, 980, 1001–1006, 1008–1009, E-2, E-4
Manchu dynasty, 459–460, 608–612, 782–788, 885
Ming dynasty, 445, 456–460, 609, 782
under Mongols, 222–229
Shang dynasty, 120–122
Sung dynasty, 207, 209, 213–215, 456–457
T'ang dynasty, 207–212, 214–215, 217, 219, 223
Yuan dynasty, 225–229, 456–457
Ch'in dynasty [chihn, cheen], 127–130, 212, 224
Ch'in Liang-yu, 459
Chin P'ing Mei, 457–458
Chola, 207
Cholula, ambush at, 421
Chopin, Frédéric [fray-day-*reek* shoh-*pan*], 680
Chou [joh] dynasty, 122–127
Chou Enlai [joh en-*lye*], 888, 1004
Christian IV, 399
Christianity, 29, 90–91, 94, 101, 135, 178, 180, 187, 195–196, 240–242, 426–428, 430–431, 465, 594, 596, 609, 611, 654, 895, 1014–1015
during Enlightenment, 545–546
medieval, 277, 282–295, 300
nineteenth century, 662–665
during Renaissance, 332, 334–336, 339, 343, 351
in Roman empire, 141–155
Christina, 400
Chrysoloras [krih-suh-*lawr*-uhs], Manuel, 334
Chuang-tzu [jwahng dzuh], 125
Chu Hsi [joo she], 214–215
Ch'ung-cheng, 460

Church of England. *See* Anglicanism
Churchill, Sarah, 493
Churchill, Winston, 710, 807, 861, 920, 924–925, 927, 930, 932, 940, 943–944, 988
Cicero [*sis*-uh-roh], Marcus Tullius, 58, 98, 100, 333, 335, 337, 349
Cid [seed], El, 279
Cistercians [sis-*tur*-shuhnz], 286–287
Civilization, defined, 9–11
Civil Rights Act, 979
Civil War (U.S.), 741–742
Clark, William, 728
Classicism, 474–475
Claudius, 90
Clay, Henry, 740
Clayton Antitrust Act, 744
Cleisthenes [*klice*-thee-neez], 48–49
Clemençeau, Georges [zhorzh klay-mahn-*soh*], 814–816, 818, 820
Clement V, 292
Clement VII, 332
Clement VIII, 396
Clement of Alexandria, 149
Cleopatra, 88–89
Cleves [kleevz], 487
Clinton, Bill, 983, 1005, 1016, E-6
Clitherow, Margaret, 394
Clovis [*kloh*-vihs] I, 300
Cluniac reforms, 286
Cochin China, 781
Code Napoléon, 585, 622, 624, 630, 686
Coen [koon], Jan Pieterszoon, 436
Coeur family, 275
Colbert, Jean Baptiste [zhahn ba-*teest* kohl-*bayr*], 482–483, 492, 518, 547
Cold War, 939–970, E-8
Coleridge, Samuel Taylor, 675–676
Coligny [ko-lee-*nyee*], Admiral de, 377
Coligny, Louise de, 391
Colleoni [koh-lay-*oh*-nee], Bartolomeo, 340–341
Colombia, 423, 628, 728, 746, 750, 1025
Colosio, Luis Donaldo, 1025

Colosseum (Rome), 94, 97
Columbus, Christopher, 101, 321, 416, 418–419
Combination Acts, 672–673
COMECON, 964, 976
Comintern, 911
Commedia dell'arte, 353
Commercial Revolution, 416, 434–435, 474
Committee of Public Safety, 582, 584, 653
Commodus [*koh*-muh-duhs], 151
Common Market. *See* European Economic Community
Commonwealth of Nations, 841–842, 903, 910, 1007, 1017
Communism, 61, 137, 673–674, 854–865, 888–890, 911, 942–943, 960, 1001–1002
Comnenus [kohm-*nee*-nuhs], Alexius, 165, 289
Comte [kohnt], Auguste, 667–668
Conceptualism, 276
Conciliar Movement, 294
Concord, battle of, 568, 572
Concordat of 1801, 622, 686, 715
Concordat of Worms, 284–285
Condillac [kohn-dee-*yak*], Etienne de, 544
Condorcet [kon-dohr-*say*], Marquis de, 545, 552
Confederacy, 741
Confucianism, 124–127, 129–134, 137, 207–209, 212–214, 226, 457, 461, 465–466, 610, 613–615, 885, 887
Confucius [kon-*few*-shus], 124–126
Congo, Belgian, 759–760, 900–901, 1017, 1020
Congo River, 234, 239, 431
Congress (U.S.), 568–570, 910, 921, 951, 979, 982–983, E-9
Congress of Berlin, 724, 799, 802
Congress of People's Deputies, 958, 962
Congress System, 638–640
Congress of Vienna, 636–640, 685–688

Einstein, Albert, 842, 844, E-2
Eisenhower, Dwight, 923, 951, 979
Eisenstein, Sergei, 865
El Alamein, battle of, 928, 930
Elamites, 14
Elba, 626
Eleanor of Aquitaine, 308, 313
Eleusinian [ee-loo-*sin*-ee-uhn] cults, 57
El Greco, 348, 408
Elizabeth (Bohemian monarch), 398, 405
Elizabeth (Russian tsarina), 491, 494
Elizabeth, Duchess of Braunschweig, 369
Elizabeth I, 353, 371, 392–397, 404
Elizabeth of Valois, 388
Ellul, Jacques, 991
El Salvador, 750, 982, 1025
Emancipation Proclamation
  Russia, 701
  United States, 742
Employers' Liability Act, 709
Ems dispatch, 698–699
Enabling Act, 874
Enclosure laws, 507–508, 515
Engels, Friedrich [*free*-drik *ehn*-guhls], 671, 673
England. *See* Britain
Enlightenment, 531–555, 561–562, 578, 620, 698
Entente Cordiale, 801
Environmental Program (U.N.), 996
Epictetus [ehp-ihk-*teet*-ehs], 101
Epicureans, 69, 98, 100
Epicurus [ehp-ih-*kyoor*-uhs], 69
Equal Rights Amendment, 995
Equiano, Olaudah, 729
Erasmus, Desiderius [des-ih-*deer*-ee-uhs ih-*rahz*-muhs], 349–351, 363, 380
Eratosthenes [er-uh-*toss*-thuh-neez], 69
Erhardt, Ludwig, 991
Eritrea [ehr-ih-*tree*-ah], 1021
Eskimos, 250
Essenes, 143–144, 149
Essex, Earl of, 396, 405
Estates-General, 310, 316, 319, 402, 485, 504, 518, 574–575

Esterhazy [*ess*-ter-hah-zee] family, 503, 714
Estonia, 837–838, 858, 922, 957, 959–960
Ethelred the Unready, 310
Ethiopia, 4, 235–236, 1021
  ancient kingdom, 240–244, 416–418, 433, 599
  Italian control, 762, 914–915, 925
  nineteenth century, 759–762
Etruscans [ih-*trus*-kenz], 76–77, 79–81, 96
Euclid [*yoo*-klid], 69, 193–194, 277
Euphrates [yoo-*fray*-teez] River, 11, 14, 17
Euripides [yoo-*rip*-ih-deez], 63
European Atomic Energy Commission, 986
European Coal and Steel Community, 986, 991
European Economic Community (EEC), 986–988, 990–992, 994–995
European Free Trade Association, 987
European Recovery Program, 945
Evans, Arthur, 42
Eware the Great, 240, 430
Extraterritoriality, 784, 790
Ezekiel, 29

Fabian Society, 674, 710
Fahd, 1016
Fa-Hsien [fah shyen], 203
Fairfax, Lord, 405–406
Faisal al-Hussein [*fye*-sahl ahl hoo-*seyn*], 894–895
Fallen Timbers, battle of, 573
Fan Changda, 215
Fanon, Frantz, 1018
Faraday, Michael, 667
Farmers Laws, 160
Farnese [fahr-*nay*-say], Alexander, 391
Farouk [fah-*rook*], 1011–1012
Fascism, Italian, 851, 865–870, 914–915
Fasilidas, 599
Fatehpur-Sikri [*fah*-teh-puhr see-kree], 455
Fatima, 180, 188, 192

Fatimids [*fat*-ih-mihdz], 192–193
Federalists, 570
Federal Reserve Act, 744
Federal Trade Commission, 744
Ferdinand I (Austrian emperor), 692
Ferdinand I (Holy Roman emperor), 388
Ferdinand I (Neapolitan king), 639
Ferdinand II, 397–399
Ferdinand VII, 639
Ferdinand of Aragon, 320–321
Ferghana [fur-*gahh*-ah], 452
Fertile Crescent, 7, 11, 34–35, 38
Feudalism, 305–307, 312
Ficino, Marsilio, 335–336
Fiefs [feefs], 306–307
Fielding, Henry, 542
Fieravanti, Aristotele, 173
Fifth Crusade, 291
Fiji [*fee*-jee], 655
Finland, 397, 637, 836–837, 858, 910, 922, 924, 941, 987
First Crusade, 192, 272, 289–290, 308
First International, 674
Fisher, John, 371
Fish River, battle of, 593
Fisk, Jim, 743
FitzGerald, Edward, 195
Fitzwilliam family, 503
Fiume [*fyoo*-may], 820, 866
Five Confucian Classics, 124, 132
Five Moral Rules, 113
Five Pillars, 185–186
Five-year plans, 862–864
Flanders, 272, 274, 308, 316, 319, 354–355, 389–391, 508
Flaubert [floh-*bair*], Gustave, 678
Fleury [flur-*ree*], Cardinal, 504–505
Flood, Henry, 573
Florence, 330–331, 334–335, 338–341, 362, 380, 434
Florida, 423, 437, 496, 567
Foch [fohsh], Ferdinand, 813–814
Fontana, Livonia, 409
Food and Agricultural Organization (U.N.), 941

Leipzig [*lype*-zihg], battle of, 585, 626
Lend-Lease Act, 927
Lenin, Nikolai, 716–718, 813, 820, 854, 856–861, 864, 888, 943, 947–948, 958
Leningrad, siege of, 927
Leo I (pope), 148, 154, 173
Leo III (emperor), 188
Leo VI (pope), 163
Leo X (pope), 364–365
Leo XIII (pope), 662–664
Leo the Isaurian, 160–161
Leonardo da Vinci [*vihn*-chee], 340, 342–343, 348
Leopold I (Belgian king), 687
Leopold I (Holy Roman emperor), 484–485
Leopold II (Belgian king), 759–760
Leopold of Tuscany, 525
Lepanto [lay-*pahn*-toh], battle of, 395
Leuger, Karl, 670
Leveller movement, 406
Lewis, Meriwether, 728
Lexington, battle of, 568, 572
Leyden [*lye*-d'n], University of, 536
Leyster, Judith, 409
Leyte Gulf, battle of, 932
Liberia, 760
Libya, 764–765, 769–770, 982, 1019
Licensing Act, 563
Li Ch'ing, 215
Liebknecht [*leep*-k'nekt], Karl, 870
Lilburne, Elizabeth, 406
Lilburne, John, 406–407
Lille [leel], 651
Lima [*lee*-mah], 425, 430
Limpopo River, 237–238
Lincoln, Abraham, 740–741
Linear A & B scripts, 42, 44
Linnaeus, Carolus (Karl von Linné), 537
Lin Tse-hsu [lin-dzeh-shoo], 785
Li Peng, 1004
Li Po, 210–211
Lister, Joseph, 666
Li Ta-chao, 888
Lithuania, 837–838, 858, 922, 957, 959–960
Li-tsung, 212

Liu Pang [lyoo bahng], 130
Liverpool, 506, 511, 520, 594, 649
Livingstone, David, 758
Livy, 78–79, 85, 99, 102, 335, 349
Lloyd George, David, 710, 814–816, 818, 820, 833
Lloyds of London, 476
Locarno pact, 911–912, 915
Locke, John, 543–546, 548, 550–553, 563, 566–567, 583
Lollards, 294
Lombard League, 324
Lombards, 152, 155, 282, 301, 303
Lombardy, 274, 694
London, 510–511, 516, 518, 520, 573, 648–649, 669, 674, 702, 834
London, treaty of, 803
London Company, 439
Long March, 888
Long Parliament, 405
Longueville [long-*veel*], Madame de, 479
Lorraine [loh-*rehn*], 305, 698, 713, 799, 806, 888
Lothair [leh-*ther*], 305
Louis VI ("the Fat"), 308
Louis VIII, 309
Louis IX, 291, 309
Louis XI, 319
Louis XIII, 397–398, 400, 475
Louis XIV, 400, 437, 473, 475–476, 479–484, 486–487, 492–493, 501–502, 504–505, 539, 543, 599
Louis XV, 494, 501–502, 504–505, 514, 521, 547, 564
Louis XVI, 521, 574–576, 579–581, 587, 621, 686,
Louis XVIII, 626, 686
Louis the Child, 322
Louis of Condé, 377
Louis the German, 305
Louis Philippe [loo-*ee* fee-*leep*], 687, 689–690
Louis the Pious, 305
Louisiana, 483, 496, 627
Louisiana Purchase, 628, 740
Louvois [loo-*vwah*], Marquis de, 483
Low, Sidney, 735
Loyola, Ignatius, 380–381
Lubbe [*loo*-beh], Marinus van der, 874

Lucretius [loo-*kree*-shuhs], 98, 100
Lucy, 4–5
Lugals, 13, 18
Lugard, Lord, 761
Lumière [loom-*yair*], Auguste, 681
Lumière, Louis-Jean, 681
Lunda empire, 598
Lung Shan culture, 120
Luo tribe, 1020
Lusitania, 813
Luther, Martin, 351, 359–360, 363–370, 373–374, 380, 408, 688
Lutheranism, 364–369, 372, 374, 389, 400, 554
Lutzen [*luht*-sehn], battle of, 387, 399
Luxembourg, 389, 698, 924, 945, 986
Luxemburg, Rosa, 870–871
Lyceum (Aristotle), 59
Lycurgus [lye-*kur*-guhs], 49–50
Lydians, 35–37, 47, 51
Ly [lee] dynasty, 468
Lyell [*lye*-el], Charles, 664

Ma (Chinese empress), 456
Mably [mah-blee], Gabriel de, 548
McAdam, John, 647
Macao [muh-*kow*], 420, 459–460, 783, 787
MacArthur, Douglas, 984
Macauley, Catherine, 545, 552
Maccabaeus [mak-kah-*bee*-uhs], Judas, 142
McCarthy, Joseph, 979, 1001
Macdonald, John A., 738
MacDonald, Ramsay, 710, 833–834
Macedonia [mass-uh-*dohn*-ya]
  ancient, 56, 65–68, 82–84, 161–162, 164
  modern, 768, 770, 802, 992
Machiavelli, Niccolò [nee-koh-*loh* ma-kyah-*vell*-ee], 55, 116, 333, 337, 345
Machu Picchu [*ma*-choo *peek*-choo], 259
Mackenzie, Alexander, 728
McKinley, William, 752, 890
McLuhan, Marshall, E-1
Macmillan, Harold, 988, 1017

Médicis, Marie de, 397
Medina [mih-*dee*-nah], 181–182, 187
Megaliths, 9–10
Megasthenes [mee-*gas*-thee-neez], 115
Megiddo [meh-*gihd*-doh], battle of, 30
Mehmet II [meh-*met*], 447, 449
Meiji [may-jee] restoration, 790–793, 882, 884
Melian massacre, 55
Menander [meh-*nah*-duh], 117
Mencius [*men*-shuhs] (Meng-tzu), 125–126
Mendel, Gregor, 665–666
Mendeleev [men-deh-*lay*-ef], Dmitri, 666
Mendelssohn, Felix, 676–677
Mendelssohn, Moses, 545
Mendez, Alfonso, 433
Menelik [*may*-neh-lihk] II, 752, 763
Menes [*may*-nayz] (Narmer), 18
Mengistu Haile Mariam, 1021
Menkaure [men-*kow*-ray], 19, 24
Mennonites, 378
Mensheviks, 717, 853–856, 859
Mercantilism, 476, 478–479, 482–483, 506–507, 519–521
Meroë [*mehr*-oh-wee], 241
Merovingians [mehr-uh-*vin*-jee-uhns], 299–301
Mesolithic culture, 6, 250
Mesopotamia, 9–18, 23
Messiah, 143–146
Methodism, 554, 662
Methodius, 162–163
Metternich [*meht*-ur-nik], Klemens von, 636–640, 688–689, 691, 721
Mexico, 252, 417, 728, 731, E-7
   Aztecs, 233, 249–250, 253–254, 256–258, 421–423, 434
   independence, 629, 746
   nineteenth century, 694, 740, 744–747
   Spanish colony, 420–423, 425–427, 429–430
   twentieth century, 747–749, 813, 840–841, 1024–1025
Mexico City, 423, 425, 430, 629, 747
Micah [*mye*-kuh] (prophet), 33

Michael (Russian tsar), 489
Michel, Claude, 540
Michelangelo Buonarroti [mee-kel-*ahn*-jel-loh bwoh-nuh-*roh*-tee], 332, 339, 342–345
Michelet [*meesh*-le], Jules, 631
Midas [*mye*-dahs], 35
Midhat Pasha, 769
Midway, battle of, 928
Midway Islands, 782
Mikoyan, Anastas, 947
Miles, William, 513
Mill, John Stuart, 633–634
Milton, John, 410
Minamoto clan, 222
Ming dynasty, 420, 445, 456–462, 609
Minoans [mih-*noh*-uhnz], 42–44
Minos [*mye*-nahs], 42
Mirandola, Pico della, 336
Miriam, 30
Missouri Compromise, 740
Mita, Ciriaco de, 993
Mithras, 109, 146
Mitterand, François, 990
Mladenov, Peter, 968
Mobutu Sese Seko [moh-*boo*-too *say*-say *say*-koh], 1020
Modernism, 679–680
Mohacs [*moh*-hahch], battle of, 447
Mohammed (Persian shah), 450
Mohenjo-Daro [moh-*hen*-joh *dahr*-oh] excavations, 107–108
Moi, Daniel arap, 1019
Moldavia, 722
Moldova, 957, 959–960, 963
Molière [moh-*lyair*], 475
Molotov, Vyacheslav [vyih-cheh-*slaff moh*-luh-toff], 922, 947
Moluccas, 436, 440, 469, 486
Mombassa, 244, 433
Momoyama period, 466
Monet [moh-*nay*], Claude, 679
Mongke Khan, 224–225, 228
Mongolia, 120, 609
Mongols, 131, 136, 166–168, 171–172, 192–193, 204, 207, 213, 222–229, 446–447, 456, 459–462, 468
Mon-Khmers, 466–467
Monmouth, battle of, 572
Monnet, Jean, 986
Monomotapa, 433–434, 598

Monotheism, 20, 23, 33, 182–184
Monroe Doctrine, 630, 744, 751
Monroe, James, 640, 744
Montague, Mary Motley, 537, 552
Montaigne [mon-*tayn*], Michel de, 333, 352
Monte Alban, 253
Montenegro [mon-te-*neh*-groh], 168, 721, 723, 768
Montespan, Madame de, 480
Montesquieu [mohn-tes-*kyoo*], Marquis de, 543, 550, 552, 563, 569
Montezuma [mahn-teh-*soo*-mah] I, 257
Montezuma II, 257, 421–422
Montfort [mohn-*for*], Simon de, 315
Montmorency family, 392
Montpensier [mohn-pahn-see-*yay*], Madame de, 479
Montreal, 437
Montserrat, 440
Moors, 157, 188, 196, 303, 320, 381, 388–389, 416, 418
Moravia [muh-*ray*-vee-uh], 162
Moravian movement, 554
More, Hannah, 554
More, Thomas, 349–351, 370–371, 380
Morelos [moh-*ray*-lohs], José Maria, 629
Morgan, John Pierpont, 746
Mori family, 463
Moro, Aldo, 993
Morocco, 418, 430
   crises (1905, 1911), 801–802
   French colony, 762, 764, 766, 898
   independence, 1011, 1019
   pirate state, 600
Moscow, 171–173, 489, 491, 625–626, 669, 701, 857–858, 911, 927
Moses, 20, 29–31, 33, 142, 180–181
Mossadeq [*moh*-sa-dek], Mohammed, 1013
Mossi states, 238, 240
Mother Goddess, 9, 42–43, 100, 108, 112, 146
Mother Lu, 132
Mount Vernon, 540

Nicholas V (pope), 332
Nicopolis [nih-*kah*-puh-lis], battle of, 166
Nigeria, 597, 905
  Biafra war, 1020–1021
  British colony, 759, 761–762, 900
  early, 235, 238, 240, 430
  independence, 1017, 1020
Niger [*nye*-jer] River, 235, 237–238, 245, 247, 430, 592, 595–596, 600
Nike [*nye*-kee] rebellion, 157
Nile River, 12, 18, 20–25, 234–235, 241, 1015
Nine-Power treaty, 884, 887
Nineva [*nihn*-uh-vuh], battle of, 159
Ning-tsing, 212
Nixon, Richard, 952, 955, 978–981, 1004
Nkrumah, Kwame [*kwah*-may en-*kroo*-muh], 905, 1019
Nobel, Alfred, 654
Nobunaga, Oda, 463, 466
Noh [noh] drama, 466
Nok culture, 235–236
Nominalism, 276
Noriega, Manuel, 1025
Normandy, 308, 311–312
Normans, 165, 269, 272, 310–312
North, Lord, 568
North American Free Trade Alliance (NAFTA), 983, 987, 1025, E-7
North Atlantic Treaty Organization (NATO), 945, 955, 962, 970, 990–992, 994–995
North German Confederation, 698
North Korea, 946
Northumberland, Duke of, 371–372
North Vietnam, 950–953
Norway, 268, 369, 637, 833, 924, 945, 987
Nova Scotia, 437, 493, 736
Novgorod [*nov*-guh-rud], 168, 171–172
Nuremberg, 367
Nuremberg war crimes trial, 940
Nzinga [en-*zihn*-gah], Anna, 433, 598

Nzinga Myemba, 431–432

Obrenovich [oh-*bren*-oh-veech], Michael, 723
Octavian, 88–89
October Manifesto, 718
Odovacar [oh-doh-*vay*-ker], 155
Odysseus [oh-*dih*-see-uhs], 62
Oil embargo, 1012
Okinawa [oh-kee-*nah*-wah], 932
Oklahoma City bombing, E-3
Olduvai Gorge fossils, 5
Oleg (Kievan ruler), 168
Olesnicka, Zofia, 377
Olga, 168
Oligarchy, 10, 47, 56, 76–78
Olive oil, 42, 44, 47–48
Olmecs [*ol*-meks], 250, 252
Olympias, 66
Olympic Games, 682
Oman [oh-*mahn*], 599, 772
Open Door Policy, 745, 787, 884
Opium trade, 783–785
Orange, house of, 404, 486–487, 636
Orange Free State, 733–734
Oregon, 740
Orenburg-Tashkent Railway, 771
Orestes [oh-*rehs*-tees], 155
Organization of American States (OAS), 1024
Organization for Economic Cooperation and Development, E-6
Organization of Petroleum Exporting Countries (OPEC), 976, 978, 1012
Orlando, Vittorio, 814–815, 820
Orléans [ohr-lay-*ahn*], house of, 687
Ormuz, 420, 451
Orwell, George, E-1, E-9
Ortega y Gasset [or-*tay*-gah ee gah-*set*], José, 839
Osaka [oh-*sah*-kah], 463, 466
Osiris [oh-*sye*-ris], 22–23, 146
Osman [*oz*-mun, os-*mahn*] I, 193
Ostracism, 49
Ostrogoths, 153, 155, 157
Otis, James, 572
Otto I ("the Great"), 322–323
Otto III, 323
Ottoman Empire, 141, 164–166, 193, 394–395, 445–451, 455,

484, 495, 600–602, 656–657, 893–894. *See also* Turkey
  disintegration of, 764, 766–770
  Napoleonic era, 621, 636, 638–639
  nineteenth century, 708, 721–724
  World War I, 797–799, 802–803, 805–807, 814, 816, 818, 820, 826
Ovid [*oh*-vihd], 99
Ovimbundu, 598
Owen, Robert, 635
Owen, Wilfrid, 811
Oxford Movement, 663
Oxford University, 278–279, 294
Oyo [*oh*-yoh] kingdom, 240, 597–598

Pachacuti [pah-cha-*koo*-tee], 260–262
Pact of Steel, 921
Padua [*pad*-yo-ah], University of, 336
Paechke [*payk*-cheh], 217
Pahlavi [*pah*-luh-vee], Mohammed Riza, 898, 1013
Pahlavi, Riza, 897–898
Paine, Thomas, 545, 547, 550, 568–569, 572
Pakistan, 107, 117, 893, 1007–1010
Palacky [*pah*-lahts-kee], Frantiek, 631
Palatine Hill (Rome), 75
Palenque [pah-*lehn*-kay], 254
Paleolithic culture, 6, 8-9, E-13
Paleologos [pay-lee-*oh*-loh-gehs] dynasty, 165
Palestine
  ancient, 20–21, 27, 29–30, 33, 142–144, 192–193, 224
  modern, 670, 816, 841, 894–895, 897, 1010–1012
Palestine Liberation Organization (PLO), 1010, 1014, 1016–1017
Palestrina, Giovanni [joh-*vahn*-nee pah-lay-*stree*-nah], 408
Paley, William, 553
Palladio, Andrea [ahn-*dray*-ah pah-*lah*-dee-oh], 408
Palm d'Aelders, Etta, 578
Palmer, Elihu, 547
Palmerston, Lord, 704

Ramayana, 109, 112
Ramses [*ram*-seez] II, 20, 25, 27
Ranke [*rahng*-kuh], Leopold von, 631, E-11
Rao, P. V. Narasimha, 1008
Rapallo pact, 911–912
Raphael [*raf*-ay-uhl] (Raffaello Sanzio), 332, 342–343, 348
Rasputin [rahs-*poo*-tyin, ras-*pew*-tin], 852–853
Ratislav, 162
Ravenna [rah-*vehn*-nah], 155, 157–158, 301
Rawlings, Jerry, 1020
Ray, John, 537
Reagan, Ronald, 982–983, 1025
Realism, 276, 678–679
Realpolitik [ray-*ahl*-poh-lih-*teek*], 685, 695, 697
Reconquista, 320–321
Reconstruction, 741–742
Red Army, 857–858, 864, 930, 943
Red Brigade, 992–993
Red Guards, 1003
Reform Bill, 709–711
Reichstag [*rikes*-tahk] (Berlin), 870, 875
Reid, Thomas, 546
Reign of Terror, 581–584
Reinsurance Treaty, 799
Remarque [ruh-*mahrk*], Erich Maria, 876, 913
Rembrandt van Rijn [rine], 409
Remus [*ree*-muhs], 76
Renoir [ruh-*nwar*], Pierre Auguste, 679
Revere, Paul, 568
Reynolds, Joshua, 539
Rhazes, 193
Rhineland, 818, 827, 911, 915
Rhode Island, 439–440, 520–521
Rhodes [rohdz], 82, 416, 447
Rhodes, Cecil, 733–735, 762, 902
Rhodesia, 598, 734, 763, 901–902, 1021
Ricci [*ree*-chee], Matteo, 460
Richard I, 290, 308, 314
Richard II, 317
Richard III, 318
Richardson, Samuel, 542
Richelieu [*ree*-sheh-lyuh], Cardinal, 397–400, 475, 479
Riebeeck, Jan van, 592

Rigaud [ree-*goh*], Hyacinthe, 480
Rig-Veda [rig ray-dah], 108–109, 111
Ripa, Father, 611
Robespierre [roh-bes-*pyair*], Maximilien, 580, 582, 584
Rockefeller, John D., 654
Rococo, 539–540
Rocroi [roh-*kwah*], battle of, 400
Rodin [roh-*danh*], Auguste, 845
Roger II, 323
Roland, 279
Romance of the Three Kingdoms, 228
Romanesque style, 280–281
Romania
    democratic, 969
    independence, 803
    Ottoman Empire, 447–448, 722–723, 768
    Soviet domination, 941, 943, 946, 968–969
    World War I, 809, 816, 820
    World War II, 925, 930
    between world wars, 837–838
Romanovs [ruh-mah-*noffs*], 489, 700
Romanus Lecapenus I, 163
Rome (ancient), 75–76, 119, 134–136, 202, 337, 339
    and Christianity, 141–155
    contributions to civilization, 90–102
    empire, 89–94, 268
    monarchy, 76–78
    republic, 78–89, 142
Rome (city), 148, 152, 157, 303, 323, 340–345, 363, 695, 719, 867
Romilly [*rah*-mih-lee], Samuel, 565
Rommel [*rah*-mehl], Erwin, 923, 927
Romulus [*rahm*-yoo-luhs], 76–77
Romulus Augustulus, 76, 155
Roosevelt, Franklin, 840–841, 846, 921, 927, 930–932, 978, 982
Roosevelt, Theodore, 744–746, 751–752
Roosevelt Corollary, 751
Rosetta Stone, 621

Rossiter, Thomas, 570
Rothschild banking firm, 649
Rousseau [roo-*soh*], Jean-Jacques, 516, 542, 544–545, 548, 550, 552–553, 580, 583–584
Rowlatt Act, 891
Roxelana, 449
Royal Society (London), 538
Rubens, Peter Paul, 409
Rubicon River, 87
Rucellai [roo-*chel*-lay] family, 331
Rudolf I, 324
Rudolf II, 398
Ruhr [roor], 827–828, 835, 911
Rule of St. Basil, 150
Rump Parliament, 406
Rupert (English prince), 405
Rush, Benjamin, 572
Russell, Bertrand, 811, E-9
Russell, Lady, 394, 397
Russia. *See also* Soviet Union
    colonial expansion, 770–773, 784, 786–787, 793
    early history, 166–173
    Industrial Revolution, 646, 648, 650, 652, 654, 656–657
    late twentieth century, 959, 962–964, 970, 997
    medieval, 268
    Napoleonic era, 621, 623–626, 636–640
    nineteenth century, 601–603, 669, 674, 685, 687, 692, 694–695, 697–698, 700–702, 707, 715–724, 744, 746
    Revolution, 813, 851–865, 882
    seventeenth and eighteenth centuries, 489–496, 502–503, 505, 510–511, 518–519, 523–524, 580, 606, 609
    World War I, 797, 799–809, 812–814, 816, 820, 826, 828
Russian Orthodox Church, 141–142, 168–173
Russian Revolution, 813, 851–865, 882
Russo-Japanese War, 718, 746, 793, 798, 802, 882
Ruth, Babe, 846
Rutherford, Ernest, 667, 842
Ruysch, Rachel, 540
Rwanda, 901, 1019

Saar [zahr], 910
Saba [*sah*-ba], 178, 241
Sadat [sah-*dot*], Anwar, 1012–1013, 1015
Sadducees, 142–143
Safavid [*sah*-fah-veed] dynasty, 446, 450–451, 602
Sahara Desert, 234–235, 245
Saigon [sye-*gon*], 950–952
St. Augustine, 423
St. Bartholomew's Eve massacre, 392–393
St. Germaine, treaty of, 820
St. Helena, 619, 626
St. Kitts, 438, 440
St. Lawrence River, 437–438, 496, 737
St. Lucia, 496
St. Peter's basilica (Vatican), 332, 342–343, 364, 409
St. Peter's Fields, 672, 702
St. Petersburg, 491–492, 523, 700–701, 717–719, 852–854, 927, 942
Saint-Simon [sahn-see-*monh*], Henri de, 635, 667, 671
Saipan [sye-*pan*], 932
Sakharov [*sah*-ka-rof], Andrei, 957
Saladin [*sal*-uh-dihn], 290–291
Salazar, Antonio de, 838, 993
Salian dynasty, 323
Salinas, Carlos, 1025
Salisbury, 734
Samad [sah-*mahd*], Abdus, 455
Samad, Khwaja Abdus, 451
Samaria, 32
Samarkand [sam-ur-*kahd*], 452
Samnite wars, 81
Sampson, Deborah, 572
Samuel (prophet), 30–31
Samurai [*sah*-muhr-eye], 220, 463, 465, 613, 788–791
San, 592
Sanches, Manuela, 630
Sandinistas, 983, 1025
San Francisco, 941
Sanhedrin [san-*hee*-drin], 142, 144
San Jacinto [san ha-*sin*-toh], battle of, 629
Sankoré mosque [san-kor-*ay*], 247, 249
San Lorenzo, 250, 252

San Martín [san mar-*teen*], José de, 628–629
San Remo Conference, 895
San Salvador Island, 419
Sanskrit, 108, 110, 207, 466
San Stefano, treaty of, 723–724
Santa Anna, Antonio Lopez de, 629, 747
Santa Fe, 423
Sao Tomé, 426, 430–431
Sao Vincente, 420
Sappho [*saff*-oh], 62
Saracens, 161, 289
Sarajevo [sah-rah-*yeh*-voh], 804–805, 970
Saratoga, battle of, 568, 573
Sardinia, 493, 581–582, 585, 636, 688, 691, 694–695, 723
Sargon I, 13
Sassanids [suh-*sah*-nidz], 178, 187
Saudi Arabia, 178, 601, 894–895, 897, 982, 1015–1016
Saul, 30–32
Savonarola [sah-voh-nah-*roh*-lah], 380
Savoy, house of, 493, 676
Saxons, 152, 154, 282, 310–312, 322–323
Saxony, 367–368, 387, 494, 636
Schiller [*shil*-er], Friedrich von, 542, 675
Schleswig-Holstein [*sles*-vig *hohl*-stine], 697–698
Schlieffen [*shleef*-ehn], Alfred von, 806
Schliemann [*shlee*-mahn], Heinrich, 44–45
Schmalkaldic [shmahl-*kahl*-dik] League, 369
Schmelling, Max, 847
Schmidt [shmidt], Helmut, 992
Schoenberg [*shen*-berg], Arnold, 844
Scholasticism, 276–277, 332–335, 363
Schönborn [*shen*-born] family, 503
Schubert [*shoo*-bert], Franz, 676–677, 680
Schumann [*shoo*-mahn], Robert (composer), 677, 680
Schumann, Robert (politician), 986

Schuschnigg [*shoosh*-nig], Kurt von, 918
Scipio [*sip*-ee-oh], 82
Scotland, 315–316, 370, 377, 392–395, 404–406, 643, 645, 649
Scott, Walter, 675, 677
Scotus, Duns [duhns *sko*-tuhs], 277
Scudéry [sko-*day*-ree], Madeleine, 410, 482
Scythians [*sith*-ee-uns], 117, 131
Second Crusade, 290
Second International, 674
Secretariat (U.N.), 941
Security Council (U.N.), 941
Seikigahara [say-kee-gah-*hah*-rah], battle of, 463
Sejong, 461
Seleucid empire [sih-*loo*-sidh], 67–68, 70, 82–83, 87, 117, 134, 143
Seleucus [sih-*loo*-kuhs], 67, 115
Selim [say-*leem*] I, 447, 450
Selim III, 601, 721, 768
Seljuk [sel-*jook*] Turks, 164–166, 192–193, 289–291
Semitic languages/culture, 12–13, 26, 34–35
Senate (Rome), 77–79, 81, 85–91, 95, 150–151, 155
Seneca, 99, 101
Senegal [say-nay-*gahl*], 905
Senegal River, 483, 592, 594, 599–600, 694
Senghor [sahn-*gohr*], Leopold Sedar, 905
Sepoy [*see*-poy] Rebellion, 779
Serbia, 168
  Balkan crises, 802–803
  disintegration of Yugoslavia, 969–970
  independence, 799
  Ottoman Empire, 601–602, 720–724, 768
  World War I, 804
Serfdom, 271, 274
Servetus [ser-*vee*-tuhs], Michael, 374
Seth, 22
Seventh Crusade, 291
Seven Years' War, 494–495, 505, 514, 520, 562, 604–605
Sèvres, treaty of, 898

Shaka [*shah*-kah], 758–759
Shakers, 554
Shakespeare, William, 98, 330, 353–354, 662
Shamash, 14, 17
Shang, Lord, 127–128
Shang [shahng] dynasty, 120–122
Shanghai [shahng-*hye*], 886, 912, 914
Sharia, 186
Sharif [shah-*reef*], Nawaz, 1010
Shaw, George Bernard, 674, 679
Sheba [*shee*-bah], 178, 241
Sheba, Queen of, 241
Shelley, Percy Bysshe, 676
Shen Chou, 459
Shen-tsung, 213
Sherif Husein [sheh-*reef* hoo-*sayn*], 894–895
Sherman Antitrust Act, 744
Shih Chi, 132–133
Shi'ites [*shee*-ites], 188–189, 449, 451, 602, 1013
Shimonoseki, treaty of, 787
Shintoism, 217, 219, 793, 882
Shishak, 21
Shiva [*shee*-vah], 112, 203
Shogun, 222, 462–463, 788–790
Shona [*shoh*-nah], 598
Short Parliament, 405
Shostakovich, Dmitri, 865
Shudra [*shoo*-drah] caste, 109–110
Shuo Wen, 133
Sibelius, Jean, 680
Siberia, 491, 606, 648, 700, 942, 947
Sicily, 81–82, 268, 323–324, 493, 695, 928
Sickingen, Franz von, 368
Sidon [*sye*-dun], 28–29, 272
Sierra Leone, 761
Sieyès [*syay*-yahs], Abbé, 621
Sigismund III, 485
Sikhs [seeks], 604, 1008–1009
Silesia [sih-*lee*-zhuh], 494–495, 818
Silk trade, 134–136, 228
Silla, 217, 460–461
Sinai [*sigh*-nigh] Covenant, 29, 31, 33
Sinai peninsula, 1011–1012
Sind, 107, 204

Singapore, 781, 914, 978, 986, 1005–1007
Singh [sing], Manmohan, 1008
Singh, V. P., 1008
Sino-Japanese War, 793
Sisters of the Common Life, 381
Sistine Chapel (Vatican), 332, 343–345
Six Articles, 371–372
Sixth Crusade, 291
Skavronska, Marfa, 489
Skeptics, 69
Slavs, 157–158, 160–162, 166–168, 172, 268, 303–304, 322, 631, 669–670, 692, 701, 723, 799, 802
Slovakia, 167, 967–968
Slovenia [slo-*veen*-yuh], 167, 970
Sluys [slo-*iss*], battle of, 316
Smeaton [*smee*-tun], John, 538
Smetana [*smeh*-ta-nah], Bedrich, 680
Smiles, Samuel, 681
Smith, Adam, 545, 548–549, 578, 632–633
Smith, Alfred E., 840
Smith, John, 439
Soares, Mario, 993
Social Darwinism, 668–669, 742, 745
Socialism, 634–636, 673–675
Social Security Act, 840
Socrates [*sahk*-ruh-teez], 57–59, 63, 68
Solari, Pietro Antonio, 173
Solidarity, 966
Solomon, 21, 32, 241
Solon [*soh*-luhn], 48, 62
Solzhenitsyn [sol-zhun-*neet*-siz], Alexander, 957
Somalia, 761, 1011, 1021
Somerset, Duke of, 371
Somme [sum], battle of the, 808–810
Songhai [sahng-*hye*] empire, 247, 430, 600
Song of Roland, 279
Soninke [sun-*in*-kay] dynasty, 245
Sonni Ali, 247
Sophia (regent), 489
Sophie (archduchess), 804–805
Sophists, 58, 63
Sophocles [*sahf*-uh-kleez], 62–63
Souligna-Vongsa, 605

South Africa, 4, 234, 655, 727–728, 731
British colony, 733–734, 758–759, 798
Dutch colony, 592–593, 732–733
early twentieth century, 801, 901, 903–904
late twentieth century, 1022–1024
Southeast Asia Treaty Organization (SEATO), 951
South Korea, 946, 978, 986, 1005–1006
South Sea Company, 505, 510
South Vietnam, 950–952
Southwest Africa, 901, 1023–1024
Southwest African Peoples' Organization (SWAPO), 1024
Soviet Union, 834–835, 838, 886, 888. *See also* Russia
late twentieth century, 939–950, 953–969, 976, 980, 982–983, 991–992, 1002–1004, 1008–1009, 1011–1012, 1015, 1021, 1024, 1026, E-7
Russian Revolution, 813, 851–865
World War II, 924, 926–932
between world wars, 910–912, 915–916, 921–922
Sovkhoz [*sohv*-kohz], 861
Spain, 153, 157, 188, 196, 256, 802, 926
civil war, 836, 838, 915–916
colonial expansion, 416–430, 434–438, 465, 469, 594, 744, 746–748, 751, 782
late twentieth century, 987, 993–994
medieval, 268, 300–301, 303, 320–321
Napoleonic era, 624–626, 628–630, 636, 639
nineteenth century, 698
Reformation, 370, 372, 381–382, 388–402
Renaissance, 344, 352–353
seventeenth and eighteenth centuries, 484, 486, 492–494, 496, 502, 507, 519–520, 525, 568, 581–583

Uitzilpochtli, 258
Ukiyo [oo-*kee*-yoh], 615
Ukraine [yew-*krayn*], 496, 511,
    837, 858, 929, 957, 959–960,
    963
Ulfilas [*uhl*-fee-lahs], 282
Ulm, battle of, 624
Ulster, 709–710
Umar [*oo*-mahr], 187
Umayyad [oo-*mah*-yahd]
    dynasty, 188–189
Umberto, 720
Ummah, 182, 186
UNESCO, 941
Union Pacific Railroad, 742
United Empire Loyalists, 737
United Nations, 930, 941–942,
    946, 983, 1011, 1015–1016,
    1022, 1025, E-6, E-7, E-8
United States, 727–728
    Civil War, 741–742
    colonial, 564, 566, 728, 890
    foreign policy, 744–746,
        751–752, 754
    imperialistic expansion,
        751–752, 754, 782, 784,
        789–790
    Industrial Revolution,
        644–645, 647–648, 650, 657,
        742–744
    late twentieth century,
        939–946,948, 950–956,
        960–961, 964, 970, 976,
        978–984, 1004–1005,
        1009–1016, 1019, 1021,
        1024–1025, E-6, E-7, E-8
    Napoleonic era, 619, 627–630,
        640
    Revolutionary war, 566–574
    territorial expansion, 739–741
    World War I, 806, 812–820
    World War II, 926–928,
        930–932, 934–935
    between world wars, 826–832,
        839–840, 910–911, 914–916,
        921
United States Steel, 744
Universal Manhood Suffrage
    Bill, 882
Unkiar Skelessi, treaty of, 722
Untouchables, 110
Upanishads [oo-*pah*-nih-shahdz]
    109–113
Ur [er], 13–14, 29

Urban II, 165, 288
Urdu, 206, 455
Ur-Nammu, 14
Ursins, Princess des, 493
Ursulines [or-soo-*leenz*],
    381–382
Uruguay, 628, 750, 1024
Uruguay Round, 978
Urukagina, 13
Usman dan Fodio [us-*mahn* don
    foh-*dee*-oh], 600, 759
Uthman, 187–188
Utopianism, 635
Utrecht [*yoo*-trekt], treaty of,
    487, 492–496, 596, 736
U-2 incident, 948
Uxmal [oosh-*mahl*], 254
Uzbegs [*uhz*-bex], 447, 450, 452,
    602–603

Vaishyas [vye-*shee*-ahs] caste,
    109–110
Vakaranga [vah-kah-*rahng*-gah]
    empire, 433–434
Valley Forge, 568
Valmy [*val*-mee], battle of, 580
Valois [vahl-*wah*], house of, 316,
    362, 388, 479
Vandals, 152–154, 157
Van Eyck, Jan [yahn van *eyk*],
    354
Van Gogh [van *goh*], Vincent,
    680
Varangians [var-*an*-jee-anz],
    167–168, 171
Varuna [vah-*roo*-nah], 109
Vasa, Gustavus, 369
Vasa dynasty, 397
Vassals, 306–307
Vedic [*vay*-dik] ages, 108–111,
    203
Velasquez [vay-*lahs*-keth],
    Diego, 409
Venezuela, 419, 428, 628, 728,
    745, 750–751, 840, 1024
Venice, 155, 164–165, 226, 272,
    290–291, 344–346, 362, 390,
    395, 408, 416, 434
Ventris, Michael, 44
Verdi [*ver*-dee], Giuseppe, 680
Verdun [ver-*duhn*], battle of,
    808–809
Verdun, treaty of, 305
Verlaine [ver-*len*], Paul, 679

Vermeer, Jan, 409
Verrazzano, Giovanni da, 437
Verrocchio [ver-*roh*-kee-yoh],
    Andrea del, 340–341
Versailles [vehr-*sye*] (palace),
    475, 479–480, 482–483,
    502, 575–576, 578, 698–699,
    712
Versailles, treaty of, 818–820,
    828, 866–867, 871, 873–875,
    887, 904, 910–912, 915
Vervins [vehr-*van*], peace of, 396
Vesalius [vih-*say*-lee-uhs],
    Andreas, 336, 533
Vespasian [veh-*spay*-zhuhn], 91,
    145
Vichy [*vee*-shee] government,
    924
Victor Emmanuel II, 691,
    694–695
Victor Emmanuel III, 867, 912
Victoria (English queen),
    655–656, 662
Vienna [vee-*ehn*-uh], 193, 511,
    649, 670, 689, 691–692
Viet Cong, 951–952
Vietminh, 950, 952
Vietnam, 208, 466, 468–469,
    605, 694, 781, 889–890,
    952–953
    North, 950–953
    South, 950–952
Vietnam War, 950–953, 956,
    979–980
Vijanyager [*vee*-zhan-yah-er],
    452
Vikings, 161, 167–168, 171,
    268–269, 305–306, 310
Viollet-le-Duc, Eugène [*oo*-zhen
    vee-oh-*let*-luh-*dook*], 677
Viracocha, 260–261
Virgil [*vehr*-jil], 77, 91–92,
    98–100, 333, 349
Virginia, 438–439, 521, 566,
    568–569, 572
Vishnu [*vish*-noo], 109, 112–114,
    203
Visigoths, 153–155, 157, 188,
    282, 300
Vladimir [*vla*-duh-meer]
    (Kievan ruler), 168–169
Vladimir Monomakh (Kievan
    ruler), 171
Volos, 168

The Reference Maps

History accounts for human activities in time, and maps depict them in space. Therefore, to understand humanity's experiences, knowledge of the planetary environment is essential. These reference maps show key areas at significant periods; they include basic physical features that affect human attempts to control the environment and their fellow beings.

Map 1: The Ancient Near East and Greece

On this map, we can trace the progressive expansion of human environmental control resulting from the invention of new tools and social institutions. The transition from food collecting to farming occurred in well-watered sites bordering the Syrian, Arabian, and Iranian deserts—such as at Jarmo in uplands to the east of the Tigris. The breakthrough from Neolithic barbarism to civilization, that is, to societies sufficiently complex to permit the emergence of urban centers, occurred in two important river basins, the Tigris-Euphrates and the Nile—linked by a Fertile Crescent with minimal natural obstacles to impede the movement of peoples and goods.

Employing primitive craft, Neolithic seafarers hugged the Mediterranean coasts and slowly pushed westward—as attested by Neolithic sites in Cyprus, Rhodes, and Crete. Improvements in maritime technology permitted the emergence of a splendid Aegean civilization centering at Knossos in Crete, Pylos on the Greek mainland, and Troy in northwest Asia Minor. Civilization's center of gravity shifted progressively northward across the eastern basin of the Mediterranean, culminating in Hellas with its sea-oriented city-states: Corinth; Thebes; and, above all, Athens. Continued advances in maritime technology enabled the Greeks to master the eastern Mediterranean and Black seas and to establish colonies, while the Phoenicians carried their mercantile ventures from their port cities of Tyre and Sidon along the North African coast. What the Tigris-Euphrates had been to the Babylonians and the Nile to the Egyptians, the Mediterranean became to the Greeks, the Phoenicians, and eventually to the Romans—the "middle of the earth."

Map 2: The Roman Empire, c. A.D. 117

This map underscores the importance of physical features in the creation of the Roman world-state. The expansion of the Roman world began with the conquest of the Italian peninsula and Great Greece (including Sicily). The Punic Wars opened up the entire western basin of the Mediterranean, while subsequent intrusion into the eastern basin extended Roman dominion over the Hellenistic world. During the first century B.C., Rome consolidated its control in Asia Minor; conquered transalpine Gaul; and annexed Egypt, Numidia, and Cyrenaica. The territorial domain was rounded out later by the acquisition of Mauretania, Dacia, Armenia, and Mesopotamia.

In this map, we see the Roman world at its broadest expanse, encompassing almost 100 million people. However, declines in population, administrative efficiency, and military power sapped the strength of the overpowered Empire. Armenia, Mesopotamia, and Dacia were abandoned, and eventually the Roman legions were recalled from Britain.

In the fourth century, the once majestic Roman Empire was polarized into two unequal segments. The western section, administered from Rome, had the weaker but spatially larger area; the eastern section, controlled from New Rome (Constantinople, formerly Byzantium), had a larger population, a more compact territory, and a stronger economy. When the two segments were split asunder by Germanic invasions, the classical world gave way to the medieval world.

Map 3: The Ancient East

Here we encounter the homelands of two major fluvial civilizations (societies originating in river basins) centering on the Indus-Ganges and the Huang Ho (Yellow River) drainage basins. The remarkable longevity of Indian and Chinese societies owes much to physical factors that inhibited alien intrusion. The Indian triangle was protected by the Indian Ocean and the Himalayas, although invasion was possible through the western passes; as for China, the obstacles posed by the Pacific Ocean, the forbidding Taklamakan and Gobi deserts, and a series of mountain ranges effectively limited entrance into the Huang Ho valley.

The map shows the boundaries of three empires: the Han in China, the Mauryan in India, and the Parthian in western Asia. Note that these empires were contemporary with the Roman world-state at its zenith. The centuries of the Han Dynasty were stable and prosperous. So too were the centuries of Mauryan rule in India. Under Ashoka, a single administration extended from the Himalayas across the Narbada River and included the Deccan—leaving only the southernmost part of the subcontinent outside its rule. To the northwest lay Bactria, where Hellenistic and Indian culture interfused, producing the Gandharan art found in Taxila.

During this era, too, the western and eastern segments of the Eurasian land mass were in commercial and cultural contact. Ships plied the Indian Ocean, and a tenuous but profitable overland Silk Route stretched from Ch'ang-an to Kashgar and Samarkand and across Parthian lands to Ecbatana, Ctesiphon, and Seleucia.

Map 4: Medieval France, Spain, and England, 1328   We can perceive here the emerging outlines of the national state system in western Europe. For example, in 1328 Edward II had to recognize Scotland officially as independent, while across the Channel, the extinction of the Capetian line set the stage for a protracted struggle over the succession to the French throne. Known as the Hundred Years' War (1337–1453), it was marked by the loss of large English holdings obtained in Plantagenet days. Meanwhile, ambitious French kings enlarged their domain from the Ile de France around Paris southward to the Mediterranean and then sought to expand their territory eastward at the expense of the fragmented Holy Roman Empire. The Iberian peninsula was also fragmented, but here the Christian kingdoms were girding to oust the Moors from Granada.

Also during this era the textile industry enriched such towns as Bruges, Lille, Ghent, Ypres, and Cambrai. The most famous medieval fairs in all Europe were held in Champagne. Narbonne in southern France and Marseilles were other thriving commercial centers.

Whereas in the classical era urban centers predominated on the coasts, in medieval Europe a large number of river-oriented towns were founded or acquired increasing importance. Roads were poor, and river transport was both economical and efficient. The Thames, Meuse, Seine, Loire, Rhone, Garonne, Tagus, Guadalquivir, and Po rivers were being constantly utilized, while the Rhine and the Danube—important as political and military boundaries in Roman times—were vital waterways throughout the medieval period.

Map 5: Europe, 1648   The year 1648 is a crucial one for it marks the end of the Thirty Years' War, which started as a religious conflict and concluded with the victory of the nation-state, which acknowledged no authority higher than its own sovereignty and interests. The map indicates the further territorial consolidation of the national state system (as compared with Map 4). Thus Scotland and England are now one political entity, while the Iberian peninsula is demarcated as Spain and Portugal, although neither is any longer a first-class power. The map also shows the nation-states Switzerland, Denmark, Sweden, Norway, Poland, and Russia.

The German and Italian states remain territorially fragmented and politically unstable, as the Holy Roman Empire has vanished in everything but name and pretensions. The situation in the flat north European plain remains fluid as the boundaries of Brandenburg, Poland, and Russia are always shifting, reflecting the fluctuating balance of power in those states. Meanwhile, despite their defeat at Lepanto in 1571, the Ottomans continue to threaten central Europe.

Map 6: Africa, A.D. 700–1500   The historical development and cultural evolution of Africa owe much to two physical features of the continent—the Sahara Desert and the Great Rift Valley. The valley is a huge depression resulting from volcanic activity that runs from the Jordan Valley in southwest Asia to the Red Sea, through Ethiopia to form the basin containing Lake Victoria, and southward through Lake Tanganyika to Lake Nyasa. The Sahara cuts off northern Africa from the rest of the continent. Northwest Africa is largely oriented to the Mediterranean and to Europe; northeast Africa has long been linked with southwest Asia and the Arabian peninsula. Sub-Saharan Africa is drained by the Niger, Congo, Zambezi, and Limpopo rivers. In this huge region, the Sudanese savanna lands, equatorial rain forest, and steppes and deserts of southern Africa succeed one another from north to south. The map depicts the major cultures of the area and the various empires that flourished during the millennium under review, as well as trade routes across the Sahara, over which caravans carried the wares of the marketplace and mind alike.

Map 7: European Empires, c. 1700 With the age of European expansion, western Europeans spread their religion, cultures, and languages to new territories. In the wake of the explorer came the missionary, merchant, and musketeer so that in time Europeans controlled most, or all, of the land surface of every other continent. Expansion intensified European national rivalries.

European states bordering the Atlantic attempted to explore and colonize lands in the New World in latitudes roughly comparable to their own. Thus, the Danes proceeded northwestward to Iceland and Greenland, the English and French competed for lands north of the Gulf of Mexico, and Spain and Portugal staked their respective claims in more southerly latitudes. Following Portuguese initiative, other Europeans sought out—and fought over—islands, coastal strips, and spheres of interest on the African and Indian coasts and in the archipelagoes of Southeast Asia.

On the map, we can see clearly the depths of European penetration. In the Americas, Europeans encountered native civilizations that were incapable of assimilating, much less fighting off, the newcomers. Consequently, European acquisition of North and South America—and later of

Australia—was complete. In contrast, in sub-Saharan Africa as well as South and East Asia, the Europeans were invariably outnumbered. Hence, although they managed to establish trading settlements along the coast and eventually acquire political ascendancy in most of these regions, they did not succeed in replacing the indigenous culture patterns.

Map 8: Europe, August 1939 As a result of the defeat of the Central Powers in World War I, Germany lost Alsace-Lorraine, half of Schleswig, three western districts to Belgium, the Polish Corridor, and a zone in the Rhineland, which was demilitarized, as well as its overseas colonies. The Austrian Empire was dismembered: the nationalist movements of the Czechs, Poles, and Slavs achieved formal territorial recognition; the remnant of the Empire was converted into the separate states of Austria and Hungary; and further Austrian territories were awarded to Italy. The Ottoman Empire was also dissected: Greece obtained nearly all of European Turkey, Syria was mandated to France, and Palestine and Iraq went to Great Britain. After the Bolshevik Revolution, Russia lost much of its western territory, resulting in the establishment of Finland, Estonia, Latvia, and Lithuania, as well as the major portion of reconstituted Poland, while Bessarabia was ceded to Romania.

In the interwar years, as the map shows, national appetites were whetted to gain new territory or reannex lost possessions. Under Hitler, Nazi Germany reoccupied the Rhineland in 1936, seized Austria and occupied Sudetenland in 1938, and the following year seized other Czech territory in addition to Memel. In 1939, too, Hungary annexed part of Slovakia, while Mussolini's Italy defeated and annexed Albania. The stage was also set for the Soviet Union to reannex territory lost after the Bolshevik Revolution.

Map 9: Africa, 1914 Africa possesses three major cultural environments, each with unique historical developments. Northeast Africa, partly cut off from the rest of the continent by the Sahara, has long been linked with southwest Asia. Africa east of the Great Rift Valley is oriented toward the Indian Ocean, toward the Arab trader, and since the last century, toward the

European who has farmed the plateaus of Kenya, Uganda, and Tanzania. The lands in the southern section of the Great Rift Valley constitute a huge area drained by the Niger, Congo, Zambezi, and Limpopo rivers. In these lands occurred Europe's great scramble for empire in the nineteenth century. By 1914 all Africa had been partitioned among European powers except for Liberia (founded by former slaves from the United States) and Abyssinia, which successfully resisted Italian attempts at conquest in 1896.

Map 10: Africa Profound political and territorial changes have occurred in Africa since 1914—undoubtedly the most spectacular to be found in any continent during the past half-century. From being a vast collection of colonial holdings, Africa has emerged as an agglomeration of national states, virtually all having minimal political stability or economic viability. During the interwar years, some major changes took place on the political landscape. German Togoland and the Cameroons were mandated to Great Britain and France; German East Africa was divided into two mandates: Ruanda-Urundi (Belgium) and Tanganyika (Great Britain); and German Southwest Africa was mandated to South Africa. Egypt became an independent kingdom but Italy's possessions in East Africa were enlarged by the conquest of Abyssinia. Since World War II, however, a spectacular alteration has occurred. The entire continent has passed into indigenous political control. The mandates mentioned above have become the independent states of, respectively, Ghana, Togo, Cameroon, Rwanda, Burundi, Tanzania, and Namibia, which gained its independence from South Africa in 1990. In 1994, the election of Nelson Mandela, leader of the African National Congress, to the presidency of South Africa symbolized the end of domination by the white minority in that country.

Map 11: Russia and Asia Dominating Eurasia, the greatest land mass on earth, is the enormous area of Russia, which occupies more than 6 million square miles and extends along a west-east axis for nearly 5000 miles. European Russia, largely a continuation of the north European plain, is drained by the Dvina, Dnieper, Don, and Volga rivers, the last three flowing southward.

East of the Urals, virtually all rivers flow north to the Arctic, except the Amur, which in its eastward journey also serves as a border with China. Asian Russia is separated from middle- and low-latitude Asia by steppes, deserts, and mountains.

Russian eastward expansion reached the Pacific by 1649. In the next two centuries, the Russians penetrated east of the Caspian into what became the Kazakh, Uzbek, and Turkmen Soviet Socialist Republics. After the collapse of the Soviet Union in 1991, the former Soviet republics became the independent states of Russia, Estonia, Latvia, Lithuania, Byelorussia, Ukraine, Moldavia, Georgia, Armenia, Azerbaijan, Kazakhstan, Turkmenistan, Uzbekistan, Tajikistan, and Kyrgyzstan.

China has continued to develop south of the Great Wall and Gobi Desert and east and north of such massive mountain ranges as the Tien Shan, Pamirs, and Himalayas. Indian society occupies the subcontinent below the Himalyas and influences the culture patterns of neighboring lands to the east and south. Southeast Asia has long been subject to recurrent cultural and military intrusions. Its highly indented coastline and physical terrain have contributed to a fragmentation of cultures and languages. Offshore in East and Southeast Asia are three archipelagoes: Japan, the most highly industrialized and prosperous of non-Western countries; the Philippines; and Indonesia.

Map 12: Latin America Latin America was first colonized by southern Europeans, notably the Spaniards and Portuguese. Exploiting the mountain ranges that run the length of Central and South America for their precious metals, the Spaniards increased their holdings until the close of the eighteenth century. They created several vice-royalties: New Spain, including Mexico and Central America; Peru, at first embracing all of Spanish South America; New Granada, in what is now Colombia and Venezuela; and La Plata, which subsequently became Bolivia, Paraguay, Uruguay, and Argentina. Brazil, discovered by the Portuguese Cabral in 1500, was made a vice-royalty in 1714.

In half a century (1776–1826) of colonial revolutions in the New World, Spanish and Portuguese America became independent (except for

Cuba and Puerto Rico, which remained Spanish until 1898).

The tropical regions of Latin America—including Mexico; Central America; and the lands drained by the Magdalena, Orinoco, and Amazon rivers—have predominantly Amerind populations. In contrast, temperate South America, comprising southern Brazil, Uruguay, Argentina, and Chile, finds Europeans in the majority.

Map 13: The Middle East This region—segmented by deserts and seas but with the latter providing interconnecting routes of travel—has long permitted maximal movement of peoples, goods, and ideas in all directions. In this area, which is unique for the convergence of three continents, we find the birthplace of "civilization" and of three major religions, as well as a continuous succession of dynasties and empires. The twentieth century has witnessed a resurgence of Islamic culture and political strength—attended by the creation of numerous independent states, including Libya, Egypt, Sudan, Syria, Lebanon, Jordan, Iraq, and Pakistan. This resurgence has capitalized on the strategic value of the region as well as on its massive oil resources.

The region has also been in a state of continuous tension and intermittent conflict since the end of World War II. When the British mandate of Palestine was terminated in 1948, the area proclaimed itself the new state of Israel. The Arab states, however, opposed recognition, and several campaigns were mounted in an effort to regain Palestine for the Muslim Arabs. Arab-Israeli hostilities erupted into war in 1967 and 1973. The Middle East in the 1990s is still the scene of considerable tension. Throughout the region, terrorist activities threaten both natives and visitors. A revolution in Iran was followed by war between Iran and Iraq. Iraq's invasion of Kuwait in 1990 touched off an international crisis and eventually led to the Persian Gulf War.

Map 14: Europe Compare this map with Map 8 to obtain a clearer picture of territorial changes resulting from the outcome of World War II. As after World War I, defeated Germany and its allies lost territory, and the Soviet Union emerged as the greatest single territorial beneficiary.

In 1945, Germany was stripped of East Prussia, while its eastern boundary was set at the Oder-Neisse rivers—the farthest line west achieved by the Slavs since the twelfth century. Moreover, postwar Germany was both ideologically and territorially split—its western segment associated in military and economic pacts with the Western world and its eastern section integrated in the Communist world and a member of the Warsaw Pact. Defeated Italy lost its overseas colonies and Albania.

The Soviet Union expanded westward, annexing part of Finland; all of Estonia, Latvia, and Lithuania; and the eastern portion of Poland, shifting that country's center of gravity westward at the expense of Germany. Stalinist policies and power created a series of "people's democracies" from the Baltic to the Black seas, resulting in the iron curtain. Yet, the region was to prove far from monolithic. Shortly after the war, Tito declared Yugoslavia an independent Communist state.

Tiny Albania was later to ally itself with China in the great split within the Communist world. By the late 1980s, Communist regimes in many Eastern European states had fallen, free multiparty elections had taken place, and democratic parties had come to power. East and West Germany were reunited into a single state. In 1991 the Soviet Union itself collapsed, leading to the emergence of fifteen new independent states from the former Soviet republics. Unfortunately, the end of the Cold War has failed to eliminate conflict. Rather, superpower rivalry has been replaced by ethnic, religious, and nationalist hostilities, most notably in Bosnia and Herzegovina.

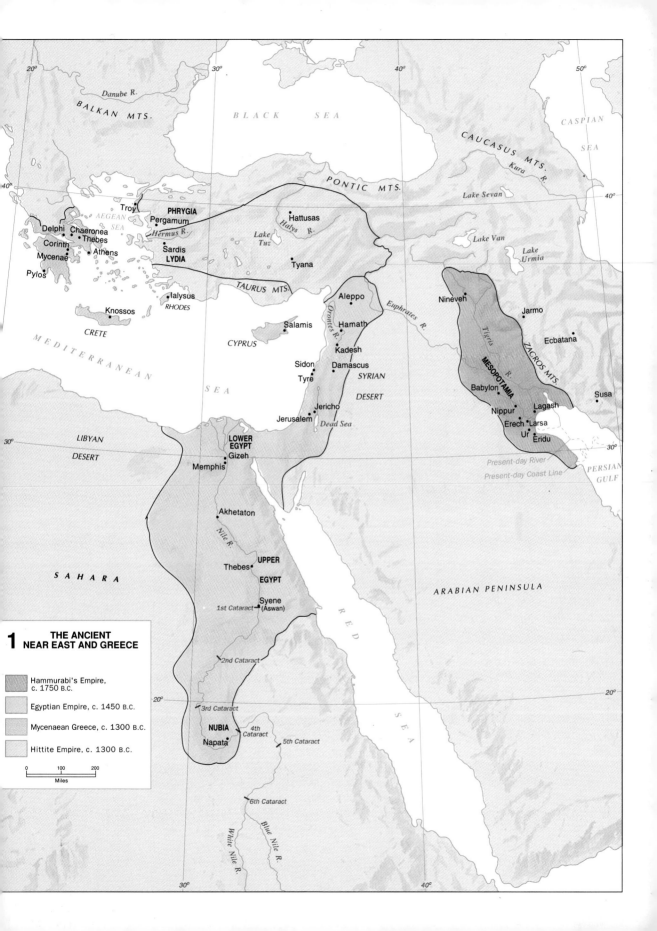

**THE ANCIENT
NEAR EAST AND GREECE**

1

Hammurabi's Empire,
c. 1750 B.C.

Egyptian Empire, c. 1450 B.C.

Mycenaean Greece, c. 1300 B.C.

Hittite Empire, c. 1300 B.C.

0   100   200
Miles

50°   **30°**   **20°**   **10°**   60°   0°   **10°**

IRELAND

NORTH SEA

Antoninus' Wall
(C. A.D. 140)

Hadrian's Wall
(C. A.D. 122)

BALTIC

York

Chester • Lincoln

BRITAIN

PENNINES

Colchester • London

Bath • Thames R.

ENGLISH CHANNEL

GERMANIA

Cologne

R.

Elbe R.

Oder R.

SUDETES

ATLANTIC OCEAN

BELGICA

Mainz

Rhine R.

Seine R.

Paris

Loire R.

GAUL

Meuse R.

Danube

Saône R.

BAY OF BISCAY

Bordeaux

Garonne R.

CENTRAL MASSIF

Lyons

Rhône R.

ALPS

CISALPINE GAUL

Po R.

ADRIATIC S

Genoa • Ravenna

CANTABRIAN MTS.

PYRENEES

Marseille

Pisa

Salonae

Douro R.

Segovia

Ebro R.

APENNINES

Tagus R.

SPAIN

CORSICA

ITALY

Guadiana R.

Toledo

Saguntum

Rome

SIERRA MORENA

Cordova

Valencia

SARDINIA

Naples • Pompeii

Guadalquivir R.

Cádiz

SIERRA NEVADA

New Carthage

BALEARIC ISLANDS

TYRRHENIAN SEA

Strait of Gibraltar

Tangier • Pillars of Hercules

MADEIRA ISLANDS

MEDITERRANEAN

Messina

SICILY

Syracuse

MAURITANIA

ATLAS MTS.

Moulouya R.

Chélif R.

Medjerda R.

Utica

Carthage

MALTA

CANARY ISLANDS

Chott Djerld

NUMIDIA

Oea • Leptis Magna

GRAND ERG OCCIDENTAL

GRAND ERG ORIENTAL

2   **THE ROMAN EMPIRE**
C. A.D. 117

0   100   200   300

Miles

AHAGGAR MTS.

SAHARA

0°   20°   10°

GOTHS

HUNS

SARMATIA

Western Dvina R.

Bug R.

Vistula R.

Dniester R.

Dnieper R.

Volga R.

Kama R.

Ural R.

URAL MTS.

Tobol R.

Don R.

Volga R.

CARPATHIANS

Olbia

SEA OF AZOV

ARAL SEA

CASPIAN SEA

Apulum

R. TRANSYLVANIAN ALPS

DACIA

Naissus

BALKAN MTS.

BLACK SEA

CAUCASUS MTS.

Kura R.

Lake Sevan

ELBURZ MTS.

Daryācheh-ye Namak

THRACE

MACEDONIA

Byzantium

Sea of Marmara

Sinope

PONTIC MTS.

Trapezus

Aras R.

Artaxata

ARMENIA

Lake Van

Lake Urmia

PLATEAU

PARTHIAN EMPIRE

OF IRAN

PONTUS

ASSYRIA

Ecbatana

Ctesiphon

ZAGROS

MTS.

Thebes

Pergamum

ASIA

Ephesus

AEGEAN SEA

Lake Tuz

Kizil R.

R.

Tarsus

CILICIA

MESOPOTAMIA

Tigris R.

Corinth

Athens

Sparta

RHODES

CYPRUS

Palmyra

Dura Europos

Euphrates R.

SYRIA

Knossos

CRETE

SEA

Sidon

Tyre

Damascus

PALESTINE

Jerusalem

Dead Sea

PERSIAN GULF

Cyrene

CYRENAICA

Alexandria

Memphis

EGYPT

Nile R.

ARABIA

LIBYAN

DESERT

Thebes

Berenice

Syene

RED SEA

3 THE ANCIENT EAST

Mauryan Empire, 320 B.C.–190 B.C.

Han Empire, 200 B.C.–A.D. 200

Parthian Empire, 200 B.C.–A.D. 226

MILES
0   200   400   600

MEDITERRANEAN SEA

BLACK SEA

CAUCASUS MTS.

CASPIAN SEA

URAL MTS.

KIRGIZ STEPPE

Lake Balkhash

ALTAI MTS.

SAYAN MTS.

YABLONOVY RANGE

GREAT KHINGAN MTS.

SIKHOTE ALIN RANGE

Danube R.
Don R.
Volga R.
Ural R.
Ob R.
Irtysh R.
Angara R.
Lena R.
Amur R.

Jerusalem
Antioch
Damascus
RED SEA
ARABIAN PENINSULA

MESOPOTAMIA
Euphrates R.
Tigris R.
Babylon
Seleucia
Ctesiphon
Ecbatana
Susa
Elam
PERSIA
Persepolis
PARTHIA
ZAGROS MTS.
DRANGIANA
PERSIAN GULF

Samarkand
Syr Darya (Jaxartes R.)
Amu Darya (Oxus R.)
BACTRIA
Bactra
Tashkurgan
HINDU KUSH
PAMIRS
Helmand R.

Mohenjo-Daro
Indus R.
THAR DESERT
Harappa
GANDHARA
Taxila
Yarkand
Kashgar
Khotan
TIEN SHAN
TAKLAMAKAN DESERT
Tarim R.
Loulan
KUNLUN MTS.
ALTYN TAGH
PLATEAU OF TIBET

ARABIAN SEA

Indraprastha
Mathura
Ganges R.
KOSALA
Pataliputra
MAGADHA
Champa
Narbada R.
Godavari R.
Krishna R.
ANDHRA
EASTERN GHATS
WESTERN GHATS
KALINGA
Mt. Everest
HIMALAYAS
Brahmaputra R.

INDIAN OCEAN

BAY OF BENGAL

Irrawaddy R.
Salween R.
Mekong R.

GOBI DESERT
Yellow R.
ORDOS DESERT
Great Wall
Yen
Shu
Pa
NAN LING
Han R. (Red R.)
Yangtze R.
Hsi R. (West R.)
Panyü
Wu
Ch'ang-an
YANG SHAO
LUNG SHAN
Loyang
Yüan
Linyüan
Chihan
Tai Mtn.
Sian Hu (Siang Hu)
Kan R.

SOUTH CHINA SEA

EAST CHINA SEA

SEA OF JAPAN

PHILIPPINE SEA

PACIFIC OCEAN

60°
80°
100°
120°
140°
20°
40°
0°

MEDIEVAL SPAIN, FRANCE, AND ENGLAND, 1328

4

England and Possessions
France
Kingdom of Navarre
Kingdom of Castile and Leon and Dependencies
Kingdom of Aragon and Dependencies
Kingdom of Granada
Portugal

0   100   200
MILES

ATLANTIC OCEAN

NORWAY

SWEDEN

DENMARK
Copenhagen

NORTH SEA

Elbe R.

Weser R.

Brandenburg

SCOTLAND
Aberdeen
Glasgow
Edinburgh
Durham
York
Lincoln
Chester

IRELAND
Galway
Limerick
Shannon R.
Wexford
Cork
Dublin
St. David's
WALES

ENGLAND
London
Bath
Winchester
Hastings
Severn R.
Thames R.

ENGLISH CHANNEL

Haarlem   Amsterdam
Rotterdam
Bruges   Ghent
FLANDERS   Louvain
Ypres   Brussels
Agincourt   Lille   Cateau-
Crécy   Cambrai   Cambrésis
Amiens   Vervins   Rocroy
Rouen   Soissons
Compiègne   Verdun
Paris   LORRAINE
Chartres   CHAMPAGNE   Toul
Clairvaux   ALSACE
Molesme   Luxeuil
Vézelay

Rhine R.
LUXEMBOURG
ARDENNES
Meuse R.

HOLY
ROMAN
EMPIRE

Danube R.

Brest
Mont St. Michel
BRITTANY
Champeaux
Carnac
NORMANDY
ANJOU
Seine R.
Loire R.
Tours
POITOU
Poitiers
FRANCE
Orléans
BURGUNDY
Cluny
Lyons
CENTRAL MASSIF
Saône R.
Rhône R.
SWITZERLAND
Po R.
VENICE
PAPAL STATES

BAY OF BISCAY
Cognac
AQUITAINE
Bordeaux
Dordogne R.
Garonne R.
GASCONY
Nimes
Marseille
Toulon
THE CORNICHE
CORSICA
SARDINIA
Cagliari

Santiago de Compostela
ASTURIAS
Oviedo
Cave of Covadonga
CANTABRIAN MTS
Leon
Miño R.
Ebro R.
Douro R.
Roncesvalles Pass
KINGDOM OF NAVARRE
PYRENEES
Toulouse
Carcassonne
Narbonne
Perpignan
Barcelona

Porto
Salamanca
Segovia
Madrid
Toledo
KINGDOM OF NAVARRE
Saragossa
KINGDOM OF ARAGON

PORTUGAL
KINGDOM OF
Lisbon
Tagus R.
CASTILE AND
Las Navas de Tolosa
LEON
Guadiana R.
Cordova
Guadalquivir R.
Seville
Granada
Cádiz
KINGDOM OF GRANADA
Strait of Gibraltar
Pillars of Hercules
Tangier

Palma
Valencia
BALEARIC ISLANDS

MEDITERRANEAN SEA

MUSLIM STATES

Segura R.

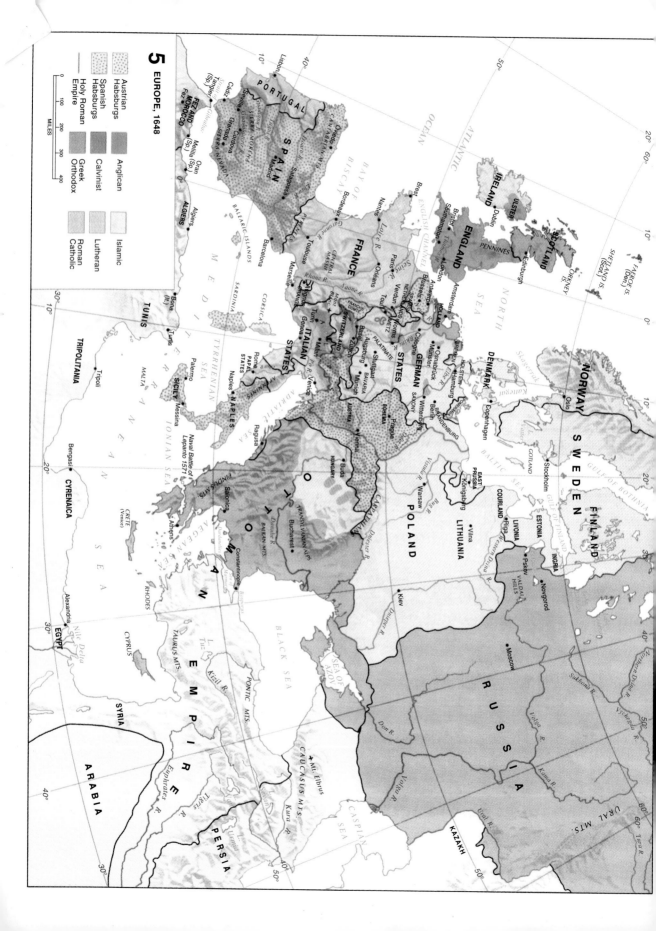

5 EUROPE, 1648

Austrian Habsburgs

Spanish Habsburgs

Holy Roman Empire

Anglican

Calvinist

Greek Orthodox

Islamic

Lutheran

Roman Catholic

0 100 200 300 400
MILES

ATLANTIC OCEAN

FAEROE IS. (Den.)

SHETLAND IS. (Scot.)

ORKNEY IS.

IRELAND
Dublin
ULSTER

SCOTLAND
Edinburgh

ENGLAND
London
Bristol
Southampton
PENNINES

NORTH SEA

ENGLISH CHANNEL

Brest

FRANCE
Nantes
Loire R.
Orléans
Paris
Seine R.
Toulouse
Bordeaux
Garonne R.
PYRENEES
CENTRAL MASSIF
Rhône R.
Saône R.
Marseille
Lyons
Grenoble
FRANCHE COMTÉ

BAY OF BISCAY

PORTUGAL
Lisbon

SPAIN
Madrid
Toledo
Oporto
CANTABRIAN MTS.
Duero R.
Saragossa
Barcelona
Valencia
SIERRA MORENA
Córdoba
Granada
SIERRA NEVADA
Cádiz
Gibraltar (Sp.)
Ceuta (Sp.)
Tangier (Sp.)
Melilla (Sp.)

BALEARIC ISLANDS

FEZ AND MOROCCO
Fez
Oran (Sp.)
Algiers
ALGIERS

MEDITERRANEAN SEA

SARDINIA

CORSICA

BALEARIC ISLANDS

Bona (It.)
Tunis
TUNIS
Tripoli
TRIPOLITANIA

SWITZERLAND
Basel
Zürich
Turin
Milan
Genoa
Venice
P.R.R.
METZ
Verdun
Toul
Worms

ITALIAN STATES
PAPAL STATES
Rome
Naples
NAPLES
APENNINES

SICILY
Palermo
Messina

MALTA

TYRRHENIAN SEA

IONIAN SEA

GERMAN STATES
Amsterdam
HOLLAND
Antwerp
Brussels
SPANISH NETH.
Cologne
Münster
Osnabrück
BREMEN
Hamburg
Elbe R.
HOLSTEIN
BRANDENBURG
Berlin
Wittenberg
SAXONY
PALATINATE
Stuttgart
Augsburg
Munich
BAVARIA
Vienna
Prague
BOHEMIA
AUSTRIA

DENMARK
Copenhagen

Skagerrak
Kattegat

NORWAY
Oslo

SWEDEN
Stockholm
GOTLAND

FINLAND

GULF OF BOTHNIA

BALTIC SEA

GULF OF FINLAND

ESTONIA
INGRIA
LIVONIA
Riga
Pskov
Novgorod
VALDAI HILLS

COURLAND
EAST PRUSSIA
Königsberg
Vilna
LITHUANIA

POLAND
Warsaw
Vistula R.
Bug R.
Kiev
Dniester R.
Dnieper R.

HUNGARY
Buda
CARPATHIANS
TRANSYLVANIAN ALPS
Danube R.
Bucharest
BALKAN MTS.

RUSSIA
Moscow
Volga R.
Kama R.
Ural R.
Don R.
URAL MTS.

KAZAKH

OTTOMAN EMPIRE
Ragusa
Salonica
ADRIATIC SEA
PINDUS MTS.
Athens
AEGEAN SEA
Constantinople
Bosporus
Sea of Marmara
Naval Battle of Lepanto 1571
CRETE (Venice)
RHODES
CYPRUS

BLACK SEA

SEA OF AZOV

CASPIAN SEA

CAUCASUS MTS.
Mt. Elbrus
Kura R.

PERSIA
Euphrates R.
Tigris R.

SYRIA
TAURUS MTS.
Kizil R.
PONTIC MTS.

EGYPT
Alexandria
Nile Delta
Nile R.

CYRENAICA
Bengasi

ARABIA

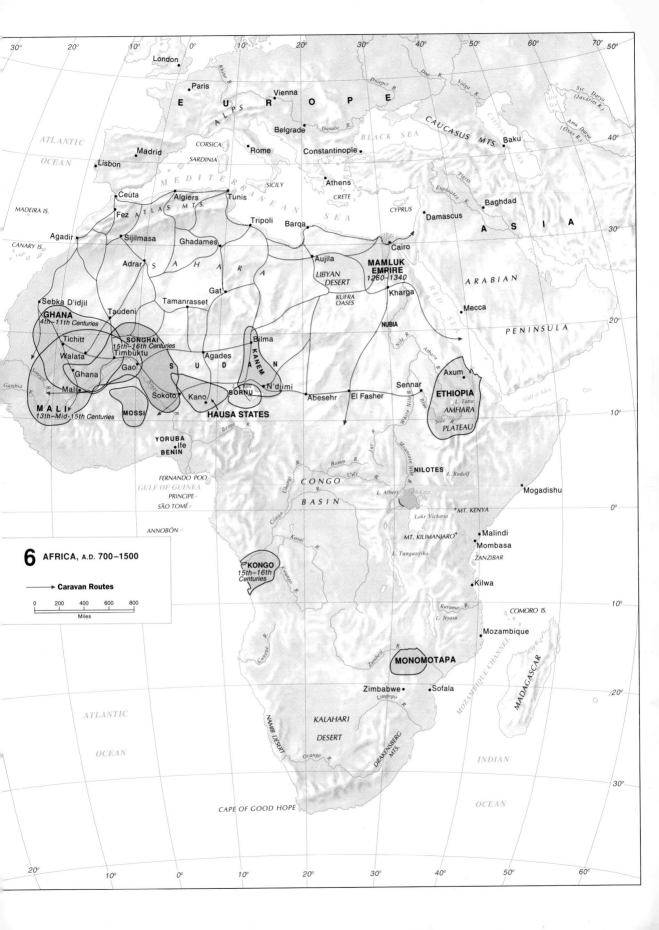

30°   20°   10°   0°   10°   20°   30°   40°   50°   60°   70°   50°

London

E U R O P E

Paris

ATLANTIC
OCEAN

Vienna

ALPS

Belgrade

Danube R.

Dnieper R.

Don R.

Volga R.

Syr Darya
(Jaxartes R.)

Aral
Sea

Amu Darya
(Oxas R.)

CAUCASUS MTS.

Baku

40°

Madrid

CORSICA

Rome

BLACK SEA

Constantinople

ASIA

Caspian Sea

Lisbon

SARDINIA

MEDITERRANEAN

SICILY

Athens

CRETE

CYPRUS

Damascus

Tigris R.

Baghdad

MADEIRA IS.

Ceuta

ATLAS MTS.

Algiers

Tunis

30°

CANARY IS.

Agadir

Fez

Sijilmasa

Tripoli

Barqa

SEA

Euphrates R.

Cairo

Ghadames

S A H A R A

Aujila

LIBYAN
DESERT

MAMLUK
EMPIRE
1260–1340

Damascus

ARABIAN

Persian Gulf

Adrar

Gat

Tamanrasset

KUFRA
OASES

Kharga

RED SEA

Mecca

PENINSULA

20°

Sebka D'idjil

Taudeni

GHANA
4th–11th Centuries

Bilma

NUBIA

Nile R.

Tichitt

Walata

SONGHAI
15th–16th Centuries

Timbuktu

Agades

K
A
N
E
M

N

Athara R.

Axum

Ghana

Gao

S U D

BORNU

N'djimi

White Nile R.

Sennar

ETHIOPIA

AMHARA

L. Tana

Gulf of Aden

Gambia R.

Senegal R.

Mali

MALI
13th–Mid-15th Centuries

MOSSI

Sokoto

Kano

HAUSA STATES

Abesehr

El Fasher

Blue Nile R.

Nile R.

Niger R.

PLATEAU

10°

YORUBA

Ife
BENIN

Benue R.

Jur R.

FERNANDO POO

GULF OF GUINEA

PRINCIPE

SÃO TOMÉ

Bomu R.

U'éc R.

NILOTES

L. Rudolf

Mogadishu

CONGO

BASIN

Ubangi R.

Congo R.

L. Albert

Lake Victoria

MT. KENYA

0°

Kasai R.

MT. KILIMANJARO

Malindi

Mombasa

ZANZIBAR

ANNOBÓN

L. Tanganyika

6 AFRICA, A.D. 700–1500

KONGO
15th–16th
Centuries

Kwango R.

Kilwa

10°

→ Caravan Routes

Ruvuma R.

COMORO IS.

0   200   400   600   800

Miles

L. Nyasa

Mozambique

MADAGASCAR

MOZAMBIQUE CHANNEL

Cunene R.

Zambezi R.

MONOMOTAPA

20°

ATLANTIC

NAMIB DESERT

Zimbabwe

Limpopo R.

Sofala

OCEAN

KALAHARI

DESERT

Orange R.

DRAKENSBERG MTS.

INDIAN

30°

CAPE OF GOOD HOPE

OCEAN

20°   10°   0°   10°   20°   30°   40°   50°   60°

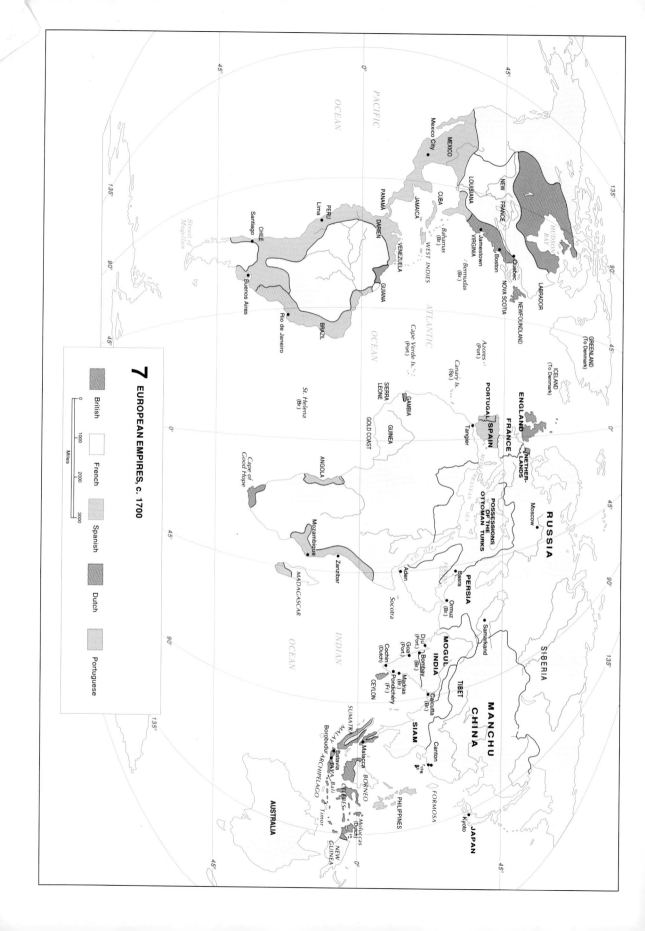

7 EUROPEAN EMPIRES, c. 1700

British
French
Spanish
Dutch
Portuguese

Miles
0
1000
2000
3000

PACIFIC OCEAN

Strait of Magellan

Mexico City
MEXICO
PANAMA
DARIEN
PERU
Lima
CHILE
Santiago
Buenos Aires
Rio de Janeiro
BRAZIL
GUIANA
VENEZUELA
JAMAICA
CUBA
Bahamas (Br.)
WEST INDIES
Bermudas (Br.)
VIRGINIA
Jamestown
Boston
Quebec
NOVA SCOTIA
NEWFOUNDLAND
LABRADOR
NEW FRANCE
LOUISIANA

HUDSON BAY

GREENLAND (To Denmark)

ICELAND (To Denmark)

ATLANTIC OCEAN

Azores (Port.)
Canary Is. (Sp.)
Cape Verde Is. (Port.)
St. Helena (Br.)
SIERRA LEONE
GAMBIA
GUINEA
GOLD COAST
Cape of Good Hope
ANGOLA
MOZAMBIQUE
MADAGASCAR
Zanzibar
Socotra

PORTUGAL
SPAIN
FRANCE
ENGLAND
NETHER-LANDS

POSSESSIONS OF THE OTTOMAN TURKS

Tangier
MEDITERRANEAN SEA
RED SEA
Aden
Basra
PERSIA
Ormuz (Br.)

Moscow
RUSSIA
SIBERIA
Samarkand

MOGUL INDIA
Diu (Port.)
Goa (Port.)
Bombay (Br.)
Cochin (Dutch)
Madras (Br.)
Pondichéry (Fr.)
CEYLON
Calcutta (Br.)
TIBET

INDIAN OCEAN

MANCHU CHINA
Canton
FORMOSA
Kyoto
JAPAN

SIAM
MALAYA
SUMATRA
Malacca
Batavia
JAVA
Borobudur
Bali
BORNEO
CELEBES
Moluccas (Dutch)
Timor
PHILIPPINES
ARCHIPELAGO
NEW GUINEA

AUSTRALIA

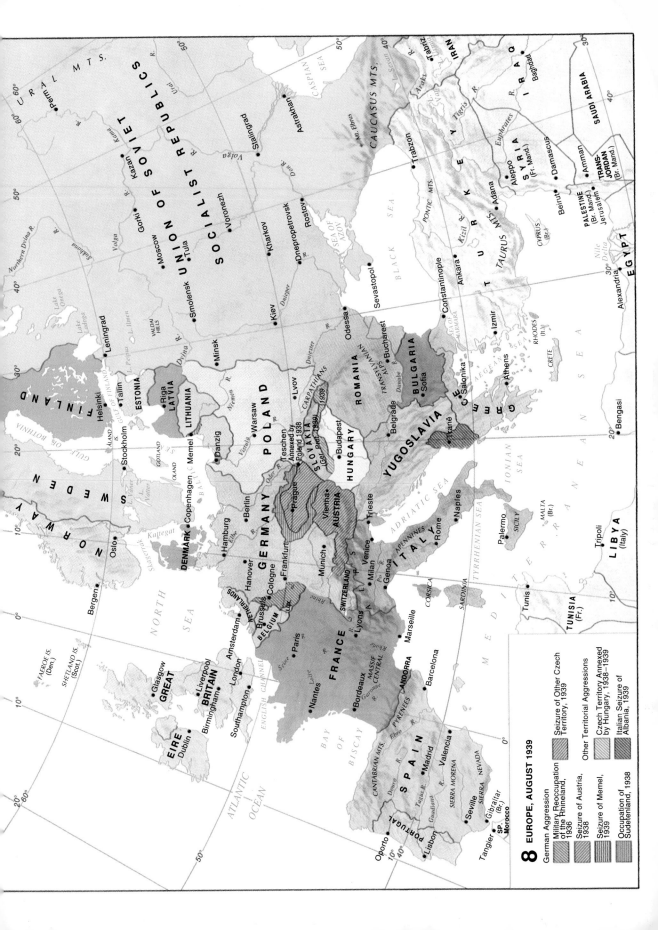

8 EUROPE, AUGUST 1939

German Aggression

Military Reoccupation of the Rhineland, 1936	Seizure of Other Czech Territory, 1939
Seizure of Austria, 1938	Other Territorial Aggressions
Seizure of Memel, 1939	Czech Territory Annexed by Hungary, 1938–1939
Occupation of Sudetenland, 1938	Italian Seizure of Albania, 1939

UNION OF SOVIET SOCIALIST REPUBLICS

URAL MTS.

Perm

Kazan

Gorki

Moscow
Tula

Smolensk

Voronezh

Stalingrad

Astrakhan

CAUCASUS MTS.

Mt. Elbrus

Volga
Don R.

Kama R.

Northern Dvina R.

Sukhona R.

Lake Onega

Lake Ladoga

L. Ilmen

L. Peipus

VALDAI HILLS

Leningrad

Helsinki

FINLAND

GULF OF FINLAND

Tallin
ESTONIA

Riga
LATVIA

LITHUANIA

Dvina

Minsk

Kharkov

Dnepropetrovsk

Rostov

Kiev

Dnieper

Dniester

Odessa

SEA OF AZOV

Sevastopol

BLACK SEA

CASPIAN SEA

Trabzon

Tabriz

IRAN

IRAQ

Baghdad

Araks R.

SAUDI ARABIA

SYRIA (Fr. Mand.)

Aleppo

Damascus

Beirut

Amman
TRANS-JORDAN (Br. Mand.)

PALESTINE (Br. Mand.)
Jerusalem

CYPRUS (Br.)

Ankara

Adana

Izmir

Constantinople

SEA OF MARMARA

AEGEAN SEA

RHODES (It.)

CRETE

TURKEY

TAURUS MTS.

PONTIC MTS.

Kizil R.

Tigris

Euphrates

EGYPT

Alexandria

Nile Delta

NORWAY

SWEDEN

Bergen

Oslo

Stockholm

Copenhagen
DENMARK

Skagerrak

Kattegat

GULF OF BOTHNIA

ALAND IS.

GOTLAND

OLAND

L. Vänern

L. Vättern

BALTIC SEA

Memel

Danzig

POLAND

Warsaw

Vistula

Teschen Annexed by Poland 1938

Lvov

CARPATHIANS

SLOVAKIA (Ger. prot. 1939)

Prague

HUNGARY

Budapest

AUSTRIA

Vienna

ROMANIA

Bucharest

TRANSYLVANIAN ALPS

Danube

Belgrade

YUGOSLAVIA

BULGARIA

Sofia

Tiranë

GREECE

Salonika

Athens

IONIAN SEA

MEDITERRANEAN SEA

GERMANY

Berlin

Hamburg

Hanover

Frankfurt

Cologne

Munich

Elbe

Oder R.

Neisse R.

Neman R.

SWITZERLAND

ALPS

Trieste

Venice

Milan

Genoa

ITALY

APENNINES

Rome

Naples

TYRRHENIAN SEA

ADRIATIC SEA

CORSICA

SARDINIA

SICILY

Palermo

MALTA (Br.)

Tunis

TUNISIA (Fr.)

Tripoli

LIBYA (Italy)

Bengasi

NETHERLANDS

Amsterdam

Brussels
BELGIUM

Lux.

FRANCE

Paris

Nantes

Bordeaux

Lyons

Marseille

MASSIF CENTRAL

PYRENEES

Seine

Loire

Garonne

Rhône

Rhine

ANDORRA

Barcelona

SPAIN

Madrid

Valencia

Seville

CANTABRIAN MTS.

SIERRA MORENA

SIERRA NEVADA

Ebro

Tagus R.

Douro

Guadiana R.

Guadalquivir R.

PORTUGAL

Lisbon

Oporto

Gibraltar (Br.)

SP. MOROCCO

Tangier

GREAT BRITAIN

Glasgow

Liverpool

Birmingham

London

Southampton

EIRE

Dublin

FAEROE IS. (Den.)

SHETLAND IS. (Scot.)

ENGLISH CHANNEL

NORTH SEA

ATLANTIC OCEAN

BAY OF BISCAY

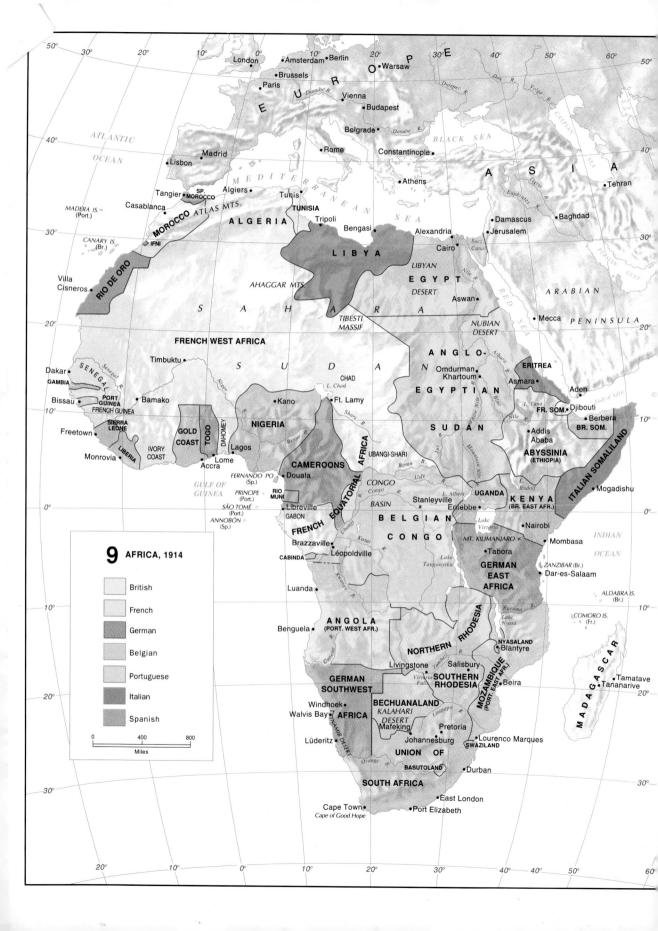

9 AFRICA, 1914

Legend:
- British
- French
- German
- Belgian
- Portuguese
- Italian
- Spanish

Scale: 0 — 400 — 800 Miles

EUROPE

London · Amsterdam · Berlin · Warsaw
Brussels
Paris · Vienna · Budapest
Belgrade · Rome · Constantinople
Madrid · Lisbon · Athens

ATLANTIC OCEAN

BLACK SEA

CASPIAN SEA

ASIA

Damascus · Baghdad
Jerusalem · Tehran

MADERA IS. (Port.)

Tangier · SP. MOROCCO · Algiers · Tunis · TUNISIA
Casablanca · MOROCCO · ATLAS MTS. · Tripoli · Bengasi · Alexandria · Cairo
CANARY IS. (Br.) · IFNI
Villa Cisneros · RIO DE ORO

ALGERIA · LIBYA · LIBYAN DESERT · EGYPT · EGYPTIAN DESERT · Aswan

ARABIAN PENINSULA · Mecca

RED SEA

AHAGGAR MTS.

SAHARA

TIBESTI MASSIF · NUBIAN DESERT

FRENCH WEST AFRICA

ANGLO-EGYPTIAN SUDAN

Dakar · SENEGAL · Timbuktu · SUDAN · Omdurman · Khartoum · ERITREA · Asmara
GAMBIA
Bissau · PORT. GUINEA · Bamako · CHAD · L. Chad · Aden
FRENCH GUINEA · Kano · Ft. Lamy · L. Tana · FR. SOM. · Djibouti · Berbera · BR. SOM.
Freetown · SIERRA LEONE · NIGERIA · Addis Ababa
IVORY COAST · GOLD COAST · TOGO · DAHOMEY · ABYSSINIA (ETHIOPIA)
Monrovia · LIBERIA · Lagos · CAMEROONS · Douala
Lome · Accra · EQUATORIAL AFRICA · UBANGI-SHARI

FERNANDO PO (Sp.)
GULF OF GUINEA · PRINCIPE (Port.) · RIO MUNI · CONGO BASIN · UGANDA · KENYA (BR. EAST AFR.) · ITALIAN SOMALILAND · Mogadishu
SÃO TOMÉ (Port.) · Libreville · GABON · Stanleyville · Entebbe
ANNOBÓN (Sp.) · FRENCH · BELGIAN CONGO · Lake Victoria · Nairobi
Brazzaville · Léopoldville · MT. KILIMANJARO · Mombasa
CABINDA · Lake Tanganyika · Tabora · GERMAN EAST AFRICA · ZANZIBAR (Br.)
Luanda · Dar-es-Salaam

INDIAN OCEAN

ALDABRA IS. (Br.)
COMORO IS. (Fr.)

ANGOLA (PORT. WEST AFR.)
Benguela · Lake Nyasa · NYASALAND · Blantyre
NORTHERN RHODESIA · Livingstone · Salisbury · MOZAMBIQUE (PORT. EAST AFR.) · Beira
SOUTHERN RHODESIA
GERMAN SOUTHWEST AFRICA · Windhoek · Walvis Bay · BECHUANALAND · KALAHARI DESERT · Mafeking · Pretoria · Johannesburg · Lourenco Marques · SWAZILAND
Lüderitz · UNION OF SOUTH AFRICA · BASUTOLAND · Durban
Cape Town · Cape of Good Hope · East London · Port Elizabeth

MADAGASCAR · Tamatave · Tananarive

MEDITERRANEAN SEA

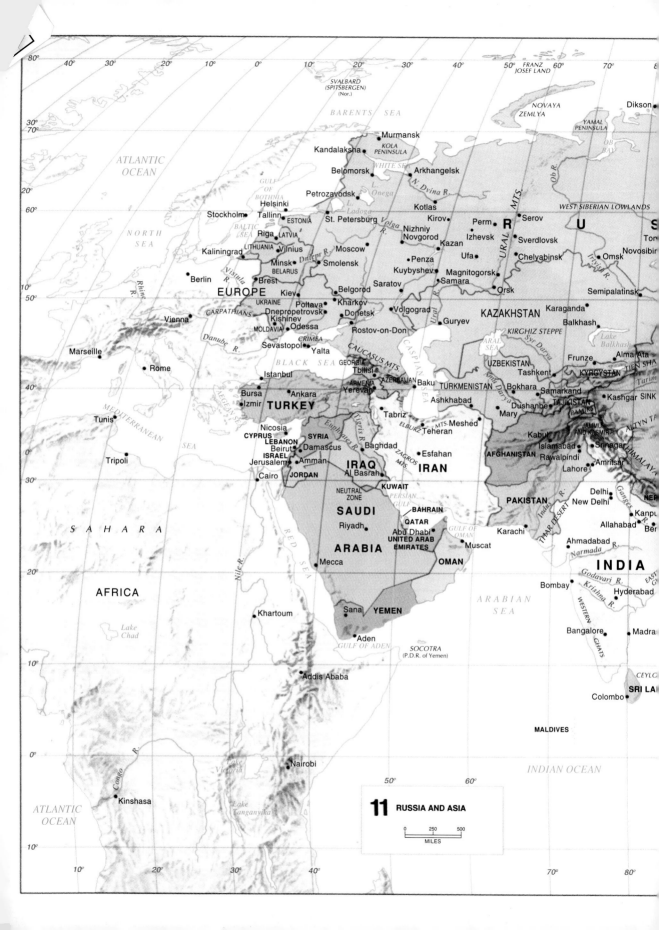

80° 40° 30° 20° 10° 0° 10° 20° 30° 40° 50° FRANZ 60° 70° 8
                                                      JOSEF LAND

SVALBARD
(SPITSBERGEN)   NOVAYA
(Nor.)   ZEMLYA   Dikson

BARENTS SEA   YAMAL
                                                      PENINSULA   OB
30°   BAY
70°   Murmansk
              Kandalaksha   KOLA
ATLANTIC   PENINSULA
OCEAN   Belomorsk   WHITE SEA   Arkhangelsk
20°   GULF   N. Dvina R.   Ob R. WEST SIBERIAN LOWLANDS
         OF   Petrozavodsk L. Onega
60°   BOTHNIA   U   S
         Helsinki L. Ladoga   Kotlas
Stockholm Tallinn St. Petersburg   Kirov   Serov
         ESTONIA   Volga R. Nizhniy   Perm Sverdlovsk   Ton
NORTH   Riga LATVIA   Moscow Novgorod Izhevsk   Novosibir
SEA   Kaliningrad LITHUANIA Vilnius   Kazan Chelyabinsk Omsk
10°   Minsk Dnepr R. Smolensk Penza Ufa   Irtysh R.
Berlin   BELARUS Brest   Kuybyshev Magnitogorsk   Semipalatinsk
50°   Vistula R. Kiev   Saratov Samara
EUROPE   UKRAINE Poltava Belgorod   Volgograd Orsk
Vienna   Rhine R. Dnepropetrovsk Kharkov   KAZAKHSTAN Karaganda
CARPATHIANS Kishinev Donetsk   Guryev   Balkhash
         MOLDAVIA Odessa   KIRGHIZ STEPPE Syr Darya Lake
Marseille Danube R. Sevastopol CRIMEA Rostov-on-Don ARAL   Balkhash
Rome   Yalta   SEA   Frunze Alma-Ata
         BLACK SEA   CAUCASUS MTS. CASPIAN UZBEKISTAN TIEN SHA
40°   Istanbul   GEORGIA Tbilisi   Tashkent KYRGYSTAN
         Bursa Ankara ARMENIA AZERBAIJAN Baku Amu Darya Bokhara Samarkand Tarim
         Izmir TURKEY   Yerevan   TURKMENISTAN   Dushanbe TAJIKISTAN Kashgar SINK
AEGEAN   Ashkhabad Mary PAMIRS
Tunis   SEA   Nicosia   Tabriz ELBURZ MTS. Meshed   Kabul   ALTYN TA
         CYPRUS SYRIA   Teheran   Islamabad JAMMU   Srinagar HIMALAYA
MEDITERRANEAN Beirut Damascus Tigris R. Baghdad ZAGROS Esfahan AFGHANISTAN Rawalpindi AND KASHMIR Amritsar
         LEBANON Euphrates R.   MTS. IRAN   Lahore
Tripoli ISRAEL Amman IRAQ   Al Basrah   PAKISTAN Delhi NEP
         Jerusalem JORDAN   KUWAIT   Indus R. New Delhi Kanpu
30°   Cairo   NEUTRAL PERSIAN BAHRAIN   Karachi THAR DESERT Allahabad Ber
         ZONE   GULF   QATAR   Ahmadabad
SAHARA   SAUDI   Abu Dhabi GULF OF Muscat   Narmada R. INDIA
                        Riyadh UNITED ARAB OMAN   Bombay
20°   ARABIA EMIRATES   OMAN   Godavari R. Hyderabad
         Mecca   WESTERN Krishna R. EAST
                                  RED SEA   ARABIAN   GHATS   G
AFRICA   Khartoum   SEA   Bangalore Madra
                                  Sana YEMEN   GHATS
                        Aden   CEYLO
10°   GULF OF ADEN SOCOTRA   Colombo SRI LA
                                  (P.D.R. of Yemen)
         Addis Ababa   MALDIVES

                                              50°   60°   INDIAN OCEAN
0°
                        Nairobi
         Congo R. Lake
         Victoria   **11** **RUSSIA AND ASIA**
ATLANTIC Kinshasa Lake
OCEAN   Tanganyika   0   250   500
10°   MILES

10°   20°   30°   40°   70°   80°

ATLANTIC

OCEAN

UNITED STATES

Great Salt Lake

ROCKY MOUNTAINS

Colorado R.

Missouri R.

Chicago

New York

Denver

St. Louis

Washington

Dallas

Mississippi R.

New Orleans

Bermuda Is. (Br.)

SIERRA MADRE OCCIDENTAL

M E X I C O

Rio Grande

Conchos R.

Guadalajara

Monterrey

Tampico

Mexico City

Veracruz

Acapulco

Oaxaca

Sta. Maria

SIERRA MADRE ORIENTAL

Bolsas

GULF OF CALIFORNIA

GULF OF MEXICO

Miami

Laredo

Mérida

Chichen Itza

Uxmal

Havana

C U B A

WEST

BAHAMAS

Port-au-Prince

DOMINICAN REPUBLIC

Santo Domingo

PUERTO RICO (U.S.)

ST. CHRISTOPHER AND NEVIS

ANTIGUA AND BARBUDA

Guadeloupe (Fr.)

Martinique (Fr.)

DOMINICA

ST. LUCIA

BARBADOS

ST. VINCENT AND THE GRENADINES

GRENADA

TRINIDAD AND TOBAGO

Port of Spain

JAMAICA

HAITI

Kingston

INDIES

BELIZE (Br.)

Belize City

Belmopan

Tikal

GAUTEMALA

Guatemala

HONDURAS

Tegucigalpa

NICARAGUA

San Salvador

EL SALVADOR

Managua

COSTA RICA

San José

PANAMA

Colón

Panamá

CARIBBEAN SEA

Barranquilla

Lake Maracaibo

Caracas

Orinoco R.

VENEZUELA

Georgetown

Paramaribo

GUYANA

SURINAME

FRENCH GUIANA

Cayenne

GUIANA HIGHLANDS

Bogotá

COLOMBIA

Buenaventura

Quito

ECUADOR

Guayaquil

Iquitos

GALAPAGOS IS. (Ec.)

Marañón R.

Ucayali R.

Japurá R.

Rio Negro

Amazon R.

Manaus

Purus R.

Madeira R.

Tapajos R.

Xingu R.

Tocantins R.

Belém

Recife

PERU

Lima

ANDES MTS.

Guaporé R.

Mamoré R.

PLATEAU OF MATO GROSSO

B R A Z I L

Brasília

Salvador

Arequipa

La Paz

BOLIVIA

Sucre

Rio Grande

Belo Horizonte

BRAZILIAN HIGHLANDS

PACIFIC

OCEAN

Antofagasta

ATACAMA DESERT

PARAGUAY

Pilcomayo R.

Asunción

Iguaçu Falls

São Paulo

Santos

Rio de Janeiro

Tucumán

Salado R.

Paraná R.

Córdoba

Santa Fé

Rosario

Mt. Aconcagua

Valparaíso

Mendoza

Santiago

C H I L E

A R G E N T I N A

Buenos Aires

URUGUAY

Montevideo

Río de la Plata

PAMPA

Colorado R.

Bahía Blanca

Valdivia

PATAGONIA

ATLANTIC

OCEAN

FALKLAND IS. (ISLAS MALVINAS) (Br.)

Punta Arenas

TIERRA DEL FUEGO

Cape Horn

SOUTH GEORGIA (Br.)

Drake Passage

SOUTH ORKNEY IS. (Br.)

ANTARCTICA

12 LATIN AMERICA

0   400   800

Miles

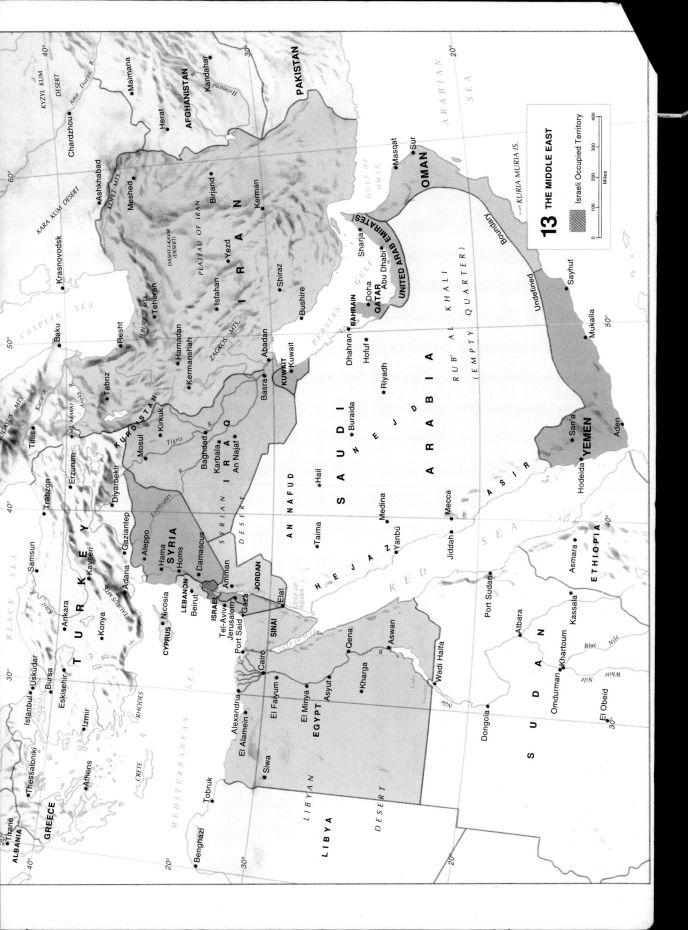

THE MIDDLE EAST

13

Israeli Occupied Territory

Boundary

Undefined

Miles
0 100 200 300 400

GREECE
ALBANIA
Tiranë
Thessaloniki
Athens
CRETE
RHODES

TURKEY
Istanbul
Üsküdar
Bursa
Eskisehir
Izmir
Ankara
Konya
Samsun
Kayseri
Adana
Gaziantep
Diyarbekir
Erzurum
Trabzon
Tiflis
CAUCASUS MTS.

BLACK SEA
MARMARA
TAURUS MTS.
Kizil R.
Kura R.
Aras R.
MT. ARARAT
KOPET MTS.

CYPRUS
Nicosia
MEDITERRANEAN SEA

LEBANON
Beirut
SYRIA
Aleppo
Hama
Homs
Damascus
ISRAEL
Tel-Aviv
Jerusalem
Gaza
JORDAN
Amman
SINAI
Elat
Port Said

SYRIAN DESERT

KURDISTAN
Mosul
Kirkuk
IRAQ
Baghdad
Karbala
An Najaf
Basra
Tigris
Euphrates

CASPIAN SEA
Baku
Resht
Tabriz
Hamadan
Kermanshah
ELBURZ MTS.
ZAGROS MTS.
Teheran
Isfahan
IRAN
PLATEAU OF IRAN
DASHT-I-KAVIR (DESERT)
Shiraz
Yezd
Kerman
Birjand
Meshed
Ashkhabad
KARA KUM DESERT
Krasnovodsk
Chardzhou
KYZYL KUM DESERT
Amu Darya R.
Maimana
Herat
AFGHANISTAN
Kandahar
Helmand R.
PAKISTAN

Abadan
Bushire
Kuwait
KUWAIT

PERSIAN GULF
BAHRAIN
Dhahran
Hofuf
QATAR
Doha
Sharja
Abu Dhabi
UNITED ARAB EMIRATES
GULF OF OMAN
Masqat
OMAN
Sur
ARABIAN SEA
KURIA MURIA IS.
Sayhut
Mukalla
Undefined

SAUDI ARABIA
NEJD
Buraida
Riyadh
Hail
AN NAFUD
Taima
Medina
Yanbū
RUB' AL KHALI
(EMPTY QUARTER)

HEJAZ
Jiddah
Mecca
ASIR
San'a
YEMEN
Hodeida
Aden

RED SEA
GULF OF AQABA
GULF OF SUEZ

EGYPT
Cairo
Alexandria
El Alamein
Siwa
El Faiyum
El Minya
Asyut
Qena
Kharga
Aswan
Wadi Halfa
Lake Nasser

LIBYA
Benghazi
Tobruk
LIBYAN DESERT

SUDAN
Dongola
Atbara
Port Sudan
Kassala
Omdurman
Khartoum
El Obeid
Blue Nile
White Nile
Nile
ETHIOPIA
Asmara

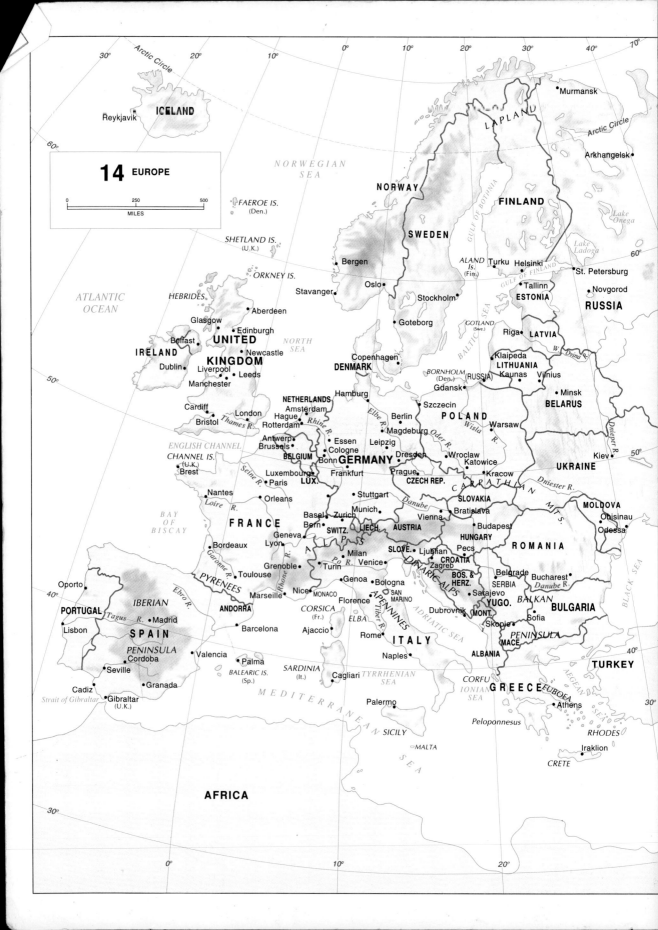

14 EUROPE

0 — 250 — 500
MILES

ATLANTIC
OCEAN

NORWEGIAN
SEA

ICELAND
Reykjavik•

FAEROE IS.
(Den.)

SHETLAND IS.
(U.K.)

ORKNEY IS.

HEBRIDES

Arctic Circle

Murmansk•

LAPLAND

Arctic Circle

NORWAY

SWEDEN

FINLAND

Arkhangelsk•

GULF OF BOTHNIA

Lake
Onega

Lake
Ladoga

Bergen•

Stavanger•

Oslo•

Goteborg•

Stockholm•

ALAND
Is.
(Fin.)

Turku• Helsinki•

GOTLAND
(Swe.)

GULF OF FINLAND

St. Petersburg•

Novgorod•

Tallinn•
ESTONIA

RUSSIA

BALTIC SEA

Riga• LATVIA

W. Drina R.

Glasgow•
•Aberdeen

Belfast• •Edinburgh

IRELAND

UNITED
KINGDOM

Dublin• Newcastle•
Liverpool•
Leeds•
Manchester•

NORTH
SEA

Copenhagen•

DENMARK

Hamburg•

BORNHOLM
(Den.)

(RUSSIA)

Klaipeda•
LITHUANIA
Kaunas• Vilnius•

Minsk•

BELARUS

Gdansk•

Szczecin•

POLAND

Wisla R.

Warsaw•

Cardiff•
Bristol•

London•

Thames R.

ENGLISH CHANNEL

CHANNEL IS.
(U.K.)
Brest•

NETHERLANDS
Amsterdam•
Hague•
Rotterdam•

Rhine R.

Antwerp•
Brussels•

BELGIUM

Essen• Berlin•
Cologne• Leipzig•

Bonn• GERMANY

Elbe R.

Magdeburg•

Oder R.

Dresden•

Wroclaw•
Katowice•

Prague•

CZECH REP.

Kracow•

CARPATHIAN MTS.

Dniester R.

UKRAINE

Kiev•

Nantes•

Loire R.

Seine R.

Paris•

LUX.

Luxembourg•

Frankfurt•

Stuttgart•

Munich•

Danube R.

Vienna•

SLOVAKIA
Bratislava•

Budapest•

MOLDOVA
Chisinau•

Odessa•

Orleans•

BAY
OF
BISCAY

FRANCE

Bordeaux•

Basel• Zurich•
Bern•
SWITZ. LIECH. AUSTRIA

A L P S

HUNGARY

Pecs•

SLOVE.

Ljubljana•
Zagreb•
CROATIA

ROMANIA

Bucharest•
Belgrade•
Danube R.

BLACK SEA

Garonne R.

PYRENEES

Toulouse•

Geneva•
Lyon•

Grenoble•

Rhone R.

Milan•
Turin•

Po R.

Venice•

Genoa• Bologna•

DINARIC ALPS

BOS. &
HERZ.
Sarajevo•

SERBIA

YUGO.

MONT.

BALKAN
PENINSULA

BULGARIA

Sofia•

Oporto•

PORTUGAL

Lisbon•

IBERIAN

Tagus R.

•Madrid

SPAIN

PENINSULA

Cordoba•

ANDORRA

Ebro R.

Barcelona•

Nice•
Marseille• MONACO

CORSICA
(Fr.)

Florence•

ELBA

APENNINES

Tiber R.

Rome•

ITALY

SAN
MARINO

ADRIATIC SEA

Dubrovnik•

Skopje•
MACE.
ALBANIA

CORFU

IONIAN
SEA

GREECE

EUBOEA

TURKEY

Cadiz•

Seville•

•Granada

Strait of Gibraltar

Gibraltar
(U.K.)

Valencia•

•Palma

BALEARIC IS.
(Sp.)

SARDINIA
(It.)

Cagliari•

TYRRHENIAN
SEA

Naples•

Palermo•

M E D I T E R R A N E A N

SICILY

MALTA•

SEA

Peloponnesus

Athens•

AEGEAN
SEA

RHODES

Iraklion•

CRETE

AFRICA